SUNDAYS

AND

SEASONS

2002

Augsburg Fortress

SUNDAYS AND SEASONS

2002, Year A

RELATED RESOURCES

Icon: Visual Images for Every Sunday (AFP 0-8066-4077-4)
Worship Planning Calendar, 2002, Year A (AFP 0-8066-9085-5)
Words for Worship, 2002, Year A (AFP 0-8066-4086-3)

ACKNOWLEDGMENTS

Scripture quotations are from the New Revised Standard Version Bible © 1989 Division of Christian Education of the National Council of the Churches of Christ in the United States of America. Used by permission.

The prayers (printed in each Sunday/festival section) may be reproduced for one-time, congregational use, provided copies are for local use only and the following copyright notice appears: From *Sundays and Seasons*, copyright © 2001 Augsburg Fortress.

Annual Materials
The Gospel of Matthew, Dennis Creswell

Seasonal and Weekly Materials
Images of the Season: Samuel Torvend (Advent), Dennis Bushkofsky (Christmas, Epiphany), Ronald Roschke (Easter Cycle), Robert Buckley Farlee (Season after Pentecost)

Environment and Art for the Season: Lynn Joyce Hunter

Preaching with the Season and Images for Preaching: Catherine Malotky (Christmas Cycle), Robert Smith (Easter Cycle), Beth Gaede (Summer), Bruce Modahl (Autumn, November)

The Prayers: Mark Strobel (Christmas Cycle), Rhoda Schuler (Easter Cycle), Karen Ball (Summer), Mark Briehl (Autumn, November)

Worship Matters: D. Foy Christopherson (Christmas Cycle), Robert Hofstad (Easter Cycle), Theodore Asta (Season after Pentecost)

Let the Children Come: Susan Briehl

Music Materials
Assembly Song for the Season: Kevin Anderson; mainstream/classic choral: Thomas Pavlechko, Carole Weatherby; children's choirs: Kathy Donlan Tunseth; keyboard/instrumental: Andrew Heller; handbell: Randy Knutson; praise ensemble: Michael Fenton, Lynn Panosh

Editors
Norma Aamodt-Nelson, Suzanne Burke, Carol Carver, Rebecca Lowe, Martin A. Seltz, and Eric Vollen

Art and Design
Art: Tanja Butler
Book Design: The Kantor Group, Inc.

Manufactured in the U.S.A.          0-8066-4084-7

1     2     3

# Introduction

Introduction . . . . . . . . . . . . . . . . . . . . . . . . . . . . . . . . . . . . . . . . . . .6

The Gospel of Matthew . . . . . . . . . . . . . . . . . . . . . . . . . . . . . . . . . .8

New Songs, Old Patterns . . . . . . . . . . . . . . . . . . . . . . . . . . . . . . .11

Worship Planning Checklist . . . . . . . . . . . . . . . . . . . . . . . . . . . . .14

Key to Music Publishers . . . . . . . . . . . . . . . . . . . . . . . . . . . . . . . .17

Music for Worship Key . . . . . . . . . . . . . . . . . . . . . . . . . . . . . . . . .18

Key to Hymn and Psalm Collections . . . . . . . . . . . . . . . . . . . . .19

Selected Publishers . . . . . . . . . . . . . . . . . . . . . . . . . . . . . . . . . . .20

# Advent

Introduction to the Season . . . . . . . . . . . . . . . . . . . . . . . . . . . . . .24

      Alternate Worship Texts . . . . . . . . . . . . . . . . . . . . . . . . . . . . .33

      Seasonal Rites . . . . . . . . . . . . . . . . . . . . . . . . . . . . . . . . . . . .34

First Sunday in Advent . . . . . . . . . . . . . . . . . . . . . . . . Dec 2, 2001 . .36

Second Sunday in Advent . . . . . . . . . . . . . . . . . . . . . . . . . . Dec 9 . .39

Third Sunday in Advent . . . . . . . . . . . . . . . . . . . . . . . . . Dec 16 . . . .43

Fourth Sunday in Advent . . . . . . . . . . . . . . . . . . . . . . . . Dec 23 . . . .46

# Christmas

Introduction to the Season . . . . . . . . . . . . . . . . . . . . . . . . . . . . . .50

      Alternate Worship Texts . . . . . . . . . . . . . . . . . . . . . . . . . . . . .57

      Seasonal Rites . . . . . . . . . . . . . . . . . . . . . . . . . . . . . . . . . . . .58

The Nativity of Our Lord/Christmas Eve . . . . . . . . . . . . . . Dec 24 . . . . .60

The Nativity of Our Lord/Christmas Dawn . . . . . . . . . . . .Dec 25 . . . . . .63

The Nativity of Our Lord/Christmas Day . . . . . . . . . . . . . .Dec 25 . . . . . .65

First Sunday after Christmas . . . . . . . . . . . . . . . . . . . . . .Dec 30 . . . . . .69

# Epiphany

Introduction to the Season . . . . . . . . . . . . . . . . . . . . . . . . . . . . . .74

      Alternate Worship Texts . . . . . . . . . . . . . . . . . . . . . . . . . . . . .82

      Seasonal Rites . . . . . . . . . . . . . . . . . . . . . . . . . . . . . . . . . . . .83

The Epiphany of Our Lord . . . . . . . . . . . . . . . . . . . . . . .Jan 6, 2002 . . . . . . . .86

The Baptism of Our Lord . . . . . . . . . . . . . . . . . . . . . . . . .Jan 13 . . . . . . .89

Second Sunday after the Epiphany . . . . . . . . . . . . . . . . .Jan 20 . . . . . . .93

Third Sunday after the Epiphany . . . . . . . . . . . . . . . . . . .Jan 27 . . . . . . .96

Fourth Sunday after the Epiphany . . . . . . . . . . . . . . . . . .Feb 3 . . . . . . . .99

The Transfiguration of Our Lord . . . . . . . . . . . . . . . . . . . .Feb 10 . . . . . . . .102

# Lent

Introduction to the Season . . . . . . . . . . . . . . . . . . . . . . . . . . . . . . . . . . . . . . . . . . .106

    Alternate Worship Texts . . . . . . . . . . . . . . . . . . . . . . . . . . . . . . . . . . . . . . . .114

    Seasonal Rites . . . . . . . . . . . . . . . . . . . . . . . . . . . . . . . . . . . . . . . . . . . . . . .115

Ash Wednesday . . . . . . . . . . . . . . . . . . . . . . . . . . . . . . . . . . . . . . . .Feb 13 . . . . . . . .118

First Sunday in Lent . . . . . . . . . . . . . . . . . . . . . . . . . . . . . . . . . . . . .Feb 17 . . . . . . . .121

Second Sunday in Lent . . . . . . . . . . . . . . . . . . . . . . . . . . . . . . . . . .Feb 24 . . . . . . . .125

Third Sunday in Lent . . . . . . . . . . . . . . . . . . . . . . . . . . . . . . . . . . . .Mar 3 . . . . . . . . 129

Fourth Sunday in Lent . . . . . . . . . . . . . . . . . . . . . . . . . . . . . . . . . . .Mar 10 . . . . . . . .132

Fifth Sunday in Lent . . . . . . . . . . . . . . . . . . . . . . . . . . . . . . . . . . . . .Mar 17 . . . . . . . 135

Sunday of the Passion/Palm Sunday . . . . . . . . . . . . . . . . . . . . . . .Mar 24 . . . . . . . .139

# The Three Days

Introduction to the Season . . . . . . . . . . . . . . . . . . . . . . . . . . . . . . . . . . . . . . . . . . .144

    Alternate Worship Texts . . . . . . . . . . . . . . . . . . . . . . . . . . . . . . . . . . . . . . . .153

    Seasonal Rites . . . . . . . . . . . . . . . . . . . . . . . . . . . . . . . . . . . . . . . . . . . . . . .154

Maundy Thursday . . . . . . . . . . . . . . . . . . . . . . . . . . . . . . . . . . . . . .Mar 28 . . . . . . . .155

Good Friday . . . . . . . . . . . . . . . . . . . . . . . . . . . . . . . . . . . . . . . . . . .Mar 29 . . . . . . . .158

The Resurrection of Our Lord/Vigil of Easter . . . . . . . . . . . . . . . . .Mar 30 . . . . . . . .161

The Resurrection of Our Lord/Easter Day . . . . . . . . . . . . . . . . . . .Mar 31 . . . . . . . .165

The Resurrection of Our Lord/Easter Evening . . . . . . . . . . . . . . . .Mar 31 . . . . . . . .168

# Easter

Introduction to the Season . . . . . . . . . . . . . . . . . . . . . . . . . . . . . . . . . . . . . . . . . . .172

    Alternate Worship Texts . . . . . . . . . . . . . . . . . . . . . . . . . . . . . . . . . . . . . . . .179

    Seasonal Rites . . . . . . . . . . . . . . . . . . . . . . . . . . . . . . . . . . . . . . . . . . . . . . .180

Second Sunday of Easter . . . . . . . . . . . . . . . . . . . . . . . . . . . . . . . . . .Apr 7 . . . . . . . .181

Third Sunday of Easter . . . . . . . . . . . . . . . . . . . . . . . . . . . . . . . . . . .Apr 14 . . . . . . . .184

Fourth Sunday of Easter . . . . . . . . . . . . . . . . . . . . . . . . . . . . . . . . . .Apr 21 . . . . . . . .187

Fifth Sunday of Easter . . . . . . . . . . . . . . . . . . . . . . . . . . . . . . . . . . . .Apr 28 . . . . . . . .190

Sixth Sunday of Easter . . . . . . . . . . . . . . . . . . . . . . . . . . . . . . . . . . .May 5 . . . . . . . .193

The Ascension of Our Lord . . . . . . . . . . . . . . . . . . . . . . . . . . . . . . . .May 9 . . . . . . . .196

Seventh Sunday of Easter . . . . . . . . . . . . . . . . . . . . . . . . . . . . . . . . .May 12 . . . . . . . .199

Vigil of Pentecost . . . . . . . . . . . . . . . . . . . . . . . . . . . . . . . . . . . . . . .May 18 . . . . . . . .202

The Day of Pentecost . . . . . . . . . . . . . . . . . . . . . . . . . . . . . . . . . . . .May 19 . . . . . . . .204

# Summer

Introduction to the Season . . . . . . . . . . . . . . . . . . . . . . . . . . . . . . . . . . . . . . . . .210
    Alternate Worship Texts . . . . . . . . . . . . . . . . . . . . . . . . . . . . . . . . . . . .218
The Holy Trinity . . . . . . . . . . . . . . . . . . . . . . . . . . . . . . . . .May 26 . . . . . . . . . .219
Second Sunday after Pentecost/Proper 4 . . . . . . . . . . . . . . . . . . . .June 2 . . . . . . . . .223
Third Sunday after Pentecost/Proper 5 . . . . . . . . . . . . . . . . . . . .June 9 . . . . . . . . .226
Fourth Sunday after Pentecost/Proper 6 . . . . . . . . . . . . . . . . . .June 16 . . . . . . . . .230
Fifth Sunday after Pentecost/Proper 7 . . . . . . . . . . . . . . . . . . .June 23 . . . . . . . . .233
Sixth Sunday after Pentecost/Proper 8 . . . . . . . . . . . . . . . . . . .June 30 . . . . . . . . .237
Seventh Sunday after Pentecost/Proper 9 . . . . . . . . . . . . . . . . .July 7 . . . . . . . . . .240
Eighth Sunday after Pentecost/Proper 10 . . . . . . . . . . . . . . . . .July 14 . . . . . . . . .244
Ninth Sunday after Pentecost/Proper 11 . . . . . . . . . . . . . . . . .July 21 . . . . . . . . .247
Tenth Sunday after Pentecost/Proper 12 . . . . . . . . . . . . . . . . .July 28 . . . . . . . . .250
Eleventh Sunday after Pentecost/Proper 13 . . . . . . . . . . . . . . .Aug 4 . . . . . . . . . .254
Twelfth Sunday after Pentecost/Proper 14 . . . . . . . . . . . . . . . .Aug 11 . . . . . . . . .257
Thirteenth Sunday after Pentecost/Proper 15 . . . . . . . . . . . . . .Aug 18 . . . . . . . . .260
Fourteenth Sunday after Pentecost/Proper 16 . . . . . . . . . . . . . .Aug 25 .Inside .263

# Autumn

Introduction to the Season . . . . . . . . . . . . . . . . . . . . . . . . . . . . . . . . . . . . . . . . . . . .268
    Alternate Worship Texts . . . . . . . . . . . . . . . . . . . . . . . . . . . . . . . . . . .275
    Seasonal Rites . . . . . . . . . . . . . . . . . . . . . . . . . . . . . . . . . . . . . . . . . .276
Fifteenth Sunday after Pentecost/Proper 17 . . . . . . . . . . . . . . . . . .Sep 1 . . . . . . . . . .279
Sixteenth Sunday after Pentecost/Proper 18 . . . . . . . . . . . . . . . . . .Sep 8 . . . . . . . . . .282
Seventeenth Sunday after Pentecost/Proper 19 . . . . . . . . . . . . . . .Sep 15 . . . . . . . . .285
Eighteenth Sunday after Pentecost/Proper 20 . . . . . . . . . . . . . . . .Sep 22 . . . . . . . . .289
St. Michael and All Angels . . . . . . . . . . . . . . . . . . . . . . . . . . . . . . .Sep 29 . . . . . . . . .292
Nineteenth Sunday after Pentecost/Proper 21 . . . . . . . . . . . . . . . .Sep 29 . . . . . . . . .295
Twentieth Sunday after Pentecost/Proper 22 . . . . . . . . . . . . . . . . .Oct 6 . . . . . . . . . .298
Twenty-first Sunday after Pentecost/Proper 23 . . . . . . . . . . . . . . .Oct 13 . . . . . . . . .302
Day of Thanksgiving (Canada) . . . . . . . . . . . . . . . . . . . . . . . . . . . .Oct 14 . . . . . . . . .304
Twenty-second Sunday after Pentecost/Proper 24 . . . . . . . . . . . .Oct 20 . . . . . . . . .305
Reformation Sunday . . . . . . . . . . . . . . . . . . . . . . . . . . . . . . . . . . . .Oct 27 . . . . . . . . .308
Twenty-third Sunday after Pentecost/Proper 25 . . . . . . . . . . . . . .Oct 27 . . . . . . . . .311

# November

Introduction to the Season . . . . . . . . . . . . . . . . . . . . . . . . . . . . . . . . . . . . . . . . . . . .316
    Alternate Worship Texts . . . . . . . . . . . . . . . . . . . . . . . . . . . . . . . . . . .323
    Seasonal Rites . . . . . . . . . . . . . . . . . . . . . . . . . . . . . . . . . . . . . . . . . .324
All Saints Sunday . . . . . . . . . . . . . . . . . . . . . . . . . . . . . . . . . . . . . .Nov 3 . . . . . . . . . .326
Twenty-fourth Sunday after Pentecost/Proper 26 . . . . . . . . . . . . .Nov 3 . . . . . . . . . .329
Twenty-fifth Sunday after Pentecost/Proper 27 . . . . . . . . . . . . . . .Nov 10 . . . . . . . . .332
Twenty-sixth Sunday after Pentecost/Proper 28 . . . . . . . . . . . . . .Nov 17 . . . . . . . . .336
Christ the King/Proper 29 . . . . . . . . . . . . . . . . . . . . . . . . . . . . . . .Nov 24 . . . . . . . . .339
Day of Thanksgiving (U.S.A.) . . . . . . . . . . . . . . . . . . . . . . . . . . . .Nov 28 . . . . . . . . .342

Bibliography . . . . . . . . . . . . . . . . . . . . . . . . . . . . . . . . . . . . . . . . . . . . . . . . . . . . . . . .346
Preparing for Worship . . . . . . . . . . . . . . . . . . . . . . . . . . . . . . . . . . . . . . .Inside back cover

# Introduction

Once again we have come full circle. In the coming

church year, as many churches begin another three-year round of

lectionary readings, *Sundays and Seasons* returns for its

seventh year. We are confident that you will find it to be a lively and valued companion in the task of preparing worship for the people of God.

## SUNDAYS

This is a resource for Sundays. For each Sunday and holy day, you will find several pages of resources, including reading citations and summaries, newly crafted prayers of the church, images for preaching, guidance in worship matters, and ideas for deepening children's participation in worship. Musical resources include suggestions for hymns and songs, choral and instrumental music, children's and handbell choirs, and praise ensembles.

## SEASONS

This is a resource for seasons. Effective worship planning is more than week-to-week and involves attention to the larger rhythms of the church's year. For each season you will find essays on seasonal images, preaching, and environment and art, as well as seasonal suggestions for the shape of worship, assembly song, and other music.

## NEW THIS YEAR

Each year *Sundays and Seasons* gathers and offers the contributions of a number of writers who serve as active practitioners of the worship arts in their various settings. We are delighted to share with you the gifts of those who have contributed new materials to this volume.

Reflections on the readings and seasonal images are valuable not only for preachers but for all who plan worship. Dennis Creswell offers another helpful gospel overview, this year based on the Gospel of Matthew. Evocative essays on seasonal images have been prepared by Ronald Roschke and Robert Buckley Farlee as well as by two former editors of this resource, Samuel Torvend

and Dennis Bushkofsky. Those who proclaim will be well served by the vivid seasonal and weekly preaching images provided by Catherine Malotky, Robert Smith, Beth Gaede, and Bruce Modahl.

Lynn Joyce Hunter has carefully woven the set of essays on seasonal environment and art, even inviting us into her conversations with some of the country's leading liturgical artists.

Practical worship matters are ably addressed by Foy Christopherson, Robert Hofstad, and Theodore Asta. Susan Briehl has brought fresh ideas to the section "Let the Children Come." Prayers for each Sunday and holy day have been prepared and edited by Mark Strobel, Rhoda Schuler, Karen Ball, and Mark Briehl.

An experienced group of musicians have provided new lists of seasonal and daily music recommendations: Thomas Pavlechko and Carole Weatherby (choral), Kathy Donlan Tunseth (children's choirs), Andrew Heller (keyboard/instrumental), Randy Knutson (handbell), and Michael Fenton and Lynn Panosh (praise ensemble). Kevin Anderson has drawn a musical thread through the year with assembly song essays that make imaginative links among seasonal emphases, ritual action, and the people's song. The introductory essay "New Songs, Old Patterns," adapted from the full music edition of *Worship & Praise*, offers help to those seeking to include materials from various genres of popular Christian song in their worship.

## RELATED RESOURCES

*Sundays and Seasons* continues its close association with other Augsburg Fortress lectionary-based resources. *Words for Worship* 2002 contains electronic files of sections within this volume that are intended for group use, in addition to complete lectionary readings and psalms. *Worship Planning Calendar* has been redesigned for 2002 to make it even more closely linked as a workbook counterpart to *Sundays and Seasons.* Users of Life Together lectionary-based curriculum resources will find many supportive connections in this volume.

Tanja Butler's wonderful art throughout this volume is available for use by congregations that purchase the CD-ROM *Icon: Visual Images for Every Sunday,* a three-year set of images for use in designing worship folders and other local materials. Selected images from this series are also featured in *Calendar of Word and Season 2002: Liturgical Wall Calendar.*

The vast majority of hymns referenced in *Sundays and Seasons* from various published collections are available in *Hymns for Worship,* a CD-ROM with text files and music graphics for over 1,400 hymns. This electronic resource also includes sound reference files, a powerful search engine, and a copyright management tool. *Hymns for Worship* will ease selection of assembly song as well as worship folder preparation.

## A WORK IN PROGRESS

*Sundays and Seasons* can never be the last word on worship planning. It is a work in progress that continues to evolve from year to year, and we are grateful for the feedback from users, which contributes to its ongoing improvement. We offer it as a collection of first words: images, ideas, and suggestions that we hope will encourage and support worship leaders and assemblies as you go about the exciting task of preparing worship in your various contexts for the year ahead.

—Martin A. Seltz, general editor

# The Gospel *of* Matthew

The Gospel of Matthew holds a special place in the church's preaching. The early Christian writer Papias of Hierapolis, who wrote in the middle of the second century after Christ,

believed Matthew was the first of the four gospels written and that it was originally written in Aramaic and later translated into Greek. The belief that it was the earliest gospel explains why it is placed first in the New Testament canon.

In several ways, Matthew has been the preferred gospel in the life of the church. For example, in the one-year lectionary, which was in use for many years in the Lutheran tradition and other traditions that used a lectionary (see, for example, *Service Book and Hymnal*, pp. 75–106), the gospel readings for twenty-two of the Sundays and major festivals are from Matthew, with the remainder divided between the other three gospels. Half of the gospel readings for the lesser festivals listed in the Revised Common Lectionary are from the Gospel of Matthew. This preference for Matthew's gospel has caused some to call it "the church's gospel."

## UNIQUE ASPECTS OF MATTHEW'S GOSPEL

Among the gospels, Matthew is unique in many ways. Only in Matthew do we find the Sermon on the Mount (chapters 5–7). The form of the Lord's Prayer that is most commonly used in the worship of the church is found only in Matthew (6:9-13), although another form of the prayer is included in Luke (11:2-4). In the stories about the birth of Jesus, several incidents—the appearance of the angel to Joseph in a dream (1:20-25), the story of the magi, the response of Herod, the holy family's flight into Egypt, and the slaughter of the innocents (2:1-18)—are recorded only in Matthew. In the accounts of Jesus' crucifixion and resurrection, only Matthew reports the opening of the tombs of the saints and their appearance in Jerusalem (27:52-53), Pilate's decision to place a guard at the tomb in order to prevent the disciples from stealing Jesus' body (27:62-66), and the false story concocted by the chief priests that the disciples came and stole Jesus' body while the guards were asleep (28:11-15). Matthew is also the only gospel that records the story of the great judgment (25:31-46) and the great commission of Jesus to his disciples (28:18-20), though Luke does record that Jesus commanded the disciples that "repentance and forgiveness of sins is to be proclaimed in his name to all nations, beginning from Jerusalem" (Luke 24:47).

Matthew gives us a genealogy different from Luke's, one that traces Jesus' lineage patrilineally, through Joseph back to Abraham, emphasizing the regularity of God's great acts since the call of Abraham: "So all the generations from Abraham to David are *fourteen generations*; and from David to the deportation to Babylon, *fourteen generations*; and from the deportation to Babylon to the Messiah, *fourteen generations*" (1:17, emphases added). The implication seems to be that God is methodical and does some great thing every fourteen generations. Luke traces the family of Jesus all the way back to "Adam, son of God" (3:37). Matthew, however, is content to show that Jesus was from the line of Abraham, through Isaac, Jacob, and Judah, and finally through David. His emphasis seems to be on Jesus as the fulfillment of the promises God made to Abraham and David.

In his genealogy of Jesus, Matthew also calls attention to four women among the ancestors of Jesus: Tamar, the widow of Judah's son, who had to trick Judah into doing what he was bound by law to do as her father-in-law—that is, to ensure that her husband would have an heir (1:3); Rahab, the prostitute in Jericho who hid the Israelite spies from the authorities and was rewarded by being spared when the city fell (v. 5); Ruth, the Moabite, who adopted her mother-in-law's country and God, and who became the grandmother of David (v. 5); and the wife of Uriah—Bathsheba—who became David's wife and Solomon's mother (v. 6). We might wonder what Matthew is up to when he mentions these four women. Why were *these* women named and not Sarah, Rebekah, Leah, or any number of others who might be considered more worthy of remembrance?

In a commentary on Matthew, Jack Dean Kingsbury points out another of Matthew's unique characteristics: Matthew alone alerts readers when actions and events fulfill the Hebrew scriptures. At 1:22-23; 2:15; 2:17-18; 2:23; 4:14-16; 8:17; 12:17-21; 13:14-15; 13:35; 21:4-5; and 27:9-10, we read some version of the words, "This took place to fulfill what had been spoken through [or, 'written by'] the prophet…." Matthew lets his hearers know that Jesus is not some new idea thought up by the God of Israel, but is, in fact, the very thing God has been working toward through all of history since choosing Abraham to be the ancestor of God's special people.

Because, as Kingsbury contends, Matthew was written for a Jewish Christian community, it was important for him to point out Jesus' continuity with what God had done in the past. Thus Mary's virginity, the place where Jesus was born, the flight into Egypt and the slaughter of the innocents, the places where Jesus grew up and began his ministry, Jesus' healing ministry, the fact that many could not understand his teaching, his speaking in parables, his rejection of the teaching of the Pharisees and scribes, his triumphal entry into Jerusalem, the adoration of Jesus by the children in the temple, the desertion of the disciples at the time of Jesus' arrest, and the price for his betrayal are all presented by Matthew as ways in which Jesus fulfills the promises of the ancient writings. These events show the continuity between what God was doing with the people of Israel in the past and what God is now doing for all people through Jesus. Jesus is the Messiah, the fulfillment of God's purpose for God's people, Israel, and the one who will carry God's purpose even further, so that all people can have a share in the kingdom of God.

## THE MATTHEAN PERICOPES IN YEAR A

The gospel readings for year A give us a picture of Jesus and his teachings, as observed and recorded by Matthew. During the festival half of the church year, the texts for year A describe the life of Jesus. Three of the four Sundays in Advent use Matthean texts, as do the first Sunday after Christmas and the feast of the Epiphany, which falls on a Sunday this year. Four of the five Sundays of the Epiphany season also use Matthean texts, including the Baptism and the Transfiguration of Our Lord. Together with the accounts of Jesus' triumphal entry into

Jerusalem and the passion account read on Passion Sunday, the gospel readings from Matthew during this half of the year highlight the major events of Jesus' life. Jesus' birth, the visit of the magi, the flight into Egypt, his baptism and the beginnings of his ministry, the transfiguration, the last supper, the agony of Gethsemane, his crucifixion and resurrection are all recounted in these texts.

The second half of the church year, beginning with Holy Trinity, is given over to the teachings of Jesus as recorded in Matthew's gospel. On the last Sundays in July, there is an opportunity to preach three weeks in a row on the parables in Matthew 13 and to speak about the different pictures of the kingdom of God that Jesus paints. The gospels for the Pentecost season are arranged in a continuous reading from Matthew 7 on the second Sunday after Pentecost through Matthew 25 on Christ the King. In November, the gospel readings for the last three Sundays of the church year, ending with Christ the King, focus on Jesus' return.

The pattern of continuous reading gives the preacher an opportunity to spend time immersed in the Gospel of Matthew and in conversation with other interpreters of Matthew, either in person or through written commentaries on these texts. The flow of the gospel is evident to those who are listening every Sunday, and that flow can be used each week to build on the previous week's sermon.

## THEMES IN MATTHEW'S GOSPEL

Each of the titles ("Christ/Messiah," "Son of God," "Son of Man," "Lord," "Son of David") given to Jesus in this gospel has significance. Looking at several texts that use the same title provides clues about what each of these titles means. "Christ/Messiah" points to the one who fulfills the scriptural prophecies. "Son of Man" evokes the book of Daniel's apocalyptic judge, who will separate the righteous from the unrighteous at the end of time. "Son of David" carries with it the history of the promise that a descendent of David will rule over God's people.

"Lord" has behind it the whole weight of the Hebrew tradition and is the circumlocution for the Hebrew *YHWH* in the Greek version of the Old Testament. To speak of Jesus as Lord is to identify him with the God who has been revealed to the people of Israel in scripture. Speaking of him as Lord also puts Jesus in con-

9

tention with the emperor, because the statement "Caesar is Lord" was used to recognize the emperor's divinity. The Jewish people were exempted in the first century from making this statement, but when the Christian community was no longer considered a Jewish sect, as was the case by the time Matthew was written, Christians lost this exemption. To say "Jesus is Lord," therefore, was an act of treason.

By far the most important title given to Jesus in Matthew is "Son of God." This title is revealed at his baptism (3:17) as he begins his ministry and is repeated at the transfiguration (17:5) as he begins his passion. It is also spoken by the centurion at the cross (27:54). At these central moments in the life and death of Jesus, he is called "Son of God." Those who interpret this gospel would do well to reflect on what Matthew means when he says that Jesus is the Son of God.

One theme that many have pointed out in the Gospel of Matthew is Jesus as the second Moses. This parallel is especially suggested by the Sermon on the Mount (5–7), when Jesus goes up the mountain and teaches the disciples what seems to be a new law. In these chapters, he takes some of the Ten Commandments and tells the disciples that the way that they have been kept does not go far enough. He amplifies them to prohibit not only the *acts*, but also the *intentions of the heart* that lead to the prohibited acts. One is guilty of breaking the commandment against murder if one is angry with one's sister or brother (5:21-26). One is guilty of breaking the commandment against adultery if one has lust in one's heart (5:27-28). In this way, Jesus increases the reach of the law, so that no one can claim to be righteous by his or her own doing. Jesus boldly summarizes his teachings in the last verse of chapter 5: "Be perfect, therefore, as your heavenly Father is perfect" (5:48).

We might be inclined to view Jesus' reinterpretation of the Mosaic Law as a blueprint for our lives. Jesus is not giving us a stricter law to keep, however. Rather, he is revealing the depth of our sin, how tightly sin has a hold on us. He reveals that not only our outward acts point out that we are not living up to God's expectations for us, but our inward thoughts and desires condemn us as well. When preaching on these texts it is important to remember that they are law, not gospel. They are not intended to provide a way for us to save ourselves, but offer a mirror, held up by our Savior, to reveal the true nature of our lives. It is according to our sinful nature that we try to earn God's favor by being good. Our redeemed nature leads us to trust that God forgives all our sins and makes it possible for us to live in such a way, as these words point out, that we do not harm our neighbor, but help our neighbor in every time of need. If we remember that the one who spoke these words was also the one who died for us because we cannot live up to them, we will have a better grasp of what Jesus intended when he spoke them.

Spending a year with the Gospel of Matthew is a challenge. As the life and teaching of Jesus unfold in this gospel, we are invited to ask just who this Jesus is. As we ask that question and seek answers in the gospel itself, we are drawn closer to Christ and to what Christ has done for us. Matthew, like all of the gospels, has at its heart the desire to bring us to faith in Jesus.

## FOR FURTHER READING

Hagner, Donald. *Word Biblical Commentary Series* (Dallas: Word Books, 1993, 1995).

Kingsbury, Jack Dean. *Matthew*, in Proclamation Commentaries, Gerhard Krodel, ed. (Philadelphia: Fortress Press, 1986).

Kingsbury, Jack Dean. *Matthew as Story*, 2d ed. (Philadelphia: Fortress Press, 1988).

Luz, Ulrich. *The Theology of the Gospel of Matthew* (Cambridge: Cambridge University Press, 1995).

Powell, Mark Allan. *God with Us: A Pastoral Theology of Matthew's Gospel* (Minneapolis: Fortress Press, 1995).

Senior, Donald. *What Are They Saying about Matthew?*, 2d ed. (New York: Paulist Press, 1996).

# New Songs, Old Patterns

A vast body of worship songs in musical styles

drawn from popular culture has emerged in the last several decades.

"Contemporary" is a shorthand term often applied

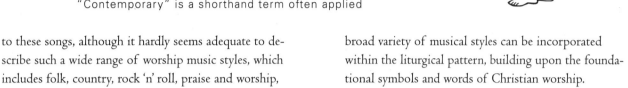

to these songs, although it hardly seems adequate to describe such a wide range of worship music styles, which includes folk, country, rock 'n' roll, praise and worship, alternative rock, guitar-based liturgical songs, older standards arranged in pop style, and more.

The sampling of these songs and musical styles in such publications as *Worship & Praise* and *With One Voice* represents some of the most widely used and most broadly useful of this literature. Even though congregations may readily use songs from either of these resources in existing worship patterns (for example, any of the orders for Holy Communion provided in *Lutheran Book of Worship* or *With One Voice*), this discussion is intended especially for pastors, musicians, and other worship leaders as they attempt to discover ways to use contemporary song resources for worship in Christian assemblies.

Both *With One Voice* and *Worship & Praise* have been developed in the context of two deep commitments: a commitment to word and sacrament as the central framework for worship, and a commitment to rich diversity in the ways that the people of God express themselves in worship and song. It is possible to hold these two commitments in a rich and complex harmony. How can the repertoire of contemporary song be used most effectively within the weekly gathering of Christians around word and sacrament?

## THE PATTERN FOR WORSHIP EMBRACES MANY STYLES

Many of the songs, from the *Worship & Praise* collection in particular, originate from theological traditions in which gatherings for worship may not be focused on word and sacrament within the context of the church's ancient and ecumenical pattern. The words and melodies of these songs can find a home, however, in other gatherings that do regularly follow such a pattern. A rich,

broad variety of musical styles can be incorporated within the liturgical pattern, building upon the foundational symbols and words of Christian worship.

What are the benefits of a consistent worship pattern that allows for rich variation?

1) By following a pattern of word and sacrament held in common by a majority of Christians and developed over the centuries, we are linked to the church around the world and throughout history.

2) We retell the Christian story over and over again, not only through the reading of scriptures, preaching, and singing, but through the recurring actions and words of the Christian assembly itself.

3) An established framework provides a base of familiarity for worshipers that enables them to be more receptive to new songs, seasonal variations, and challenging presentations of the word.

4) A practical consideration: because worship follows a structured pattern, it is not necessary to begin anew each week. With the time saved, elements that make up the pattern can be enriched.

## THE PATTERN FOR SUNDAY

The foundational pattern for Christian worship begins with Sunday, the primary day on which Christians gather. On this day of Jesus' resurrection and his appearance to the disciples, the people of God gather to hear the word, to pray for those in need, to offer thanks to God for the gift of salvation, to receive the bread of life and the cup of blessing, and to be renewed for the daily witness of faith, hope, and love.

A common fourfold structure makes up this ecumenical pattern: gathering, word, meal, and sending. Each section of the structure allows for considerable variety. The following suggestions are offered to help worship planners use the resources of *Worship & Praise* and *With One Voice* within this pattern.

11

GATHERING

Amid a culture rich with sound and activity, many worshiping communities gather in intentional and reflective silence. Other Christian assemblies embrace a more participatory gathering, which includes a time of singing using medleys or song sets, in any number of musical styles. In selecting appropriate music, it is helpful to observe how the words of the songs work together, in addition to musical relationships such as meter and key.

After the people have assembled with singing, silence, and/or instrumental music, the elements of the gathering pattern for Sunday might include an entrance song, a biblical greeting ("The grace of our Lord Jesus Christ…"), a song of petition for God's mercy, a hymn of praise ("Glory to God" and "This is the feast"), and the prayer of the day.

This pattern is easily enriched with contemporary song. For a song of petition the following might be considered:

Kyrie    WOV 601, 602, 604
Señor, ten piedad    WOV 605
Kyrie eleison    W&P 81

The hymn of praise is traditionally a song that glorifies God for the saving work of Christ. Songs that reflect this emphasis are not difficult to find. The following might be considered:

Glory and praise to our God    W&P 43
Glory to God/You alone are the Holy    W&P 45
Lift up your heads    W&P 88
The trumpets sound, the angels sing    W&P 139
We bow down    W&P 149
This is the feast of victory    W&P 142
We will glorify    W&P 154
Glory to God    WOV 606, 607
This is the feast of victory    WOV 608
Glory to God, we give you thanks    WOV 787
Alabaré    WOV 791

The prayer of the day concludes the gathering section, often illustrating a theme of the day or season and helping to focus the congregation on hearing the word of God that follows.

WORD

The proclamation of the word within the Sunday worship pattern has a responsive shape inherited from our ancestors in faith among the Hebrew people. God's word is proclaimed to us, and we respond in song. This natural rhythm still works today. The ecumenical order of this section includes a first reading (usually from the Hebrew scriptures), a psalm, a second reading (usually from the New Testament letters), a gospel acclamation, a reading from the gospels, a sermon, a hymn of the day, a creed, and the prayers.

Contemporary worship songs may be used for sung responses to the word. Many settings of psalms and psalm verses are included in *With One Voice* and *Worship & Praise*; see the scriptural indexes of each volume for listings. For the gospel acclamation, a song that welcomes Christ who is present in the proclamation of the gospel, the following might be considered:

Alleluia    W&P 6
Alleluia. Lord, to whom shall we go?    W&P 7
Praise to you, O Christ, our Savior    W&P 118, WOV 614
What a mighty Word God gives    W&P 155
Hallelujah/Heleluyan    WOV 609
Alleluia    WOV 610
Halle, halle, hallelujah    WOV 612
Celtic Alleluia    WOV 613
Return to the Lord    WOV 615

Scripture songs, such as "Good soil" (W&P 52, WOV 713), "Listen, God is calling" (WOV 712), "Open your ears, O faithful people" (WOV 715), and "For God so loved" (W&P 39), may also be incorporated into the rhythm of speaking and singing the word.

The hymn of the day is an important element in the Lutheran tradition of worship. This hymn or song usually follows the sermon and stands beside the reading of scripture and preaching as a proclamation or response to the word of God. Several possibilities for a hymn of the day are listed in *Sundays and Seasons*. A wide range of other hymns and songs for various other places in the liturgy are provided for each week as well.

MEAL

Following the word and prayers, the gathered community is invited to give thanks to God and to partake of the bread of life and cup of blessing. Elements of the eucharistic meal pattern include a greeting of peace, the gathering and presentation of gifts, a prayer of thanksgiving, the Lord's Prayer, the communion of the people, and a song and prayer after the communion. Songs from this collection can be used wherever singing is part of the pattern.

Music may accompany the gathering of money and other gifts, and is especially appropriate for the presentation of the gifts at the table. Songs that give thanks for God's gifts to us, and that refer to the dedication of our selves, our time, and our possessions to God are most helpful. The following might be considered:

 Create in me a clean heart W&P 34, 35; WOV 732

 We are an offering W&P 146

 We bring the sacrifice of praise W&P 150

 What have we to offer? W&P 156

 As the grains of wheat WOV 705

 Come to us, creative Spirit WOV 758

 Accept, O Lord, the gifts we bring WOV 759

 For the fruit of all creation WOV 760

 Now we offer WOV 761

Many contemporary settings of "Holy, holy, holy Lord" (Sanctus) and "Lamb of God" (Agnus Dei) are available for use with the prayer of thanksgiving. A few possibilities are:

 Holy, holy, holy Lord W&P 63, 64; WOV 616a, 617a,
  618a, 619a

 Lamb of God W&P 82, 83; WOV 621, 622

 Jesus, Lamb of God W&P 76

Singing is natural as people come to share the communion. Songs with easily remembered refrains are espe-

cially useful, allowing worshipers to sing without books or papers as they come to receive the bread and cup. Several possibilities in both books are listed in the topical indexes under "Holy Communion."

After all have communed, a song of thanksgiving for God's gifts and a brief prayer may conclude the meal. If a song is not to be sung at the conclusion of the service, a song here could send worshipers from the table into the world. The following might be considered:

 Give thanks W&P 41

 Go in peace and serve the Lord W&P 46

 Praise to you, O God of mercy W&P 119

 The trees of the field W&P 138

 We are called W&P 147

 Thankful hearts and voices raise WOV 23

 Now, Lord, you let your servant go in peace
  WOV 624, 625

 Hallelujah! We sing your praises WOV 722

 Let us talents and tongues employ WOV 754

 Thine the amen, thine the praise WOV 801

SENDING

Words of dismissal such as "Go in peace. Serve the Lord" are perhaps best spoken after any sending song. After receiving God's blessing and these words of sending, the assembly is sent out to participate in God's mission to the world.

## FOR FURTHER READING

*Gathered and Sent: An Introduction to Worship.* Participant book by Karen Bockelman. Leader guide by Roger Prehn. Minneapolis: Augsburg Fortress, 1999. For inquirers and general adult instruction on the basic structure and meaning of worship.

Adapted from "Using Worship & Praise" in *Worship & Praise* (Minneapolis: Augsburg Fortress, 1999), and "Holy Communion: All Times and Places, Setting 6" in *With One Voice* (Minneapolis: Augsburg Fortress, 1995).

13

# Worship Planning Checklist

### ADVENT

- Purchase materials needed for the Advent wreath (four candles and enough greens to cover the wreath). Perhaps more than one wreath will be desired for your congregation if Sunday school students and other groups gather for worship during the season in locations other than the sanctuary.
- Arrange for the Advent wreath to be set up one or two days before the first Sunday in Advent (December 2 this year).

### CHRISTMAS

- Arrange for purchase or donation of a Christmas tree.
- Locate any decorations that are in storage from previous years for the Christmas tree, the crèche, the chancel, and other interior or exterior areas. Repair or replace decorations as needed.
- Decide on a date and time for Christmas decorating, and solicit volunteer help.
- Prepare extra communion elements and communionware that may be needed for additional worshipers at Christmas services.
- Prepare a sign-up list for those who wish to sponsor additional flowers or poinsettia plants at Christmas.
- Plan for removal of Christmas decorations following the twelve days. Decide whether festive decorations will remain in place for Epiphany, which falls on a Sunday, or whether you will remove them beforehand.
- If handheld candles are used by worshipers on Christmas Eve, determine how many candles and holders can be used from previous seasons and how many new candles and holders will be needed.
- Order special bulletin covers if needed for services on Christmas Eve or Christmas Day.

### EPIPHANY

- Determine what (if any) Epiphany decorations are needed.
- If incense is to be used for a service on the festival of the Epiphany, purchase a small quantity of it (along with self-lighting charcoal).

- If the Baptism of Our Lord (January 13) is to be observed as a baptismal festival, publicize the festival through congregational newsletters and bulletins; arrange for baptismal preparation sessions with parents, sponsors, and candidates; and when the day arrives set out the following:
  - Towel (baptismal napkin) for each person baptized
  - Baptismal candle for each person baptized
  - Shell (if used)
  - Oil for anointing (also a lemon wedge and a towel for removing oil from the presiding minister's hands)
  - Baptismal garment for each person baptized (if used)
  - Fresh water in a ewer (pitcher) or the font

### LENT

- If ashes are used on Ash Wednesday, arrange for someone (perhaps one or two altar guild members) to burn palms from the previous Passion Sunday. (Ask members to bring in their own from home if they also saved them.) Or contact a church supply store for a supply of ashes. (A small quantity of ashes mixed with a small amount of olive oil will go a long way.)
- Determine whether any Lenten decorations other than Lenten paraments are to be used.
- If crosses or images are draped in purple during the Lenten season, recruit volunteers to do this between the Transfiguration of Our Lord (February 10) and Ash Wednesday (February 13).
- Order enough palm branches to distribute to worshipers on Passion Sunday. (Additional palm branches or plants may be used as decorations that day.) If the long individual palm fronds are used, they will need to be separated ahead of time. Make sure that they are fresh.

- Make sure worshipers know where to gather for a procession with palms liturgy. Prepare signs to direct them. Determine how those with physical disabilities will participate in the procession or be seated ahead of time.
- Reserve leftover palm branches to be burned for ashes next Ash Wednesday.
- Order worship participation leaflets if used for the Ash Wednesday liturgy or Passion Sunday processional liturgy.
- Order additional bulletin covers if needed for any special Lenten services (especially midweek liturgies).

## THE THREE DAYS

- Schedule special rehearsals for the liturgies on these days. The liturgies in this week are unique, so all worship leaders, even those who have been involved in previous years, need to prepare for their roles.
- Be sure that altar guild members are well equipped and informed about their tasks for these busy days.
- Locate one or more basin and pitcher sets for the Maundy Thursday liturgy. Towels are also needed for drying the feet of participants.
- Determine how participants will be recruited for the footwashing. Even if all in the congregation are invited, several people should be specifically prepared to participate.
- If the altar and the rest of the chancel is to be stripped on Maundy Thursday, recruit helpers (sacristans/altar guild members, even children) for this task.
- If you ring bells to announce services or chimes to mark times of the day, consider silencing them from the beginning of the Maundy Thursday liturgy until the hymn of praise at the Easter Vigil (or the first celebration of Easter).
- Keeping in mind that all of the liturgies of the Three Days are considered to be as one, do not plan a procession of worship leaders for Good Friday. All worship leaders simply find their own way to their respective places before the service.
- If a rite of procession and veneration of the cross is to be used on Good Friday, find or construct a rough-hewn cross, and determine how it will be placed in the chancel ahead of time or carried in procession.

- Prepare to thoroughly clean the worship space sometime between the Maundy Thursday liturgy and the Easter Vigil.
- If handheld candles are to be used by worshipers at an Easter Vigil, determine how many candles and holders can be used from previous seasons, and how many new candles and holders will need to be purchased.
- Well before the Easter Vigil, purchase a paschal candle (or arrange to make one) that will fit your congregation's stand. When the candle is received or finished, check to be sure it fits the stand snugly yet without being forced into place.
- Prepare materials needed to start a fire at the beginning of the Easter Vigil (kindling, wood, brazier, matches). Also, recruit someone to start and extinguish the fire properly.
- Prior to the Easter Vigil, place the paschal candle stand in the chancel for use throughout the fifty days of Easter.
- Make sure worshipers know where to gather for the service of light at the Easter Vigil. If you plan to gather outside, be sure to make backup plans in case you have inclement weather.
- Decide how light will be provided so assisting ministers and lectors can see to read during the Easter Vigil service. Determine what level of light is needed so all members of the congregation can participate during this liturgy. Practice setting lighting levels (at night) with the person who will be responsible for this during the vigil.
- Plan how the readings of the Easter Vigil will be proclaimed. Consider having a different person proclaim each of the readings to enliven the readings for the assembly.
- Prepare extra communion elements and communionware that may be needed for additional worshipers at Holy Week and Easter services.
- Order worship participation leaflets if used for the Maundy Thursday, Good Friday, or Easter Vigil liturgies.
- Order bulletin covers if needed for any Holy Week liturgies.
- It is helpful to prepare printed materials for worship leaders for the Three Days. Consider placing all the texts and musical resources needed by worship lead-

15

ers into three-ring binders (half-inch binders purchased at office supply stores work well). Highlight speaking parts and instructions for each worship leader in individual copies.

- If the Easter Vigil (or Easter Sunday) is to be observed as a baptismal festival, publicize the festival through congregational newsletters and bulletins; arrange for baptismal preparation sessions with parents, sponsors, and candidates; and when the day arrives set out the following:
  - Towel (baptismal napkin) for each person baptized
  - Baptismal candle for each person baptized
  - Shell (if used)
  - Oil for anointing (also a lemon wedge and a towel for removing oil from the presiding minister's hands)
  - Baptismal garment for each person baptized (if used)
  - Fresh water in a ewer (pitcher) or the font
  - Evergreen branches for sprinkling
- Prepare a sign-up list for people who wish to sponsor Easter lilies or other flowers for Easter Day (and throughout the season of Easter).
- Order extra bulletin covers for additional worshipers on Easter Day.

## EASTER

- Determine whether special flowers are to be used on Pentecost. (Some churches order red geraniums to be placed around the church grounds or given away following Pentecost services.)
- If Pentecost is to be observed as a baptismal festival, publicize the festival through congregational newsletters and bulletins; arrange for baptismal preparation sessions with parents, sponsors, and candidates; and when the day arrives set out the following:
  - Towel (baptismal napkin) for each person baptized
  - Baptismal candle for each person baptized
  - Shell (if used)
  - Oil for anointing (also a lemon wedge and a towel for removing oil from the presiding minister's hands)
  - Baptismal garment for each person baptized (if used)
  - Fresh water in a ewer (pitcher) or the font

- On Pentecost, seven votive candles in red glass holders may be lit and placed on or near the altar to recall the gifts of the Spirit.

## SUMMER

- If the worship schedule changes, notify local newspapers and change listings on exterior signs and church answering machines.
- Consider ways to make worshipers cooler during warm weather.
- If the congregation worships outside one or more times during the summer, decide how worshipers will know where to gather and how they will be seated.

## AUTUMN

- For worship schedule changes, notify local newspapers and change listings on exterior signs and church answering machines.
- If a harvest festival is scheduled, determine what (if any) additional decorations are to be used and who is to do the decorating.
- If one or more food collections are to be received, notify the congregation about them in advance, and arrange to deliver food to the appropriate agency within a day or two after the collection.

## NOVEMBER

- Provide a book of remembrance or another way to collect the names of those who have died and who are to be remembered in prayers this month (or only on All Saints Sunday).
- If All Saints is to be observed as a baptismal festival, publicize the festival through congregational newsletters and bulletins; arrange for baptismal preparation sessions with parents, sponsors, and candidates; and when the day arrives set out the following:
  - Towel (baptismal napkin) for each person baptized
  - Baptismal candle for each person baptized
  - Shell (if used)
  - Oil for anointing (also a lemon wedge and a towel for removing oil from the presiding minister's hands)
  - Baptismal garment for each person baptized (if used)
  - Fresh water in a ewer (pitcher) or the font

16

# Key *to* Music Publishers

| | | | | | | | |
|---|---|---|---|---|---|---|---|
| ABI | Abingdon | FLA | Flammer (Shawnee) | MSM | MorningStar Music |
| AFP | Augsburg Fortress | GAL | Galaxy | NOV | Novello (Shawnee) |
| AG | Agape (Hope) | GIA | GIA Publications | NPM | National Association of |
| AGEHR | AGEHR Inc. | GS | GlorySound | | Pastoral Musicians |
| ALF | Alfred | Gsch | G. Schirmer | OCP | Oregon Catholic Press |
| AMC | Arista | HAL | Hal Leonard: G. Schirmer | OXF | Oxford University Press |
| AMSI | AMSI | HIN | Hinshaw | PAR | Paraclete |
| AUR | Aurole | HOP | Hope | PET | Peters |
| BBL | Broude Brothers | HWG | H.W. Gray (Warner) | PLY | Plymouth |
| BEC | Beckenhorst | INT | Integrity (Word) | PRE | Presser |
| BEL | Belwin (Warner) | JEF | Jeffers | PVN | Pavane (Intrada) |
| BNT | Brentwood–Benson Music | KIR | Kirkland House | RME | Randall M. Egan |
| B&H | Boosey & Hawkes | KJO | Kjos | SEL | Selah |
| BRN | Bourne | LAK | Lake State | SGM | Stained Glass Music |
| CEL | Celebration Press | LAW | Lawson-Gould Publishing | SHW | Shawnee |
| CFI | Carl Fischer | LB | Lutheran Brotherhood | SMP | Sacred Music Press (Lorenz) |
| CFP | C.F. Peters | LED | Leduc | VIV | Vivace |
| CG | Choristers Guild (Lorenz) | LEM | Lemoine (Presser) | WAL | Walton |
| CHA | Chantry (Augsburg Fortress) | LIL | Lillenas (Royal Marketing) | WAR | Warner (Plymouth) |
| CHE | Chester | LOH | Live Oak | WJK | Westminster John Knox |
| CPH | Concordia | LOR | Lorenz | WLP | World Library |
| DUR | Durand (Presser) | MAR | Maranatha | WRD | Word Music |
| ECS | E.C. Schirmer | MAY | Mayhew | | |
| FB | Fred Bock Music Co. | MCF | McAfee Music Corp. (Warner) | | |

17

# Music *for* Worship Key

| | | | | | | | |
|---|---|---|---|---|---|---|---|
| acc | accompaniment | hc | handchimes | qrt | quartet |
| bar | baritone | hp | harp | rec | recorder |
| bng | bongos | hpd | harpsichord | sax | saxophone |
| bsn | bassoon | hrn | horn | sop | soprano |
| cant | cantor | inst | instrument | str | strings |
| ch | chimes | kybd | keyboard | synth | synthesizer |
| cl | clarinet | M | medium | tamb | tambourine |
| cong | congregation | MH | medium high | tba | tuba |
| cont | continuo | ML | medium low | tbn | trombone |
| cym | cymbal | mxd | mixed | timp | timpani |
| DB | double or string bass | narr | narrator | trbl | treble |
| dbl | double | ob | oboe | tri | triangle |
| desc | descant | oct | octave | tpt | trumpet |
| div | divisi | opt | optional | U | unison |
| drm | drum | orch | orchestra | vc | violoncello |
| eng hrn | English horn | org | organ | vcs | voices |
| fc | finger cymbals | perc | percussion | vla | viola |
| fl | flute | picc | piccolo | vln | violin |
| glock | glockenspiel | pno | piano | ww | woodwind |
| gtr | guitar | pt | part | xyl | xylophone |
| hb | handbells | qnt | quintet | | |

# Key *to* Hymn *and* Psalm Collections

ASF — *A Singing Faith: The hymns of Jane Parker Huber.* Louisville: Westminster/John Knox Press, 1987.

ASG — *As Sunshine to a Garden: Hymns and Songs of Rusty Edwards.* Mpls: Augsburg Fortress, 1999.

BAS — *Bach for All Seasons Choirbook.* Mpls: Augsburg Fortress, 1999.

BC — *Borning Cry: Worship for a New Generation.* Waverly, IA: New Generation Publishers, 1992.

BL — *Bread of Life: Mass and Songs for the Assembly.* Mpls: Augsburg Fortress, 2000.

BH — *Baptist Hymnal.* (Southern Baptist Convention). Nashville, TN: Convention Press, 1991.

DH — *Dancing at the Harvest: Songs of Ray Makeever.* Mpls: Augsburg Fortress, 1997.

GC — *Gather Comprehensive.* Chicago: GIA Publications, 1994.

GS2 — *Global Songs 2: Bread for the Journey.* Mpls: Augsburg Fortress, 1997.

H82 — *The Hymnal 1982* (Episcopal). New York: The Church Pension Fund, 1985.

HFW — *Hymns for Worship.* Mpls: Augsburg Fortress, 2001.

ISH — *In Search of Hope & Grace: The Hymns of Sylvia G. Dunstan.* Chicago: GIA, 1991.

LBW — *Lutheran Book of Worship.* Mpls: Augsburg; Philadelphia: Board of Publication, LCA, 1978.

LEV — *Lift Every Voice and Sing II.* New York: The Church Pension Fund, 1993.

LLC — *Libro de Liturgia y Cántico.* Mpls: Augsburg Fortress, 1998.

LS — *LifeSongs.* Mpls: Augsburg Fortress, 1999.

LW — *Lutheran Worship* (Lutheran Church–Missouri Synod). St. Louis: Concordia Publishing House, 1982.

MBW — *Moravian Book of Worship* (Moravian Church in America). Bethlehem, PA: Interprovincial Board of Publications and Communications, 1995.

NCH — *The New Century Hymnal* (United Church of Christ). Cleveland: The Pilgrim Press, 1995.

NSR — *New Songs of Rejoicing.* Kingston, NY: Selah Publishing Co., Inc., 1994.

OBS — *O Blessed Spring: Hymns of Susan Palo Cherwien.* Mpls: Augsburg Fortress, 1997.

PCY — *Psalms for the Church Year.* 8 vol. Chicago: GIA Publications.

PH — *The Presbyterian Hymnal* (PC-USA). Louisville: Westminster John Knox Press, 1990.

PS — *Psalm Songs.* 3 vol. Mpls: Augsburg Fortress, 1998.

PsH — *Psalter Hymnal* (Christian Reformed). Grand Rapids, MI: CRC Publications, 1987.

PW — *Psalter for Worship.* 3 vol. (Cycles A, B, C.) Mpls: Augsburg Fortress.

REJ — *Rejoice in the Lord* (Reformed Church in America). Grand Rapids, MI: William B. Eerdmans Publishing Co., 1985.

RS — *RitualSong: A Hymnal and Service Book for Roman Catholics.* Chicago: GIA Publications, Inc., 1996.

STP — *Singing the Psalms.* 3 vol. Portland: OCP Publications.

TFF — *This Far by Faith.* Mpls: Augsburg Fortress, 1999.

TP — *The Psalter: Psalms and the Canticles for Singing.* Louisville: Westminster/John Knox Press.

TWC — *The Worshiping Church.* Carol Stream, IL: Hope Publishing Company, 1990.

UMH — *The United Methodist Hymnal.* Nashville: The United Methodist Publishing House, 1989.

W3 — *Worship: A Hymnal and Service Book for Roman Catholics.* Third ed. Chicago: GIA 1986.

WAO — *We Are One in Christ: Hymns, Paraphrases, and Translations by Gracia Grindal.* Kingston: Selah Publishing Co., Inc., 1996.

WGF — *The Word Goes Forth: The Hymns of Herman Stuempfle.* Chicago: GIA, 1993.

WOV — *With One Voice.* Mpls: Augsburg Fortress, 1995.

W&P — *Worship & Praise.* Mpls: Augsburg Fortress, 1999.

# Selected Publishers

**AMSI**
3706 East 34th Street
Minneapolis MN 55406
612/724-1258 General
612/729-4487 Fax

**ABINGDON PRESS**
201 8th Avenue South
PO Box 801
Nashville TN 37202
800/251-3320 Customer Service
800/836-7802 Fax

**AGEHR, INC.**
1055 E. Centerville Station Road
Dayton OH 45459
800/878-5459
937/438-0085

**ALFRED PUBLISHING CO., INC.**
Box 10003
16380 Roscoe Boulevard
Van Nuys CA 91410-0003
800/292-6122 Customer Service
800/632-1928 Fax
818/891-5999 Direct

**AMERICAN LUTHERAN PUBLICITY BUREAU**
PO Box 327
Delhi NY 13753-0327
607/746-7511 General

**ARISTA MUSIC**
PO Box 1596
Brooklyn NY 11201

**AUGSBURG FORTRESS**
PO Box 1209
Minneapolis MN 55440-1209
800/328-4648 Ordering
800/421-0239 Permissions
612/330-3300 General

**BECKENHORST PRESS**
PO Box 14273
Columbus OH 43214
614/451-6461 General
614/451-6627 Fax

**BOOSEY & HAWKES, INC.**
35 East Twenty-first Street
New York NY 10010
212/358-5300 General
212/358-5301 Fax

**BOSTON MUSIC CO.**
215 Stuart Street
Boston MA 02116
617/426-5100 Retail
617/528-6141 Fax

**BOURNE COMPANY**
5 West 37th Street
New York NY 10018
212/391-4300 General
212/391-4306 Fax

**BRENTWOOD-BENSON MUSIC, INC.**
Order from: Provident Music
741 Cool Springs Boulevard
Franklin TX 36067
800/333-9000 ext 3300

**BROUDE BROTHERS LTD.**
141 White Oaks Road
Williamstown MA 01267
413/458-8131

**BROADMAN HOLMAN GENEVOX**
Customer Accounts Center
127 Ninth Avenue North
Nashville TN 37234
800/251-3225 General
615/251/3870 Fax

**C F PETERS CORPORATION**
Building 36, Atlas Terminal
70-30 80th Street
Glendale NY 11385
718/416-7800 General
718/416-7805 Fax

**CHANGING CHURCH FORUM/ PRINCE OF PEACE PUBLISHING**
200 E. Nicollet Boulevard.
Burnsville MN 55337
800/874-2044

**CHESTER MUSIC**
Contact Hal Leonard Corp
Music Dispatch

**CHURCH PENSION**
445 5th Avenue
New York NY 10016-0109
800/223-6602 General
212/779-3392 Fax

**CONCORDIA PUBLISHING HOUSE**
3558 South Jefferson Avenue
Saint Louis MO 63118
800/325-3391 Sales
800/325-3040 Customer Service
314/268-1329 Fax
314/268-1000 General

**E. C. SCHIRMER MUSIC CO.**
138 Ipswich Street
Boston MA 02215
800/777-1919 Ordering
617/236-1935 General
617/236-0261 Fax
614/236-1935

**EUROPEAN AMERICAN MUSIC DIST.**
Note Service Department
15800 Northwest 48th Avenue
Miami FL 33014
800/628-1528

**CARL FISCHER, INC.**
Order from local music store

**GIA PUBLICATIONS, INC.**
7404 South Mason Avenue
Chicago IL 60638
800/442-1358 General
708/496-3800 General
708/496-3828 Fax

**GALAXY COMMUNICATIONS**
Contact E. C. Schirmer Music Co

**HINSHAW MUSIC CO, INC.**
PO Box 470
Chapel Hill NC 27514-0470
919/933-1691 General
919/967-3399 Fax

**HAL LEONARD CORP**
PO Box 13819
7777 West Bluemound Road
Milwaukee WI 53213
414/774-3630 General
800/637-2852 Music Dispatch

20

HOPE PUBLISHING CO.
380 South Main Place
Carol Stream IL 60188
800/323-1049 General
630/665-3200 General
630/665-2552 Fax

ICEL (INTERNATIONAL COMMISSION
ON ENGLISH IN THE LITURGY)
1522 K Street Northwest
Suite 1000
Washington DC 20005-4097
202/347-0800 General

IONIAN ARTS, INC.
PO Box 259
Mercer Island WA 98040-0259
206/236-2210 General

THE LITURGICAL CONFERENCE
415 Michigan Avenue Northeast
Suite 65
Washington DC 20017
800/394-0885 Ordering
202/832-6520 General
202/832-6523 Fax

THE LITURGICAL PRESS
St. John's Abbey
PO Box 7500
Collegeville MN 56321-7500
800/858-5450 General
800/445-5899 Fax
320/363-2213 General
320/363-3299 Fax

LITURGY TRAINING PUBLICATIONS
1800 North Hermitage Avenue
Chicago IL 60622-1101
800/933-1800 Ordering
800/933-4779 Customer Service
800/933-7094 Fax

LIVE OAK HOUSE
3211 Plantation Rd.
Austin TX 78745-7424
512/282-3397

THE LORENZ CORPORATION
PO Box 802
Dayton OH 45401-0802
800/444-1144 General

LUDWIG MUSIC PUBLISHING CO.
557 East 140th Street
Cleveland OH 44110-1999
800/851-1150 General
216/851-1150 General
216/851-1958 Fax

MARANATHA!
PO Box 1077
Dana Point, CA 92629
800/245-7664 Retail

MASTERS MUSIC PUBLICATIONS,
INC.
PO Box 810157
Boco Raton FL 33481-0157
561/241-6169 General
561/241-6347 Fax

MORNINGSTAR MUSIC PUBLISHERS
1727 Larkin Williams Road
Fendon MD 63026
800/647-2117 Ordering
314/305-0121 Fax

MUSICA RUSSICA
27 Willow Lane
Madison CT 06443
800/326-3132

NEW GENERATION PUBLISHERS
Box 321
Waverly IA 50677
319/352-4396

NORTHWESTERN PUBLISHING
HOUSE
1250 North 113th Street
Milwaukee WI 53226-3284
800/662-6093

OREGON CATHOLIC PRESS
5536 Northeast Hassalo
Portland OR 97213
800/547-8992 General
800/462-7329 Fax

OXFORD UNIVERSITY PRESS
2001 Evans Road
Cary NC 27513
800/451-7556 General
919/677-1303 Fax

PARACLETE SOCIETY
INTERNATIONAL
1132 Southwest 13th Avenue
Portland OR 97205

PLYMOUTH MUSIC CO.
170 Northeast 33rd Street
Fort Lauderdale FL 33334
954/563-1844 General
954/563-9006 Fax

RANDALL M. EGAN, PUBLISHERS
2024 Kenwood Parkway
Minneapolis MN 55405-2303
612/377-4450 General
*51 Fax

SHAWNEE PRESS
PO Box 690
49 Waring Drive
Delaware Water Gap PA 18327-1699
800/962-8584 General
570/476-0550 General
570/476-5247 Fax

THEODORE PRESSER CO.
1 Presser Place
Bryn Mawr PA 19010
610/527-4242 Retail
610/527-7841 Fax

WARNER BROTHERS PUBLICATIONS
15800 Northwest 48th Avenue
Miami FL 33014
800/327-7643 General
305/621-4869 Fax

WESTMINSTER/JOHN KNOX PRESS
100 Witherspoon Street
Louisville KY 40202-1396
800/523-1631 General
800/541-5113 Fax

WORD MUSIC CO.
3319 West End Avenue, Suite 201
Nashville TN 37203
888/324-9673

WORLD LIBRARY PUBLICATIONS
3825 North Willow Road
Schiller Park IL 60176
800/621-5197 General
847/678-0621 General
847/671-5715 Fax

21

# ADVENT

*We light our candles for the Messiah*

*who has already come*

# Images *of the* Season

Although many of us relish the brightness and warmth

of summer's long days, the cooler nights and fewer hours

of daylight in autumn can make it difficult to linger outdoors.

Each season of the year, however, offers its own grace if we would but watch for it. Let us then take ourselves outside in the days of December to see the deep blue that fills the sky some minutes after the sun has set. Look westward as the heavens begin to darken. The faint whiteness of the departing sun may still linger as a line marking the horizon. But then, look up. The sky will turn into a deep azure field flecked with stars, a parament of blue, open and stretched from west to east. Turn toward the east and gaze upon blue turning to purple. Darkness is covering the oceans and shores of eastern lands. If you are the sort, however, who rises at the first light, then crawl out of bed even earlier, and find a window facing east. Gaze upon the lingering shadows of night's fleeting darkness until the black sky dissolves under the light's impress.

In the days of Advent, the church welcomes the blues and purples of dusk and dawn as the Christian community gathers under an evergreen crown and prays for the coming of God's gracious light in our time and place. Perhaps we hear this plaintive lyric: "Light one candle to watch for Messiah: let the light banish darkness. He shall bring salvation to Israel, God fulfills the promise" (WOV 630). When receiving such words as our own, we find ourselves in an odd position, perhaps a paradox. Amid Advent's blues and purples, we light our candles for the Messiah who has already come and dwells among us. And yet our lives and our world cry out for the fulfillment of the promise that God's justice and peace will flourish in our midst.

Some people might advise us to put away the color of night, exchange the wavering candle for brighter and better lights. "Get rid of blue," they say, "it is too cool, too distant for our happy winter gatherings. Don't worry, be happy, the Savior is coming!" Christian faith, however, is rooted in death and resurrection and sees all of life—indeed, each season of the year—from the viewpoint of this central mystery. Such faith is far more realistic and

truthful. When we wrap ourselves in Advent's blue, we give color to the deep longing that is so frequently muffled in our land and—truth be told—in our churches. We give voice to our yearning for a world marked by a deeper justice, a land resting under a blue mantle of peace.

If we hold, then, to this more realistic grace, what is central in keeping the weeks of Advent? Of course, it is the liturgy itself. The people gather in the name of God and hear the prayer that marks the purpose of the gathering. The word of God is proclaimed in readings, psalm, acclamation, preaching, and song. The needs of the world and the church, informed by the word of God, are voiced or sung in prayer. With its presider, the assembly offers thanksgiving over bread and cup and then receives these gifts. With God's blessing, all are sent into the world, especially to those who are absent from the liturgy and those in need. Christians do not celebrate the liturgy nor keep the seasons in a vacuum. Rather, the readings, preaching, and singing, the greeting of peace, thanksgiving at table, and sharing of the supper take place in a world still yearning for that time when "nation shall not lift up sword against nation" (Isa. 2:4).

Thus, what is central are the primary elements of the liturgy, for through them the worshiping assembly rehearses the words and deeds of the one who "shall judge the poor, and decide with equity for the meek of the earth" (Isa. 11:4). They rehearse the baptized faithful in the promise of the one who strengthens weak hands and makes firm the feeble knees, who opens the eyes of the blind and the ears of the deaf (Isa. 35:3, 5).

Central to the liturgy in Advent are biblical images of the one who leads us from the table of word and supper to labor for God's justice and peace in this troubled world. Because we know that Christ has been born, has died, is risen, and will come again, the central thing of Advent cannot be our preparation for a birth that has already taken place. Might it not be our preparation for his continuing incarnation among us as the Prince of Peace

24

and the Sun of justice? And yet we know that if we ask what makes for justice in our land, we will be met with opposition. It is easier to celebrate a liturgy of nostalgia that simply and safely looks back to a birth in the distant past. It is easier to celebrate Christian charity than the prophets' call to act with God's own holy justice.

Central to the liturgy in Advent is the increasing darkness of our days and our yearning for light—images in the skies, our dreams, and the scriptures. Here,

in this brief season, the profound mythic and psychological power of the darkness turning to light is transformed in the liturgy to speak about our baptism, our enlightenment in Christ, and the ways in which this assembly is a sign of God's mercy for those who dwell in shadows and the darkness of death. Let us be clothed then in deep blue, the color of our waiting and our struggling for a peace "as deep as Sheol or high as heaven" (Isa. 7:11).

# Environment *and* Art *for the* Season

At seven o'clock on a Monday morning in early December,

two young children take their place at the breakfast table.

Heat rises from their bowls of oatmeal and cups of hot chocolate,

teasing their still-sleepy eyes awake. The younger child looks upward and notices the view out a high window. The sky is an inky blue, a deep indigo, and the silhouette of a great tree in the yard cuts across the almost emerging dawn as a rough black stripe. "Mom," he says, suddenly alert, "look at the sky. It's the same color as the Advent candles!"

In Advent, we turn our eyes upward. The smoky blue threshold of night that blankets North America during these weeks can feel oppressive, so that emotionally we may feel "blue." But this vast celestial canopy can also inspire awe. Advent blue marks this tension between our smallness, our sleepiness, our vulnerable place in the cosmos and the way the heavenly promise of redemption stirs and quickens us. As the scriptures urge us to "keep awake," we respond with vigilance.

The Advent wreath is said to have its origins in the practices of our pre-Christian ancestors in northern Europe. As northern nights lengthened to the point that there was little or no daylight, the work of the people came to a halt. As a sign of this dormancy, wagon wheels were brought indoors and decorated with greens. This fallow time without light was also a time of longing and expectation for the sun's return.

It is no wonder the Advent wreath is such a beloved

symbol of Advent waiting. The lighting of candles each week on this wheel of time speaks to primitive, unconscious yearnings within us. As Christians, we prepare again to receive the light of the world in God's incarnation as Christ Jesus. We prepare again for a renewal of the cosmos, a renewal in which the human will receive and bear the divine.

An Advent wreath is not required in worship during this season. Greens need not be arranged in a wreath, and even the greens themselves are not necessary. The primary symbol is the light of the candles, whether they are blue, purple, or white. Liturgical artist Tanja Butler describes the new wreath in her church:

> The church commissioned a member of the congregation to create a large, elegant, cast iron wreath to be suspended as a crown from the ceiling. It looked quite stunning with simple white candles. This relieved the visual clutter of the large evergreen display we used to place next to the altar and created new symbolic associations, with a window to heaven opened up above the congregation.

A cast iron wreath might also reinforce the primitive wheel imagery.

In another church, lit candles are placed within glass globes affixed to the top of poles and are carried like

25

processional torches into the dark worship space. The procession leads to a hanging wreath, where the poles are placed upright in floor stands. The procession also includes an incense bearer, who carries a bowl of burning incense, which is placed in the center of the candles, so the smoke rises through the wreath. Another option is to place four standing torches around a wreath on a pedestal.

The most important considerations when designing an Advent wreath are its scale, proportion, and the quality of materials used. The wreath must be large enough in scale to relate to the space where it is placed. In some churches, it will be as large as six feet in diameter. If creating a large, beautiful wreath is difficult, consider using a smaller one in a different spot. In some churches, a smaller wreath is placed in the narthex, where it is lit before worship. Whatever the size, be sure that the candles are in proportion to the greens. Consider the quality of the greens and candles. Always favor natural elements such as beeswax candles and fresh evergreens. A florist or other knowledgeable person can recommend greens that will look fresh and not lose needles during the season. The scent of balsam and other conifers can enhance the worship environment, especially if the greens are refreshed or replaced as the season progresses.

When designing an Advent wreath, always remember to consult with those responsible for planning the liturgy. Ask whether the candles will be lit before the liturgy or during the entrance rite. This decision may affect significantly both placement and design of the wreath.

Many liturgical artists speak of Advent as a season of the church year that tends to get overlooked or that is undermined by the encroachment of inappropriate Christmas decoration. This time of symbolic gestation holds wonderful artistic opportunities for the parish community that are seldom realized. Liturgical artist Jane Pitz speaks of her vision for Advent:

> I would like to work into the environment [of my church] wonderful, beautiful hangings from the colonnades surrounding the worship space, which would gather the assembly in an intimate way during this season. The hope would be to create a sense of being surrounded and enclosed—held.

Without words, the assembly might be led to a sense of hopeful incubation.

Tanja Butler's art and environment group designed a series of abstract pieces:

> The first piece was introduced on the first Sunday, flanked by two new pieces the second, and so on, until all seven were displayed. The unity of the design was evident when all were installed. The individual designs related to the readings for the day. For example, the first was reminiscent of the curtain parting and light descending. Short descriptive texts were included in the bulletin to help the congregation make connections with the abstract designs.

The change from week to week built expectation, although each installment had its own integrity.

Butler also suggests developing an Advent activity focusing on the prophetic promises of the Hebrew Scriptures:

> I recently found a variation of the stations of the cross published for use during Advent, using Old Testament prophetic promises as the stations. I would love to develop imagery for this kind of group activity, with people sharing in readings and prayers at different places [within the church].

If the art for such a project is not appropriate as seasonal art for Sunday liturgies, it could remain on display in some other space throughout the season.

Artist Nancy Chinn, in her book *Spaces for Spirit: Adorning the Church* (Chicago: LTP, 1998), describes her fabric installation of polyester basted onto nylon net. Stylized angel images represent the four elements of earth, fire, air, and water. She writes, "There is no sentimentality here: Advent is also about judgment and the final things, about this world passing away and the new one being born" (Chinn, p. 28). As part of another Advent installation, Chinn designed a canopy of Mylar stars to hang over large, abstract painted works.

Working with celestial imagery can be captivating, but if it is not executed well, it can appear childish. To install a cascade of stars or the suggestion of clouds hanging above the assembly without an artist's design and direction is probably unwise. On the other hand, many artists are available and eager to expand the church's use of art in worship. Does your church have an art and environment committee? Do you know whether any parishioners are artists? One fine resource for locating liturgical artists is Christians in the Visual Arts

(CIVA), P.O. Box 18117, Minneapolis, MN 55418-0117; www.civa.org.

Twilight blue is the color of vestments and paraments in Advent. Some churches have traditionally favored purple, perhaps as a reminder that Advent is a time of inwardness and preparation. Blue vestments will distinguish this season from Lent and are more suggestive of night and cold and even of the promise of kindling—the blue fire that yields to white flame.

We live in a culture that forces Christmas into view before its time. Be aware of this tendency when using evergreens or other materials that might suggest Christmas. Keep evergreens simple and to a minimum. This is the season of Jesse's shoot rather than of the decorated Christmas tree. Bare trees (birches, aspens) are appropriate and can appear dramatic and unconventionally beautiful. This imagery can provide a welcome antidote to the Christmas trimmings that decorate the commercial world during Advent. Another helpful practice for keeping Advent is to wait until the fourth Sunday of Advent to put out the manger. (Like the Advent wreath, the manger display is entirely optional.) Although a cow or other farm animals can be displayed now, wait until Christmas Eve to place human figures or angels in the manger. (Children, especially, enjoy watching and waiting for the additional figures.)

John the Baptist is prominent in Advent scriptures. Advent is a wonderful opportunity to display an icon or other image of the Baptizer. A font near the gathering space is a fine spot for this art. Place the art on a small table, easel, or stand. Perhaps the church has a permanent image of John, depicted in stained glass or some other media. This might be highlighted with lights, votive candles, or flowers.

Many churches collect toys, clothing, and other goods for those in need during Advent. In some churches, these gifts are brought to the altar during the liturgy. This is a powerful practice that signifies the worshiping community's solidarity with the poor and hungry. Provide large baskets or attractive bins for these gifts, so that they can be moved to the narthex or another appropriate spot during the week. Moving the gifts leaves the altar area uncluttered and encourages donations throughout the week. Rather than have yet another tree ("the mitten tree") to lessen the impact of the Christmas evergreen, why not create a "mitten board" as part of a collection corner? Colorful paper "people" could be mounted on the board and mittens would be attached or hung from the hands of the paper figures. In this incarnational cycle of the church year, joining hands with those who are underprivileged can be a meaningful gesture for children.

Any effective outdoor décor must be weatherproof and durable. Some churches have successfully placed an Advent wreath in front of the church, using fire-safe torches designed for outdoor use. Blue bunting over doorways is a gracious statement to the community that Christmas has not yet arrived and that the church is engaged in something else—the keeping of Advent.

27

# Preaching *with the* Season

In Advent, Christians wait for the coming of Christ.

At the same time, the culture of which we are a part

prepares us for something quite different: the holidays.

During this holiday preparation, we witness a general welling up of goodwill and generosity, and a pervasive focus on decorating, shopping, and connecting through gifts and food, cards and visiting. The world's Advent is also full of anticipation. What Christians anticipate is so different from the object of the world's longing, though.

The surrounding culture's lights are turned up bright during Advent. The music is nostalgic—about remembering, not proclaiming. We try to do the same things we did as children, to reenact old holiday traditions, to recreate feelings we used to have or at least imagine we should have.

Liturgical rhythms are rarely as out of sync with the world around us as they are during Advent. Trying to strike the proper balance between the songs of Advent and the carols of Christmas during these four weeks is a sign of how hard it is to be countercultural in this season. But we are impoverished if we do not wait in Advent as the season bids us.

Although many people seem to prefer a brightly lit Advent, for Christians the season of Advent is dark and quiet. It is subdued and earnest, not blatant or glittery. It is so much more like those final months of pregnancy, when one simply must wait for God's time and temper impatience.

Advent is a time of promise, imagining, and hoping. So the first Sunday's texts invite us to hear the imagination of the faithful, to wonder what it will be like when Jesus comes again in glory. How will the world change? How might we make ourselves ready? Nowhere in these texts are we holding soft swaddling clothes or hearing a cooing baby, freshly changed and content. We are given a glimpse of the transformation of long-held human patterns, as war turns to peace (in Isaiah's vision), as the favor of God overturns all human expectations (in Matthew). These readings are about anything but chestnuts roasting by an open fire.

The second Sunday's readings speak of the power of the one who will come again. The reading from Isaiah unfolds image after image expressing the justice and mercy that will come with him. Matthew captures John the Baptist's confrontation of tradition and the perceived privilege of lineage. While Isaiah saturates his images with comfort and hope, John's words are a clarion call to God's justice and mercy. Life will change from what we know. Yes, indeed! A Christian Advent is less about the past and more about what is to come. We live facing both directions at once. We look to the past not for its own sake but because we are eager to glean wisdom for the future. The past is not something to be captured and repeated year after year, like once again closing the Christmas Eve service with "Silent Night," as beautiful and wonderful as that practice may be. The past gives witness to God's faithfulness, but we cannot be redeemed in the past, only today and tomorrow. So John calls us to repent, to turn around and see before us, to seek wisdom.

Hope is again the foundation of the first reading for the third Sunday in Advent. Be strong and do not fear! God's coming brings the promise of water for those who thirst. We will be welcomed home, and we will be safe. In the reading from Matthew, we hear John ask Jesus whether he is indeed the one long promised. Jesus bids him look at the results of his ministry. John will see that the promise is being fulfilled. The eyes of the blind are opened, weak hands are strengthened, burning sand becomes a pool. We dare not miss the vision, because we tend to look for what we have seen before. Salvation is a whole new thing. The Messiah comes as quite a surprise.

So when the world looks for dazzle, we Christians look for surprise. We look for hope in the womb of an unwed teen. We look for a theophany in a stable, not in a palace. We look for the creator of the whole universe to be present in our time and our space, among us, as one of us. Will we notice God's surprise in the cacophony of the cultural holidays or the busy-ness of frantic preparation?

28

We need dark and quiet to appreciate the nuances of Mary's burden, and Joseph's, too. We need to wait until the baby is born to sing and dance. We need to wait.

Advent's gift to us is this: we get to imagine, to hope, and to grasp the promise and wait for its fulfillment. In our countercultural Advent stillness, we get to see a glimmer of God's justice and mercy for ourselves and the whole creation—a world of peace and dignity and abundance for all. In Advent we get to pray, "God, we thank you that you would come to be one of us; that you would love us this much; that you would take such a risk—to become flesh and bone as we are." Until then, in Advent, we savor the promise. In Advent, we lean, yearning, toward the Savior.

# Shape *of* Worship *for the* Season

## BASIC SHAPE OF THE EUCHARISTIC RITE

- Confession and Forgiveness: see alternate worship text for Advent in *Sundays and Seasons*

### GATHERING

- Greeting: see alternate worship text for Advent
- Use the Kyrie
- Omit the hymn of praise

### WORD

- Use the Nicene Creed
- The prayers: see alternate forms and responses for Advent

### MEAL

- Offertory prayer: see alternate worship text for Advent
- Use the proper preface for Advent
- Eucharistic prayer: in addition to the four main options in *LBW*, see "Eucharistic Prayer A: The Season of Advent" in *WOV* Leaders Edition, p. 65
- Invitation to communion: see alternate worship text for Advent
- Post-communion prayer: see alternate worship text for Advent

### SENDING

- Benediction: see alternate worship text for Advent
- Dismissal: see alternate worship text for Advent

## OTHER SEASONAL POSSIBILITIES

### BLESSING THE ADVENT WREATH

The gathering rite for either the first week or all the weeks in Advent may take the following form of lighting the Advent wreath. Following the entrance hymn and the greeting, one of the prayers of blessing in the seasonal rites section may be spoken. A candle on the wreath may then be lit during the singing of an Advent hymn, such as "Light one candle to watch for Messiah" (WOV 630). The service then continues with the prayer of the day. On the remaining Sundays in Advent, the number of candles lit before the service would be the total number lit the previous week. One new candle is then lit each week during the service.

Alternatively, candles of the Advent wreath may simply be lit before the service, without any special prayer of blessing. Candles may also be lit during the singing of an entrance hymn, the Kyrie, or the psalm for the day, without any special accompanying prayers or music.

### EVENING PRAYER FOR ADVENT

Consider holding an evening prayer service one weeknight each week throughout the Advent season. All the events might take place in a fellowship hall around tables. A possible format for the gatherings:

29

- Light candles placed at tables as worshipers begin singing a hymn of light ("Joyous light of glory" [*LBW,* p. 143], "O Trinity, O blessed Light" [LBW 275], "Light one candle to watch for Messiah" [WOV 630], "O Light whose splendor thrills" [WOV 728], among others). Follow with a table prayer.
- Have a simple meal, perhaps consisting only of soup, bread, and salad.
- Prepare gifts to be given to homebound people or others in need.
- Close with an abbreviated form of evening prayer:
  - a psalm (especially 141)

- a short scripture reading
- the Song of Mary (Canticle 6 in *LBW,* or "My soul now magnifies the Lord" [LBW 180], or "My soul proclaims your greatness" [WOV 730])
- brief prayers of intercession
- the Lord's Prayer
- dismissal
- Other possibilities for musical settings of evening prayer include *Joyous Light Evening Prayer* (Ray Makeever) and *Holden Evening Prayer* (Marty Haugen).

Try to focus in these gatherings on things that people of all ages can do together, so that families are brought together during this time of year.

# Assembly Song *for the* Season

As the days shorten and the nights grow longer,

the church gathers to prepare for the coming dawn

of God's reign. The quiet watching and waiting of Advent

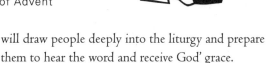

is in stark contrast to the hustle and bustle of many people's lives.

### GATHERING

The gathering can serve as the place where people gradually make the transition from the stress of daily life to the patient preparation of the church. Let the gathering unfold gradually and quietly. Instead of beginning the service with a prelude, invite the congregation to sing as they gather. "Wait for the Lord" (Taizé), "Come by here" (TFF 42 or 43), or "Jesus, name above all names" (W&P 77) can serve to bring people together in sung prayer.

Continue preparing for worship by lighting the Advent wreath as you sing the appropriate stanza of "Light one candle to watch for Messiah" (WOV 630). A period of silent prayer may follow. The confession and forgiveness, greeting, Kyrie, and prayer of the day may follow. Save the more complex hymns for later in the liturgy. This prayerful form of gathering, led in an unhurried and gracious manner by the presiding minister,

will draw people deeply into the liturgy and prepare them to hear the word and receive God' grace.

### WORD

The appointed verses intimately relate to the gospel readings of Advent. If you normally sing a setting of the general gospel acclamation "Alleluia. Lord to whom shall we go?" consider singing the appointed verse instead. Create a gospel acclamation for Advent quickly and easily by following this model. A cantor sings the final phrase of "Let all mortal flesh keep silence" (LBW 198): "Alleluia! Alleluia! Alleluia, Lord most high!" The congregation repeats the phrase with the cantor. Then, the cantor intones the appointed verse to *LBW* psalm tone 2. Finally, the cantor and congregation repeat the phrase from "Let all mortal flesh keep silence." The verses can be found in the leaders edition of *With One Voice,* pages 74–75.

### MEAL

Worship planners vary the liturgy from season to season with good reason. They consider not only the celebration of the particular season, but also take into account what has come before and what will follow. There is a balance between what is familiar and what is new. One way to make larger connections within the church year is to carry certain liturgical elements throughout a cycle. Music during the meal can serve to connect the Christmas cycle—the Advent, Christmas, and Epiphany seasons—by providing a unified setting of the great thanksgiving.

Choose a musical setting of the great thanksgiving to be used throughout the Christmas cycle, then consider these seasonal modifications. During Advent, speak the preface dialog and proper preface. Sing the "Holy, holy, holy Lord" fully but with a simple accompaniment. If the eucharistic prayer includes acclamations, let them be spoken. During the Christmas season, sing the preface dialog and proper preface. Add instruments and bells to the "Holy, holy, holy Lord." Include sung acclamations in the eucharistic prayer. Finally, during the Epiphany

season, retain the festive treatment of the great thanksgiving on the Sundays of the Baptism of Our Lord and the Transfiguration of Our Lord. The other Sundays should receive a more moderate musical treatment.

### SENDING

One feature of Lutheran liturgies is the inclusion of a post-communion canticle. In keeping with this tradition, each of these three canticles from the gospel of Luke—the Magnificat (1:46-55), the Benedictus (Luke 1:68-79), and the Nunc dimittis (Luke 2:29-32)—could be used during the Christmas cycle. The Magnificat is fitting during Advent. Choose one setting to be used for all four Sundays. Many settings of the Magnificat exist and include: "My soul does magnify the Lord" (TFF 168), "My soul proclaims your greatness" (WOV 730), "My soul proclaims the greatness of the Lord" (*LBW*, pp. 147–48), "My soul now magnifies the Lord" (LBW 180), or "Canticle of the turning" (W&P 26).

31

# Music *for the* Season

## VERSE AND OFFERTORY

Cherwien, David. *Verses for the Sundays in Advent.* U, org, opt hb. MSM 80-001.

*Gospel Acclamations.* Cant, choir, cong, inst.   MAY 0862096324.

Haas, David. *Advent/Christmas Gospel Acclamations.* 2 pt, org, gtr, solo inst.   OCP 8732GC.

Hillert, Richard. *Verses and Offertory Sentences, Part 1: Advent through Christmas.* U, kybd.   CPH 97-5509.

Krentz, Michael. *Alleluia Verses for Advent.* SAB, org. AFP 0800647041.

Schiavone, J. *Gospel Acclamation Verses for the Sundays of Advent.* GIA G-2110.

Wetzler, Robert. *Verses and Offertories: Advent 1–Baptism of Our Lord.* SATB, kybd.   AFP 0800648994.

## CHORAL

Bach, J.S. "Comfort, Comfort Ye My People."   CPH 98-2045 (U); 98-2046 (str, fl, ob).

Bach, J.S. "Savior of the Nations, Come" in *Bach for All Seasons.* SATB, kybd.   AFP 080065854X.

Burkhardt, Michael. "Lost in the Night." SATB, org. MSM-60-7013.

Carter, John. "Blessed Be the God of Israel." SATB, org, opt cong. AFP 0800659147.

Christiansen, Paul. "My Song in the Night." SATB.   WAR 8036.

Gibbons, Orlando. "This Is the Record of John." SAATB, T solo, org. OXF TCM42.

Haugen, Kyle. "Lost in the Night." SAB, pno.   AFP 0880659244.

Holst, Gustav. "Let All Mortal Flesh Keep Silence." SATB, org, opt orch.   GAL S.& B.2309.

Hopson, Hal H. "Thou Shalt Know Him When He Comes." SATB, org.   FLA A-6009.

Janzen, Janet L. "Thou Shalt Know Him When He Comes." SATB, kybd, opt tpt.   MSM-50-0021.

Jean, Martin. "Advent Hymn." SATB.    AFP 0800656628.

Jennings, Carolyn. "Climb to the Top of the Highest Mountain."
SATB, opt ch choir/solo, kybd.    CURTIS. C8118.

Johnson, David N. "The Hills Are Bare at Bethlehem." SATB, org.
AFP 6000103409.

Ley, Henry G. "Come, Thou Long Expected Jesus" in *The Oxford Easy
Anthem Book.* SATB, org.    OXF.

Lovelace, Austin. "The Comings of the Lord." SAB, kybd.
CPH 98-3210.

Mitchell, Tom. "People Look East."    CG CGA-505 (SAB, pno, fc);
CGA-571 (opt fl, ob, cl, glock).

Niedmann, Peter. "Lift Up Your Heads." SATB, org.
AFP 0800656350.

Powell, Robert J. "Adam Lay Ybounden." SATB, org.
AFP 0800659104.

Schalk, Carl. "As the Dark Awaits the Dawn." SATB, org.
AFP 0800658450.

Shute, Linda Cable. "Come, Jesus, Come Morning Star." SATB, org.
AFP 0800659163.

Sirett, Mark G. "Thou Shalt Know Him." SATB.
AFP 0800655206.

Taule, Alberto. "Toda la Tierra." (All Earth Is Waiting). SSA, pno.
CPH 98-3233.

Thoburn, Crawford R. "The Linden Tree." SATB, kybd.
AFP 0800652134.

Walker, David. "The Hills Are Bare at Bethlehem." U/2 pt, Orff.
AFP 6000118457.

### CHILDREN'S CHOIRS

Eggert, John. "Hosanna Now through Advent." U, kybd, opt C inst.
AFP 0800674146.

Ellingboe, Bradley. "We Light the Advent Candles." U, kybd, Orff.
AFP 0800674243.

Hopson, Hal H. "A Star, a Song." U, kybd.    CG CGA-167.

Levinson, Doron/arr. Ed. Lojeski Ed. "Lay Down Your Arms." 2 pt,
kybd, fl.    HAL 08602173.

### KEYBOARD/INSTRUMENTAL

Archer, Malcolm. *A Year of Praise.* Org.    MAY 0-86209-155-1.

*Augsburg Organ Library: Advent.* Org.    AFP 0800658957.

Leupold, Wayne. *The Church Organist's Library, vol. 3: Advent and Christmas.*
Org/Pno.    BEL DM253.

Uehlein, Christopher. *A Blue Cloud Abbey Christmas Organ Book.* Org.
AFP 0800659791.

Wasson, Laura. *A Christmas Season Tapestry for Piano.* Pno.
AFP 080065725X.

Wold, Wayne L. *Light One Candle.* Org.    AFP 0800655745.

Young, Jeremy. *Gathering Music for Advent.* Pno, 2 solo inst, DB/vc.
AFP 0800656598.

### HANDBELL

Afdahl, Lee J. "Prepare the Royal Highway." 3-5 oct. L2+.
AFP 080065577X.

Biggs, Susan. "Come, Thou Long Expected Jesus." 2 oct. L2.
AFP 0800659872.

Honoré, Jeffrey. "The King of Glory." 3-5 oct. L3.    CPH 97-6528.

Mathis, William H. "O Come, O Come, Emmanuel." 3-6 oct. L3.
JEF FB BG0947.

Nelson, Susan T. "Two Hymns in Renaissance Style." 3 oct. L2.
AMSI HB-33.

Waugh, Timothy. "Huron Carol." 3 oct. L1+.    JEF JHS 9181.

### PRAISE ENSEMBLE

Besig, Don. "Come, Emmanuel, Come." SATB, kybd.    FLA A6499.

Besig, Don. "Emmanuel Is Coming!" SATB, kybd.    FLA A7401.

Drennan, Patti. "Every Valley."    ALF 18379 (SATB, kybd, opt
soloists, fl); 18380 (SAB).

Robinson, Marc A. "Prepare Ye." SATB, kybd, perc.    KJO Ed. 8830.

# Alternate Worship Texts

## CONFESSION AND FORGIVENESS

It is time to wake from sleep. Salvation is near!
Let us make confession to God.

*Silence for reflection and self-examination.*

Faithful God,
we confess that in thought, word, and deed,
we have turned away from you.
We have not eagerly expected your coming.
We have been slow to serve you and our neighbor.
Restore us, God of might.
Let your face shine upon us,
and we shall be saved. Amen

Lay aside the works of the night;
put on the Lord Jesus Christ.
Strengthen your hearts,
for God is with us to save us from our sins.
Almighty God grant you forgiveness,
keep you in the grace of Christ Jesus,
and by the power of the Holy Spirit
fill you with joy and hope.
**Amen**

## GREETING

Beloved of God,
called to be saints:
Grace, mercy, and peace be with you all.
**And also with you.**

## OFFERTORY PRAYER

God of abundance,
we bring before you
the precious fruits of your creation,
and with them our very lives.
Teach us patience and hope
as we care for all those in need
until the coming of your Son, our Savior. Amen

## INVITATION TO COMMUNION

God is with us, our Immanuel.
Come to the table of grace.

## POST-COMMUNION PRAYER

God of the promise,
you give food to those who hunger
and justice to those who are oppressed.
As you have nourished us in this meal,
send us to proclaim
the coming of your righteous reign;
through Jesus Christ, our Lord.
**Amen**

## BLESSING

May God grant you
to live in harmony with one another
in accordance with Christ Jesus;
and the blessing of almighty God,
the Father, the ✚ Son, and the Holy Spirit,
be among you and remain with you forever.
**Amen**

## DISMISSAL

The night is far gone, the day is near.
Go in peace. Serve the Lord.
**Thanks be to God.**

33

# Seasonal Rites

## Blessing of the Advent Wreath

### FIRST SUNDAY IN ADVENT

We praise you, O God, for this evergreen crown
that marks our days of preparation for Christ's advent.
As we light the first candle on this wreath,
rouse us from sleep, that we may be ready to greet our Lord
when he comes with all the saints and angels.
Enlighten us with your grace,
and prepare our hearts to welcome him with joy.
Grant this through Christ our Lord,
whose coming is certain and whose day draws near.
**Amen**

*Light the first candle.*

### SECOND SUNDAY IN ADVENT

We praise you, O God, for this circle of light
that marks our days of preparation for Christ's advent.
As we light the candles on this wreath,
kindle within us the fire of your Spirit,
that we may be light shining in the darkness.
Enlighten us with your grace,
that we may welcome others as you have welcomed us.
Grant this through Christ our Lord,
whose coming is certain and whose day draws near.
**Amen**

*Light the second candle.*

### THIRD SUNDAY IN ADVENT

We praise you, O God, for this victory wreath
that marks our days of preparation for Christ's advent.
As we light the candles on this wreath,
strengthen our hearts as we await the Lord's coming in glory.
Enlighten us with your grace,
that we may serve our neighbors in need.
Grant this through Christ our Lord,
whose coming is certain and whose day draws near.
**Amen**

*Light the third candle.*

### FOURTH SUNDAY IN ADVENT

We praise you, O God, for this wheel of time
that marks our days of preparation for Christ's advent.
As we light the candles on this wreath,
open our eyes to see your presence
in the lowly ones of this earth.
Enlighten us with your grace,
that we may sing of your advent among us
in the Word made flesh.
Grant this through Christ our Lord,
whose coming is certain and whose day draws near.
**Amen**

*Light the fourth candle.*

34

# Lessons and Carols for Advent

### ENTRANCE HYMN
Fling wide the door   LBW 32
Lift up your heads, O gates   WOV 631

### DIALOGUE
The Spirit and the church cry out:
**Come, Lord Jesus.**
All those who wait his appearance pray:
**Come, Lord Jesus.**
The whole creation pleads:
**Come, Lord Jesus.**

### OPENING PRAYER
The Lord be with you.
**And also with you.**
Let us pray.
Eternal God, at the beginning of creation you made the light that scatters all darkness. May Christ, the true light, shine on your people and free us from the power of sin and death. Fill us with joy as we welcome your Son at his glorious coming; for he lives and reigns with you and the Holy Spirit, one God, now and forever.
**Amen**

### LESSONS AND CAROLS
First Reading: Isaiah 40:1-11
Comfort, comfort now my people   LBW 29
All earth is hopeful   WOV 629, TFF 47
Shout to the Lord   W&P 124

Second Reading: Isaiah 35:1-10
Your kingdom come, O Father   LBW 384
Awake, awake, and greet the new morn   WOV 633
Come, we that love the Lord   WOV 742, TFF 135

Third Reading: Baruch 4:36—5:9
A multitude comes from east and west   LBW 313
People, look east   WOV 626
I've got a robe   TFF 210

Fourth Reading: Isaiah 11:1-9
Hail to the Lord's anointed   LBW 87
O day of peace   WOV 762
The king of glory   W&P 136

Fifth Reading: Isaiah 65:17-23
The King shall come   LBW 33
Soon and very soon   WOV 744, TFF 38

Sixth Reading: 1 Thessalonians 5:1-11, 23-24
Wake, awake, for night is flying   LBW 31
Light one candle to watch for Messiah   WOV 630
Freedom is coming   TFF 46

Seventh Reading: Luke 1:26-38
Savior of the nations, come   LBW 28
The angel Gabriel from heaven came   WOV 632
Canticle of the turning   W&P 26

### RESPONSIVE PRAYER
Blessed is the one who comes in the name of the Lord.
**Hosanna in the highest.**
Show us your mercy, O Lord,
**and grant us your salvation.**
Give peace, O Lord, in all the world;
**for only in you can we live in safety.**
Let not the needy, O Lord, be forgotten,
**nor the hope of the poor be taken away.**
Shower, O heavens, from above,
**and let the skies rain down righteousness.**
Come, O Lord, at evening, with light,
**and in the morning, with your glory,**
**to guide our feet in the way of peace.**

### THE LORD'S PRAYER

### BLESSING AND DISMISSAL
Let us bless the Lord.
**Thanks be to God.**
May Christ, the Sun of righteousness, shine upon you and scatter the darkness from your path. Almighty God, Father, ✛ Son, and Holy Spirit, bless you now and forever.
**Amen**

### SENDING HYMN
Lo! He comes with clouds descending   LBW 27
I want to walk as a child of one light   WOV 649

35

# December 2, 2001

First Sunday in Advent

## INTRODUCTION

Of one thing we can be certain: our fragile, mortal lives will come to an end. We know neither the day nor the hour. Yet with our hearts enlightened by faith, we know that Christ—our life and our resurrection—is already with us in his word, his baptismal promise, his body and blood, his community of faith. We have been grasped and held for all time with Christ's steadfast love. In these gifts of grace, the people of God rejoice. Indeed, if there is any urgency, it concerns our mission in this fragile, broken world that yearns for light, life, and salvation.

## PRAYER OF THE DAY

Stir up your power, O Lord, and come. Protect us by your strength and save us from the threatening dangers of our sins, for you live and reign with the Father and the Holy Spirit, one God, now and forever.

## READINGS

Isaiah 2:1-5

The visionary message presented in this reading focuses on a future day when God establishes universal reign. At that time, the Lord will be recognized as God of all the earth. The prophet calls God's people to trust in the certainty of that reign even now.

Psalm 122

I was glad when they said to me, "Let us go to the house of the Lord." (Ps. 122:1)

Romans 13:11-14

Paul compares the advent of Christ to the coming of the dawn. We should anticipate his arrival and prepare for it as we would prepare to greet the new day.

Matthew 24:36-44

Jesus describes his second coming as a sudden unexpected event that will bring salvation or judgment upon people caught up in the usual affairs of daily life. Therefore, he urges people to be alert and expectant.

## COLOR Blue *or* Purple

## THE PRAYERS

Watchful at all times, let us pray in joyful anticipation for the advent of our God.

*A BRIEF SILENCE.*

That weapons of war be turned to instruments of peace and the long night of violence give way to the dawn of a new day, let us pray to the Lord.

**Lord, reveal your mercy.**

That the church may stand open as a house where all people are fed with the wisdom made known in word and sacrament, let us pray to the Lord.

**Lord, reveal your mercy.**

That those living with depression, loneliness, or illness, and all who wait for health and healing (especially) may find hope in the presence of Christ, let us pray to the Lord.

**Lord, reveal your mercy.**

That this assembly may watch for Christ's presence at all times and lay aside quarreling and jealousy in our life together, let us pray to the Lord.

**Lord, reveal your mercy.**

*HERE OTHER INTERCESSIONS MAY BE OFFERED.*

That the witness of the saints may strengthen us all until the day we stand together in the house of God, let us pray to the Lord.

**Lord, reveal your mercy.**

Sustain us in your promises, faithful God, as we watch for you, and gather us into the peaceful reign of your Son, Jesus Christ our Lord.

**Amen**

## IMAGES FOR PREACHING

What will happen on that day when Jesus stirs up his power and comes? Will we witness swirling cosmic forces? Will he come in the blink of an eye and make new everything that was familiar? Will the unleashed powers of nature create firestorm, cyclone, and earthquake?

These powers belong to God, the one who could not stay away from us but had to take on flesh to be close to us. God's power is the power of redemption, persistent love, fierce justice, and mercy—all at the same time. How will this power change us? This we know—we will be no less God's after that day and that hour. We will still be claimed by one who loves us. We will quake, but we can also trust God's embrace.

So we stay awake and watch for that power, here among us and still to come, now and not yet. We expect God's great power to break through everywhere—in the joy of laughter, the beauty of love, the reliability of the sun and moon, the redemptive power of forgiveness to link and heal, the miracle of growth and learning. We turn our faces expectantly toward the stirring wind. We see the first swirls of dust and remember that dust is both our end and our beginning. He is coming. The Savior of the whole world is coming.

## WORSHIP MATTERS

Assemblies suffer when their leaders do not prepare for worship. It is the height of hubris for worship leaders to think their years of experience exempt them from the need to prepare. Musicians and actors know that continual preparation and rehearsal is critical to keeping skills sharp.

Sometime during the week, pray the prayers for the coming liturgy to make them your own. Plan movements, gestures, and placement of participants and liturgical objects. Speak the texts aloud. How will you use the leader's book? Will your hands need to be free? Will you memorize anything? Consider scheduling a rehearsal for other worship leaders. None of this preparation will prevent spontaneity or exclude the Spirit. All of this planning will make you a more comfortable, gracious worship leader—for the sake of the people, for the sake of the gospel.

## LET THE CHILDREN COME

Let the children come before Sunday to help prepare the worship space for Advent. The wreath needs to be hung, blue or purple paraments put into place, perhaps a Jesse tree "planted" in the narthex or elsewhere upon which children could hang symbols of our ancestors in the faith throughout the season. Many children enjoy working behind the scenes to ready the place for worship. This activity increases their sense of participation in the liturgy, the work of the people. Share with them things they might like to know about the season, its moods, music, colors, symbols, and meanings. End the event by singing familiar and new Advent hymns.

## HYMNS FOR WORSHIP
### GATHERING

Wake, awake, for night is flying    LBW 31
Awake, awake, and greet the new morn    WOV 633

### HYMN OF THE DAY

Savior of the nations, come    LBW 28

### ALTERNATE HYMN OF THE DAY

Soon and very soon    WOV 744, TFF 38, W&P 128
Hark! A thrilling voice is sounding! (MERTON)    HFW
A story for all people    W&P 2

### COMMUNION

Lo! He comes with clouds descending    LBW 27
All earth is hopeful    WOV 629, TFF 47

### SENDING

Grant peace, we pray, in mercy, Lord    LBW 471
O Zion, haste    LBW 397
Soon and very soon    WOV 744, TFF 38, W&P 128

### ADDITIONAL HYMNS AND SONGS

My Lord, what a morning    WOV 627, TFF 40
I was glad    W&P 68
Emmanuel    TFF 45, W&P 36
I want to be ready    TFF 41
Stir up your power    ASG 38

## MUSIC FOR THE DAY
### SERVICE MUSIC

In the season of Advent, it is customary to sing the Kyrie in the entrance rite and to omit the hymn of praise.

### PSALMODY

Farrell, Bernadette. "I Rejoiced" in PS 1.
Joncas, Michael. "Let Us Go Rejoicing"    GIA G-3437.
Let us go rejoicing    TFF 17
Proulx, Richard. "I Rejoiced When I Heard Them Say" Choir, cong, kybd, fl, opt bass.    GIA G-3780.
Walker, Christopher. "Ps. 122: I Rejoiced" in STP, vol. 2.
Witte, Marilyn.  PW A.

### CHORAL

Bach, J.S. "Zion Hears the Watchmen Singing" in *Bach for All Seasons*. U, kybd, opt C inst.    AFP 080065854X.

37

Busarow, Donald. "I Was Glad." AFP 6000101597 (SATB); 11-4646 (3 fl).

Butler, Eugene. "I Was Glad." SATB, pno/org. AG EB9200.

Howells, Herbert. "O, Pray for the Peace of Jerusalem." SATB, org. OXF 42.064.

McAfee, Don. "But in the Last Days." SATB, opt pno/org. BRN 842.

McIntyre, John Samuel. "Advent Procession on 'Savior of the Nations, Come.'" SATB, org, 3 oct hb, ch, fc. AFP 0800654579.

Parry, C. Hubert. "I Was Glad When They Said unto Me." SSATTB, org. HWG GCMR 2404.

Proulx, Richard. "I Rejoiced When I Heard Them Say." 2 pt mxd, cong, fl, opt DB. GIA G-3780.

Shute, Linda Cable. "Come, Jesus, Come Morning Star." SATB, org. AFP 080065916-3.

Thomas, André. "Keep Your Lamps!" SATB, conga drm. HIN HMC-577.

Willan, Healey. "Rejoice, O Jerusalem, Behold, Thy King Cometh." SATB, org. CPH 98-1506.

### CHILDREN'S CHOIRS

Ellingboe, Bradley. "We Light the Advent Candles." U, kybd, Orff inst. AFP 0800674243.

Hopson, Hal H. "Come to Us, Lord Jesus." U/kybd. CG CGA-449.

Liebergen, Patrick. "African Call to Peace." 2 pt, kybd, perc. ALF 6154.

### KEYBOARD/INSTRUMENTAL

Bach, J.S. "Nun komm, der Heiden Heiland" in *Orgelbüchlein*. Org. Peters 10635.

Burkhardt, Michael. "Nun komm, der Heiden Heiland" in *Festive Hymn Settings, Set 3*. Org, cong. MSM 10-128.

Dahl, David P. "Nun komm, der Heiden Heiland" in *Hymn Interpretations for Organ*. Org. AFP 0800658248.

Distler, Hugo, Paul Sifert, and Helmut Walcha. "Nun komm, der Heiden Heiland" in *Augsburg Organ Library: Advent*. Org. AFP 0800658957.

Dupré, Marcel. "Mighty Creator of the Stars" in *Sixteen Chorales*. Org. BEL GB 197.

Manz, Paul. "Nun komm, der Heiden Heiland" in *Improvisations for the Christmas Season, set 1*. Org. MSM 10-100.

Oliver, Curt. "Nun komm, der Heiden Heiland" in *Advent Keyboard Seasons*. Pno. AFP 0800655788.

Rose, Richard. "Nun komm, der Heiden Heiland" in *Hymnal Companion for Woodwinds, Brass and Percussion, Series 1*. Org, inst. CPH 97-6710.

Sedio, Mark. "Nun komm, der Heiden Heiland" in *How Blessed This Place*. Org. AFP 0800658035.

### HANDBELL

Lamb, Linda R. "The Morning Trumpet." 3-5 oct. L3. CG CGB 225.

Music, David W. "O Come, O Come, Emmanuel." 2-3 oct. L3. SEL 845-101.

### PRAISE ENSEMBLE

Crouch, Andraé. "Soon and Very Soon." HOP GC 952 (SATB, kybd); GC 952C (reh/perf cass).

Zschech, Darlene/arr. Jay Rouse. "Glory to the King" in *Hillsongs Choral Collection*. SATB, kybd. INT 16996.

# Thursday, December 6

## NICHOLAS, BISHOP OF MYRA, C. 342

Though Nicholas is one of the church's most beloved saints, little is known about his life. In the fourth century he was a bishop in what is now Turkey. Legends that surround Nicholas tell of his love for God and neighbor, especially the poor. One famous story tells of Nicholas secretly giving bags of gold to the three daughters of a father who was going to sell them into prostitution because he could not provide dowries for them. Nicholas has become a symbol of anonymous gift giving.

In some countries gifts are given on this day, and may include a visit from Nicholas himself. One of the ways Nicholas can be remembered is to have the congregation or families within it gather to prepare gifts that will be given anonymously as a way to remind us of the tradition of giving gifts as a sign of God's love given freely to all.

# Friday, December 7

## AMBROSE, BISHOP OF MILAN, 397

Ambrose was a governor of northern Italy and a cate-chumen when he was elected bishop of Milan. He was baptized, ordained, and consecrated a bishop all on the same day. While bishop he gave away his wealth and lived in simplicity. He was a famous preacher and is largely responsible for the conversion of St. Augustine.

He is also well known for writing hymns. On one occasion, Ambrose led people in a hymn he wrote while the church in which they were secluded was threatened by attack from Gothic soldiers. The soldiers turned away, unwilling to attack a congregation that was singing a hymn. Ambrose's hymn "Savior of the nations, come" (LBW 28) could be sung during these first weeks in Advent when the apocalyptic readings on Sundays encourage believers to stand firm in their faith.

# December 9, 2001

## Second Sunday in Advent

## INTRODUCTION

In the scripture, prayers, and hymns of Advent, John the Baptist brings us to the Jordan River and the waters of baptism. He calls us to repent, for the reign of God is near. The Baptizer calls us to the font of new birth, where we have been grafted into God's branch, the root of Jesse. He calls us to the holy supper, where we receive forgiveness in the life-giving fruit of Christ's body and blood. From the celebration of word and sacrament—from the center of our worship—we are called to go forth as a people whose mission is the proclamation of God's mercy for our suffering world.

## PRAYER OF THE DAY

Stir up our hearts, O Lord, to prepare the way for your only Son. By his coming give us strength in our conflicts and shed light on our path through the darkness of this world; through your Son, Jesus Christ our Lord, who lives and reigns with you and the Holy Spirit, one God, now and forever.

## READINGS

### Isaiah 11:1-10

In the previous chapter Isaiah portrays God's judgment as the felling of a great forest. In today's reading the prophet describes the ideal ruler who will come in the future as a green shoot springing from the dead stump (David's royal line) of Jesse (David's father). The reign of this monarch will be experienced as paradise regained.

### Psalm 72:1-7, 18-19

In his time the righteous shall flourish. (Ps. 72:7)

### Romans 15:4-13

Paul encourages Christians to welcome diversity and live in harmony with one another. In particular, the writings of the Hebrew scriptures promise that Gentiles will be welcome among God's people.

### Matthew 3:1-12

Just before Jesus began his public ministry, John the Baptist appeared, calling people to live in accordance with their words and speaking of the powerful one who was to come.

## COLOR  Blue *or* Purple

## THE PRAYERS

Watchful at all times, let us pray in joyful anticipation for the advent of our God.
*A BRIEF SILENCE.*

For leaders of nations, states, and cities, that they serve their people with wisdom and justice, let us pray to the Lord.
**Lord, reveal your mercy.**
For the church, that it may be stirred up to new life, follow the path of Christ, and bear the fruit that comes from repentance, let us pray to the Lord.
**Lord, reveal your mercy.**

39

For those who are poor and forgotten, and for victims of violence and injustice, that the nearness of Christ's reign give them reason to hope, let us pray to the Lord.

**Lord, reveal your mercy.**

For those who are alone or homebound, for the despairing and the sick (especially), that they may find strength in Christ's coming among us, let us pray to the Lord.

**Lord, reveal your mercy.**

For this community of faith, that we may glorify God with one voice, live in harmony with one another, and welcome others as we have been welcomed by God, let us pray to the Lord.

**Lord, reveal your mercy.**

HERE OTHER INTERCESSIONS MAY BE OFFERED.

In thanksgiving for the witness of John the Baptist and all the saints, and that we may be gathered with them into the great harvest of eternal life, let us pray to the Lord.

**Lord, reveal your mercy.**

Sustain us in your promises, faithful God, as we watch for you, and gather us into the peaceful reign of your Son, Jesus Christ our Lord.

**Amen**

## IMAGES FOR PREACHING

When it has been very dry, the scent of water is poignant. It promises renewal, life, refreshment. When our every cell is thirsty, we feel as if, like frogs, we could soak in the moisture through our very pores.

John the Baptist preached in the dust, but he baptized in the water. Though he wore rough skins and suffered scuffed feet, dried hands, and sun-bleached hair, John's rough life was soothed in the waters of the Jordan. In the water his hands became pliant, his feet softened, his sun-glazed skin cooled.

John preached repentance, and people came to hear him through the dust of their lives. People woke up to their own raspy souls, stiff hands, and dry eyes. They came to him in the wilderness to find themselves, the selves they truly were, not the ones they projected or held out for others to see. They came to face the truth about themselves, to turn around and see the one God sees.

Parched and worn, they walked with John into the river Jordan. They went down into the water, water that could kill as well as bring life. They went down into the water, and it moved over them as the Spirit had moved over the waters in those first moments of creation. That water cleared away their pretenses and lies, cleansed their festering spiritual wounds, and nourished them with promise.

We experience the same healing in baptism, but it is Jesus who calls our name as the water washes over us. The Spirit breathes over the water that cleanses us, and the water soaks into our very pores. In that swirling water, we are held and shaped into children of God, never to be let go. We are washed, never to be the same again. Once baptized, the scent of water will always be near.

## WORSHIP MATTERS

Is your worship folder a worship aid, a hospitality tool, an announcement sheet, a newsletter, a billboard, a devotional, or a worship education handout? Is it all of these? Or perhaps something more? The Sunday bulletin usually serves many functions. Does yours provide more or less information about the service order than the assembly needs? Does it include prayer concerns? Is it necessary for worshipers to have a list of the week's activities in their hands during worship? What do you wish your weekly folder included but presently is left out because of space concerns? Is the space in the folder allocated to match your congregation's understanding of its mission?

This week sit down with leaders in your congregation and reflect on what you wish to accomplish with this publication. Prioritize the list. Are there other vehicles for some of these tasks? How can your folder be reshaped to fit the congregation's needs and call?

## LET THE CHILDREN COME

"Come, Lord Jesus" is a phrase familiar to the many children who have learned to pray it at the family table. Although it is a common congregational acclamation in the eucharistic prayer, children might need a little help connecting the prayer they offer before a meal at home to the one prayed at the church's table. Teach them the word *maranatha* and the Advent acclamation, "Come, Lord Jesus." Plan to incorporate the acclamation into the eucharistic prayer for the season, and then ask children to listen carefully for the moment when they can speak "their line."

## HYMNS FOR WORSHIP
### GATHERING
Hark, the glad sound!   LBW 35

All earth is hopeful   WOV 629, TFF 47

The King of glory   W&P 136

### HYMN OF THE DAY
Comfort, comfort, now my people   LBW 29

### ALTERNATE HYMN OF THE DAY
O day of peace   WOV 762

On Jordan's stormy banks   TFF 49

### COMMUNION
Father, we thank you   WOV 704

Now we join in celebration   LBW 203

One bread, one body   WOV 710, TFF 122, W&P 111

### SENDING
Mine eyes have seen the glory   LBW 332, TFF 297

Let justice flow like streams   WOV 763, TFF 48

### ADDITIONAL HYMNS AND SONGS
A ram's horn blasting barren hills   OBS 89

For the coming of the Savior   AYG 13

Prepare the way of the Lord   GC 336

Wild and lone the prophet's voice   PH 409

## MUSIC FOR THE DAY
### PSALMODY
Cooney, Rory. "Let us go rejoicing" in STP, vol. 4.

Hallock, Peter. "Psalm 72" in TP.   WJK.

Haugen, Marty. "Every Nation on Earth Will Adore You" in PCY.

Hail to the Lord's anointed   LBW 87

Jesus shall reign   LBW 530

Ogden, David. "In His Days" in PS 1.

Schoenbachler, Tim. "Ps. 72: Justice Shall Flourish" in STP, vol. 3.

Witte, Marilyn.   PW A.

### CHORAL
Busarow, Donald. "On Jordan's Bank the Baptist's Cry." SATB, cong, ob, org.   CPH 98-2639.

Distler, Hugo. "Lo! How a Rose E'er Blooming" in the *Chantry Choirbook.* SATB.   AFP 0800658558.

Ferguson, John. "Comfort, Comfort." SATB, opt insts.   AFP 08000646355.

Hopp, Roy. "And a Little Child Shall Lead Them." SATB, kybd, opt cong.   AFP 0800674006.

Howells, Herbert. "A Spotless Rose" in *100 Carols for Choirs.* SATB, T or B solo.   OXF.

Jean, Martin. "Advent Prayer." SATB.   AFP 0800658469.

Kosche, Kenneth T. "Comfort, My People." 2 pt mxd, kybd, C inst, opt cong.   AFP 0800674081.

Powell, Robert J. "O Day of Peace." SATB, org.   CPH 98-3565.

Praetorius, Michael. "Lo, How a Rose E'er Blooming." SATB.   GSCH 2484.

Scholz, Robert. "Lo, How a Rose E'er Blooming." 2 pt choir and SATB, fl, hb, pno/synth, org, opt 2 fl, bell tree.   MSM-50-1034.

Thomas, Paul Lindsley. "Hark the Glad Sound." SATB, org.   CPH 98-2999.

### CHILDREN'S CHOIRS
Bostrom, Sandra. "Christ Is Coming." 2 pt, kybd.   CG CGA691.

Eggert, John. "Hosanna Now Through Advent." U, kybd, opt C inst.   AFP 0800674146.

Thompson, J. Michael/arr. Barry L. Bobb. "He Came with His Love." U, org.   AFP 0800654668.

### KEYBOARD/INSTRUMENTAL
Albrecht, Timothy. "Comfort, Comfort Ye My People" in *Grace Notes II.* Org.   AFP 080065305X.

Busarow, Donald. "Freu dich sehr" in *Five Chorale Preludes for Organ and Two Instruments, vol. III.* Org, inst.   CPH 97-5665.

Dengler, Lee. "Comfort, Comfort Now My People" in *Advent Piano Variations.* Pno.   CPH 97-6749.

Sedio, Mark. "Comfort, Comfort Now My People" in *A Global Piano Tour.* Pno.   AFP 0800658191.

### HANDBELL
Behnke, John A. "Suite for Advent." 2-3 oct. L4.   CPH 97-6248.

Larson, Katherine. "Wake, Awake, for Night Is Flying." 5 oct. L4.   AFP 0800655109.

### PRAISE ENSEMBLE
Martin, Joseph M. "Prepare!"   FLA A7400 (SATB, kybd); LB 5597 (orch); MD 5087 (CD track).

Page, Sue Ellen. "Creation Will Be at Peace."   ALF 4248 (SATB, kybd); ALF 5890 (SAB); ALF 12392 (hb).

41

# Tuesday, December 11

## LARS OLSEN SKREFSRUD, MISSIONARY TO INDIA, 1910

Lars Olsen Skrefsrud was born in Norway in 1840. When he was nineteen years old, he and some friends robbed a bank. In prison he began to read religious books. Visits with a pastor who came to the prison revived Skrefsrud's earlier desire to become a pastor. In 1863 he began work among the Santals of northern India. His work among them included providing a written language, translating the gospels and the Small Catechism, and writing hymns in that language. He also taught agriculture and carpentry methods to raise the Santals' standard of living. The Christian community he founded there continues to flourish.

Consider ways in which Skrefsrud's life echoes the prophetic work of Isaiah and John the Baptist, who prepared the way of the Lord. In what ways can a congregation's proclamation of the gospel and its work for justice point the way to the coming Christ?

# Wednesday, December 12

## OUR LADY OF GUADALUPE

Many Mexican and Mexican American Christians, as well as many others of Central and South America, commemorate Mary, mother of our Lord, on this day. In a famous painting found on the cloak of Juan Diego, a sixteenth-century Mexican Christian, Mary is depicted as an indigenous native, head bowed in prayer and pregnant with the Word of God. As a sign of the blending of the Aztec and European culture, as a sign of God's identification with the poor and powerless, and as an evangelical sign of the coming of the gospel to the new world, Our Lady of Guadalupe can be a powerful symbol of Advent longing for the Word of God among the poor in this hemisphere. Images for preaching on this day might arise from Revelation 12, Luke 1:39-56, or Luther's Commentary on the Magnificat.

# Friday, December 14

## JOHN OF THE CROSS, RENEWER OF THE CHURCH, 1591
## TERESA OF AVILA, RENEWER OF THE CHURCH, 1582

John and Teresa were both members of the Carmelite religious order. John met Teresa when she was working to reform the Carmelite Order and return it to a stricter observance of its rules, from which she believed its members had departed. John followed Teresa's lead and encouraged others to follow her reform. He was imprisoned when he encountered opposition to the reform. Both John and Teresa's writings reflect a deep interest in mystical thought and meditation. Their emphasis on contemplation can guide us in our Advent worship as we watch for the coming Christ.

Both John and Teresa believed that authentic prayer leads to greater love of neighbor and service to those in need. Teresa wrote, "Christ has no body now but yours...yours are the eyes through which he looks in compassion on the world." In one of John's poems, "The Spiritual Canticle," he cried, "Oh, that my griefs would end! Come, grant me thy fruition full and free!"

# December 16, 2001

## THIRD SUNDAY IN ADVENT

### INTRODUCTION

In today's gospel reading, Jesus points to signs of God's reign: the blind see, the lame walk, lepers are cleansed, the deaf hear. Echoing these words of Jesus, the prayer of the day asks God to open our eyes and ears so that we might see and hear God's strong and saving presence among us today: in word and holy supper, in the church and in our homes, in the silence of prayer and in the events of daily life. Strengthen your hearts, the Lord is near.

### PRAYER OF THE DAY

Almighty God, you once called John the Baptist to give witness to the coming of your Son and to prepare his way. Grant us, your people, the wisdom to see your purpose today and the openness to hear your will, that we may witness to Christ's coming and so prepare his way; through Jesus Christ our Lord, who lives and reigns with you and the Holy Spirit, one God, now and forever.

*or*

Lord, hear our prayers and come to us, bringing light into the darkness of our hearts; for you live and reign with the Father and the Holy Spirit, one God, now and forever.

### READINGS

Isaiah 35:1-10

The prophet uses the image of the wasteland becoming a garden to describe the restoration of the exiled people of Judah to their homeland.

Psalm 146:4-9 (Psalm 146:5-10 [NRSV])

The Lord lifts up those who are bowed down. (Ps. 146:7)

*or* Luke 1:47-55

My spirit rejoices in God my Savior. (Luke 1:47)

James 5:7-10

The faith of Christians who are waiting for their Lord should be marked by patience and by trust in God's compassion and mercy.

Matthew 11:2-11

In the early days of his ministry, John the Baptist proclaimed the advent of God's reign and bore witness to Jesus as the promised one of God. But even John had his doubts later, when Jesus demonstrated that God's reign was present in merciful deeds among the poor, rather than a terrifying day of judgment.

### COLOR Blue *or* Purple

### THE PRAYERS

Watchful at all times, let us pray in joyful anticipation for the advent of our God.

*A BRIEF SILENCE.*

That all nations and peoples may follow the path of wisdom and truth, and blossom with the fruits of justice and peace, let us pray to the Lord.

**Lord, reveal your mercy.**

That those who serve in the church's ministries and all the baptized may be a steadfast witness to those with fearful hearts, let us pray to the Lord.

**Lord, reveal your mercy.**

That all who are depressed, lonely, and ill (especially) find comfort in those who care for them as they await the healing presence of Christ, let us pray to the Lord.

**Lord, reveal your mercy.**

That the ministry and work of charities be blessed as they open our hearts to strangers in need and reach out to the poor, let us pray to the Lord.

**Lord, reveal your mercy.**

That during these busy days of preparation our hearts find calm in the gifts of patience, stillness, and hope, let us pray to the Lord.

**Lord, reveal your mercy.**

*HERE OTHER INTERCESSIONS MAY BE OFFERED.*

That the witness of all the saints, those who have died and entered Zion singing and those baptized who stand next to us, nourish our faith, let us pray to the Lord.

**Lord, reveal your mercy.**

Sustain us in your promises, faithful God, as we watch for you, and gather us into the peaceful reign of your Son, Jesus Christ our Lord.

**Amen**

### IMAGES FOR PREACHING

The people had waited for so long. Generations of waiting, hoping, and imagining preceded the promised one. Even John could not make out for sure in the darkness of unfulfilled hopes whether Jesus was the one. The figures were too shadowy.

Jesus knew, however, that when it is dark, we can see the periphery better than the center. "Tell John what you hear and see," Jesus told John's disciples. Don't look at me directly, look at what happens around me: "the blind receive their sight, the lame walk, the lepers are cleansed, the deaf hear, the dead are raised, and the poor have good news brought to them" (Matt. 11:5).

Are we surprised that we cannot see Jesus with clarity when we look straight on? Our ancient forebears believed they would die if they looked at the face of God. God is so far beyond our imagining. How can we see through the darkness of the unknown? How shall we know God in Jesus if even John needed to ask?

Yet God is here, among us. The Messiah in the flesh was announced by John. And God is still enfleshed among us in the community of God's people, the body of Christ. We can learn about John from Jesus' questions of the crowds. Do we expect to see someone wearing soft robes and living in a royal palace—or someone in an Armani suit ensconced in a boardroom? Whatever we expect to see, we will see more when we do not try to look straight on. We must look to the peripheries, to the places where opposites live—where the blind see, the lame walk, the sick are healed, the deaf hear, the dead rise, the poor hear good news. That is where God is, redeeming and bringing life out of death and light into the darkness. Come, Lord Jesus, teach us to see you.

### WORSHIP MATTERS

The Sunday morning liturgy begins with the Saturday night bath. How can we assist the assembly to prepare for worship? What do they need from us? What does "prepare for worship" mean to them? Perhaps there is a catechetical opportunity here. As a worship leader or planner, what do you do to provide for the preparation of the assembly? Have texts or reflections been sent home so they can meditate during the week on the themes of the day? Are devotional materials or opportunities provided for the assembly? What is the assembly's expectation for the moments before worship? Do we need to support that expectation or challenge it? Review the environment that greets worshipers. How can musicians and artists assist us in this task?

### LET THE CHILDREN COME

By the third grade, many children are able to read a Bible passage clearly and meaningfully. When possible, schedule children to serve as reader on Sundays when the readings will easily make sense to them. The second reading for this Sunday is such a passage. Children need the same instruction and practice adults need. In addition, they might need a stool to stand on at the ambo and a good microphone. Teach them how to introduce the reading and to allow silence for reflection following the reading. Instruct them to close with the phrase "The word of the Lord," so the assembly, including the children, can respond, "Thanks be to God."

### HYMNS FOR WORSHIP

#### GATHERING

On Jordan's banks the Baptist's cry    LBW 36
People, look east    WOV 626
Open our eyes    TFF 98, W&P 113

#### HYMN OF THE DAY

Prepare the royal highway    LBW 26

#### ALTERNATE HYMN OF THE DAY

Herald, sound the note of judgment    LBW 556,
    HFW (Regent Square)
The King of glory    W&P 136

#### COMMUNION

Once he came in blessing    LBW 312
Surely it is God who saves me    WOV 635

#### SENDING

Hark, the glad sound!    LBW 35
The Spirit sends us forth to serve    WOV 723

#### ADDITIONAL HYMNS AND SONGS

For all people Christ was born    DH 52
The angel Gabriel from heaven came    WOV 632
There's a voice in the wilderness crying    H82 75
When the King shall come again    W3 355

## MUSIC FOR THE DAY

### PSALMODY: PSALM 146

Haas, David. "As long as I Live."   GIA G-4681.

Haugen, Marty. "Bless the Lord, My Soul." SATB, cant, gtr, kybd, cong.   GIA G-3339.

Martens, Mason. "Psalm 146" in TP. Cant, hb.

Praise the Almighty   LBW 539

Ridge, M.D. "Praise the Lord, my soul" in STP, vol. 4.

Sing unto the Lord   DH 47

Wellicome, Paul. "Maranatha, Alleluia!" in PS 1.

### PSALMODY: LUKE 1:47-55

Canticle of the turning   W&P 26

My soul now magnifies the Lord   LBW 180

My soul proclaims your greatness   WOV 730

Schalk, Carl. "A Parish Magnificat." U, cong, org.   CPH 98-288.

Smith, Alan. "Magnificat" in PS 1.

Tell out, my soul, the greatness of the Lord!   W3 534.

Toolan, Suzanne. "My Soul Proclaims." SATB, cant, cong, kybd, gtr, 2 solo insts, fl, ob, vc trio.   OCP 10580.

Witte, Marilyn.   PW A.

### CHORAL

Distler, Hugo. "Maria Walks Amid the Thorn" in *Chantry Choirbook*. SAB.   AFP 0800657772.

Elgar, Edward. "The Spirit of the Lord Is Upon Me." SATB, org. NOV 29 0216.

Ferguson, John. "Advent Processional." SATB.   AFP 080065238X.

Gibbs, C. Armstrong. "Bless the Lord, O My Soul" in *The Oxford Easy Anthem Book*. SATB in 2 pts, org.   OXF.

Helgen, John. "Prepare the Royal Highway." SATB, pno. AFP 0800674227

Jennings, Carolyn. "A New Magnificat." SATB, opt cong. AFP 080065255X.

Laster, James. "Sing of Mary, Pure and Lowly." SATB, org. AFP 0800674235.

Pfautsch, Lloyd. "Go and Tell John." SAB.   HOP CY3342.

Posegate, Maxcine W. "The Lord Will Come." SATB.   RME.

Schalk, Carl. "As the Dark Awaits the Dawn." SATB, org. AFP 0800658450.

Schalk, Carl. "Hail, O Favored One." SATB, opt solo. AFP 080064705X.

Scott, K. Lee. "Tell Out My Soul." SATB, fl, hb, org. CPH 98-3096.

### CHILDREN'S CHOIRS

Antholz, Jan. "Praise Rondo." 2 pt, kybd.   AMSI 465.

Patterson, Mark. "With One Heart." U, kybd, fl.   CG CGA804.

### KEYBOARD/INSTRUMENTAL

Dupré, Marcel. "Magnificat I" in *Fifteen Pieces for Organ*. Org. HWG GB 188.

Oliver, Curt. "Prepare the Royal Highway" in *Advent Keyboard Seasons*. Kybd.   AFP 0800655788.

Ore, Charles. "Prepare the Royal Highway" in *Eleven Compositions, Set V.* Org.   CPH 97-6107.

### HANDBELL

Afdahl, Lee J. "Prepare the Royal Highway." 3-5 oct. AFP 080065577X.

Dobrinski, Cynthia. "O Come, O Come, Emmanuel." 3-5 oct. L3. AG 1399.

Matheny, Gary. "Puer Nobis." 3 oct. L2.   AMSI HB-3.

### PRAISE ENSEMBLE

Lowry, Mark and Buddy Green/arr. Bruce Greer. "Mary, Did You Know?" SATB, kybd.   WRD 301 0723 164

Nolan, Douglas. "Come with Shouting." SAB, kybd.   FLA D5501.

**45**

# Sunday, December 16

### LAS POSADAS

Las Posadas, "lodgings," is celebrated in homes of Mexican heritage and is becoming a popular parish practice as well. Families or groups of people wander through the neighborhood to mark the journey of Mary and Joseph to Bethlehem. They knock on doors, asking to come in, but a rude voice says that there is no room. The visitors either respond that Mary is about to give birth to the king of heaven, or they sing an Advent carol foretelling his birth. Eventually the door is opened, and everyone is welcomed into a great party of traditional Mexican holiday food and singing.

The traditional songs of this celebration are included in *Libro de Liturgia y Cántico* (284–86). Prepare a special package or offering for a shelter or halfway house. Las Posadas can be a strong reminder of Christ's humble birth among the poor and the importance of extending hospitality.

## Friday, December 21

ST. THOMAS, APOSTLE

Thomas is perhaps best remembered as "Doubting Thomas." But alongside this doubt, the Gospel of John shows Thomas as fiercely loyal: "Let us also go, that we may die with him" (John 11:16). And John's gospel shows Thomas moving from doubt to deep faith. Thomas makes one of the strongest confessions of faith in the New Testament, "My Lord and my God!" (John 20:28). From this confession of faith, ancient stories tell of Thomas's missionary work to India where Christian communities were flourishing a thousand years before the arrival of sixteenth-century missionaries.

Though we hear about Thomas each year on the second Sunday of Easter, Thomas can also serve as an Advent saint. He watched for the risen Christ and looked for the signs of Christ's incarnation. In Advent we, too, watch. We look for the coming of Christ in our lives, his risen presence in the sacraments, and his incarnation soon to be celebrated at Christmas.

# December 23, 2001

Fourth Sunday in Advent

INTRODUCTION

We do well to acknowledge that one of the reasons we celebrate the festivals and seasons of the year is our tendency to forget God's merciful presence. In word and sacrament we are not only reminded of God's promises, we also encounter the very presence of Jesus Christ. The liturgy of Advent names him Immanuel, "God is with us." God comes to us in ordinary ways, offering extraordinary gifts: new life in baptism, gracious words to guide us on life's path, welcome food for the journey of faith. Let us not forget: God is with us now.

PRAYER OF THE DAY

Stir up your power, O Lord, and come. Take away the hindrance of our sins and make us ready for the celebration of your birth, that we may receive you in joy and serve you always; for you live and reign with the Father and the Holy Spirit, now and forever.

READINGS

Isaiah 7:10-16

An Israelite and Aramean military coalition presents a serious threat to King Ahaz of Judah. In response, Ahaz decides to secure his throne and kingdom by asking mighty Assyria for help. In today's reading, Isaiah reminds him that human attempts to establish security will only fail. The prophet repeats the promise that God alone will make God's people secure.

Psalm 80:1-7, 16-18 (Psalm 80:1-7, 17-19 [NRSV])

Show the light of your countenance and we shall be saved. (Ps. 80:7)

Romans 1:1-7

Paul's letter to the Romans is devoted to presenting the gospel (or "good news") of God, which provides salvation for all who believe. This theme is introduced already in the opening words of the letter, where Paul expands the typical salutation to include a statement of faith.

Matthew 1:18-25

Matthew's story of Jesus' birth focuses on the role of Joseph, who adopts the divinely begotten child into the family of David and obediently gives him the name Jesus, which means, literally, "God saves."

COLOR  Blue *or* Purple

THE PRAYERS

Watchful at all times, let us pray in joyful anticipation for the advent of our God.

*A BRIEF SILENCE.*

For the church, that it may not grow weary of proclaiming Christ at work in the world and present in word and sacrament, let us pray to the Lord.

**Lord, reveal your mercy.**

For the nations of the world, that all who govern may be led by wisdom and serve the common good, let us pray to the Lord.

**Lord, reveal your mercy.**

For those awaiting the birth of a child, that their hearts be filled with peace and their fears be turned to joy, let us pray to the Lord.

**Lord, reveal your mercy.**

For those who are homeless and hungry, lonely and depressed, sick or near death (especially), that fear may give way to trust and hope, let us pray to the Lord.

**Lord, reveal your mercy.**

For all gathered here, that we may be drawn to the mystery of Christ's gracious presence in our lives, let us pray to the Lord.

**Lord, reveal your mercy.**

*HERE OTHER INTERCESSIONS MAY BE OFFERED.*

In thanksgiving for the witness of Mary and Joseph, and that Immanuel find welcome in our hearts until we join all the saints in heavenly glory, let us pray to the Lord.

**Lord, reveal your mercy.**

Sustain us in your promises, faithful God, as we watch for you, and gather us into the peaceful reign of your Son, Jesus Christ our Lord.

**Amen**

## IMAGES FOR PREACHING

This picture is not soft around the edges. This picture is filled with shame and broken dreams. This picture is about unraveling, or at least it starts that way.

It begins as a story of a man and woman who follow the rules. They are engaged. They have entered into the propriety of betrothal. The exchange of property is begun. They will be married, bear children, and live good and decent lives.

Then the story is interrupted. The pattern the storyteller was beginning to weave is suddenly altered. She is with child, before they have lived together. This is the beginning of shame. Given the rules established long ago, he must leave her, quietly and without bringing more shame into the picture than already drowns it. He could do more. He could expose her, and himself, to public disgrace, but he will not. The broken pattern need not become any uglier.

Then the story is interrupted more profoundly. The warp and woof are lifted from the loom and totally undone. He is asked to begin again, to take her as his wife. The Spirit has been let loose and created a whole new fabric. This child will be "God with us," a blessing. Instead of a constant reminder of their failure, this child will redeem the whole world. This child will bear the sin and shame of the universe on himself and in the end, bring new life, order, and hope.

Joseph and Mary were freed to begin again, to weave a life that was blessed by God. In Jesus, we too are raised above our sin and shame. Out of our broken patterns, Jesus weaves a wholeness. In the fabric of our lives, God's justice and mercy are revealed.

## WORSHIP MATTERS

Are you prepared for an emergency during worship? Where is your first aid kit? Is it up to date and complete? Who knows where it is kept? What other medical equipment is called for? Where are the fire-fighting supplies? Are there people in the congregation who can be identified as "first responders"? Are ministers of hospitality and worship trained to lead the congregation in a time of crisis? Under what circumstances does the congregation continue with the service, pause, pray, or evacuate? Are these procedures reviewed annually?

## LET THE CHILDREN COME

Following worship today, children and others could be invited to stay to prepare the worship space for Christmas. Greens could be brought in and the white paraments made ready. Because this Sunday is the day before Christmas Eve, perhaps the tree has already been set up and allowed to stand in its unadorned natural beauty. Now the children might bring in the crèche and the appropriate figures to place near the tree. After the worship space is prepared, take a tour of your building and point out the Christmas symbols present in carvings, stained glass, paintings, and textile art throughout the building.

## HYMNS FOR WORSHIP
GATHERING

Let all mortal flesh keep silence    LBW 198
Lift up your heads, O gates    WOV 631
Emmanuel    W&P 36, TFF 45

47

HYMN OF THE DAY

Oh, come, oh, come, Emmanuel    LBW 34

ALTERNATE HYMN OF THE DAY

Peace came to earth    LBW 99

Lift up your heads    W&P 88

COMMUNION

Lo, how a rose is growing    LBW 58

Holy Child within the manger    WOV 638

When long before time    WOV 799

SENDING

Joy to the world    LBW 39

O Savior, rend the heavens wide    LBW 38

What feast of love    WOV 701

ADDITIONAL HYMNS AND SONGS

Christ is coming!    TWC 271

Hills of the north, rejoice    W3 365

Jesus, child of God    DH 53

Sing of Mary, pure and lowly    WOV 634

## MUSIC FOR THE DAY

PSALMODY

Behold and tend this vine    DH 39

Furlong, Sue. "God of Hosts, Bring Us Back" in PS 1.

Haas, David. "Holy Is Your Name."    GC 147.

Haugen, Marty. "Lord, Make Us Turn to You" in PCY, vol. 2.

Jenkins, Stephen. "An Advent Psalm." SATB/U, cant, org, cong.
MSM 80-003.

Schaffer, Robert J. "Psalm 80" in *Psalms for the Cantor*, vol. III.
WLP 2504.

Smith, Timothy R. "Lord, Make Us Turn to You" in STP, vol. 4.

Witte, Marilyn.    PW A.

Ylvisaker, John. "Restore Us, O Lord" in BC.

CHORAL

Busarow, Donald. "Savior of the Nations, Come." SAB, fl, cong.
AFP 3-8305.

Dawson, William. "Mary Had a Baby." SATB, S solo.    KJO T 142.

Ferguson, John. "He Comes to Us as One Unknown." SATB.
AFP 0800656008.

Ferguson, John. "O Come, O Come, Emmanuel." SSATBB, vla.
MSM 50-0015.

Handel, G.F. "Behold a Virgin Shall Conceive" and "O Thou That
Tellest" in *Messiah*. SATB, A solo, kybd.    Various ed.

Hopson, Hal H. "Advent Prayer." 2 pt mxd, kybd, opt solo.
AFP 0800658469.

Keesecker, Thomas. "All Earth Is Hopeful." U, 2, or 3 pt trbl, pno.
AFP 0800657411.

Shakarian, Roupen. "Oh, Come, Oh, Come, Emmanuel. SATB, fl/ob.
AFP 0800646428.

Wetzler, Robert. "Take of the Wonder." SATB, pno, fl, opt qtr.
AFP 0800644222.

CHILDREN'S CHOIRS

Handel, G.F./arr. John F. Wilson. "Sweet Is the Name of Jesus."
U, kybd.    HOP A391.

Kemp, Helen. "A Waiting Carol." U, kybd, fl, drm.    CG CGA-555.

KEYBOARD/INSTRUMENTAL

Biery, Marilyn. "Veni, Emmanuel" in *Augsburg Organ Library: Advent*.
Org.    AFP 0800658957.

Manz, Paul. "The Angel Gabriel from Heaven Came" in *Six Advent
Improvisations*. Org.    MSM 10-002.

Organ, Anne Krentz. "Veni, Emmanuel" in *Advent Reflections*. Pno, inst.
AFP 0800657284.

Rowley, Alec. "Benedictus" in *Augsburg Organ Library: Advent*. Org.
AFP 0800658957.

Young, Jeremy. "Veni, Emmanuel" in *Gathering Music for Advent*. Kybd, 2
solo inst, DB/vc.    AFP 0800656598.

HANDBELL

Biggs, Susan. "Come, Thou Long Expected Jesus." 2 oct hb.
AFP 0800659872.

Kinyon, Barbara Baltzer. "O Sing a Song of Bethlehem." 3 oct. L1.
ALF 12387.

Lamb, Linda R. "People, Look East." 2-3 oct. L2+.    AG 2139.

Larson, Katherine Jordahl. "Let All Mortal Flesh Keep Silence."
3-5 oct. L3+.    AMSI HB-28.

PRAISE ENSEMBLE

Liebergen, Patrick. "He Shall Come in Love to Us." SATB, kybd, fl.
FLA A6655.

Smith, Michael W. and Dennis Allen. "Our God Is with Us."
GVX 0-7673-9676-6 (SATB, kybd); 0-7673-9615-4 (orch).

48

# CHRISTMAS

*Jesus has come to us purely out of grace*

# Images *of the* Season

Although observing Advent seems countercultural

to many of us, celebrating Christmas during this season's

twelve days may seem less so. For many people this season

is quieter than the hectic days leading up to December 25. Many office and factory workers take extra time off—especially between Christmas Day and New Year's Day. Families and friends may gather more frequently for unstructured activity together. In a word, the world feels more at peace. The words we read from the Bible in these days are finally more in tune with our general mood.

Christmas Eve is ushered in with words about peace, though we may be too excited—or exhausted—to hear them. "Glory to God in the highest, and peace to God's people on earth!" These were the words sung by an angel choir, and they announce Christ's mission from the outset. Perhaps greetings of peace are not new for any of us in this season, but have we really heard them? Or have they been buried in an avalanche of cards, bills, and wrapping paper? Are the glad tidings now lost in demands on our time, wallets, and personal space?

If we cannot quite hear words of peace on Christmas Eve, we have another opportunity at Christmas Dawn. Though few people might assemble for early morning services, the words from the second reading (Titus 3:4-7) remind us that Christ has come to us purely through grace, "not because of any works of righteousness that we had done" (v. 5). Whether or not we had time to do everything that we thought we had to do before our holiday celebrations began, we can take great delight in the news that Christ has come to us despite our preparedness or lack thereof. It does not matter how well we have shopped or cleaned or studied. Jesus has come to us purely out of grace.

Words from the first reading for Christmas Day, Isaiah 52:7-10, speak again of peace: "How beautiful upon the mountains are the feet of the messenger who announces peace" (v. 7). Worshipers' minds might be focused on other things than the reading, a holiday meal to put in the oven or a last-minute gift to deliver, but this prophecy tells of a glorious event. Imagine the ruins of Jerusalem rejoicing at the return of righteous rule and

salvation after decades of destruction and exile. We, too, may rejoice, for the message of this day is peace and healing for the damaged places in our lives.

The gospel for Christmas Day is pure poetry (John 1:1-14). This reading may well be the crown jewel of Christmas Day worship. If you cannot gather with other worshipers on this day, then ask one of those who may be gathered to read this passage aloud. This story goes back to the beginning of time. (Do we not hear a bit of Genesis 1 in these words?) Slow down. Pause. Take time to *listen* to the words. John's gospel does not include a manger, or shepherds, or wise men, but this is the Christmas story just the same. When we get to the end of the reading—a passage filled with centuries of anticipation—we can revel in the sound of this: "And the Word became flesh and lived among us, and we have seen his glory, the glory as of a father's only son, full of grace and truth" (v. 14). Peace comes to dwell in our very midst in the person of Jesus Christ.

By December 30, the first Sunday after Christmas, we might at last be in a better frame of mind for listening to stories. The day's first reading begins "I will recount the gracious deeds of the Lord,...because of all that the Lord has done for us" (Isa. 63:7). The passage goes on to speak about God's great mercy and steadfast love. Even if we have failed to hear it before, we have a chance to receive the message today: God loves us! It does not matter what we finished or failed to finish this past year. God saves and redeems us purely because that is just what God wants to do for us.

Take time in this season's often quieter days to revel in truly good gifts—the kind that do not have to be purchased or wrapped or opened. Take time to hear the words from the scriptures that announce God's reign of peace and grace. Take time to celebrate the things that you have (and are they not really the *big* things?)—the goodness of God, the embrace of loved ones, the company of sisters and brothers in Christian community.

# Environment *and* Art *for the* Season

Writer Gretel Ehrlich, spending a winter in Greenland,

describes a moment of "utter breathlessness" as the first pale light

of *Solfest* removes the cloak of night from the town:

"House by house, the dead windows come alive." The community gathers on the town's highest cliff, counting down the waning darkness, until the sun appears. "For six minutes," she writes, "the sun burns…like a flame." [citation?] For the first time in months, the people can see their own shadows, as if the sun bestows proof that their bodies exist in a physical world. Afterward, families and friends return to their homes to share a feast.

At Christmas, we celebrate the incarnation, the coming of Christ as the light of the world. We enter again the mystery of our salvation, the wondrous good news that our gracious God has entered the life of the world as a human being, and that human beings have become bearers of the divine. During these twelve days of Christmas, we feast.

The color of pure, blazing light is white—the totality of all colors in the light spectrum. White vestments and paraments are appointed for Christmas Eve and Christmas Day, as well as for the first Sunday after Christmas. If lesser festivals are celebrated within the season, the liturgical color for the martyrs (St. Stephen and the Holy Innocents) is red, and St. John the Evangelist remains white.

When planning the environment for the Christmas season, be aware that Easter, not Christmas, is the primary festival of the church year, and the worship environment should reflect their relative importance. The festive (though brazenly commercial) displays within the dominant culture at this time can tempt churches to compete with inappropriately fussy or cute decorations. Artist Nancy Chinn states that any time the church environment gets too decorative, "it ceases to hold meaning." Overblown decoration becomes a distraction to worship, rather than an enhancement. And yet, Christmas is a time when the worshiping community has certain expectations. Maybe poinsettias are a nonnegotiable element in the Christmas decor. Perhaps church decorators in years past, nostalgic for a Bing Crosby "white Christmas," have fa-

vored fluffy simulated snow. We can respect these expectations if we work them into an overall plan that does not compromise the worship activities of the assembly.

The Christmas tree is a sign of enduring life. In Ehrlich's essay on the winter *Solfest*, she writes that the people toast the return of the sun as a triumph of their own survival. Despite the darkness and brokenness of our Advent gestation, we are alive in body and spirit through the grace of God. To avoid the tendency to overdecorate, either limit the number of trees in the worship environment to one or decorate only one. Choose a tree that will stay green as it dries. Pines and firs retain their color and needles better than spruces or hemlocks. White lights on the Christmas tree will lift up the significance of white during this season.

If bare trees were brought into the worship space during Advent, perhaps they can be attractively embellished with candles, flowers, berries, or evergreens. If the outcome of this decoration is anything less than splendid, remove the bare trees from the worship space and focus instead on the Christmas tree.

Holly, ivy, mistletoe, and other greens can be used as garlands. Red and white poinsettias and other white and gold flowers (amaryllis, paperwhite, chrysanthemum) may be grouped in pots on the floor or placed in hanging baskets, trimmed with evergreens and ribbon. Candlesticks may be ornamented with greens or flowers. Flowers and greens should look beautiful throughout the twelve days of Christmas, if not also into the Epiphany season.

The use of a crèche in the worship environment is a tradition in many congregations. If the crèche has been placed near the altar in past years, people are likely to expect it to remain there. However, the altar is rarely, if ever, the best place for it. Consider placing the crèche in a more accessible spot that invites prayer, reflection, and cheery visits from adults and children alike. On Christmas Eve, place within the manger the figures of Jesus,

51

Mary, Joseph, the shepherds and their sheep, angels, and other animals. Pay attention to the size of the crèche. It should be in proportion to the space in which it is displayed. The manger and figures should be clean and in good repair. Wonderful, imaginative figures crafted by indigenous peoples in other countries are a delightful option for a new crèche.

The celebration of the Lord's incarnation among us is an especially meaningful time for sacred movement. In one church, the liturgy opens with children in simple white robes processing ahead of dancers. The children carry poles from which long, thin strips of white and gold fabric sway. Following the children, several dancers dressed in gold perform choreographed moves, flanked by two dancers carrying candles in front of and behind them. Sacred movement could also be incorporated in the offertory procession.

During Christmas and Epiphany, the use of vessels fashioned of pewter, silver, gold, or other precious metals reminds us of the gifts of the magi. For churches that are uncomfortable with or opposed to using these expensive materials, beautiful earthenware vessels are always appropriate. During the Christmas season, simple, elegant materials can remind us of the humble birth of the King of kings.

Candles can be used to highlight any permanent art within the church that is especially significant during the Christmas season. If the church has a panel of stained glass depicting the nativity, candles and flowers can draw viewer's attention to this. Likewise, images within the church of St. Stephen, St. John, or the Holy Innocents could be highlighted.

Christmas is regularly trivialized in our society, both by its commercialization and by a mistaken, sentimental emphasis on the infancy of Jesus. Christ's incarnation is his coming into the world as savior. The story of Jesus' birth is incomplete without reference to his death. A traditional icon of the nativity can provide good visual instruction on the meaning of Christ's incarnation. The traditional imagery would depict the infant Jesus in swaddling clothes that are meant to suggest the bands of cloth that would wrap him for burial. The manger in which the child Christ lies resembles a coffin. Mary and Joseph, instead of being drawn into the glow of the holy infant, seem to turn inward, as if pondering in their hearts what the future may hold for this child.

The church might display a fine, traditional icon in the gathering space, near the font, or in the narthex. Place the icon on a small table or easel with a candle alongside it. Include in your worship folder a short explanation of the icon's symbolism and forms. Two good books that might be consulted are Leonid Ouspensky and Vladimir Lossky's *The Meaning of Icons* (Crestwood, N.Y.: St. Vladimir's Seminary Press, 1982) and Jim Forest's *Praying with Icons* (Maryknoll, N.Y.: Orbis Books, 1997). Icons of St. Stephen, St. John, and the Holy Innocents could also be added. A good source for quality, inexpensive icons is Bridge Building Images (www.BridgeBuilding.com; phone 800-325-6263).

In many churches, toys were collected during Advent and distributed before Christmas. Do not allow the giving season to end simply because Santa has returned to the North Pole. Maintain collection bins for food and clothing in the same area where the donations of toys were made. A corner of the narthex permanently designated for charitable giving reminds worshipers of ongoing needs in the community and contributes to the church's identification with the poor.

Whether or not your climate permits a "white Christmas" of freshly fallen snow, walkways must remain clear of ice, snow, or mud and be sufficiently lit. For Christmas Eve, consider lining the paths with luminaria. Luminaria can be created by filling white paper bags a third to one-half full with sand and placing a votive candle into the sand. Because luminaria are becoming increasingly popular in home decorating, the bags and candles can often be found in craft stores.

How will the church send to the wider community its message that Christmas has arrived and God is with us? If the church has growing on the grounds a large evergreen that can be handsomely lit, then allow this to be the focal point of outdoor decoration. Every door of the church can display a festive wreath, festooned with berries and ribbons. A single, illuminated star can be an eloquent announcement that the light of the world is with us.

# Preaching *with the* Season

At Christmas, it is finally time to sing out loud.

Our hopeful waiting has turned into joyous dancing.

The child we have imagined and longed for is here!

Liturgically, Christmas is an astoundingly short season. It begins with joy at the birth of Jesus, but turns, almost immediately, to the first episode of the world's resistance to God's great love come to us—Herod's paranoid slaughter of the innocents. The flow of the season allows precious little time simply to rejoice. We hear the singing of the angels, but almost before the last notes have faded, we hear the keening of Rachel, crying in the wilderness for her dead children. Jesus' sojourn on earth will incite resistance as well as good.

Those who come to worship Jesus during the Christmas season go home to a world that quickly forgets. Our challenge in worship is to celebrate Christmas *during* the season rather than *before* it. How might we sustain joy in the midst of the Christmas clearance? And what a downer to have to recall the dreadful story of Herod's tyranny! We are called to go deeper than a simplistic joy, however. We are called to praise and sing even with the specter of death nearby. Jesus did not come just to be nice. He came because we and the whole world badly need redemption.

The Christmas Eve texts promise an endless peace under the child who bears authority and is called the Prince of Peace, among other titles of honor. If such a thing were within our grasp, we would not need him. But *we* cannot establish justice and righteousness. We need *him*. It is the zeal of the Lord of hosts that will do this. God is not a passive spectator, launching a board game that will eventually play itself out. God is zealous to establish peace for us all. Coursing through Luke's story, as sweetly as we may read it, are undertones of this need. That Mary and Joseph must travel when Mary is so close to giving birth is a sign that their world was not about nurture and grace. Certainly, as cozy as we may picture the stable where he was born, it was not a hospitable community welcoming the laboring woman and her husband into competent and sure hands. That it was shepherds who first heard the angels' glorias is no

less a sign of the world's need for peace. Shepherds were hardly a desirable crew. This is a God who holds joy and sorrow close together, as if they could not live without each other.

Here is the beauty of this season, for if we have lived at all, we hold some difficulty or grief at bay, and it is when we expect ourselves to be most happy and whole that we feel most acutely death's dark shadows. So the texts of Christmas Dawn promise salvation. Isaiah says we shall be called "'The Holy People, the Redeemed of the Lord'; and you shall be called 'Sought Out, A City Not Forsaken'" (Isa. 62:12). This baby born is one who knows full well the depths in which we might dwell. This baby came to fill the empty places, even if we have tried all our lives to fill them with gifts or tradition or wealth or fame or love or whatever other idol we might choose.

The texts for Christmas Day give us a moment to reflect on the meaning of this birth. In this baby, God has bared a holy arm that all the ends of the earth might see salvation (Isaiah). In John we trace this child back to the very beginning, when the Word was with God and was God. This baby is not a sudden flare-up of God's compassion, a mere sign of God's persistence. Without this Word, not one thing came into being, and it is this Word we welcome. Dare we welcome God into our world of time and space and flesh? In this baby we see God's glory, full of grace and truth. Fragile life and indomitable power are gathered together in this little one. This is a reality beyond our imagining.

So we know this will be a story unlike any other. On the first Sunday after Christmas, we hold our breath as Joseph bundles his wife and son off to Egypt, lest they have to face Herod and his sword. Isaiah confesses God's faithfulness—the gracious deeds of the Lord, according to the abundance of his steadfast love. We are promised God's redemption. The story turns us to face the unfolding of our salvation history, God at work, calling us and the whole creation to life.

53

# Shape *of* Worship *for the* Season

## BASIC SHAPE OF THE EUCHARISTIC RITE

- Confession and Forgiveness: see alternate worship text for Christmas in *Sundays and Seasons*

### GATHERING

- Greeting: see alternate worship text for Christmas
- Use the Kyrie, particularly for the most festive liturgies during this season
- Use the hymn of praise ("Glory to God")

### WORD

- Use the Nicene Creed
- The prayers: see alternate forms and responses for Christmas

### MEAL

- Offertory prayer: see alternate worship text for Christmas
- Use the proper preface for Christmas
- Eucharistic prayer: in addition to the four main options in *LBW,* see "Eucharistic Prayer B: The Season of Christmas" in *WOV* Leaders Edition, p. 66
- Invitation to communion: see alternate worship text for Christmas
- Post-communion prayer: see alternate worship text for Christmas

### SENDING

- Benediction: see alternate worship text for Christmas
- Dismissal: see alternate worship text for Christmas

## OTHER SEASONAL POSSIBILITIES
### PROCLAMATION OF THE BIRTH OF CHRIST

The services on Christmas Eve may begin with the proclamation of the birth of Christ (see text in the seasonal rites section), taken from the ancient martyrology. The proclamation should be understood as the announcement of the incarnation within human history rather than a literal counting of years. The lights may be turned down, and, following a period of silence, the proclamation may be read or sung on one note by a leader standing at the entrance to the church. Following the proclamation, the lights are turned on as the entrance hymn is begun.

## CANDLELIGHTING OPTIONS FOR CHRISTMAS EVE
### OPTION 1

- The liturgy may begin with a service of light as at evening prayer. The congregation may face the entrance to the church, and handheld candles may be lit. As the procession passes during the Christmas versicles, all turn to face forward.
- Christmas versicles *LBW,* p. 175
- Hymn of light (LBW 45, 56, or WOV 638)
- Thanksgiving for light (see *LBW,* p. 144)
- The service may then continue with the greeting, followed by the hymn of praise and the prayer of the day.

### OPTION 2

Another option is to light handheld candles at the reading of the gospel. A hymn, such as "The first Noel" (LBW 56) or "Angels, from the realms of glory" (LBW 50), may be sung as handheld candles are lit. The gospel may be read from the midst of the people. "Silent night, holy night!" (LBW 65) may be sung following the gospel, after which handheld candles are extinguished.

### OPTION 3

- A third option is to light handheld candles at the close of the service. Following the post-communion canticle (or at a service without communion, following the offering and the prayers), handheld candles are lit. Instrumental or choral music may accompany the candlelighting.
- Hymn: "Silent night, holy night!" (LBW 65:1–2; or another hymn of light, as listed in option 1)
- Reading from John 1:1-14. A gospel procession may move to the midst of the assembly.
- LBW 65:3 (or the final stanza of another hymn of light)
- Benediction and dismissal

# Assembly Song *for the* Season

After several weeks of waiting and preparing,

Christmas seems to come and go very quickly. Whereas the celebration

of Easter is extended over seven Sundays,

the Christmas season in compacted into twelve days. Indeed, the Christmas season is time of intense celebration. Additional worship opportunities are common in Advent. Why not during Christmas? A service of Christmas lessons and carols or the nightly observance of a simple service of evening prayer will add to the festive nature of the season.

The abundance of beloved carols is both a blessing and a curse for worship planners. It seems there are too many carols to sing and too little time to sing them. Some carols are so beloved people want to sing them several times. The Christmas Eve liturgy can contain only so many carols. A good way to incorporate additional carols is to use them as liturgical music.

### GATHERING

Sing familiar carols in place of the prelude. An informal gathering on the first Sunday after Christmas might allow worshipers to choose the carols to be sung. A traditional and important aspect of the gathering during Christmas is the singing of the hymn of praise "Glory to God in the highest," echoing the song of the angels and placing Christ's birth within the salvation story. "Hark! The herald angels sing" (LBW 60), "Angels we have heard on high" (LBW 71), or "Gloria en las alturas" (LLC 297) could serve as the hymn of praise also.

### WORD

Sing "Let our gladness have no end" (LBW 57) or "Hush, little Jesus boy" (TFF 56) as the gospel acclamation. Consider using a gospel procession to emphasize the incarnate Word living and dwelling among us. Sing one or two stanzas before the reading as the procession moves into the congregation and one stanza following the reading.

### MEAL

As the gifts are presented, sing "What feast of love" (WOV 701) or stanza 3 of "What child is this" (LBW 40). Continue the musical setting of the great thanksgiving begun in Advent, but now with a more festive tone. Sing the preface dialog and proper preface. Add instruments and bells to the "Holy, holy, holy Lord," and include sung acclamations in the eucharistic prayer. Additional carols can be sung during the distribution.

### SENDING

Continue singing the series of Lukan canticles by choosing a setting of the Benedictus (Luke 1:68-79) as the post-communion canticle. "Blessed be the God of Israel" (WOV 725), "Blessed be the Lord God of Israel" (W&P 20), or the setting from Morning Prayer (*LBW,* pp. 134–36) are three settings in different musical styles. "Good Christian friends, rejoice" (LBW 55) is an appropriate carol to use as a post-communion song.

55

# Music *for the* Season

## VERSE AND OFFERTORY

Boehnke, Paul. Festive *Verse Settings for Christmas, Epiphany and Transfiguration.* SATB, opt kybd.   MSM-80-100.

Haas, David. *Advent/Christmas Gospel Acclamations.* 2 pt, org, gtr, solo inst.   OCP 8732GC.

Hillert, Richard. *Verses and Offertory Sentences I: Advent through Christmas.* U.   CPH 97-5501.

Schiavone, J. *Gospel Acclamation Verses for the Christmas Season.* GIA G-2111.

Wetzler, Robert. *Verses and Offertories: Advent 1—Baptism of Our Lord.* SATB, kybd.   AFP 0800648994.

## CHORAL

Bach, J.S. "From Heaven Above to Earth I Come" in *Bach for All Seasons.* SATB.   AFP 080065854X.

Benson, Robert. "The Snow Lay on the Ground." SATB, org. AFP 0800674294.

Brooks, Barrington. "Betelehemu" (Nigerian Carol). SATB, drms. LAW 52744.

Carnahan, Craig. "The Christ Child Lay on Mary's Lap." SATB, pno/harp.   AFP 0800659260.

Ellingboe, Bradley. "Jesus, Jesus, Rest Your Head." SATB. AFP 0800655796.

Kadidlo, Philip. "In the Bleak Midwinter." SATB, pno. AFP 0800674162.

Kastalsky-Norden. "God Is with Us." SSATTB.   BEL F. E. C. 4138.

Niedmann, Peter. "Wexford Carol." SATB, org.   AFP 0800659279.

Schalk, Carl. "Where Shepherds Lately Knelt." SATB. AFP 0800646525.

Shepperd, Mark. "Shepherd, Play Your Pipes Tonight." SATB, kybd, ob.   AFP 0800655826.

Shute, Linda Cable. "Glory in the Highest/Gloria en las alturas." SATB, pno, opt perc.   AFP 088065918X.

Sirett, Mark G. "What Sweeter Music." SATB.   AFP 0800659287.

## CHILDREN'S CHOIRS

Bedford, Michael. "Twas in the Moon of Wintertime." 2 pt trbl, kybd, S rec or fl, Orff.   AFP 0800674316.

Chilcott, Bob. "The Child." U, kybd.   OXF U170.

Collins, Dori Erwin. "Hurry to the Stable." U, kybd. AFP 0800674154.

Grotenhuis, Dale. "Infant Holy, Infant Lowly." 2 pt, kybd, fl. MSM-50-1402.

## KEYBOARD/INSTRUMENTAL

Carlson, J. Bert. *Carols from Many Lands.* Pno.   AFP 0800659767.

Hildebrand, Kevin. *Triptych on Forest Green.* Org/vln.   MSM 20-165.

Lind, Robert. *On December Five and Twenty!* Org.   AFP 0800653351.

Mann, Adrian. *'Tis the Season: Preludes for Treble Instrument and Keyboard.* Kybd, inst.   AFP 0800659848.

Moore, David W. *Three Carols for Piano and Solo Instrument.* Pno, inst. AFP 0800659082.

Osterland, Karl. *I Wonder as I Wander.* Org.   AFP 0800657225.

Pelz, Walter. "Variations on 'From Heaven Above.'" Org. AFP 080064798X.

## HANDBELL

Bloedow, Mark E. "The Holly and the Ivy." 3-5 oct. L2. CPH 97-6747.

Moklebust, Cathy. "Still, Still, Still." 5-7 oct. L5.   ALF 18568.

Smith, James. "Christmas a la Carte." 3-4 oct. L2.   JEF RO 3210.

Tucker, Margaret. "Swedish Christmas Medley." 3-5 oct. L3. AFP 0800659953.

Wagner, Douglas E. "What Child Is This." 3-4 oct. L2. LOR 20/1061L.

Young, Philip M. "Four Christmas Lullabies for Handbells." 3-5 oct. L3.   AFP 0800657349.

## PRAISE ENSEMBLE

Cloninger, Claire and Paul Baloche. "You Are Emmanuel" in *The Ultimate Youth Choir Book.* SATB, kybd.   WRD 0 80689 33017 9.

Grant, Amy and Chris Eaton. "Breath of Heaven (Mary's Song)." SATB, kybd.   HAL 08595535

Mason, Babbie and Donna Douglas/arr. Jack Schrader. "King Jesus Is His Name." SATB, kybd.   HOP GC 953

56

# Alternate Worship Texts

## CONFESSION AND FORGIVENESS

Rejoicing in the good news
that God and sinners are reconciled in Christ,
let us confess our need for forgiveness.

*Silence for reflection and self-examination.*

God of everlasting love,
we confess that we have lived
in captivity to the fear of death.
By our actions and by our neglect,
we have resisted
your good and gracious will.
Free us from anxiety and distraction;
cast out our sin, and enter in;
give us a new birth of hope
as we welcome the child born to save,
Christ the Lord. Amen

"You are my children;
I am your Savior," says our God,
who has redeemed us,
who lifts us up and carries us all our days.
In mercy and lovingkindness
God forgives us all our sins
for the sake of Jesus,
who delights to call us sisters and brothers.
**Amen**

## GREETING

Good news of great joy,
light and life, grace and peace
be with you all.
**And also with you.**

## OFFERTORY PRAYER

Good and loving God,
we rejoice in the birth of Jesus,
who came among the poor
to bring the riches of your grace.
Bless the gifts we offer this day,
and let them be blessing for others.
With the trees of the field,
with all earth and heaven,
we shout for joy
at the coming of your Son. Amen

## INVITATION TO COMMUNION

Come to Bethlehem, the house of bread.
Receive the living God.

## POST-COMMUNION PRAYER

Great and gracious God,
we thank you that in this holy meal
the true Light has come to dwell in us.
As we return into the world you love,
may we take to all people
the good news of Jesus Christ,
in whose name we pray. Amen

## BLESSING

Almighty God,
the One who is and who was and who will be,
the ☩ Word made flesh,
the holy and life-giving Spirit,
bless you and keep you
now and forever.
**Amen**

## DISMISSAL

Go out with joy to the world.
Serve in the name of Christ.
**Thanks be to God.**

57

# Seasonal Rites

## Blessing of the Nativity Scene

*This blessing may be used after the sermon or after the communion of the people on Christmas Eve.*

O Lord our God, with Mary and Joseph, angels and shepherds, and the animals in the stable, we gather around your Son, born for us. Bless us with your holy presence, and inspire us to help those who have no place to dwell. Be with us that we might share Christ's love with all the world, for he is our light and salvation. Glory in heaven and peace on earth, now and forever.
**Amen**

## Proclamation of the Birth of Christ

Today, the twenty-fifth day of December,
unknown ages from the time when God created the heavens
and the earth and then formed man
and woman in his own image.

Several thousand years after the flood,
when God made the rainbow shine forth
as a sign of the covenant.
Twenty-one centuries from the time of Abraham and Sarah;
thirteen centuries after Moses led the people of Israel out of
    Egypt.

Eleven hundred years from the time of Ruth and the Judges;
one thousand years from the anointing of David as king;
in the sixty-fifth week according to the prophecy of Daniel.

In the one hundred and ninety-fourth Olympiad;
the seven hundred and fifty-second year from the foundation
of the city of Rome.

The forty-second year of the reign of Octavian Augustus;
the whole world being at peace,
Jesus Christ, the eternal God and Son of the eternal Father,
desiring to sanctify the world by his most merciful coming,
being conceived by the Holy Spirit,
and nine months having passed since his conception,
was born in Bethlehem of Judea of the Virgin Mary.

Today is the nativity of our Lord Jesus Christ according to the
    flesh.

## Lessons and Carols for Christmas

*This service may be used during the twelve days of Christmas.*

### ENTRANCE HYMN
Oh, come, all ye faithful   LBW 45
Once in royal David's city   WOV 643
Jesus, the Light of the World   TFF 59

### DIALOG
The people who walked in darkness have seen a great light.
**The light shines in the darkness,**
**and the darkness has not overcome it.**
Those who dwelt in the land of deep darkness,
on them light has shined.
**We have beheld Christ's glory,**
**glory as of the only Son from the Father.**
To us a child is born, to us a Son is given.
**In him was life, and the life was the light of all people.**

### OPENING PRAYER
The Lord be with you.
**And also with you.**
Let us pray.
Almighty God, you have filled us with the new light of the Word who became flesh and lived among us. Let the light of our faith shine in all we do; through your Son, Jesus Christ our Lord, who lives and reigns with you and the Holy Spirit, one God, now and forever.
**Amen**

### LESSONS AND CAROLS
First Reading: Isaiah 9:2-7
Lo, how a rose is growing   LBW 58
Emmanuel   TFF 45, W&P 36
Lo, how a rose e'er blooming   HFW

Second Reading: Micah 5:2-5a
O little town of Bethlehem   LBW 41, HFW (FOREST GREEN)
There's a star in the East   WOV 645, TFF 58

Third Reading: Luke 1:26-35, 38
What child is this   LBW 40
Sing of Mary, pure and lowly   WOV 634
Jesus, what a wonderful child   TFF 51

Fourth Reading: Luke 2:1-7
Away in a manger   LBW 67, WOV 644
I wonder as I wander   WOV 642, TFF 50
The virgin Mary had a baby boy   TFF 53

Fifth Reading: Luke 2:8-16
Infant holy, infant lowly   LBW 44
Before the marvel of this night   WOV 636
Mary had a baby   TFF 55

Sixth Reading: Luke 2:21-36
In his temple now behold him   LBW 184; HFS (Regent Square)
That boy-child of Mary   TFF 54

Seventh Reading: Matthew 2:1-11
The first Noel   LBW 56
We three kings of Orient are   WOV 646
Sister Mary   TFF 60

Eighth Reading: Matthew 2:13-18
Oh, sleep now, holy baby   WOV 639
Oh, Mary, gentle poor Mary (María, pobre María)   LLC 310

Ninth Reading: John 1:1-14
Of the Father's love begotten   LBW 42
Let our gladness have no end   LBW 57
He came down   TFF 37

**RESPONSIVE PRAYER**

Glory to God in the highest,
**and peace to God's people on earth.**
Blessed are you, Prince of peace.
**You rule the earth with truth and justice.**
Send your gift of peace to all nations of the world.
Blessed are you, Son of Mary. You share our humanity.
**Have mercy on the sick, the dying,**
**and all who suffer this day.**
Blessed are you, Son of God.
**You dwell among us as the Word made flesh.**
Reveal yourself to us in word and sacrament
**that we may bear your light to all the world.**

**THE LORD'S PRAYER**

**BLESSING AND DISMISSAL**
Let us bless the Lord.
**Thanks be to God.**

May you be filled with the wonder of Mary, the obedience of Joseph, the joy of the angels, the eagerness of the shepherds, the determination of the magi, and the peace of the Christ child. Almighty God, Father, ✛ Son, and Holy Spirit bless you now and forever.
**Amen**

**SENDING HYMN**
LBW 60   Hark! The herald angels sing
TFF 59   Jesus, the Light of the world

# December 24, 2001

### Christmas Eve (I)

## INTRODUCTION

Three great vigils mark the festivals of the year: Easter, Pentecost, and Christmas. At this vigil celebration, we join with Christians throughout the world to celebrate the great mystery of our faith: God speaks to us in our words so that we might know God's mercy; God comes to us in human flesh—in Christ's body and blood—so that we might share in God's unfailing love.

It is not a baby's birth we celebrate, but the light of redemption. As Paul reminds us, the grace of God has appeared bringing salvation to all. Christ unites himself to our fragile, mortal lives so that we might know he is with us, always offering us life, health, and salvation. With the heavenly host we sing, "Glory to God in the highest."

## PRAYER OF THE DAY

Almighty God, you made this holy night shine with the brightness of the true Light. Grant that here on earth we may walk in the light of Jesus' presence and in the last day wake to the brightness of his glory; through your only Son, Jesus Christ our Lord, who lives and reigns with you and the Holy Spirit, one God, now and forever.

## READINGS

### Isaiah 9:2-7

Originally, this poem was written to celebrate either the birth or the coronation of a new Davidic king. After the fall of Jerusalem, this poem came to be viewed as an expression of the hope that eventually God would raise up a new ruler who would possess the qualities described in the text.

### Psalm 96

Let the heavens rejoice and the earth be glad. (Ps. 96:11)

### Titus 2:11-14

The appearance of God's grace is an invitation for God's people to live with zeal and energy for good deeds in the new age inaugurated by Jesus

### Luke 2:1-14 [15-20]

Luke tells the story of Jesus' birth with reference to rulers of the world because this birth has significance for the whole earth, conveying a divine offer of peace.

## COLOR White

## THE PRAYERS

As the heavens and earth are filled with the grace and peace of the Word made flesh, let us pray for the church, the world, and all those in need.

*A BRIEF SILENCE.*

Mighty God, Sovereign of peace, strengthen the leaders of nations in their service, that all the corners of the earth may be filled with your justice and righteousness. God of grace and peace,

**hear us, we pray.**

Give voice to your church, that we may proclaim Christ in our midst and live out the good news of his birth among us. God of grace and peace,

**hear us, we pray.**

Shelter those who are homeless, poor, lonely, and despised of the world. Break the yoke of their burdens and grant them your joy. God of grace and peace,

**hear us, we pray.**

Console those who are homebound, hospitalized, and sick (especially). Enfold them with your light and healing. God of grace and peace,

**hear us, we pray.**

Make room in our hearts for all who join us in worship, and call to mind those absent from us, that our common bonds of faith may be strengthened. God of grace and peace,

**hear us, we pray.**

Enliven this congregation with the Word made flesh in bread and wine, that we may be signs of Christ's presence in the world. God of grace and peace,

**hear us, we pray.**

*HERE OTHER INTERCESSIONS MAY BE OFFERED.*

Hold us in unity with all the saints, that together we may share in the joyful song of the heavenly hosts. God of grace and peace,

**hear us, we pray.**

Hear our prayer, gracious God, as we rejoice in the Word made flesh, your Son, Jesus Christ our Lord.

**Amen**

60

## IMAGES FOR PREACHING

The sounds of a birth. Rustling straw, shifting bodies, a hard-breathing woman, mumbled comfort, the strain of labor stretching even the air, resting, stroking, cramping again, gasping, resting, animals restless with her effort to bring new life, straining, groaning, a cry—small at first, joyful weeping, wrapping, holding, suckling.

Then, in the distance, the sound of a choir more glorious than ever before heard, singing the ecstasy of the whole universe. Glory to God in the highest heaven! Glory to God in the highest heaven! To you is born this day a Savior!

Footsteps alert the tired mother and father. Shepherds come to see what was told them and then to tell: this manger child is the one for whom we have waited. He is the Messiah, the Lord. Admiring, cooing, thanking.

Then the quiet again. Animals stir. The deep breathing of sleep settles through the stable. And Mary hears the precious sounds of her newborn, the Savior of the world. Lord Jesus, you have come.

## WORSHIP MATTERS

This is the season when we celebrate the incarnation. The presence of the word of God in our midst is a sign of the incarnation of the Word. How is Christ, the living Word, honored in your community? Is the place of the word dignified and easily identified as a primary center in the worship space? What does the book used for public proclamation look like? Is it large enough to be seen easily by the whole community? Is it beautifully bound? Is it in good repair? Does it look like the most important book in the room? How is it given visual importance? Would the congregation readily identify it as "their family Bible"? Luther spoke of the Bible as the manger in which the Christ is laid. How might you honor the Word in this incarnational season?

## LET THE CHILDREN COME

"O Lord, how shall I receive you?" the old Christmas hymn asks. Tonight and throughout this season, offer gentle table instructions to children and other communicants. Show them how to make a manger with their open hands so as to receive the gift of Christ.

## HYMNS FOR WORSHIP
### GATHERING

Hark! The herald angels sing   LBW 60
Once in royal David's city   WOV 643

### HYMN OF THE DAY

Lo, how a rose is growing   LBW 58

### ALTERNATE HYMN OF THE DAY

From heaven above   LBW 51
A stable lamp is lighted   LBW 74

### COMMUNION

Away in a manger   LBW 67, WOV 644
I am so glad each Christmas Eve   LBW 69
Your little ones, dear Lord   LBW 52

### SENDING

Silent night, holy night!   LBW 65
Night of silence   W&P 101
I wonder as I wander   WOV 642, TFF 50

### ADDITIONAL HYMNS AND SONGS

Angels we have heard on high   LBW 71
Jesus, child of God   DH 53
Pastores: a Belén/Oh, come to Bethlehem   LLC 305
That boy-child of Mary   TFF 54
The virgin Mary had a baby boy   TFF 53

## MUSIC FOR THE DAY
### SERVICE MUSIC

This is the night to take the congregation's best-known version of the Gloria in excelsis and "dress it up" so that it is sung with special festivity.

### PSALMODY

Christopherson, Dorothy. "The Lord Is King." U, cong, kybd. AFP 0800650611.

Great is the Lord   W&P 53.

Haas, David and Marty Haugen. "Psalm 96: Proclaim to All the Nations" in GC.

Inwood, Paul. "Psalm 96: Today Is Born Our Savior" in STP, vol. 1.

Let the heavens rejoice   TFF 10

Ollis, Peter. "Today a Saviour Has Been Born" in PS 1.

Shout to the Lord   W&P 124

Wetzler, Robert.   PW A.

61

## CHORAL

Carnahan, Craig. "The Christ-Child Lay on Mary's Lap." SATB, pno/hp.   AFP 0800659260.

Jennings, Kenneth. "All My Heart." SATB, 2 fl/2 rec.   AFP 11-1597.

Laster, James. "Oh, Sleep Now, Holy Baby." SATB.   AFP 0800646851.

Ledger, Philip. "On Christmas Night." SATB div, org.   OXF 42.480.

Niedmann, Peter. "Wexford Carol." SATB, org.   AFP 0800659279.

Pelz, Walter L. "While by My Sheep." SATB.   AFP 11-2057.

Praetorius, Michael. "Psallite" in *Chantry Choirbook*. SATB.   AFP 0800657772.

Purcell, Henry. "O Sing unto the Lord." SATB, soloists, str, org.   NOV 29 0146 03.

Reger, Max. "The Virgin's Slumber Song." SSA, kybd.   GSCH HL50482659.

Rutter, John. "Christmas Night." SATB.   OXF 84.316.

Schalk, Carl. "Cradle Hymn." SATB, org, fl.   AFP 080067412X.

Scott, K. Lee. "Infant Holy, Infant Lowly." SATB.   AFP 0800650271.

Sedio, Mark. "This Night Did God Become a Child." SATB.   MSM-50-1019.

Shute, Linda Cable. "Glory in the Highest." SATB.   AFP 080065918X.

Vantine, Bruce. "All My Heart Rejoices." SATB, opt kybd.   MSM-50-1043.

Victoria, Tomas Luis de. "O Magnum Mysterium." SATB. Various ed.

Wetzler, Robert. "God Woke the Stars." SATB.   AMSI 727.

Willcocks, David. "Sussex Carol." SATB.   OXF X75.

## CHILDREN'S CHOIRS

Bedford, Michael. "'Twas in the Moon of Wintertime." U or 2 pt, kybd, Orff.   AFP 0800674316.

Collins, Dori Erwin. "Hurry to the Stable." U, kybd.   AFP 0800674154.

Martinson, Joel. "Alepun." U, org.   CG CGA657.

Rogers, Cheryl Jones. "One Star." U, kybd, fl.   CG CGA-460.

## KEYBOARD/INSTRUMENTAL

Albrecht, Timothy. "Es ist ein Ros" in *Grace Notes VIII*. Org.   AFP 0800658264.

Langlais, Jean. "La Nativité" in *Poemes Evangeliques*. Org. Herelle p 32.359.

Leavitt, John. "Es ist ein Ros" in Christmas Suite. Org.   AFP 0800657217.

Lovinfosse, Dennis. "Es ist ein Ros" in *A New Liturgical Year*. Org.   AFP 0800656717.

Sedio, Mark. "Oh, Come to Bethlehem" in *A Global Piano Tour*. Pno.   AFP 0800658191.

Young, Jeremy. "Roses and Angels" in *Pianoforte Christmas*. Kybd.   AFP 0800655702.

## HANDBELL

Afdahl, Lee J. "Once in Royal David's City." 3-5 oct. L4.   AFP 0800658892.

Dobrinski, Cynthia. "Joy to the World." 3-5 oct. L3.   AG 2157.

Dobrinski, Cynthia. "Silent Night." 3-5 oct. L2.   AG 1586.

Larson, Lloyd. "Carol of the Bells/God Rest Ye Merry Gentlemen." 3-5 oct. L3+.   AG 1912.

Maggs, Charles. "Away in a Manger." 3 oct. L1.   AG GP 1024.

McFadden, Jane. "Pastorale on Lo, How a Rose E'er Blooming." 5 oct.   AFP 0800654021.

Waugh, Tim. "Kolyada." 3-4 oct. L2.   JEF JHS9196.

## PRAISE ENSEMBLE

Baloche, Paul and Gary Sadler. "Rise Up and Praise Him" in *Hosanna Music Songbook 13*. SAT[B], kybd.   INT 13576.

Berry, Cindy. "Heaven Rejoices Tonight (with Joy to the World)." HAL 08742515 (SATB, kybd); 08742516 (inst); 08742517 (CD).

Fettke, Tom. "For Unto Us a Child Is Born."   LIL AN-3928 (2 pt, kybd); MU-2458D (choraltrax); MU-5519T (CD); OR-2458 (orch).

Meece, David and David Emerson. "One Small Child." HAL 4032614 (SAB, kybd); 40326127 (SATB, 2 pt inst); 40326127 (cass).

Sleeth, Natalie. "Jazz Gloria." SATB, kybd, tpt, bass, perc.   CFI CM7752.

# December 25, 2001

Christmas Dawn (II)

## INTRODUCTION

The liturgy proclaims, "To you is born this day a Savior!" The scriptures announce the presence of God among the people of the earth. At the festive table of communion we meet the child born of Mary, our crucified and risen Lord. Through baptism we have become children of the true Light. We go forth to proclaim this news of great joy: God is with us.

## PRAYER OF THE DAY

Almighty God, you have made yourself known in your Son, Jesus, redeemer of the world. We pray that his birth as a human child will set us free from the old slavery of our sin; through Jesus Christ our Lord, who lives and reigns with you and the Holy Spirit, one God, now and forever.

## READINGS

Isaiah 62:6-12

When Israel returned from exile and Jerusalem still lay in ruins, the prophet invited God's people to imagine the city's restoration.

Psalm 97

Light has sprung up for the righteous. (Ps. 97:11)

Titus 3:4-7

Salvation is a free and gracious gift from God. In baptism, God's people have a new birth with Christ.

Luke 2:[1-7] 8-20

The world's deep night is shattered by the light of God's new day. Shepherds not only come to the manger to see what has happened; they also return to share the good news with others.

## COLOR White

## THE PRAYERS

As the heavens and earth are filled with the grace and peace of the Word made flesh, let us pray for the church, the world, and all those in need.

*A BRIEF SILENCE.*

God of goodness and lovingkindness, draw all peoples to your path of salvation, that your wisdom may be known to the ends of the earth. God of grace and peace,
**hear us, we pray.**

Form your church, a people you make holy through baptism, into a great company of disciples to live out the mercy that is born today. God of grace and peace,
**hear us, we pray.**

Remember those who live with fear, poverty, anxiety, or illness (especially), that the light of Christ's birth may scatter their darkness and bring renewed hope. God of grace and peace,
**hear us, we pray.**

Gather the outcasts and those easily overlooked, that with the shepherds they may hear the good news of your love for all the world. God of grace and peace,
**hear us, we pray.**

Reveal your wonder to us in the midst of our Christmas celebration, that we may ponder with Mary all that God has done for us. God of grace and peace,
**hear us, we pray.**

*HERE OTHER INTERCESSIONS MAY BE OFFERED.*

Gather us together with all your saints, the people you have sought out and made holy, and bring us to the dawn of your eternal day. God of grace and peace,
**hear us, we pray.**

Hear our prayer, gracious God, as we rejoice in the Word made flesh, your Son, Jesus Christ our Lord.
**Amen**

## IMAGES FOR PREACHING

The sun rises on a new world! Jesus is born! God is among us! In the promise of a new day, the cries of a newborn can raise the dead. On this day, it is the angels who fill the sky with sound. It is the shepherds who set the pace. This child changes everything.

What kind of world did God see as Jesus entered time and space? What kind of world did Jesus come to announce? Imagine a world without war, poverty, hunger, class distinctions, or strife. Imagine a world in balance, where all God's creatures are respected, the earth as well as human beings.

63

Imagine a world where every child is wanted and nourished into the fullness of life, where the old are cherished and know how to bless. Imagine a world where the gifts of everyone are welcomed and given a place to grow. Imagine such a world, so unlike the one we know.

Imagine the promise in this new child, how through him our imaginations and even we ourselves are lifted from despair. Imagine a great multitude, all moving toward God's abundance. Imagine each one welcomed, scooped up, and soothed. Imagine a God of justice, who wills that all people, all creation, live to the fullest. Imagine a God who promises, even if such a world never happens within the confines of time, that such a world will be ours, for eternity.

To you is born this day in the city of David a Savior, who is the Messiah, the Lord.

### WORSHIP MATTERS

We often speak of the congregation as the Body of Christ active in the world. In this image, we link the assembly to the eucharistic meal. But how often have you heard the congregation referred to as the Word of God active in the world, thus linking the assembly to the liturgy of the word? There is opportunity here to help the congregation deepen its self-understanding. We lift up Christ's presence in meal, bath, word, and assembly. Make the connection between word and assembly a little stronger this season.

### LET THE CHILDREN COME

"Glory to God in the highest!" This morning we sing the angels' song. The gospel tells the story that the assembly recalled in song as the liturgy began. Remind the children of this. Give them small brass bells to ring as they sing with the angels. Gather the bells as the children leave the nave and use them for the Gloria every Sunday through the Baptism of Our Lord.

### HYMNS FOR WORSHIP
#### GATHERING
Rejoice, rejoice, this happy morn  LBW 43
The bells of Christmas  LBW 62

#### HYMN OF THE DAY
Good Christian friends, rejoice  LBW 55

### ALTERNATE HYMN OF THE DAY
Once in royal David's city  WOV 643
There's a star in the East  WOV 645, TFF 58

### COMMUNION
Infant holy, infant lowly  LBW 44
Oh, come, all ye faithful  LBW 45
Peace came to earth  WOV 641

### SENDING
Once again my heart rejoices  LBW 46
When Christmas morn is dawning  LBW 59

### ADDITIONAL HYMNS AND SONGS
Hear the angels  W&P 57
Gloria, gloria, gloria  WOV 637
Christians, awake, salute the happy morn  H82 106
On Christmas day  BC

## MUSIC FOR THE DAY
### PSALMODY
Beckett, Debbie. "This Day New Light Will Shine" in PS 1.
Cooney, Rory. "The Lord Is King" in STP, vol. 4.
Haas, David. "Our God Is here."  GIA G-5041.
Hopson, Hal H. "Psalm 97" in TP. Cant, cong.
Kreutz, Robert E. "Psalm 97" in *Psalms for the Cantor*, vol. III. WLP 2504.
The Dameans. "A Light will Shine/Lord Today" in PCY, vol. 6.
Wetzler, Robert.  PW A.

### CHORAL
Bach, J.S. "Break Forth, O Beauteous Heavenly Light" in *Bach for All Seasons*. SATB, kybd.  AFP 080065854X.
Benson, Robert. "The Snow Lay on the Ground." SATB, org. AFP 0800674294.
Burt, Alfred. "All on a Christmas Morning" in *The Alfred Burt Carols, Set 1*. SATB or solo, kybd.  SHW A-449.
Nelson, Ron. "Choral Fanfare for Christmas." SATB or TTBB, org/brass.  B&H OCTB5337.
Praetorius, Michael. "Psallite" in *Chantry Choirbook*. SATB.  AFP.
Scott, K. Lee. "When Christmas Morn Is Dawning." SATB, org. MSM-50-1010.
Shaw, Martin. "Fanfare for Christmas Day." SATB, org, 2 tpt. GSCH 8745.
Shute, Linda Cable. "Glory in the Highest." SATB, pno, opt perc. AFP 080065918X.

64

Sirett, Mark G. "What Sweeter Music." SATB.   AFP 0800659287.

Werner, Gregor Joseph-Oberdoerffer. "Puer Natus in Bethlehem." SATB, vln/fl, cont.   CPH 98-2313.

## CHILDREN'S CHOIRS

Goetze, Mary, arr. "Dormi, Dormi." U, kybd.   B&H OCTB6128.

Gritton, Eric. "Welcome, Jule!" U, kybd.   GAL I.5140.

## KEYBOARD/INSTRUMENTAL

Burkhardt, Michael. *Three Carols for Oboe and Organ.*   MSM 20-164.

Dupré, Marcel. "In dulci jubilo" in *A New Liturgical Year.* Org. AFP 0800656717.

Held, Wilbur. "In dulci jubilo" in *Six Carol Settings.* Org. CPH 97-4985.

Mulet, Henry. "Noel" in *Esquisses Byzantines.* Org.   LED BL 631.

Uehlein, Christopher. "Bring a Torch, Jeanette, Isabella" in *A Blue Cloud Abbey Christmas Organ Book.* Org.   AFP 0800659791.

Wold, Wayne L. "Once in Royal David's City" in *God with Us.* Org. AFP 0800658213.

## HANDBELL

Beck, Theodore. "In Dulci Jubilo." 3 oct. L2.   AFP 0800654005.

Behnke, John A. "Of the Father's Love Begotten." 3-5 oct. L3. CPH 97-6844.

McChesney, Kevin. "The Holly and the Ivy." 3 oct. L2. CG CGB137.

Moklebust, Cathy. "Infant Holy, Infant Lowly." 2-3 oct. L2. CG CGB222.

## PRAISE ENSEMBLE

Black, Lee, and Cindi Ballard. "Emmanuel, Emmanuel."   HAL 08742471 (SATB, kybd); 08742472 (inst); 08742473 (CD).

Watson, Wayne. "Child of Bethlehem" in *The Ultimate Youth Choir Book Christmas.* SAB, kybd. CD available.   WRD 0 80689 33017 9.

65

# December 25, 2001

## Christmas Day (III)

## INTRODUCTION

Since the beginning of time, the coming of light has been a sign of life and hope. The sun and the stars transform the darkness into an inhabitable space. On the festival of the Lord's nativity, the church gathers to celebrate the light of God's grace present in Christ. In the holy bath of baptism, Christ enlightens and claims us as brothers and sisters. In the holy word of scripture, Christ speaks to us of God's love for each human being. In the holy meal of the eucharist, Christ gives us the bread of eternal life. From this festive liturgy we go forth to be light-bearers in the ordinary rhythms of daily life.

## PRAYER OF THE DAY

Almighty God, you wonderfully created and yet more wonderfully restored the dignity of human nature. In your mercy, let us share the divine life of Jesus Christ who came to share our humanity, and who now lives and reigns with you and the Holy Spirit, one God, now and forever.

## READINGS

Isaiah 52:7-10

Changing events in Babylon inspire this announcement of hope and joy to the people of Judah near the end of their exile. "Your God reigns," says the prophet. It is the dawn of comfort, redemption, and the salvation of our God.

Psalm 98

All the ends of the earth have seen the victory of our God. (Ps. 98:4)

Hebrews 1:1-4 [5-12]

This rich and stately New Testament letter begins with a strong affirmation of Jesus as the Son of God. To call Jesus God's Son is to recognize that he is superior even to prophets and angels.

John 1:1-14

The prologue to the gospel of John describes Jesus as the Word of God made flesh, God's true presence among us, the one whose very existence reveals God, "full of grace and truth."

COLOR  White

THE PRAYERS

As the heavens and earth are filled with the grace and peace of the Word made flesh, let us pray for the church, the world, and all those in need.

*A BRIEF SILENCE.*

Ever-present God, strengthen your church to be a messenger of peace, that through its proclamation and life it may bring good news to all who are disheartened. God of grace and peace,
**hear us, we pray.**

Uphold all who strive for justice and freedom, that their work for peace may shine with your saving love. God of grace and peace,
**hear us, we pray.**

Raise up those who are lowly and powerless, that Christ's humble birth may shine hope within their hearts and lead us to care for all in need. God of grace and peace,
**hear us, we pray.**

Surround with your love the lonely, bereaved, and all for whom this day is a burden, that they may know the arms of your mercy. God of grace and peace,
**hear us, we pray.**

Let your healing presence be the oil of gladness for all who are sick (especially), that they may be comforted and lifted up. God of grace and peace,
**hear us, we pray.**

Gladden our hearts through our sharing of word and sacrament, and let your grace and truth fill all our days. God of grace and peace,
**hear us, we pray.**

*HERE OTHER INTERCESSIONS MAY BE OFFERED.*

Unite us with all the saints in the light of your baptismal grace, until we join them in the brightness of heavenly glory. God of grace and peace,
**hear us, we pray.**

Hear our prayer, gracious God, as we rejoice in the Word made flesh, your Son, Jesus Christ our Lord.
**Amen**

IMAGES FOR PREACHING

And the Word became flesh. Not a chimera, not ephemera, not a sixth-sense "presence." The Word became flesh. What is the value of being able to see, touch, smell, and taste? What does it mean that we are irretrievably temporal? And why did God come to be with us, in the flesh, sharing our physical senses but also our inevitable limits?

Imagine this miracle and believe. The creator of the whole universe chose to step into the vulnerabilities of flesh—to hurt, tire, hunger, thirst, anguish, praise, and love—most of all, to love. We who are limited to flesh, who know life only within our own flesh, we must be met in the flesh. God knows this. It was God's imagination that it should be so. So a baby is born. So a man heals and holds. So comes a death, and—here is the greatest miracle of all—then comes a rising. When it was his hour to leave time and space, he left us his body and blood. In this holy food, a sacrament of love, God is ever incarnate, God is always "in the flesh."

Now he lives in each of us, in our hurt and hunger, in our anguish and joy, in our love for each other and the world. God has declared our flesh good and ours to treasure. Today we see his fleshly glory, full of grace and truth. Now we rejoice in the birth of a child, God and yet one of us.

WORSHIP MATTERS

Art can be incarnational. The Word became flesh and dwelt among us. Through human flesh, we have come to know God. We also meet God in other parts of creation. Reflect with your worship committee on the use of incarnational arts in your congregation. Do the visual arts in your community make Christ known? How do you use these arts to form Christians? Evaluate fine arts in your congregation aesthetically, theologically, and pastorally. Lutherans have a great heritage of using music both to proclaim and to transform. The works of other artists—carpenter, painter, potter, weaver, dancer, designer, and actor—are also important tools in our ministry tool kit. Honor these gifts. Learn to use them in worship, proclamation, and formation.

LET THE CHILDREN COME

What is it about candles that draws children and the child in each of us to their flickering mystery? Today's gospel shines with the very Light of whom it speaks. Plan a simple but dignified gospel procession. Instruct four older children, grades four and above, to carry substantial pillar candles, two preceding the book bearer and presider and two following. Another child could hold the book. Depending on the shape of your worship space, there might be room for the candle-bearers to stand in a circle, forming a "wreath" of flame around the word, the light no darkness can overcome.

## HYMNS FOR WORSHIP
### GATHERING

Let our gladness have no end   LBW 57

What feast of love   WOV 701

### GOSPEL SEQUENCE HYMN

All praise to you, eternal Lord   LBW 48

Glory to God, glory in the highest   WOV 788

### HYMN OF THE DAY

Holy child within the manger   WOV 638

### ALTERNATE HYMN OF THE DAY

Hark! The herald angels sing   LBW 60

Jesus, the light of the world   TFF 59

### COMMUNION

Of the Father's love begotten   LBW 42

The first Noel   LBW 56

### SENDING

Go tell it on the mountain   LBW 70, TFF 52

There's a star in the East   WOV 645, TFF 58

### ADDITIONAL HYMNS AND SONGS

He came down   TFF 37

The King of glory   W&P 136

Love came down at Christmas   H82 84

When God's time had ripened   NSR 8

## MUSIC FOR THE DAY
### PSALMODY

Joy to the world   LBW 39

Smith, Timothy R. "The Lord has revealed" in STP, vol. 4.

Wetzler, Robert.   PW A.

### CHORAL

Bach, J.S. "Gloria in excelsis Deo" in *Bach for All Seasons*. SATB, kybd.
AFP 080065854X.

Bouman, Paul. "A Babe Is Born." SATB.   CPH CH1058.

Carter, Andrew. "Hodie Christus natus est." SATB, org.
OXF X382.

Hovland, Egil. "The Glory of the Father." SATB.   WAL W2973.

Jennings, Carolyn. "In the Beginning Was the Word." SSAATB, hb.
AFP 6000101619.

Johnson, David N. "Praise Be the Lord This Day" in *A Service of Nine Lessons and Carols*. SATB, fl.   AFP 0800648617.

Praetorius, Michael. "Enatus est Emmanuel" in the *Chantry Choirbook*.
SATB.   AFP 0800657772.

Roberts, Paul. "The Word Became Flesh." SATB, fl.
AFP 0800657659.

Schweizer, Mark. "Let All the Rivers Clap Their Hands." SATB, kybd.   CPH 98-3427.

Sweelinck, J.P. "Hodie Christus Natus Est." SSATB.
HWG GCMR01855.

Werner, Gregor Joseph-Oberdoerffer. "Puer natus in Bethlehem."
SATB, vl/fl, cont.   CPH 98-2313.

Zimmermann, Heinz Werner. "And the Word Became Flesh." SATB.
CPH 98-2177.

### CHILDREN'S CHOIRS

Davis, Katherine K. "Sing Gloria." U, kybd.   WAR 4309-4.

Walters, Edmund. "The Cuckoo Carol." U, kybd.
B&H OCTB5721.

### KEYBOARD/INSTRUMENTAL

Glick, Sara. "Holy Child within the Manger" in *Piano Music for Ministry: Advent, Christmas, Epiphany*. Pno.   AFP 0800659783.

Groom, Lester. "Prelude on 'Divinum Mysterium'" in *Six Organ Preludes*. Org.   BEL GB 654.

Purvis, Richard. *Greensleeves*. Org.   MCA 01326-012.

Uehlein, Christopher. *A Blue Cloud Abbey Christmas Organ Book*. Org.
AFP 0800659791.

### HANDBELL

Afdahl, Lee. "Three Spanish Carols for Bells." 2-3 oct. L3.
AFP 0800658108.

Morris, Hart. "On This Day Earth Shall Ring." 3-5 oct. L3.
CPH 97-6681.

Taylor, Jeffery. "God Rest Ye Merry, Gentlemen." 3 oct. L3.
AG 2149.

### PRAISE ENSEMBLE

Althouse, Jay. "Joyful, Joyful to the World."   ALF 18324 (SATB, kybd, tpt); 18325 (SAB); 18326 (2 pt); 18328 (brass); 1832 (CD).

Carey, Mariah. "Jesus Born on This Day." HAL 08742056 (SATB, kybd); 08742057 (orch).

Harlan, Benjamin. "Fanfare for Christmas Day." HAL 08742411 (SATB, kybd); 08742485 (brass); 08742486 (CD).

# Wednesday, December 26

## ST. STEPHEN, DEACON AND MARTYR

Stephen was a deacon and the first martyr of the church. He was one of those seven upon whom the apostles laid hands after they had been chosen to serve widows and others in need. Later, Stephen's preaching angered the temple authorities, and they ordered him to be put to death by stoning.

The Christmas song "Good King Wenceslas" takes place on the feast of Stephen. The king sees a peasant gathering wood near the forest and sends his page to invite the peasant to a feast. The song, with its theme of charity to the poor, can be a way to remember Stephen, who cared for widows and those in need. Congregations and families within them can be invited to include gifts to charitable organizations during these days of Christmas in honor of Stephen.

# Thursday, December 27

## ST. JOHN, APOSTLE AND EVANGELIST

John, the son of Zebedee, was a fisherman and one of the twelve. John, his brother James, and Peter were the three who witnessed the light of the Transfiguration. John and James once made known their desire to hold positions of power in the kingdom of God. Jesus' response showed them that service to others was the sign of God's reign in the world. Though authorship of the gospel and the three epistles bearing his name has often been attributed to the apostle John, this tradition cannot be proven from scriptural evidence.

John is a saint for Christmas through his proclamation that the Word became flesh and dwelt among us, that the light of God shines in the darkness, and that we are called to love one another as Christ has loved us. According to an early story about John, his enemies once tried to murder him with poisoned wine. On this day, many Christians in Europe will toast one another with the words "I drink to the love of John."

# Friday, December 28

## THE HOLY INNOCENTS, MARTYRS

In a culture where Christmas is overcommercialized and sentimentalized, the commemoration of the Holy Innocents, Martyrs on the fourth day of Christmas must come as something of a shock. How could the birth of a baby be the occasion for the death of anyone? Yet these martyrs were the children of Bethlehem, two years old and younger, who were killed by Herod, who worried that his reign was threatened by the birth of a new king. St. Augustine called these innocents "buds, killed by the frost of persecution the moment they showed themselves." Those linked to Jesus through their youth and innocence encounter the same hostility Jesus encounters later in his ministry.

Remembering all innocent victims and taking up the words of the prayer of the day, which ask God to "frustrate the designs of evil tyrants and establish your rule of justice, love, and peace," can mark this commemoration.

# December 30, 2001

### First Sunday after Christmas

## INTRODUCTION

The gospel reading for this day juxtaposes the birth of Christ with the death of innocent children. Indeed, whenever we sentimentalize the nativity of the Lord, we need to hear this story of the slaughter of the Holy Innocents. Christian faith does not lead us out of the world of evil rulers, injustice, and death. Rather, the gift of faith strengthens us to contend with any force that threatens the life God has created.

Here is this potent sign: in the holy supper we receive the body and blood of the one who accompanies us in this broken and fragile world.

## PRAYER OF THE DAY

Almighty God, you have made yourself known in your Son, Jesus, redeemer of the world. We pray that his birth as a human child will set us free from the old slavery of our sin; through Jesus Christ our Lord, who lives and reigns with you and the Holy Spirit, one God, now and forever.

*or*

Almighty God, you wonderfully created and yet more wonderfully restored the dignity of human nature. In your mercy, let us share the divine life of Jesus Christ who came to share our humanity, and who now lives and reigns with you and the Holy Spirit, one God, now and forever.

## READINGS

### Isaiah 63:7-9

These verses sing of thanksgiving and praise because of God's "gracious deeds" and "steadfast love" (v. 7). Both of these terms are translations of the Hebrew word *hesed*. It is not a romantic love that grows cold. Rather, this love always treats the other person with unselfish kindness, respect, and loyalty.

### Psalm 148

The splendor of the Lord is over earth and heaven. (Ps. 148:13)

### Hebrews 2:10-18

Though Christmas is a joyous season, its meaning can-

not be separated from the message of Holy Week. Jesus became like us in order to suffer with us and to destroy the power of death.

### Matthew 2:13-23

Matthew describes the terrible slaughter of young Bethlehem boys as a sign of evil present in the world, and to highlight the relationship between the Hebrew scriptures and Jesus' life.

## COLOR  White

## THE PRAYERS

As the heavens and earth are filled with the grace and peace of the Word made flesh, let us pray for the church, the world, and all those in need.

*A BRIEF SILENCE.*

Guide the church in its mission and ministry, that like Joseph and Mary, your people may be led with faith and hope. God of grace and peace,

**hear us, we pray.**

Make the leaders of nations, states, and communities to be lovers of goodness and truth, that all your children may be nurtured and protected. God of grace and peace,

**hear us, we pray.**

Free those caught in political bondage or personal addiction, that they may find new life in Christ, who shares in their suffering and pain. God of grace and peace,

**hear us, we pray.**

Comfort and heal all who are sorrowful or sick (especially), that they may be embraced by your steadfast love. God of grace and peace,

**hear us, we pray.**

Watch over our families and friends, and protect all who travel, that their way may be kept safe and their homecomings made joyful. God of grace and peace,

**hear us, we pray.**

*HERE OTHER INTERCESSIONS MAY BE OFFERED.*

Bless us with the witness of all your saints, that together with them we may delight in the one who calls us brothers and sisters. God of grace and peace,

**hear us, we pray.**

69

Hear our prayer, gracious God, as we rejoice in the Word made flesh, your Son, Jesus Christ our Lord.
**Amen**

## IMAGES FOR PREACHING

The sounds associated with Christmas do not include wailing. We prefer to be spared reminders of suffering when we are rejoicing in the birth of Jesus—as we anticipate the miracle of his life among us. But Jesus did not come just to shine on our happy times. It would not have been so astounding that God would take on flesh if God had come only to join us in joy. In Jesus, God also takes on the risks of being among us, with us, one of us.

Joseph and Mary will escape with Jesus this time. Jesus will be spared an infant's death, but others will not be. Wailing and loud lamentation are heard in Jesus' day, as in ours. Rachel's voice from history bears the anguish of mothers whose children have been stolen. In Rachel's voice from Ramah is carried the weeping of all those who have lost their little ones to the snarls of power and dominion.

Immediately we are forced to ask, Is this the world God has chosen to save? This world of callous ambition is the one God loves so recklessly? Even as the singing of angels fades in the sky, evil rears its head. Jesus was protected in his parents' arms this time, but soon he will not escape suffering and death.

Soon he will walk toward the blind and lame. Soon he will chastise the ruling powers. Soon he will stand before Pilate and say nothing as he is accused. Soon he will suffer and die.

Jesus is here not merely to rejoice with us. He is here not merely to commiserate. He is here to save, to call us into life, to be irrevocably God with us.

## WORSHIP MATTERS

Lectionary inserts may be convenient tools for the assembly, especially for those who want to take home a reminder of the week's proclamation or who have difficulty hearing or seeing. They are not tools for the lector or reader, however. The words embodied by the reader are no ordinary words. They are the word of life. The reader's tools are the book of life, the body, and the voice. Does the book from which your worship leaders read fit the scale of the worship space, and is it of a quality that dignifies its contents? This book forms the focus for the liturgy of the word. Encourage lectors to so embody and proclaim the words that the assembly is drawn into engagement with the living Word, not left to follow the lectionary insert. This lively proclaiming is the very Word of God in our midst.

## LET THE CHILDREN COME

Much of North American culture has finished its midwinter festival of consumerism and consumption, while the church is in the middle of its celebration of the incarnation. Encourage the people of your parish to keep their homes awash with the light of their Christmas trees, their walkways or doorways illumined, and their tables brightened with candles until Epiphany. This helps children see that they are keeping the same feast at home and at church.

## HYMNS FOR WORSHIP
### GATHERING

Good Christian friends, rejoice    LBW 55
Cold December flies away    LBW 53
He came down    TFF 37

### HYMN OF THE DAY

I wonder as I wander    WOV 642, TFF 50

### ALTERNATE HYMN OF THE DAY

Let all together praise our God    LBW 47
Sister Mary    TFF 60

### COMMUNION

O little town of Bethlehem    LBW 41
It came upon the midnight clear    LBW 54
Oh, sleep now, holy baby    WOV 639

### SENDING

Hark! The herald angels sing    LBW 60
Rejoice, rejoice, this happy morn    LBW 43
There's a star in the East    WOV 645, TFF 58

### ADDITIONAL HYMNS AND SONGS

The King of glory    W&P 136
Hush, little Jesus boy    TFF 56
'Twas in the moon of wintertime    LBW 72
María, pobre María/Oh, Mary, gentle poor Mary    LLC 310

## MUSIC FOR THE DAY
### PSALMODY

Haas, David. "Praise in the Heights."   GIA G-5041.

Handel, G.F./arr. Hal H. Hopson. "Praise God, Oh, Bless the Lord." SATB, org.   AFP 6000131798.

Ogden, David. "Let All Creation Sing" in PS 1.

Powell, Robert J. "Praise the Lord from the Heavens." U, kybd. SEL 422-772.

Praise the Lord of heaven!   LBW 541

Rorem, Ned. "Psalm 148" in *Cycle of Holy Songs for Voice and Piano*. Solo. Peer 01-073794-212.

Wetzler, Robert.   PW A.

### CHORAL

Bass, Claude L. "At Bethlehem." SATB, pno.   AFP 080065742X.

Bishop, Dorothy. "Lullay, Thou Little Tiny Child." SATB. CFI CM7070.

Eccard, Johann. "Raise a Song, Let Praise Abound" in the *Chantry Choirbook*. SATTB.   AFP 0800657772.

Ferguson, John. "Let All Together Praise Our God." SATB, org/2 tpt. CPH 98-2651.

Johnson, David N. "Judah's Land." SATB.   AFP 0800652606.

Pelz, Walter. "Coventry Carol." SATB, hp/kybd. AFP 0800646088.

Shaw, Martin. "Coventry Carol" in *100 Carols for Choirs*. SATB.   OXF.

Vaughan Williams, Ralph. "The Blessed Son of God" in *Two Chorals from the Cantata 'This Day' (Hodie)*.   OXF 43.929. Or *Carols for Choirs 1*. SATB.   OXF.

Warland, Dale. "Coventry Carol." SATB.   CPH 98-1928.

Wyton, Alec. "Lullaby after Christmas." SATB, fl, marimba, org. AUR AE32.

### CHILDREN'S CHOIRS

Bertaux, Betty. "This Is the Truth." U, kybd, tri, tamb, fc, drm, jingle bells.   B&H MO51471294.

Mitchell, Tom. "Sing and Rejoice." 2 pt, org.   CG CGA-584.

### KEYBOARD/INSTRUMENTAL

Carlson, J. Bert. "I Wonder" in *Carols from Many Lands*. Kybd. AFP 0800659767.

Glick, Sara. "I Wonder" in *Piano Music for Ministry: Advent, Christmas, Epiphany*. Pno.   AFP 0800659783.

"I Wonder" in *Let It Rip at the Piano*. Kybd.   AFP 0800659066.

Lovelace, Austin. "Mendelssohn" in *Variations on Seven Christmas Hymns*. Org.   AFP 11-9098.

Osterland, Karl. "I Wonder" in *I Wonder as I Wander*. Org. AFP 0800657225.

Walther, J.G. "Lobt Gott, ihr Christen" in *80 Chorale Preludes*. Org/pno.   PET 11354.

### HANDBELL

McChesney, Kevin. "In You Is Gladness." 3-5 oct. L3. CPH 97-6510.

Sherman, Arnold B. "An English Carol." 3-5 oct. L3+.   AG 1433.

Thompson, Martha Lynn. "Good King Wenceslas." 3-5 oct. L2. AG 2093.

### PRAISE ENSEMBLE

Condon, Mark/arr. Mark Condon and J. Daniel Smith. "Marvelous Things" in *Marvelous Things Choral Collection*. SATB, kybd. INT 18256.

Hayes, Mark. "Behold! Rise Up! Go Tell! Shine!"   ALF 18045 (SATB, kybd); 18046 (SAB); 18300 (brass); 18047 (acc cass).

71

# Tuesday, January 1

## THE NAME OF JESUS

The observance of the octave (eighth day) of Christmas has roots in the sixth century. Until the recent past, Lutheran calendars called this day "The Circumcision and Name of Jesus." The emphasis on circumcision is the older emphasis. Every Jewish boy was circumcised and formally named on the eighth day of his life. Already in his youth, Jesus bears the mark of a covenant that he makes new through the shedding of his blood, now and on the cross. That covenant, like Jesus' name, is a gift to us and marks us as children of God. Baptized into Christ, we begin this new year in Jesus' name. Sustained by the gift of his body and blood, we will find that this year, too, we will be sustained by the gift of Christ's body and the new covenant in Christ's blood.

# Wednesday, January 2

JOHANN KONRAD WILHELM LOEHE, PASTOR, 1872

Loehe was a pastor in nineteenth-century Germany. From the small town of Neuendettelsau he sent pastors to North America, Australia, New Guinea, Brazil, and the Ukraine. His work for a clear confessional basis within the Bavarian church sometimes led to conflict with the ecclesiastical bureaucracy. Loehe's chief concern was that a parish finds its life in the eucharist, and from that source evangelism and social ministries would flow. Many Lutheran congregations in Michigan, Ohio, and Iowa were either founded or influenced by missionaries sent by Loehe, and the chapel at Wartburg Theological Seminary is named in his honor.

Loehe's vision to see the eucharist at the center of parish life can lead us on to think about ways that the incarnate presence of Christ in holy communion sends us out in a life of ministry and mission.

72

# Saturday, January 5

KAJ MUNK, MARTYR, 1944

Munk, a Danish Lutheran pastor and playwright, was an outspoken critic of the Nazis who occupied Denmark during the Second World War. His plays frequently highlighted the eventual victory of the Christian faith despite the church's weak and ineffective witness. The Nazis feared Munk because his sermons and articles helped to strengthen the Danish resistance movement. In one of his sermons for New Year's Day he wrote, "The cross characterizes the flags of the North [Nordic countries].... Lead us, thou cross in our flag, lead us into that Nordic struggle where shackled Norway and bleeding Finland fight against an idea which is directly opposed to all our ideals" (*Four Sermons*, trans., J. M. Jensen. Blair, NE: Lutheran Publishing House, 1944).

Munk's life and death invite us to ponder the power of the gospel in the midst of social and political conflicts. Offer prayers for those who face persecution and for those who resist and challenge tyranny.

# EPIPHANY

*Nations shall come to your light,*

*and kings to the brightness of your dawn*

# Images *of the* Season

Christians in the Northern Hemisphere have long

associated midwinter's decreased amount of natural light

with the gloom overcome by Christ's birth.

Matthew's story of the magi traveling to Bethlehem guided by a star is certainly one biblical event that encourages our use of the light metaphor in this season whenever we speak of Christ's effect on the world. Epiphany is a time to celebrate the presence of Christ as light. It is also a season for focusing on a few central teachings of the Christian faith. By doing so, we hope to discover what is most important in our faith and in the Christian mission throughout the world.

The arrival of the magi at Jesus' home (Matt. 2:1-12) established his worldwide significance. Isaiah 60:1-6 (the first reading for the festival of Epiphany) proclaims, "Nations shall come to your light, and kings to the brightness of your dawn" (v. 3). Jesus fulfills this ancient promise. Though born in Judea, Jesus became a treasure for the whole human race.

How Epiphany came to be known as the festival celebrating the revelation of Christ to the nations, and more particularly the arrival of three kings, is a peculiar development. Perhaps associating the Isaiah 60 passage with the Matthew 2 story gave Christians the notion that the magi were kings (the story in Matthew does not mention that they were). Furthermore, Matthew's account of the magi does not indicate how many of them there were, though Isaiah 60:6, which speaks about camels coming from Midian, Ephah, and Sheba, may have suggested to people that there were three. The three gifts presented to the Christ child in Matthew 2:11 (gold, frankincense, and myrrh) may have led to a tradition that assigned one bearer to each gift. Regardless of its accuracy, a story about three foreign kings coming a long distance to bow down and worship before a child has drawing power. That a child of such humble origins can be the focus of so much attention asks for our wonder-filled consideration.

The spotlight continues to stay on Jesus as we move throughout the season after Epiphany. At Jesus' baptism the spotlight is accompanied by a dove and a voice from heaven. Not only is Jesus special, he is the Son of God.

In following weeks, as we continue the gospel readings, we notice that Jesus caused a stir wherever he went. Two of John's disciples turned and instead followed Jesus. Then the two sons of Zebedee were added to their number. Jesus caught people's attention as he taught in synagogues and healed diseases (Matt. 4:23). And, in the fifth chapter of Matthew, Jesus attracted a large crowd and delivered the famed sermon on the mount.

Finally we reach Jesus' transfiguration on a high mountain in the presence of Peter, James, and John. In the story Jesus was not only in the spotlight, but "his face shone like the sun, and his clothes became dazzling white" (Matt. 17:2). Peter was so struck by this occasion, and by the presence of Moses and Elijah along with Jesus, that he wanted to build three shrines. But Jesus did not stay there for long. He took the disciples down the mountain, while telling them not to talk about what they had seen until after the resurrection.

The biblical scenes in the weeks after Epiphany keep pointing us back to the person whom the magi came to worship in Bethlehem. Jesus is the center of attention; the spotlight keeps focusing on him and on his mission. All of these events lead to the main part of the drama: Jesus' death and resurrection. Jesus' birth, baptism, and the beginning of his public ministry represent act 1. The coming weeks will take us into act 2. The spotlight will again be focused on Jesus, with more intensity and brilliance.

Can we stay with the story as it unfolds? Can we also focus all of our energies as congregations on proclaiming Christ to the world? Week in and week out, it is Christ who is the center of our focus. He is our gift, our leader, and our teacher. Come, and see what he provides. See where his light leads us to serve others who are in darkness. Invite others to join you as you gather around the light.

# Environment *and* Art *for the* Season

Every year on January 6, Regina pulls out a

stepstool. Carefully, she climbs the steps and stretches

her ninety-two-year-old body to reach the lintel above

a doorway in her home. With chalk in hand, she marks the threshold of another year of the new millennium on the wooden doorframe: 20 + C + M + B + 02. She will leave the chalk marking on the lintel until it wears off.

Having immigrated to the United States from Poland when she was a little girl, Regina maintains this custom from her early years in Europe. When one of her great-grandchildren asks her why she does this, she does not hesitate to explain: "I like to remember how far I've traveled in my life. And like the three kings, I like to remind myself that I am traveling to Jesus."

The word *epiphany* comes from the Greek word *epiphania*, meaning "manifestation" or "revelation." In the season after Epiphany, we take the light of Christ that has come into the world and carry it as a gift on our outward journeys. We give witness to the revelation of Christ as King of kings by manifesting this good news in our homes, in our communities, and on our travels. It is fitting that Epiphany arrives during the first week of the New Year. The celebration of the New Year is a time to evaluate the old boundaries that keep our lives and faith in isolation, and to recognize opportunities for new doorways that will lead us to greater Christian witness and fuller sharing of our lives.

In the year 2002, the church receives the gift of Epiphany falling on a Sunday. This is a marvelous opportunity for members of the church community to celebrate this ancient festival together. An Epiphany party might be planned, with an open invitation to the wider community. New Orleans is famous for its Epiphany parties, which begin on "Twelfth Night" (the evening before Epiphany) and continue throughout the season, culminating in Mardi Gras revelry. The "king's cake" is central to these festivities. A dried lima bean (or more often, a tiny plastic figure of an infant) is baked within the cake. Whoever finds the bean in his or her cake is crowned and robed "king." Following the crowning and robing come games and pageantry. The parties are delightful for both young and old.

An Epiphany party or other community celebration during the season after Epiphany might have a multicultural or ecumenical focus. The Week of Prayer for Christian Unity falls within this season (January 18 through January 25) as does the commemoration of Martin Luther King Jr. (January 15, with the national holiday celebrated on January 21). A congregation might hold an international potluck supper, asking members to bring dishes native to their origins or a place they have visited. In this season of Christ making his home with us, we are mindful of those without homes. The winter months of January and February are a time for inviting the hungry into our parish home and feeding them.

Christmas decorations—evergreens, poinsettias, ribbons, and candles—may remain in the worship space for this Sunday Epiphany celebration. Any flowers or greens that are dried or wilting should be removed. Doorways may be decorated or embellished with wreaths or swags. The traditional chalk markings described above might be incorporated as part of the liturgy; for example, the congregation might gather outside the main church door after the post-communion prayer and use an adapted form of the Blessing of the Home at Epiphany (in the seasonal rites section).

During the season after Epiphany, an increased display of light is in order to signify that the light of the world shines forth from God's people. Perhaps members of the assembly hold votive candles, or the liturgy begins with a festive procession of people holding candles, waving flags, and performing sacred movement. A robust parade of children with fire-safe lanterns is another option. One church, fortunate enough to have a resident sacred dance group, featured dancers wearing costumes from around the world and carrying lanterns.

Waving flags or processional banners creates a festive atmosphere. White is the color of vestments and paraments for this day, but white and gold flags dressed with multicolor ribbon would be appropriate. Liturgical

75

artist Jane Pitz describes a design for banners that can be carried in procession or displayed on stationary bases:

> The standards were made by a local carpenter from a sketch. The height of the two companion standards was calculated to match heights of other church furniture/elements, e.g., the crosspiece of the very large cross, which is moveable within the worship space. The top of the standard is a wheel shape, solid pine, and hook-and-loop fabric strips (Velcro) have been applied to the topmost surface. Ribbons of varying, seasonal colors are hung from the strips. The effect is wonderful and as they are being carried they move with the wind of the walk. They draw the assembly's attention to the procession and help us welcome and focus. When not used during a particular season, they are set in a base that matches the other furniture.

On the Epiphany of Our Lord, who will bring the gifts to the altar? Perhaps members of the church community who come from other countries or cultures might wear costumes from their homeland. Small children holding baskets of white flowers or votive candles might accompany those who represent the diverse cultures on whom Christ's light shines. If the church owns vessels fashioned of precious metals, by all means use these for this Epiphany celebration. Incorporate incense into ritual, both in memory of the gift of frankincense and to heighten the solemnity and beauty of the offerings.

On Epiphany the magi reach their destination in Bethlehem. Now is the time to add the three kings and their camels to the manger scene. An Epiphany star could be hung from the ceiling or a high point in the building. A three-dimensional star, such as a Moravian star, would be most effective and could be constructed from metallic paper (such as Mylar). The star should be in proportion to the room as a whole.

The week following Epiphany, we celebrate the Baptism of Our Lord. The color for the vestments and paraments for this liturgy remains white. Now we are in mid-January. The crèche, as well as any specifically Christmas seasonal decorations, such as red and gold ribbons or a wreath, can be removed from the worship space. The natural green palette of evergreens can remain if they continue to look fresh. In the coming weeks, these greens could be redressed with seasonal flowers. Beware of leaving the worship space looking "picked over," as if left in the wake of a party!

The focus of ornamentation for the Baptism of Our Lord is the font. If the font is moveable, put it in a prominent place. This festival is a wonderful day for the community to gather around the sacrament of baptism. Even if no baptism takes place in the church on that day, the font can be decorated with white candles and flowers. Any additional candles should not compete with or obscure the primary significance of the lighted paschal candle, however. In addition, an icon or other appropriate framed art of the baptism of Christ could be positioned on an easel near the font. Other icons that could be displayed throughout this season include the wedding at Cana, Jesus' presentation at the temple, and the transfiguration, as well as suitable portraits in honor of the Confession of Peter (January 18) and the Conversion of Paul (January 25). The worship folder provides a good opportunity for commentary on this art.

For the next three weeks, we enter a period of "green Sundays." In late January and early February, a deep forest green seems more appropriate than the brighter greens of summer. If your church owns only one set of "summery" green vestments, consider purchasing a second set. This set could also be worn in autumn. Continue to prune the worship environment of dried greens or any other vestiges of Christmas.

Just as this season might open with festivities on Twelfth Night and Epiphany, your church may choose to celebrate the season's close with a Mardi Gras party. Gertrude Mueller Nelson writes about Mardi Gras revelry as a playful time "to discover or engage the most hidden shadow self within." In *To Dance with God*, she provides information on planning carnival activities that serve to engage our shadows. This end of Epiphany and eve of Lent is a fitting time to give attention to our shadow selves, because shadows are most sharply defined by bright light.

# Preaching *with the* Season

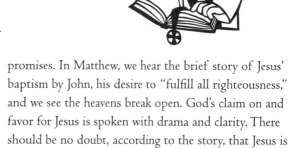

Jesus goes public in Epiphany. The cloistered beauty

of Christmas gives way to public display. Ancient calendars

indicated the winter solstice fell on January 6.

Our fourth-century European forebears established their celebration of Jesus' birth on the winter solstice, which by then was understood to be December 25. Contemporary astronomers have determined the winter solstice occurs on or near December 22. Exact date aside, for those of us in the Northern Hemisphere, the natural world reflects the images of the season. The light is growing longer now, and we begin to see more and more of Jesus, from his birth in the flesh to his ongoing revelation during the season of Epiphany.

Historically the celebration of Epiphany has been complicated and different in the East than in the West. The celebration of Epiphany appears to have predated the establishment of Christmas and was a combined celebration of the birth and baptism of Jesus. Remnants of this complexity reside throughout the Christian world. In some Latin American cultures, for example, Epiphany, not Christmas, is the day for gifts and parties. Light came in the star of Bethlehem. We have chosen to distinguish between Christmas and Epiphany by observing who comes to worship. At Christmas, the angels and shepherds come to the Light, and at Epiphany, the wise ones from the East do.

So on January 6, the texts for the day celebrate the coming of the light and the power of the light to draw us to God. Isaiah calls on us to arise and shine, to see the people gathering from all the nations in the light of God. Matthew tells the story of the magi from the East following the light of the star to pay homage to Jesus. This gospel reading falls chronologically before last week's text, so we also hear the foreshadowing of Herod's terrible paranoia. We sense that the coming of the light will unveil evil even as it reveals the goodness and glory of God.

We turn next to the baptism of Jesus. Consistent with our understanding of baptism as both God's claim on us and God's sending, we hear God claim the Servant in Isaiah and send him in fulfillment of long-standing

promises. In Matthew, we hear the brief story of Jesus' baptism by John, his desire to "fulfill all righteousness," and we see the heavens break open. God's claim on and favor for Jesus is spoken with drama and clarity. There should be no doubt, according to the story, that Jesus is the one foretold.

The ramifications of God's claim on Jesus now begin to be seen. Isaiah declares that the Servant is not just for the chosen people, but is a light to the nations. In the Gospel of John, the Baptizer gives witness to the heavens opening and the coming of the Holy Spirit. John's role is clarified. He came to prepare the way, that Jesus might be revealed. It is in this story that Jesus' first disciples answer *his* call. Others now begin to confess that Jesus is the Messiah.

In the texts for the third Sunday after the Epiphany, we read that Zebulun and Naphtali, the first tribes to fall to foreign domination, were ordered into exile in Assyrian provinces a full decade before the rest of Israel. Matthew reminds us again that the ancient messianic promise finds continuity in Jesus, and we also see God's compassion. The first to dwell in darkness will be the first to see the great light. Jesus gathers his disciples, and we get a glimpse of his purpose—"I will make you fish for people" (Matt. 4:19). Lest we wonder about the nature of fishing, however, we hear immediately that Jesus' work was to teach, proclaim the good news of the coming of God's dominion, and to heal. This was not about creating a revolutionary movement or establishing some sort of social club. This was about bringing light into the darkness.

Are teaching, preaching, and healing tasks for all the followers of Jesus? The texts for February 3 would say so. In Micah we hear that worship and disciplines of faith, even finely done, do not fulfill God's requirement to do justice, love kindness, and walk humbly with God. In Micah, the reprimand is direct. In Matthew, the gentleness of the beatitudes is good news

77

for those who struggle, and a stark, though indirect, reminder about which spirit and actions are linked to God's blessing.

As the season of Epiphany unfolds, it becomes increasingly clear that we are also to be bearers of light into the darkness. But lest we think it is all up to us, we are reminded by the transfiguration of our Lord that Jesus is still our beacon. He, God incarnate, breaks through the shadows first. Peter, James, and John watched the light fill him until he shone like the sun. No one else can be the savior. No one else breaks open the heavens. No one else is God with us. As Moses met God on the heights of Mt. Sinai and carried the law to God's people, mortals met God as Jesus was transfigured. Rather than come down the mountain to reveal God's law, however, Jesus comes down the mountain to reveal God's unstoppable, unflappable love. Even in the face of the cross and death, God wills life for us. After the transfiguration, we turn our faces with Jesus toward Jerusalem.

# Shape *of* Worship *for the* Season

## BASIC SHAPE OF THE EUCHARISTIC RITE

- Confession and Forgiveness: see alternate worship text for Epiphany in *Sundays and Seasons*

### GATHERING

- Greeting: see alternate worship text for Epiphany
- Consider omitting the Kyrie on Sundays after the Epiphany, but use the Kyrie on the festivals of the Epiphany, the Baptism of Our Lord, and the Transfiguration of Our Lord
- Use the hymn of praise throughout Epiphany ("Glory to God")

### WORD

- Use the Nicene Creed for festival days and Sundays in this season; use the Apostles' Creed for the Sundays after the Epiphany
- The prayers: see alternate forms and responses for Epiphany

### BAPTISM

- Consider having a baptismal festival on the Baptism of Our Lord (January 13)

### MEAL

- Offertory prayer: see alternate worship text for Epiphany
- Use the proper preface for Epiphany

- Eucharistic prayer: in addition to the four main options in *LBW*, see "Eucharistic Prayer C: The Season of Epiphany," *WOV* Leaders Edition, p. 67
- Invitation to communion: see alternate worship text for Epiphany
- Post-communion prayer: see alternate worship text for Epiphany

### SENDING

- Benediction: see alternate worship text for Epiphany
- Dismissal: see alternate worship text for Epiphany

## OTHER SEASONAL POSSIBILITIES

- Celebrate the festival of the Epiphany (January 6), which falls on a Sunday this year, with Holy Communion. It is a fitting occasion to use incense. *Worship Wordbook* (pp. 103–104), *Manual on the Liturgy* (pp. 279–82), and *Altar Guild and Sacristy Handbook* (p. 81) are three possible resources to consult for instructions on using incense.

- One way to observe this week is by using the service in the seasonal rites section. For Lutherans celebrating with one or more congregations of the Episcopal Church, *Guidelines and Worship Resources for the Celebration of Full Communion*, available from Augsburg Fortress (6000132018), may be consulted. Similar resources are available for Lutheran-Reformed celebrations (600010362X) and Lutheran-Moravian celebrations (6000117167).

- The blessing of homes is customary in the season after the Epiphany. See Blessing of a Dwelling, *Occasional Services*, p. 186, Blessing of a Home at Epiphany in the seasonal rites section of *Sundays and Seasons*, or Bendición de una residencia, *Ritos Ocasionales*, p. 179.

# Assembly Song *for the* Season

Planning music for the Epiphany season can be

a challenge. Unfortunately, Epiphany can seem like a season

of recovery from Christmas or one of marking time until Lent.

How can the season be seen as the culmination of the Christmas cycle, the revealing of God's glorious light to all nations? What can be planned to give the season a character of its own and yet keep it connected to the Advent and Christmas seasons? One aural manifestation of Christ's "epiphany" to all nations is present in the music of world cultures. The diversity of the Christian witness is evident in the variety of ways people express their Christian experience through music.

The Epiphany season is long enough to teach the congregation new repertoire through weekly repetition. Perhaps music from other cultures not normally represented in your particular congregation could be used within the liturgy for the entire season. Often this requires extra work on the part of the parish musician. Introducing music in unfamiliar styles requires careful planning and preparation. Parish musicians must do some studying and a lot of listening to begin to discover how this music should sound. A good place to start is *Leading the Church's Song*. This is a practical guide to leading congregational song in a variety of musical styles including African American, Latino, African, and Asian. Know your congregation's abilities and limits when it comes to incorporating new music into the liturgy. Some congregations will relish the opportunity to worship using culturally diverse music while others will be challenged with one new song. The goal is to learn, appreciate, understand, respect, and love a new song—to encounter Christ in a culture not your own.

A large selection of music from diverse cultures is widely available for use in Lutheran congregations. *With One Voice* contains a number of songs from many cultures. *Libro de Liturgia y Cántico* is a Spanish worship resource containing a number of bilingual hymns. *This Far by Faith* is an African American resource for worship. Both the Spanish and African American books contain a wide variety of liturgical music and hymns for the whole church, not just those communities. Remember to obtain appropriate copyright permission if you reprint music from these resources in a worship folder.

## GATHERING

Gathering songs for the season include "We are marching in the Light of God" (TFF 63, WOV 650), "Come all you people" (TFF 138, WOV 717), "This little light of mine" (TFF 65), "Jesus, we are gathered" (TFF 140), "Let us go now to the banquet" (LLC 410), and "I am the light of nations" (LLC 319). Since Epiphany is most likely the season in which the Gloria is sung every week, this is a good opportunity to reintroduce the congregation to a setting they already know but have not sung for a while, or learn a new one. *This Far by Faith* contains three settings of the Gloria in gospel and jazz styles (pp. 28–29, 46–47, and no. 24). *Libro de Liturgia y Cántico* contains one bilingual setting of the Gloria (no. 189) and several settings in Spanish.

### WORD

Numerous gospel acclamations from various cultures can be found in the service music sections of *With One Voice*, *Libro de Liturgia y Cántico*, and *This Far by Faith*. "Holy is our God" (LLC 273, TFF 203, W&P 61) or "Listen, God is calling" (WOV 712, TFF 130) are good hymn substitutes for the gospel acclamation.

### MEAL

Two excellent offertory hymns are "Now we offer" (WOV 761, TFF 129) and "Grains of wheat" (WOV 708, LLC 392). Both hymns express the unity all Christians share in the communion meal. Continue using the same musical setting of the great thanksgiving begun in Advent as a means of musically connecting the Christ-

mas cycle. The preface dialog and proper preface can be sung or spoken. Additional instruments and bells could be added again to heighten the celebration of the two feast days that are bookends for the season—the Baptism of Our Lord and the Transfiguration of Our Lord. The congregation could speak or sing the acclamations in the eucharistic prayer.

### SENDING

The final canticle from Luke that might be used in a Christmas cycle of canticles is the Nunc dimittis (Luke 2:29-32). "Lord, now you let your servant go in peace" is one of the post-communion canticle options of the service of Holy Communion in *Lutheran Book of Worship* (pp. 73, 93–94, and 116). Additional settings can be found in *With One Voice* (pp. 26–27 and no. 625) and *Libro de Liturgia y Cántico* (no. 248). Other sending songs for the season include "The Lord now sends us forth" (LLC 415), "Send me, Jesus" (TFF 244, 245), and "Let us talents and tongues employ" (WOV 754).

# Music *for the* Season

### VERSE AND OFFERTORY

Boehnke, Paul. *Festive Verse Settings for Christmas, Epiphany and Transfiguration.* SATB, opt kybd.   MSM 80-100.

Cherwien, David. *Verses for the Epiphany Season.* U, opt hb, org.   MSM 80-200.

Johnson, David N. *Verses and Offertories for Epiphany 2 through Transfiguration.* U, kybd.   AFP 0800649028.

*Verses and Offertory Sentences, Part II: Epiphany through Transfiguration.* CPH 97-5502.

### CHORAL

Bach, J.S./arr. Hal H. Hopson. "The Only Son From Heaven." SATB, kybd.   AFP 0800647092.

Bach, J.S. "The Only Son From Heaven."   CPH 98-2033 (SATB, vln, ob/fl, org); 98-2034 (complete inst pts).

Bengtson, Bruce. "Behold My Servant." SATB, org, opt cong.   AFP 0880659120.

Busarow, Donald. "O Morning Star, How Fair and Bright." SAB, cong, trbl inst, org.   CPH 98-2819.

Candlyn, T. Frederick. "Christ, Whose Glory Fills the Skies." SATB, org.   CFI CM622.

Christianson, F. Melius. "Beautiful Savior." SATB.   AFP 0800652584.

Ehret, Walter. "Rejoice and Be Merry." SATB, kybd.   CPH 98-3502.

Ferguson, John. "Jesus! Name of Wondrous Love" in *St. John Passion.* SATB, org.   AFP 0800658582.

Forsberg, Charles. "Fairest Lord Jesus." SATB, pno.   AFP 0800656962.

Helgen, John. "Brighter Than the Sun." SATB, kybd.   AFP 0800659155.

Kosche, Kenneth T. "Rejoice and Be Merry." SATB.   MSM-50-1080.

Larkin, Michael. "Jesus! Name of Wondrous Love." SATB, kybd.
CPH 98-3560.

Martinson, Joel. "Arise, Shine." SATB, org.    AFP 0800652401.

Music, David W. "We Three Kings." SATB, trbl inst, kybd.
CPH 98-2940.

Pelz, Walter. "Arise, O God, and Shine." SATB, org.    CPH 98-1718.

Tallis, Thomas. "O Nata Lux." SATTB.    OXF 43.228.

Willan, Healy. "Arise, Shine." SATB, org.    CPH 98-1508.

## CHILDREN'S CHOIRS

Bågenfelt, Susanne. "There's a Light in the World." U, opt 2 pt, kybd.
AFP 0800674286.

Bedford, Michael. "Star Bright" in *Songs and Seasons*. U, kybd, hb.
CG CGA-540.

Farrell, Bernadette. *Share the Light*. 2 pt, kybd, gtr, opt inst.
OCP 11307CC.

Kemp, Helen, arr. "Follow the Star." U, kybd, perc.    CG CGA-484.

McRae, Shirley, arr. "Midnight Stars Make Bright the Sky" in *Songs From the East Wind*. U, xyl, rec, perc.

## KEYBOARD/INSTRUMENTAL

Carlson, J. Bert. *This Little Light of Mine: Piano Collection*. Pno.
AFP 0800659503.

Kolander, Keith. *Three Arias for Piano and Solo Instrument*. Kybd, solo inst.
AFP 0800658175.

Linker, Janet. *Three Epiphany Pieces*. Org.    AFP 0800658221.

Manz, Paul. *Improvisation on "I Want to Walk as a Child of the Light."* Org.
MSM 10-520.

Pelz, Walter. "Deo Gracias" in *Hymn Settings for Organ and Brass*.
AFP 0800650697.

Sedio, Mark. *Dancing in the Light of God*. Pno.    AFP 0800656547.

Wold, Wayne L. *Suite on "Bright and Glorious Is the Sky."* Org.
AFP 0800659023.

## HANDBELL

Hussey, William. "Let All Mortal Flesh Keep Silence." 3-5 oct. L4.
MSM 30-804.

Kinyon, Barbara B. "All Things Bright and Beautiful." 2-3 oct. L2+.
AG 1733.

Larson, Katherine Jordahl. "Beautiful Savior." 3-4 oct. L3.
AFP 0800653963.

McChesney, Kevin. "O For a Thousand Tongues to Sing." 3-5 oct.
L3.    LOR 20/1037.

Tucker, Sondra. "I Want to Walk as a Child of the Light." 3-5 oct.
L2.    AFP 0800658868.

Wagner, Douglas E. "For the Beauty of the Earth (Dix)." 2 oct. L3.
AG 1436.

Young, Philip M. "In Thee Is Gladness." 4-5 oct. L3.
AFP 0800665001.

## PRAISE ENSEMBLE

Hallquist, Gary. "People of Light."    WRD 0 80689 32627 1
(SATB, kybd); 0 80689 63024 8 (choraltrax);
0 80689 32447 5 (orch).

Kendrick, Graham. "Shine, Jesus, Shine!" SATB, kybd.
HOP GC 937.

LeBlanc, Lenny. "You Are the One I Love" from *Extravagant Grace Songbook*. SAT[B], kybd.    INT 16737.

Smith, Michael W. and Deborah D. Smith. "Shine On Us."
WRD 301 0876 165 (SATB, kybd); 301 7547 086 (choraltrax); 301 0593 252 (orch).

Williams, J. Paul and Joseph M. Martin. "Arise! Shine!"    GS A 7063
(SATB, kybd); MC 5189 (cass); LB 5360 (orch).

81

# Alternate Worship Texts

## CONFESSION AND FORGIVENESS

Let us draw near to God in humility and confidence, confessing our sin.

*Silence for reflection and self-examination.*

God of truth and light,
we confess our trust and reliance
on human wisdom and strength.
We acknowledge the things that divide us
within the church, among the nations,
and in our own relationships.
Pour out your great light on us.
Through the power and wisdom of the cross,
heal our brokenness
and forgive our foolish ways,
that your light may shine through us
and we may give glory to you. Amen

The boundless riches of Christ
are the gift of God's grace to all people.
As a called and ordained minister of the church of Christ,
and by his authority, I declare to you
the entire forgiveness of all your sins,
in the name of the Father, and of the ✝ Son,
and of the Holy Spirit.
**Amen**

## GREETING

The grace, the wisdom, and the power of God
be with you all.
**And also with you.**

## OFFERTORY PRAYER

God of glory,
with great joy we worship you
and lay before you these gifts.
Let our lives serve you only,
and lead us always to our dearest treasure,
Jesus Christ, the bright and morning star.
Amen

## INVITATION TO COMMUNION

Blessed are they
who hunger and thirst for righteousness,
for they shall be filled.

## POST-COMMUNION PRAYER

We thank you, O God,
that you have strengthened our hearts
through this feast of life and salvation.
Be the light for our path,
that we may do justice,
love kindness,
and walk humbly with you,
now and forever.
**Amen**

## BLESSING

God's blessing be with you,
Christ's peace be with you,
the Spirit's outpouring be with you,
now and always.
**Amen**

## DISMISSAL

Go forth as light into the world,
rejoicing in the power of the Spirit.
**Thanks be to God.**

82

# Seasonal Rites

## Lessons and Carols for Epiphany

**ENTRANCE HYMN**
Good Christian friends, rejoice   LBW 55
The first Noel   LBW 56

**DIALOG**
The people who walked in darkness have seen a great light.
**The light shines in the darkness,**
**and the darkness has not overcome it.**
Those who dwelt in the land of deep darkness,
on them light has shined.
**We have beheld Christ's glory,**
**glory as of the only Son from the Father.**
For to us a child is born, to us a Son is given.
**In him was life, and the life was the light of all people.**

**OPENING PRAYER**
*See the prayer of the day for Epiphany.*
**LESSONS AND CAROLS**
First Reading: John 1:1-14
Of the Father's love begotten   LBW 42
Let our gladness have no end   LBW 57
He came down   TFF 37

Second Reading: John 1:18-25
Infant holy, infant lowly   LBW 44
Away in a manger   LBW 67, WOV 644
Jesus, the light of the world   TFF 59

Third Reading: Matthew 2:1-12
Bright and glorious is the sky   LBW 75
We three kings of Orient are   WOV 646
The magi who to Bethlehem did go   LLC 317
Sister Mary   TFF 60

Fourth Reading: Matthew 2:13-23
By all your saints in warfare (st. 9)   LBW 177
Oh, sleep now, holy baby   WOV 639
Oh, Mary, gentle poor Mary   LLC 310

Fifth Reading: Luke 2:41-51
In a lowly manger born   LBW 417
Once in royal David's city   WOV 643
The virgin Mary had a baby boy   TFF 53

Sixth Reading: Matthew 3:13-17
When Christ's appearing was made known   LBW 85
When Jesus came to Jordan   WOV 647
Wade in the water   TFF 114

Seventh Reading: John 2:1-11
Now the silence   LBW 205
Jesus, come! for we invite you   WOV 648

**RESPONSIVE PRAYER**
Glory to God in the highest,
**and peace to God's people on earth.**
Blessed are you, Prince of Peace.
**You rule the earth with truth and justice.**
Send your gift of peace to all nations of the world.
**Blessed are you, Son of Mary. You share our humanity.**
Have mercy on those who are sick, dying,
**and all who suffer this day.**
Blessed are you, Son of God.
**You dwell among us as the Word made flesh.**
Reveal yourself to us in word and sacrament,
**that we may bear your light to all the world.**

**THE LORD'S PRAYER**

**BLESSING AND DISMISSAL**
Let us bless the Lord.
**Thanks be to God.**
May you be filled with the wonder of Mary, the obedience of Joseph, the joy of the angels, the eagerness of the shepherds, the determination of the magi, and the peace of the Christ child. Almighty God, Father, ✛ Son, and Holy Spirit bless you now and forever.
**Amen**

**SENDING HYMN**
LBW 90   Songs of thankfulness and praise
TFF 61   The Lord is my light

83

# Blessing of the Home at Epiphany

*Matthew writes that when the magi saw the shining star stop overhead, they were filled with joy. "On entering the house, they saw the child with Mary his mother" (2:10-11). In the home, Christ is met in family and friends, in visitors and strangers. In the home, faith is shared, nurtured, and put into action. In the home, Christ is welcome.*

*Twelfth Night (January 5) or another day during the season of Epiphany offers an occasion for gathering with friends and family members for a blessing of the home, using the following as a model. Someone may lead the greeting and blessing, while another person may read the scripture passage. Following an eastern European tradition, a visual blessing may be inscribed with white chalk above the main door; for example, 20+CMB+02. The numbers change with each new year. The three letters stand for either the ancient Latin blessing Christe mansionem benedica, which means, "Christ, bless this house," or the legendary names of the magi (Caspar, Melchior, and Blather).*

### GREETING
May peace be to this house and to all who enter here. By wisdom a house is built and through understanding it is established; through knowledge its rooms are filled with rare and beautiful treasures.
*See Proverbs 24:3-4.*

### READING
As we prepare to ask God's blessing on this household, let us listen to the words of scripture.

In the beginning was the Word, and the Word was with God, and the Word was God. He was in the beginning with God. All things came into being through him, and without him not one thing came into being. What has come into being in him was life, and the life was the light of all people. The Word became flesh and lived among us, and we have seen his glory, the glory as of a father's only son, full of grace and truth. From his fullness we have all received, grace upon grace.
*See John 1:1-4, 14, 16.*

### INSCRIPTION
*This inscription may be made with chalk above the entrance:*

20 + C M B + 02

The magi of old, known as
C   Caspar,
M   Melchior, and
B   Balthasar
    followed the star of God's Son who came to dwell among us
20 two thousand
02 and two years ago.

✝ Christ, bless this house,
✝ and remain with us throughout the new year.

### PRAYER
O God, you revealed your Son to all people by the shining light of a star. We pray that you bless this home and all who live here with your gracious presence. May your love be our inspiration, your wisdom our guide, your truth our light and your peace our benediction; through Christ our Lord. Amen

*Then everyone may walk from room to room, blessing the house with incense or by sprinkling with water, perhaps using a branch from the Christmas tree.*

Adapted from *Come, Lord Jesus: Devotions for the Home* (Augsburg Fortress, 1996).

# Ecumenical Service during the Week of Prayer for Christian Unity

### CONFESSION AND FORGIVENESS
We gather as the people of God
to offer our repentance and praise,
to pray for the unity of the church
and the renewal of our common life.
Trusting in God's mercy and compassion,
let us ask for the forgiveness of our sins.

*Silence for reflection and self-examination.*

Lord Jesus, you came to reconcile us
to one another and to the Father:
Lord, have mercy on us.
**Lord, have mercy on us.**

Lord Jesus, you heal the wounds
of pride and intolerance.
Christ, have mercy on us.
**Christ, have mercy on us.**
Lord Jesus, you pardon the sinner
and welcome the repentant.
Lord, have mercy on us.
**Lord, have mercy on us.**
May almighty God grant us pardon and peace,
strengthen us in faith,
and make us witnesses to Christ's love.
**Amen**

## HYMN OF PRAISE

## PRAYER OF THE DAY
God our Father, your Son Jesus prayed that his followers might
be one. Make all Christians one with him as he is one with you,
so that in peace and concord we may carry to the world the
message of your love; through your Son, Jesus Christ our Lord,
who lives and reigns with you and the Holy Spirit, one God, now
and forever.
**Amen**

## READINGS
Isaiah 2:2-4
Psalm 133
Ephesians 4:1-6
John 17:15-23

## SERMON

## HYMN OF THE DAY

## THANKSGIVING FOR BAPTISM
*The people remain standing after the hymn as the minister(s)
gather at the font. After the prayer, the people may be sprinkled
with water from the font. Or at the conclusion of the service,
they may be invited to dip their hands in the font and trace the
sign of the cross over themselves.*

The Lord be with you.
**And also with you.**
Let us give thanks to the Lord our God.
**It is right to give our thanks and praise.**

Holy God and mighty Lord, we give you thanks,
for you nourish and sustain us and all living things
with the gift of water.
In the beginning your Spirit moved over the waters,
and you created heaven and earth.
By the waters of the flood you saved Noah and his family.
You led Israel through the sea out of slavery
into the promised land.
In the waters of the Jordan
your Son was baptized by John and anointed with the Spirit.
By the baptism of his death and resurrection
your Son set us free from sin and death
and opened the way to everlasting life.

We give you thanks, O God,
that you have given us new life in the water of baptism.
Buried with Christ in his death,
you raise us to share in his resurrection
by the power of the Holy Spirit.
May all who have passed through the water of baptism
continue in the risen life of our Savior.
To you be all honor and glory, now and forever.
**Amen**

## CONFESSION OF FAITH
There is one Lord, one faith, and one baptism.
United in Christ, let us confess the faith we hold in common.
*The people recite the Apostles' Creed.*

## THE PRAYERS
*At the conclusion, the people pray the Lord's Prayer.*

## GREETING OF PEACE
The Lord Jesus prayed for the unity of his disciples.
We look for the day when the church will shine forth
in unity at his holy supper.
The peace of the Lord be with you always.
**And also with you.**
*The people exchange a sign of Christ's peace.*

## BLESSING AND DISMISSAL

## SENDING HYMN

85

# January 6, 2002

### The Epiphany of Our Lord

## INTRODUCTION

On this day the church celebrates its catholic nature and mission. In worship we pray that the Holy Spirit would make our lives radiant with the brightness of Christ. From the Lord's table the church goes forth into the world as a witness to Christ's merciful presence. As the stars light up the darkness of night, so the baptized are called to be light in the world.

## PRAYER OF THE DAY

Lord God, on this day you revealed your Son to the nations by the leading of a star. Lead us now by faith to know your presence in our lives, and bring us at last to the full vision of your glory, through your Son, Jesus Christ our Lord, who lives and reigns with you and the Holy Spirit, one God, now and forever.

## READINGS

### Isaiah 60:1-6

The long years of darkness are over. The prophet announces the end of exile in Babylon and looks forward to the restoration of the city of Jerusalem. God's light, reflected in Israel, will draw caravans bearing treasure from all the nations who freely come to praise the Lord.

### Psalm 72:1-7, 10-14

All kings shall bow down before him. (Ps. 72:11)

### Ephesians 3:1-12

Though it had been hidden for years, Paul now reveals the secret that has shaped his apostolic witness: in Jesus Christ, God's salvation extends beyond the Jews to include all people. The light of Christ shines upon Jew and Gentile alike.

### Matthew 2:1-12

The rich symbolism of this story—the magi, a star in the east, Herod's plots—announces the prophetic hope for an epiphany or revelation that God has entered into our history as one of us.

## COLOR White

## THE PRAYERS

Let us pray that the dawn from on high will shine for the church, the world, and all those in need.

*A BRIEF SILENCE.*

That the church may be radiant with the gospel and draw all people to the boundless riches of your glory revealed in Jesus Christ; God of light and life:

**hear us, we pray.**

That nations will be led by your wisdom and leaders serve with justice and righteousness to scatter the clouds of hatred and oppression; God of light and life:

**hear us, we pray.**

That all who are depressed, lonely, or sick (especially) may be nursed by your healing power and rest in the arms of your comfort; God of light and life:

**hear us, we pray.**

That we would share our abundance of wealth and grace with those who live in poverty of riches and spirit; God of light and life:

**hear us, we pray.**

That those whose lives and cultures differ from our own may find welcome among us at the table of the Lord; God of light and life:

**hear us, we pray.**

That those who are filled with doubt and struggle to believe may be led by the Holy Spirit to acclaim your love incarnate in Jesus Christ; God of light and life:

**hear us, we pray.**

*HERE OTHER INTERCESSIONS MAY BE OFFERED.*

That those who have died and now behold your great epiphany may surround us until we come to the brightness of your dawning; God of light and life:

**hear us, we pray.**

God of splendor and light, hear our prayer and illumine us with the radiance of your glory shown in Jesus Christ our Lord.

**Amen**

## IMAGES FOR PREACHING

Who is Jesus? Certainly he was an unlikely candidate to be the Messiah. After such a lowly birth, who would believe he was God's anointed? The angels proclaimed it, though. The shepherds believed it and saw their own salvation in him. But the wise? The powerful? Would they believe?

At the Epiphany, God turned up the lights on everyone who saw Jesus. The shining star pointed the way for wise ones to find him and offer their praise. Herod, however, was frightened by the light of the star. For those who conspire in shadowed corners, the light, even a star shining in the night, is not good news.

Jesus was already beginning to cause the established order to waver. Jesus was already turning things upside down, surprisingly like the promised Messiah. And yet, who was up and who was down? Who was in and who was out? Here we find the surprise. Wise ones from the East, foreigners, recognized the star. They saw the light. They came from the outside but were welcomed in.

Herod, king and leader, could only be afraid. He thought himself to be on the inside but saw a threat in the star. It pointed to the king of the Jews, a king beyond his control. The star illumined a world much bigger than Herod imagined. In his posturing to be up, he was down and could not see the world Jesus promised.

Perhaps when we see the light we also at first feel fear. Perhaps we also are afraid to let God be the one in charge, to let Jesus upset the careful structure of our lives. Perhaps we resist following the star and worshiping him. God will be patient. The star will show us the way.

## WORSHIP MATTERS

Intercessory prayer, the prayer of the church, the prayer of the faithful, concerns itself with all of creation. The historic shape of the prayer blankets the whole earth. We offer petitions for the world, the church, the nation or community, and those in special need, and finally we offer our thanksgiving for those who have died in faith. On this day when we celebrate the revelation of God's Son to the whole earth, reflect on the depth and breadth of the intercessory prayers as they are gathered in your assembly. Are the concerns expressed as broad as today's texts? How does the assembly own and participate in this prayer? How and by whom is it led?

## LET THE CHILDREN COME

Epiphany on a Sunday offers opportunities for greater participation in this festive day. Create a procession of stars. Depending on the number of children in the assembly, including visitors, the procession will vary from a small constellation to a multitude. Cut bright white, shiny silver, and glittery gold stars from tag board, and attach them to dowels. Thread ribbons through holes punched in the points of the stars. One star must be "brightest and best," guiding all the others in the entrance procession to the place where "our infant redeemer is laid." The children lead the worshipers out of the nave at the close of the liturgy, for in the world, among the least and little ones, Christ is present today.

## HYMNS FOR WORSHIP

### GATHERING

As with gladness men of old   LBW 82

Arise, your light has come!   WOV 652

Shine, Jesus, shine   WOV 651, TFF 64, W&P 123

### HYMN OF THE DAY

O Morning Star, how fair and bright!   LBW 76

### ALTERNATE HYMN OF THE DAY

I want to walk as a child of the light   WOV 649

Hear the angels   W&P 57

### COMMUNION

The first Noel   LBW 56

Beautiful Savior   LBW 518

We three kings of Orient are   WOV 646

### SENDING

Christ, whose glory fills the skies   LBW 265

There's a star in the East   WOV 645, TFF 58

We are marching in the light of God   WOV 650, TFF 63, W&P 148

### ADDITIONAL HYMNS AND SONGS

All hail King Jesus   W&P 3

In the morning   W&P 75

Los magos/The magi who to Bethlehem did go LLC 317

87

## MUSIC FOR THE DAY

### PSALMODY

Cooney, Rory. "Justice Shall Flourish" in STP, vol. 4.

Della Picca, Angelo A. *Psalms for the Cantor*, vol. III. WLP 2504.

Guimont, Michael. "Psalm 72: Justice Shall Flourish" in RS.

Hail to the Lord's anointed LBW 87

Haugen, Marty. "Every Nation on Earth Will Adore You" in PCY.

Hobby, Robert. PW C.

Jesus shall reign LBW 530

Smith, Dave. "Let His Glory Fill the Earth" in PS I.

### CHORAL

Bach, J.S. "O Morning Star, How Fair and Bright" in *Bach for All Seasons*. SATB. AFP 080065854X.

Bender, Mark. "Arise, Shine; for Your Light Has Come." 2 pt mxd, org. CPH 98-2707.

Cornelius, Peter. "The Three Kings" in *100 Carols for Choirs*. SATB, T solo. OXF.

Hirten, John Carl. "For Glory Dawns Upon You." 2 pt mxd, kybd. AFP 0800655257.

Jennings, Kenneth. "Arise, Shine, for Thy Light Has Come." SATB. AFP 6000101902 and 0800656784.

Johnson, David N. "On This Day Earth Shall Ring" in *A Service of Nine Lessons and Carols*. SATB, fl, org. AFP 0800648617.

Nelson, Ronald A. "For Your Light Has Come." SATB, 2 tpt, opt timp & cym. AFP 6000107803.

Neswick, Bruce. "Epiphany Carol" in *Augsburg Choirbook*. U, org. AFP 0800656784.

Praetorius, Michael. "O Morning Star, How Fair and Bright" in *Chantry Choirbook*. SSATB. AFP 0800657772.

Running, Joseph. "Epiphany." SATB, opt tpt. AFP 0800646878.

Weaver, John. "Epiphany Alleluias." SATB, org. B&H OCTB5683.

### CHILDREN'S CHOIRS

Jennings, Carolyn, arr. "Oh, How Beautiful the Sky." U, kybd, fl, hb/glock. AFP 6000097824.

Scott, K. Lee. "Guiding Star." U/2 pt, kybd. AMSI 541.

### KEYBOARD/INSTRUMENTAL

Hassell, Michael. "Houston" in *More Folkways*. Pno. AFP 0800656679.

Leavitt, John. "Wie schön leuchtet" in *Hymn Preludes for the Church Year*. Org. AFP 0800620328.

Leupold, A. W. "Wie schön leuchtet der Morgenstern" in *An Organ Book*. Org. CHA 603.

Pelz, Walter. "O Morning Star, How Fair and Bright." Org. MSM 10-520.

Sadowski, Kevin. "Pastorale on O Morning Star, How Fair and Bright." Org. CPH 97-6045.

### HANDBELL

Honoré, Jeffrey. "Dance Africana on 'Dix.'" 3-5 oct. L2. CPH 97-6745.

Kinyon, Barbara. "O Morning Star, How Fair and Bright." 3 oct. L2. HOP 1690.

McChesney, Kevin. "Arise, Shine, thy Light has Come." 3-5 oct. L4. JEF JHS9108.

Sherman, Arnold B. "We Three Kings." 3-5 oct. L3. RR HB0014.

### PRAISE ENSEMBLE

Pote, Allen. "Arise, Shine, for Your Light Has Come." SATB, kybd. PRE 392-41548.

Smith, Michael W. and Deborah D. Smith. "Shine On Us." WRD 301 0876165 (SATB, kybd); 301 7547 086 (choraltrax); 301 0593 252 (orch).

Williams, J. Paul and Joseph M. Martin. "Arise! Shine!" GS A 7063 (SATB, kybd); MC 5189 (cass); LB 5360 (orch).

# Wednesday, January 9

ADRIAN OF CANTERBURY, TEACHER, C. 710

African by birth, Adrian (or Hadrian) worked with Theodore, archbishop of Canterbury, in developing the church in England, particularly through his direction of an influential school where many church leaders were instructed.

The growing awareness of the multicultural life of the church leads many to discover surprises in the church's history; for example, that an African missionary such as Adrian would have been influential in the development of the church in England, a church sometimes perceived only as Western and European in its history. Within parish groups, use the example of Adrian to explore the cross-cultural influence within the ancient church.

# January 13, 2002

The Baptism of Our Lord
First Sunday after the Epiphany

## INTRODUCTION

In the waters of the Jordan, Jesus is baptized by John. The Spirit descends on him and a voice from heaven says, "You are my beloved." Here is the pattern for our entrance into Christ's community and mission: we come to the waters of the font, our Jordan; we are washed by the Word and anointed by the Spirit; we are named God's beloved children. With Christ we are chosen to proclaim God's mercy in a suffering world. With Christ we are made public witnesses to God's justice. With Christ we are called to do good and relieve the suffering of the oppressed.

## PRAYER OF THE DAY

Father in heaven, at the baptism of Jesus in the River Jordan you proclaimed him your beloved Son and anointed him with the Holy Spirit. Make all who are baptized into Christ faithful in their calling to be your children and inheritors with him of everlasting life; through your Son, Jesus Christ our Lord, who lives and reigns with you and the Holy Spirit, one God, now and forever.

## READINGS

### Isaiah 42:1-9

The Lord's transformation of something old (something expected) into something new is a major theme of Isaiah 40–55. Today's reading begins with the familiar language of the Lord bringing justice (or "the true way") through a chosen one. What is new is how the Lord brings that about: the servant is not a triumphant warrior, but is one who works quietly and patiently.

### Psalm 29

The voice of the Lord is upon the waters. (Ps. 29:3)

### Acts 10:34-43

Peter's sermon to the Roman centurion Cornelius tells how the message of God's inclusive salvation came to expression in the ministry of Jesus following John's baptism.

### Matthew 3:13-17

Before Jesus begins his ministry, he is baptized by John, touched by the Spirit, and identified publicly as God's child.

## COLOR  White

## THE PRAYERS

Let us pray that the dawn from on high will shine for the church, the world, and all those in need.

*A BRIEF SILENCE.*

For all who are baptized in Christ and anointed with the Holy Spirit, that their mission and ministry may be a light to the nations; God of light and life:

**hear us, we pray.**

For all who govern and serve, that justice and peace be established in all corners of the earth; God of light and life:

**hear us, we pray.**

For those weakened by age or illness (especially), that you take them by the hand and uphold them with your Spirit; God of light and life:

**hear us, we pray.**

For all who doubt that they are your sons and daughters, that they may be assured by the voice of your promise; God of light and life:

**hear us, we pray.**

For our congregation, that we will not grow weary or faint as we share your grace and forgiveness with all people; God of light and life:

**hear us, we pray.**

*HERE OTHER INTERCESSIONS MAY BE OFFERED.*

In thanksgiving for all the saints, that your light upon their lives may guide us also to be instruments of healing and peace; God of light and life:

**hear us, we pray.**

God of splendor and light, hear our prayer and illumine us with the radiance of your glory shown in Jesus Christ our Lord.

**Amen**

## IMAGES FOR PREACHING

Who entered the waters of the Jordan with John to be baptized? And who emerged from those waters? Jesus could have been any other devout Jew heeding John's call to repentance, to turn around and live a new life. He could have been.

89

But when he came up from the water, the heavens opened and the Spirit of God descended on him like a dove. John preached fire and brimstone. John demanded repentance. Jesus submitted for the sake of righteousness. But here the Spirit of God was more like a dove than a hail of fire. It settled on him, dove-like—gently, not with force or power or coercion. It simply claimed him.

The voice confirmed the claim. This one who stood dripping in the river was not just anyone but was God's own Son, the one promised long ago, the one who would follow in God's footsteps, who would continue God's work of justice and mercy. God was well pleased with him.

Now he does not quiver in swaddling clothes in a stable's dark night. Now he is not bundled away in secrecy to Egypt. Now he does not settle with his parents only where it is safe. Now he is proclaimed by voice and Spirit as God's chosen, God's promised, God's beloved. Now he is presented to the world in the full light of day. Now the heavens are opened. In Jesus, God walks with us.

## WORSHIP MATTERS

"Water…is used generously in Holy Baptism….A baptismal font filled with water, placed in the assembly's worship space, symbolizes the centrality of this sacrament for faith and life" (*The Use of the Means of Grace: A Statement on the Practice of Word and Sacrament* [Chicago: Evangelical Lutheran Church in America, 1997], principles 26–27). This application is made: "As congregations are able, they may consider the creation of fonts of ample proportions filled with flowing water, or baptismal pools which could allow immersion. The location of the font within the church building should express the idea of entrance into the community of faith, and should allow ample space for people to gather around." Use this week to reflect with your community on the centrality of baptism in your life together.

## LET THE CHILDREN COME

This is the first of four major baptismal festival days in the church year. The Vigil of Easter, Pentecost, and All Saints Day will follow. On these days, or whenever baptisms are planned, let the children come to the font during the hymn of the day. They can carry the things needed for baptism: the candle, robe, towel, shell, and oil. Have a child carry a pitcher of water that can be poured into the font during the thanksgiving for baptism, thus connecting sight and sound and word. The children will have a great view of the action, and perhaps they will be splashed a little during this great bath.

## HYMNS FOR WORSHIP
### GATHERING
We know that Christ is raised    LBW 189
We were baptized in Christ Jesus    WOV 698

### HYMN OF THE DAY
I bind unto myself today    LBW 188

### ALTERNATE HYMN OF THE DAY
When Jesus came to Jordan    WOV 647
From God the Father, virgin-born    HFW (Puer nobis)

### COMMUNION
God, whose almighty word    LBW 400
Thy holy wings    WOV 741
Waterlife    W&P 145

### SENDING
Let all things now living    LBW 557
I've just come from the fountain    WOV 696
Wade in the water    TFF 114

### ADDITIONAL HYMNS AND SONGS
He came to be baptized    BC
On Jordan's banks the Baptist's cry    LBW 36
Song over the waters    W&P 127
To Jordan came the Christ, our Lord    LBW 79

## MUSIC FOR THE DAY
### SERVICE MUSIC
If there are baptisms on this day, consider using the baptismal song "I saw water" from *Bread of Life* (Jeremy Young, AFP 0806638699).

## PSALMODY
Batastini, Robert. "Psalm 29: The Lord Will Bless His People" in RS.
Booth, Tom. "The Lord Will Bless His People" in STP, vol. 4.
Haas, David.    PCY, vol. VIII.
Hobby, Robert.    PW C.
Marshall, Jane. *Psalms Together*, vol. II.    CGA. CGC-21.
Smith, Geoffrey Boulton. "Give Strength to Your People, Lord" in PS I.

90

Song over the waters    W&P 127

Wetzler, Robert.    PW A.

## CHORAL

Bach, J.S. "The Only Son from Heaven" (alt. text for "Bring Low Our Ancient Adam") in *Bach for All Seasons.* SATB, kybd, opt inst. AFP 0800656784.

Bengtson, Bruce. "Behold My Servant." SATB, org, opt cong. AFP 0800659120.

Biery, James. "The Waters of Life." SATB, org.    AFP 0800657683.

Busarow, Donald. "The Baptism Carol." SATB, kybd. CPH 98-3223.

Cleobury, Stephen. "Joys Seven" in *100 Carols for Choirs.* SATB, org. OXF.

Ferguson, John. "Jesus! Name of Wondrous Love" in *St. John Passion.* SATB, org.    AFP 0800658582.

Helman, Michael. "Christ When You Were Baptized." SAB, kybd. AFP 0800674507.

Nystedt, Knut. "This Is My Beloved Son." SAB, org.    CPH 98-1805.

Schramm, Charles W., Jr. "You Are My Son." SA(T)B, org. CPH 98-3571.

Thompson, J. Michael. "Come, You Lovers of the Feasts." SATB, org. AFP 0800653823.

## CHILDREN'S CHOIRS

Estes, Jerry. "Our Gift for You." 2 pt, kybd, desc, sign language. ALF 11365.

Ferguson, John. "Jesus, My Lord and God." U, org. AFP 0800646193.

## KEYBOARD/INSTRUMENTAL

Billingham, Richard. "I've Just Come from the Fountain" in *Seven Reflections on African American Spirituals.* Org.    AFP 0800656229.

Hassell, Michael. "I've Just Come from the Fountain" in *Jazz All Seasons.* Pno.    AFP 0800656830.

Schaffner, John Hebden. "St. Patrick's Breastplate" in *Organ Music for the Seasons.* Org.    AFP 0800657233.

Sowerby, Leo. "Prelude on 'St. Patrick'" in *Ten Preludes on Hymn Tunes.* Org.    HWG GB 651.

## HANDBELL

Hibbard, Suzanne M. "Borning Cry." 3-5 oct. L2.    CPH 97-6761.

Thompson, Martha Lynn. "Thy Holy Wings." 3-5 oct. L2. ALF API9005.

## PRAISE ENSEMBLE

Foley, John. "Come to the Water." SATB, kybd, gtr, cong, solo inst. OCP 9489.

Hayes, Mark. "Wade in the Water." SATB, kybd.    ALF 5810.

# Sunday, January 13

### GEORGE FOX, RENEWER OF SOCIETY, 1691

Fox severed his ties among family and friends in search of enlightenment. He found no comfort in the traditional church, and he became an itinerant preacher. His preaching emphasized the abiding inward light given by God to believers as the real source of comfort and authority. His preaching led to the establishment of preaching bands of women and men known as the "Publishers of the Truth." In time, these preachers established local communities that came to be known as the Society of Friends, or Quakers. During visits to the Caribbean and North America, Fox witnessed the evil of the slave trade, and he founded the abolitionist movement in England.

Quakers are known for the long period of silence in their meetings. Consider growing into the practice of silence in worship. Be mindful of the ways that silence breaks the hectic pace of life and leads us to attend to the wisdom of God in spoken word and through service to others.

# Monday, January 14

### EIVIND JOSEF BERGGRAV, BISHOP OF OSLO, 1959

In 1937, Berggrav was elected bishop of Oslo and primate of Norway. In 1940, he was asked to negotiate with the Nazi regime in order to ascertain its intentions regarding the social and religious life of the Norwegian people. Rejecting any compromise with the occupation forces, he left the negotiations and demanded that the Nazis recognize the rights of the Jews and the autonomy of the church. Deprived of his episcopal title in 1943, he was placed under arrest, only to escape and remain in hiding in Oslo until the end of the war.

During the season of Epiphany, the life of Berggrav is another witness to the light of Christ. His life raises questions for believers today about the readiness to risk title, power, and prestige to speak for victims of injustice and seek truth in the midst of evils that face us in the world.

91

# Tuesday, January 15

MARTIN LUTHER KING JR.,
RENEWER OF SOCIETY, MARTYR, 1968

Martin Luther King Jr. is remembered as an American prophet of justice among races and nations, a Christian whose faith undergirded his advocacy of vigorous yet nonviolent action for racial equality. A pastor of churches in Montgomery, Alabama, and Atlanta, Georgia, his witness was taken to the streets in such other places as Birmingham, Alabama, where he was arrested and jailed while protesting against segregation. He preached nonviolence and demanded that love be returned for hate. Awarded the Nobel Peace Prize in 1964, he was killed by an assassin on April 4, 1968.

Congregations may choose to remember King by singing "We shall overcome" (TFF 213) or "Holy God, you raise up prophets" (TFF 299).

# Thursday, January 17

ANTONY OF EGYPT, RENEWER OF THE CHURCH, C. 356

Antony was born in Qemen-al-Arous, Upper Egypt, and was one of the earliest Egyptian desert fathers. Born to Christian parents from whom he inherited a large estate, he took personally Jesus' message to sell all that you have, give to the poor, and follow Christ. After making arrangements to provide for the care of his sister, he gave away his inheritance and became a hermit. Later, he became the head of a group of monks that lived in a cluster of huts and devoted themselves to communal prayer, worship, and manual labor under Antony's direction. The money they earned from their work was distributed as alms. Antony and his monks also preached and counseled those who sought them out.

Antony and the desert fathers serve as a reminder that certain times and circumstances call Christians to stand apart from the surrounding culture and renounce the world in service to Christ.

# Friday, January 18

THE CONFESSION OF ST. PETER
WEEK OF PRAYER FOR CHRISTIAN UNITY BEGINS

The Week of Prayer for Christian Unity is framed by two commemorations, today's Confession of St. Peter and next week's Conversion of St. Paul. Both apostles are remembered together on June 29, but these two days give us an opportunity to focus on key events in each of their lives. Today we remember that Peter was led by God's grace to acknowledge Jesus as "the Christ, the Son of the living God" (Matt. 16:16).

This confession is the common confession that unites us with Peter and with all Christians of every time and place. During these weeks of Epiphany, with their emphasis on mission, consider holding an ecumenical worship service with neighboring congregations to embody the unity we share in our confession of Christ, a unity granted us in our one baptism, a unity we yearn to embody more fully. The hymn "We all are one in mission" (WOV 755) could be sung at this service.

# Saturday, January 19

HENRY, BISHOP OF UPPSALA,
MISSIONARY TO FINLAND, MARTYR, 1156

Henry, an Englishman, became bishop of Uppsala, Sweden, in 1152, and is regarded as the patron of Finland. He traveled to Finland with the king of Sweden on a mission trip and remained there to organize the church. He was murdered in Finland by a man whom he had rebuked and who was disciplined by the church. Henry's burial place became a center of pilgrimage. His popularity as a saint is strong in both Sweden and Finland.

Today is an appropriate day to celebrate the Finnish presence in the Lutheran church. Consider singing "Lost in the night" (LBW 394), which uses a Finnish folk tune. During Epiphany we celebrate the light of Christ revealed to the nations, and martyrs such as Henry continue to reveal that light through their witness to faith.

# January 20, 2002

## Second Sunday after the Epiphany

## INTRODUCTION

Here is a simple pattern for the church's celebration during Epiphany: Christ is revealed as the servant of all people; Christ is baptized for his mission; Christ proclaims his message in word and deed until he goes up to Jerusalem. Here the season and the readings set forth a pattern for the community of faith: we enter this church, shaped and sustained by the sacraments, with a mission to serve the world. We are called to invite others to come and see the Lord. Come and touch the waters of new life, we say. Come and hear the words of good news. Come and taste the bread of life and the cup of mercy. Let your lives be shaped and sustained by these good things of God's grace.

In addition to the observance of Martin Luther King Jr.'s birthday (USA) tomorrow, the Week of Prayer for Christian Unity continues through January 25.

## PRAYER OF THE DAY

Lord God, you showed your glory and led many to faith by the works of your Son. As he brought gladness and healing to his people, grant us these same gifts and lead us also to perfect faith in him, Jesus Christ our Lord.

## READINGS

### Isaiah 49:1-7

Today's reading again picks up the theme of God's transformation of the old into something new. The imagery is familiar: the appointed one is called before birth and equipped to do God's work. The new thing is that the servant will not only do God's work for the benefit of Israel, but will also work for the benefit of the nations.

### Psalm 40:1-12 (Psalm 40:1-11 [NRSV])

I love to do your will, O my God. (Ps. 40:9)

### 1 Corinthians 1:1-9

Paul's letters to Corinth are addressed to a church beset by many problems. Still, he begins this epistle by emphasizing the faithfulness and grace of God, whose strength will see them through.

### John 1:29-42

John the Baptist's witness to Jesus initiates a chain of testimony as his disciples begin to share with others what they have found.

## COLOR  Green

## THE PRAYERS

Let us pray that the dawn from on high will shine for the church, the world, and all those in need.

*A BRIEF SILENCE.*

For the mission of the church, that we live as a light to the nations and invite others to join our worship and witness; God of light and life:

**hear us, we pray.**

For the leaders of nations, cities, and states, that they may serve with wisdom and courage and provide for the needs of all people; God of light and life:

**hear us, we pray.**

For those who are homebound and sick in our community (especially), that our words and care for them may show your love and compassion; God of light and life:

**hear us, we pray.**

For all who live in poverty or who suffer abuse, that you hold them in your mercy and rescue them from the grip of despair; God of light and life:

**hear us, we pray.**

For those newly born and for those about to die, that they find honor and strength in you; God of light and life:

**hear us, we pray.**

*HERE OTHER INTERCESSIONS MAY BE OFFERED.*

In thanksgiving for Martin Luther King Jr. and all who struggle for racial equality and the renewal of society, that we may be led by their example; God of light and life:

**hear us, we pray.**

God of splendor and light, hear our prayer and illumine us with the radiance of your glory shown in Jesus Christ our Lord.

**Amen**

93

## IMAGES FOR PREACHING

Will we know Jesus when we see him? Some did. John the Baptist declared him the Lamb of God, the one John came to reveal. How gracious of John. In our world, the first and famous rarely point to their successors. Yet John saw in Jesus the liberator of his people, the Passover lamb who came to save.

John not only saw him. John gave witness to what he saw. His words and testimony were the light that drew others to see and know Jesus. John confessed to two of his disciples, Here is "'the one who baptizes with the Holy Spirit.' And I myself have seen and have testified that this is the Son of God" (John 1:33-34). Because of John's testimony, those disciples wanted to know more, so they followed Jesus.

"What are you looking for?" Jesus asked. "Where are you staying?" the disciples wondered aloud (v. 38). Jesus invited them to come and see. The text says nothing about their conversation, only that they remained with Jesus for that day. But in that time, they saw John's witness come true. Andrew went to find his brother, Simon, and became a witness himself. "We have found the Messiah" (v. 41).

Jesus might ask all of us, What are you looking for? Do we seek a rescuer? A conqueror? A pal? A confidant? Through what images do we think of God? In what light do we see Jesus?

In the Spirit's light, these early believers gave witness to the Jesus they saw—the one long awaited, the one who abides with the Spirit, the one who is intimately connected with God. They came to see him as more than "Rabbi" but as Lord.

In the Spirit's light, we will see Jesus for who he is. Will we be able to be silent in the face of that grace and glory?

## WORSHIP MATTERS

The need for a rite to recognize in the worshiping assembly the life and stillbirth of a child has been expressed by many. Some have offered rites for consideration. Today's first reading is an appropriate text for such a time: "The Lord called me before I was born, while I was in my mother's womb he named me" (Isa. 49:1b). The text honors this one whom we did not have opportunity to know or baptize, but who is known and loved by the God of us all. How do you surround in prayer and support those who have experienced miscarriage or stillbirth? How might you ritualize this loss in the worshiping assembly?

## LET THE CHILDREN COME

In today's gospel reading, we find the scriptural source of a liturgical song, "Lamb of God," the Agnus Dei. The brief introduction to this reading from the Gospel of John could include an invitation to the children in the congregation to listen for these words later in the liturgy: "Lamb of God, you take away the sin of the world." As the assembly sings, an older sibling, parent, or other caring adult can point to the words in the worship book for children learning to read.

## HYMNS FOR WORSHIP

### GATHERING

Rise, shine, you people!   LBW 393
Now the feast and celebration   WOV 789

### HYMN OF THE DAY

Jesus, come! for we invite you   WOV 648

### ALTERNATE HYMN OF THE DAY

Son of God, eternal Savior   LBW 364
The Lamb   TFF 89

### COMMUNION

Now the silence   LBW 205
I, the Lord of sea and sky   WOV 752, TFF 230
Lamb of God, come take away   DH 25
Cup we bless   BL

### SENDING

All hail to you, O blessed morn   LBW 73
Angels from the realms of glory   LBW 50
We all are one in mission   WOV 755

### ADDITIONAL HYMNS AND SONGS

Dearest Jesus, at your word   LBW 248
Listen! You nations of the world   LBW 14
Jesus has come and brings pleasure eternal   LW 78
Jesus, Lamb of God   W&P 76
O God of light   LBW 237

94

## MUSIC FOR THE DAY
### PSALMODY

Chepponis, James J. "Here Am I, O Lord." SATB, solo, cong, gtr, kybd, opt C inst, hb.   GIA G-3295

Cooney, Rory. "Psalm 40: Here I Am" in STP, vol. 3.

Make me a servant   W&P 96

Nelson, Ronald A.   PW A.

Ylvisaker, John. "I've Waited Calmly for You" in *Borning Cry*.   NGP.

### CHORAL

Basler, Paul. "Agnus Dei." SATB, pno, hrn, perc.   PLY PJMS-106.

Bouman, Paul. "Behold the Lamb of God." SA, org.   CPH 98-1088.

Christiansen, F. Melius. "Lamb of God." SATB.   AFP 11-0133.

Christiansen, O.C. "Light Everlasting." SATB.   KJO 5110.

Goss, John. "These Are They Which Follow the Lamb" in *Anthems for Choirs 1*. SATB, org.   OXF.

Handel, G.F. "Behold the Lamb of God" in *Messiah*. SATB, org. Various ed.

Moore, Undine Smith. "I Believe This Is Jesus" in *The Augsburg Choirbook*. SATB.   AFP 0800656784.

Morley, Thomas. "Agnus Dei." SATB.   KJO 21.

Roth, John D. "Agnus Dei." SATB, kybd.   CPH 98-3261.

Slawson, Thomas H.B. "O Lamb of God." SATB, kybd.   AFP 0800659678.

### CHILDREN'S CHOIRS

Hopson, Hal H. "You Are My Child." U, kybd, fl.   CG CGA-480.

Lutz, Deborah. "Loving Jesus, Gentle Lamb." U, kybd.   MSM-50-9500.

### KEYBOARD/INSTRUMENTAL

Bach, J.S. "Herr Christ, der einig Gotts Sohn" in *Orgelbüchlein*. Org.   PET 10635.

Biery, James. "Union Seminary" in *Tree of Life*. Org.   AFP 0800655370.

Osterland, Karl. "Union Seminary" in *Lift One Voice*. Org.   AFP 0800659007.

Sedio, Mark. "Siyahamba/Thuma Mina" in *Dancing in the Light of God*. Pno.   AFP 0800656547.

### HANDBELL

Hollander, Lynne. "Brightly Sound the Chimes." 2-3 oct. L1.   JEF RO 3222.

Ward, Robert J. "Siyahamba." 4-6 oct. L3.   AGEHR AG46014.

### PRAISE ENSEMBLE

Chisum, John and George Searcy/arr. Don Harris. "Come and Behold Him." SATB, kybd.   INT 01217.

Haas, David. "Come and Journey With Me." SATB, kybd, solo, cong, C inst.   GIA G-4082.

Jernigan, Dennis/arr. Bruce Greer. "You Are My All in All." SATB, kybd.   WRD 301 0937 164.

# Friday, January 25

THE CONVERSION OF SAINT PAUL
WEEK OF PRAYER FOR CHRISTIAN UNITY ENDS

Today the Week of Prayer for Christian Unity comes to an end. The church remembers how a man of Tarsus named Saul, a former persecutor of the early Christian church, was led by God's grace to become one of its chief preachers. The risen Christ appeared to Paul on the road to Damascus and called him to proclaim the gospel. The narratives describing Paul's conversion in the Acts of the Apostles, Galatians, and I Corinthians inspire this commemoration, which was first celebrated among the Christians of Gaul.

# Saturday, January 26

TIMOTHY, TITUS, AND SILAS

Following the celebration of the Conversion of Paul, we remember his companions. Today, we remember Timothy, Titus, and Silas. They were missionary coworkers with Paul. Timothy accompanied Paul on his second missionary journey and was commissioned by Paul to go to Ephesus, where he served as bishop and overseer of the church. Titus was a traveling companion of Paul, accompanied him on the trip to the council of Jerusalem, and became the first bishop of Crete. Silas traveled with Paul through Asia Minor and Greece, and was imprisoned with him at Philippi, where they were delivered by an earthquake.

This festival invites the church to remember Christian leaders, bishops, pastors, and teachers—both men and women—who have been influential in the lives of individual members as gospel signs of the light of Epiphany.

95

# January 27, 2002

## Third Sunday after the Epiphany

### INTRODUCTION

Today's gospel reading narrates a strange fishing expedition. Jesus utters simple words that change human lives: "Follow me and I will make you fish for people." No glitz, no slick marketing, no extravagant claim; only these words: "Follow me."

Here is the mission that flows from the watery pool of our baptism into Christ. The Christian community goes forth and invites others to see what good things God offers in the waters of rebirth, in the scriptures, in the holy supper, in the community of faith. People can be "caught" in many things. What happens when they are caught in the net of God's mercy?

### PRAYER OF THE DAY

Almighty God, you sent your Son to proclaim your kingdom and to teach with authority. Anoint us with the power of your Spirit, that we, too, may bring good news to the afflicted, bind up the brokenhearted, and proclaim liberty to the captive; through your Son, Jesus Christ our Lord.

### READINGS

Isaiah 9:1-4

The people in the northern parts of Israel have experienced "gloom" and "darkness" because of the destruction wrought by Assyrian military forces. To these people, the prophet announces the shining of a great light of salvation. Matthew equates this light with the beginning of Jesus' ministry in Galilee.

Psalm 27:1, 5-13 (Psalm 27:1, 4-9 [NRSV])

The Lord is my light and my salvation. (Ps. 27:1)

1 Corinthians 1:10-18

Three of the most highly respected missionaries in the early church were Paul, Apollos, and Cephas (also known as Simon Peter). Still, as Paul himself attests, respect for any human leader is misplaced if it becomes divisive or obscures devotion to Christ.

Matthew 4:12-23

John the Baptist called everyone to repent, including the ruler Herod, who had him thrown in prison. It was at this point that Jesus began his public ministry, proclaiming the nearness of the reign of God.

### COLOR Green

### THE PRAYERS

Let us pray that the dawn from on high will shine for the church, the world, and all those in need.

*A BRIEF SILENCE.*

That our unity in Christ may lead all Christians to unity at the Lord's table and in mission and ministry to the world; God of light and life:

**hear us, we pray.**

That nations, peoples, and homes shadowed by conflict and violence may come to reconciliation and the dawn of peace; God of light and life:

**hear us, we pray.**

That all who live with grief, anxiety, loneliness, or illness (especially) may find hope in the wisdom of the cross; God of light and life:

**hear us, we pray.**

That we may proclaim the nearness of Christ's rule by promoting health and healing in our communities; God of light and life:

**hear us, we pray.**

That our congregation with its diverse gifts may offer hospitality to those of other faiths, those who doubt, and those who differ from us; God of light and life:

**hear us, we pray.**

*HERE OTHER INTERCESSIONS MAY BE OFFERED.*

In thanksgiving for the saints united with us through our baptism into Christ, that we may be brought with them to your land of glory; God of light and life:

**hear us, we pray.**

God of splendor and light, hear our prayer and illumine us with the radiance of your glory shown in Jesus Christ our Lord.

**Amen**

### IMAGES FOR PREACHING

When John was arrested, deeper shadows descended. Yes, they had already settled over the land in the hardness of Herod's heart. But when John was arrested, the darkness deepened.

Jesus, however, was the light to shine in the dark-

96

ness. What did he do first? He went to the land of Zebulun and Naphtali—the first tribes to fall to foreign domination, the first to become outsiders. He settled near a land of Gentiles, outsiders all, and began to proclaim that the kingdom of heaven had come near.

Now, in hindsight, we confess that Jesus himself was God incarnate. Now we see in him the way God works—to settle first with those who are outside. But then, who knew? Who knew that soon he would be crucified? Who knew that he would rise from the dead in triumph and promise?

Jesus began to proclaim that God's will and way were near, and then he called James and John to follow. He called them away from the life they knew, and they went. He went throughout Galilee teaching, preaching the good news of God's presence and welcome, and healing those in need.

Here is the light in this world's gloom. Jesus asks us to turn around, to witness to God's presence, to grow, and to heal. Here is the light for our path. No one else could show us the way.

## WORSHIP MATTERS

A well-prepared reader is familiar with the text, its context, the specific translation to be read, and the format in which the text is printed, as well as the light switch, microphone, and other mechanics of the ambo or reading desk. Provide readers with an exact copy of the page from the ritual edition of the Bible or lectionary used in your congregation. Encourage them to practice with the actual book, reading desk, and sound system in place. If necessary, use self-adhesive notes to mark the beginning and end of the lectionary passage. Ritual introductions and conclusions can be written on these notes.

Most ritual edition Bibles and lectionaries include ribbon markers. Use them to mark the pages for the day's readings. Ribbon markers are best used in the order they are bound into the spine, and are most functional if the loose ends extend from the side of the book, rather than the bottom, and are arranged with the marker for each succeeding reading placed lower down the page.

## LET THE CHILDREN COME

Let an older child lift high the cross in a procession as the people gather to hear the word and share the meal, and then let the child carry the cross out of the sanctuary when worship ends. Indeed, the cross can be carried out the front door of the church and into the parking lot or onto the sidewalk. Let the children lead the others, who follow the cross and follow Jesus into the world, into the places they are sent to live and serve.

## HYMNS FOR WORSHIP
### GATHERING

From God the Father, virgin-born    LBW 83
You servants of God    LBW 252
Each morning brings us    WOV 800

### HYMN OF THE DAY

Lift every voice and sing    LBW 562, TFF 296

### ALTERNATE HYMN OF THE DAY

You have come down to the lakeshore    WOV 784, TFF 154
The Lord is my light    TFF 61

### COMMUNION

O Master, let me walk with you    LBW 492
One bread, one body    WOV 710, TFF 122, W&P 111
The summons    W&P 137

### SENDING

I love to tell the story    LBW 390, TFF 228
We all are one in mission    WOV 755
Go, make disciples    W&P 47

### ADDITIONAL HYMNS AND SONGS

O Jesus, I have promised    LBW 503
Christ calls us now, as long ago    ASF 29
Those who love and those who labor    RS 805

## MUSIC FOR THE DAY
### PSALMODY

DeBruyn, Randall. "The Lord Is My Light" in STP, vol. 4.
Kreutz, Robert E. "The Lord Is My Light" in *Psalms and Selected Canticles*.  OCP.
The Lord is my light    TFF 61
Nelson, Ronald A.    PWA.
*Psalms for All Seasons: An ICEL Collection*.  NPM.
Soper, Scott. "Ps 27: The Goodness of the Lord" in STP, vol. 3.

### CHORAL

Ferguson, John. "He Comes to Us as One Unknown." SATB, org.
AFP 0800656008.
Handel, G.F. "His Yoke Is Easy" in *Messiah*. SATB, org.    Various ed.

97

Handel, G.F. "The People That Walked in Darkness" in *Messiah*.
B solo.    Various ed.

Kopylow-Wilhousky. "Heavenly Light." SATB.    CFI CM 497.

Erickson, Richard. "I Want to Walk as a Child of the Light." SATB,
org.    AFP 0800658396.

Helgen, John. "Brighter Than the Sun." SATB, kybd.
AFP 0800659155.

Manz, Paul. "I Want to Walk as a Child of the Light." SATB, org, opt
cong.    MSM-60-9019.

Roff, Joseph. "Shine within My Soul." SATB, opt hb, kybd.
MSM-50-9044.

Zimmermann, Heinz Werner. "The Lord Is My Light." SATB.
CPH 98-2174.

## CHILDREN'S CHOIRS

Bagenfelt, Susanne. "There's a Light in the World." U, opt 2 pt, kybd.
AFP 0800674286.

Christopherson, Dorothy. "The Lord Is My Light." U, kybd, fc.
AFP 0800647475.

Story, Donald, arr. "O Splendor of God's Glory Bright." 2 pt,
kybd, fl.    KJO 406806.

## KEYBOARD/INSTRUMENTAL

Behnke, John. Partita on "I Want to Walk as a Child of the Light."
Org.    CPH 97-6595.

Diemer, Emma Lou. "Jesus Calls Us" in *AGO Anthology of American
Organ Music*. Org.    OXF 87-754295.

## HANDBELL

Afdahl, Lee J. "Two Spanish Tunes for Handbells." 3-5 oct. L3.
AFP 0800657381.

Bettcher, Peggy. "Shine, Jesus, Shine." 2-3 oct. L2.    AG 2069.

## PRAISE ENSEMBLE

Besig, Don. "United in Christ." SATB, kybd, tpt.    FLA A 7302.

Evans, Darrell. "Whom Shall I Fear?" in *Hosanna Music Songbook 13*.
SAT[B], kybd.    INT 13576.

Moen, Don/arr. Tom Brooks. "My Love and My Light." SATB,
kybd.    INT 14637.

Rice, Chris. "Go Light Your World." SATB with duet, kybd.
WRD 301 0883 161.

# Sunday, January 27

## LYDIA, DORCAS, AND PHOEBE

Today we remember three women in the early church who were companions in Paul's ministry. Lydia was Paul's first convert at Philippi in Macedonia. She was a merchant of purple-dyed goods, and because purple dye was extremely expensive, it is likely that Lydia was a woman of some wealth. Lydia and her household were baptized by Paul, and for a time her home was a base for Paul's missionary work. Dorcas is remembered for her charitable works, particularly making clothing for needy widows. Phoebe was a *diakonos*, a deacon in the church at Cenchreae, near Corinth.

Today provides an opportunity for congregations to reflect the ministry of women, ordained and lay, wealthy and poor, who have given of themselves in service to the ministry of the gospel in their congregations.

# Saturday, February 2

## THE PRESENTATION OF OUR LORD

Forty days after the birth of Christ we mark the day Mary and Joseph presented him in the temple in accordance with Jewish law. There in the temple, a prophet named Anna began to speak of the redemption of Israel when she saw the young child. Simeon also greeted Mary and Joseph. He responded to the presence of the consolation of Israel in this child with the words of the Nunc dimittis. His song described Jesus as a "light for the nations."

Because of the link between Jesus as the light for the nations, and because an old reading for this festival contains a line from the prophet Zephaniah, "I will search Jerusalem with candles," the day is also known as Candlemas, a day when candles are blessed for the coming year.

# February 3, 2002

Fourth Sunday after the Epiphany

## INTRODUCTION

What does the Lord ask of us? To do justice, to love kindness, and to walk humbly with God. These are simple words from today's first reading that, nonetheless, remain a challenge for anyone who recognizes the injustice and suffering that mark and mar much of human existence. In the gospel reading, Jesus teaches his disciples a way of seeing those who are blessed in God's sight: the poor, mourners, the meek, those who hunger for righteousness, the merciful, the pure in heart, the peacemakers. These are the people to whom Jesus has constant recourse in his ministry. How does this congregation serve them?

Today the church's calendar invites us to remember Ansgar, ninth century missionary to Denmark and Sweden.

## PRAYER OF THE DAY

O God, you know that we cannot withstand the dangers which surround us. Strengthen us in body and spirit so that, with your help, we may be able to overcome the weakness that our sin has brought upon us; through Jesus Christ, your Son our Lord.

## READINGS

Micah 6:1-8

With the mountains and the foundations of the earth as the jury, God brings a lawsuit against Israel. Acting first as plaintiff, God charges that though the Lord has provided constant care for the people, they have not responded appropriately. Acting as judge, God indicts Israel for bringing burnt offerings instead of justice and mercy.

Psalm 15

Lord, who may abide upon your holy hill? (Ps. 15:1)

1 Corinthians 1:18-31

In the city of Corinth, many Christians prided themselves on their sophistication and learning. Paul reminds them that God identifies with what is considered foolish, weak, and despised. This message is the wisdom of the cross.

Matthew 5:1-12

Jesus opens the sermon on the mount by describing God's care for those who are blessed in the reign of God.

## COLOR Green

## THE PRAYERS

Let us pray that the dawn from on high will shine for the church, the world, and all those in need.
*A BRIEF SILENCE.*

For the church, that living in the blessedness of the commonwealth of heaven, we may show care for those who are lowly and downtrodden; God of light and life:
**hear us, we pray.**

For those persecuted for their faith, that they will find strength in the message of Christ crucified and have their hope sustained; God of light and life:
**hear us, we pray.**

For the leaders of nations, that they serve their people as peacemakers and messengers of reconciliation; God of light and life:
**hear us, we pray.**

For the poor in spirit, for all who suffer depression, poverty, or illness (especially), that you lift them to new life and health; God of light and life:
**hear us, we pray.**

For those who mourn and grieve the loss of loved ones, that you would comfort and console them; God of light and life:
**hear us, we pray.**

*HERE OTHER INTERCESSIONS MAY BE OFFERED.*

Remembering Ansgar and all the saints who have cared for the poor and lived humbly with justice and kindness, that their example sustain our ministry; God of light and life:
**hear us, we pray.**

God of splendor and light, hear our prayer and illumine us with the radiance of your glory shown in Jesus Christ our Lord.
**Amen**

99

## IMAGES FOR PREACHING

Jesus did not come to be a soft, fuzzy light. Sometimes his is the light of a bare bulb, glaring and baring our damaged vision. He shows us for what we are—so often a selfish, mean-spirited, covetous people. Jesus reveals the ways we will not and cannot live as God intended in creating us.

So Jesus reveals God's reversals. "Blessed are those who…" For those who see themselves in his words, Jesus teaches sweet comfort. But for the rest, those who are haughty, for example, or those who do not hunger and thirst for righteousness, or those who make war or persecute or revile or utter all kinds of evil—for these, Jesus' words are anything but comforting.

In God's reversals, the light will shine on those who are so often overshadowed, who understand themselves to live in darkness. They will receive blessing in the realm of God.

Yet the light also shines to reveal how all of us fall short of God's glory, how far we are from the standard expressed in Micah's words: "and what does the Lord require of you but to do justice, and to love kindness, and to walk humbly with your God?" (6:8).

When we know how we have failed, we mourn for lost opportunity, humble ourselves in the face of our failings, hunger and thirst for righteousness in ourselves and in the world. When we acknowledge how we have failed, we discover mercy, restoration, peace. And we hear Jesus' word of blessing. In him, we see God.

## WORSHIP MATTERS

Among other things, the liturgy is a dialog between leaders and assembly. One cannot effectively communicate in a dialog until both parties are ready to hear. We often forget that fact during the liturgy of the word. Readers can hinder communication if they begin to speak before the assembly is ready to listen. Waiting until the assembly is ready to listen before proclaiming the scriptures honors both the word and those who will hear it. Encourage each lector to move to the place of reading, assume a posture and establish a presence for a moment, and take control of the worshipers' attention. The reader should wait there peacefully, make eye contact with the assembly until people have settled into comfortable postures and centered their minds, and their eyes meet the reader's. Then the people of God are ready to receive the word of life.

## LET THE CHILDREN COME

Why do we stand for the gospel reading? Because each time the gospel words are read, it is as if Jesus comes among us to speak the word of life. Just as in today's gospel reading the great multitude of people gathered to hear Jesus, we rise to greet the one who speaks God's blessing to us. Encourage children to stand (perhaps even on the pew, with safe support) and to turn their bodies and eyes toward the gospel reader. We are all paying close attention to the words of Jesus.

## HYMNS FOR WORSHIP

### GATHERING

Bright and glorious is the sky   LBW 75

Rejoice in God's saints   WOV 689

### HYMN OF THE DAY

Blest are they   WOV 764

### ALTERNATE HYMN OF THE DAY

Where cross the crowded ways of life   LBW 429

We are called   W&P 147

### COMMUNION

Now we join in celebration   LBW 203

Eat this bread, drink this cup   WOV 706

He came down   TFF 37

Be thou my vision   WOV 776

### SENDING

Renew me, O eternal light   LBW 511

Let justice flow like streams   WOV 763, TFF 48

### ADDITIONAL HYMNS AND SONGS

I want Jesus to walk with me   TFF 66

Songs of thankfulness and praise   LBW 90

O loving God   DH 82

O God, to whom we turn   H82

## MUSIC FOR THE DAY

### PSALMODY

Batastini, Robert. "The Just Will Live" in *RitualSong*.   GIA.

Bengtson, Bruce.   PW B.

Gelineau, Joseph. "Psalm 15" in *RitualSong*.   GIA.

Hass, David/arr. Jeanne Cotter. "They Who Do Justice" in PCY, vol. III.

Proulx, Richard/arr. Gelineau.   TP

Pulkingham, Betty. *Celebrate the Church Year with Selected Psalms and Canticles.* Cong, choir, kybd, gtr, inst.   PLY MB 94218.

## CHORAL

Bisbee, B. Wayne. "O Splendor of God's Glory Bright." 2 pt trbl or mxd, pno.   AFP 0800659252.

Bush, Gladys Blakely. "With What Shall I Come Before the Lord." SATB.   CPH 98-3398.

Gore, Richard T. "The Beatitudes." SATB.   CHA COA 512.

Haas, David. "Blest Are They." U or SAB, kybd, opt cong, 2 C inst, gtr.   GIA G-4269.

Handel, G.F. "Exceeding Glad" in *Coronation Anthems.* SATB, org. OXF.

Pelz, Walter. "Who Shall Abide." SAB, fl, gtr.   AFP 11-0617.

Wood, Dale. "Rise, Shine" in *The Augsburg Choirbook.* SATB, org. AFP 0880656784.

## CHILDREN'S CHOIRS

Barker, Michael. "Miriam's Song." U, kybd, tamb.   CG CGA740.

Cox, Joe. "Blessed to Be a Blessing." U/2 pt, kybd. MSM MSM-50-9409.

## KEYBOARD/INSTRUMENTAL

Cherwein, David. "O Jesus, Joy" in *Interpretations Book III.* Org. AMSI OR-6.

Cotter, Jeannie. "Blest Are They" in *After the Rain.* Pno.   GIA.

Keesecker, Thomas. "Partita on 'Blest Are They.'" Org. CPH 97-6546.

Kolander, Keith. "Aria I" in *Three Arias for Piano and Solo Instruments.* AFP 0800658175.

Wold, Wayne L. "Suite on 'Bright and Glorious Is the Sky.'" AFP 0800659023. Org.

## HANDBELL

Honoré, Jeffrey. "A Prayer on SLANE." 2-3 oct. L2.   CPH 97-6846.

Manz, Paul/arr. Martha Lynn Thompson. "God of Grace." 4-5 oct. L3.   MSM 30-810.

## PRAISE ENSEMBLE

Baroni, David and John Chisum/arr. Dave Williamson. "O Mighty Cross." SATB, kybd.   INT 11037.

Larson, Lloyd. "The Lord Desires These Things." SATB, kybd. BEC BP 1530.

Nolan, Douglas. "Teach Me, O Lord." 2 pt, kybd.   GS EA5147.

# Sunday, February 3

## ANSGAR, ARCHBISHOP OF HAMBURG, MISSIONARY TO DENMARK AND SWEDEN, 865

A traditional emphasis during the weeks after Epiphany has been the mission of the church. Ansgar was a monk who led a mission to Denmark and then later to Sweden, where he built the first church. His work ran into difficulties with the rulers of the day, and he was forced to withdraw into Germany, where he served as a bishop in Hamburg. Despite his difficulties in Sweden, he persisted in his mission work and later helped consecrate Gothbert as the first bishop of Sweden. Ansgar also had a deep love for the poor. He would wash their feet and serve them food provided by the parish.

The Church of Sweden honors Ansgar as an apostle. His persistence in mission and his care for the poor invite congregations to reflect on their own ministry of bearing the light of Christ during the days after Epiphany.

101

# Tuesday, February 5

## THE MARTYRS OF JAPAN, 1597

In the sixteenth century, Jesuit missionaries, followed by Franciscans, introduced the Christian faith in Japan. But a promising beginning to those missions—there were perhaps as many as 300,000 Christians by the end of the sixteenth century—met complications from competition between the missionary groups, political difficulty between Spain and Portugal, and factions within the government of Japan. Christianity was suppressed. By 1630, Christianity was driven underground.

Today we commemorate the first martyrs of Japan, twenty-six missionaries and converts, who were killed by crucifixion. Two hundred and fifty years later, when Christian missionaries returned to Japan, they found a community of Japanese Christians that had survived underground. The witness of the Martyrs of Japan invites us to pray for the church's own witness to the gospel and encourages us to trust that the church is sustained in times of persecution.

# February 10, 2002

The Transfiguration of Our Lord
Last Sunday after the Epiphany

## INTRODUCTION

This festival concludes the Christmas cycle that began in Advent. Today's gospel reading is the inspiration for this feast. On one level it celebrates the manifestation of Jesus as God's beloved child and servant (an echo of the Christmas, Epiphany, and baptism festivals). At the same time, the church's calendar is influenced by the gospel story: after his transfiguration, Jesus announces his impending death in Jerusalem. From the festival of the transfiguration, the church turns this week to Ash Wednesday and its baptismal journey to Christ's death and resurrection celebrated during the Three Days of Maundy Thursday, Good Friday, and the Vigil of Easter/Easter Sunday.

## PRAYER OF THE DAY

Almighty God, on the mountain you showed your glory in the transfiguration of your Son. Give us the vision to see beyond the turmoil of our world and to behold the king in all his glory; through your Son, Jesus Christ our Lord, who lives and reigns with you and the Holy Spirit, one God, now and forever.

*or*

O God, in the transfiguration of your Son you confirmed the mysteries of the faith by the witness of Moses and Elijah, and in the voice from the bright cloud you foreshadowed our adoption as your children. Make us with the king heirs of your glory, and bring us to enjoy its fullness, through Jesus Christ our Lord, who lives and reigns with you and the Holy Spirit, one God, now and forever.

## READINGS

### Exodus 24:12-18

In the Bible, mountains often serve as places of revelation. Moses' six-day wait on the mountain covered by the cloud is a way of telling the reader that something important is about to be revealed: God's law. Similarly the experience of Jesus, Peter, James, and John on a mountain reveals something important: God's Son.

### Psalm 2

You are my son; this day have I begotten you. (Ps. 2:7)

*or* Psalm 99

Proclaim the greatness of the Lord; worship upon God's holy hill. (Ps. 99:9)

### 2 Peter 1:16-21

At the transfiguration of Jesus, Peter heard the voice of God speak from heaven. This same voice speaks to us from the holy word.

### Matthew 17:1-9

Shortly before he enters Jerusalem, where he will be crucified, Jesus is revealed to his disciples in a mountaintop experience of divine glory called the transfiguration.

## COLOR  White

## THE PRAYERS

Let us pray that the dawn from on high will shine for the church, the world, and all those in need.
*A BRIEF SILENCE.*

That the rulers of nations govern and serve with a vision of the world at peace, so that no one lives in fear or terror; God of light and life:

**hear us, we pray.**

That the church hear your word in Jesus Christ, behold the mystery of his presence in the eucharist, and live as a witness to your grace; God of light and life:

**hear us, we pray.**

That all who suffer (especially) find comfort in the healing touch of Christ, that their sickness may be turned to joy and health; God of light and life:

**hear us, we pray.**

That those who live with doubt and those who are overcome by fear might behold the vision of Christ's glory and be upheld with a renewed hope; God of light and life:

**hear us, we pray.**

That those who care for the poor, the deprived, and the easily forgotten may be supported by your presence in their ministry and service; God of light and life:

**hear us, we pray.**

*HERE OTHER INTERCESSIONS MAY BE OFFERED.*

In communion with all the saints, transfigure us into your likeness as we live out your grace in word and deed; God of light and life:

**hear us, we pray.**

God of splendor and light, hear our prayer and illumine us with the radiance of your glory shown in Jesus Christ our Lord.

**Amen**

## IMAGES FOR PREACHING

In Jesus, we see God. The ancient ones believed that seeing God meant certain death. Yet, in Jesus, we see God.

Peter, James, and John—faced with the transfigured Jesus—tried to make sense of a face that shone like the sun and clothes that dazzled. Moses and Elijah appeared with him, making visible his continuity with the deep history of faith.

But Peter seemed to know what the moment meant. He sought to capture this moment of seeing so luminously. He tried to hang on to this fleeting experience. Perhaps building booths would work—camping out, there on the mountaintop. Then the voice from the bright cloud overshadowed them all and named the truth about Jesus. He was not just dazzling. He was not just a fulfillment of ancient prophecy. "This is my Son, the Beloved.... Listen to him!" (Matt. 17:5).

Can it be true? In Jesus, we see God. In the face of Jesus we do not see death but new life. Perhaps we know fear, as the disciples did. In Jesus, we see both God's judgment and God's mercy. Fear and awe, yes, but above all, promise and dazzling grace. The God of the whole universe is with us. The light of Christ shows us the way.

## WORSHIP MATTERS

The transfiguration shows forth the incarnate Word in all his glory. All things—including this saving Word among us—are from God's goodness. In the offertory we acknowledge that we are totally dependent on this goodness of God. Reflect on the reception and presentation of the gifts as it is practiced in your congregation. Is it clear that the gifts are received, not taken? Is it clear that the gifts are symbols of our total dependence on God's generosity? Do the gifts that are brought forward occasionally or regularly include symbols other than the symbol of money? What other symbols seem appropriate? Is it clear to the assembly that they have nothing to offer God but their thanksgiving for these gifts already given? How do they embody, speak, pray, and sing this thanksgiving?

## LET THE CHILDREN COME

Today we stand on a mountain from which we can see both the path we have taken and the road yet to be traveled. We hear again God's words of promise first spoken at the baptism of Jesus, "This is my Son, the Beloved." At the entrance rite, invite the children to come to the font to trace on their forehead with water the sign of the cross, the sign that they are beloved of God. Tell them that on Wednesday, the sign will be traced again, then in ashes, the sign that we are Christ's even when we are little, weak, frail, or dying.

## HYMNS FOR WORSHIP

### GATHERING

Beautiful Savior   LBW 518

When morning gilds the skies   LBW 545, 546

Shine, Jesus, shine   TFF 64, WOV 651, W&P 123

### HYMN OF THE DAY

Jesus on the mountain peak   WOV 653

### ALTERNATE HYMN OF THE DAY

O Morning Star, how fair and bright!   LBW 76

There is a Redeemer   W&P 140

### COMMUNION

Thy strong word   LBW 233

I want to walk as a child of the light   WOV 649

My chosen one   BL

### SENDING

In thee is gladness   LBW 552

We are marching in the light of God   WOV 650, TFF 63, W&P 148

Alleluia, song of gladness   WOV 654

### ADDITIONAL HYMNS AND SONGS

Jesus, take us to the mountain   NCH 183

Open our eyes, Lord   W&P 113, TFF 98

In the desert, on God's mountain   OBS 88

Come to the mountain   W&P 32

103

## MUSIC FOR THE DAY
### SERVICE MUSIC

As the last festival in the Christmas cycle, this day invites special attention to the Gloria in excelsis and the Alleluia before these service elements are set aside during the season of Lent.

### PSALMODY: PSALM 2

Hopson, Hal H. *Psalm Refrains and Tones.*   HOP 425.
Wetzler, Robert.   PW A.

### PSALMODY: PSALM 99

Hopson, Hal H. *Psalm Refrains and Tones.*   HOP 425.
Seltz, Martin.   PW C.
*The Psalter: Psalms and Canticles for Singing.*

### CHORAL

Bach, J.S. "Alleluia" in *Bach for All Seasons.* SATB, kybd.
AFP 080065854X.
Bairstow, Edward C. "Jesu, the Very Thought of Thee." SATB.
OXF 43.003.
Bertalot, John. "Christ upon the Mountain Peak." 2 pt mxd, org,
ob/fl.   AFP 0800653793.
Bouman, Paul. "Christ upon the Mountain Peak." SATB, org.
CPH 98-2856.
Busarow, Donald. "Farewell to Alleluia." SATB, org, ob, opt cong.
CPH 98-2995.
Christiansen, F. Melius. "Beautiful Savior." SSAATTBB or SATB,
A solo.   AFP 0800645138.
Farlee, Robert Buckley. "Farewell to Alleluia." U, opt tpt, opt cong.
AFP 0800649486.
Forsberg, Charles. "Fairest Lord Jesus." SATB, pno.
AFP 0880656962.
Helman, Michael. "Go Up to the Mountain of God." SATB, pno,
opt fl.   AFP 0880658353.
Nystedt, Knut. "This Is My Beloved Son." SAB, org.
CPH 98-1805.
Schramm, Charles W., Jr. "You Are My Son." SA(T)B, org.
CPH 98-3571.

Thompson, Randall. "Alleluia." SATB.   ECS 1786.
Uhl, Dan. "This Is My Beloved Son" in *The Augsburg Choirbook.* SATB,
org.   AFP 0800656784.
White, David Ashley. "Alleluia." SSAATTBB.   SEL 410-931.

### CHILDREN'S CHOIRS

Bågenfelt, Susanne. "There's a Light in the World." U, opt 2 pt, kybd.
AFP 0800674286.
Behnke, John A. "Three Psalms for Unison Choir." U, kybd.
CPH 98-3578.
Harris, Robert A., arr. "This Little Light of Mine." 2 pt, kybd.
B&H OCTB6921.

### KEYBOARD/INSTRUMENTAL

Carlson, J. Bert. "This Little Light of Mine" in *This Little Light of Mine:
Piano Collection.* Pno.   AFP 0800659503.
Fields, Tim. "All Hail the Power of Jesus' Name." Org.
AFP 0800658736.
Hobby, Robert. "Christ Is the World's Light" in *Six Preludes for the
Church Year.* Org.   MSM 10-716.
Tambling, Christopher. "Antiphon—Send Forth Your Light" in *Accla-
mation.* Org.   MAY 1400015.

### HANDBELL

Larson, Katherine Jordahl. "Beautiful Savior." 3-4 oct. L2.
AFP 0806653965.
McKechnie, D. Linda. "When Morning Gilds the Skies." 3-5 oct. L3.
AG 1528.
Morris, Hart. "All Hail the Power of Jesus' Name" 3-4 oct. L2.
RR HB0011.

### PRAISE ENSEMBLE

Cull, Robert/arr. Jack Schrader. "Open Our Eyes, Lord." SATB,
kybd.   HOP C5042.
Kendrick, Graham/arr. Jack Schrader. "Shine, Jesus, Shine."
HOP GC 937 (SATB, kybd); GC937C (cass).

104

# LENT

*Coming to Lent means coming to life*

# Images *of the* Season

Coming to Lent means coming to life. In North

America the weeks of Lent mark the poleward drift of green

across the continent. Daylight is growing; the sun

is reasserting itself. Because of Christianity's development in the Northern Hemisphere, the shape of liturgical seasons is still influenced by the rhythm of sun and moon and stars.

In our own time, however, the rhythm of spring's return seems to be shifting, perhaps coming earlier now. Yes, it is wonderful to feel the warmth of the returning sun. But an early spring may also be an invitation to consider the prospect of global warming and the deadly toxins of our technological success stories. Are we tinkering with the earth's delicate balance, not so much by design but by neglect?

The contemporary concern for ecology of creation may suggest a similar dynamic for a postmodern Lenten discipline: we might consider this a season for *spiritual ecology*. It is time for us to wake from our winter deathsleep, to make an honest appraisal of our spiritual health and take actions that lead to life. These are the themes intoned for us at Lent's beginning, Ash Wednesday. The cross of ashes placed on our forehead is both "flashforward" and flashback. The flashforward catapults us to a day in the future. Imagine such a day for yourself. Perhaps you will be lying on a hospital bed, immediate family surrounding you. The pastor enters the room and everyone is glad to see her. She visits for a few moments, offers some ancient prayers, dips her thumb into a stock of oil, and traces the cross on your forehead. This act is an echo of another, which happened years before. Again, immediate family circled you and the pastor was there, tracing a cross on your forehead, recently cleansed with baptismal water.

Those two crosses form the bookends of our identity as disciples. In between is life—the time given us as a gift—days when action may be taken, amendments made, courses changed, itineraries updated. The ashen cross invites us to live the now in light of our beginnings and endings. Yes, we come from dust and return to dust. But we also are born from grace. We have come this far by faith. We are headed for a cross and open tomb. Knowing this, how shall we live in the present? What will

we do today to lessen death and affirm life—not only for ourselves, but for those we love, for the stranger, for others who are waiting to be born?

The disciplines of Lent are the tools for transformation. Each is an indispensable part of a spiritual ecology. We are called to *the Lenten fast*. Fasting is an ecological concern, a matter of keeping life in balance. Overconsumption is as bad for the soul as it is for the waistline. Lent is the season for spring training of the soul. We need to name the toxins that are poisoning us. We need to determine what is essential, let go of the extra baggage, and focus on the one or two chief tasks that deserve our greatest effort—here, now.

We are also called to *a life of prayer*. A genuine spiritual ecology does not happen in isolation; ecological balance is always holistic, and that means we must be in communication with others. A world cut off from God can never hope to be a place of life. Lent is the time for us to have a deep heart-to-heart with the creator who made us, the redeemer who claims us, the sanctifier who brings us to renewal. Lent is a time for listening and speaking, for entering the cycle of communication that will lead to life.

We are also called to *acts of kindness* toward others. The ecological dialogue into which we enter with God naturally leads to our deep connection with those around us. During Lent we ask more seriously, "Why are we doing it? For whom are we Christian? Only for ourselves?" Although Lent invites a deeper inward discipline, it also moves us beyond ourselves and toward others. Following the lead of Jesus, we are to be for others in a way that is transforming not only for us, but for those about whom we are concerned.

Over all this Lenten activity hovers the great Greek word of the season: *metanoia*, the "new mind" that is the fruit of the Spirit, the turn-around repentance that brings our old life to an end and prepares us for the new life that comes from Jesus' open tomb.

Come to Lent. The light is growing. It is time to come to life!

106

# Environment *and* Art *for the* Season

Karen is a single mother of a teenaged son.

She holds a professional, full-time job and has owned

her own home for more than ten years. She has struggled

over the years to rid herself of perfectionist tendencies, especially in the area of housekeeping. One winter, however, she found herself encountering a new challenge to her loosened standards. Karen had taken on too many responsibilities and was beginning to feel overwhelmed and stressed. She began to have dreams that dust was piling up around her. She dreamed that the broom was out of reach and she could not find the vacuum. After several nights of dreaming about dust accumulating, she decided to take action by dusting and vacuuming the rooms of her home.

Karen did not dream about dust the night after she cleaned the house. In the morning she awakened with a fresh sense of clarity and well-being. Karen says, "Somehow the dreams were telling me that I needed to clean out and reorganize my life. Although the message wasn't about the literal dust in my house, it mattered somehow to do that actual cleaning. I realized I had become slightly depressed, and I needed to exercise control over my environment."

Many of us have had similar experiences. Writers often find they simply cannot write if the room in which they work is messy. Their immediate environment needs to be ordered so that they feel free to let the wildness of the creative unconscious emerge.

Literature often speaks of the human need for cleansing or purgation as preparation for spiritual transformation. One of the most famous poems of the last century, T.S. Eliot's *The Wasteland*, speaks of contemporary life as a desert wasteland in need of redemption. The hallmark of a mythic wasteland is the absence of water. In Eliot's poem and in other mythic literature, the presence of water is the primary symbol of renewal and restoration of the proper order of life. Only water can give birth to springtime.

The look or shape of Lent facilitates an internal dance of the spirit: the uncluttered soul, stripped of its winter cover, lifts itself toward God with renewed vigor. This is perhaps the key requirement of the church environment for Lent.

Begin with a thorough spring cleaning of the church before Ash Wednesday. This may be a huge undertaking, so recognize the need for volunteers. Perhaps the volunteers are invited to stay for pizza or sandwiches after the work is completed. Remove clutter and anything that interferes with plainness and simplicity in the worship environment. Keep in mind that the seasons of Lent, the Three Days, and Easter together form a unity, what the church calls "the paschal cycle." Flowers are discouraged in Lent, so that their appearance is all the more vivid at the Vigil of Easter or Easter Sunday.

The unity of the paschal cycle is experienced in the journey to the waters of baptism. The tradition in many churches is to empty and cover the font during Lent, and to put the paschal candle away. (The candle would be used during this season only for funerals.) Some churches choose to keep water in the font during Lent, a practice that lifts up baptism as the primary focus of the paschal cycle. The practice in other churches of sealing or covering the font as a sign of the Lenten desert journey is also a sign of preparation by the community for the bath that is celebrated at the Vigil of Easter.

Another way to emphasize the baptismal character of the Lenten season is to introduce to the assembly those who are preparing for baptism or reception into the church. Catechumens and affirmers might be introduced to the community during worship, and their photos might be displayed in the narthex or other appropriate spot. In one parish, a liturgical artist renders in lovely calligraphy the names of those who will be baptized and received into the community at the Vigil of Easter. The names are painted on large, white cloth banners that are hung in the gathering space above the font. (This practice is an exception to the norm that banners should communicate images rather than words. It can be argued that the name of an individual is an image of the person.)

The Lenten gospels of year A reveal the sacramental efficacy of baptism. Jesus' night dialogue with Nicodemus, his conversation at the well with the Samaritan

107

woman, the healing of the man born blind, and the raising of Lazarus—any of these would be appropriate subjects for an art display near the font. Choose an icon of good quality or framed fine art by a gifted artist, and place it with a votive candle on a pedestal near the font.

As of Ash Wednesday, the Lenten church can be completely stripped of decoration. The color of vestments is purple or black on Ash Wednesday and remains purple throughout the season. (From Passion Sunday through Maundy Thursday, scarlet vestments and paraments may be used as a sign of Christ's passion and death.) Fabrics in neutral or desert colors, such as beige or taupe, convey wilderness aridity and can be effective accents to purple. For outdoor bunting over doorways, use a weatherproof purple fabric, and perhaps add a touch of scarlet to this for the first days of Holy Week.

Use materials that come from the earth and are made by human hands. Given Ash Wednesday's emphasis on human mortality, consider using vessels for the distribution of ashes that are crafted from clay, stone, or bone. Keep the amount of ornamentation or embellishment within the worship space to a minimum. Some churches arrange bare tree branches against purple, black, or neutral fabric. Such imagery is most effective when the symbolism is polyvalent; that is, capable of bearing more than one meaning and therefore devoid of literalism. What meanings do bare tree branches evoke? To some, these branches will communicate a barren desert. To others, the wood of the tree will imply the wood of the cross. Still others will appreciate the naked branches as an emblem of spiritual cleansing.

A good plan for the liturgical environment during the paschal cycle is one that views the seasons of Lent, the Three Days, and Easter as a whole. Artist Nancy Chinn, in her book *Spaces for Spirit* (Chicago: LTP, 1998), shows a design that accomplishes this. Bare branches are depicted on transparent nylon backgrounds and hung during Lent from the ceiling of the church. For the Easter season, the fabric panels are turned upside down and returned to their places. What had appeared as disparate, bare branches now appeared as elegant, slender trees that swayed upward. Behind each of these transparent nylon panels is hung a second transparent panel on which flowers are painted. This hanging installation conveys both the joy and the awe of Easter renewal.

How will the cross be displayed during Lent? Liturgical artist Jane Pitz explains that the stripping of her church on Ash Wednesday allows the cross to become the central focus of the environment:

> For the season of Lent, the space is emptied. The in-the-floor baptismal font, which usually welcomes the assembly with the sound of water, is emptied. Plants, except for flower bulbs in the niches that hold the three vessels of oil (which are taken out for Lent), are also removed. The cross, which is not hung but arises from the floor to a great height, dominates as the only liturgical element.

Artist Lucinda Naylor follows a similar plan but adds a dramatic swatch of purple near the altar to enhance the penitential mood.

Some churches dress a processional cross with seasonal flowers, grasses, or vines throughout the year. During Lent, dried grasses or pussy willows might be appropriate for this purpose. On Palm Sunday, the cross might be dressed with palm fronds.

Lenten programs offer wonderful opportunities for the visual arts. One church exhibited paintings by a church member for use as stations of the cross. The large paintings, done in a loose, "painterly" style, are representations of Christ's face during the passion. Tanja Butler's art has been displayed during Lent within her church. Her paintings of the passion refer to Passover events. An artist's exhibition of work in his or her own church is vitalizing for both artist and parish community alike.

# Preaching *with the* Season

What is Lent supposed to do for us? Why the purple?

Why no flowers? Why the avoiding of "alleluia"? Why all the talk

of fasting and self-examination and discipline?

In earlier times, back in the first centuries of the church's existence, what we call "Lent" was referred to as "the forty days" or "the quadragesimal fast." It was a solemn season of preparation preceding the joyous celebration of the Lord's resurrection. For catechumens, it was a time to learn the fundamentals of the Christian faith in preparation for their baptism at the Easter Vigil. For others, it was a time to do public penance after confessing some notorious sin. For all, if we are to believe the canons and decrees of church councils and the meditations of early church writers, it was a season of abstention.

According to the Apostolic Canons approved by the Eastern Church in the late seventh century, bishops, priests, deacons, lectors, or singers who neglected to fast during Lent were to be deposed from their offices. Laity who failed to fast faced excommunication. However, if Eastern Christians made the mistake of fasting on a Sunday (as was happening in "the city of the Romans"), then the canons directed that they should be deposed.

Armenian Christians were a bit too lax for some of their other Eastern brothers and sisters. They ate eggs and cheese on the Sabbath and Lord's Day in Lent. That practice was condemned in the late seventh century. Although eating food was commended on the Sabbath and Sunday, it was still widely regarded as improper to eat the flesh of animals or any other product of an animal on Sundays in the Lenten season.

Likewise it was forbidden to kneel (a penitential position) for prayers or for receiving communion on the Sundays during Lent, because those days were in but not of Lent and should have their own, altogether joyous character.

Earlier, the fourth century council of Laodicea had decreed that Christians must not celebrate marriages during Lent, a prohibition that has remained in effect in some communions to the present day. The birthdays of princes and other rulers were not to be celebrated in Lent but were transferred to other times when the rau-

cous behavior known to attend such celebrations would be acceptable.

Fasting was a pious custom taken over by the church from Judaism. The Day of Atonement was marked with a solemn fast (Lev. 16). Fasting was thought to strengthen the prayer of petitioners (Jer. 14:12; Acts 13:3) and was practiced as preparation for entering into God's presence (Exod. 34:28; Dan. 9:3). Jesus speaks of fasting in the sermon on the mount (Matt. 6:16-18), and the Didache, an early Christian document, recommends that Christians fast twice every week.

Ancient monks of the Eastern deserts earned a reputation for the most rigorous forms of fasting. In the spring of 587, at a time when Constantinople still ruled vast stretches of what we call the Middle East, two monks emerged from the monastery of Mar Theodosius outside of Bethlehem. John Moschus set off with his pupil Sophronius on a tour of the world of Byzantine monasticism. They intended to visit all the well-known holy men and women—monks, hermits, and ascetics— whom they could find.

British writer William Dalrymple was fascinated with John's account of his travels, and in 1994 he set off to visit all the places that John wrote about nearly 1,400 years earlier. He meditated on John's adventures and his own as he went. Dalrymple then recorded his observations in his book *On the Holy Mountain.*

Dalrymple writes in wonderful detail concerning the ancient monks. They took fasting and other ascetic practices to lengths that strike us as eccentric in the extreme. Some took literally Jesus' counsel that we should be like the birds of the air. They wove nests in trees and spent their entire life amid lofty branches. From this habit, they came to be called "dendrites." Better known than these tree-dwellers are the many who, like one named Simeon, lived out their life atop a stone pillar, earning for themselves the name "stylites." These saints were always devising what they thought of as "new tests of

109

endurance." Some built for themselves wooden cages to live in. They quite deliberately constructed their cages so that they were too small for the monks to stand upright. The monks forced themselves to spend all their days in a stooped position. Such contrivances sound like tortures perpetrated by conquerors upon their unwilling prisoners of war, but these monks believed that they were inflicting relatively mild punishments upon their bodies in this life so that their punishments in the next life might be fewer and lighter.

Dalrymple warns against viewing the habits of these hermits as little more than bizarre circus acts. He tries to penetrate the power that such practices exerted over the more traditionally pious. Byzantine Christians, he writes, looked on these practitioners of heroic asceticism as intermediaries, people who had already in this life crossed the boundary and gained direct access to the divine. They had denied their flesh to such an extent that they had become transparencies through which the invisible world could be glimpsed. Contact with the saint put one into contact with the spiritual and the heavenly.

Those ancient Christian ascetics, inhabiting caves

and cages, living in trees and on pillars, are our ancestors in the faith. Their practices are not ours, but their actions raise a pertinent and perhaps troubling question: To what practices of faith do we devote our energies in this Lenten season and in the rest of our lives—not as means to grace but as ways of growing in the grace in which we stand, of claiming and exercising the direct access to the divine that is God's gift to us in Christ?

Of course, those Eastern monks were not the first to retreat to the desert. Jesus himself, immediately after being baptized, was led into the desert by the Holy Spirit. There he fasted for forty days and forty nights, and he wrestled with Satan, who attempted to sway Jesus from his vocation. Then, and this is good news, Jesus did not remain in the desert. He left behind the fasting of those days and, strengthened by his desert sojourn, once more took up life in village and town. He did not seek the solitude of desert cave or lofty pillar but walked among us, practicing the deep compassion that issues from the heart of God. The only tree he dwelt in was the tree of the cross, where he finished his work of loving the world to the uttermost.

# Shape *of* Worship *for the* Season

## BASIC SHAPE OF THE EUCHARISTIC RITE

- Confession and Forgiveness: see alternate worship text for Lent in *Sundays and Seasons*

### GATHERING

- Greeting: see alternate worship text for Lent
- Use the Kyrie during Lent
- Omit the hymn of praise during Lent

### WORD

- For dramatic readings based on lectionary passages, use *Scripture Out Loud!* (AFP 0806639644) for Ash Wednesday and the fourth Sunday in Lent
- For contemporary dramas based on lectionary passages, use *Can These Bones Live?* (AFP 0806639652) for Ash Wednesday, the fifth Sunday in Lent, and Passion Sunday

- Use the Nicene Creed
- The prayers: see the prayers for Ash Wednesday and each Sunday

### MEAL

- Offertory Prayer: see alternate worship text for Lent
- Use the proper preface for Lent
- Use the proper preface for Passion beginning with Passion Sunday
- Eucharistic prayer: in addition to four main options in *LBW,* see "Eucharistic Prayer D: The Season of Lent" in *WOV* Leaders Edition, p. 68
- Invitation to communion: see alternate worship text for Lent

110

- Post-communion prayer: see alternate worship text for Lent

SENDING

- Benediction: see alternate worship text for Lent
- Dismissal: see alternate worship text for Lent

OTHER SEASONAL POSSIBILITIES

- Ash Wednesday liturgy: see *LBW* Ministers Edition, pp. 129–31; congregational leaflets available from Augsburg Fortress (AFP 080660574X)
- Enrollment of Candidates for Baptism (for First Sunday in Lent): see *Welcome to Christ: Lutheran Rites for the Catechumenate*, pp. 18–21

- Midweek Lenten worship: see order for evening prayer services in seasonal rites section
- Blessing of Candidates for Baptism (for third, fourth, and fifth Sundays in Lent): see *Welcome to Christ: Lutheran Rites for the Catechumenate*, pp. 22–34
- Procession with Palms liturgy for Passion Sunday: see *LBW* Ministers Edition, pp. 134–35; congregational leaflets available from Augsburg Fortress (AFP 0806605766)
- Blessing of oil: for synodical gatherings (and other groups of congregations wishing to celebrate this order), see Dedication of Worship Furnishings in *Occasional Services*, pp. 176–77

# Assembly Song *for the* Season

Lent is the "springtime" of the church, our wet

season in which we are surrounded again by the refreshing

waters of baptism. The gospel texts are the classic baptismal

texts used for centuries during Lent. The thirsty people are called to the font and wellspring of life, there to encounter Jesus as the "resurrection and the life" into which we are baptized. Use the season as a time of liturgical renewal. Often the liturgy can become cluttered with layers of local tradition that cloud the important central elements. Uplift the liturgical core of word and meal and strip away peripheral music and actions. The music and liturgy should be simple and concise in form and function.

### GATHERING

Save the festive organ stops, bells, and cymbals for the Easter Vigil. Let the music speak simply and clearly. This can be a time to cleanse our ears in preparation for the sumptuous sonic feast of Easter. Hymn accompaniments should be strong, energizing, and supportive without being overly fancy. Occasionally use the choir to lead the congregation in singing interior hymn stanzas without accompaniment in either unison or four parts. As an alternative to

an instrumental prelude, consider having the congregation sing a few contemplative songs prior to a period of silent prayer. Following silent prayer, lead the confession from the font, omit the entrance hymn, and do a simple entrance procession during the singing of the Kyrie. Use a familiar setting of the Kyrie for the season, or perhaps use a different setting each week, or learn a new setting.

### WORD

Involve the congregation in the proclamation of the word. If you normally speak the psalm, consider using a psalm antiphon, sung first by the cantor then repeated by the congregation. The appointed verses for Lent are familiar texts. Create your own gospel acclamation by using "Gospel Acclamation: Lent" (WOV 611b) as the refrain. The cantor sings the refrain first followed by the congregation. The cantor sings the verse to a psalm tone (such as *LBW* tone 2), and then all repeat the refrain. Another option is to sing one or two stanzas of "Praise to you, O Christ, our Savior" (WOV 614, W&P 118).

111

### MEAL

"Create in me," a portion of the Psalm 51 text from Ash Wednesday, can serve as the offertory. Choose a musical setting of the great thanksgiving to use throughout the Easter cycle (Lent, Three Days, and Easter). Keep the accompaniment simple during Lent. Speak the preface dialogue and proper preface as well as any congregational responses in the eucharistic prayer. The "Lamb of God" is especially appropriate to sing during the Easter cycle. Consider using a more elaborate choral setting to be sung by the choir. A fine setting in Spanish with an English translation is "Cordero de Dios" (LLC 240). If your assembly normally sings hymns during the distribution, try using simple refrains for the Lenten season. Encourage people to memorize these simple refrains and sing them as they process to communion. The choir or a cantor should sing the verses. These types of songs include "Jesus, remember me" (WOV 740), "Now in this banquet" (W&P 104, using the Lent refrain), "Now we remain" (W&P 106), or "Eat this bread" (WOV 709, TFF 125).

### SENDING

We are sent forth from the Sunday celebration of the resurrection to continue on our Lenten journey throughout the week. The sending music should support and encourage the congregation as they strive to carry out the Lenten discipline or continue with baptismal preparations. Seasonal sending songs include "I want Jesus to walk with me" (TFF 66, WOV 660), "You are mine" (W&P 158), "Guide me ever, great Redeemer" (LBW 343), "The Summons" (W&P 137), "He who began a good work in you" (W&P 56), and "Lead me, guide me" (TFF 70). Postludes can be a festive touch to the liturgy but sometimes they are no more than background sound. Intentional silence at the conclusion of the liturgy can be a reminder of the cleansing and renewing purpose of the season.

# Music *for the* Season

### VERSE AND OFFERTORY

Busarow, Donald. *Verses and Offertories, Part III—Ash Wednesday through Maundy Thursday.* SATB, org.    CPH 97-5503.

Cherwien, David. *Verses for the Sundays in Lent.* U/2 pt, org.    MSM 80-300.

Farlee, Robert Buckley. *Verses and Offertories for Lent.* U/SATB.    AFP 0800649494.

*Gospel Acclamations.* Cant, choir, cong, inst.    MAY 0862096324.

Schalk, Carl. "Return to the Lord, Your God." SATB, opt kybd.    MSM 50-3033.

Schiavone, J. *Gospel Acclamation Verses for the Sundays of Lent.*    GIA G-2160.

Schramm, Charles. *Verses for the Lenten Season.* SATB, opt org.    MSM 80-301.

### CHORAL

Bach, J.S. "Bring Low Our Ancient Adam" in *Bach for All Seasons.* SATB, org, opt inst.    AFP 080065854X.

Bach, J.S. "Jesu meine Freude" in *Bach for All Seasons.* SATB, opt kybd.    AFP 080065854X.

Candlyn, T. Frederick H. "Thee We Adore." SATB, org.    CFI CM 492.

Christiansen, Paul. "Wondrous Love." SATB.    AFP 0800652665.

Farrant, Richard. "Lord, for Thy Tender Mercy's Sake" in *The Parish Choir Book.* SATB.    CPH CH1137.

Ferguson, John. "Ah, Holy Jesus." SATB, org, opt cong.    AFP 0800654528.

Friedell, Harold. "Jesus So Lowly." SATB.    HWG 2018.

Goudimel, Claude. "As the Deer, For Water Yearning" in *Chantry Choirbook.* SATB.    AFP 0800657772.

Hampton, Keith. "Give Me Jesus." SATB, S solo.    AFP 0800659554.

Hopson, Hal H. "A Lenten Walk" in *The Augsburg Choirbook.* 2 pt mxd, org, opt timp, opt hb.    AFP 0800656784.

Hopson, Hal H. "A Psalm of Confession." SATB, solo.
AFP 080065952X.

Hopson, Hal H. "O Lord, from the Depths I Cry." SA/TB, org.
AFP 0800659686.

Lindh, Jody W. "If Thou but Suffer God to Guide Thee." 2 pt mxd,
org. CPH 98-2081.

Oldroyd, George. "Prayer to Jesus." SATB, org. OXF A 73.

Pasquet, Jean. "Create in Me a Clean Heart." SAB, kybd.
AFP 600010121X.

Rutter, John. "Thy Perfect Love." SATB, org. OXF 42.392.

Schiavone, John. "Wilt Thou Forgive?" SATB. CPH 98-2119.

Schulz-Widmar, Russell. "Sweet Spirit, Comfort Me." SATB, fl, ob,
bsn; or 2 vln, vc; or kybd. CPH 98-3066.

Slawson, Thomas H.B. "O Lamb of God." SATB, kybd.
AFP 0800659678.

Stanford, C. V. "O for a Closer Walk with God." Collegium Mus.
Pub. SATB, org. COLCD 118.

Terry, Sir R.R. "Richard de Castre's Prayer to Jesus." SATB.
GSCH 8624.

Willcocks, Jonathan. "O Holy Jesus (Prayer of St. Richard of Chi-
chester)." SATB, org. SMP 10/1937S.

## CHILDREN'S CHOIRS

Bedford, Michael. *Seven Songs for the Church Year.* U, opt hb.
CG CGA 693.

Bedford, Michael. *Singing the Seasons.* U, opt hb. CG CGA854.

Farrell, Bernadette. *Share the Light.* 2 pt, kybd, gtr, opt inst.
OCP 11307CC.

Owens, Sam Batt. "Alone You Once Went Forth." 2 pt, org.
MSM-50-3504.

## KEYBOARD/INSTRUMENTAL

*Augsburg Organ Library: Lent.* Org. AFP 0800658973.

Ferguson, John. *Thy Holy Wings.* Org. AFP 0800647955.

Gabrielson, Stephen. *We Are Your Own Forever.* Org.
AFP 0800652517.

Hassell, Michael. *Jazz Lenten Journey.* Pno. AFP 080065949X.

Manz, Paul. *Improvisations for the Lenten Season.* Org. MSM 10-300.

Miller, Aaron David. *Triptych for Lent and Easter.* Org.
AFP 0800659457.

Mozart, W.A. *Adagio in C.* Org/Eng hrn. CPH 97-5429.

Organ, Anne Krentz. *Global Piano Reflections.* Pno, opt inst/perc.

Porter, Emily Maxson. *Hymn Images for Lent and Easter.* Org.
CPH 97-6680.

Speller, Frank. "Herzliebster Jesu" in *Three Preludes Based on Hymn Tunes,
set 2.* Org. CPH 97-5934.

Young, Jeremy. *At the Foot of the Cross.* Pno. AFP 0800655397.

## HANDBELL

Edwards, Dan R. "Meditation." 2-3 oct. L2. CG CGB 220.

Larson, Katherine Jordahl. "A Scottish Melody." 3-5 oct, opt ch, inst.
AFP 0800656318.

McChesney, Kevin. "Land of Rest." 3-5 oct. L2. CG CGB215.

McFadden, Jane. "Two More Swedish Melodies (BLOTT EN DAG)."
3-4 oct, opt ch. AFP 0800657357.

Nelson, Susan T. "Plainchant Meditation and Morning Suite." 3 oct.
AFP 080065546X.

Sanders, Patricia A. "Medley on the Cross." 3-5 oct. L3. AG 1421.

Wagner, H. Dean. "Fantasy on Kingsfold" 3-5 oct. L2+.
AG 2135.

## PRAISE ENSEMBLE

Espinosa, Eddie. "Change My Heart, O God." SATB, kybd.
MAR 301 0813 163.

Larson, Lloyd. "A Lenten Prayer (O Lord Throughout These Forty
Days)." SATB, kybd. LOR 10/1794L.

Larson, Lloyd, arr. "I Want Jesus to Walk with Me." SATB, kybd.
GS A 7172.

Nockels, Nathan and Christy Nockels. "My Heart, Your Home" in
*Extravagant Grace Songbook.* SAT[B], kybd. INT 16737.

Zschech, Darlene/arr. Jay Rouse. "The Potter's Hand" in *Hillsongs
Choral Collection.* SATB, kybd. INT 16996.

113

# Alternate Worship Texts

## CONFESSION AND FORGIVENESS

Let us return to our gracious and merciful God,
confessing our need for healing.

*Silence for reflection and self-examination.*

Tender-hearted God,
through the gift of baptism
you give new birth to your children
by water and the Spirit.
Yet we question your wisdom for us,
thirst for what can never satisfy,
and wander in the ways of death.
Turn us again, O God.
Forgive us our sin,
gather us into your embrace,
and teach us the way that we should go. Amen

Almighty God, just and compassionate,
grant you remission of all your sins
for the sake of Jesus Christ,
true repentance, amendment of life,
and the grace and consolation of the Holy Spirit.
Amen

## GREETING

The gift of peace through our Lord Jesus Christ,
the love of God poured into our hearts,
and the renewing grace of the Spirit of life
be with you all.
And also with you.

## OFFERTORY PRAYER

Holy God,
you provide us with every gift of creation,
and you quench our thirst with living water.
Receive these tokens of your goodness to us.
May our lives be bread for the hungry
and streams in the wilderness,
signs of the abundance of your grace
in Jesus Christ. Amen

## INVITATION TO COMMUNION

God has prepared a table before you.
Goodness and mercy are yours this day.

## POST-COMMUNION PRAYER

We bless you, O God, for the free gift
of righteousness and peace in Jesus Christ,
whose body and blood have nourished us here.
Lead us out from this house of prayer
to the places you will show us,
so that we will be a blessing to others
in the name of Christ, our redeemer.
Amen

## BLESSING

May God restore in you the joy of salvation,
strengthen your love for your neighbor,
and grant you to live in harmony with all creation;
and the blessing of almighty God,
the Father, ✚ the Son, and the Holy Spirit,
be among you and remain with you forever.
Amen

## DISMISSAL

Go in peace. Make known the Savior of the world.
Thanks be to God.

114

# Seasonal Rites

## Midweek Evening Prayer for Lent

*This flexible order of evening prayer may be celebrated as a midweek service during Lent. It is an adaptable form of vespers with readings and music that highlight five of the readings from the Easter Vigil. These stories are among the most prominent of passages that announced hope and salvation to the ancient Hebrew people. For Christians these readings are regarded as "types" of the salvation brought to us through the death and resurrection of Christ. Because of their traditional use in the Easter Vigil, the primary liturgy for baptism, these readings also have a strong baptismal association for Christians.*

*Contemporary dramatizations of these same five readings are available in* Can These Bones Live? Contemporary Dramas for Lent and Easter *by David Kehret (AFP 0806639652).*

### OVERVIEW: MIDWEEK THEMES BASED ON READINGS FROM THE EASTER VIGIL

FIRST WEEK
Genesis 1:1—2:4a
Creation

SECOND WEEK
Genesis 7:1-5, 11-18; 8:6-18; 9:8-13
The Flood

THIRD WEEK
Genesis 22:1-18
The Testing of Abraham

FOURTH WEEK
Exodus 14:10-31; 15:20-21
Israel's Deliverance

FIFTH WEEK
Ezekiel 37:1-14
The Valley of the Dry Bones

### SERVICE OF LIGHT
*A lit vesper candle may be carried in procession during the following versicles and placed in its stand near the altar.*

*These versicles may be sung to the tones given in Evening Prayer, LBW, p. 142.*

Behold, now is the accept- | able time;
**now is the day of sal- | vation.**
Turn us again, O God of | our salvation,
**that the light of your face may shine on | us.**
May your justice shine | like the sun;
**and may the poor be lifted | up.**

### HYMN OF LIGHT
*One of the following hymns may be sung.*
Dearest Jesus, at your word    LBW 248
O Light whose splendor thrills    WOV 728
Christ, mighty Savior    WOV 729
I heard the voice of Jesus say    TFF 262
Joyous light of glory    W&P 79

### THANKSGIVING FOR LIGHT
*This is set to music in LBW, p. 144.*

The Lord be with you.
**And also with you.**
Let us give thanks to the Lord our God.
**It is right to give our thanks and praise.**
Blessed are you, O Lord our God, king of the universe,
who led your people Israel by a pillar of cloud by day
and a pillar of fire by night:
Enlighten our darkness by the light of your Christ;
may his Word be a lamp to our feet and a light to our path;
for you are merciful, and you love your whole creation,
and we, your creatures, glorify you, Father, Son, and Holy Spirit.
**Amen**

115

## PSALMODY

*The first psalm may be Psalm 141, as printed in LBW, pp. 145–46; or another setting of this psalm may be used.*

*An additional psalm or canticle may be used for each of the weeks during Lent (see Psalter for Worship):*

### FIRST WEEK
Psalm 136:1-9, 23-26

### SECOND WEEK
Psalm 46

### THIRD WEEK
Psalm 16

### FOURTH WEEK
Exodus 15:1b-13, 17-18 (Song of Moses and Miriam)

### FIFTH WEEK
Psalm 143

## HYMN

*Possibilities for hymns related to the readings for each of the weeks follow.*

### FIRST WEEK
How marvelous God's greatness   LBW 515
When long before time   WOV 799
God the sculptor of the mountains   TFF 222

### SECOND WEEK
Oh, happy day when we shall stand   LBW 351
Thy holy wings   WOV 741
'Tis the old ship of Zion   TFF 199

### THIRD WEEK
A multitude comes from the east and the west   LBW 313
Day by day   WOV 746
The summons   W&P 137

### FOURTH WEEK
When Israel was in Egypt's land   WOV 670, TFF 87
Glories of your name are spoken   LBW 358
Wade in the water   TFF 114

### FIFTH WEEK
Love divine, all loves excelling   LBW 315
The Word of God is source and seed   WOV 658
You are mine   W&P 158

## OTHER HYMN OPTIONS INCLUDE:
All who believe and are baptized   LBW 194
Lord, thee I love with all my heart   LBW 325
We were baptized in Christ Jesus   WOV 698
O blessed spring   WOV 695
A wonderful Savior is Jesus   TFF 260
Amazing love   W&P 8

## READINGS FOR EACH OF THE WEEKS OF LENT

### FIRST WEEK
Genesis 1:1—2:4a

### SECOND WEEK
Genesis 7:1-5, 11-18; 8:6-18; 9:8-13

### THIRD WEEK
Genesis 22:1-18

### FOURTH WEEK
Exodus 14:10-31; 15:20-21

### FIFTH WEEK
Ezekiel 37:1-14

*A homily or meditation may follow the reading.*

*Silence is kept by all.*

*The silence concludes:*
Long ago, in many and various ways,
God spoke to our ancestors by the prophets;
**but in these last days God has spoken to us by the Son.**

## GOSPEL CANTICLE
My soul now magnifies the Lord   LBW 180
My soul proclaims your greatness   WOV 730
My soul does magnify the Lord   TFF 168
Canticle of the turning   W&P 26

## LITANY

*The music for the litany in LBW, p. 148, may be used with the following.*

In peace, let us pray to the Lord.
**Lord, have mercy.**
For the peace from above, let us pray to the Lord.
**Lord, have mercy.**
For the peace of the whole world, for the well-being of the church of God, and for the unity of all, let us pray to the Lord.
**Lord, have mercy.**
For those who are preparing for the Easter sacraments, let us pray to the Lord.
**Lord, have mercy.**
For the baptized people of God and for their varied ministries, let us pray to the Lord.
**Lord, have mercy.**
For those who are poor, hungry, homeless, or sick, let us pray to the Lord.
**Lord, have mercy.**
Help, save, comfort, and defend us, gracious Lord.

*Silence is kept by all.*
Rejoicing in the fellowship of all the saints, let us commend ourselves, one another, and our whole life to Christ, our Lord.
**To you, O Lord.**

## PRAYER OF THE DAY
*From the previous Sunday if a service is held during the week.*

## THE LORD'S PRAYER

## BLESSING
*For a musical setting, see LBW, p. 152.*

Let us bless the Lord.
**Thanks be to God.**

The almighty and merciful Lord, the Father, the Son, and the Holy Spirit, bless and preserve us.
**Amen**

# Service of the Word for Healing in Lent

*An order for Service of the Word for Healing is presented in the seasonal materials for autumn. It may also be adapted for use during Lent in the following ways:*

## DIALOG
Behold, now is the acceptable time;
**now is the day of salvation.**
Return to the Lord, your God,
**who is gracious and merciful, slow to anger,**
**and abounding in steadfast love.**
God forgives you all your sins
**and heals all your infirmities.**
God redeems your life from the grave
**and crowns you with mercy and lovingkindness.**
God satisfies you with good things,
**and your youth is renewed like an eagle's.**
Bless the Lord, O my soul,
**and all that is within me bless God's holy name.**

FIRST READING: Isaiah 53:3-5
PSALM: Psalm 138
GOSPEL: Matthew 8:1-3, 5-8, 13-17

## THE PRAYERS

## HYMNS
*Either of these hymns may be used when the Service of the Word for Healing occurs during Lent:*
Jesus, refuge of the weary   LBW 93
In the cross of Christ I glory   LBW 104

117

# February 13, 2002

Ash Wednesday

## INTRODUCTION

Christians gather on this day to mark the beginning of Lent's baptismal preparation for Easter. On this day, the people of God receive an ashen cross on the forehead (a gesture rooted in baptism), hear the solemn proclamation to keep a fast in preparation for Easter's feast, and contemplate anew the ongoing meaning of baptismal initiation into the Lord's death and resurrection. While marked with the ashes of human mortality, the church hears God's promise of forgiveness and tastes God's mercy in the bread of life and the cup of salvation. From this solemn liturgy, the church goes forth on its journey to the great baptismal feast of Easter.

## PRAYER OF THE DAY

Almighty and ever-living God, you hate nothing you have made and you forgive the sins of all who are penitent. Create in us new and honest hearts, so that, truly repenting of our sins, we may obtain from you, the God of all mercy, full pardon and forgiveness; through your Son, Jesus Christ our Lord, who lives and reigns with you and the Holy Spirit, one God, now and forever.

## READINGS

### Joel 2:1-2, 12-17

The context of this reading is a liturgy of communal lamentation. The prophet has called the temple-community to mourn a devastating plague of the past and to announce a day of darkness, the day of the Lord. The community is called to repent, to return to God who is gracious and merciful.

*or* Isaiah 58:1-12

### Psalm 51:1-18 (Psalm 51:1-17 [NRSV])

Have mercy on me, O God, according to your lovingkindness. (Ps. 51:1)

### 2 Corinthians 5:20b—6:10

Out of love for humankind, the sinless one experienced sin and suffering so that the redemptive power of God could penetrate the most forbidding and tragic depths of human experience. No aspect of human life is ignored by the presence of God's grace. Because of this, Paul announces that this day is a time to turn toward God's mercy.

### Matthew 6:1-6, 16-21

This passage sets forth a vision of genuine righteousness illustrated by three acts of Jewish devotion: almsgiving, prayer, and fasting. Jesus does not denounce the acts—in his time they were signs of singular devotion to God. Rather, he criticizes those who perform them to gain a sense of self-satisfaction or public approval. Care for the poor, intense prayer, and fasting with a joyous countenance are signs of loving dedication to God.

## COLOR  Black *or* Purple

## THE PRAYERS

As we journey to Easter's fountain of life, let us pray for the world, the church, and for all people according to their needs.

*A BRIEF SILENCE.*

For the church and its bishops, pastors, leaders, and all the baptized, that we may seek reconciliation with you and each other, let us pray to the Lord.

**Lord, have mercy.**

For all those around the world preparing for baptism at Easter, that they may be brought to repentance and new life, let us pray to the Lord.

**Lord, have mercy.**

For those afflicted by poverty, oppression, or discrimination, that we respond with justice and compassion, let us pray to the Lord.

**Lord, have mercy.**

For all who seek healing, comfort, and peace, and for all who suffer in mind or body (especially), that you give them endurance and hope, let us pray to the Lord.

**Lord, have mercy.**

For this congregation, that our Lenten pilgrimage renew our commitment to you, to each other, and to the needs of our community, let us pray to the Lord.

**Lord, have mercy.**

*HERE OTHER INTERCESSIONS MAY BE OFFERED.*

For ourselves, that with all those marked with the holy cross and baptized into Jesus' death we may come into the full glory of his resurrection, let us pray to the Lord.

**Lord, have mercy.**

Hear our prayers, O merciful God, as we eagerly await the day of resurrection, through Jesus Christ our Lord. **Amen**

## IMAGES FOR PREACHING

Jesus warns his disciples in the opening line of today's gospel reading concerning the way they practice their piety. "Piety" is a good, old word, but it conjures up in many minds a narrow set of behaviors having to do with strictly personal acts. The Greek word behind "piety" is better rendered as "righteousness," already mentioned half a dozen times in Matthew's gospel (beginning in 3:15 and continuing in 5:6, 10, and 20).

Humankind has been restored to "righteousness" or right relationship with God by the fresh outburst of grace in the life, death, and resurrection of Jesus. In the gospel for this day, Jesus declares that this "righteousness" just naturally expresses itself in such outward acts as almsgiving, prayer, and fasting.

The beginning of Lent each year brings us face-to-face with these ancient religious practices that seem to belong to another time and place. Have these practices outlived their usefulness? From one angle, these three are oddly relevant to the deepest spiritual needs of our nation at the beginning of the twenty-first century.

Almsgiving has to do with money and budgets and social responsibility. Prayer woos us from our self-absorption and self-congratulation, because through it we exercise our relationship with God and fix our life on its proper center. Fasting is a healthy alternative to ordinary patterns of consumption in a nation that is increasingly overweight, in more ways than one.

This day, together with the whole of Lent, calls us to step back and examine the ways in which the dominant culture of North America lulls our spirits and lures us into an unthinking consumerist lifestyle. Lent bids us to experiment for a brief season with spiritual exercises such as almsgiving, prayer, and fasting. If we covenant together, not only as individuals but also as families and congregations, to withdraw for a short time from ordinary patterns of living and freely adopted such alternative practices, others might not immediately "glorify God." The first reaction might be, "Those people are odd." But we have to ask ourselves, would it be so bad to be at odds with the self-indulgence of our culture?

## WORSHIP MATTERS

Ashes in worship carry dual symbolism: they are a reminder of our mortality and a sign of repentance. Certain scripture texts, such as this one from Genesis 3:19, come to mind: "You are dust, and to dust you shall return." These words are spoken as the sign of the cross is marked with ash on our foreheads. They remind us that we belong to the creation in all its fullness—both living and finite.

We also read in Job 42:6: "I despise myself and repent in dust and ashes." Ashes call us to lifelong repentance and conversion. When we repent, we turn our face to a new voice and begin walking in a new direction. All of these implications are carried in our Ash Wednesday worship, brought to life by way of rich liturgy, honest confession, and strong proclamation.

## LET THE CHILDREN COME

Do not be afraid to mark the foreheads of children, even babies, with ashes. Our finitude may frighten us, but it is a fact. Children are not unaware of death or loss or weakness, nor are their parents blind to the vulnerability of their little ones. Let us not pretend, but let us speak the truth that is more enduring than death: the love of God in Christ crucified and risen.

## HYMNS FOR WORSHIP
### HYMN OF THE DAY
Out of the depths I cry to you    LBW 295

### ALTERNATE HYMN OF THE DAY
O Sun of justice    WOV 659
Softly and tenderly Jesus is calling    WOV 734, TFF 155

### COMMUNION
Come to Calvary's holy mountain    LBW 301
I received the living God    WOV 700
Just as I am, without one plea    LBW 296

### SENDING
Abide with me    LBW 272
Restore in us, O God    WOV 662
Give thanks    TFF 292, W&P 41

### ADDITIONAL HYMNS AND SONGS
Our Father, we have wandered    WOV 733
Create in me a clean heart    W&P 35

119

## MUSIC FOR THE DAY

### PSALMODY

Create in me a clean heart   W&P 35

Create in me a clean heart, O God   WOV 732

Haugen, Marty. "Be Merciful, O Lord."   RS 83.

Hurd, Bob. "Create in Me." Cant, choir, kybd, gtr, sax.
OCP 10251CC.

Joncas, Michael. "Be Merciful, O Lord." SAB/U, gtr, kybd, inst, cong.
GIA G-3433.

Rees, Elizabeth. "O Lord, You Love Sincerity of Heart" in PS 2.

Schwarz, May.   PW A.

Walker, Christopher. "Psalm 51: Give Me a New Heart, O God" in
STP, vol. 3.

### CHORAL

Brahms, Johannes. "O World So Vain" in *Chantry Choirbook.* SATB.
AFP 0800657772.

Brahms, Johannes. "Create in Me a Clean Heart." SATBB.   GSCH
7504.

Chepponis, James J. "Lenten Proclamation." 3 pt equal vcs or mxd,
opt hb.   GIA G-2761.

Clokey, Joseph W. "Treasures in Heaven." SATB, org.
WAR SBCH9310.

Ferguson, John. "Psalm 130." SATB, org.   AFP 0800656075.

Graham, Michael. "Treasure."   SATB, pno, vc/bsn. CPH 98-3541.

Hopson, Hal H. "O Lord, from the Depths I Cry." ST/TB, org.
AFP 088065968-6.

Leaf, Robert. "Out of the Depths I Cry to Thee." SATB, org, opt 2
tpt, 2 tbn.   AFP 0800647505.

Rotermund, Donald. "Have Mercy in Your Goodness, Lord." U/2 pt,
org, opt hb, opt rec.   CPH 98-3037.

Schalk, Carl. "Out of the Depths." SAB, org.   MSM-50-3410.

Schiavone, John. "Be Merciful, O Lord." 2 pt equal/mxd, org/pno, fl,
opt gtr.   GIA G-2845.

Scott, K. Lee. "Out of the Depths I Cry to Thee." 2 pt mxd, kybd.
AFP 0800647327.

White, David Ashley. "Psalm 51." SATB, org.   RME EC-254.

### CHILDREN'S CHOIRS

Marshall, Jane. "Create in Me, O God." U, kybd.   CG CGA750.

Pooler, Marie. "Wondrous Love." U, kybd.   AFP 0800645685.

Reeves, Jeff. "Create in Me a Clean Heart." U/2 pt, pno.
CG CGA879.

### KEYBOARD/INSTRUMENTAL

Bach, J.S. "Aus tiefer Not" in *Organ Works.* Org.   Various ed.

Callahan, Charles. *A Lenten Prelude.* Org/fl.   MSM 20-360.

Drischner, Max. "Aus tiefer Not" in *Augsburg Organ Library: Lent.* Org.
AFP 0800658973.

Organ, Anne Krentz. "Savior, When in Dust to You" in *Christ, Mighty
Savior.* Pno.   AFP 0800656806.

### HANDBELL

Smith, James C. "Welsh Tune (ABERYSTWYTH)." 3-5 oct. L3.
HIN HHB-34.

Ullom-Berns, Susan. "Impressions on an Advent Carol (ABERYST-
WYTH)." 2 oct. L2.   LOR 20/1082L.

Wagner, Douglas E. "What Wondrous Love Is This?" 3-5 oct. L2+.
AG 1312.

### PRAISE ENSEMBLE

Althouse, Jay. "Lord, I Stretch My Hands to You." SATB, kybd.
HOP PP131.

Bannister, Brown. "Create in Me a Clean Heart." SAB, kybd.
WRD 301 0346 166.

Leavitt, John. "Call on Him." SATB with inst, kybd.
HAL 08596405.

# Thursday, February 14

CYRIL, MONK, 869; METHODIUS, BISHOP, 885;
MISSIONARIES TO THE SLAVS

These two brothers from a noble family in Thessalonika
in northeastern Greece were priests and missionaries. After
some early initial missionary work by Cyril among the
Arabs, the brothers retired to a monastery. They were later
sent to work among the Slavs, the missionary work for
which they are most known. Since Slavonic had no written
form at the time, the brothers established a written language with the Greek alphabet as its basis. They translated
the scriptures and the liturgy using this Cyrillic alphabet.
The Czechs, Serbs, Croats, Slovaks, and Bulgars regard the
brothers as the founders of Slavic literature. The brothers'
work in preaching and worshiping in the language of the
people is honored by Christians in both East and West.

# February 17, 2002

First Sunday in Lent

## INTRODUCTION

In the early church, those to be baptized at the Easter Vigil were given intense preparation in the preceding weeks. This catechetical process is the origin and purpose of the Lenten season: a time for the church and its baptismal candidates to ponder the meaning of baptism into the death and resurrection of the Lord. The forty days—a scriptural image of testing and renewal—invite us to return to holy baptism.

The weeks of Lent invite us to speak the truth about the keeping of our baptismal promises. The weeks of Lent invite us to hear and taste God's abundant forgiveness in word and sacrament.

## PRAYER OF THE DAY

Lord God, you led your ancient people through the wilderness and brought them to the promised land. Guide now the people of your Church, that, following our Savior, we may walk through the wilderness of this world toward the glory of the world to come; through your Son, Jesus Christ our Lord, who lives and reigns with you and the Holy Spirit, one God, now and forever.

*or*

Lord God, our strength, the battle of good and evil rages within and around us, and our ancient foe tempts us with his deceits and empty promises. Keep us steadfast in your Word and, when we fall, raise us again and restore us through your Son, Jesus Christ our Lord, who lives and reigns with you and the Holy Spirit, one God, now and forever.

## READINGS

### Genesis 2:15-17; 3:1-7

Human beings were formed with great care, to be in relationship with the Creator, creation, and one another. This passage recounts the first in a series of stories that depict the nature of human sin—wanting to be like God.

### Psalm 32

Mercy embraces those who trust in the Lord. (Ps. 32:11)

### Romans 5:12-19

Paul describes the effect of Jesus' obedience as analogous to that of Adam's disobedience. Through Christ, God has reversed the consequences of sin and death to offer the free gift of eternal life.

### Matthew 4:1-11

Jesus experiences anew the temptations that Israel faced in the wilderness. As the Son of God, he endures the testing of the evil one.

## COLOR  Purple

## THE PRAYERS

As we journey to Easter's fountain of life, let us pray for the world, the church, and for all people according to their needs.

*A BRIEF SILENCE.*

For the church, that with Christ we may resist evil and be obedient to your word, let us pray to the Lord.

**Lord, have mercy.**

For all who will be baptized or received into the church at Easter, that you may be their strength in all temptation, let us pray to the Lord.

**Lord, have mercy.**

For all nations torn by war or internal strife, that they may know your peace and reconciliation, let us pray to the Lord.

**Lord, have mercy.**

For all those suffering from hunger in our community and throughout the world, that they may eat and be satisfied, let us pray to the Lord.

**Lord, have mercy.**

For all walking in the wilderness of loneliness, despair, or sickness (especially), that they may be fed and strengthened with the bread of life, let us pray to the Lord.

**Lord, have mercy.**

*HERE OTHER INTERCESSIONS MAY BE OFFERED.*

We give you thanks for all the faithful ones who have traveled through the wilderness and now dwell in your paradise. Bring us with them to the eternal Easter feast of joy. Let us pray to the Lord.

**Lord, have mercy.**

Hear our prayers, O merciful God, as we eagerly await the day of resurrection, through Jesus Christ our Lord.

**Amen**

## IMAGES FOR PREACHING

Fyodor Dostoyevsky once said, "If every copy of the Bible were destroyed, and we had only the single page which tells the story of Jesus' temptation in the wilderness, it would be enough." Enough for what? Enough to save us, to heal us, to make us whole. How can that be?

We do not need books and sermons to teach us of temptation or evil. Evil we can see and hear and feel. Even the most casual review of the twentieth century must cause us to stumble at the violent outbursts of evil in war and mayhem on an unprecedented scale. The awful power of evil threatens to overwhelm our confidence in the goodness of God.

The question arises, Can anything hold evil in check? Government exists to do just that. Every government struggles with the evil that breaks out between nations and within communities. The larger question is this: Can evil be defeated? Can it be trampled under foot?"

Dostoyevsky was celebrating the fact that this single page of scripture announces that evil has met its master in Jesus of Nazareth. We have in this one narrative the record of how Jesus refused to serve himself or the devil and relied totally on God. The path that Jesus chose led him through acts of healing and compassion to the cross. And then God raised him up, a sign of the ultimate victory of compassion and divine love over every evil.

Tradition has it that Jesus' temptation took place in the wilderness on the cliffs above Jericho. An old monastery marks the spot. It was once nearly inaccessible, but a Swiss company built a cable car that now whisks people from ground zero at Jericho to the top of the cliff in a matter of seconds. The ascent is swift and painless. So tourists follow in the footsteps of Jesus, but they travel to Jericho in air-conditioned buses and then ascend to the place of victory by mechanical means. The fast track to bliss! The way of Jesus was longer, harder, and more effective, and every Lenten pilgrim knows it.

## WORSHIP MATTERS

Lent is a time of baptismal preparation. The catechumens—those preparing for baptism at the great Vigil of Easter—look forward to the time when they will be joined to Jesus Christ in the sacrament of baptism. This baptismal preparation comes by way of regular worship, prayer, scripture study, and blessings bestowed by the worshiping community.

For the baptized—those already part of the body of Christ—Lent can be a time of baptismal renewal. Here baptismal symbols are important. The sign of the cross is a reminder of the cross of Christ marked on our brow in baptism. The paschal candle reminds us of the presence of the risen Christ with us. And the white funeral pall covering a casket evokes memory of the white garment—Christ's own righteousness—covering us in baptism.

## LET THE CHILDREN COME

To encourage children to participate in the offering and to understand how our gifts become signs of God's gracious love for others, place a large basket in the chancel and invite children to bring nonperishable food items to worship each week during Lent. While the offering plates are being passed, let the children come and place their gifts in the basket. Keep a stash of canned goods for visiting children, so they can participate as well.

At the end of the season, older children can sort, box, and deliver these gifts to a local food bank, hospitality house, or homeless shelter. A church school class could spend a Saturday afternoon volunteering in such a place. In small ways like these, children learn what it means to dedicate their lives to the care and redemption of all that God has made.

## HYMNS FOR WORSHIP
### GATHERING

Guide me ever, great Redeemer    LBW 343
Our Father, we have wandered    WOV 733
Lead me, guide me    TFF 70, W&P 84

### HYMN OF THE DAY

I want Jesus to walk with me    WOV 660, TFF 66

### ALTERNATE HYMN OF THE DAY

A mighty fortress is our God    LBW 228, 229
If Jesus Christ be for me    HFW

### COMMUNION

O Jesus, I have promised    LBW 503
Eat this bread    WOV 709, TFF 125
Yield not to temptation    TFF 195

### SENDING

Oh, that the Lord would guide my ways    LBW 480
The glory of these forty days    WOV 657

122

## ADDITIONAL HYMNS AND SONGS

If God himself be for me   LBW 454

As the sun with longer journey   WOV 655

Forty days and forty nights   H82 150

Jesus tempted in the desert   RS 548

Weary of all trumpeting   WOV 785

You are my hiding place   W&P 160

## MUSIC FOR THE DAY

### SERVICE MUSIC

Use the litany (*LBW*, p. 168) in place of the confession, gathering hymn, and Kyrie; its themes echo the readings for this day and call to mind the church's "desert journey" during this season. Establish a rhythmic cadence with a slight overlapping of the bids and responses; with choral leadership and a strong cantor, this can be sung a cappella.

### PSALMODY

Cooney, Rory. "Psalm 32" in PCY, vol. 4.

Howard, Julie. *Sing for Joy: Psalm Settings for God's Children*.   LTP.

Schwarz, May.   PW A.

Stewart, Roy James.   PCY, vol. 5.

### CHORAL

Below, Robert. "The Glory of These Forty Days." SATB, org. AFP 600010152X.

Bender, Jan. "Begone, Satan." SA/TB, org.   CPH 98-1848.

Busarow, Donald. "Provençal Carol." SATB, kybd.   CPH 98-3221.

Ferguson, John. "Jesus Walked This Lonesome Valley." SATB, solo or cong, fl.   GIA G-3279.

Haan, Raymond. "I Want Jesus to Walk with Me." SATB, pno. MSM 50-9002.

Handel, G.F. "Since by Man Came Death" in *Messiah*. SATB, org.

Hassler, Hans L. "A Mighty Fortress Is Our God" in *Chantry Choirbook*. SATB.   AFP 0800657772.

Mengel, Dana. "Lord, Who throughout These Forty Days." SATB, kybd.   CPH 98-3343.

Ord, Boris. "Adam Lay Ybounden" in *100 Carols for Choirs*. SATB. OXF.

Powell, Robert. "Adam Lay Ybounden." SATB, org. AFP 0800659104.

Trinkley, Bruce. "I Want Jesus to Walk with Me." SATB, pno. AFP 800657071.

### CHILDREN'S CHOIRS

Beech, Jay. "Out in the Wilderness."   W&P 115

Eilers, Joyce, arr. "Them Bones Gonna Rise Again." 2 pt, kybd. HAL 40225058.

## KEYBOARD/INSTRUMENTAL

Bach, J.S. "Christus, der uns Selig Macht" in *Orgelbüchlein*. Org.   PET 10635.

Billingham, Richard. "Sojourner" in *Seven Reflections on African American Hymns*. Org.   AFP 0800656229.

Cherwein, David. "Seelenbräutigam" in *Interpretations Book III*. Org. AMSI OR-6.

Glick, Sara. "Sojourner" in *Piano Arrangements for Worship: Lent, Easter, Spring*. Pno, opt inst.   AFP 0800658809.

Hassell, Michael. "Sojourner" in *Traveling Tunes*. Pno, inst. AFP 0800656199.

Hobby, Robert. "Sojourner" in *Three Lenten Hymn Settings for Organ, Set 3*. Org.   MSM 10-322.

## HANDBELL

McChesney, Kevin. "Beach Spring." 2-3 oct. L2. AFP 080065885X.

Nelson, Susan T. "Lenten Prayer." 3 oct. L2.   CPH 97-6616.

Page, Anna Laura. "A Mighty Fortress Is Our God." 3-5 oct, opt ch. L2-3.   AFP 0800658841.

Wagner, Douglas E. "On Eagle's Wings." 3-5 oct. L3.   AG 1715.

## PRAISE ENSEMBLE

Evans, Timothy. "Accept the Gift." SATB, kybd.   GS A7165.

Green, Melody and Benjamin Harlan. "There Is a Redeemer." SATB, kybd, fl.   HAL 08742224.

Mauldin, Russell, arr. "God So Loved the World." SATB, kybd. BNT 25986-0754-7.

123

# Monday, February 18

## MARTIN LUTHER, RENEWER OF THE CHURCH, 1546

For those in the habit of remembering the work of Martin Luther on Reformation Day, this commemoration may seem out of place. But it is a custom to remember saints on the day of their death, their "heavenly birthday." On this day Luther died at the age of 62. For a time, he was an Augustinian monk, but it is his work as a biblical scholar, translator of the Bible, reformer of the liturgy, theologian, educator, and father of German vernacular literature, which holds him in our remembrance. In Luther's own judgment, the greatest of all of his works was his catechism written to instruct people in the basics of faith. And it was his baptism that sustained him in his trials as a reformer.

If a congregation has catechumens who will be baptized at the Easter Vigil, they might receive the catechism during the Enrollment of Candidates on the first Sunday in Lent. If there are no catechumens, a congregation might study the catechism during Lent to renew its own baptismal faith.

## Wednesday, February 20

### RASMUS JENSEN, THE FIRST LUTHERAN PASTOR IN NORTH AMERICA, 1620

Jensen came to North America in 1619 with an expedition sent by King Christian IV of Denmark and Norway. The expedition took possession of the Hudson Bay area, naming it Nova Dania. Within months of their arrival, most of the members of the expedition died, including Jensen. After this expedition, much Danish missionary activity was concentrated in India and the Virgin Islands.

Today would be an appropriate time to give thanks for the church in Canada, which flourished even after its early struggles. It would also be an opportunity to pray for missionaries who face difficulty in their tasks.

## Saturday, February 23

### POLYCARP, BISHOP OF SMYRNA, MARTYR, 156

Polycarp was bishop of Smyrna and a link between the apostolic age and the church at the end of the second century. He is said to have been known by John, the author of Revelation. In turn he was known by the Iranaeus, bishop of Lyon in France, and Ignatius of Antioch. At the age of eighty-six he was martyred for his faith. When urged to save his life and renounce his faith, Polycarp replied, "Eighty-six years I have served him, and he never did me any wrong. How can I blaspheme my king who saved me?" The magistrate who made the offer was reluctant to kill a gentle old man, but he had no choice. Polycarp was burned at the stake, his death a testimony to the cost of renouncing temptation.

## Saturday, February 23

### BARTHOLOMAEUS ZIEGENBALG, MISSIONARY TO INDIA, 1719

Bartholomaeus Ziegenbalg was a missionary to the Tamils of Tranquebar on the southeast coast of India. The first convert to Christianity was baptized about ten months after Ziegenbalg began preaching. His missionary work was opposed both by the local Hindus and also by Danish authorities in that same area. Ziegenbalg was imprisoned for his work on a charge of converting the natives. The Copenhagen Mission Society that opposed him wanted an indigenous church that did not reflect European patterns or show concern for matters other than the gospel. Ziegenbalg, in contrast, argued that concern for the welfare of others is a matter of the gospel. Today, the Tamil Evangelical Lutheran Church carries on his work.

Ziegenbalg's missionary work can lead us into Lent with the reminder that we are called to live in service to others.

# February 24, 2002

Second Sunday in Lent

## INTRODUCTION

In today's gospel, Jesus directs our attention to the font of baptism. By water and the word, the Holy Spirit gives us new birth. Freely, out of love, we are made sons and daughters of God, brothers and sisters of the Lord Jesus, messengers of the Holy Spirit. From the waters of baptism we rise as a people blessed by God. We are sent forth into the world, not to condemn but to offer mercy.

## PRAYER OF THE DAY

Eternal God, it is your glory always to have mercy. Bring back all who have erred and strayed from your ways; lead them again to embrace in faith the truth of your Word and to hold it fast; through Jesus Christ your Son our Lord, who lives and reigns with you and the Holy Spirit, one God, now and forever.

## READINGS

Genesis 12:1-4a

Genesis 1–11, often called the "primeval history," provides the background for today's reading. The repeated pattern of human rebellion and God's response ends with the Tower of Babel incident (11:1-9). In today's reading, God begins the relationship with humanity anew, starting with the person of Abram.

Psalm 121

It is the Lord who watches over you. (Ps. 121:5)

Romans 4:1-5, 13-17

Paul has taught that Jews and Gentiles alike are made right with God through faith, and he insists that this has been true since Abraham, the great ancestor of the Jewish people. For this reason, people of "many nations" may share in God's promises to Abraham through faith.

John 3:1-17

The ministry of Jesus drew ambiguous responses from the religious leaders of his day. Some were offended by his challenge to their traditions and rejected him. Others, like Nicodemus, recognized the work of God in him, but needed his teaching to understand how to respond to him and God.

COLOR Purple

## THE PRAYERS

As we journey to Easter's fountain of life, let us pray for the world, the church, and for all people according to their needs.

*A BRIEF SILENCE.*

That all nations and families of the earth be blessed through the church's witness of your love, let us pray to the Lord.

**Lord, have mercy.**

That those who will be born of water and the Spirit at Easter may grow in grace and faith, let us pray to the Lord.

**Lord, have mercy.**

That those who are homeless and all refugees of war may find safety and relief from their suffering, let us pray to the Lord.

**Lord, have mercy.**

That all who suffer in mind, body, or spirit (especially) may be strengthened and encouraged in the knowledge of God's love for them, let us pray to the Lord.

**Lord, have mercy.**

*HERE OTHER INTERCESSIONS MAY BE OFFERED.*

That we may follow all the saints who have trusted in Christ, who was lifted on the cross for our salvation, let us pray to the Lord.

**Lord, have mercy.**

Hear our prayers, O merciful God, as we eagerly await the day of resurrection, through Jesus Christ our Lord.

**Amen**

## IMAGES FOR PREACHING

Nicodemus was an educated man, a teacher of Israel, and he was anxious to talk with Jesus, whom he recognized as a fellow teacher. Nicodemus arrived for what appears to be an evening colloquium, a sharing of views, a discussion of the issues. But he grossly underestimated Jesus. After all, what is it that God offers in Jesus? A little more information—or rebirth? More data—or life itself? And how shall we describe this Jesus? Is he, as Nicodemus assumed, a teacher like Nicodemus and

125

other teachers, only a bit more clever and somewhat more charismatic—or is he the Son of the living God?

The opening exchange mystified Nicodemus. He did not grasp Jesus' talk about rebirth and the blowing of the wind. Then Jesus referred to the topics discussed in that entire first part of their conversation as "earthly things." If Nicodemus failed to catch Jesus' meaning up to that point, how could he possibly understand the infinitely more difficult matter that Jesus calls the "heavenly things"?

How strange that Jesus should use the phrase "earthly things" to describe rebirth and the Spirit's working. How can they be easy or elementary? It is simply a fact that many religions and philosophies speak confidently about being reborn and about essential matters that are unseen and nonmaterial. These topics are commonly addressed. Nicodemus could no doubt converse comfortably about such matters with gurus and sages of many stripes.

But Jesus moves the conversation beyond those common topics to what he calls "heavenly things." What is he talking about? What is the hard and heavenly core of the teaching? Jesus speaks of a serpent being lifted up, and he speaks of his own lifting up. Here is the heart of the hard and heavenly teaching: God gives life to the world in the one who is lifted up on the cross. God gives victory in the one who seemed defeated at the cross. God gives rebirth and pours out the Spirit through this one whose life is poured out on the cross.

## WORSHIP MATTERS

The Lenten gospel texts in year A carry a clear baptismal emphasis. These Lenten texts are particularly appropriate for study and reflection whenever there are catechumens in the congregation—adults preparing for baptism at the Vigil of Easter. The gospel story of Nicodemus's nocturnal visit to Jesus read on the second Sunday in Lent is a primary text—along with others such as Romans 6:3-4—that shapes our baptismal theology. The gospel texts for the third, fourth, and fifth Sundays in Lent—the woman at the well, the man born blind, and the raising of Lazarus—give glimpses into the life-changing transformation for which those about to be baptized are preparing.

Through preaching, teaching, and liturgical celebration, catechumens—and all the baptized as well—are given living water, granted new eyes to see, and raised to new life in Christ.

## LET THE CHILDREN COME

On this and the next three Sundays we read stories from John's gospel. See in these stories, as the early church did, images of our coming to faith and to new life in Christ. Hear water flowing through, spilling over, and leaping in these words. If yours is a church that keeps the font full of water throughout this season of baptismal preparation and renewal, fill a ewer with water and have a child who is tall enough and attentive enough pour water into the font during the gospel reading, letting it spill and splash when water is mentioned: "No one can enter the kingdom of God without being born of water and the Spirit." Do you hear the birth waters breaking? In baptism we are born anew.

## HYMNS FOR WORSHIP
### GATHERING

O Savior, precious Savior    LBW 514

Blessed assurance    WOV 699, TFF 118

Step by step    W&P 132

### HYMN OF THE DAY

All who believe and are baptized    LBW 194

### ALTERNATE HYMN OF THE DAY

God loved the world    LBW 292, HFW (Duke Street)

How to reach the masses    TFF 227

### COMMUNION

Amazing grace, how sweet the sound    LBW 448

I want Jesus to walk with me    WOV 660

Waterlife    W&P 145

### SENDING

How firm a foundation    LBW 507

We all are one in mission    WOV 755

I shall not be moved    TFF 147

### ADDITIONAL HYMNS AND SONGS

Lord, thee I love with all my heart    LBW 325

O Sun of justice    WOV 659

Wind of the Spirit    W&P 157

Sometimes I feel like a motherless child    LEV 169

For God so loved the world    ASG 10

## MUSIC FOR THE DAY

### PSALMODY

Beall, Mary Kay. *Sing Out! A Children's Psalter.*   WLP 7191.

Callahan, Charles. "Psalm 121." SSA, kybd.   MSM 50-9600.

Cooney, Rory. "Our Help." 2 pt, kybd, gtr, fl.   OCP 5296CC.

Cotter, Jeanne.   PCY, vol. 3.

Joncas, Michael. "Guiding Me." SATB, cong, gtr, kybd, opt 2 C inst.
GIA G-3438.

Ogden, David. "I Lift Up My Eyes" in PS3.

Schwarz, May.   PW A.

Unto the hills   LBW 445

### CHORAL

Berger, Jean. "I to the Hills Lift Up Mine Eyes." SATB.
AFP 0800645448.

Distler, Hugo. "For God So Loved the World" in *Chantry Choirbook.*
SAB.   AFP 0800657772.

Mendelssohn, Felix. "Lift Thine Eyes" in *Elijah.* SSA.   Various ed.

Pote, Allen. "I Lift Up Mine Eyes." SATB, fl, ob, kybd
HOP A 595.

Schütz, Heinrich. "God So Loved the World" in *Chantry Choirbook.*
SATTB.   AFP 0800657772.

Stainer, John. "God So Loved the World" from *The Crucifixion.* SATB.
GSCH, octavo 3798.

Young, Gordon. "I Will Lift Up Mine Eyes." SATB, kybd.
FLA A-5618.

### CHILDREN'S CHOIRS

Bouman, Paul. "I Will Lift My Eyes to the Hills." 2 pt, org.
B&H OCTB6550.

Lovelace, Austin. "Psalm 121." U, kybd, fl.   CG CGA-361.

### KEYBOARD/INSTRUMENTAL

Albrecht, Mark. "My God and I" in *Timeless Hymns of Faith.* Pno.
AFP 0800657276.

Behnke, John A. "Es ist das Heil" in *Variations for Seven Familiar Hymns.*
Org.   AFP 0800655605.

Bingham, Seth. "Toplady" in *Twelve Hymn Preludes, set 1.* Org.
HWG GB 151.

Callahan, Charles. *Prelude in C.* Org.   MSM 10-913.

Kolander, Keith. "Es ist das Heil" in *All Things Are Thine.* Org.
AFP 0800658000.

Webster, Richard. "Bred dina vida vingar" in *Augsburg Organ Library:*
*Lent.* Org.   AFP 0800658973.

Wold, Wayne L. "Beach Spring" in *Augsburg Organ Library: Lent.* Org.
AFP 0800658973.

### HANDBELL

Afdahl, Lee J. "For as the Rain Comes Down." 3-5 oct, opt ch, fc,
perc.   AFP 0800658159.

Sherman, Arnold B. "Ballade." 3-5 oct. L3+.   AG 2073.

Waldrop, Tammy. "How Firm a Foundation." 3-4 oct. L1+.
RR BL5005.

### PRAISE ENSEMBLE

Brown, Scott Wesley and Jeff Nelson. "Grace Alone."
WRD 0 80689 81027 5 (SATB, kybd); WRD 0 80689 66524
(acc cass); 0 80689 81047 3 (orch).

Bullock, Geoff and Gail Dunshea. "You Are My God." SATB, kybd.
MAR 301 0891 164.

Hayes, Mark, arr. "The Gospel of Grace (Amazing Grace and I'm
New Born Again)."   ALF 17899 (SAB); 17898 (SATB);
17900 (perf/acc cass); 17901 (inst).

Morgan, Reuben/arr. J. Daniel Smith. "Touching Heaven, Changing
Earth" in *Hillsongs Choral Collection.* SATB, kybd.   INT 16996.

127

# Monday, February 25

## ST. MATTHIAS, APOSTLE (TRANSFERRED)

After Christ's ascension, the apostles met in Jerusalem to choose a replacement for Judas. Matthias was chosen over Joseph Justus by the casting of lots. Little is known about Matthias, and little is reported about him in the account of his election in Acts 1:15-26. Matthias had traveled among the disciples from the time of Jesus' baptism until his ascension. His task, after he was enrolled among the eleven remaining disciples, was to bear witness to the resurrection.

During the weeks of Lent, congregations with catechumens will have a chance to learn stories of how people have been called, some in unusual ways like Matthias.

# Monday, February 25

## ELIZABETH FEDDE, DEACONESS, 1921

Fedde was born in Norway and trained as a deaconess. In 1882, at the age of thirty-two, she was asked to come to New York to minister to the poor and to Norwegian seamen. Her influence was wide ranging, and she established the Deaconess House in Brooklyn and the

Deaconess House and Hospital of the Lutheran Free Church in Minneapolis. She returned home to Norway in 1895 and died there.

Fedde was an example of selfless service to those in need. How does your congregation reach out to those who are sick, in need, or forgotten? Perhaps ways to reach out that have been overlooked can easily be incorporated in your congregation's ministry.

## Friday, March 1

GEORGE HERBERT, PRIEST, 1633

As a student at Trinity College, Cambridge, George Herbert excelled in languages and music. He went to college with the intention of becoming a priest, but his scholarship attracted the attention of King James I. Herbert served in parliament for two years. After the death of King James and under the influence of a friend, Herbert's interest in ordained ministry was renewed. He was ordained a priest in 1630 and served the little parish of St. Andrew Bremerton until his death. He was noted for unfailing care for his parishioners, bringing the sacraments to them when they were ill, and providing food and clothing for those in need.

Herbert was also a poet and hymnwriter. One of his hymns, "Come, my way, my truth, my life" (LBW 513),

invites an intimate encounter with Christ through a feast that "mends in length" and could be included as a communion hymn on a Sunday close to March 1.

## Saturday, March 2

JOHN WESLEY, 1791; CHARLES WESLEY, 1788; RENEWERS OF THE CHURCH

The Wesleys were leaders of a revival in the Church of England. Their spiritual discipline of frequent communion, fasting, and advocacy for the poor earned them the name "Methodists." The Wesleys were missionaries in the American colony of Georgia for a time but returned to England discouraged. Following a conversion experience while reading Luther's preface to the Epistle to the Romans, John was perhaps the greatest force in eighteenth-century revival. Their desire was that the Methodist Societies would be a movement for renewal in the Church of England, but after their deaths the societies developed a separate status.

Charles wrote more than six hundred hymns, twelve of which are in *Lutheran Book of Worship* and one of which is in *With One Voice*. Three of Charles's hymns are especially appropriate for Lent: "Christ, whose glory fills the skies" (LBW 265), "Love divine, all loves excelling" (LBW 315), and "Forth in thy name, O Lord, I go" (LBW 505).

# March 3, 2002

Third Sunday in Lent

## INTRODUCTION

In the early church, immediate preparation for baptism at Easter was heightened by the proclamation of gospel stories chosen especially for the last Sundays in Lent. We hear these readings today and in the Sundays to come.

Today's gospel is the story of the Samaritan woman asking Jesus for water. It is an image of our great thirst for God's mercy, grace, and forgiveness. It is an image of God's grace freely given to us in scripture, baptism, the holy supper, and the faith of our brothers and sisters. The church invites all who seek God to come to these good things where we encounter the one who gives us life-giving water.

## PRAYER OF THE DAY

Eternal Lord, your kingdom has broken into our troubled world through the life, death, and resurrection of your Son. Help us to hear your Word and obey it, so that we become instruments of your redeeming love; through your Son, Jesus Christ our Lord, who lives and reigns with you and the Holy Spirit, one God, now and forever.

*or (year A)*

Almighty God, your Son once welcomed an outcast woman because of her faith. Give us faith like hers, that we also may trust only in your love for us and may accept one another as we have been accepted by you; through your Son, Jesus Christ our Lord, who lives and reigns with you and the Holy Spirit, one God, now and forever.

## READINGS

Exodus 17:1-7

Today's reading is one of several that tell of experiences during the wilderness wandering. In this case, the people complain because they have a legitimate need and God responds by providing for them. Later in their wanderings, when the people complain because of their wants, God responds with anger.

Psalm 95

Let us shout for joy to the rock of our salvation. (Ps. 95:1)

Romans 5:1-11

Through Jesus' death on the cross, sinners have been put right with God through faith. But being made right with God produces results—ultimately, sure hope for the future produced by God's Spirit.

John 4:5-42

In the culture of Jesus' time, Jews tended to avoid dealings with Samaritans, and men did not converse with women in public. When Jesus crosses these boundaries to speak with a Samaritan woman, he makes himself known as the agent of God who knows all.

## COLOR  Purple

## THE PRAYERS

129

As we journey to Easter's fountain of life, let us pray for the world, the church, and for all people according to their needs.

*A BRIEF SILENCE.*

Strengthen the church to share the water of life with all who thirst for the gospel. Let us pray to the Lord.

**Lord, have mercy.**

Grant peace and reconciliation to all nations and peoples who are estranged from one another. Let us pray to the Lord.

**Lord, have mercy.**

Refresh with your healing waters all those who are discouraged, fearful, or ill (especially). Let us pray to the Lord.

**Lord, have mercy.**

Pour out your grace on all those to be baptized at Easter, and all who will renew their baptismal vows. Let us pray to the Lord.

**Lord, have mercy.**

Satisfy the thirst of all who long for a deeper sense of your presence in their lives. Let us pray to the Lord.

**Lord, have mercy.**

*HERE OTHER INTERCESSIONS MAY BE OFFERED.*

Bring us with all the saints to the river of life in our eternal home. Let us pray to the Lord.

**Lord, have mercy.**

Hear our prayers, O merciful God, as we eagerly await the day of resurrection, through Jesus Christ our Lord. **Amen**

## IMAGES FOR PREACHING

One of the prayers for this day speaks of the Samaritan woman as "an outcast woman." That is a time-honored view, but it is probably wrong. To identify her as an "easy" or promiscuous woman has no doubt served the needs of many moralizing preachers, but it constitutes a rush to judgment.

But what about all those husbands she has had, and then there is the man, not her husband, with whom she is currently living. What about them?

It helps to remember that this talk of "five husbands" is not the first time that the fourth gospel has used the imagery of marriage. Jesus performed his first sign in John's gospel for the benefit of a wedding party at Cana (John 2). When the followers of John the Baptist complained to their leader that Jesus was baptizing more folks than he was, John called Jesus the "bridegroom" and described himself in more humble terms as "best man" at the bridegroom's wedding (John 3:29).

Now Jesus, passing from Judea to Galilee, arrives in the land of the Samaritans and sits at a well. Soon enough a woman approaches and gives him water. We should be hearing echoes here of the stories of Isaac and Rebekah (Gen. 24), Jacob and Rachel (Gen. 29), and Moses and Zipporah (Exod. 2). Those are all stories of a stranger from another country meeting a woman at a well. And each of those encounters continues with a report to the family about the stranger, followed by the offer of hospitality. Each narrative also concludes with a wedding.

John depicts Jesus as the heavenly bridegroom traveling to alien territory. He arrives at the well and woos this woman—woos her in a spiritual sense, woos her and her fellow Samaritans to the true, spiritual worship of God. And God in Christ continues to woo, seeking to win our allegiance and to bless us with the water of life.

## WORSHIP MATTERS

Silence is a rare thing in our worship. In the press of time and with increasing pressure to add more to the service—announcements, temple talks, children's sermons—time for silence seems to be a rare commodity.

Yet silence is also a rich treasure. It allows time for individual prayer and reflection. It heightens both the spoken word and the sung response. Through silence the Holy Spirit can speak to us in a new way.

When is silence appropriate in worship? Certainly following a scripture reading or the proclamation of the word—after the readings and the sermon. It is also appropriate during the confession—allowing ample time for individual confession of sin. Silence can also mark the transitions in the basic order of our worship—between gathering, word, meal, and sending. Silence in worship can be a source of both variety and renewal.

## LET THE CHILDREN COME

Again this Sunday let a child pour water into the font during the gospel reading. The pouring can begin quietly when Jesus asks the Samaritan woman for a drink of water. Then it can become louder during their conversation, becoming loudest when Jesus says, "The water I will give will become in them a spring of water gushing up to eternal life." Do you see the leaping, living, spring of Christ's gift of life? In baptism the gift of God's wisdom flows through us, and the grace of God's Holy Spirit springs up within us like a fountain.

## HYMNS FOR WORSHIP

GATHERING

Come, thou Fount of every blessing    LBW 499

We bow down    W&P 149

There's a sweet, sweet Spirit in this place    TFF 102

The Lord is my song    WOV 772

HYMN OF THE DAY

O Jesus, joy of loving hearts    LBW 356

ALTERNATE HYMN OF THE DAY

I heard the voice of Jesus say    LBW 497

All the way my Savior leads me    TFF 255

COMMUNION

Draw near and take the body of the Lord    LBW 226

Rock of Ages, cleft for me    LBW 327

I received the living God    WOV 700

Cup we bless    BL

## SENDING

Guide me ever, great Redeemer   LBW 343

I've just come from the fountain   WOV 696

## ADDITIONAL HYMNS AND SONGS

Jesus, Christ, my sure defense   LBW 340

Dona nobis pacem   WOV 774

All was not well   DH 58

Let justice roll like a river   W&P 85

## MUSIC FOR THE DAY
### PSALMODY

Dobry, Wallace. "A Trio of Psalms."   MSM 80-706.

Geary, Patrick. "Listen to the Voice of the Lord" in PS 2.

Haugen, Marty, and David Haas. "If Today You Hear His Voice" in PCY.

How, Martin. "O Come, Let Us Sing Unto the Lord." 2 pt, org. MSM 50-73012.

Hurd, Bob. "If Today." Cong, SATB, pno, gtr, fl.   OCP 10249CC.

Schwarz, May.   PW A.

### CHORAL

Callahan, Charles. "O Dearest Lord." SAB, org.   CPH 98-2912.

Christiansen, Paul. "Wondrous Love." SATB.   AFP 0800652665.

Farlee, Robert Buckley. "O Blessed Spring." SATB, org, ob (vln or vc), opt cong.   AFP 0800654242.

Handel, G.F. "Surely He Hath Borne Our Griefs" in Messiah. SATB. Various ed.

Hobby, Robert. "I've Just Come from the Fountain." SATB. AFP 0800659198.

Mendelssohn, Felix. "O Come, Every One that Thirsteth" in Elijah. SATB, org.   GSCH ed 34.

Pooler, Marie. "Wondrous Love." SAB, org/pno. AFP 0800645685.

Rachmaninoff, Sergei. "O Come Let Us Worship" from All Night Vigil in Songs of the Church. SSAATTBB.   HWG GB 640.

Rorem, Ned. "Sing, My Soul, His Wondrous Love." SATB. PET 6386.

### CHILDREN'S CHOIRS

Haugen, Marty. "Come, O Come, Let Us Sing." U, kybd, ww. GIA G-4275.

Hopson, Hal H. "A Lenten Walk." 2 pt, org, opt solo, timp, hb. AFP 080065448X.

## KEYBOARD/INSTRUMENTAL

Albrecht, Timothy. "Walton" in Grace Notes VIII. Org. AFP 0800658264.

Hailstork, Adolphus. "We Shall Overcome" in Four Spirituals. Org. MSM 10-896.

Harmon, Christina. "When I Survey the Wondrous Cross" in Joyful, Joyful: Preludes and Postludes for Organ. Org.   VIV 325.

Porter, Rachel Trelstad. "Give Me Jesus" and "Rockingham" in Praise, My Soul. Pno.   AFP 0800659511.

Sadowski, Kevin. "Walton" in Six Hymn Preludes. Org. CPH 97-6044.

## HANDBELL

Dobrinski, Cynthia. "Come, Thou Fount of Every Blessing." 3-5 oct. L3.   AG 1832.

Sherman, Arnold B. "What Wondrous Love Is This" 2-3 oct or 4-5 oct. L2+.   RR HB0020B.

## PRAISE ENSEMBLE

DeShetler, Jacque. "We Have Come" in Hosanna Music Songbook 13. SAT[B], kybd.   INT 13576.

Foley, John. "Come to the Water." SATB, kybd, gtr, solo inst. OCP 9489.

Founds, Rick/arr. Gary Rhodes. "Lord, I Lift Your Name On High." WRD 301 0805 160 (SATB, kybd); 301 7278 084 (choraltrax); 301 0510 25X (orch).

131

# Thursday, March 7

### PERPETUA AND FELICITY AND COMPANIONS, MARTYRS AT CARTHAGE, 202

In the year 202 the emperor Septimius Severus forbade conversions to Christianity. Perpetua, a noblewoman, Felicity, a slave, and other companions were all catechumens at Carthage in North Africa. They were imprisoned and sentenced to death. Perpetua's father, who was not a Christian, visited her in prison and begged her to lay aside her Christian convictions in order to spare her life and spare the family from scorn. Perpetua responded and told her father, "We know that we are not placed in our own power but in that of God."

Congregations that do not have catechumens can pray for those who do as they approach their own death and rebirth in the waters of baptism at the Easter Vigil and are clothed with the new life of Christ.

## Thursday, March 7
### THOMAS AQUINAS, TEACHER, 1274

Thomas Aquinas was a brilliant and creative theologian of the thirteenth century. He was first and foremost a student of the Bible and profoundly concerned with the theological formation of the church's ordained ministers. As a member of the Order of Preachers (Dominicans), he worked to correlate scripture with the philosophy of Aristotle, which was having a renaissance in Aquinas's day. Some students of Aristotle's philosophy found in it an alternative to Christianity. But Aquinas immersed himself in the thought of Aristotle and worked to explain Christian beliefs in the philosophical culture of the day. The contemporary worship cultural studies done by the Lutheran World Federation resonate with Aquinas's method.

Aquinas was also a hymnwriter. His hymn "Thee we adore, O hidden Savior" (LBW 199) is traditionally sung on Maundy Thursday and might also be sung this Sunday as a communion hymn.

# March 10, 2002

Fourth Sunday in Lent

132

## INTRODUCTION

The gospel for this Sunday is the story of a blind man healed by Christ. It is a profound image of our human condition: we seek after greater clarity and light. It is also a baptismal image of washing and receiving sight, of Christ's desire to enlighten us with the truth of who we are: God's beloved daughters and sons.

## PRAYER OF THE DAY

God of all mercy, by your power to heal and to forgive, graciously cleanse us from all sin and make us strong; through your Son, Jesus Christ our Lord, who lives and reigns with you and the Holy Spirit, one God, now and forever.

## READINGS
### 1 Samuel 16:1-13

In chapter 15, Saul's failings have finally caused the Lord to regret having made Saul king over Israel. Now, the Lord directs the prophet Samuel to see to the replacement of Saul, who was made king by popular acclamation of the people. The new king, this time chosen by God, is a simple shepherd boy from Judah.

### Psalm 23

You have anointed my head with oil. (Ps. 23:5)

### Ephesians 5:8-14

The letter to the Ephesians teaches that through baptism Christians live in God's light. Therefore, we ought to live by doing those things that reflect the light of Christ.

### John 9:1-41

Some people in Jesus' day regarded infirmities as signs of divine punishment, and a few even thought Jesus was wrong to help afflicted people. When Jesus is criticized for healing a man born blind, the question arises as to whether such attitudes are not themselves a form of blindness, thereby showing that the heart is far from God.

## COLOR Purple

## THE PRAYERS

As we journey to Easter's fountain of life, let us pray for the world, the church, and for all people according to their needs.

*A BRIEF SILENCE.*

For God's holy people, that the light of Christ shine in their words and deeds, let us pray to the Lord.

**Lord, have mercy.**

For those who govern and lead, that they be anointed with your Spirit of justice and compassion, let us pray to the Lord.

**Lord, have mercy.**

For those preparing for baptism, that they be enlightened with your grace and mercy, let us pray to the Lord.

**Lord, have mercy.**

For all who live with poverty, discrimination, anxiety, or illness (especially), that you guide and comfort them, let us pray to the Lord.

**Lord, have mercy.**

For ourselves, that you open our eyes to your presence in our lives, and to the needs of all of who suffer, let us pray to the Lord.

**Lord, have mercy.**

HERE OTHER INTERCESSIONS MAY BE OFFERED.

For all the saints who have lived as children of light, we give you thanks. Bring us out from the shadows to the unending light of Easter. Let us pray to the Lord.

**Lord, have mercy.**

Hear our prayers, O merciful God, as we eagerly await the day of resurrection, through Jesus Christ our Lord.

**Amen**

## IMAGES FOR PREACHING

From start to finish, John 9 is a treatise on sin. Various forms of the word occur nine times in this one chapter. What is sin? Nowhere in the fourth gospel does Jesus exhibit any interest in the ordinary sins that bedevil society. He offers no convenient classification of sins according to their severity, categories like venial versus mortal, misdemeanors versus felonies. He never comments on the seven deadly sins derived from Isaiah 11. He does not reinterpret sin as an immature stage on the road of universal progress or speak of sin as an inappropriate action based on unresolved childhood conflicts.

Jesus is not pictured here as a judge of human failings who assigns harsher or more lenient penalties depending on the seriousness of the crime. He nowhere speaks of suspended sentences, time off for good behavior, or credit for days already spent behind bars. All of that is the language of human courts and human judges, but it is not the language of Jesus.

So who is Jesus, and what is sin? In the opening scenes of the gospel, John the Baptist called Jesus "the Lamb of God who takes away the sin of the world" (John 1:29). Jesus is no commentator or lawyer. He has arrived on the scene as sin's nemesis and destroyer.

But once again, what is sin? John may have been very much concerned about the incidence in his society of theft, adultery, assault, perjury, kidnapping, and murder. But in his gospel he gives his entire attention to the sin that lurks in the hidden depths beneath all of sin's manifestations. In John's gospel, "sin" is unbelief or bad faith. It is a faulty orientation of one's life and being.

John presents Jesus as the one who cracks through our doubt, our wavering, our anxiety, our hardness of head and heart, our bad believing, or our misplaced trust. John's gospel shows Jesus leading the blind man from darkness to light, to a fresh orientation of his whole being, so that his life rests henceforth on new and reliable ground.

## WORSHIP MATTERS

Liturgical hospitality is both a gift and an art. Yes, worship leaders must be sufficiently prepared, so they do not trip over words or stumble over actions. And they must be gracious and welcoming. But liturgical hospitality is more than that; it is more than the sum of its parts.

Hospitality has as much to do with what is not done as what is done. A hospitable worship leader allows worshipers to relax and be calm by not hurrying or rushing the liturgy. Hospitality depends on leaders using gestures and postures that are not obtrusive to worship or offensive to worshipers. By waiting patiently when it is helpful, by allowing calm and graciousness to prevail, liturgical hospitality can be an art that is both practiced and demonstrated.

## LET THE CHILDREN COME

By this week the children, and others, will be watching, waiting, listening for the sound of water splashing during the reading of the gospel. "Go wash in the pool of Siloam," Jesus says to the man born blind. "Go wash in the waters of the Sent One," we hear. Water again washes our eyes, and we see in Jesus the One sent from God, our Savior and our Lord. In baptism the eyes of our hearts are opened to the wonder of God's gift to us and to the whole world in Christ Jesus.

## HYMNS FOR WORSHIP

GATHERING

Give to our God immortal praise   LBW 520
Be thou my vision   WOV 776

HYMN OF THE DAY

Word of God, come down on earth   WOV 716

ALTERNATE HYMN OF THE DAY

God, whose almighty word   LBW 400
Awake, O sleeper!   DH 63

COMMUNION

What wondrous love is this   LBW 385
There is a balm in Gilead   WOV 737

SENDING

Jesus, the very thought of you    LBW 316
Forth in thy name, O Lord, I go    LBW 505
Send me, Jesus    WOV 773, TFF 244/TFF 245

ADDITIONAL HYMNS AND SONGS

Healer of our every ill    WOV 738
What a friend we have in Jesus    LBW 439
That priceless grace    TFF 68

## MUSIC FOR THE DAY

### PSALMODY

Behnke, John. "The Lord's My Shepherd." Cong, choir, kybd.
    CPH 98-3400.

Burkhardt, Michael. "Psalm 23." SATB, opt cong, C inst, org.
    MSM 50-9051.

Cherwien, David. "Psalm 23: The Lord Is My Shepherd." U, cong,
    org.    MSM 80-840.

Glynn, John. "My Shepherd Is the Lord" in PS 2.

Haugen, Marty. "Shepherd Me, O God." cong, kybd, C inst, opt
    glock/str.    GIA G-2950. SATB,

Ollis, Peter. "The Lord Is My Shepherd" in PS 2.

Smith, Timothy R.    STP, vol. 4.

The King of love my shepherd is    LBW 456

The Lord's my shepherd    LBW 451

My good shepherd is the Lord    ASG 23

### CHORAL

Bertalot, John. "Amazing Grace." SATB, org.    AFP 0800649141
    and 0800656784.

Hassler/Handel. "Our Father We Have Wandered". SATB, 2 fl, kybd.
    AFP 6000001398.

Haydn, Franz Joseph. "Lo, My Shepherd's Hand Divine." SATB, org.
    ECS 1019.

Hurd, David. "Psalm 23." SATB, kybd, opt cong.    AFP 0800650603.

Macfarlane, Will C. "Open Our Eyes." SATB, opt org.
    GSCH HL50297400.

Manz, Paul. "I Want to Walk as a Child of the Light." SATB, org, opt
    cong.    MSM-60-9019.

Manz, Paul. "On My Heart Imprint Thine Image." SATB.
    MSM-50-3037.

Moore, Undine Smith. "I Believe This Is Jesus" in *The Augsburg Choir-
    book*. SATB.    AFP 0800656784.

Pavlechko, Thomas. "Within a Womb of Darkness" in *The Collected
    Hymns of Joy Patterson*. U, kybd.    HOP 1628.

Rutter, John. "The Lord Is My Shepherd" in *Requiem*. SATB, ob, org,
    opt orch.    HIN MH-164.

Schütz, Heinrich. "O Lord, I Trust Your Shepherd Care" in *Chantry
    Choirbook*. SATB.    AFP 0800657772.

### CHILDREN'S CHOIRS

Lowenberg, Kenneth. "Blessed Are the Poor in Spirit." U/2 pt, kybd.
    SEL 410-557.

Smith, Gregg. "The Lord Is My Shepherd." 2 pt, kybd.
    GSCH 12325.

### KEYBOARD/INSTRUMENTAL

Bach, J.S. "Liebster Jesu, wir sind hier" in *Orgelbüchlein*. Org.
    CPH 97-5774.

Carlson, J. Bert. "Candler" in *A New Look at the Old*. Org.
    AFP 0800658760.

Cherwein, David. "There Is a Balm in Gilead" in *Amazing Grace*. Pno.
    AFP 0800659031.

Oliver, Curt. "Liebster Jesu, wir sind hier" in *Built on a Rock*. Kybd.
    AFP 080065496X.

Organ, Anne Krentz. "Christ, the Life of All the Living" in *Christ,
    Mighty Savior*. Pno.    AFP 0800656806.

Wolff, S. Drummond. "Liebster Jesu, wir sind hier" in *Hymn Descants*,
    Set III. Org, inst.    CPH 97-6197.

### HANDBELL

Polley, David J. "Two Lenten Hymns for Handbells." 3 oct. L3.
    MSM 30-300.

Rogers, Sharon Elery. "How Great Thou Art." 3-5 oct. L2.
    AFP 0800659937.

Sherman, Arnold B. "Prayer." 3-5 oct. L3.    LOR 20/1147L.

Young, Philip. "There Is a Balm in Gilead." 3-4 oct. L2.
    AFP 0800653572.

### PRAISE ENSEMBLE

Hallquist, Gary. "People of Light."    WRD 0 80689 32627 1
    (SATB, kybd); 0 80689 63024 8 (choraltrax);
    0 80689 32447 5 (orch).

McDonald, Mary. "Holy, True and Faithful God." SATB, solo, kybd.
    LOR 10/1456M.

Morgan, Reuben. "My Heart Will Trust" in *Shout to the Lord 2000 Song-
    book*. SAT[B], kybd.    INT 14247.

Schrader, Jack, arr. "Amazing Grace."    HOP GC 1006 (SATB (div),
    kybd); 1006C (reh/perf cass).

134

## Tuesday, March 12

### GREGORY THE GREAT, BISHOP OF ROME, 604

Gregory was born into a politically influential family. At one time he held political office, and at another time he lived as a monk, all before he was elected to the papacy. Gregory's work was extensive. He influenced public worship through the establishment of a lectionary and prayers to correlate with the readings. He established a school to train church musicians, and Gregorian chant is named in his honor. He wrote a treatise underscoring what is required of a parish pastor serving a congregation. He sent missionaries to preach to the Anglo-Saxons who had invaded England. And at one time he organized distribution of grain during a shortage of food in Rome.

Gregory's life serves as an example of the link between liturgy and social justice. His Lenten hymn, "O Christ, our king, creator, Lord" (LBW 101), sings of God's grace flowing out from the cross to all creation.

# March 17, 2002

## Fifth Sunday in Lent

### INTRODUCTION

Today's gospel is the story of Jesus raising Lazarus from the dead. With Martha and Mary we stand at the graves of our beloved dead and hear Jesus say, "I am the resurrection and the life." His words give hope to all who dwell in the shadows of death. But also they are words spoken next to the font of baptism, where we die to death and rise to life in Christ.

At the font we sing with St. Patrick, "I bind unto myself today…[Christ's] cross of death for my salvation, his bursting from the spiced tomb" (LBW 188).

### PRAYER OF THE DAY

Almighty God, our redeemer, in our weakness we have failed to be your messengers of forgiveness and hope in the world. Renew us by your Holy Spirit, that we may follow your commands and proclaim your reign of love; through your Son, Jesus Christ our Lord, who lives and reigns with you and the Holy Spirit, one God, now and forever.

### READINGS

Ezekiel 37:1-14

Ezekiel's earlier vision of the glory of the Lord departing from the temple (10:18ff.) symbolizes Israel's defeat by Babylon and subsequent exile. Now, his vision of the valley of dry bones is a promise that Israel as a nation, though dead in exile, will live again in their land through God's life-giving Spirit.

Psalm 130

With the Lord there is mercy and plenteous redemption. (Ps. 130:6-7)

Romans 8:6-11

Paul contrasts two ways of living: The unspiritual life may seek to please God but cannot do so, for it is marked by self-reliance. The spiritual life begins with our justification by God and continues in the power of the Spirit who raised Christ from the dead.

John 11:1-45

The raising of Lazarus is presented as the last and greatest sign in John's gospel. It reveals Jesus as the giver of life. But as John 11:45-53 makes clear, this sign leads to the plan to execute Jesus.

### COLOR  Purple

### THE PRAYERS

As we journey to Easter's fountain of life, let us pray for the world, the church, and for all people according to their needs.

*A BRIEF SILENCE.*

For the church, that inspired by the missionary zeal of St. Patrick, it may witness boldly to the world, let us pray to the Lord.

135

**Lord, have mercy.**

For all those around the world preparing for baptismal death and resurrection at Easter, let us pray to the Lord.

**Lord, have mercy.**

For the leaders of nations, that they may seek the life and dignity of all people, let us pray to the Lord.

**Lord, have mercy.**

For those who weep over the loss of loved ones, and all whose lives are marked by despair, addiction, abuse, or illness (especially), that they may be filled with hope, let us pray to the Lord.

**Lord, have mercy.**

For ourselves, that our Lenten pilgrimage would renew our faith in the promise of resurrection and new life, let us pray to the Lord.

**Lord, have mercy.**

HERE OTHER INTERCESSIONS MAY BE OFFERED.

For all the saints who have died in the blessed hope of sharing in Christ's resurrection, we give thanks. Keep us steadfast in faith until you bring us from death to the eternal life of Easter. Let us pray to the Lord.

**Lord, have mercy.**

Hear our prayers, O merciful God, as we eagerly await the day of resurrection, through Jesus Christ our Lord.

**Amen**

### IMAGES FOR PREACHING

So what became of this Lazarus once he emerged alive from his four days asleep in the tomb? Nikos Kazantzakis, in his *Last Temptation of Christ*, describes the resurrected Lazarus as hovering in a half-dead, half-living state. The sun hurt his eyes, and his skin had a decidedly green cast to it. He mostly crouched in the darkest corner of his house in Bethany and showed few signs of life. Once he made the mistake of venturing out when Barabbas was skulking in the neighborhood, looking for Lazarus, whom he regarded as a more or less living reminder of the power by which Jesus attracted people to himself and diverted them from following Barabbas. In a fit of fury Barabbas seized Lazarus by the arm and tugged on that strangely sponge-like appendage until he wrenched it off his body. Aghast at what he had done, Barabbas threw that arm into the underbrush and fled the scene.

A different story is told in old traditions of the Greek Orthodox Church. They speak of how Lazarus

and his sisters Mary and Martha were set adrift in a leaky boat by enemies of the young Christian movement. Their boat was swept along by friendly winds, however, and they were at length deposited safely onto the shores of the island of Cyprus. There Lazarus enjoyed a long and productive second life as a bishop on the eastern end of the island. Taxi drivers in Larnaca proudly tell travelers, "Don't forget to visit the Church of St. Lazarus!"

These stories raise the question, How lively (or lifeless) are Christians after their rebirth in the waters of baptism? The basic mystery in the Lazarus story, however, remains the baffling but beautiful message that raising Lazarus from death cost Jesus his own life (John 11:45-53). Life given up for life. John calls us to ponder the mystery that the gift of life to all of us Lazaruses costs God dearly. It is God's "glory" (John 11:4) to be such a giver.

### WORSHIP MATTERS

How does one prepare to lead worship? For a pastor on Sunday morning—after the sermon is written and the liturgy is in order—this may be the last question to be asked. After all, worshipers arrive with a flood of prayer requests and last-minute announcements to be remembered. Other worship leaders await instructions. Still, this question is not unimportant: How does one prepare for worship amid a barrage of requests and information?

Perhaps in the moments while vesting and before worship, our preparation may consist of only a quiet prayer spoken in silence. But other actions can help: breathe deeply and exhale as you vest; relax your neck and rotate your shoulders as you pray. Prepare to lead the gathered assembly by stopping—if only momentarily—to calmly give thanks for being alive and for the privilege of leading the people of God in worship.

### LET THE CHILDREN COME

"Wait," you say, "there is no water in the story of the raising of Lazarus." Look again. Listen more closely. Jesus weeps. The salty water of his grief and suffering fills the font today. But we find more water. The opening of the tomb is the breaking open of the womb-waters, and the sound of his name is reviving water to Lazarus. Life, a fountain of fresh water, leaps up within him. In baptism we do not only wash in the water of the Sent One. We drown and die in those waters and are raised

136

with Christ to new life. Let the water flow today, and let it carry the children all the way through the Three Days to Easter's resurrection!

## HYMNS FOR WORSHIP
### GATHERING

Christ, whose glory fills the skies    LBW 265

Awake, O sleeper    WOV 745

Spirit of the living God    TFF 101

### HYMN OF THE DAY

I am the Bread of life    WOV 702

### ALTERNATE HYMN OF THE DAY

Breathe on me, breath of God    LBW 488

I bind unto myself today    LBW 188

### COMMUNION

You are the way    LBW 464

You satisfy the hungry heart    WOV 711

Taste and see    BL

### SENDING

Let us ever walk with Jesus    LBW 487

What a fellowship, what a joy divine    WOV 780

Abide with me    LBW 272

### ADDITIONAL HYMNS AND SONGS

Come, my way, my truth, my life    LBW 513

I know of a sleep in Jesus' name    LBW 342

Martha sent unto the Savior    WAO 44

Only by grace    W&P 112

Weary of all trumpeting    WOV 785

When Lazarus lay within the tomb    NSR 37

## MUSIC FOR THE DAY
### PSALMODY

Chepponis, James. "Out of the Depths." GIA G-2308.

Foley, John. PCY, vol. 7.

Haugen, Marty. "With the Lord There Is Mercy" in RS.

Out of the depths I cry to you    LBW 295

Sadowski, Kevin. "Psalm 130." 2 pt mxd, cong, org.    CPH 98-3058.

Schwarz, May. PW A.

Smith, Alan. "From the Depths I Call To You" in PS 2.

### CHORAL

Burarow, Donald. "Not Unto Us, O Lord." SATB, org, opt cong. AFP 0800659651.

Carter, John. "I Am the Resurrection." SATB.    PRE 312-41655.

Dressler, Gallus. "I Am the Resurrection" in *Chantry Choirbook*. SATB. AFP 0800657772.

Ferguson, John. "Psalm 130." SATB, org.    AFP 0800656075.

Hildebrand, Kevin. "I Am the Resurrection." SATB. MSM-50-4032.

Leaf, Robert. "Out of the Depths I Cry to Thee." SATB, org, opt 2 tpt, 2 tbn.    AFP 0800647505.

Rutter, John. "Agnus Dei" in *Requiem*. SATB, org, opt orch. HIN MH-164.

Rutter, John. "Out of the Deep" in *Requiem*. SATB, org, vc, opt orch. HIN MH-164.

Schalk, Carl. "Out of the Depths." SAB, org.    MSM-50-3410.

Toolan, S. Suzanne. "I Am the Bread of Life." SATB, kybd. GIA GI693.

### CHILDREN'S CHOIRS

Althouse, Jay. "More Like You, Lord." 2 pt, kybd.    ALF 4213.

Hopson, Hal H. "Dry Bones." U, kybd, perc.    KIR 15/1137.

### KEYBOARD/INSTRUMENTAL

Barber, Samuel. *Wondrous Love*. Org.    Schirmer 44477.

Bender, Jan. "Variations on a Theme by Hugo Distler." Org. AFP 0800673697.

Bernthal. John. "I Am the Bread of Life" in *Lift High the Cross*. Org, opt tpt.    AFP 0800657314.

Callahan, Charles. "The Divine Sacrifice" in *A Lenten Suite*. Org. MSM 10-312.

Hassell, Michael. *Jazz Plain and Simple*. Pno.    AFP 0800657268.

### HANDBELL

Behnke, John A. "O Dearest Jesus." 2-3 oct. L2.    CPH 97-6820.

Sherman, Arnold B. "Ah, Holy Jesus." 3-5 oct. L3.    AG 1612.

### PRAISE ENSEMBLE

Courtney, Craig. "Be Not Afraid." SATB, kybd.    BEC BP 1388.

Fisher, Lucy. "Breathe on Me" in *Shout to the Lord 2000 Songbook*. SAT[B], kybd.    INT 14247.

Harris, Don. "Only God for Me" in *Only God for Me Songbook*. SAT[B], kybd.    INT 15297.

Harris, Don. "What You Are" in *Only God for Me Songbook*. SAT[B], kybd.    INT 15297.

Hayes, Mark. "Dry Bones."    ALF 17792 (SATB, kybd); 17794 (inst).

137

## Sunday, March 17

PATRICK, BISHOP, MISSIONARY TO IRELAND, 461

At sixteen, Patrick was kidnapped by Irish pirates and sold into slavery in Ireland. He himself admitted that up to this point he cared little for God. He escaped after six years, returned to his family in southwest Britain, and began to prepare for ordained ministry. He later returned to Ireland, this time to serve as a bishop and missionary. He made his base in the north of Ireland and from there made many missionary journeys with much success. In his autobiography he denounced the slave trade, perhaps from his own experience as a slave.

Patrick's famous baptismal hymn to the Trinity, "I bind unto myself today" (LBW 188), can be used as a meditation on Lent's call to return to our baptism.

## Tuesday, March 19

JOSEPH, GUARDIAN OF OUR LORD

The gospels are silent about much of Joseph's life. We know that he was a carpenter or builder by trade. The gospel of Luke shows him acting in accordance with both civil and religious law by returning to Bethlehem for the census and by presenting the child Jesus in the temple on the fortieth day after his birth. The Gospel of Matthew tells of Joseph's trust in God, who led him through visionary dreams. Because Joseph is not mentioned after the story of a young Jesus teaching in the temple, it is assumed that he died before Jesus reached adulthood.

Congregations might consider a Sicilian tradition to commemorate Joseph that combines the three Lenten disciplines of fasting, almsgiving, and prayer. The poor are invited to a festive buffet called "St. Joseph's Table." Lenten prayers and songs interrupt the course of the meal. What other ways can a congregation's almsgiving and charity be increased during Lent?

## Friday, March 22

JONATHAN EDWARDS, TEACHER,
MISSIONARY TO THE AMERICAN INDIANS, 1758

Edwards was a minister in Connecticut and has been described as the greatest of the New England Puritan preachers. One of Edwards's most notable sermons has found its way into contemporary anthologies of literature. In this sermon, "Sinners in the Hands of an Angry God," he spoke at length about hell. Throughout the rest of his works and his preaching, however, he had more to say about God's love than God's wrath. His personal experience of conversion came when he felt overwhelmed with a sense of God's majesty and grandeur rather than a fear of hell. Edwards served a Puritan congregation. He believed that only those who had been fully converted ought to receive communion; his congregation thought otherwise. Edwards left that congregation and carried out mission work among the Housatonic Indians of Massachusetts. He became president of the College of New Jersey, later to be known as Princeton.

# March 24, 2002

Sunday of the Passion
Palm Sunday

## INTRODUCTION

On this day Christians throughout the world begin the great and holy week that culminates in the central celebration of our faith: the Lord's passage from death to new life celebrated in the Three Days. Today's reading of Christ's passion sets forth the central act of God's love for humankind. In the reception of the Lord's body and blood, the church receives this life-giving love. In prayer, hymns, and readings, we hear the great paradox of our faith: Christ is proclaimed the mighty one who reigns from the tree of life.

## READINGS FOR PROCESSION WITH PALMS

Matthew 21:1-11

Psalm 118:1-2, 19-29

Blessed is he who comes in the name of the Lord. (Ps. 118:26)

## PRAYER OF THE DAY

Almighty God, you sent your Son, our Savior Jesus Christ, to take our flesh upon him and to suffer death on the cross. Grant that we may share in his obedience to your will and in the glorious victory of his resurrection; through your Son, Jesus Christ our Lord, who lives and reigns with you and the Holy Spirit, one God, now and forever.

## READINGS FOR LITURGY OF THE PASSION

Isaiah 50:4-9a

The image of the servant of the Lord is one of the notable motifs in Isaiah 40–55. Today's reading is a self-description of the mission of the servant. This motif became even more important in the early church for understanding the suffering and death of Jesus.

Psalm 31:9-16

Into your hands, O Lord, I commend my spirit. (Ps. 31:5)

Philippians 2:5-11

To illustrate the great self-giving of Christ's passion—the motive for Christian love—Paul quotes an early Christian hymn.

Matthew 26:14—27:66

The story of Jesus' crucifixion in Matthew's gospel emphasizes his rejection by the political and religious insti-

tutions of the day. But the events surrounding his death show that he overcame the powers of death. Even the soldiers who crucify him recognize him as "the Son of God."

*or* Matthew 27:11-54

COLOR Scarlet *or* Purple

## THE PRAYERS

As we journey to Easter's fountain of life, let us pray for the world, the church, and for all people according to their needs.

*A BRIEF SILENCE.*

For the church, that its life and mission may be renewed in the celebration of Jesus' death and resurrection, let us pray to the Lord.

**Lord, have mercy.**

For all preparing for baptism at Easter, that they may follow Christ in the journey from death to life, let us pray to the Lord.

**Lord, have mercy.**

For the leaders of nations, that they may strive to serve their people in humility and without self-interest, let us pray to the Lord.

**Lord, have mercy.**

For those who are sick or dying (especially), that in their suffering they may know that God is with them, let us pray to the Lord.

**Lord, have mercy.**

For our community of faith, that following the pattern of Jesus we may empty ourselves for the sake of those who are poor, vulnerable, or in need, let us pray to the Lord.

**Lord, have mercy.**

*HERE OTHER INTERCESSIONS MAY BE OFFERED.*

We give thanks for all the saints who have walked the way of the cross. Bring us with them to the endless joy and victory of Easter. Let us pray to the Lord.

**Lord, have mercy.**

Hear our prayers, O merciful God, as we eagerly await the day of resurrection, through Jesus Christ our Lord.

**Amen**

139

## IMAGES FOR PREACHING

"Blood is thicker than water," and we hear about both blood and water (but mostly about blood) in Matthew's passion narrative. One dictionary defines blood as "the red oxygen-bearing liquid circulating in the bodies of animals." That is fine for starters, but blood is more than that. Neolithic people smeared red ochre on skeletons as a prayer for the return of life to dry bones, and in earliest times blood was manipulated at countless altars to heal the breech between humans and their God. Scripture says life is in the blood (Gen. 9:4; Lev. 17:11). Goethe got it exactly right: "Blood is a very special juice."

Pilate was neither the first nor the last to plunge bloody hands into water in an effort to make them clean. He took a defiant tone, declaring, "I am innocent of this man's blood." His audience responded, "His blood be on us!" (Matt. 27:24-25).

Matthew wants us to ponder "this man's blood," and he actually wants Jesus' blood to be not only *on* us but also *in* us, because it is *for* us. At the last supper (26:26-29), Jesus took bread and wine and gave them to the disciples, urging them to eat and drink not just these good fruits of the earth, that is, the good yield from the sowing of grains of wheat and tending of vines of grape. He declared these to be his body and his blood, his self, his life force, given and poured out like food for us.

Judas, seeing that he had "betrayed innocent blood," returned the thirty pieces of silver. The priests shrunk back, calling those terrible coins "blood money." With them they purchased a field to bury strangers and foreigners. So they called that place "Field of Blood." Matthew wants us to see how the blood of Jesus benefited not only the disciples in the upper room but also those strangers and foreigners. And the blood of Jesus still benefits strangers and sinners and all manner of folk, including ourselves.

## WORSHIP MATTERS

Making the sign of the cross is both a reminder of and a living witness to the cross of Christ signed on our brow at baptism. In worship, making the sign of the cross is appropriate at many points—for example, whenever the name of the Trinity is invoked or proclaimed as part of the liturgy.

One such moment is during communion preparation. Consider inviting worshipers to dip their fingers in the waters of the baptismal font and trace a small cross

on their forehead as they come to communion. When the font is placed conveniently, making the sign of the cross can be a natural and unobtrusive action. As worship leaders, we can ease people's fears by emphasizing that this is both a voluntary act and a faith discipline that has been practiced throughout the history of Christ's church.

## LET THE CHILDREN COME

Children love a parade, and this day the whole assembly participates. The procession with palms or other branches, whether done outside of the building, throughout the building, or inside the nave, allows worshipers to walk and sing and wave their branches. Choose a hymn, such as "All glory, laud, and honor" (LBW 108), with a refrain that is easily memorized, or, if outside, an ostinato hosanna that can be sung accompanied by hand-carried instruments. Then people need not carry a book and even those who do not read can join in the singing.

The reading of the passion narrative, using a variety of voices with readers stationed around the nave, will engage the attention of children. Let them look around as the story unfolds. Sitting still is not the highest good. Consider breaking up the narrative with a simple sung refrain the children could easily learn.

## HYMNS FOR WORSHIP

### GATHERING

All glory, laud, and honor   LBW 108
O Lord, how shall I meet you   LBW 23
Lift up your heads, O gates   WOV 631
Ride on, King Jesus   TFF 182

### HYMN OF THE DAY

There in God's garden   WOV 668

### ALTERNATE HYMN OF THE DAY

O sacred head, now wounded   LBW 116
Were you there   TFF 81

### COMMUNION

Beneath the cross of Jesus   LBW 107
Ah, holy Jesus   LBW 123

### SENDING

Go to dark Gethsemane   LBW 108
Stay here   WOV 667

140

ADDITIONAL HYMNS AND SONGS

A Lamb goes uncomplaining forth   LBW 105

God of love, have mercy   DH 10

Jerusalén, ciudad de Dios/Jerusalem, the city of
God   LLC 335

Mantos y palmas/Filled with excitement   LLC 333

My song is love unknown   LBW 94, WOV 661

Of the glorious body telling   LBW 120

Strange King   DH 61

## MUSIC FOR THE DAY

### PROCESSION WITH PALMS

Shaw, Robert. "Ride On, King Jesus." SATB.   LAW 51106.

Vaughan Williams, R. "At the Name of Jesus." SATB, org.
OXF 40.100.

### SERVICE MUSIC

On the Sunday of the Passion, one of the traditional ways in which
music has played a significant role in the observance of the day is in
the chanting of the Passion narrative. Two simple settings, sung to the
classic chant formulas, are available, one in the NRSV translation, the
other in the NAB translation:

Kern, Jan. "Chants of the Passion." 3 solo vcs (NAB).
GIA G-1795.

Plater, Ormonde. "The Passion Gospels." 3 solo vcs (NRSV).
Church Hymnal Corporation 164-8.

A further expanded form of the Matthew Passion for singing is:

Bertalot, John. "Passion of Our Lord According to St. Matthew."
SATB, 6 solo vcs, org, cong (in Passiontide hymns) (NRSV).
AFP 0800651391.

### PSALMODY

Cooney, Rory. "I Place My Life." SATB, cant, cong, gtr, kybd,
str qrt, fl.   GIA G-3613.

Farlee, Robert Buckley.   PW A.

Haas, David. "I Put My Life in Your Hands." Cant, cong, SATB, gtr,
opt C inst, vc/bsn.   GIA G-3949.

Haugen, Marty. "Psalm 31" in *Gather Comprehensive.*

Hopson, Hal H. *Psalm Refrains and Tones.*   HOP 425.

Smith, G. Boulton. "Father, Into Your Hands" in PS 2.

### CHORAL

Bach, J.S. "Crucifixus" from "Mass in B Minor" in *Bach for All Seasons.*
SATB, org.   AFP 0800656784.

Candlyn, T. Frederick. "Ride On! Ride On in Majesty." SATB, org.
HWG 643.

Ferguson, John. "Ah, Holy Jesus." SATB, div, vla.   MSM-50-3012.

Ferko, Frank. "Motet for Passion Sunday." SATB.   ECS 4916.

Gounod, Charles. "Blessed Is He Who Cometh." SATB, solo, org.
GSCH 3423.

Hopson, Hal H. "A Lenten Walk" in *The Augsburg Choirbook.* 2 pt mxd,
org, opt hb, opt timp.   AFP 0800656784.

Jennings, Carolyn. "Ride On, Ride On in Majesty." SATB, org.
BEL SCHCH 07725.

Johnson, Carolyn. "Spread Branches." SATB, org/pno.
AFP 0800659724.

Music, David W. "Hosanna in the Highest." SATB, perc, kybd, opt
children's choir.   CPH 98-2797.

Nystedt, Knut. "Hosanna! Blessed Is He." SAB, org.
AFP 11-1410.

Scott, K. Lee. "The Holy Lamb of God." SATB, org.   MSM-50-3004.

Tchaikovsky, Peter. "The Crown of Roses" in *100 Carols for Choirs.*
SATB.   OXF.

Victoria, Tomas Luis. "Hosanna to the Son of David." SATB.
CPH 98-1993.

Voorhaar, Richard E. "Lamb of God." U, 2/3 pt, hb, xyl, pno, org.
AFP 0800651758.

### CHILDREN'S CHOIRS

Hopson, Hal H. "Song of Zechariah." U, kybd.   FLA-5018.

Smith, G. Alan. "Antiphonal Hosanna." 2 pt, kybd.   HOP F973.

### KEYBOARD/INSTRUMENTAL

Cherwien, David. "Shades Mountain" in *O God Beyond all Praising.* Org.
AFP 0800657241.

Farlee, Robert Buckley. "Shades Mountain" in *Many and Great.* Org.
AFP 0800658949.

Guilmant, Alexandre. "Marche Religieuse" in *The Organ Music of
Alexandre Guilmant,* vol. 1. Org.   MCF DM 240.

Organ, Anne Krentz. "Shades Mountain" in *Woven Together.* Pno, inst.
AFP 0800658167.

Vaughan Williams, Ralph. "Rhosymedre" in *Augsburg Organ Library:
Lent.* Org.   AFP 0800658973.

Young, Jeremy. "Shades Mountain" in *At the Foot of the Cross.* Pno.
AFP 0800655397.

### HANDBELL

Afdahl, Lee J. "Gethsemane." 3-5 oct.   AFP 080065367X.

Gramann, Fred. "Herzliebster Jesu." 4-7 oct. L5.
AGEHR AG47002.

Kerr, J. Wayne. "There in God's Garden." 3-5 oct. L2.   MSM 30-820.

Parrish, Mary Kay. "Praise and Reflection." 3-5 oct. L4.
JEF JHS 9030.

Starks, Howard F. "Beside Still Waters." 3 oct. L3.   AG 1047.

141

PRAISE ENSEMBLE

Borop and Sprague/arr. Tom Fettke. "Via Dolorosa." SATB, kybd.
WRD 301 086416 7.

Courtney, Craig. "Procession and Hymn for Palm Sunday." SATB,
children's choir, org, cong.    BEC BP1536.

## Sunday, March 24

OSCAR ARNULFO ROMERO,
BISHOP OF EL SALVADOR, MARTYR, 1980

Romero is remembered for his advocacy on behalf of
the poor in El Salvador, though it was not a characteristic of his early priesthood. After being appointed as
bishop he preached against the political repression in his
country. He and other priests and church workers were
considered traitors for their bold stand for justice, especially defending the rights of the poor. After several
years of threats to his life, Romero was assassinated
while presiding at the eucharist. During the 1980s thousands died in El Salvador during political unrest.

Romero is remembered as a martyr who gave his life
in behalf of the powerless in his country. Our Lenten
journey of conversion calls us to be bold in our witness
to Christ, work on behalf of the powerless, and speak on
behalf of justice and equality for all people, who are created in the image of God.

## Monday, March 25

MONDAY IN HOLY WEEK

PRAYER OF THE DAY

O God, your Son chose the path which led to pain before
joy and the cross before glory. Plant his cross in our
hearts, so that in its power and love we may come at last
to joy and glory; through your Son, Jesus Christ our Lord.

READINGS

Isaiah 42:1-9

The servant brings forth justice

Psalm 36:5-11

Your people take refuge under the shadow of your
wings. (Ps. 36:7)

Hebrews 9:11-15

The redeeming blood of Christ

John 12:1-11

Mary anoints the feet of Jesus

## Tuesday, March 26

TUESDAY IN HOLY WEEK

PRAYER OF THE DAY

Lord Jesus, you have called us to follow you. Grant that
our love may not grow cold in your service, and that we
may not fail or deny you in the hour of trial.

READINGS

Isaiah 49:1-7

The servant brings salvation to earth's ends

Psalm 71:1-14

From my mother's womb you have been my strength.
(Ps. 71:6)

1 Corinthians 1:18-31

Christ crucified, the wisdom of God

John 12:20-36

The hour has come

## Wednesday, March 27

WEDNESDAY IN HOLY WEEK

PRAYER OF THE DAY

Almighty God, your Son our Savior suffered at human
hands and endured the shame of the cross. Grant that we
may walk in the way of his cross and find it the way of
life and peace; through your Son, Jesus Christ our Lord.

READINGS

Isaiah 50:4-9a

The servant is vindicated by God

Psalm 70

Be pleased, O God, to deliver me. (Ps. 70:1)

Hebrews 12:1-3

Look to Jesus, who endured the cross

John 13:21-32

The departure of Jesus' betrayer

# THE THREE DAYS

*This is the center of the story,*

*the source from which all else flows*

# Images *of the* Season

Three days—seventy-two hours and their immediate

aftermath. This is the center of the story, the source from which

all else flows as well as the great ocean into which all things

eventually are gathered. The liturgy of the Three Days is the most dramatic of all the liturgies of the year, not only in its intensity but also in its form. A helpful exercise for focusing on this shortest season is to consider the tangible objects used in the course of these days. This is a hands-on, action-oriented liturgy, and being aware of how these objects are handled, arranged, and displayed might help to release their power in the worshiping community as conveyers of gospel and signs of grace.

Some of these objects occur in balanced pairs. The bowl is a good example. It figures prominently in the Maundy Thursday liturgy, where it is used for footwashing. Set in the context of first-century eastern Mediterranean culture, the washing basin would have been a familiar sign of hospitality as well as hygiene. Footwashing was an entrance rite that allowed a person to change identity from traveler to guest. But more importantly, the foot basin also defined fixed social roles: those who did the washing and those who were washed. The shock of the Maundy Thursday footwashing is the intentional violation of those social boundaries. The master becomes servant, and the servant becomes one who is served. This new arrangement is declared to be not a chance occurrence but rather the inauguration of a new social reality supported by a new kind of law, a "command" (in Latin, *mandatum*, from which the day takes its name). Even as the first scene of the Three Days opens, we know a significant revolution is taking place.

The bowl reappears on day three for the Vigil of Easter and Easter Day. Christ's community gathers around a baptismal font. Again, the bowl serves as a marker for both an entrance rite and a fundamental shift in roles. Again, people are being cleansed and assuming new identities. Again, boundaries are being violated, but this time the revolution cuts even deeper, now slicing through realities of life and death. Like the open door to Jesus' tomb, the baptismal bowl becomes a declaration

that a hole has been punched through our most basic understanding of how the world operates. What started two days earlier as a redefinition of social roles has now become a cosmic quake shaking the foundations of reality and opening up a doorway through which we are invited to walk as daughters and sons of God and heirs of the promise of eternal life.

Other objects are paired during the Three Days. There is a pair of meals—both including a loaf of bread and a cup. On Thursday, the meal is a sign of impending treachery—"the night in which he was betrayed." It is a before-the-fact interpretation of what will happen on Good Friday: betrayal at the hands of one who shares the bread and dips from the common bowl, body broken, blood spilled. On Saturday night and Sunday, however, the eucharistic meal not only looks back at the wonder of the entire drama now unfolded, but becomes for the community a foretaste of the feast to come, the beginning of a great victory banquet that celebrates the new cosmic order already flowing out of the command, the cross, and the open tomb.

In the very center of the liturgy of the Three Days, in the middle of day two, stands the cross. The Good Friday liturgy may include a rough-hewn cross carried into the assembly. It is a cross of contradiction—the grizzly instrument of a torturous death and the sign of the world's salvation. Here is where the old order is "crossed out" and a new world comes into being. Here is where this darkest of all days becomes for the faithful a good Friday. Here is where bowl and towel, bread and wine, servant and slave suddenly are thrown together by God's grace. One life ends; another begins.

As you approach the Three Days, think about the objects used in this central liturgy. These simple things help to draw us into God's new story, a story that takes us with Jesus, slays and raises us with Christ, gives us a new identity, and catapults us into resurrection life.

144

# Environment *and* Art *for the* Season

imaginative and well-delivered, and the church environment was gracious and beautiful. Even sacred movement had been incorporated into the liturgy of the Three Days. Greeting a young family after the Vigil of Easter, the pastor asked the youngest child, "Did you manage to stay awake tonight?"

"Yes, Pastor!" the little girl replied. "My favorite parts were the bonfire and then when the people get baptized. I wish I could have been baptized here again tonight. When I grow up, I'm going to have my children baptized at the Easter Vigil!"

In our worship during these days, our Lenten thirst for God is slaked by the celebration of our entrance into the life of Christ. Understandably, we want these days to be magnificent. Rather than strive for novelty or extravagance, however, those who successfully plan for the Three Days begin with an appreciation for the power of the primary symbols of these days. Otherwise, we may find ourselves lavishing attention on the wrong priorities. Proclaiming the word, washing the elect in the waters of baptism, and sharing the bread and wine of the eucharist are the central actions of the liturgy. All else is secondary.

Artist Jane Pitz describes the way one church gives focus to the primary symbols for these days:

> The environment for the Three Days is simplified. For each day, the symbols that are used are placed in the center of the assembly. (This worship space is in the round.) On Thursday, large woven empty baskets that are to be filled with foodstuffs for a local clinic and outreach center are placed at the doors. Bowls, towels, and water pitchers for the footwashing are set up early and are very evident as the assembly enters for the service. The altar table is adorned with a full white cloth. On Friday, the large cross is moved to the center of the space between altar and ambo and placed as the only element in evidence. On Holy Saturday, in preparation for the Easter vigil, the font is again filled with water, as are the niches with oils, and green plants are placed at the base of the fountain which rises over the font.

It is wise to plan the environment for the Three Days within the context of the whole paschal cycle of Lent, the Three Days, and Easter. The Triduum begins at sundown on Maundy Thursday. By this time, Lenten purple should be removed from the church. If the worship space was embellished with scarlet for the Sunday of the Passion, this might be left in place for Maundy Thursday, especially if the same scarlet vesture will be used. However, there are two good reasons to consider removing all vestiges of Lent before the service begins. First, the ritual stripping of the altar on Maundy Thursday will not be complete if scarlet trimmings are left within the worship space. Unless all scarlet hangings can be removed as a part of this ritual, it is better to remove them before the liturgy. Second, an effective worship environment for these Three Days underscores the unity of these days as one continuous liturgy, rather than emphasizing any connection with the Lenten season.

Where will the ritual action of the footwashing take place? Liturgical artist Tanja Butler notes that by performing the footwashing not at the altar but in the middle of the gathered congregation, the communal aspect of the ritual is emphasized. Some churches create stations throughout the worship space, placing two or more chairs at various points within the nave. It is important when planning the footwashing not to stage this action as if it were a spectacle for the assembly to watch. Place the washbasin, pitcher of water, and towels on a small table near each station. Be sure to have enough towels. The water in the basin should be warm. Earthenware vessels will maintain the water temperature better than glass or metals. Remember to include additional basins, so ministers who will participate in the celebration of the eucharist can wash their hands.

If a church has never used fresh bread for communion, the Three Days is a fine time to begin this practice. Organize volunteers to bake enough bread to last

145

throughout the Three Days. The change from wafers is sure to be noticed and appreciated by the assembly.

The stripping of the altar at the end of the Maundy Thursday service is a powerful symbolic action, emblematic of Christ's self-emptying in his passion and death. Invite participants of all ages to assist in this. Rehearse the specific tasks assigned to each participant. Everything from the altar should be removed, leaving only the table (without altar linen), the ambo, and chairs. If possible, even candlesticks and cross should be removed.

There is no liturgical color assigned to Good Friday, because the altar has been stripped and the paraments have been removed. No embellishment is necessary to convey the solemnity of this day. The emptied worship space conveys this mood.

On Good Friday, the passion narrative will be proclaimed. Strong voice projection, crisp articulation, and a good sound system will ensure that the story will be heard. It is also important that the readers be seen. Make sure they are positioned so that they are not blocked from the assembly's view.

How will the cross be reverenced on Good Friday? Many churches have a large cross that is brought out of storage and used especially for this liturgy. Other churches use the processional cross or another cross that has been used by the congregation during Lent. There is a wonderful continuity in venerating the same cross that has been in view during the Lenten season or throughout the liturgical year. The cross may be moved before the service or carried to its place within the worship space during the liturgy. If the cross is large, several people may be needed to carry it carefully in procession. These people (if they are strong and hardy) can hold the cross at an angle of forty-five degrees or so while the assembly participates in its veneration. Reverencing the cross may evoke strong emotions as people touch, stroke, and kiss the wood. So that people do not feel rushed or self-conscious as they reverence the cross, some churches prop it at a low angle off the ground, leaning it against large, dignified pillows. The most important concern is that the cross be stable, because people will tend to lean on it.

The Vigil of Easter begins with an outdoor bonfire. This outdoor rite should be carefully rehearsed and prepared, preferably on another evening with the same level of ambient light. If inclement weather makes an outdoor

bonfire impossible or ill-advised, then the paschal candle can be lit in the narthex. The paschal candle should be new and beautiful, with the year inscribed, and large enough to last throughout the liturgical year. It should be clear from its scale and beauty that this is the primary candle within the church. From the paschal candle, votive candles may be lit for the assembly. If the bonfire takes place outdoors, worshipers may light votive candles from the fire and then process into the church holding lit candles, an image of the chosen people in the desert following the pillar of fire by night. Another option is to hand the unlit candles to worshipers as they enter the church. Once the paschal candle is lit, the light is shared from candle to candle until the seated assembly is a sea of lights within the darkness.

The Easter Vigil readings are wondrous revelations. Some churches unfurl banners or wave flags at the beginning of the readings. One parish, fortunate enough to have a principal dancer from a sacred dance troupe as well as a respected musical composer among its members, choreographed sacred movement to original music written to dramatize one of the readings. Flowers also might be brought gracefully into the worship space and placed in appointed spots before each reading.

For this night of all nights, uncover the font and fill it with clean, warm water. Plants and flowers are appropriate around the font as long as they do not overwhelm it or distract attention from the water, which is the primary element of baptism.

Artist Lucinda Naylor describes an art installation she created for the Easter Vigil. The installation emphasizes the baptismal character of the Easter season:

> Our most current [Easter] installation runs two rivers of blue ribbon that cascade the length of the church—rising on one side, falling on the other—the front falling side pointing to the Easter baptismal font. These Easter installations reflect the emphasis that is placed on our baptismal promises throughout all the Sundays of Easter—beginning with the baptism by immersion of the neophytes at the great Easter Vigil.

Bonfire and candlelight, service of readings, holy washing, holy meal of the Lord's supper: in the rich actions of this night of nights, we pass over with Christ from death into new life. What more could we want? Alleluia!

# Preaching *with the* Season

Children enjoy playing connect-the-dots, creating

a picture from what looked like a random scattering of dots on a

page. As adults, we do the same thing every day of our lives.

Almost unconsciously, we connect all the billions of dots of our lives to construct a meaningful narrative, so that a coherent story begins to take shape out of the mass of our daily experiences.

We get our basic stories from some teacher in our culture. At an early age, we are told stories about George Washington cutting down the cherry tree or Abraham Lincoln walking miles to return two pennies. Or we enjoy the drama of *The Little Engine That Could.* These stories promise us that we will be successful if only we will shape our lives in accord with the virtues of truth telling or honesty or patient endurance and believing in ourselves. Of course, when we grow up, we may outgrow the youthful naivete and idealism of those stories, as other stories take control.

The advertising industry beats the drum of happiness through consumption, the purchase of a sufficient supply of the goods spread before us in glossy magazines and slick television commercials. We are also bombarded by stories of power. Holding a position in the upper levels of any pyramid (business, industry, politics, school, or even church) is certain to bring us the good life, we are told.

Live theater has been called "the temple of the story." Good drama strives to cut through the haze of superficialities served up in a thousand forms by the popular culture so that we might see something of the mysterious, sometimes frightening, always awesome depths of human existence.

At its best, "the temple of the story" is a place where stories are enacted that challenge the shallow, platitudinous tales that finally fail to deliver on their promises. So what is the church? Perhaps it is "the temple of the really good story." The church has been entrusted with God's story—and if there is a season of the year when we are at the heart of God's story, it is during our observance of the Three Days. Jesus comes as climax of God's story, and these days set before our eyes the essence of the story of Jesus. The Easter Vigil with its dozen readings rehearses God's entire story from creation to Jesus and new creation, and it not only tells the story but draws us into the story.

Central to the church's vocation is telling the story in such a way that we see God in all of our stories—our personal, ecclesiastical, and national stories. Telling God's story involves both critical and constructive tasks. God's story critiques our stories when they are inadequate. And God's story confirms our stories when we are living from God and in Christ and toward the neighbor.

It has been twenty years since literary critic Northrop Frye wrote his book *The Great Code: The Bible and Literature.* On the one hand, Frye spoke of the Bible as a "huge, sprawling, tactless book." Why "tactless"? Maybe because the Bible just tells the truth, even when the word it speaks makes us squirm. "Sprawling" seems to indicate that the plot is hard to get hold of. And yet Frye insists that the Bible is a unified work. He finds the overall structure of the Bible to be a great parabola (a U-shaped form). It is the narrative of humanity's fall from grace, followed by suffering, repentance, and deliverance. Perhaps "sprawling" reflects the fact that it contains so many characters and kinds of literature—story and psalm and parable and vision—and covers so many centuries.

This huge sprawling book has the shape of a great parabola. And that parabola of fall and eventual rescue, death and resurrection, is the shape not only of the whole narrative, but of story after story between Genesis and Revelation. Those parabola-shaped stories hold the promise of renewal for our own lives, even when our stories take their most tragic turns downward.

Maundy Thursday, Good Friday, and the Resurrection of Our Lord bring together potent stories and potent acts (like footwashing and sharing bread and wine). Those stories and those actions tell us the truth, and they have power to illumine and enliven our lives.

147

# Shape *of* Worship *for the* Season

## BASIC SHAPE OF THE MAUNDY THURSDAY LITURGY

- See Maundy Thursday liturgy in *LBW* Ministers Edition, pp. 137–38; also available as a congregational leaflet from Augsburg Fortress (AFP 0806605758)

### GATHERING

- The sermon may begin the liturgy
- An order for corporate confession and forgiveness may be used (*LBW*, pp. 193–95)
- The peace follows the order for confession and forgiveness

### WORD

- The washing of feet may follow the reading of the gospel
- For a dramatic reading based on the gospel use *Scripture Out Loud!* (AFP 0806639644)
- For a contemporary drama based on the second reading, use *Can These Bones Live?* (AFP 0806639652)
- No creed is used on Maundy Thursday
- The prayers: see the prayers for Maundy Thursday in *Sundays and Seasons*

### MEAL

- Offertory prayer: see alternate worship text for the Three Days in *Sundays and Seasons*
- Use the proper preface for Passion
- Eucharistic prayer: in addition to the four main options in *LBW*, see "Eucharistic Prayer D: The Season of Lent" in *WOV* Leaders Edition, p. 68
- Invitation to communion: see alternate worship text for the Three Days
- Post-communion prayer: see alternate worship text for the Three Days
- No post-communion canticle
- Stripping of the altar follows post-communion prayer
- No benediction on Maundy Thursday
- No dismissal on Maundy Thursday

## BASIC SHAPE OF THE GOOD FRIDAY LITURGY

- See Good Friday liturgy in *LBW* Ministers Edition, pp. 139–43; also available as a congregational leaflet from Augsburg Fortress (AFP 0806605774)

### WORD

- The Passion according to St. John is read; a version involving readers and congregation may be used (AFP 0806605707)
- For a reading based of the passion interspersed with choral music, use *St. John Passion* (AFP 0800658582)
- The bidding prayer for Good Friday may be used (*LBW* Ministers Edition, pp. 139–42)
- Adoration of the Crucified may be used (*LBW* Ministers Edition, p. 142)
- No communion for Good Friday
- No benediction for Good Friday
- No dismissal for Good Friday

## BASIC SHAPE OF THE RITE FOR THE EASTER VIGIL

- See Vigil of Easter in *LBW* Ministers Edition, pp. 143–53; *WOV* Leaders Edition, pp. 88–89; Vigil of Easter—Music Edition (AFP 0806605782); also see congregational leaflet from Augsburg Fortress (AFP 0806605790)

### LIGHT

- The service of light may begin outside at the lighting of a new fire
- The congregation processes into the darkened nave following the lit paschal candle
- A cantor sings the Easter proclamation (Exsultet)

### WORD

- Twelve readings appointed for the Easter Vigil (each of which may be followed by a sung response and a prayer) are listed in *WOV* Leaders Edition, pp. 88–89
- Canticle of the Sun (a version is printed in the autumn seasonal rites section) may conclude the service of readings
- For dramatic readings based on two of the appointed

passages, see *Scripture Out Loud!* (AFP 0806639644)

- For contemporary dramas based on five of the passages, see *Can These Bones Live?* (AFP 0806639652)

## BAPTISM

- If no candidates will be baptized, a congregational renewal of baptism may be used; notes for this portion of the liturgy are printed in *LBW* Ministers Edition, p. 152

## MEAL

- The Litany of the Saints in the seasonal rites section may be sung during movement from font to the place of the meal
- Hymn of praise (traditionally "Glory to God")
- During the hymn of praise, lights may be turned on, accompanied by the ringing of bells
- The prayers: see the prayers for Vigil of Easter in *Sundays and Seasons*
- Offertory prayer: see alternate worship text for the Three Days
- Use the proper preface for Easter
- Eucharistic prayer: in addition to four main options in *LBW*, see "Eucharistic Prayer E: The Season of Easter" in *WOV* Leaders Edition, p. 69
- Invitation to communion: see alternate worship text for the Three Days
- Post-communion prayer: see alternate worship text for the Three Days
- Benediction: see alternate worship text for the Three Days
- Dismissal: see alternate worship text for the Three Days

## BASIC SHAPE OF THE RITE FOR EASTER DAY

- Confession and Forgiveness: see alternate worship text for the Easter season

## GATHERING

- Greeting: see alternate worship text for the Three Days
- Use the Kyrie

- Use the hymn of praise ("This is the feast of victory")

## WORD

- For a dramatic reading based on the gospel according to John, use *Scripture Out Loud!* (AFP 0806639644)
- Use Nicene Creed
- The prayers: see the prayers for Easter Day in *Sundays and Seasons*

## MEAL

- Offertory prayer: see alternate worship text for the Three Days
- Use the proper preface for Easter
- Eucharistic prayer: in addition to four main options in *LBW*, see "Eucharistic Prayer E: The Season of Easter" in *WOV* Leaders Edition, p. 69
- Invitation to communion: see alternate worship text for the Three Days
- Post-communion prayer: see alternate worship text for the Three Days

## SENDING

- Benediction: see alternate worship text for the Three Days
- Dismissal: see alternate worship text for the Three Days

## OTHER SEASONAL POSSIBILITIES
### PASCHAL VESPERS

- If you are able to gather for worship on Easter Evening, a festival form of evening prayer may be desired. Although it is printed as a part of morning prayer, consider appending the paschal blessing to evening prayer (*LBW*, pp. 138–41) anytime in the Easter season. See notes for this order in *LBW* Ministers Edition, p. 16, and *Manual on the Liturgy*, pp. 294–95. A hymn, such as "We know that Christ is raised" (LBW 189), "I bind unto myself today" (LBW 188), or "O blessed spring" (WOV 695), may replace the canticle "Te Deum," which is customarily associated with morning prayer.

149

# Assembly Song *for the* Season

The complex liturgy of the Three Days requires

that music be used creatively and in a variety of ways

within the liturgy. The liturgy is filled with symbolic actions

(footwashing, stripping of the altar, adoration of the cross), the movement of worshipers (individual absolution, communion, paschal procession, baptism), various other processions, and lengthy prayers and readings. Appropriate music must be chosen that supports and enhances these different liturgical actions. The music should focus the worshipers on the liturgical action without calling attention to the music itself. Consider everything that is happening in the liturgy at the moment, as well as what has just taken place and what will follow, before deciding whether a hymn, psalm, anthem, refrain, song, or silence is most appropriate. The coordination of all aspects of the liturgy is critical to successfully planning the Three Days.

### MAUNDY THURSDAY

The Maundy Thursday rite may begin with a sermon. An anthem or hymn that sets the stage for the entire service may be sung before the sermon. Simple music that does not distract from the powerful gestures of laying on of hands or footwashing may accompany these events. The Maundy Thursday absolution ends the time of penance begun with the Ash Wednesday confession. A simple refrain paraphrasing Psalm 51 such as "Create in me a clean heart" (W&P 35) could be repeated during the laying on of hands to subtly make that connection. The footwashing is a profound gesture of love, servanthood, and humility. Various musical possibilities might include a choral or congregational setting of the ancient text "Ubi caritas et amor" (LBW 126, WOV 665) or "Jesu, Jesu, fill us with your love" (TFF 83, WOV 765). As the table is cleared following communion, the congregation may sing the refrain and the choir or cantor the verses of "Now we remain" (W&P 106). The song connects the celebration of the meal with the journey to the cross. Psalm 22 is very effective if sung by a single voice to *LBW* psalm tone 7.

### GOOD FRIDAY

Silence may be the most profound music on this day. The liturgy should begin and end in silence. Silence for prayer should occur between the readings, within the bidding prayer, and during the veneration of the cross. If at all possible, the organ, piano, and other instruments should be used as little as possible with a focus on unaccompanied song. The choir's primary role is to lead the congregational singing. Sing in unison unless the people are comfortable singing in harmony. Many Taizé refrains are appropriate for use on Good Friday. Some traditions sing the Trisagion (see WOV 603 for text and one musical setting) during or following the procession of the cross. If the Trisagion is sung by the choir or cantor alone, then the congregation can focus on the mystery of salvation accomplished on the cross.

### VIGIL OF EASTER

Like the paschal light that spreads throughout the church, ever growing in brightness, the music of the vigil begins quietly and steadily grows in brilliance until the resurrection alleluias resound once again. Gather around the fire in silence. Keep the musical response ("The light of Christ. Thanks be to God.") simple. Process into the church in silence. Let the moment speak for itself. Once in place, the Easter proclamation is sung by the assisting minister using the light of the paschal candle. Sung with confidence and quiet joy, the ancient melody (see settings by Mark Bangert in *Music for the Vigil of Easter,* AFP) is perhaps still the best alternative.

The Revised Common Lectionary suggests psalms or canticles as responses to each of the Old Testament readings. Since some readings are quite lengthy, it is a good idea to involve the congregation in the responses. Remember that the church is dark. Simple responses, refrains, and familiar hymns are the best choices. Some solo or choral pieces could be included as long as they serve as a response and not an event in themselves.

150

Baptisms are always a joyful moment, but especially at the vigil. Joyful alleluias (WOV 612 and 613, LBW 135 and 139 first system only) with bells and instruments, repeated several times after each baptism, can heighten this joyful moment. Following the baptisms, the congregation may renew their faith with the affirmation of baptism. The people may be sprinkled with water during the singing of "Song over the waters" (W&P 127) or "We know that Christ is raised" (LBW 189). The Litany of Saints (see *Welcome to Christ: Lutheran Rites for the Catechumenate*, AFP) can be a dramatic conclusion to the baptismal rite.

The remainder of the music surrounding the celebration of the eucharist should be full and joyful. Christ is risen! But remember, there is still Easter morning! Save the big anthems and instrumental music for that liturgy.

## EASTER DAY

The liturgical complexities of the previous days give way to the familiar Sunday liturgy of Easter Day. Whereas the complex rites required simple music,

Easter Day is a time for "pulling out all the stops." The liturgy is full, with all the appropriate options included, and celebrated in style. Now is the time to include the grandest Easter anthems and add the congregation's instrumentalists and handbells to hymns, liturgical songs, preludes, or postludes. Elaborate hymn arrangements must be well rehearsed so that they can clearly lead congregational singing. Make sure the beginnings of stanzas are clearly identified and that descants or sudden harmonic shifts will not throw the congregation off track. Many visitors or occasional worshipers will come to Easter worship. Be hospitable and sing some familiar Easter favorites. Also show that the congregation is moving and growing by singing something in a new or different musical style.

The Three Days might seem overwhelming for a congregation beginning to celebrate the entire liturgy for the first time. The key is to keep the music simple and straightforward. Begin with a few new musical selections and build a repertoire over the years. The awesome nature of the liturgy will speak for itself.

151

# Music *for the* Season

*See the Easter section for additional music appropriate for the Resurrection of Our Lord.*

## CHORAL

Byrd, William. "The Passion According to St. John." SAB, solos. CPH 97-486.

Elgar, Edward. "Ave verum corpus" in *The New Church Anthem Book.* SATB, opt S solo, kybd.   OXF 0193531097 or octavo HWG GCMR 00039.

Ferguson, John. "St. John Passion." SATB, org.   AFP 0800658582.

Johnson, David N. "Saw Ye My Savior?" SATB, org, opt fl. AFP 6000098189.

Mozart, W. A. "Agnus Dei." SATB, org/pno.   CFI CM8174.

Mozart, W. A. "Ave verum corpus" in *Chantry Choirbook.* SATB. AFP 0800657772.

Nelson, Ronald A. *Three Pieces for Lent and Easter* ("Surely He Hath Borne Our Griefs," "Christ Hath Humbled Himself," "When I Awake"). SAB/SATB, org.   AFP 11- 2196.

Organ, Anne Krentz. "Love One Another." SATB.   AFP 0800659643.

Scott, K. Lee. "The Tree of Life." SATB, org.   MSM 50-3000.

Van, Jeffrey. "Lamb of God." SATB.   AFP 0800649958.

Victoria, Tomas Luis de'. "The Passion According to St. John." SATB, solos.   CPH 97-5430.

Williams, David H. "What Wondrous Love Is This." 2 pt mxd, org. AMSI 205.

Yarrington, John. "O Savior of the World." SATB, org. AFP 0800673158.

## CHILDREN'S CHOIRS

Bertalot, John. "There Is a Green Hill." 2 pt trbl, kybd, fl. AFP 0800654137.

Bouman, Paul. "Behold the Lamb of God." 2 pt, kybd. CPH 98-1088.

Linder, Jane. "Christ Is Risen." U, kybd, opt hb.    CG CGA767.

Purcell, Henry/arr. Dolores Hruby. "Celebrate This Happy, Holy
Day." U, kybd, C inst.    CG CGA-587.

Schalk, Carl. "Where Charity and Love Prevail." 2 pt, ob, kybd.
CPH 98-2701.

## KEYBOARD/INSTRUMENTAL

Albrecht, Mark. *Early American Hymns and Tunes for Flute and Piano.* Pno,
solo inst.    AFP 0800656911.

*Augsburg Organ Library: Lent.* Org.    AFP 0800658973.

Cherwien, David. *Now All the Vault of Heaven Resounds.* Org/brass.
Summa/AMSI 2042-FS.

Hassell, Michael. *Jazz Lenten Journey.* Pno.    AFP 080065949X.

Nicholson, Paul. "Were You There?" Org, fl.    AFP 0800654080.

Sedio, Mark. *Music for the Paschal Season.* Org.    AFP 0800656237.

Uhl, Daniel. *Easter Suite: For Trumpet, Organ and Optional Timpani.*
AFP 0800655419.

## HANDBELL

Dobrinski, Cynthia. "Outbursts of Joy." 3-5 oct. L3.    LAK HB009.

Fauré, Gabriel/arr. Kevin McChesney. "Pavane." 3 oct. L2.
AFP 0800551669.

Sherman, Arnold B. "Song of Joy."    AG 1422 (3-4 oct. L2+); 1425
(5 oct. L3).

Sherman, Arnold B. "Were You There?" 3-4 oct. L3.    AG 1267.

Starks, Howard F. "God's Amazing Grace." 3-5 oct. L2.
FLA HP 5370.

## PRAISE ENSEMBLE

Evans, Darrell and Chris Springer. "Redeemer, Savior, Friend" in *The
Smithton Outpouring Songbook.* SAT[B], kybd.    INT 15727.

Haugen, Marty. "Tree of Life." SATB, kybd.    GIA G-2944.

Kendrick, Graham/arr. Wilson. "Amazing Love." SATB, kybd.
HOP C 5043.

Martin, Joseph M. "Behold the King." SATB, kybd.    FLA A 7340.

Morgan, Reuben. "My Redeemer Lives" in *Shout to the Lord 2000 Songbook.* SAT[B], kybd.    INT 14247.

Rodgers, Dawn and Eric Wyse. "Wonderful, Merciful, Savior" in *Extravagant Grace Songbook.* SAT[B], kybd.    INT 16737.

152

# Alternate Worship Texts

## GREETING (EASTER DAY)

Alleluia! Christ is risen.

**Christ is risen indeed. Alleluia!**

The grace of our risen Savior,
the love of God,
and the communion of the Holy Spirit
be with you all.
**And also with you.**

## OFFERTORY PRAYER (MAUNDY THURSDAY)

Gracious God,
**you gave us the gift of your dear Son,**
**who humbled himself as a servant before us.**
**Receive the gifts we offer**
**as signs of our whole lives**
**returned to you in humble service to our neighbor,**
**in the name of Jesus Christ our Lord. Amen**

## OFFERTORY PRAYER (EASTER VIGIL/DAY)

God of light and word, water and life,
**as we come to your table,**
**receive us and these gifts**
in thanksgiving for the resurrection and the life,
**Jesus Christ, our risen Lord. Amen**

## INVITATION TO COMMUNION
## (MAUNDY THURSDAY)

Come to the supper of the Lord.
Share in the bread and cup of salvation.

## INVITATION TO COMMUNION (EASTER VIGIL/DAY)

Alleluia! God has prepared a holy feast for us.
Happy are those who are called to the supper of the Lamb

## POST-COMMUNION PRAYER (MAUNDY THURSDAY)

Lord God, in a wonderful sacrament
you have left us a memorial of your suffering and death.
May this sacrament of your body and blood so work in us
that the way we live
will proclaim the redemption you have brought;
for you live and reign with the Father and Holy Spirit,
one God, now and forever.
**Amen**

## POST-COMMUNION PRAYER (EASTER VIGIL/DAY)

We give you thanks, almighty God,
that you have brought us from darkness to light,
from slavery to freedom, from death to rebirth.
Transform our lives with this heavenly food,
that we may shine with your love
and take to the world the risen life of your Son,
Jesus Christ our Lord.
**Amen**                                                        153

## BLESSING

Alleluia! Christ is risen.
**Christ is risen indeed. Alleluia!**
Almighty God, Father, ✠ Son, and Holy Spirit,
bless you and raise you to newness of life,
now and forever.
**Amen**

## DISMISSAL

Go in peace. Serve the risen Christ.
**Thanks be to God. Alleluia, alleluia!**

# Seasonal Rites

## Litany of the Saints

Lord, have mercy.
**Lord, have mercy.**
Christ, have mercy.
**Christ, have mercy.**
Lord, have mercy.
**Lord, have mercy.**

Be gracious to us.
**Hear us, O God.**
Deliver your people.
**Hear us, O God.**

You loved us before the world was made:
**Hear us, O God.**
You rescued the people of your promise:
**Hear us, O God.**
You spoke through your prophets:
**Hear us, O God.**
You gave your only Son for the life of the world:
**Hear us, O God.**

For us and for our salvation he came down from heaven:
**Great is your love.**
And was born of the virgin Mary:
**Great is your love.**
Who by his cross and suffering has redeemed the world:
**Great is your love.**
And has washed us from our sins:
**Great is your love.**
Who on the third day rose from the dead:
**Great is your love.**
And has given us the victory:
**Great is your love.**
Who ascended on high:
**Great is your love.**
And intercedes for us at the right hand of God:
**Great is your love.**

For the gift of the Holy Spirit:
**Thanks be to God.**
For the one, holy, catholic, and apostolic church:
**Thanks be to God.**
For the great cloud of witnesses into which we are baptized:
**Thanks be to God.**

For Sarah and Abraham, Isaac and Rebekah:
**Thanks be to God.**

For Gideon and Deborah, David and Esther:
**Thanks be to God.**
For Moses and Isaiah, Jeremiah and Daniel:
**Thanks be to God.**
For Miriam and Rahab, Abigail and Ruth:
**Thanks be to God.**
For Mary, mother of our Lord:
**Thanks be to God.**
For John, who baptized in the Jordan:
**Thanks be to God.**
For Mary Magdalene and Joanna, Mary and Martha:
**Thanks be to God.**
For James and John, Peter and Andrew:
**Thanks be to God.**
For Paul and Apollos, Stephen and Phoebe:
**Thanks be to God.**
*Other names may be added*
For all holy men and women, our mothers and fathers in faith:
**Thanks be to God.**
For the noble band of the prophets:
**Thanks be to God.**
For the glorious company of the apostles:
**Thanks be to God.**
For the white-robed army of martyrs:
**Thanks be to God.**
For the cherubim and seraphim, Michael and the holy angels:
**Thanks be to God.**

Be gracious to us.
**Hear us, O God.**
Deliver your people.
**Hear us, O God.**

Give new life to these chosen ones by the grace of baptism:
**Hear us, O God.**
Strengthen all who bear the sign of the cross:
**Hear us, O God.**
Clothe us in compassion and love:
**Hear us, O God.**
Bring us with all your saints to the river of life:
**Hear us, O God.**

Lord, have mercy.
**Lord, have mercy.**
Christ, have mercy.
**Christ, have mercy.**
Lord, have mercy.
**Lord, have mercy.**

154

# March 28, 2002

Maundy Thursday

## INTRODUCTION

On this day the Christian community gathers to share in the holy supper Christ gave the church to reveal his unfailing love for the human family. In the actions of this liturgy, Christ demonstrates this love by speaking his faithful word, washing our feet, and giving us his body and blood. From this gathering we are sent to continue these actions in daily life: to serve those in need, to offer mercy, to feed the hungry.

This first liturgy of the Three Days has no ending; it continues with the worship of Good Friday and concludes with the Resurrection of Our Lord. Together the Three Days proclaim the mystery of our faith: Christ has died. Christ is risen. Christ will come again.

## PRAYER OF THE DAY

Holy God, source of all love, on the night of his betrayal, Jesus gave his disciples a new commandment: To love one another as he had loved them. By your Holy Spirit write this commandment in our hearts; through your Son, Jesus Christ our Lord, who lives and reigns with you and the Holy Spirit, one God, now and forever.

*or*

Lord God, in a wonderful Sacrament you have left us a memorial of your suffering and death. May this Sacrament of your body and blood so work in us that the way we live will proclaim the redemption you have brought; for you live and reign with the Father and the Holy Spirit, one God, now and forever.

## READINGS

Exodus 12:1-4 [5-10] 11-14

Israel remembered its deliverance from slavery in Egypt by celebrating the festival of Passover. This festival featured the slaughter, preparation, and consumption of the Passover lamb, whose blood was used to protect God's people from the threat of death. The early church described the Lord's supper using imagery from the Passover, especially in portraying Jesus as the lamb who delivers God's people from sin and death.

Psalm 116:1, 10-17 (Psalm 116:1-2, 12-19 [NRSV])

I will take the cup of salvation and call on the name of the Lord. (Ps. 116:11)

1 Corinthians 11:23-26

The only story from the life of Jesus that Paul recounts in detail is this report of the last supper. His words to the Christians at Corinth are reflected today in the liturgies of churches throughout the world.

John 13:1-17, 31b-35

The story of the last supper in John's gospel recalls a remarkable event not mentioned elsewhere. Jesus performs the duty of a slave, washing the feet of his disciples and urging them to do the same for each other.

COLOR  Scarlet *or* White

155

## THE PRAYERS

Gathered around the table of the Lord and united in love, let us pray for the church, the world, and all those in need.

*A BRIEF SILENCE.*

That the church may be one at the eucharistic table and in service to the world, let us pray to the Lord.

**Lord, have mercy.**

That the leaders of nations may seek reconciliation and justice wherever there is conflict and oppression, let us pray to the Lord.

**Lord, have mercy.**

That those who are unloved, weary, sick, or hospitalized (especially) may be strengthened through your gifts of grace and our care for them, let us pray to the Lord.

**Lord, have mercy.**

That our participation in this holy meal may deepen our faith toward you and our commitment to serve those who are hungry and poor, let us pray to the Lord.

**Lord, have mercy.**

That all who gather to celebrate these days, especially those who will be baptized at Easter, may partake in these holy mysteries with joy and awe, let us pray to the Lord.

**Lord, have mercy.**

*HERE OTHER INTERCESSIONS MAY BE OFFERED.*

That you would gather us with the saints of every time and place to the Passover feast of the Lamb, let us pray to the Lord.

**Lord, have mercy.**

Hear our prayers, O merciful God, as we eagerly await the day of resurrection, through Jesus Christ our Lord.

**Amen**

### IMAGES FOR PREACHING

Jesus rose from the table (we hear nothing of bread and wine in John's account) and "took off his outer robe," a gesture designed to make vivid his laying aside his life (see John 10:11-18). He divests himself of his own life on behalf of his own people. Then he "tied a towel around himself" (see 21:18-19), girding himself for the work to be completed at the cross. John does not say here that Jesus "poured out" his life or "poured wine" for his disciples but broadly hints at that when he writes that Jesus "poured water" into a basin.

John pictures Jesus as girded with a towel, kneeling with a basin of water, ready to perform the central action of that night. Jesus begins to wash the feet of his disciples. Peter draws back, refusing this service that Jesus wishes to offer him. Jesus tells Peter that this is a "washing" without which Peter cannot share in the circle of Jesus' fellowship.

Just what is this washing that Jesus offers? It is more than a humble act designed to serve as an object lesson that teaches humility. Note that Jesus performs this act of washing during the meal, at a point when we expect to hear of a loaf and a cup, of a body broken and life outpoured. This washing is nothing less than initiation into the company of Jesus, into friendship with Jesus and so into fellowship with God. This indispensable flood is the outpoured life of Jesus. When Peter catches on to all of that, he becomes marvelously enthusiastic about receiving the washing.

Jesus' dying washes and sanctifies his own, thoroughly and completely, qualifying them for entrance into the presence of God. When that has been said, then the evangelist can go on to say, Oh, yes, and this washing can serve also as an example (13:12-17).

### WORSHIP MATTERS

In the history of the church, several rites have been associated with Maundy Thursday, including the washing of feet, the blessing of holy oils, and the reconciliation of the penitents. For congregations that use oils ritually for healing or sealing—at the time of baptism, for example—Maundy Thursday is an opportune time for blessing those oils in preparation for their use. This rite allows the gathered community to participate, even when—as in the case of a private anointing of the sick—the anointing is not part of the community's regular worship.

A formal act of reconciliation might be foreign to the experience of many congregations, yet the opportunity holds much promise. For the congregation to surround, for example, those who have recently been part of a broken relationship or those who may have caused harm or injury to others can be a powerful experience of confession and forgiveness.

### LET THE CHILDREN COME

You hardly need to welcome children into this liturgy. The readings, the music, the footwashing, the meal, and the stripping of the altar engage every sense. The meaning of servanthood is not lost on the young when another bends to wash their feet in warm water. Let children carry the gifts of bread and wine to the table. Eight- to eleven-year-olds are often drawn to the solemnity of this night. With adequate rehearsal, they and older children could help with the stripping of the table (and the dressing of the table at the Vigil of Easter).

### HYMNS FOR WORSHIP
GATHERING

Lord Jesus Christ, we humbly pray   LBW 225

Lord, who the night you were betrayed   LBW 206

When twilight comes   WOV 663

HYMN OF THE DAY

Great God, your love has called us   WOV 666

ALTERNATE HYMN OF THE DAY

Around you, O Lord Jesus   LBW 496

One in the bread   BL 510

COMMUNION

Let us break bread together   LBW 212, TFF 123

Lord Jesus Christ, you have prepared   LBW 208

Eat this bread   WOV 709, TFF 125

Here is bread   W&P 58

156

## ADDITIONAL HYMNS AND SONGS

Thee we adore, O hidden Savior   LBW 199

This is my body   WOV 707, TFF 121

It happened on that fateful night   LBW 127

That we may be filled   W&P 134

## MUSIC FOR THE DAY

### PSALMODY

Brown, Teresa. "The Blessing Cup" in PS 2.

Cooney, Rory. "Our Blessing Cup." U, str, pno, gtr.   OCP 5895CC.

Farlee, Robert Buckley.   PW A.

Glynn, John. "Lord, How Can I Repay" in PS 2.

Haugen, Marty. "Ps. 116: Our Blessing Cup" in RS.

Schalk, Carl. "Now I Will Walk at Your Side" in *Sing Out! A Children's Psalter*.   WLP 7191.

### CHORAL

Antes, John. "Go, Congregation, Go!" S solo, org/pno.   B&H 5303.

Bouman, Paul. "Lord of Lords, Adored by Angels." SATB, org.   MSM-50-9025.

Duruflé, Maurice. "Ubi Caritas." SATB.   PRE 312-41253.

Elgar, Edward. "Ave Verum." SATB, org.   NOV 29 0164 01.

Griglak, Robert G. "Where Charity and Love." SATB.   AFP 080064994X.

Hopson, Hal H. "Canticle of Love" (*Ubi Caritas*). SATB, org.   AFP 0800657799.

Leighton, Kenneth. "Solus ad Victimam" (Alone to Sacrifice). SATB, org.   OXF 42.384.

Music, David W. "An Upper Room with Evening Lamps Ashine." SATB, kybd, opt cong.   AFP 0800652983.

Organ, Anne Krentz. "Love One Another." SATB.   AFP 0800659643.

Proulx, Richard. "Ubi Caritas et Amor." SATB, hb.   GIA G-1983.

Saint-Saens, Camille. "Ave Verum Corpus." SATB, opt kybd.   MSM-50-3005.

Walton, William. "A Litany" (Drop Slow Tears). SATB.   OXF 43.349.

Zipp, Friedrich. "Soul, Adorn Yourself with Gladness" in *Chantry Choirbook*. SATB, kybd.   AFP 0800657772.

### CHILDREN'S CHOIRS

Powell, Robert J. "A Lenten Prayer." U, kybd, fl.   CG CGA-159.

Schalk, Carl. "Where Charity and Love Prevail." 2 pt, org.   CPH 98-2701.

### KEYBOARD/INSTRUMENTAL

Albrecht, Mark. "Communion Meditation on Three Tunes" in *Three for Piano and Sax*. Pno, C or E-flat inst.   AFP 0800657977.

Biery, Marilyn. "Ubi caritas" in *Augsburg Organ Library: Lent*. Org.   AFP 0800658973.

Farlee, Robert Buckley. "Song 1" in *Augsburg Organ Library: Lent*. Org.   AFP 0800658973.

Langlais, Jean. "Meditation" (Communion) in *Suite Medievale*. Org.   Salabert RL 12360.

Messiaen, Olivier. *Le Banquet Celeste*. Org.   LED A.L. 22.893.

Sedio, Mark. "Ryburn" in *Organ Tapestries*, vol. 2. Org.   CPH 97-6861.

### HANDBELL

Afdahl, Lee J. "Gethsemane." 3-5 oct. L2.   AFP 080065367X.

McChesney, Kevin. "Jesu, Jesu, Fill Us with Your Love." 2-3 oct. L2.   AFP 0800658116.

### PRAISE ENSEMBLE

Jernigan, Dennis/arr. Bruce Greer. "You Are My All in All." SATB, kybd.   WRD 301 0937 164.

Pote, Allen. "The Last Supper" from *Share the Good News, He Is Risen!* SATB, kybd, opt bass.   CGA-532.

Red, Buryl. "In Remembrance" from *Celebrate Life!* SATB, kybd, C inst.   GEN 4565-35.

157

# March 29, 2002

Good Friday

## INTRODUCTION

On this day the church gathers to hear the proclamation of the Passion, to pray for the life of the world, and to meditate on the life-giving cross. The ancient title for this day—the triumph of the cross—reminds us that the church gathers to offer thanksgiving for the wood of the tree on which hung our salvation.

## PRAYER OF THE DAY

Almighty God, we ask you to look with mercy on your family, for whom our Lord Jesus Christ was willing to be betrayed and to be given over to the hands of sinners and to suffer death on the cross; who now lives and reigns with you and the Holy Spirit, one God, forever and ever.

*or*

Lord Jesus, you carried our sins in your own body on the tree so that we might have life. May we and all who remember this day find new life in you now and in the world to come, where you live and reign with the Father and the Holy Spirit, now and forever.

## READINGS

### Isaiah 52:13—53:12

Today's reading reinterprets the common idea that suffering is God's punishment for sin: "You get what you deserve." What is new is the idea that the innocent sufferer brings benefits for the community. The suffering and death of the servant serve God's purposes: the redemption of God's people.

### Psalm 22

My God, my God, why have you forsaken me? (Ps. 22:1)

### Hebrews 10:16-25 *or* Hebrews 4:14-16; 5:7-9

The writer to the Hebrews uses the Hebrew scriptures to understand the meaning of Christ's death on the cross. Like a great priest, Jesus offered his own blood as a sacrifice for our sins so that now we can worship God with confidence and hope.

### John 18:1—19:42

On Good Friday, the story of Jesus' passion—from his arrest to his burial—is read in its entirety from the Gospel of John.

## THE PRAYERS

On Good Friday, the church's ancient Bidding Prayer is said or sung. See *LBW,* Ministers Edition, pp. 139–42; or *Book of Common Worship,* pp. 283–86.

## IMAGES FOR PREACHING

Tenebrae services were once all the rage, and "services of shadows" are still celebrated with progressive darkening of sanctuaries, signaling the gradual expiration of Jesus in his final hours. Acolytes extinguish candles one by one as readings and prayers marking the progress of this Pilgrim to his prophesied end.

But no shadows fall in John's passion narrative. We hear nothing of darkness from noon till three. And Jesus shows no progressive tiring or weakening. Instead of darkness, light. Instead of weakness, regal authority.

According to John, Jesus was crucified at high noon, at a time when the sun stands high in the sky, at its zenith (19:14). The crucifixion is not Jesus' darkest moment; it is the hour of his glory. Glory means bright, shining, dazzling. And that is how John sees Jesus' death. He speaks of Jesus' crucifixion not as his humiliation but as his glorification (7:39 and elsewhere), not the moment when he "went down" to death and grave but the instant when he "ascended" (3:13 and elsewhere) and "was lifted up" or "exalted" (3:14 and elsewhere) not merely up onto the cross but all the way up into the heart of God.

The only candles or torches we hear about in John's narrative are those carried by the soldiers and police who went out to arrest Jesus (18:3). What delicious irony! Those opponents of Jesus relied on dinky human lamps and lights as they ventured out into the night, groping around in the dark for the Light of the world! They approached with pitiful confidence in the power of their iron weaponry, thinking to terrify and seize the one "through whom all things came into being" (1:3). There in the garden, Jesus confronted his would-be captors and spoke a simple "I am." Instantly they all stumbled in their darkness and fell backwards to the ground (18:6).

Standing over them, Jesus unilaterally announced the

158

terms of his "capture": If you want me, let these others go! (18:8). Here again is that strange exchange, that mysterious equation: life freely and joyously given up for life results in new life.

## WORSHIP MATTERS

Should worship leaders rehearse for their roles? If "rehearse" means to learn and follow a script so that worship can be led without thinking, the answer is no. If, on the other hand, rehearsal means becoming comfortable leading worship—so there is neither awkwardness nor embarrassment—then the answer is yes.

Rehearsal for those who do not regularly lead worship—lectors, acolytes, ushers, and others—is particularly appropriate at two points: when there is movement and when there is transition. To physically walk through movements in advance and to learn how to handle transition—for example, from the reading of scripture to the chanting of a psalm—can be comforting and reassuring to worship leaders, and ultimately to the worshiping community as well.

## LET THE CHILDREN COME

We often tell children to "be quiet in church," but do we teach them about silence? Are there spaces for silence in weekly worship following the invitation to prayer, the reading of scripture, and the sermon that would prepare children for the silences in the liturgy? Even hyperactive children have some capacity for silence, and all children need it. Help children enter silence by showing them how to breathe slowly and deeply, touch their chests and feel their heart beat, or listen for the "music" silence makes in their minds.

## HYMNS FOR WORSHIP
### GATHERING

*The liturgy begins in silence on Good Friday.*

### HYMNS FOR THE PASSION READING

Deep were his wounds   LBW 100
On my heart imprint your image   LBW 102
My heart is longing   LBW 326
O sacred head, now wounded   LBW 116/7
In the hour of trial   LBW 106
Stay here   WOV 667

### HYMN OF THE DAY

Were you there   LBW 92, TFF 81

### ALTERNATE HYMN OF THE DAY

There in God's garden   WOV 668
Calvary   TFF 85

### ADDITIONAL HYMNS AND SONGS

Jesus, Lamb of God   W&P 76
At the foot of the cross   W&P 11
Jesus, I will ponder now   LBW 115
Jesus, remember me   WOV 740
They crucified my Lord   TFF 80

## MUSIC FOR THE DAY
### PSALMODY

Cooney, Rory. "Why Have You Abandoned Me." U, kybd, gtr, fl. OCP 1463CC.
Farlee, Robert Buckley.   PW A.
Haugen, Marty.   PCY, vol. 1.
Schiavone, John. "My God, My God, Why Have You Abandoned Me" in STP, vol. 3.
Smith, Alan. "My God, My God" in PS 2.

### CHORAL

Bach, J.S. "Crucifixus" from Mass in B minor in *Bach for All Seasons.* SATB, org.   AFP 080065854X.
Carnahan, Craig. "Bright Joining." SATB, org.   AFP 0800658639.
Distler, Hugo. "A Lamb Goes Uncomplaining Forth" in *Chantry Choirbook.* SATB.   AFP 0800657772.
Fleming, Larry L. "Sing and Ponder." SATB, hb. AFP 0800653491.
Fountain, Claude. "A Litany" (*Drop, Drop, Slow Tears*). SATB. PVN P1059.
Handel, G.F. "Surely He Hath Borne Our Griefs" in *Messiah.* SATB, org.   Various ed.
Janzen, Janet L. "Drop, Drop, Slow Tears." SATB, kybd. MSM-50-3040.
Kihlken, Henry. "We Adore You, Christ Our King." SATB, org. AFP 0800684722.
Manz, Paul O. "I Caused Thy Grief." SATB, org.   MSM 50-3036.
Palestrina, G.P. "Adoramus Te Christe." SATB.   CFI CM6578.
Proulx, Richard. "Were You There." SATB, S solo, opt cong. AFP 080065451X.
Shute, Linda Cable. "What Language Shall I Borrow." SATB, org. AFP 0800657055.

159

Schütz, Heinrich. "Praise to You, Lord Jesus" in *Chantry Choirbook.*
SATB.    AFP 0800657772.

Willan, Healey. "Behold the Lamb of God." SATB, org.
CPH 98-1509.

### CHILDREN'S CHOIRS

Fauré, Gabriel/arr. Marie Stultz. "Pie Jesu." U, kybd.
MSM 50-9906.

Ferris, William. "When I Survey the Wondrous Cross." U, org.
OXF 94.509.

McIver. "Pie Jesu." U, opt. inst.    CG CGA 815.

Mozart, W. A. (Nancy Telfer, ed). "Agnus Dei." U, kybd.
KJO 8736.

### KEYBOARD/INSTRUMENTAL

Brahms, Johannes. "Herzlich tut mich verlangen" in *Eleven Chorale Pre-ludes.* Org.    Mercury 453-00260.

Nicholson, Paul. "Were You There." Org, fl.    AFP 0800654080.

Sowerby, Leo. "Were You There" in *Ten Preludes on Hymn Tunes.* Org.
BEL GB 651.

Young, Jeremy. "Were You There" in *At the Foot of the Cross.* Pno.
AFP 0800655397.

### HANDBELL

Behnke, John. "The Lamb." 3-5 oct.    CPH 97-6869.

Dobrinski, Cynthia. "Were You There?" 3-5 oct. L2.    AG 1551.

Sherman, Arnold B. "He Never Said a Mumbalin' Word." 3-5 oct.
L3.    AG 1844.

Sherman, Arnold. "Were You There?" 3 oct. L2.    HOP 1267.

### PRAISE ENSEMBLE

Barbour, Anne and Marsha Skidmore. "The Holy Heart." SATB,
kybd.    MAR 301 0838 166.

Cymbala, Carol. "Calvary." SAT[B] with solo, kybd.
WRD 0 80689 92727 0.

Goetz, Marty. "The Love of God." SATB, kybd.
WRD 0 80689 33527 3.

Hussey, Kirkpatrick/arr. Hart. "Lead Me to Calvary." SATB, kybd.
WRD 0 80689 37527 9.

# Friday, March 29

## HANS NIELSEN HAUGE,
## RENEWER OF THE CHURCH, 1824

Hans Nielsen Hauge was a layperson who began preaching about "the living faith" in Norway and Denmark after a mystical experience that he believed called him to share the assurance of salvation with others. At the time itinerant preaching and religious gatherings held without the supervision of a pastor were illegal, and Hauge was arrested several times. He also faced great personal suffering: his first wife died, and three of his four children died in infancy.

Some might remember Hauge by singing the Norwegian hymn "My heart is longing" (LBW 326), with its devotional response to the death of Christ.

# March 30, 2002

The Resurrection of Our Lord
Vigil of Easter

## INTRODUCTION

This liturgy's Easter Proclamation announces, "This is the night in which all who believe in Christ are rescued from evil and the gloom of sin, are renewed in grace, and are restored to holiness." It is the very foundation of our Christian faith, and it is what makes this the crowning moment of the church's year. This night the church celebrates the presence of the risen Lord as he brings us to new life in baptism, gives us his body and blood, speaks his word of promise, and comes to us in the Christian community.

## PRAYER OF THE DAY

O God, who made this most holy night to shine with the glory of the Lord's resurrection: Stir up in your Church that Spirit of adoption which is given to us in Baptism, that we, being renewed both in body and mind, may worship you in sincerity and truth; through Jesus Christ our Lord, who lives and reigns with you, in the unity of the Holy Spirit, one God, now and forever.

## READINGS

Creation: Genesis 1:1—2:4a
Response: Psalm 136:1-9, 23-36
> God's mercy endures forever. (Ps. 136:1b)

The Flood: Genesis 7:1-5, 11-18; 8:6-18; 9:8-13
Response: Psalm 46
> The Lord of hosts is with us; the God of Jacob is our stronghold. (Ps. 46:4)

The Testing of Abraham: Genesis 22:1-18
Response: Psalm 16
> You will show me the path of life. (Ps. 16:11)

Israel's Deliverance at the Red Sea: Exodus 14:10-31; 15:20-21
Response: Exodus 15:1b-13, 17-18
> I will sing to the Lord who has triumphed gloriously. (Exod. 15:1)

Salvation Freely Offered to All: Isaiah 55:1-11
Response: Isaiah 12:2-6
> With joy you will draw water from the wells of salvation. (Isa. 12:3)

The Wisdom of God: Proverbs 8:1-8, 19-21; 9:4b-6
or Baruch 3:9-15, 32—4:4
Response: Psalm 19
> The statutes of the Lord are just and rejoice the heart. (Ps. 19:8)

A New Heart and a New Spirit: Ezekiel 36:24-28
Response: Psalm 42 and Psalm 43
> My soul is athirst for the living God. (Ps. 42:2)

The Valley of the Dry Bones: Ezekiel 37:1-14
Response: Psalm 143
> Revive me, O Lord, for your name's sake. (Ps. 143:11)

The Gathering of God's People: Zephaniah 3:14-20
Response: Psalm 98
> Lift up your voice, rejoice and sing. (Ps. 98:5)

The Call of Jonah; Jonah 3:1-10
Response: Jonah 2:1-3 [4-6] 7-9
> Deliverance belongs to the Lord. (Jonah 2:9)

The Song of Moses: Deuteronomy 31:19-30
Response: Deuteronomy 32:1-4, 7, 36a, 43a
> The Lord will give his people justice. (Deut. 32:36)

The Fiery Furnace: Daniel 3:1-29
Response: Song of the Three Young Men 35-65
> Sing praise to the Lord and highly exalt him forever. (Song of the Three Young Men 35b)

## NEW TESTAMENT READING

Romans 6:3-11
> Christians are baptized into the death of Christ, and are also joined to Christ's resurrection.

Response: Psalm 114
> Tremble, O earth, at the presence of the Lord. (Ps. 114:7)

## GOSPEL

Matthew 28:1-10
> Christ's resurrection is an earthshaking story. News of it spreads with urgency.

COLOR    White or Gold

161

## THE PRAYERS

Rejoicing in the resurrection, let us remember in prayer the church, the world, and all those in need.

*A BRIEF SILENCE.*

Bring your church safely through the waters to the promised land; we pray:

**Hear us, living God.**

Nourish the newly baptized with your life-giving food and drink; we pray:

**Hear us, living God.**

Strengthen the leaders of nations to work for the freedom of all who are oppressed; we pray:

**Hear us, living God.**

Deliver from suffering all who live with poverty, abuse, or illness (especially); we pray:

**Hear us, living God.**

Send favorable weather throughout the world for successful planting and a bountiful harvest; we pray:

**Hear us, living God.**

Feed us at your table, and use us to declare the glorious triumph of your resurrection; we pray:

**Hear us, living God.**

*HERE OTHER INTERCESSIONS MAY BE OFFERED.*

Bring us, with all your saints whose vigil has now ended, to the eternal victory of the Lamb's high feast; we pray:

**Hear us, living God.**

Receive our prayers and hopes, O God, and fill us with the risen life of Christ our Lord.

**Amen**

## IMAGES FOR PREACHING

At the heart of the Vigil of Easter is a chain of carefully selected texts arranged to present the entirety of God's story in one splendid rush, surrounded and supported by lights kindled in the dark and water poured out for the renewing of human life.

But what exactly is God's story? What is the theme running through all the readings and words and acts? It would be unfortunate if all we had was a scattering of interesting dots with nothing linking them into a significant pattern.

God's story is more than a match for our deepest spiritual needs, but the match needs articulating. Paul Tillich spoke of the fundamental anxieties of the human situation as threefold: the anxiety of death, guilt, and meaninglessness. He even dared to say that the earliest church grew precisely because it addressed an age obsessed with death by speaking clearly and convincingly of the new life offered by God in Jesus' death and resurrection. The Reformation of the sixteenth century succeeded where earlier efforts to change the church had not, because Luther correctly understood his age as one burdened by guilt and so spoke powerfully of God's freely given grace and forgiveness. The modern era, said Tillich, in spite of all its powers and wealth, is haunted by the specter of meaninglessness, people's sense that they are unable to connect the dots of daily life into any deeply satisfying pattern. Our contemporary culture desperately needs to hear God's good word of community and compassion.

God's story must be told and can be told in such ways that we see our lives touched and embraced by God's story. Then we can begin to reword our own stories and find the strength to resist the blandishments of all the deficient stories that call out to us, tempting us to accept their distorted portraits of reality.

## WORSHIP MATTERS

The great Vigil of Easter is a time to let words, actions, symbols, and gestures speak. There are times when instructions and announcements are appropriate and even necessary. For example, it makes sense to offer words about care of candles and open flame at the lighting of the bonfire. But for most of this rich and full worship service, additional words are neither helpful nor appropriate. As worship leaders, much of our work as God's people—liturgy—is to allow the Vigil to speak for itself by not getting in the way.

## LET THE CHILDREN COME

The great readings "around the fire" are the stories of our life. Tell them in living ways: Punctuate the creation story with the acclamation, "It is good." Recruit the best storyteller in the parish to tell about Noah and the ark. Invite children to shake tambourines and sing with Miriam after crossing the Red Sea. Let dancers bring to life the dry bones in the valley. Let the children see and hear, touch and taste as much of this night as possible.

## HYMNS FOR WORSHIP

### HYMN OF THE DAY

The day of resurrection!    LBW 141, HFW (Ellacombe and Lancashire)

### ALTERNATE HYMN OF THE DAY

Come away to the skies    WOV 669
All creatures, worship God most high!    HFW

### COMMUNION

Now the green blade rises    LBW 148
Christ has arisen, alleluia    WOV 678, TFF 96

### SENDING

Shout for joy loud and long    WOV 793
We know that Christ is raised    LBW 189

### ADDITIONAL HYMNS AND SONGS

Brighter than the sun    DH 64
Come, you faithful, raise the strain    LBW 132
Let all things now living    LBW 557
Wade in the water    TFF 114

## MUSIC FOR THE DAY

### AROUND THE GREAT FIRE

Berthier, Jacques. "Within Our Darkest Night" in *Songs and Prayers from Taizé*.    GIA G-3719.
Haugen, Marty. "At the Dawn of Creation" in *Up From the Waters: Music for Christian Initiation*.    GIA G-4835.
Sedio, Mark. "O Night More Light." SATB, solo.    SEL 405-531.
Schutte, Dan. "Most Holy Night" in *Easter Praises*. SAB, kybd, gtr.    OCP 11059GC.

### AROUND THE LIGHT OF CHRIST

Batastini, Robert. "Exsultet (Easter Proclamation)." U chant.    GIA G-2351.
"The Exsultet" in *The Psalter: Psalms and Canticles for Singing*.    WJK.
Frese, Everett. "Exsultet." Trinity Publications. SATB, cant, cong, opt timp, tpt, hp, gtr, str bass, kybd.
"Rejoice Now, All Heavenly Choirs" in *Music for the Vigil of Easter*.    AFP 0806605790.
Repulski, John. "Exsultet" in *Easter Praises*. Cant, SATB, hb.    OCP 11059GC.

### AROUND THE READINGS

Reponses to all readings in PW C.

#### FIRST READING

Erickson, Richard. "When Long Before Time." SATB, org, fl.    AFP 0800656768.
Haugen, Marty. "The Song and the Silence."    GIA G-5068.
Hopson, Hal. "O Praise the Lord Who Made All Beauty." U, kybd.    CGA 143.
Morning has broken    W&P 98
Smith, Alan. "God's Love Is Forever!" in PS 2.
We bow down    W&P 149

#### SECOND READING

Cherwien, David. "God Is Our Refuge and Strength." U, org.    MSM 80-800.
Our confidence is in the Lord    W&P 114
The Lord of hosts is with us    TFF 6

#### THIRD READING

Cherepponis, James. "You are my inheritance, O Lord."    GIA G-3321.
Haas, David. "Show Me the Path of Life."    GIA G-4579.
Inwood, Paul. "Centre of My Life" in PS 2.

#### FOURTH READING

Barker, Michael. "Miriam's Song." U, kybd, opt tamb.    CGA 740.
Daw, Carl, Jr. "Metrical Canticles Nos. 25 and 26" in *To Sing God's Praise*. Cong, kybd.    HOP 921.
Gibbons, John. "Canticle of Moses" in PS2.
Hughes, Howard. "Exodus Canticle" (Let Us Sing to the Lord).    GIA G-3102.
Pulkingham, Betty Carr. "The Song of Moses" (and Miriam).    GIA G-1771.
When Israel was in Egypt's land    WOV 670, TFF 87

#### FIFTH READING

Lindh, Jody. "Behold, God Is My Salvation." U/2 pt, org.    CPH 98-3193.
Rusbridge, Barbara. "Sing a Song to the Lord" in PS 1.
Surely it is God who saves me    WOV 635

#### SIXTH READING

Cox, Joe. "Psalm 19" in *Psalms for the People of God*. Cant, choir, cong, kybd.    SMP 45/1037S.
Ogden, David. "You, Lord, Have the Message of Eternal Life" in PS 2.

#### SEVENTH READING

As pants the heart for cooling streams    LBW 452
As the deer    W&P 9
Cox, Joe. "Psalm 43" in *Psalms for the People of God*. Cant, choir, cong, kybd.    SMP 45/1037S.

163

Howells, Herbert. "Like as the Hart." SATB, org.    OXF 42.066.

Hurd, Bob. "As the Deer Longs" in PS 2.

*EIGHTH READING*

Great is the Lord    W&P 53

Show me the way    DH 45

*NINTH READING*

Johnson, Alan. "All the Ends of the Earth" in PS 1.

Jothen, Michael. "O Sing Ye!" U, kybd.    BEC BP1128.

Marshall, Jane. "Psalm 98." U, kybd.    CG CGA-427.

*TENTH READING*

I, the Lord of sea and sky    WOV 752

*TWELFTH READING*

All you works of the Lord    LBW 18

Daw Jr., Carl. "Metrical Canticles 13 and 14" in *To Sing God's Praise.* Cong, kybd.    HOP 921.

Gelineau, Joseph. "Canticle of the Three Young Children." GIA G-1703.

Jennings, Kenneth. "All You Works of the Lord, Bless the Lord" in *The Augsburg Choirbook.* SATB, org.    AFP 0800656784.

Proulx, Richard. "Song of the Three Children." U, opt 2 pt, cant, cong, perc, org.    GIA G-1863.

## AROUND THE FONT

"A Litany of the Saints" and "Springs of water, bless the Lord" in *Welcome to Christ: Lutheran Rites for the Catechumanate.*    AFP 3-142.

Batastini, Robert J. "You Will Draw Water." Cong, hb, opt choir. GIA G-2443.

Fellows, Donald K. "Springs of Water."    GIA 3639.

Moore, Bob. "Sweet Refreshment." SATB, cant, gtr, opt vln, DB. GIA G-4937.

Taylor-Howell, Susan. "You Have Put on Christ." U/3 pt, opt Orff. CGA 325. [See WOV 694.]

Trapp, Lynn. "Music for the Rite of Sprinkling." SATB, org. MSM 80-901.

## PSALM 114

Farlee, Robert Buckley.    PW C.

Hopson, Hal. *Psalm Refrains and Tones.*    HOP 425.

*The Psalter—Psalms and Canticles for Singing.*    WJK.

## CHORAL

Fedak, Alfred V. "Begin the Song of Glory Now." SATB, org, opt brass.    MSM-50-4014.

Handel, GF. "Since by Man Came Death" in *Messiah.* SATB, org. Various ed.

Hayes, Mark. "Alleluia! Christ Is Risen!" SATB, kybd, opt tpts. AFP 0800659538.

Keesecker, Thomas. "Washed Anew." SAB/SATB, kybd, opt hb, opt cong.    AFP 6000001355.

Leavitt, John. "Begin the Song of Glory Now." SATB, org, perc. AFP 6000001258.

Macfarlane, Will C. "Christ Our Passover." SATB, org. PRE 322.35139.

Rachmaninoff, Sergei. "Today Hath Salvation Come" from *All Night Vigil* in *Songs of the Church.* SSAATTB.    HWG GB 640.

Scott, K. Lee. "Let Your Alleluias Rise." SATB, S/T solo. AFP 0800646908.

## CHILDREN'S CHOIRS

Berry, Cindy. "A New Heart." 2 pt, kybd.    BEL BSCM0002.

McRae, Shirley. "Now the Green Blade Rises." U, fl, hb, tamp, kybd. CG CGA 795.

## KEYBOARD/INSTRUMENTAL

Burkhardt, Michael. " O Sons and Daughters of the King" in *Five Easter Season Hymn Improvisations, set 2.* Org.    MSM 10-407.

Johnson, David N. "Herzlich tut mich erfreuen" in *Music for Worship for Manuals.* Kybd.    AFP 080064851X.

King, Larry. "Resurrection" in *AGO Anthology of American Organ Music.* Org.    OXF 754295.

Sedio, Mark. "Come Away to the Skies" in *Two on a Bench.* Kybd (2 players).    AFP 0800659090.

Thomas, David Evan. "Middlebury" in *Augsburg Organ Library: Easter.* Org.    AFP 0800659368.

## HANDBELL

Nelson, Susan T. "Easter Alleluia" (O Filii et Filiae). 3-5 oct. L2. CG CGB216.

Geschke, Susan E. "A Joyous Alleluia." 3 oct. L2.    CG CGB226.

Tucker, Sondra. "Come Away to the Skies." 3-5 oct. L3. CPH 97-6739.

## PRAISE ENSEMBLE

Nystrom, Martin/arr. John Wilson. "As the Deer." SATB, kybd. HOP A 677.

Foley, John. "Come to the Water." SATB, kybd, gtr, solo C inst. OCP 9489.

Sadler, Gary. "Wind of God" in *Hosanna Music Songbook 13.* SAT[B], kybd.    INT 13576.

# March 31, 2002

The Resurrection of Our Lord
Easter Day

## INTRODUCTION

Today is the day God began creation, transforming darkness into light. Today is the day Jesus Christ rose from the darkness of the grave to new life. Today is the day when the church celebrates its birth from the waters of baptism and its new life in the holy supper. Though suffering, injustice, and sin continue to mark the world in which we live, the Christian community goes forth from font and table with Christ's mission to heal, liberate, and forgive. In the fifty days of Easter rejoicing, the church asks the question: How does our baptism send us forth in joyful service to the world?

## PRAYER OF THE DAY

O God, you gave your only Son to suffer death on the cross for our redemption, and by his glorious resurrection you delivered us from the power of death. Make us die every day to sin, so that we may live with him forever in the joy of the resurrection; through Jesus Christ our Lord, who lives and reigns with you and the Holy Spirit, one God, now and forever.

*or*

Almighty God, through your only Son you overcame death and opened for us the gate of everlasting life. Give us your continual help; put good desires into our minds and bring them to full effect; through Jesus Christ our Lord, who lives and reigns with you and the Holy Spirit, one God, now and forever.

## READINGS

Acts 10:34-43

Peter's sermon, delivered at the home of Cornelius, a Roman army officer, is also a summary of the essential message of Christianity: Everyone who believes in Jesus, whose life, death, and resurrection fulfilled the words of the prophets, "receives forgiveness of sins through his name."

*or* Jeremiah 31:1-6

Jeremiah tells of the day when God's people will be restored, using images reminiscent of the exodus: merry-making with tambourine and dance as at the Red Sea, the entry into the promised land and planting of pleasant vineyards, the rebuilding of the city of God.

Psalm 118:1-2, 14-24

On this day the Lord has acted; we will rejoice and be glad in it. (Ps. 118:24)

Colossians 3:1-4

Easter means new life for us as well as for Christ! The Lord has risen to become our life, which is no longer linked to the uncertainties of this world but is securely "hidden" with Christ in God.

*or* Acts 10:34-43

*See above.*

John 20:1-18

John's gospel describes the confusion and excitement of the first Easter morn: the stone is moved and the tomb is empty; disciples race back and forth, while angels speak to a weeping woman. Finally, Jesus himself appears as the Lord in unity with God.

*or* Matthew 28:1-10

Christ's resurrection is an earthshaking story. News of it spreads with urgency.

## COLOR  White *or* Gold

## THE PRAYERS

Rejoicing in the resurrection, let us remember in prayer the church, the world, and all those in need.

*A BRIEF SILENCE.*

That the newly baptized and all who renew their baptismal vows may walk in newness of life, we pray:

**Hear us, living God.**

That all who work for justice and peace in the world may be encouraged and strengthened in their vocations, we pray:

**Hear us, living God.**

That all who are unloved and forgotten, poor and hungry, hospitalized and sick (especially) may find hope in the healing power of the resurrection, we pray:

**Hear us, living God.**

165

That we may be liberated by the power of the gospel from partiality and prejudice to share the hope of the resurrection with all, we pray:

**Hear us, living God.**

*HERE OTHER INTERCESSIONS MAY BE OFFERED.*

That we, in thanksgiving for all the witnesses of the resurrection, may unite our voices with theirs until we join them at the great and promised feast, we pray:

**Hear us, living God.**

Receive our prayers and hopes, O God, and fill us with the risen life of Christ our Lord.

**Amen**

## IMAGES FOR PREACHING

The whole world is turned upside down on Easter. In John's resurrection narrative, two angels in a semi-dark, cave-like place, seated opposite one another over a bench or slab, conjure up the image of the Holy of Holies in the tabernacle and temple. In the inner sanctum of the tabernacle and temple, cherubim facing one another spread their wings over the mercy seat, the place where God promised to meet the people and speak to them (Exod. 25:17-22).

Part of what John sees in Jesus' resurrection is that Jesus' tomb has become the new inner sanctum. Tombs in the first century, even more than today, were places of pollution, contamination, and dread. Tombs were fit habitation only for demons and madmen. But Easter says that Jesus' tomb has become, strangely, a place of new life. The death of Jesus, the wounds of Jesus, the place of Jesus' burial mean not failure and defeat but God's own victory, God's outpouring of rivers of life in the most startling of ways.

Each gospel tells the story of Jesus as beginning in a desert and ending in a tomb. Desert and tomb bracket the ministry of Jesus. Those places look so unpromising, so dry, so sterile, so impossible. But the evangelists invite us to look harder and deeper, to see the hand and breath of God and the power of God in things that seem at first to be weak and foolish and even dead. They invite us to see the power and the life of God in the love that led Jesus from the hot sand of the desert to the hard wood of the cross and the cold stone of the tomb. With one voice they insist that Jesus' love is unconquered, invincible, immortal. In the love of Jesus Christ, received by us and shared, we step into the Holy of Holies. We experience the presence of God.

## WORSHIP MATTERS

Why is Easter morning so special? Certainly because we celebrate the victory over death and the grave of our Lord Jesus Christ. Christ is risen! Christ is risen indeed! But there is more. Easter is distinctive because all of our senses are awakened by symbols of the resurrection. We hear the joyful strains of trumpets. We smell the sweet fragrance of lilies. We see vibrant Easter colors. We taste the richest bread and wine of the Lord's supper. We feel the joyful embrace of our fellow worshipers. Our senses are brought to life on Easter morning.

Easter acts to remind us of the important place of all the senses in worship. Frequently our worship is so monosensual—primarily auditory—that our other senses might as well have stayed in bed. Easter, and Christmas like it, remind us to consider all the senses when planning worship.

## LET THE CHILDREN COME

Before the greeting ("The grace of our Lord Jesus Christ…"), repeat three times the Easter greeting, "Alleluia. Christ is risen!" and the assembly's response, "Christ is risen indeed. Alleluia!" Repeat the Easter greeting and responses at the sending, immediately before the dismissal. Children will learn their part quickly and respond gladly, even exuberantly, if given permission. Use this acclamation throughout the season to draw children into Easter's joyful proclamation.

With a note in the bulletin, encourage people to use this acclamation before their prayer at meals. In this setting a child could declare the opening line, all gathered would respond, and a connection would be made between the language of the church and the life of faith in the home.

## HYMNS FOR WORSHIP
### GATHERING

Now all the vault of heaven resounds    LBW 143

Alleluia! Jesus is risen!    WOV 674, TFF 91

The trumpets sound, the angels sing    W&P 139

### HYMN OF THE DAY

Christ has arisen, alleluia    WOV 678, TFF 96

### ALTERNATE HYMN OF THE DAY

The strife is o'er, the battle done    LBW 135

They crucified my Savior (He rose)    TFF 90

## COMMUNION

Christ the Lord is risen today; Alleluia!    LBW 128

At the Lamb's high feast we sing    LBW 210

Low in the grave he lay    TFF 94

## SENDING

Good Christian friends, rejoice and sing!    LBW 144

Alleluia, alleluia, give thanks    WOV 671

## ADDITIONAL HYMNS AND SONGS

Now the green blade rises    LBW 148

Alleluia Canon    WOV 677

He is exalted    W&P 55

This joyful Eastertide    LBW 149, WOV 675

This is the day    TFF 262, W&P 141

Welcome, happy morning!    LBW 153

## MUSIC FOR THE DAY

### SERVICE MUSIC

All too often the great musical acclamations of the liturgy (the hymn
of praise, alleluia at the gospel, Sanctus) seem anticlimactic amidst all
the musical hoopla given to Easter hymns on this day. Strive for balance; consider one of the following embellished versions of the *LBW*
liturgies:

Cherwien, David. "Alternatives Within." Org, opt inst.
    AFP 0800654870.

Farlee, Robert Buckley. *Great and Promised Feast: Festival Music for Holy
    Communion.* Cong, SATB, soloist, org, opt brass, hb, timp.
    AFP 0800659309.

Ferguson, John. *Festival Setting of the Communion Liturgy (LBW, setting 2).*
    Org, SATB, opt brass.    CPH 6127 (full score); 98-2994
    (choir).

Hillert, Richard. *Festival Setting of the Communion Liturgy (LBW, setting
    1).* U with desc, org, brass, ob, timp, 3 oct hb.    CPH 97-5939
    (full score); 97-2755 (choral desc); 97-5958 (hb).

### PSALMODY

Farlee, Robert Buckley.    PW A.

Geary, Patrick. "Rejoice and Be Glad" in PS 2.

Haas, David. "Alleluia, alleluia" in *Gather Comprehensive.*

Hommerding, Alan J. *Sing Out! A Children's Psalter.*    WLP 7191.

Hopson, Hal H. "Psalm 118" in *10 Psalms.* SATB, cong, org.
    HOP HH 3930.

Hurd, Bob. "This Is the Day." SATB, cong, pno, gtr, 2 tpt.
    OCP 9458.

Shields, Valerie. "Psalm for Easter." SATB, cong, org, opt tpt, hb,
    tamb, tri.    MSM 80-405.

Smith, Bob. "Give Thanks to the Lord" in STP, vol. 4.

### CHORAL

Benson, Robert. "Good Christians All Rejoice and Sing." SATB, org,
    brass qrt.    AFP 0800659597.

Billings, William. "Easter Anthem." SATB.    GSCH 9949.

Brahms, Johannes. "Magdalena." SATB.    GSCH 9953.

Busarow, Donald. "Become to Us the Living Bread" (also "Good
    Christian Friends, Rejoice and Sing"). SAB, C inst, org.
    MSM-50-4406.

Cruger, Johann. "Awake, My Heart, with Gladness" in *Chantry Choir-
    book.* SATB, 2 C insts.    AFP 0800657772.

Ellingboe, Bradley. "Mary at the Tomb." SATB, pno.
    AFP 0800656946.

Englert, Eugene. "He Is Risen, Alleluia!" 2 equal/mxd vc, org.
    GIA G-1969.

Ferguson, John. "Christ the Lord Is Risen Today!" SATB, snare drm,
    picc.    AFP 0800646363.

Gallus, Jacob. "This Is the Day the Lord Has Made." SSAATTBB,
    opt brass qrt.    CPH 98-1702.

Goemanne, Noel. "Fanfare for Festivals." SATB, org, 3 tpts, timp.
    AG 298 (score & inst pts); AG 7137 (choral pts).

Handel, G.F. "Alleluia" (two choruses) in *Coronation Anthems.* SAATB,
    org.    OXF.

Mardirosian, Haig. "Christians to the Paschal Victim." SATB,
    org/brass.    MSM-50-4006.

Mendelssohn, Felix. "Jesus Christ, My Sure Defense-Alleluia" in *Chantry
    Choirbook.* SATB.    AFP 0800657772.

Robinson, McNeil. "Spice She Brought and Sweet Perfume." SATB,
    opt S solo, org.    PRE 312-41437.

Rutter, John. "Christ the Lord Is Ris'n Again." SATB, org.
    OXF 42.362.

Schalk, Carl. "Be Known to Us, Lord Jesus." SATB, opt brass, org.
    CPH 98-3202.

Schalk, Carl. "Day of Arising." SATB, org.    AFP 0800658671.

Sjolund, Paul. "Christ Is Risen." SATB, org/pno.    WAL W2160.

Stanford, Charles Villiers. "Ye Choirs of New Jerusalem" in *Anthems
    for Choirs 1.* SATB, org.    OXF.

Vulpius, Melchior. "Arisen Is Our Blessed Lord" in *Chantry Choirbook.*
    SATB, dbl chorus/instr.    AFP 0800657772.

Wolff, S. Drummond. "Christ the Lord Is Risen Today; Alleluia!"
    SAB, opt kybd.    MSM-50-4400.

Young, Carlton. "Hearts and Voices Raise." SATB, tri, tamb.
    AFP 6000097182.

167

## CHILDREN'S CHOIRS

Beck, W. Leonard. "An Easter Carillon." U, kybd.    OXF.

Hruby, Dolores. "Christ the Lord Is Risen." U, kybd.
AFP 11-0325.

Lau, Robert. "This Is the Day." U, kybd, fl.    CG CGA-552.

McRae, Shirley W. "Now the Green Blade Rises." 2 pt, kybd, fl, hb,
tamb.    CG CGA795.

## KEYBOARD/INSTRUMENTAL

Albrecht, Mark. "Alleluia! Jesus Is Risen" in *Timeless Tunes for Flute and
Piano*. Kybd, fl.    AFP 0800659074.

Leavitt, John. *A Little Easter Suite.* Org.    CPH 97-6646.

Manz, Paul. *Improvisations for the Easter Season.* Org.    MSM 10-402.

Neswick, Bruce. "Fortunatus" in *Augsburg Organ Library: Easter.* Org.
AFP 0800659368.

Organ, Anne, Krentz. "Earth and All Stars" in *Let it Rip! At the Piano.*
Pno.    AFP 0800659066.

Rutter, John. *Variations on an Easter Theme (O filii et filiae).* Org duet.
OXF 19-375715.

Vogt, Emanuel. "Mfurahini, haleluya" in *Augsburg Organ Library: Easter.*
Org.    AFP 0800659368.

## HANDBELL

Afdahl, Lee J. "Jesus Christ Is Risen Today." 3-5 oct. L3.
AFP 0800659899.

Dobrinski, Cynthia. "Hope Eternal." 3-5 oct. (w/fl) L3.
AG 1553.

Helman, Michael. "Jesus Christ Is Risen Today." L3+.
LOR 20/1156L.

McChesney. Kevin. "Come, Ye Faithful, Raise the Strain." 3-5 oct.
L5.    CPH 97-6744.

Simpson, F. Thomas. "A Trumpet Chorale." 2-3 oct. L2.    AG 2137.

Thompson, Martha Lynn. "Thine Is the Glory." 4-5 oct. L2.
CPH 97-5891.

## PRAISE ENSEMBLE

Brewster, Lincoln, Danny Chambers and Israel Houghton. "All I
Need" in *Hosanna Music Songbook 13.* SAT[B], kybd.
INT 13576.

Evans, Darrell. "Trading My Sorrows" in *Only God for Me Songbook.*
SAT[B], kybd.    INT 15297.

Fragar, Russell. "Friends in High Places" in *Shout to the Lord 2000 Songbook.* SAT[B], kybd.    INT 14247.

Harris, Ron and Carol Harris. "In This Very Room."
INT RH 0202 (SATB, kybd, also available SSA); RH C0202
(reh/perf cass).

Howard, Rob. "Christ the Lord Is Risen Today."
WRD 0 80689 37327 5.

Kenoly, Ron/arr. Dan Burgess. "Jesus Is Alive."    INT 41120C
(SATB, kybd); 4112TX (choraltrax); 41120R (orch).

Larson, Lloyd. "We Walk by Faith." SATB, kybd.    BEC BP 1537.

Lister, Mosie. "Love Was in the Room."    LIL AN-1871 (SATB,
kybd); MU-2429D (choraltrax); MU-5512 T (CD);
OR-2429 (orch).

Pethel, Stan. "We Have Seen the Risen Lord."    HOP BC 970
(SATB, kybd); GC 970C (reh/perf cass).

Pote, Allen. "This Is a Day of Rejoicing."    HOP C 5074 (SATB,
div, opt brass/timp); C 5074 B (SATB, kybd).

# March 31, 2002

### The Resurrection of Our Lord
### Easter Evening

## INTRODUCTION

The news of God's salvation, brought to the world in the
death and resurrection of Christ, is worthy of the grandest of celebrations. The gospel from Luke 24 may remind
us that the meal we receive in the sacrament of communion is a share in Christ's death and resurrection. Like the
disciples who met with the Lord on the evening of his resurrection, Christ's words and his supper burn in us as well.

## PRAYER OF THE DAY

Almighty God, you give us the joy of celebrating our
Lord's resurrection. Give us also the joys of life in your
service, and bring us at last to the full joy of life eternal;
through your Son, Jesus Christ our Lord, who lives and
reigns with you and the Holy Spirit, one God, now and
forever.

## READINGS

Isaiah 25:6-9

God prepares a splendid feast on the holy mountain. All peoples will toast God's salvation.

Psalm 114

Hallelujah. (Ps. 114:1)

1 Corinthians 5:6b-8

Christ clears out the old yeast in all people, making ready for the purity of the new.

Luke 24:13-49

The resurrected Christ makes himself known to two of the disciples in the breaking of bread.

## COLOR  White

## THE PRAYERS

Rejoicing in the resurrection, let us remember in prayer the church, the world, and all those in need.

*A BRIEF SILENCE.*

Guide the newly baptized and all who renew their baptismal vows to walk in newness of life; we pray:

**Hear us, living God.**

Pour out your wisdom on all who work for justice and peace in our world; we pray:

**Hear us, living God.**

Give hope through the healing power of the resurrection to all who are unloved and forgotten, poor and hungry, hospitalized and sick (especially); we pray:

**Hear us, living God.**

Free us from prejudice and empower us to share the good news of the resurrection without partiality; we pray:

**Hear us, living God.**

Open our eyes to recognize you in this eucharist and in the suffering and joy of daily life; we pray:

**Hear us, living God.**

*HERE OTHER INTERCESSIONS MAY BE OFFERED.*

Unite our voices with all your saints until we join them at the great and promised feast; we pray:

**Hear us, living God.**

Receive our prayers and hopes, O God, and fill us with the risen life of Christ our Lord.

**Amen**

## IMAGES FOR PREACHING

Here at the conclusion to Luke's gospel, beyond the Emmaus story, Jesus once more takes food. It is not enough to say that by offering his hands to the disciples' touch and by eating a bit of fish, he banished their doubts about the reality of his return. He desired to do more than elicit a response such as, "Ah, yes, it really is Jesus back from the dead, looking rather healthy and able to take nourishment again!"

Eating food is the most ordinary of physical acts, but sharing food is always a spiritual event. The simple act of eating the fish the disciples offered him signaled the renewal of fellowship between Jesus and his own.

But then, instead of stopping right there with what would have been a typical happy ending, the narrative explodes far beyond that room in Jerusalem, beyond the intimate gathering of old friends, beyond the sharing of a tentative touch and a bit of fish. The story does not end when the disciples' doubts are cancelled and their fears are calmed.

Jesus looks back over the whole of Israel's sacred story and then looks forward to the continuation of that story with the ingathering of all nations. The disciples should remain for the moment in Jerusalem, but soon enough divine power will descend upon them and send them out to cross borders and boundaries they have no way of imagining as yet.

So Luke remembers Easter night not simply as the warm reunion of Jesus and his disciples in the intimacy of a house in Jerusalem. He sees their Easter experience not as an end but as a beginning. He wants us to study that tiny fellowship gathered around the resurrected Jesus, sharing a scrap of fish. That small company is infinitely hospitable. The table of the Lord is set for all nations. Scripture as read and interpreted by the resurrected Jesus demands it, desires it, offers it.

## HYMNS FOR WORSHIP
### SUGGESTED HYMNS

That Easter day with joy was bright   LBW 154

Abide with us, our Savior   LBW 263

Stay with us   WOV 743

Alleluia! Jesus is risen   WOV 674, TFF 91

### ADDITIONAL HYMNS AND SONGS

As I walked home to Emmaus   LLC 362

Day of arising   OBS 54

Open our eyes, Lord   W&P 113, TFF 98

169

## MUSIC FOR THE DAY

### CHORAL

De Majo, Gian Francesco/ed. Ronald A. Nelson. "Alleluia." U, kybd. CPH 98-3474.

Hovland, Egil. "Stay with Us." SATB, org.   AFP 11-11019.

Pelz, Walter. "Stay with Us." SATB, fl, org.   CPH 98-2920.

Praetorius, Michael. "Stay with Us" in *Chantry Choirbook*. SATB.

Shute, Linda Cable. "This Joyful Eastertide." 2 pt, hb, perc. AFP 11-10750.

### KEYBOARD/INSTRUMENTAL

Keesecker, Thomas. "Stay with Us" in *Piano Impressions for Easter*. Pno. CPH 97-6695.

Powell, Robert. "Earth and All Stars" in *Sing a New Song*. Org. AFP 11-10766.

# Monday, April 1

### THE ANNUNCIATION OF OUR LORD (TRANSFERRED)

Nine months before Christmas we celebrate the annunciation. In Luke we hear how the angel Gabriel announced to Mary that she would give birth to the Son of God and she responded, "Here am I, the servant of the Lord." Ancient scholars believed that March 25 was also the day on which creation began and the date of Jesus' death on the cross. Thus from the sixth to eighth centuries, March 25 was observed as New Year's Day in much of Christian Europe.

### JOHN DONNE, PRIEST, 1631 (TRANSFERRED)

This priest of the Church of England is commemorated for his poetry and spiritual writing. Most of his poetry was written before his ordination and is sacred and secular, intellectual and sensuous. He saw in his wife, Anne—a marriage that resulted in his imprisonment— glimpses of the glory of God and a human revelation of divine love. In 1615 he was ordained, and seven years later he was named dean of St. Paul's Cathedral in London. By that time his reputation as a preacher was firmly in place.

# Thursday, April 4

### BENEDICT THE AFRICAN, CONFESSOR, 1589

Born a slave on the island of Sicily, Benedict first lived as a hermit and labored as a plowman after he was freed. When the bishop of Rome ordered all hermits to attach themselves to a religious community, Benedict joined the Franciscans, where he served as a cook. Although he was illiterate, his fame as a confessor brought many visitors to the humble and holy cook, and he was eventually named superior of the community. A patron saint of African Americans, Benedict is remembered for his patience and understanding when confronted with racial prejudice and taunts.

# Friday, April 6

### ALBRECHT DÜRER, PAINTER, 1528;
### MICHELANGELO BUONARROTI, ARTIST, 1564

These two great artists revealed through their work the mystery of salvation and the wonder of creation. Dürer's work reflected the apocalyptic spirit of his time, when famine, plague, and social and religious upheaval were common. He was sympathetic to the reform work of Luther but remained Roman Catholic. At his death, Luther wrote to a friend, "Affection bids us mourn for one who was the best." Michelangelo was a sculptor, painter, poet, and architect. His works such as the carving of the Pieta and the statue of David reveal both the tenderness and the grandeur of humanity.

# EASTER

*A holy openness is at the heart*

*of the good news*

# Images *of the* Season

If you were to choose an image for this season,

what would it be? An Easter lily? Certainly flowers will bedeck

many Christian sanctuaries on the day of resurrection.

Flowers splash color and fragrance on our celebration of the end of winterdeath, the warmth of spring and the promise of summer to come. They tie the salvation-history feast to the annual passage of seasons that calls to mind death and rebirth. A lily could be an Easter image, but there was no lily that first Easter.

Or would you choose a trumpet? The lily flute suggests it and reminds us that Easter is a celebration. We will probably have festal music and perhaps more people than at any time during the year at Easter worship in our church. The hymns will be sung with gusto. A trumpet might be nice, but there was no trumpet and no special music that first Easter.

A biblical image for Easter leads us in an entirely different direction. It is a cavity—an empty space, an open tomb. How about negative space for Easter? Negative space is the blank interval between things, the hollow between the words, the gap begging to be filled with something. The negative space of Easter is "the place where his body lay"—a place now strangely, surprisingly empty, vacated.

The music of negative space is silence—or, better yet, a gasp! You sing this involuntary song when air rushes into a vacuum in your lungs. What now? Just when you thought it had gotten as bad as it possibly could.... The gospel narratives of Easter focus on this negative space. In Matthew the angel directs the women by saying, "Come, see the place where he lay"—the place where he is not. In John, bookend angels define the limits of an absent corpse, but the shelf is empty except for cloths that once wrapped a now missing body.

Nature, they say, abhors a vacuum. Something is always waiting to fill it up. So it is with narrative, too. Something waits to fill this story-vacuum. Do not even plan to have it completed on Easter Day! The church gives us a whole season—fifty days—to do it. A full seventh of a year. An entire season to begin to fill the emptiness that Jesus' missing body creates. But even fifty days is not enough. How many Easters have you passed through? Are you finished yet? Ours is the hundredth generation of disciples who have tried to plumb the meaning of the vacuum and still we are not done with it.

A holy openness is at the heart of the good news that centers on Jesus of Nazareth, God's Christ. Tombs are meant to be conclusions—the end punctuation on the sentence of a human story. The Greek word for "tomb" is the same as the word for "remembrance." What remains after we are done living is someone to remember us, at least for a little while. In Jesus, however, God removes the final stop to the story-sentence and then does even more. The risen Jesus meets disciples and breathes resurrection breath into them. Christ invites them to follow on the road of discipleship, to begin by sharing in his baptismal drowning and rebirth. By placing his Spirit inside them, Christ entrusts his name to them and gives them new identity. Christ is now in them, as they are in Christ. Breaking bread with them, Christ offers himself as food to sustain a new way of living, a new kind of life in the world. But most of all, Christ blows wide open the endings of all our stories. The bookends of Jesus' vacated burial shelf are finally taken away to reveal a new life without limits, one marked by forgiveness and raised from the dead for new possibilities.

Even fifty days will not be enough now! This story continues, on and on, spiraling into God's future. On Easter Day the empty tomb gapes nakedly open, confounding all our sense of endings. The vacuum stands as cosmic contradiction to all that we believe to be real and true. What will get blown into this vacuum? What will fill it? The answer is God's best surprise. The answer is this: you and me. We are now a continuation of God's Easter story. The risen Lord goes before us, calling us to adventures yet to begin. But even more, the risen Lord goes *with* us, because he is in us as we are in him. God's story calls us on. The vacuum beckons!

172

# Environment *and* Art *for the* Season

Students of interior design learn that the focal point

of a room is not the furniture or the view, but rather the people

in the room. All seating, tables, lamps, wall coverings, rugs,

and framed art are placed with respect to the utility, comfort, and enjoyment of the people who will use the room. Another design insight is that "we are what we put on our walls." More than almost anything else within a room, the art that hangs on our walls reveals who we are.

These insights from the secular world are applicable to the environment of the church. In the Easter season, we celebrate our new life in Christ as the baptized people of God. In the worship space, the assembly of living people joined in prayer and thanksgiving is a sign of Christ's victory over death. In Easter, we would do well to image the resurrection in the midst of the assembly. The art we place on the walls of the nave or suspend from the ceiling above the worshiping assembly will celebrate who we are.

We see an image of the resurrection in the springtime rebirth of the earth, and flowers and gardens as natural signs of the new Eden of the resurrection. Like poinsettias at Christmas, the trumpet lily is a traditional Easter element for most churches. This familiar white flower is just one among many lily varieties, however. Consider using Casa Blanca or Calla lilies in groupings throughout the worship space as accents to the traditional trumpet lilies. The gold and orange of tiger lilies is another option for a more vivid accent.

Along with lilies, spring flowers from parishioners' gardens can be spread throughout the church, rather than clustered near the altar. Common white garden perennials include David phlox, Pee Gee hydrangea, Powis Castle artemesia, and Itsaul White dianthus. Baskets of white flowers can look stunning hung along the walls of the nave. The cross, the paschal candle, and the font can all be ornamented with flowers. The cross might be adorned with a floral wreath. Some churches create a floral cross that is placed outdoors as a sign of the resurrection. This complete floral coverage of the cross is less appropriate within the worship space. Any ornamentation of the cross within the worship space should not overwhelm or obscure its primary identity. The paschal candle can

be dressed with a ring of flowers or fragrant leaves, and cut flowers or potted plants can grace the font. Even the water in the baptismal font can be moderately scented with a natural floral essence.

Spring tree blossoms are delightful. One church hung bare branches against a purple backdrop during Lent and then replaced these branches with flowering forsythia for Easter. Another option for churches that use bare branches during Lent is to keep the same branches but dress them with flowers and herbs for Easter. This undertaking is not for the novice designer, however. Unless the bare branches can be artfully adorned with a look of abundant splendor, the effect can be haphazard or silly.

The whites and golds of Easter vestments and paraments should look fresh, crisp, and beautiful. If a fabric is yellowed or stained, it is better not to use it at all. The altar tablecloth does not have to be ornate. A fine, simple white linen will look handsome and perhaps more successfully convey that the Lord's supper is our common meal than an elaborate, brocaded cloth.

The Easter gospels are visually interpreted in traditional iconography. Either by the font or in the narthex, an icon of the *Anastasis* might be displayed. This icon depicts Christ opening the gates of hell and releasing Adam and Eve into salvation. Icons depicting Christ's appearances to his disciples in the upper room, at Emmaus, or as the Good Shepherd may be used during this season, as well. Pentecost is a wonderful subject for visual art, whether depicted in traditional iconography or in a more abstract, contemporary style. In this season of the resurrection and the ascension of our Lord, we may wish to create an environment that draws our eyes upward. Banners might be unfurled or flags waved to punctuate our alleluias. Children or dancers might carry in procession high poles from which long strips of white and gold fabric or ribbon cascade. White, diaphanous fabrics might be hung to allow light to pass through. Nancy Chinn's book *Spaces for Spirit* (Chicago: LTP, 1998) has many

173

color plates showing the effective use of sheer fabrics.

You can use white or gold bunting outdoors if your climate and weather will allow. Use these (weatherproof) fabrics only if they will look fresh and withstand spring rain and winds. Seasonal outdoor wreaths on doors and potted spring plants near doorways are joyful signs of welcome.

Some churches plan major art installations during the Easter season or for the Day of Pentecost. Lucinda Naylor creates a large installation in her church each year to announce the movement from Lent to Easter rejoicing. Her work is always designed to enhance the worship experience. Says Naylor:

> People are always looking for meaning in art—especially religious art. Meaning doesn't have to come from a literal telling or representation.... It can come from making people's imaginations fly. And in liturgy the well-placed use of color, symbol, form, can help people's imagination flow towards the divine. But we, as artists, have to be liturgically and theologically educated enough to plant the right kind of imaginative seeds,...which at Easter might mean resurrection, renewal, baptism, etc., but so much more than "think spring."

Naylor, like many artists, finds that her wildest, most daring installations are created for the Day of Pentecost. (These installations then remain in the church throughout the summer.) Naylor admits that she does not always achieve her original goal when taking risks. One year she designed an installation of "tongues of fire" ribbons to dance over the heads of the congregation. The volunteers who worked to hang the ribbons on a grid of fishing line strung the ribbon too tightly. The outcome was a jumbled mess of tangled ribbon that was, in Naylor's words, "a monstrosity." In the end, the fishing line that was to have been invisible to the eye became an integral part of the final installation. The work's ultimate form conveyed fishing and net imagery along with the flames—an effect that the pastor found inspiring.

The moral to Naylor's story is twofold. On the one hand, it speaks to a need for flexibility and resilience when working with volunteers on art projects. On the other hand, it is a cautionary tale about the requirements of successful designs—appropriate ways to install materials, sufficient volunteers to do the work, and enough time to solve problems. For many seasonal installations, proper lighting is also crucial.

Good planning for seasonal installations also depends on good communication with other church staff and volunteers. One artist had secured both approval and budget from the church staff for a particular plan for Pentecost. She bought a red fabric that she used to wrap around the beams of the church. The altar guild members, who had not been consulted about the plan, were unhappy with it and experienced the installation as an intrusion into their role as caretakers of the church environment.

Many churches have permanent images of Pentecost inside the church. Tanja Butler describes a Pentecost installation that makes use of a permanent element within the church.

> [Pentecost this year] featured an arrangement of diaphanous strips of red and yellow material radiating from the stained glass roundel of a descending dove, looping up to the small crown portion taken from the cast iron Advent wreath, and descending with ribbons and wind chimes into the congregation.

Stained glass window depictions of the Spirit as dove or of tongues of fire descending can be highlighted with votive candles and flowers.

Bright red and orange flowers in the worship space can contribute to a vibrant Pentecost environment. Use whatever local flowers are in season: peonies, wild roses, poppies, bleeding hearts, and geraniums. Another way to create a red environment is to ask the assembly to dress in red on the Day of Pentecost. This is a simple but powerful statement that the Spirit dwells within the community of believers.

Pentecost is a fitting time for a parish community festival, perhaps with a multicultural focus. In fact, it is a traditional day for picnics. These activities recall the origin of Pentecost as a harvest festival, the Feast of Weeks. In Jewish practice, the first fruits of the harvest were offered to God at this festival, fifty days after Passover. For this reason, wheat or other grains might be incorporated into the environment for worship, while strawberries or other first fruits might be included on the picnic menu.

A windsock is a fine outdoor image of the Spirit. Often these can be found in the shape of colorful fish or birds. Hung with wind chimes or ribbon, a windsock flying in the wind can be a delightful invitation to the larger community to join the church in its renewed mission and ministry.

174

# Preaching *with the* Season

The earthly ministry of Jesus begins in a desert

and ends at a tomb. All four of our evangelists narrate

the story in such a way that desert and tomb bracket

the public life of Jesus. Those places look so dry, so sterile, so unpromising. A desert is a wasteland, lacking the rainfall necessary to generate and sustain life. Water has been described as the amniotic fluid of planet earth, and a desert simply lacks that life-giving and life-sustaining fluid.

In biblical parlance, the desert is called "a land not sown" (Jer. 2:2), a place that is "empty of human life" (Job 38:26), a "howling wilderness waste" (Deut. 32:10). Deserts are lonely and unforgiving places, not fit for human habitation. Biblical writers speak of the desert as home only for jackals and vultures and wild asses—and for strange people like John the Baptist. What did Jesus see stirring and welling up in John that he went out to the desert to meet him?

Tombs are as forbidding as the desert. Tombs are signs and markers of mortality and weakness. They speak bluntly of death, which Paul called "the last enemy." According to Mosaic law, contact with a tomb, as with a corpse, rendered a person not sinful but unclean, impure, and in need of cleansing before that person can participate in worship at the sanctuary. So pious people went out before Passover and the other pilgrimage festivals and painted the tombs on the outskirts of their communities with whitewash. They wanted pilgrims, unfamiliar with their territory, to be able to avoid contamination as they marched up to Jerusalem and the temple.

Ordinary people avoided tombs, but the demon-possessed were not ordinary people. Mark tells of a man with an unclean spirit who lived among the tombs, howling on the mountainside, resisting the effort to tame him (Mark 5:1-20).

The desert in the beginning and the tomb at the end of Jesus' ministry are exceedingly unpromising locations. All deserts and tombs exist at the outer edge of human life. In fact, they are beyond the outer edge. Life exists only on this side of the desert and on this side of

the tomb. Here as always, the evangelists invite us to look harder, deeper, and see the hand and breath and power of God in things and places that seem at first to be weak and foolish and even dead.

Jesus walked the narrow way that led from the hot sand of the desert to the hard wood of the cross and the stone cold slab of the tomb. The evangelists beckon us to see the power of God and the love of God leading Jesus all the way along that path. And then they gather us round the tomb and with one voice insist that the love of God in Jesus is unconquered, invincible, immortal.

At the tomb of Jesus, the whole world is turned upside down. Each gospel has a different way of giving utterance to that great overturning worked by God.

In Matthew's gospel a deep quaking disturbs "the old eternal rocks" and guards fall to the ground like dead men. The angel of the Lord descends to the tomb and, putting shoulder to stone, rolls it back. The guards take money and agree to spread a lie, thus continuing the politics of the old age. The resurrected Jesus inaugurates a new age and a new community consisting of all nations joined in a common discipleship.

John pondered long and hard on the old story of women at the tomb on the first Easter morning. For John, the resurrection transformed the tomb of Jesus from an impure receptacle for a corpse into a new Holy of Holies. He views that dark space where they laid the body of Jesus as the new inner sanctum of the universe. His crucified and resurrected body is the new Ark of the Covenant, the place where heaven touches earth, where God comes to touch, heal, and dwell within humankind.

To believe in the resurrection means to make disciples out of all the badly fragmented nations (Matthew), to enter into the death and resurrection of Jesus and to let him enter into us and dwell deeply in us (John). Easter beckons us to new and expanded life.

175

# Shape *of* Worship *for the* Season

## BASIC SHAPE OF THE EUCHARISTIC RITE

- Confession and Forgiveness: see alternate worship text for Easter in *Sundays and Seasons*
- Or, use Confession and Forgiveness with sprinkling from the seasonal rites section

## GATHERING

- Greeting: see alternate worship text for Easter
- Use the Kyrie throughout Easter
- As the hymn of praise, use "This is the feast of victory"

## WORD

- For dramatic readings based on lectionary passages, use *Scripture Out Loud!* (AFP 0806639644) for the second and third Sundays of Easter and Pentecost Day
- For contemporary dramas based on lectionary passages, use *Can These Bones Live?* (AFP 0806639652) for the second and fourth Sundays of Easter and Pentecost Day
- Use the Nicene Creed
- The prayers: see the prayers in the Easter section of *Sundays and Seasons*

## BAPTISM

- Consider observing Pentecost Day (May 19) as a baptismal festival

## MEAL

- Offertory prayer: see alternate worship text for Easter
- Use the proper preface for Easter; use the proper preface for Pentecost on Pentecost Day
- Eucharistic Prayer: in addition to four main options in *LBW,* see "Eucharistic Prayer E: The Season of Easter" in *WOV* Leaders Edition, p. 69; and "Eu-

charistic Prayer F: The Day of Pentecost" in *WOV* Leaders Edition, p. 70

- Invitation to communion: see alternate worship text for Easter
- Post-communion prayer: see alternate worship text for Easter

## SENDING

- Benediction: see alternate worship text for Easter
- Dismissal: see alternate worship text for Easter

## OTHER SEASONAL POSSIBILITIES
### ROGATION BLESSING

- See seasonal rites section; may be used to conclude worship on the sixth Sunday of Easter (traditionally, rogation days are the Monday, Tuesday, and Wednesday before Ascension Day) or at another time when such a blessing is appropriate

### VIGIL OF PENTECOST

- A celebration for this evening could be modeled on the Easter Vigil, but using these elements:
  - Service of Light (from *LBW,* pp. 142–44)
  - Service of Word (from the prayer of the day through the hymn of the day)
  - Service of Baptismal Affirmation (from *LBW,* pp. 199–201, with the congregation gathering around the font, space permitting; water may be sprinkled from the font during the recitation of the creed)
  - Service of Communion (from the offering through the dismissal)

# Assembly Song *for the* Season

Easter Day resounds with joyous alleluias that

reverberate for the weeks to come. The Easter season

is the culmination of a liturgical journey that began in Advent.

In the preceding seasons, various portions of the liturgy have been highlighted while other portions have been absent. The resurrection of Jesus Christ fulfills God's promise of salvation and brings wholeness to all of creation—a theme reflected in the liturgy celebrated in all its fullness and glory. "This is the feast of victory for our God. Alleluia!"

## GATHERING

Choose service music that can be elaborated in various ways for the next seven weeks through Pentecost. If you prepared elaborate settings of liturgical songs for Easter Day, get the most out of your effort by using those settings throughout the season. Plan ahead so that various instrumentalists, handbells, or choir descants can be included each week. Use both the Kyrie and hymn of praise in the gathering rite. Remind people it is still Easter by singing a well-known Easter hymn as the entrance hymn.

## WORD

Alleluias can serve as congregational refrains to the psalms and proper verses. The alleluias from "The strife is o'er, the battle done" (LBW 135), "Good Christian friends, rejoice and sing" (LBW 144), or "O sons and daughters of the King" (LBW 139) make excellent psalm refrains. The reading of the Easter gospels is a highlight of the proclamation of the word. Surround it with an abundance of alleluias before and after the reading. Several acclamations with multiple alleluias can be found in the service section of *With One Voice, Libro de Liturgia y Cántico,* and *This Far by Faith.* Expand your musical horizon a little bit. Remember, everyone can sing *¡Aleluya!* in Spanish!

## MEAL

The Easter season is a time to continue the focus on the meal begun during the Three Days. Send a clear message to the congregation that this is the victory feast. The presentation of the gifts can be done in a more elaborate way than usual. If you normally set the table in a simple manner, consider presenting the gifts in an offertory procession. A processional cross, banners, or bells might accompany the gifts in the procession. As the gifts are presented sing "The trumpets sound, the angels sing" (W&P 139) or "At the Lamb's high feast we sing" (LBW 210). Sing the preface dialogue and proper preface, add handbells, brass, or descants to the "Holy, holy, holy Lord," and sing the acclamations of the eucharistic prayer. During the distribution, continue singing alleluias. Mozart's "Alleluia canon" (WOV 677), the South African "Alleluia" (WOV 610, TFF 26), or "Alleluia, alleluia, give thanks" (WOV 671) are easily sung without music as the congregation moves to communion.

## SENDING

The breadth of the Easter liturgy requires a full sending rite as well to balance and bring to a conclusion that which has gone before. This may be the one season to use both a post-communion song and a sending hymn. Use the post-communion song to clear the table in as festive a way as the table was set. Consider learning a new setting of "Thank the Lord/Thankful hearts" or sing "Hallelujah! We sing your praises" (WOV 722, TFF 158) as the post-communion song. Following the blessing, sing another Easter hymn prior to the dismissal. Send the people out on a joyful note with a festive postlude that could include additional instruments or have the people sing a reprise of a favorite alleluia refrain from the liturgy as they leave.

177

# Music *for the* Season

## VERSE AND OFFERTORY

Cherwien, David. *Verses for the Sundays of Easter.* U, org.    MSM 80-400.

Farrell, Bernadette. "Eastertide Gospel Acclamation."
    OCP 7172CC.

*Gospel Acclamations.* Cant, choir, cong, inst.    MAY 0862096324.

Pelz, Walter L. *Verses and Offertories: Easter—The Holy Trinity.* SATB, org.
    AFP 0800649044.

Schalk, Carl. *Verses and Offertory Sentences: Part IV, Easter Day through
    Easter 7.*    CPH 97-5504.

Willan/Gunther. *Verses for the Easter Season.* SATB, kybd.
    CPH 98-3057.

## CHORAL

Bouman, Paul. "Jesus Christ, the Lord of Joy." SATB, org, opt brass.
    CPH 98-4896.

Collins, Dori Erwin. "Offering." SATB, U, pno, fl, opt hb.
    AFP 0800659694.

Hassler, Hans L. "Cantate Domino" in *Chantry Choirbook.* SATB.
    AFP 0800657772.

Helman, Michael. "We Walk by Faith." SATB, pno, opt fl, hb.
    AFP 0800659759.

Hopp, Roy. "God of Grace and God of Laughter." SATB, ob,
    hp/pno.    AFP 0800659570.

Jennings, Kenneth. "With a Voice of Singing." SATB.
    AFP 0800645669.

Jordan, Alice. "See the Land, Her Easter Keeping." SATB, org.
    RME EC92-107.

Kallman, Daniel. "In Thee Is Gladness." SATB, kybd, opt fl/C inst.
    MSM-50-9058.

Kosche, Kenneth T. "It Is a Good Thing." SATB.
    AFP 0800659635.

Schalk, Carl. "Thine the Amen." SATB, org, opt cong.
    AFP 0800646126.

St. Thomas Moore Group. *Easter Mysteries.* SATB, kybd, gtr, inst.
    OCP 9858GC.

## CHILDREN'S CHOIRS

Burkhardt, Michael, arr. "Come Holy Ghost, Our Souls Inspire."
    2 pt, hb.  MSM-50-5551.

Cherwien, David, arr. "O Holy Spirit Enter In." U/2 pt/SATB, org.
    CPH 983484.

Ramseth, Betty Ann and Melinda Ramseth Hoiland. *A Child's World.*
    U, Orff, opt gtr.    AFP 0800653173.

Sleeth, Natalie. *Bread and Wine: Eight Pieces for the Communion Service.*
    CG CGC8.

## KEYBOARD/INSTRUMENTAL

Albrecht, Mark. *Festive Processionals.* Org, tpt.    AFP 0800657985.

*Augsburg Organ Library: Easter.* Org.    AFP 0800659368.

Burkhardt, Michael. "Come, You Faithful, Raise the Strain" (Varia-
    tions). Org.    MSM 10-414.

Callahan, Charles. "An Easter Prelude for Flute and Organ." Org, fl.
    MSM 20-460.

Leavitt, John. *A Little Easter Suite.* Org.    CPH 97-6646.

Manz, Paul. *Improvisations for the Easter Season.* Org.    MSM 10-402.

Rutter, John. *Variations on an Easter Theme.* Org duet.
    OXF 0-19-375715.

Webster, Richard. *Paschal Suite for Organ and Trumpet.* Org, tpt.
    AFP 080065692X.

## HANDBELL

Helman, Michael. "Gift of Finest Wheat." 3-5 oct. L3.
    AFP 0800657365.

Rogers, Sharon Elery. "Easter Medley." 3-5 oct. L3+.
    JEF JHS9266.

Thompson, Martha Lynn. "Hymn of Promise." 3-5 oct.    AG 1519.

Young, Philip. "Good Christians, Rejoice and Sing." 2-3 oct.
    AFP 080065627X.

## PRAISE ENSEMBLE

Founds, Rick/arr. Gary Rhodes. "Lord, I Lift Your Name on High."
    SATB, kybd.    WRD 301 0805 160.

Pethel, Stan. "Celebrate the Victory." SATB, kybd.
    LOR 10/2334LA.

Pote, Allen. "On the Third Day."    HOP F1000 (SATB, kybd, hb);
    F1000B (brass).

178

# Alternate Worship Texts

## CONFESSION AND FORGIVENESS

Blessed be God, who chose us in Christ.
Let us come to the fountain of mercy.

*Silence for reflection and self-examination.*

Living God,
in the light of the resurrection
we rejoice to see our Lord Jesus,
by whose wounds we have been healed.
Trusting in your promise of mercy,
we repent of our sins.
Forgive our quickness to turn from you
and our slowness of heart to believe.
Renew in us the grace of baptism,
and guide us in the way of truth and life. Amen

In great mercy God has given us
a new birth into a living hope
through the resurrection of Jesus Christ.
In obedience to our Lord's command,
I forgive you all your sins
in the name of the Father, and of the ✙ Son,
and of the Holy Spirit.
Amen

## GREETING

Alleluia! Christ is risen.
**Christ is risen indeed. Alleluia!**

The grace of our risen Savior,
the love of God,
and the communion of the Holy Spirit
be with you all.
**And also with you.**

## OFFERTORY PRAYER

Blessed are you, O God,
ruler of heaven and earth.
Day by day you shower us with blessings.
As you have raised us to new life in Christ,
give us glad and generous hearts,
ready to praise you and to respond to those in need. Amen

## INVITATION TO COMMUNION

When we eat this bread we share the body of Christ.
When we drink this cup we share the blood of Christ.
Reveal yourself to us, O Lord,
in the breaking of bread,
as once you revealed yourself to your disciples.

## POST-COMMUNION PRAYER

We have tasted your goodness, O God,
in your gifts of word and sacrament.
May our hearts burn within us,
that we may proclaim your mighty acts
and joyfully live as your chosen people;
through Jesus Christ, our Lord.
**Amen**

179

## BLESSING

The God of all grace,
who has called you to eternal glory in Christ,
✙ restore, support, and strengthen you
through the power of the Holy Spirit,
now and forever.
**Amen**

## DISMISSAL

Go in peace. Serve the risen Christ.
**Thanks be to God. Alleluia, alleluia!**

# Seasonal Rites

## Confession and Forgiveness with Sprinkling

*The order may be used before the entrance hymn or in conjunction with the entrance hymn (in procession). People are invited to turn and face the baptismal font or the place where the sprinkling bowl is located. All stand.*

St. Paul writes, "As many of you as were baptized into Christ have clothed yourselves with Christ" (Gal. 3:27). As we are clothed with Christ, we are clothed with God's mercy. Standing under that mercy, we freely confess that we have sinned and fallen short of the glory of God.

*Silence for reflection and self-examination.*

In the waters of Holy Baptism
God liberated us from sin and death,
joining us to the death and resurrection
of our Lord Jesus Christ.
**Our life in Christ is nothing more
than a constant return to our baptism.
We daily die to sin and rise to newness of life.**

### THANKSGIVING OVER THE WATER
Gracious God,
from age to age
you made water a sign of your presence among us.
In the beginning your Spirit brooded over the waters,
calling forth life that was good.
You led the people of Israel safely through the Red Sea
and into the land of promise.
In the waters of the Jordan,
you proclaimed Jesus Beloved,
the One upon whom your favor rests.

By water and the Spirit
you adopted us as your daughters and sons,
making us heirs of the promise,
and laborers for the Reign of God.

In the sprinkling of this water,
remind us of our baptism.

Shower us with your Spirit ✝,
so that we may experience anew
your forgiveness,
your grace,
and your love.
**Amen**

*An ordained minister sprinkles the people with water, in silence or during the entrance hymn (in procession). The singing of Psalm 51 in Lent and Psalm 117 in Easter, with an appropriate antiphon, may be used in place of the entrance hymn. After the sprinkling, the liturgy of Holy Communion continues with the greeting (Kyrie or hymn of praise), and prayer of the day.*

Reprinted by permission from *Worship '99* (January) Chicago: Division for Congregational Ministries, Evangelical Lutheran Church in America.

## Rogation Blessing

### PRAYER FOR SEEDS
*Hold seeds aloft.*
Creating God, you have given seed to the sower and bread to the people. Nourish, protect, and bless the seeds which your people have sown in hope. By your loving and bountiful giving, may they bring forth their fruit in due season, through Jesus Christ our Lord. Amen

### PRAYER FOR THE SOIL
*Hold soil aloft.*
Giver of life, we give you thanks that in the richness of the soil, nature awakens to your call of spring. We praise you for the smell of freshly tilled earth, the beauty of a cleanly cut furrow, and a well-plowed field. We ask that you help us to be good stewards of this land. In the name of the one who gives us new life, Jesus Christ our Lord. Amen

### PRAYER FOR WATER AND RAIN
*Hold water aloft.*
Sustaining God, we receive the fruits of the earth from you. We give you thanks for the smell of the earth after rain, for its welcome cooling, and its necessary hydration for the land. We ask that the rain come as often as it is needed so that the crops may flourish and the coming harvest be indeed bountiful. Amen

From *Worship from the Ground Up: A Worship Resource for Town and Country Congregations.* Dubuque, Iowa: Center for Theology and Land, University of Dubuque and Wartburg Theological Seminaries, 1995. Contact 319/589-3117 for reprint permission.

# April 7, 2002

Second Sunday of Easter

## INTRODUCTION

In today's gospel reading, the risen Christ appears to the disciples who have locked themselves into a house. In the midst of their fear he offers his peace so that they might go forth to proclaim God's victory over death. In this Sunday liturgy, Christ offers us his peace anew as we prepare to come to the table where he gives us his body and blood. As we receive bread and cup he says, Do not doubt but believe that I am with you. He sends us forth to be his peacemakers in a community and a world locked in by fear and injustice.

## PRAYER OF THE DAY

Almighty God, with joy we celebrate the festival of our Lord's resurrection. Graciously help us to show the power of the resurrection in all that we say and do; through your Son, Jesus Christ our Lord, who lives and reigns with you and the Holy Spirit, one God, now and forever.

## READINGS

### Acts 2:14a, 22-32

After the Holy Spirit came to the apostles on Pentecost, Peter preaches the gospel to the gathered crowd. He tells them that Jesus, who obediently went to his death according to God's plan, was raised from the dead by God. Finally, he appeals to scripture, quoting Psalm 16:8-11, to show that Jesus is the Messiah: though crucified, the risen Jesus is now enthroned.

### Psalm 16

In your presence there is fullness of joy. (Ps. 16:11)

### 1 Peter 1:3-9

This epistle was written to encourage Christians who were suffering for their faith. It begins by praising God for the resurrection of Jesus, which produces hope, then and now.

### John 20:19-31

One week after Easter, Christ still comes to those who believe in him; he seeks any who may have missed his offer of peace and life through his resurrection.

## COLOR White

## THE PRAYERS

Rejoicing in the resurrection, let us remember in prayer the church, the world, and all those in need.

*A BRIEF SILENCE.*

For the church, born anew to a living hope, that it may joyfully proclaim the resurrection, we pray:

**Hear us, living God.**

For nations divided by war, those living under oppression, and peoples separated by conflict, that you bless them with peace, justice, and reconciliation, we pray:

**Hear us, living God.**

For all who suffer (especially), that amid their pain they may rejoice in a living hope, we pray:

**Hear us, living God.**

For those who face trials and those who struggle with doubt or unbelief, that your presence, peace, and forgiveness may be made known to them, we pray:

**Hear us, living God.**

For this assembly, that freed from fear and united at your holy table, we may be strengthened in faith for ministry to the world, we pray:

**Hear us, living God.**

*HERE OTHER INTERCESSIONS MAY BE OFFERED.*

In thanksgiving for Thomas and all the saints who have confessed the crucified and risen Christ, that inspired by their faith, we may praise you on earth until we receive our eternal inheritance in heaven, we pray:

**Hear us, living God.**

Receive our prayers and hopes, O God, and fill us with the risen life of Christ our Lord.

**Amen**

## IMAGES FOR PREACHING

In Thomas's response to the disciples' announcement, "We have seen the Lord," he is quite specific. Note what he does not say. He does not demand to touch Jesus to assure himself that Jesus is solid. He does not say that he wants to study Jesus' profile or hear Jesus recite some familiar words or watch Jesus break bread or perform some

181

other familiar act. His request goes beyond merely establishing that this post-Easter Jesus is the same one whom he had known previously.

Thomas goes on and on about Jesus' wounds. That is what is on his mind. Conventional wisdom is that God should conquer death and devil by superior force and with incredible ease, by divine fiat, by speaking a word, by a flick of the wrist or a snap of the fingers. Thomas's request raises for us the most profound question: Does God really gain the victory by means of wounds—the wounds on the body of Jesus, the wounds on the body of the church? That is to say, instead of throwing the divine weight around and bludgeoning the opposition with superior force, does God gain the victory through the cross, through wounds, through self-giving love?

The story of Thomas tells us that Easter faith is more than saying, "God has reversed the death of Jesus." It is more than declaring, "Jesus lives and breathes again!" The resurrected Jesus continues to be the crucified Jesus. The Easter Jesus still bears in his hands and side the marks of his wounding. His hands and side have not healed. Indeed, the wounds will never go away. The Easter gospel is that the universe is held secure in wounded hands of unimaginably deep love and compassion.

## WORSHIP MATTERS

In the communion liturgy, the peace of Christ is shared. It is more than a time of meeting, greeting, and sharing a handshake, hug, or smile. The sharing of the peace of Christ—particularly when it takes place immediately before the offering—is brought into sharp focus by the words of Matthew's gospel: "So when you are offering your gift at the altar, if you remember that your brother or sister has something against you, leave your gift there before the altar and go; first be reconciled to your brother or sister, and then come and offer your gift" (5:23-24). First and foremost, the sharing of the peace is an act of reconciliation—mending broken relationships, sharing forgiveness, and receiving from Christ the gift of peace. In the course of teaching and preaching about the peace, we can help others to make this connection.

## LET THE CHILDREN COME

"Peace be with you," the risen Christ declares to the gathering of fearful disciples, as he opens his hands to show them his wounds. Presiders, to help children see

that Christ's gift of peace given to the disciples is the same gift given now, put down the book, look at the people, be graceful and generous in opening your arms and hands to proclaim the peace of the Lord. Invite members of the assembly to greet one another with the same graceful, generous gift of peace.

## HYMNS FOR WORSHIP
### GATHERING

Come, you faithful, raise the strain   LBW 132

Now the feast and celebration   WOV 789

### HYMN OF THE DAY

Jesus lives! The victory's won!   LBW 133

### ALTERNATE HYMN OF THE DAY

We walk by faith and not by sight   WOV 675

Christ is risen! Shout hosanna!   HFW (AUSTRIA)

### COMMUNION

O sons and daughters of the King   LBW 139

Spirit of the living God   TFF 101, W&P 129

Stay with us   WOV 743

### SENDING

Peace, to soothe our bitter woes   LBW 338

Hallelujah! We sing your praises   WOV 722, TFF 158

Spirit song   TFF 105, W&P 130

### ADDITIONAL HYMNS AND SONGS

God has spoken, bread is broken   BL

Make songs of joy   LBW 150

Shalom   WOV 724

Shout to the Lord   W&P 124

Show me your hands, your feet, your side   ISH 21

Good news, alleluia!   DH 65

## MUSIC FOR THE DAY
### PSALMODY

Haas, David. "Show Me the Path." GIA G-4579.

Howard, Julie. *Sing for Joy: Psalm Settings for God's Children*. LTP.

Inwood, Paul. STP, vol. 5

Marshall, Jane. *Psalms Together*. CGA. CGC-18.

Peña, Donna. "Sing Unto the Lord" in *Canten al Señor*. Choir, cong, gtr. GIA G-3352.

Sedio, Mark. PW A.

## CHORAL

Cherwien, David. "Blessing Be and Glory to the Living One." U, opt desc, org, 2 C inst.   AFP 0800657861.

Clemens, James E. "Although the Doors Were Closed." SATB. CPH 98-3394.

Couperin-Vree. "In Thee O Lord Is Fullness of Joy." SA, org. CPH 98-2059.

Gieschen, Thomas. "Jesus Stood Among Them." SATB, org. AFP 6000101686.

Hassler, Hans Leo. "Because You Have Seen Me, Thomas" in *Ten Renaissance Motets.* SATB.   WLP ESA-1635-8.

Helman, Michael. "We Walk by Faith." SATB, pno, opt fl/hb. AFP 0800659759.

Hillert, Richard. "Image of the Unseen God." SATB, org. AFP 0800659627.

Marenzio, Luca. "Because You Have Seen Me, Thomas." SATB. CPH 98-2617.

## CHILDREN'S CHOIRS

Conlon, Joan. "Come, Enjoy God's Festive Springtime." U, kybd, opt C inst.   AFP 0800646487.

Mendelssohn, Felix/arr. Patrick Liebergen. "Sing with a Joyful Heart." 2 pt, kybd.   HWG CMR9505.

## KEYBOARD/INSTRUMENTAL

Held, Wilbur. "O filii et filiae" in *Augsburg Organ Library: Easter.* Org. AFP 0800659368.

Kloppers, Jacobus. "Jesus, meine Zuversicht" in *Five Chorale Preludes.* Org.   CPH 97-5733.

Leupold, Anton Wilhelm. "Jesus, meine Zuversicht" in *Augsburg Organ Library: Easter.* Org.   AFP 0800659368.

Manz, Paul. "Jesus, meine Zuversicht" in *Improvisations for the Easter Season.* Org.   MSM 10-402.

Pelz, Walter. *A Festive Intrada.* Org.   CPH 97-6675.

## HANDBELL

Dicke, Martin. "Rondo for Bells." 2 oct. L3.   AFP 0800659945.

McChesney, Kevin. "Festiva." 3-5 oct. L3.   LAK HB93029.

Wagner, Douglas E. "A Joyous Ring." 3-5 oct. L4.   AG 1468

Wagner, Douglas E. "Peals of Joy." 3 oct. L2+.   LOR 20/1157L.

## PRAISE ENSEMBLE

Carter/arr. Hayes. "Standing on the Promises."   ALF 16163 (SATB, kybd); 16167 (choraltrax); 16164 (orch).

Davis, Geron and Becky Davis/arr. Camp Kirkland. "Mercy Saw Me."   INT 12117 (SATB, kybd); 12118 (choraltrax); 12115 (orch).

Zschech, Darlene. "Shout to the Lord."   INT 09707 (SATB, kybd); 09708 (choraltrax); 09705 (orch).

# Tuesday, April 9

### DIETRICH BONHOEFFER, TEACHER, 1945

Bonhoeffer was a German theologian who, at the age of twenty-five, became a lecturer in systematic theology at the University of Berlin. In 1933, and with Hitler's rise to power, Bonhoeffer became a leading spokesman for the confessing church, a resistance movement against the Nazis. He was arrested in 1943. He was linked to a failed attempt on Hitler's life and sent to Buchenwald, then later to Schoenberg prison. After leading a worship service on April 8, 1945, at Schoenberg, he was taken away to be hanged the next day. His last words as he left were, "This is the end, but for me the beginning of life."

A hymn written by Bonhoeffer shortly before his death includes the line, "By gracious powers so wonderfully sheltered, and confidently waiting come what may, we know that God is with us night and morning, and never fails to greet us each new day" (WOV 736). Bonhoeffer's courage is a bold witness to the paschal mystery of Christ's dying and rising.

# Wednesday, April 10

### MIKAEL AGRICOLA, BISHOP OF TURKU, 1557

Agricola was consecrated as the bishop of Turku in 1554 without papal approval. As a result, he began a re-form of the Finnish church along Lutheran lines. He translated the New Testament, the prayerbook, hymns, and the mass into Finnish and through this work set the rules of orthography that are the basis of modern Finnish spelling. His thoroughgoing work is particularly remarkable in that he accomplished it in only three years. He died suddenly on a return trip after negotiating a treaty with the Russians.

183

# April 14, 2002

### Third Sunday of Easter

## INTRODUCTION

In this story from Luke's gospel, the risen Christ joins two disciples overcome by the apparent loss of one who was "a prophet mighty in deed and word" (Luke 24:19). Here Luke presents us with two things: our yearning to see the risen Christ, and the Lord's response to that yearning. In word (interpreting the scriptures) and sacrament (breaking the bread) he reveals himself to them and to us. In these two central actions—readings with preaching and thanksgiving with communion—our eyes are opened to see the risen Lord in our midst. Here is the center of our weekly gathering on the Lord's Day.

## PRAYER OF THE DAY

184

O God, by the humiliation of your Son you lifted up this fallen world, rescuing us from the hopelessness of death. Grant your faithful people a share in the joys that are eternal; through your Son, Jesus Christ our Lord, who lives and reigns with you and the Holy Spirit, one God, now and forever.

## READINGS

Acts 2:14a, 36-41

Today's reading is the conclusion of Peter's sermon preached following the giving of the Holy Spirit to the apostles on the day of Pentecost. The center of his preaching is the bold declaration that God has made the crucified Jesus both Lord and Christ.

Psalm 116:1-3, 10-17 (Psalm 116:1-4, 12-19 [NRSV])

I will call upon the name of the Lord. (Ps. 116:11)

1 Peter 1:17-23

The First Letter of Peter uses the image of "exile" to describe the experience of new Christians who are no longer at home in the non-Christian world. Their faith in the risen Christ distinguishes them from their ancestors and neighbors and calls them to place their faith and hope in God.

Luke 24:13-35

The colorful story of Jesus' appearance to two disciples on the road to Emmaus answers the question of how Jesus is to be recognized among us. Here, he is revealed through the scriptures and in the breaking of bread.

## COLOR  White

## THE PRAYERS

Rejoicing in the resurrection, let us remember in prayer the church, the world, and all those in need.

*A BRIEF SILENCE.*

Rekindle the hearts of church leaders and all the baptized to study the holy scriptures with diligence; we pray:

**Hear us, living God.**

Open the hearts of those welcomed into the church at Easter to the surprising gifts of your grace; we pray:

**Hear us, living God.**

Inspire the leaders of nations to discover new ways of overcoming divisions and mistrust; we pray:

**Hear us, living God.**

Open our eyes to your presence among us as we share our bread with the hungry; we pray:

**Hear us, living God.**

Comfort with your abiding love those living with sorrow, loneliness, chronic pain, or sickness (especially); we pray:

**Hear us, living God.**

Reveal yourself to this assembly in the proclamation of the word and the breaking of the bread; we pray:

**Hear us, living God.**

*HERE OTHER INTERCESSIONS MAY BE OFFERED.*

Stay with us, O Lord, until we join all the saints at your heavenly feast of unending joy; we pray:

**Hear us, living God.**

Receive our prayers and hopes, O God, and fill us with the risen life of Christ our Lord.

**Amen**

## IMAGES FOR PREACHING

Two nearly anonymous disciples are walking down a road. This idea is not really in the text, but the story seems to imply that the disciples are on a downward path, down in the dumps. They are described as "looking sad," but that is too mild a rendering of the original. Their hopes had been shattered, they thought, by the crucifixion of Jesus. So they are slouching along, with faces turned not to the rising sun but toward the setting sun, toward deepening darkness.

As they walk that path, and it is a familiar one, the unrecognized resurrected Jesus joins them. When they arrive at Emmaus, Jesus starts down the road by passing their village. They hold him back with words later formed into a hymn, "Abide with us, fast falls the eventide."

So Jesus enters the house, sits at the table, and assumes the role of head of the family. He, not they, takes bread, blesses and breaks it, and gives it to them. It finally dawns on them. The guest is Jesus. And their hearts burn within them while he is with them.

What is revealed to disciples today in this story? That Jesus is alive? Surely, but it is more than that. In the breaking of the bread it is revealed that God liberates us through life that is crucified, through life that is broken like bread and given for others to eat. And we begin to see the alternative: Life is cursed and killed when we grasp and hoard and are unwilling to share, or, worse yet, when we try to use and dominate the lives of others. What dawns on us is the triumph of the Crucified, the victory and the power of suffering love.

In our pilgrimage we often wander off the path into the dark, but God in Christ keeps on showing up in our lives, questioning and conversing, illuminating and guiding, abiding and not abandoning. The Emmaus story prods us to ponder from where we have come, where we are going, and with whom we are traveling.

## WORSHIP MATTERS

In the Emmaus story from Luke 24, two travelers do not recognize the risen Christ until Jesus shares a meal with them. "When he was at the table with them, he took bread, blessed and broke it, and gave it to them. Then their eyes were opened, and they recognized him" (vv. 30-31).

Likewise, we who do not recognize the face of Jesus Christ in our neighbors can have our eyes opened in the sharing of the Lord's supper. Especially when the breaking of bread is supported by strong preaching and worshipful celebration, and when worship leadership is provided by people of all ages, both male and female, and people from a variety of backgrounds and positions, our eyes can be opened to the face of Jesus in those very people with whom we worship. This, in turn, can open our eyes to Jesus in the face of those who are not part of our worshiping community.

## LET THE CHILDREN COME

In communion, Jesus invites us to remember him by taking the simple things of the earth, giving thanks for them as part of the bounty of God's creation, and sharing in and with them the body and blood of Christ given for each of us. We are not about the business of historical reenactment, however, and so we do not break the bread at the moment in the institution narrative where that action of Jesus is recounted because it is not yet time to distribute the bread and wine that has been blessed for us. Rather, the bread is broken following the Lord's Prayer, when it is time to share this meal of the kingdom. Teach children to watch for the breaking of the bread.

## HYMNS FOR WORSHIP
### GATHERING

Hallelujah! Jesus lives   LBW 147
We come to the hungry feast   WOV 766
We bring the sacrifice of praise   W&P 150

### HYMN OF THE DAY

Stay with us   WOV 743

### ALTERNATE HYMN OF THE DAY

With high delight let us unite   LBW 140
As I walked home to Emmaus   LLC 362

### COMMUNION

Come with us, O blessed Jesus   LBW 219,
    HFW (inclusive text)
For the bread which you have broken   LBW 200
Here is bread   W&P 58

### SENDING

Let us talents and tongues employ   WOV 754, TFF 232
Shout for joy loud and long   WOV 793
This joyful Eastertide   LBW 149, WOV 676

### ADDITIONAL HYMNS AND SONGS

You satisfy the hungry heart   WOV 711
Come, risen Lord   LBW 209
Day of arising   OBS 54

## MUSIC FOR THE DAY

### PSALMODY

Cooney, Rory. "Our Blessing Cup" in *Cries of the Spirit.*
OCP 5270GC.

Cooney, Rory and Gary Daigle.    PCY, vol. 4.

Glynn, John, in PS 2.

Howard, Julie. *Sing for Joy: Psalm Settings for God's Children.*    LTP.

Joncas, Michael.    STP, vol. 2.

Sedio, Mark.    PW A.

### CHORAL

Bach, J.S. "Christ Is Arisen" in *Bach for All Seasons.* SATB, kybd.
AFP 080065854X.

Busarow, Donald. "Become to Us the Living Bread." SAB, C inst, org.
MSM-50-4406.

Cruger, Johann. "Awake, My Heart, with Gladness" in *Chantry Choirbook.* SATB, C inst, org.    AFP 0800657772.

Hovland, Egil. "Stay with Us." SATB, org/pno.
AFP 0800658825.

Lovelace, Austin. "What Shall I Render to My God?" SATB, org.
SMP Canyon 5503.

Schalk, Carl. "Be Known to Us, Lord Jesus." SATB, opt brass, cong, org.    CPH 98-3202.

Tiefenbach, Peter. "What Shall I Render to the Lord?" in the *Augsburg Choirbook.* SATB.    AFP 0800656784.

Praetorius, Michael. "Stay with Us, Lord" in *Chantry Choirbook.* SATB.
AFP 0800657772.

Schalk, Carl. "Day of Arising." SATB, org.    AFP 0800658671.

### CHILDREN'S CHOIRS

Christopherson, Dorothy. "The Lord Is My Light." U, kybd, fc.
AFP 0800647475.

Ellen, Jane. "Love One Another." 2 pt, kybd, fl.    KJO 6271.

### KEYBOARD/INSTRUMENTAL

Cherwien, David. "This Joyful Eastertide," in *Amazing Grace: Four for Piano.* Pno.    AFP 0800659031.

Cherwien, David. "Stay with Us" in *Eight for Eighty-Eight.* Pno.
AFP 0800659058.

Ferko, Frank. "Orientis partibus" in *Augsburg Organ Library: Easter.* Org.
AFP 0800659368.

Haan, Raymond. *Canonic Variations on "With High Delight."* Org.
CPH 97-6167.

Keesecker, Thomas. "Stay with Us" in *Piano Impressions for Easter.* Kybd.
CPH 97-6695.

### HANDBELL

Hall, Jeffery H. "I Am the Bread of Life." 3-5 oct. L3.    CPH 97-6659.

Helman, Michael. "Let Us Talents and Tongues Employ." 3-5 oct. L3.
AFP 0800659937.

Kinyon, Barbara Baltzer. "A Gift of Joy." 2-3 oct. L3.    CG CGB202.

Moklebust, Cathy. "Come, Let Us Eat." 3-5 oct. L2.    CG CGB152.

### PRAISE ENSEMBLE

Green, Melody/arr. Benjamin Harlan. "There Is a Redeemer." SATB,
kybd.    HAL 08742224.

Morgan, Reuben/arr. Richard Kingsmore. "I Give You My Heart" in
*Hillsongs Choral Collection.* SATB, kybd.    INT 16996.

# Friday, April 19

OLAVUS PETRI, PRIEST, 1552;
LAURENTIUS PETRI, ARCHBISHOP OF UPPSALA, 1573;
RENEWERS OF THE CHURCH

These two brothers are commemorated for their introduction of the Lutheran movement to the Church of Sweden after studying at the University of Wittenberg. They returned home and, through the support of King Gustavus Vasa, began their work. Olavus published a catechism, hymnal, and a Swedish version of the mass. He resisted attempts by the king to gain royal control of the church. Laurentius was a professor at the university in Uppsala. When the king wanted to abolish the ministry of bishops, Laurentius persuaded him otherwise, and the historic episcopate continues in Sweden to this day. Together the brothers published a complete Bible in Swedish and a revised liturgy in 1541.

The Easter hymn "Praise the Savior, now and ever" (LBW 155) uses a Swedish folk tune and can be sung to commemorate the contributions of the Petris and the Swedish church to our worship life.

186

# April 21, 2002

Fourth Sunday of Easter

## INTRODUCTION

To some contemporary Christians, the image of Christ as shepherd appears outdated. Yet the continuing popularity of this "Good Shepherd Sunday" and the tender psalm appointed for the liturgy begs the question, Why are moderns attracted to a shepherd? Is it not that we yearn for guidance, protection, and strength in a world filled with much chaos, violence, and fast-paced change? The liturgy this day offers the image of our God as shepherd: the one who guides us—not out of this world, but in and through it with staff and overflowing cup, with word and holy supper.

Today the church remembers a faithful shepherd of God's flock, Anselm, archbishop of Canterbury in the eleventh century.

## PRAYER OF THE DAY

God of all power, you called from death our Lord Jesus, the great shepherd of the sheep. Send us as shepherds to rescue the lost, to heal the injured, and to feed one another with knowledge and understanding; through your Son, Jesus Christ our Lord, who lives and reigns with you and the Holy Spirit, one God, now and forever.

*or*

Almighty God, you show the light of your truth to those in darkness, to lead them into the way of righteousness. Give strength to all who are joined in the family of the Church, so that they will resolutely reject what erodes their faith and firmly follow what faith requires; through your Son, Jesus Christ our Lord, who lives and reigns with you and the Holy Spirit, one God, now and forever.

## READINGS

### Acts 2:42-47

Today's reading is a description of life in the community following Peter's sermon on the day of Pentecost, when the Spirit was outpoured on God's people. This new community is founded on the teachings of the apostles and sustained in the breaking of the bread.

### Psalm 23

The Lord is my shepherd; I shall not be in want. (Ps. 23:1)

### 1 Peter 2:19-25

The First Letter of Peter addresses the theme of suffering. Jesus, the shepherd and guardian of our souls, models for Christians how one suffers for doing what is right.

### John 10:1-10

Jesus uses an image familiar to the people of his day to make a point about spiritual leadership. Good shepherds bring people to life through Jesus, but those who avoid Jesus are dangerous to the flock.

## COLOR White

## THE PRAYERS

Rejoicing in the resurrection, let us remember in prayer the church, the world, and all those in need.

*A BRIEF SILENCE.*

For all who gather to hear the voice of the shepherd and feast at his table, that you make them one in ministry to the world, we pray:

**Hear us, living God.**

For bishops, pastors, and all who serve as shepherds, that they remain faithful to the apostles' teachings and to the breaking of bread, we pray:

**Hear us, living God.**

For all who govern the nations and all in positions of power over others, that they seek justice and the welfare of all people, we pray:

**Hear us, living God.**

For all who live without adequate food, clothing, or shelter, that your abundance be shared among the people of the world, we pray:

**Hear us, living God.**

For all who walk through valleys of fear, loneliness, violence, loss, or illness (especially), that you anoint them with your comfort and love, we pray:

**Hear us, living God.**

For this assembly, that the daily refreshment of our baptism lead us to extend the loving care of our good shepherd to those in need, we pray:

**Hear us, living God.**

HERE OTHER INTERCESSIONS MAY BE OFFERED.

For Anselm, archbishop of Canterbury, and all the saints who followed Christ the shepherd in life and in death, we give thanks and praise. Make us faithful in our calling all the days of our lives, until we dwell with them in your house forever; we pray:

**Hear us, living God.**

Receive our prayers and hopes, O God, and fill us with the risen life of Christ our Lord.

**Amen**

## IMAGES FOR PREACHING

In ancient Sumeria, Babylonia, Assyria, and Egypt, kings and generals and gods were regularly described as the "shepherds" of the people. In Israel, Yahweh was described as the shepherd who went before the flock (the people), guiding them to pasture, protecting them with the staff, whistling to the straying and gathering them, carrying the lambs.

Jeremiah 23 and Ezekiel 34 and 37 speak of the current crop of Israelite leaders as unfaithful shepherds. But the prophets promise that the day is coming when Yahweh will personally assume the role of shepherd or will set over the flock one shepherd, namely the coming messianic son of David.

Shepherding is a political term. It is all about a community of people and their leaders. It is a traditional image of kingship or generalship. Jesus seizes it and declares that he is the good leader for whom people long hungered.

Others who claim to be shepherd seek a different kind of glory and wish to exercise a different kind of leadership. The false shepherds want to be leaders over the flock without a cross, without self-giving, without love. They are not givers of life. They come "only to steal and kill and destroy" (John 10:10).

Military historians coined the expression "chateau generals" to describe those high officers on both sides of the First World War who lived the lives of country gentlemen a safe distance from the horror of the trenches. They commandeered comfortable chateaux, dined every night on hot food and excellent wine, and slept between clean sheets, far from the battles in which their flocks of young soldiers went like sheep to the slaughter.

The Good Shepherd is no chateau general, and people have known it through the centuries. They hear him calling them to follow on a path that he himself travels, the path of weakness and vulnerability, of service and openness to others. The journey seems so dangerous, but he promises that the path leads to abundant life.

## WORSHIP MATTERS

Jesus said, "[The shepherd] calls his own sheep by name and leads them out.... He goes ahead of them, and the sheep follow him because they know his voice" (John 10:3-4). We recognize the voice of God and hear our name called in the reading of God's word—the Bible. Scripture reading is at the heart of our worship as the body of Christ.

How scripture is read is important, because such reading gives human voice to the word of God. Lectors must be trained, so that the word of God will be read well. Congregations might consider whether providing a written scripture insert dulls the human voice as our ears give way to our eyes. Worship planners might also make use of a variety of reading methods—including unison reading, antiphonal reading, and reading in narrative parts—to enrich the reading of scripture.

## LET THE CHILDREN COME

Our names are dear to us. We know we are at home when a familiar voice tenderly calls us by name. The Good Shepherd calls his own sheep by name, and they know his voice. They belong to him. Do you know the children in your parish by name? Before or after worship, have greeters or other worship leaders welcome each child by name.

## HYMNS FOR WORSHIP
### GATHERING

Praise the Lord, rise up rejoicing    LBW 196
What a fellowship, what a joy divine    WOV 780
Step by step    W&P 132

### HYMN OF THE DAY

Savior, like a shepherd lead us    LBW 481

### ALTERNATE HYMN OF THE DAY

The King of love my shepherd is    LBW 456
Lead me, guide me    W&P 84

## COMMUNION

At the Lamb's high feast we sing   LBW 210
Draw us in the Spirit's tether   WOV 703
Precious Lord, take my hand   WOV 731

## SENDING

With God as our friend   LBW 371
I'm so glad Jesus lifted me   WOV 673

## ADDITIONAL HYMNS AND SONGS

Shall we gather at the river   WOV 690
God, here is my life and my will   BL
Our Paschal Lamb, that sets us free   WOV 679
Have no fear, little flock   LBW 476
My shepherd will supply my need   HFW

## MUSIC FOR THE DAY

### PSALMODY

*See listing for the fourth Sunday in Lent.*

### CHORAL

Bairstow, Edward C. "The King of Love My Shepherd Is." SATB, org. OXF A46.

Callahan, Charles. "Feed My Sheep." Solo, org.   MSM 40-901.

Handel, G.F. "All We Like Sheep Have Gone Astray" in *Messiah*. SATB, org.   Various ed.

Handel, G.F. "And With His Stripes We Are Healed" in *Messiah*. SATB, org.   Various ed.

Handel, G.F. "He Shall Feed His Flock" in *Messiah*. S/A solo. Various ed.

Leavitt, John. "The Lord Is My Shepherd." SATB, kybd. CPH 98-3594.

Pelz, Walter. "The King of Love My Shepherd Is." SATB, org, fl, opt cong.   AFP 0800646010.

Sateren, Leland B. "They Follow Me." SATB.   AFP 6000102550.

Thompson, Randall. "The Lord Is My Shepherd." SATB, pno, org/hp.   ECS 2688.

Thomson, Virgil. "My Shepherd Will Supply My Need." SATB. HWG 2046.

### CHILDREN'S CHOIRS

Hopson, Hal H. "Gentle Shepherd, Kind and True." U, opt. hb. CG CGA 687.

Leavitt, John. "Blessed Are They." U, 2 pt, kybd.   CPH 98-35550.

Roberts, William Bradley. "Savior, Like a Shepherd Lead Us." U, kybd, opt C inst.   AFP 0800646983.

Wagner, Douglas. "Brother James' Air." 2 pt, kybd.   BEL BSC9921.

### KEYBOARD/INSTRUMENTAL

Bach. J.S. "Sheep May Safely Graze" in *The Biggs Book of Organ Music*. Org.   H. W. Gray GB 645.

Biery, James. "Union Seminary" in *Tree of Life*. Org. AFP 0800655370.

Harbach, Barbara. "Crimond" in *Augsburg Organ Library: Easter*. Org. AFP 0800659368.

Tambling, Christopher. "Pastorale" in *Fifteen Pieces for Organ*. Org. MAY 1400015.

### HANDBELL

Afdahl, Lee J. "The Lord's My Shepherd." 3-5 oct. AFP 0800659902.

Geisler, Herbert. "Safely in the Shepherd's Arms." 2-3 oct. MSM 30-816.

Kinyon, Barbara B. "My Shepherd Will Supply My Need." 3-5 oct. L4-.   BEC HB200.

O'Kelly, Niamh. "In Pastures Green." 2 oct. L2.   LOR 20/1190L.

### PRAISE ENSEMBLE

Martin, Angerman. "Footprints in the Sand."   FLA A 6998 (SATB, kybd); MC 5180 (cass track); LB 5351 (orch).

Morgan, Reuben. "My Heart Will Trust" in *Shout to the Lord 2000 Songbook*. SAT[B], kybd.   INT 14247.

Roth, John. "David's Song." 2 pt, kybd.   CPH 98-3184.

# Sunday, April 21

## ANSELM, ARCHBISHOP OF CANTERBURY, 1109

This eleventh-century Benedictine monk stands out as one of the greatest theologians between Augustine and Thomas Aquinas. He is counted among the medieval mystics who emphasized the maternal aspects of God. Of Jesus, Anselm says, "In sickness you nurse us and with pure milk you feed us." He is perhaps best known for his theory of atonement, the "satisfaction" theory. In this theory he argued that human rebellion against God demands a payment, but because humanity is fallen, it is incapable of making that satisfaction. Therefore, God takes on human nature in Jesus Christ in order to make the perfect payment for sin.

# April 28, 2002

### Fifth Sunday of Easter

## INTRODUCTION

The gospel readings for the last Sundays of Easter shift the focus from Christ's presence among the disciples to his care for those who will continue his mission in the world. While the scriptural context is obvious, Christ addresses his contemporary disciples as well. To the community that bears his name he says, You will also do the works that I do. The church keeps Easter's fifty days in order to discern anew its baptismal witness in the world. In our community, at this time, with these gifts, what witness can we offer to the one who is our way, our truth, and our life?

## PRARYER OF THE DAY

O God, form the minds of your faithful people into a single will. Make us love what you command and desire what you promise, that, amid all the changes of this world, our hearts may be fixed where true joy is found; through your Son, Jesus Christ our Lord, who lives and reigns with you and the Holy Spirit, one God, now and forever.

## READINGS

### Acts 7:55-60

Stephen was one of the seven men chosen by the apostles to serve tables so that the apostles could be free to serve the word (Acts 6:1-6). Stephen does more than distribute food, however. For his preaching of God's word, Stephen becomes the first martyr of the faith.

### Psalm 31:1-5, 15-16

Into your hands, O Lord, I commend my spirit. (Ps. 31:5)

### 1 Peter 2:2-10

The First Letter of Peter has spoken of Christians as people reborn through the resurrection of Christ. Now, those who have experienced this new birth in baptism are encouraged to seek the nourishment of scripture that provides spiritual growth.

### John 14:1-14

John's gospel records here some of Jesus' final words to his disciples before his departure. As the one through whom God is known, he promises always to go before them and to continue to act on their behalf.

## COLOR White

## THE PRAYERS

Rejoicing in the resurrection, let us remember in prayer the church, the world, and all those in need.
*A BRIEF SILENCE.*

For bishops, pastors, and all leaders in the church, that they may faithfully equip the baptized to fulfill their calling as the priesthood of all believers, we pray:
**Hear us, living God.**

For leaders in the world, that they may defend the rights of all people to practice their religious faith, we pray:
**Hear us, living God.**

For the unemployed, the underemployed, and for those demeaned or victimized by their work, that they may find new opportunities for joy and satisfaction, we pray:
**Hear us, living God.**

For those who live with illness or whose hearts are troubled (especially), that they may find comfort in Christ the way, the truth, and the life, we pray:
**Hear us, living God.**

For this assembly, that nourished with the body and blood of Christ, we may declare the deeds of the one who called us out of darkness into marvelous light, we pray:
**Hear us, living God.**

*HERE OTHER INTERCESSIONS MAY BE OFFERED.*

For Stephen and for all the martyrs and saints who have lived and died in faith, we give thanks. Bring us with them to the dwelling place prepared for us; we pray:
**Hear us, living God.**

Receive our prayers and hopes, O God, and fill us with the risen life of Christ our Lord.
**Amen**

## IMAGES FOR PREACHING

Years ago Scottish theologian James Moffatt, in his translation of the New Testament, rendered John 14:6 with these words, "I am the true and living Way." That translation accurately captures the relationship among the three nouns *way, truth,* and *life.* The topic of the para-

190

graph is "the way," and each sentence in the paragraph comments on the way from a different angle.

In ancient as in modern times, the term *way* has been used to identify goat paths in the mountains, streets and avenues in developed cities, roads traveled by marching armies, routes taken by religious pilgrims, and the course followed by ships at sea. The same word is used figuratively to speak of human conduct, as in "way of life."

Taking their cue from Isaiah 40 ("Prepare the way of the Lord"), the people associated with the Dead Sea called themselves "the Way" and described their members as those who "have chosen the Way" and apostates as having "turned aside from the Way." They called their community rules "the regulations of the Way." The earliest believers in Christ also described themselves as "belonging to the Way" (Acts 9:2; 19:9, 23; 22:4; 24:14, 22).

Human life is a swift voyage or passage between birth and death. For too many people, life is a mindless migration, a series of wrong turns, a wandering in circles, a groping in the dark, a trudging on a treadmill. Jesus calls out to all travelers, inviting them to know him as "the way." Many of us are fascinated with short cuts and the fast track, but experience teaches that those easy paths often lead to dead ends. In Christ the human journey becomes intentional and compassionate, a pilgrimage toward holiness, toward God, toward real life.

## WORSHIP MATTERS

Our understanding of Christian liturgy as the "work of the people" means in part that there is more than one leadership role. Two of the most prominent roles are those of presiding minister and assisting minister. What happens when the presiding minister is uncomfortable leading some portion of the liturgy—for example, chanting the dialogue of the eucharistic prayer because he or she cannot carry a tune? Is it better for a presider who cannot chant to give this portion of the liturgy to an assisting minister who can? In this case, the answer is no. The logic of the eucharistic prayer is that greeting the congregation from the table, inviting the people to give thanks, and leading them in the prayer of thanksgiving is a unified action carried out by the presider. Speaking the dialogue and preface is a perfectly acceptable alternative to chanting, and preserves the sensible differentiation of leadership roles.

## LET THE CHILDREN COME

Jesus is our teacher in prayer. Pay special attention to the intercessions. How can children be encouraged to add their voices when the people pray?

## HYMNS FOR WORSHIP
### GATHERING

Awake, my heart, with gladness    LBW 129
Christ is made the sure foundation    LBW 367, WOV 747

### HYMN OF THE DAY

Come, my way, my truth, my life    LBW 513

### ALTERNATE HYMN OF THE DAY

Now all the vault of heaven resounds    LBW 143
Alleluia, alleluia, give thanks    WOV 671

### COMMUNION

Jesus, thy boundless love to me    LBW 336
To go to heaven    TFF 181
Be my home    W&P 16

### SENDING

I know that my Redeemer lives    LBW 352
Soon and very soon    WOV 744

### ADDITIONAL HYMNS AND SONGS

You are the way    LBW 464
Father, we thank you    WOV 704
God of love, have mercy    DH 10
We are God's people    BH 383

## MUSIC FOR THE DAY
### PSALMODY

DeBruyn, Randall.    STP, vol. 4
Hopson, Hal H. *Psalm Refrains and Tones*.    HOP 425.
Sedio, Mark.    PW A.
Smith, G. Boulton, in PS 2.

### CHORAL

Cherwien, David. "Blessing Be and Glory to the Living One." U or
   2 pt, org, 2 C insts.    AFP 0800657861.
Hampton, Keith. "He's Got the Whole World." SATB, solo.
   AFP 0800659600.
Haydn, F. J. "In Thee, O Lord." SATB, pno/org.    Sam Fox PS 103.
Hobby, Robert. "You Are a Chosen Race." SATB.    CPH 98-3537.

Mendelssohn, Felix. "Jesus Christ, My Sure Defense—Alleluia" in *Chantry Choirbook.* SATB.    AFP 0800657772.

Pelz, Walter. "Peace I Leave with You." SATB.    AFP 0800645650.

Scott, K. Lee. "The Call" in *Sing a Song of Joy: Vocal Solos for Worship.*
AFP 0800652827 (ML); 0800647882 (MH).

Vaughan Williams, Ralph. "O Taste and See." SATB, org.
OXF 44.415.

Vaughan Williams, Ralph. "The Call" in *Five Mystical Songs.* B solo,
kybd.    GAL I.5038.

### CHILDREN'S CHOIRS

Drexler, Richard/arr. Rusty Edwards. "O Lord, I Worship You."
U, kybd, opt C inst.    AFP 0800674219.

Sleeth, Natalie. "God Is Like a Rock." U, kybd.    CG CGA-395.

Vaughan Williams, Ralph. "This Is the Truth." 2 pt, kybd.
OXF 44.087.

Vaughan Williams, Ralph/ed. Marie Stultz. "The Call." U, kybd.
MSM 50-9912.

### KEYBOARD/INSTRUMENTAL

Burkhardt, Michael. "Truro" in *Four Hymn Improvisations for Holy Week.*
Org.    MSM 10-318.

Miller, Aaron David. "Morgenlied" in *Triptych for Lent and Easter.* Org.
AFP 0800659457.

Nixon, June. "March on 'Lasst uns Erfreuen'" in *Festival Finales.* Org.
MAY 0-86209-353-8.

Sedio, Mark. "Lasst uns erfreuen" in *Music for the Paschal Season.* Org.
AFP 0800656237.

Walther, Johann. "Jesus, meine Zuversicht" in *80 Chorale Preludes.* Org.
Peters 11354.

### HANDBELL

Burroughs, Bob. "Processional Alleluia." 3 oct. L2.    ALF 8623.

Kinyon, Barbara B. "Christ Is Alive." 3-5 oct. L3+.    AG 2070.

Tucker, Sondra. "Crosswind." 3-5 oct.    AFP 0800659880.

### PRAISE ENSEMBLE

Baloche, Paul, Geoffrey Cueller, Sandy Hoffman, and Ed Kerr.
"Deeper in Love." SATB, kybd.    INTI4667.

Byerly/arr. Kirkland. "Giver of Life."    Allegis AG-I08I (SATB,
kybd); M-5039T (CD); OR 2460 (orch).

Mengel, Dana. "Lord of Love." SATB, kybd.    ABI 06323X.

# Monday, April 29
## CATHERINE OF SIENA, TEACHER, 1380

Catherine of Siena was a member of the Order of Preachers (Dominicans), and among Roman Catholics she was the first woman to receive the title Doctor of the Church. She was a contemplative and is known for her mystical visions of Jesus. Catherine was a humanitarian who worked to alleviate the suffering of the poor and imprisoned. She was also a renewer of church and society and advised both popes and any uncertain persons who told her their problems.

# Wednesday, May 1
## ST. PHILIP AND ST. JAMES, APOSTLES

Philip, one of the first disciples of Jesus, after following Jesus invited Nathanael to "come and see." According to tradition, he preached in Asia Minor and died as a martyr in Phrygia. James, the son of Alphaeus, is called "the Less" to distinguish him from another apostle named James, commemorated July 25. Philip and James are commemorated together because the remains of these two saints were placed in the Church of the Apostles in Rome on this day in 561.

# Thursday, May 2
## ATHANASIUS, BISHOP OF ALEXANDRIA, 373

Athanasius attended the Council of Nicea in 325 as a deacon and secretary to the bishop of Alexandria. At the council and when he himself served as bishop of Alexandria, he defended the full divinity of Christ against the Arian position held by emperors, magistrates, and theologians. Because of his defense of the divinity of Christ he was considered a troublemaker and was banished from Alexandria on five separate occasions.

Athanasius is an appropriate saint to be remembered at Easter. His name means "deathless one," though he himself lived in threat of death because of his theological stands. We are made in God's likeness, Athanasius affirmed. By the resurrection we are remade in the likeness of the Son, who has conquered death.

## Saturday, May 4

MONICA, MOTHER OF AUGUSTINE, 387

Monica was married to a pagan husband who was ill-tempered and unfaithful. She rejoiced greatly when both her husband and his mother became Christian. But she is best known because she is the mother of Augustine. Monica had been a disciple of Ambrose, and eventually Augustine came under his influence. Almost everything we know about Monica comes from Augustine's Confessions, his autobiography. Her dying wish was that her son remember her at the altar of the Lord, wherever he was.

Monica's life bore witness to the vital role that parents play in the faith formation of their children. Consider how the church supports parents in that task.

# May 5, 2002

### Sixth Sunday of Easter

## INTRODUCTION

In today's gospel reading, Jesus speaks clearly of the Spirit he will send to his disciples of every generation. Earlier in John's gospel, Jesus announces that a person comes to birth as a child of God through water and the Spirit. In this reading he calls the Spirit another advocate, the one who will speak to the heart of the baptized who listen in silence for his voice.

In their prayers, hymns, and preaching, Western Christians have tended to place greater emphasis on Christ than the Holy Spirit. In these Sundays, when the role of the Spirit in Christian life is highlighted, it may be appropriate to reflect on our understanding of this seemingly silent yet ever-present person of the Holy Trinity.

## PRAYER OF THE DAY

O God, from whom all good things come: Lead us by the inspiration of your Spirit to think those things which are right, and by your goodness help us to do them; through your Son, Jesus Christ our Lord, who lives and reigns with you and the Holy Spirit, one God, now and forever.

## READINGS

Acts 17:22-31

In Athens, Paul faces the challenge of proclaiming the gospel to Greeks who know nothing of either Jewish or Christian tradition. He proclaims that the "unknown god" whom they worship is the true Lord of heaven and earth who will judge the world with justice through Jesus, whom God has raised from the dead.

Psalm 66:7-18 (Psalm 66:8-20 [NRSV])

Be joyful in God, all you lands. (Ps. 66:1)

1 Peter 3:13-22

The First Letter of Peter calls Christians, who may be overwhelmed by the challenges of living and working in a non-Christian world, to use their way of life and their words to witness to the power of Easter manifested to them through baptism.

John 14:15-21

John's gospel is concerned with the faith of disciples who no longer have Jesus with them physically. Jesus promises that they will receive the Spirit and that he will continue to reveal himself to those who love him.

COLOR  White

## THE PRAYERS

Rejoicing in the resurrection, let us remember in prayer the church, the world, and all those in need.
*A BRIEF SILENCE.*
Send your Spirit to the church, that your disciples may love you and faithfully keep your commandments; we pray:
**Hear us, living God.**
Send your Spirit to the nations, that governing officials lead with integrity and honesty; we pray:
**Hear us, living God.**
Send your Spirit to all who suffer for their faith, that

they may be strengthened by your word and holy supper;
we pray:

**Hear us, living God.**

Send your Spirit to those who seek after you, that they
may find assurance and truth in the risen Christ; we pray:

**Hear us, living God.**

Send your Spirit to all struggling with addiction, all living in nursing homes and care facilities, and all who are
ill (especially), that your presence abide with them; we
pray:

**Hear us, living God.**

Send your Spirit to the pastor(s) and leaders of this congregation, that they may grow in love and servanthood;
we pray:

**Hear us, living God.**

*HERE OTHER INTERCESSIONS MAY BE OFFERED.*

We give you thanks for all the faithful ones who have
lived abiding in the Spirit of truth. Bring us with them
to the great and promised day when we will see you face-
to-face; we pray:

**Hear us, living God.**

Receive our prayers and hopes, O God, and fill us with
the risen life of Christ our Lord.

**Amen**

## IMAGES FOR PREACHING

John 14 as a whole addresses the disciples' fear of being
abandoned by Jesus. Jesus speaks of his dying as going
away to the Father's house (vv. 2-3). Earthly monarchs
have their palaces, and God is often pictured as living in
an enormous heavenly house with rooms beyond number, rooms for all. Jesus is going to prepare a place for
his disciples in that house of God.

The image is a homely, traditional one. Jesus uses it
as a text for a sermon, a springboard for new revelation.
He says, "I will not leave you orphaned; I am coming to
you" (v. 18). That, too, sounds traditional, but he does
not continue by promising to return with the clouds of
heaven, accompanied by angelic hosts, to the music of a
great trumpet fanfare. He uses none of the imagery we
often associate with the second coming.

Instead Jesus speaks the language of spiritual in-
dwelling. As he approaches death, he anticipates his
withdrawal from the world of touch and sight and
sound. He sees in dying his going home to God, and his
dying is the preparation for the spiritual homecoming of

the disciples. Because of his dying, the disciples will be
able to be in Jesus and Jesus in them. In fact, Jesus declares that he and the Father will come and make their
home with the disciples (v. 23).

To the unbelieving eye, Jesus' departure on the cross
seemed like the destruction of Jesus. But the eye of faith
sees more clearly. At the cross he finished his work of
pouring love into the world (13:1; 19:30). In his dying
and rising he is freed to return to his disciples as godly
energy and presence, fulfilling God's own deep desire to
dwell with people and to have them dwell in God.

## WORSHIP MATTERS

A common shape for baptismal fonts is the octagon—the
eight-sided bath or stand. If your font is octagonal, there
is a built-in baptismal lesson close at hand. Eight-sided
fonts are a sign of the eighth day, the day of perfection—
a completing and perfecting of God's work in creation. It
is this eighth day that is promised in our own baptism.

In addition, the words of I Peter 3:20-21 come to
mind: "God waited patiently in the days of Noah, during the building of the ark, in which a few, that is, eight
persons, were saved through water. And baptism, which
this prefigured, now saves you...." The eight-sided font
also points to these eight persons—and us as well—for
whom the waters of the flood became the waters of new
life. This image holds possibilities for theological and
liturgical education and can be used in a variety of
venues, from children's sermons to commentary on the
readings at the Vigil of Easter.

## LET THE CHILDREN COME

Children could learn and sing "You have put on Christ"
(WOV 694) as the gospel acclamation. This simple two-
line song based on Galatians 3:27 could be repeated by
the whole assembly in canon after the gospel reading.

## HYMNS FOR WORSHIP

### GATHERING

Come, thou almighty King    LBW 522

All things bright and beautiful    WOV 767

Awesome God    W&P 13

### HYMN OF THE DAY

Shout for joy loud and long    WOV 793

## ALTERNATE HYMN OF THE DAY

Dear Christians, one and all   LBW 299

No longer strangers   W&P 102

## COMMUNION

Alleluia, alleluia, give thanks   WOV 671

Waterlife   W&P 145

Love divine, all loves excelling   LBW 315

## SENDING

O Zion, haste   LBW 397

Oh, sing to the Lord   WOV 795

## ADDITIONAL HYMNS AND SONGS

Come, O come, our voices raise   H82 430

God, you spin the whirling planets   PH 285

I saw water   BL

Like the murmur of the dove's song   WOV 685

Many and great, O God, are your works   WOV 794

## MUSIC FOR THE DAY
### PSALMODY

Cooney, Rory.   STP, vol. 4

Foley, John.   PCY, vol. 7.

Jothen, Michael. *Sing Out! A Children's Psalter.*   WLP 7191.

Marshall, Jane. *Psalm Together.*   CGA CGC-18. U.

Proulx, Richard.   TP WJK.

Sedio, Mark.   PW A.

### CHORAL

Coombs, Francis. "If Ye Love Me, Keep My Commandments." SATB, org.   CPH 98-1215.

Running, Joseph. "I Will Not Leave You Comfortless." SATB.   AFP 080065045X.

Scott, K. Lee. "So Art Thou to Me." SATB, kybd.   AFP 0800674308.

Scholz, Robert. "Children of the Heavenly Father." SATB.   AFP 0800659110.

Shute, Linda Cable. "If You Can Walk." SAB, org.   AFP 0800659619.

Tallis, Thomas. "If Ye Love Me." SATB.   OXF 42.60.

Wilby, Philip. "If Ye Love Me." SSATB, org.   Banks Mus Pub ECS 191.

## CHILDREN'S CHOIRS

Mitchell, Tom. "Everyone Praise the Lord." U, kybd, fl.   CG CGA792.

Powell, Robert. "Awake, Awake." 2 pt trbl, kybd.   AFP 0800674146.

## KEYBOARD/INSTRUMENTAL

Callahan, Charles. *Voluntary on "Engelberg."* Org.   MSM 10-702.

Hobby, Robert A. "Personent Hodie" in *Six Preludes for the Church Year.* Org.   MSM 10-716.

Manz, Paul. "Personent Hodie" in *Three Hymn Improvisations.* Org.   MSM 10-867.

Moore, David W. *Dona Nobis Pacem.* Pno, solo inst.   AFP 0800659392.

Organ, Anne Krentz. "Tryggare kan ingen vara" in *Let It Rip! At the Piano.* Pno.   AFP 0800659066.

Powell, Robert J. "Personent Hodie" in *Sing a New Song.* Org.   AFP 0800656261.

## HANDBELL

Dobrinski, Cynthia. "Canticle of Hope."   AG 1150 (3 oct) L3; 1167 (5 oct) L3.

McChesney, Kevin. "Festival Fanfare on Engelberg." 3-5 oct. L3.   CPH 97-6843.

## PRAISE ENSEMBLE

Coates, John. "Almighty Medley."   WRD 25986-0516-7 (SATB, kybd); 25986-0516-5 (acc cass); 25986-0516R (orch).

Klein, Laurie/arr. Jack Schrader. "I Love You, Lord."   HOP GC 936 (SATB, kybd); GC 936C (reh/perf cass).

Sadler, Gary. "Wind of God" in *Hosanna Music Songbook 13.* SAT[B], kybd.   INT 13576.

Zschech, Darlene. "Shout to the Lord."   INT 09707 (SATB, kybd); 09708 (choraltrax); 09705 (orch).

# Wednesday, May 8

## VICTOR THE MOOR, MARTYR, 303

Known also as Victor Maurus, this native of the African country of Mauritania was a Christian from his youth. He served as a soldier in the Praetorian Guard. Under the persecution of Maximian, Victor died for his faith at Milan. Few details are known about his life, but many churches in the diocese of Milan are dedicated to him.

# May 9, 2002

## The Ascension of Our Lord

### INTRODUCTION

The risen Lord enters the invisible presence of God in order to be present in all times and in all places to the church and to the world. Where shall we find the risen and ascended Lord today? In his word and his bread, in his people and his washing with water and the Spirit, and in all who cry out for mercy.

### PRAYER OF THE DAY

Almighty God, your only Son was taken up into heaven and in power intercedes for us. May we also come into your presence and live forever in your glory; through your Son, Jesus Christ our Lord, who lives and reigns with you and the Holy Spirit, one God, now and forever.

### READINGS

#### Acts 1:1-11

Before he is lifted into heaven, Jesus promises that the missionary work of the disciples will spread out from Jerusalem to all the world. His words provide an outline of the book of Acts.

#### Psalm 47

God has gone up with a shout. (Ps. 47:5)

#### or Psalm 93

Ever since the world began, your throne has been established. (Ps. 93:3)

#### Ephesians 1:15-23

After giving thanks for the faith of the Ephesians, Paul prays that they might also see the power of God, who in the ascension has now enthroned Christ as head of the church, his body.

#### Luke 24:44-53

At the time of his ascension, Jesus leaves the disciples with the promise of the Holy Spirit and an instruction that they should await the Spirit's descent.

### COLOR White

### THE PRAYERS

Rejoicing in the resurrection, let us remember in prayer the church, the world, and all those in need.

*A BRIEF SILENCE.*

Enliven the church with your Spirit, that it may be a witness of the saving power of Jesus Christ to the ends of the earth; we pray:

**Hear us, living God.**

Guide the leaders of nations, that they may exercise their power and authority for the good of all people; we pray:

**Hear us, living God.**

Raise up those who are poor, discouraged, depressed, sick, or who live without hope (especially), that they may know the abiding presence of Christ; we pray:

**Hear us, living God.**

Deepen our care for the earth, that we may be faithful stewards of its resources and be mindful of generations still to come; we pray:

**Hear us, living God.**

Enlighten the eyes of our hearts, and grant us a deeper understanding of your word, that we may press onward toward the hope to which you have called us; we pray:

**Hear us, living God.**

*HERE OTHER INTERCESSIONS MAY BE OFFERED.*

We give thanks for all the saints now sharing in the riches of your glorious inheritance. Clothe us with power from on high, that we may proclaim the crucified and risen one until we join them in glory; we pray:

**Hear us, living God.**

Receive our prayers and hopes, O God, and fill us with the risen life of Christ our Lord.

**Amen**

### IMAGES FOR PREACHING

"Power from on high" stands in sharp contrast to the powers we humans ordinarily wheel out in times of conflict. Once conflicts were handled by striking directly with sword or spear at the enemy, who was within arm's reach. The introduction of gunpowder gave rise to a revolution in warfare. Suddenly chemical power enabled soldiers to project their destructive force over thousands of yards. In most recent times combatants have had at their disposal sophisticated weaponry including jet-propelled aircraft and rockets guided by computers, lasers, and heat sensors. These have given armies the deadly ability to strike enemies not just thousands of yards but thousands of miles distant from one another and to do so with lethal effect.

When Jesus speaks of power from on high, he has in mind power of a different order altogether. He is not talking about God punishing the earth with comets and meteors or with frightening flows of lava or the sudden snapping of tectonic plates. He is speaking of the enigmatic power of the Spirit of God. It is enigmatic because it is clear that the power of the Spirit is the continuation in time of the power of the cross. To speak of the "power of the cross" might seem like an oxymoron, but it is by that power that the promises of scripture regarding Jesus are fulfilled (Luke 24:44-45). By that power God will "redeem Israel" (v. 21) and indeed "all the nations" (v. 47). By that power God will grant peace.

On the Mount of Olives, Jesus lifted his hands in blessing, and while he was blessing the disciples, he parted from them. This vision of a deeply benevolent, universal sovereign is desperately needed today. Jesus holds out a promise that reaches beyond limitations of human leadership. In that final view of the crucified and now resurrected Jesus, the disciples, and we with them, are granted a vision of "all nations" as one great human family under the hands of Christ upraised in blessing.

## WORSHIP MATTERS

Offerings of freshly cut flowers are common additions to a worship space. Cut flowers symbolize both the beauty and frailty of creation. Bouquets and arrangements frequently adorn the altar or chancel. For variety consider arranging flowers around the baptismal font when appropriate—on Sundays with a baptismal emphasis, for example, or whenever the community celebrates Holy Baptism. Another possibility is to consider using live plants as a permanent baptismal decoration. Living greenery is a visual reminder of the new life that is ours in baptism. Plants and flowers are a sign of our baptismal theology.

## LET THE CHILDREN COME

Ascension Day is still a national holiday in Denmark. Though many do not keep the feast, they do leave work to picnic. Perhaps this outing allows them a moment to look up and to look around. Some children who are full

of daydreams are living signs of wonder among us. They remind us to look up in awe. Other children, whose lives are so difficult that daydreaming is a form of survival, call us to look around at the needs and hurts of the world and to respond. After the liturgy, invite everyone outside to look up and find pictures in the clouds and to look around at the needs of the neighborhood.

## HYMNS FOR WORSHIP
### GATHERING

Look, the sight is glorious   LBW 156
Come away to the skies   WOV 669
Open our eyes, Lord   TFF 98, W&P 113

### HYMN OF THE DAY

A hymn of glory let us sing   LBW 157

### ALTERNATE HYMN OF THE DAY

Lord, you give the great commission   WOV 756
How lovely on the mountains   TFF 99

### COMMUNION

Beautiful Savior   LBW 518
Blessed assurance   WOV 699, TFF 118
Shout to the Lord   W&P 124

### SENDING

Give to our God immortal praise!   LBW 520
Hallelujah! We sing your praises   WOV 722, TFF 158

### ADDITIONAL HYMNS AND SONGS

Alleluia! Sing to Jesus   LBW 158
See the Conqueror mounts in triumph   H82 215
Hail the day that sees him rise   HFW
Up through endless ranks of angels   LBW 159

## MUSIC FOR THE DAY
### PSALMODY

Brown, Teresa. "God Goes Up" in PS 2.
Haugen, Marty.   PCY, vol. 1.
Kogut, Malcolm.   PCY, vol. 10.
Palmer. "Ps 47: God Mounts His Throne." Cant, choir, kybd, tpt. GIA G-4063.
Pelz, Walter.   PW A.
Clap your hands! Shout for joy!   ASG 6

197

## CHORAL

Cherwien, David. "Up through Endless Ranks of Angels." SAB, org, opt tpt/cong.   AFP 0800658817.

Croft, William. "God Is Gone Up with a Merry Noise." SSAATB, org.   NOV 88 0034 00.

Diercks, John. "Clap Your Hands." U, opt SATB, pno/org. CG A-199.

Forsberg, Charles. "Fairest Lord Jesus." SATB, pno. AFP 0800656962.

Hutchings, Arthur. "God Is Gone Up with a Merry Noise." in *Shorter Anthems*. SATB.   NOV 296.

Mathias, William. "Lift Up Your Heads" in *Anthems for Choirs 1*. SATB, org.

Moore, Philip. "The Ascension" (Lift Up Your Heads). SATB, org PVN 1006. .

Riegel, Friedrich Samuel. "See God to Heaven Ascending" in *Chantry Choirbook*. AFP 0800657772.

Rohlig, Harald. "O Clap Your Hands." SATB.   AFP 6000097727.

Rutter, John. "O Clap Your Hands." SATB, org.   OXF 42.378.

Vaughan Williams, Ralph. "O Clap Your Hands." SATB, org. GAL 2222.

## CHILDREN'S CHOIRS

Lightfoot, Mary Lynn. "Sing Joyful Praise." 2 pt, kybd. Raymond A. Hoffman Company H2045.

Owens, Jimmy. "Clap Your Hands, All You People."   LS 182

Page, Anna Laura. "Clap Your Hands with Joy." 2 pt, kybd. FLA EA-5093.

## KEYBOARD/INSTRUMENTAL

Carlson, J. Bert. "Hyfrydol" in *A New Look at the Old*. Org. AFP 0800658760.

Honoré, Jeffrey. "Hyfrydol" in *Classic Embellishments*. Org, opt inst. AFP 0800658728.

Lloyd, Richard. "Pavilioned in Splendour" in *Festival Finales*. Org. MAY 0-86209-358-8.

Messiaen, Olivier. "Alleluias Sereins" in *L'Ascension*. Org.   Leduc 30.

Wasson, Laura E. "Hyfrydol" in *A Piano Tapestry*. Pno. AFP 0800656822.

## HANDBELL

Helman, Michael. "Processional in C." 3-5 oct, opt tpt. AFP 0800656288.

Hopson, Hal H. "Fantasy on 'Hyfrydol.'"   AG 2078 (3-5 oct); 1048 (2 oct) L 2+.

McChesney, Kevin. "Rejoice, the Lord Is King!" 3-5 oct. L2.   LOR HB312.

## PRAISE ENSEMBLE

Hayford, Jack/arr. Jack Schrader. "Majesty."   HOP GD 868 (SATB, kybd); GC 868C (reh/perf cass).

Morgan, Reuben/arr. Richard Kingsmore. "Hear Our Praises" in *Hillsongs Choral Collection*. SATB, kybd.   INT 16996.

Price, Nancy and Don Besig. "A New and Glorious Song." GS A7337 (SATB, kybd); 5051 (CD track); 5547 (inst).

Price, Nancy and Don Besig. "Go Out and Serve Him!" GS A 7365 (SATB, kybd, opt cong); 5062 (CD track); 5554 (inst).

# May 12, 2002

Seventh Sunday of Easter

## INTRODUCTION

"Holy Father, protect them in your name…so that they may be one" (John 17:11). With these words, Jesus prays for the unity of his disciples in every age, for their life, and for their mission in the world. Throughout these last days of Easter leading to Pentecost, we could readily pray these words: Holy Father, protect us in your name so that we may be one. In the midst of much economic, ethnic, and cultural diversity, there is ample room for letting what is distinctive about us become divisive. Yet, as Christians, our deepest identity is discovered in baptism, proclaimed in the word, and nourished in the holy supper: we are one people who struggle for the unity that God intends for the entire human family.

## PRAYER OF THE DAY

Almighty and eternal God, your Son our Savior is with you in eternal glory. Give us faith to see that, true to his promise, he is among us still, and will be with us to the end of time; who lives and reigns with you and the Holy Spirit, one God, now and forever.

*or*

God, our creator and redeemer, your Son Jesus prayed that his followers might be one. Make all Christians one with him as he is one with you, so that in peace and concord we may carry to the world the message of your love; through Jesus Christ our Lord, who lives and reigns with you and the Holy Spirit, one God, now and forever.

## READINGS

Acts 1:6-14

Today's reading is part of the introduction to the narrative of the outpouring of the Spirit on Pentecost. These verses tell of the risen Lord's conversation with his disciples on the eve of his ascension.

Psalm 68:1-10, 33-36 (Psalm 68:1-10, 32-35 [NRSV])

Sing to God, who rides upon the heavens. (Ps. 68:4)

1 Peter 4:12-14; 5:6-11

Christians should expect to be persecuted, the First Letter of Peter says, whether by violence, ostracism, or simply name-calling. Firm faith is based on hope in God in defiance of such opposition.

John 17:1-11

John records Jesus' final prayer to his Father before his crucifixion. He prays that his followers, who continue his work in this world, will live in unity.

## COLOR  White

## THE PRAYERS

Rejoicing in the resurrection, let us remember in prayer the church, the world, and all those in need.

*A BRIEF SILENCE.*

That the communities of faith scattered throughout the world may be one in you, just as you and the Son are one, we pray:

**Hear us, living God.**

That those who govern may serve with humility and with genuine concern for all who face poverty or injustice, we pray:

**Hear us, living God.**

That all who suffer for their faith in Christ may be upheld and strengthened by the hope of glory you have promised, we pray:

**Hear us, living God.**

That those who suffer in body, mind, or spirit (especially) may cast their anxieties on you and know your care for them, we pray:

**Hear us, living God.**

That our land may be blessed with seasonable weather, so that the earth may yield food for all the people of the earth, we pray:

**Hear us, living God.**

That mothers and all who care for children may be held in honor by all and may find blessings in their service, we pray:

**Hear us, living God.**

That the gifts of church musicians and all who sing in choirs may enrich the corporate praise and deepen the faith of this congregation, we pray:

**Hear us, living God.**

199

That we who are gathered around word and table may witness to the unity God desires for the whole human family, we pray:
**Hear us, living God.**
*HERE OTHER INTERCESSIONS MAY BE OFFERED.*
That we may one day be joined with all the faithful departed who share your eternal glory, we pray:
**Hear us, living God.**
Receive our prayers and hopes, O God, and fill us with the risen life of Christ our Lord.
**Amen**

## IMAGES FOR PREACHING

After the last supper and before his arrest, Jesus prays. In his praying he fixes his own attention (and ours also) on the hour of his death. He has been speaking of that hour since the wedding at Cana (John 2:4). That mysterious hour has now come. But what kind of hour is it? For Mark, Matthew, and Luke, it is his darkest hour. But in John's gospel, when Jesus speaks of the end of his earthly path, he never speaks of dying or of being humiliated or forsaken. Quite the opposite. In his prayer he speaks of being glorified.

John in his gospel is at pains to help us see that Jesus' end really is glorious. Jesus is crucified not at nine in the morning as in the other gospels but at high noon, when the sun is at its zenith, and there is no hint of darkness shrouding the whole earth. For John, the moment of crucifixion is Jesus' shining hour. At the cross Jesus completes the work of glorifying God that he had been carrying out all along. The cross is no detour, no sudden downturn.

The entire work of Jesus, from first to last, was to be God's Word in and for the world. Throughout his life, his every breath and movement made God known, and at the cross he revealed God and the love of God most fully.

What is the purpose of that full and glorious display of God's heart? What is the intended accomplishment of the display? Jesus speaks of oneness as the point of it all. As the sun shines on the earth and draws plants upwards out of the earth and toward the sky, so Jesus, lifted high on the cross, would draw all people up to himself and through himself into the life of God, into oneness with God. By the glory of his cross he would draw us away from darkness, away from the lie, away from death, up into light and truth and life.

## WORSHIP MATTERS

Many congregations recognize members' birthdays by sending cards or printing names in the newsletter. Another possibility is to recognize and celebrate baptismal birthdays. A personal or public recognition can act both as an affirmation of belonging to the family of God and as a reminder of what it means to live out our baptism.

Creativity knows no bounds at this point. Cards and newsletters certainly are appropriate. But computer databases also open the possibility of assigning worship leadership roles—lector, acolyte, bearer of bread and wine for the eucharist—on or near baptismal birthdays. Such recognition can sometimes make a significant difference in worship participation during the crucial years of a young person's growth in faith.

## LET THE CHILDREN COME

The fifty days of Easter are coming to an end. Yet, for the Day of Pentecost, continue to use the Easter acclamation, which the children know by heart now. Ring the bells. Sing a song of resurrection. Carry fragrant spring flowers into the nave. If the season of Easter dwindles to a whimper, the eyes and ears and noses of the children will pick up no clues that the season is about to change.

## HYMNS FOR WORSHIP
### GATHERING
Hail thee, festival day! (Ascension)   LBW 142
A hymn of glory let us sing!   LBW 157
Alabaré   WOV 791, LLC 582
Soon and very soon   WOV 744, TFF 38, W&P 128

### HYMN OF THE DAY
Crown him with many crowns   LBW 170

### ALTERNATE HYMN OF THE DAY
Oh, love, how deep   LBW 88
Thine the amen, thine the praise   WOV 801

### COMMUNION
You satisfy the hungry heart   WOV 711
Lord, who the night you were betrayed   LBW 206
Lord Jesus Christ, we humbly pray   LBW 225

SENDING

The church's one foundation    LBW 369

Bind us together    WOV 748, W&P 18

ADDITIONAL HYMNS AND SONGS

The head that once was crowned    LBW 173

Hail the day that sees him rise    HFW

Like the murmur of the dove's song    WOV 685

We will glorify    W&P 154

**MUSIC FOR THE DAY**

PSALMODY

Cooney, Rory. "You Have Made a Home."    CG.

Marshall, Jane. *Psalms Together II.*    CGC-21. U.

Sedio, Mark.    PW A.

CHORAL

Biery, James. "The Waters of Life." SATB, org.    AFP 0800657683/ *The Augsburg Choirbook* 0800656784.

Ferguson, John. "The Head That Once Was Crowned with Thorns." SATB, org, brass qrt.    GIA G-3750.

Handel, G.F. "Glory and Worship" in *Coronation Anthems.* SAATTBB, org.    OXF.

Johnson, David. "The Lone, Wild Bird" in *The Augsburg Choirbook.* SATB.    AFP 0800656784.

Pelz, Walter L. "Crown Him with Many Crowns." SATB, cong, org, 3 tpts.    AFP 080064803X.

Purcell, Henry. "O God the King of Glory" in *Anthems for Choirs 1.* SATB, opt org.    OXF.

Schalk, Carl F. "O Love, How Deep, How Broad, How High." SATB, 3 tpts or org.    CPH 98-1524.

Schalk, Carl. "Thine the Amen, Thine the Praise." SATB, org, opt cong.    AFP 0800646126.

Wolff, S. Drummond. "Crown Him with Many Crowns." SATB, org. CPH 98-2332.

CHILDREN'S CHOIRS

Althouse, Jay. "Be Joyful and Sing to the Lord." 2 pt, kybd, desc. ALF 17904.

Althouse, Jay. "Each and Every Day." 2 pt, kybd.    ALF 18001.

Bedford, Michael. "Go, Therefore, and Make Disciples." U, org. CPH 98-3270.

KEYBOARD/INSTRUMENTAL

Albrecht, Timothy. "Diademata" in *Grace Notes, Vol. 6.* Org. AFP 080065865.

Brahms, Johannes. "My Jesus Leadeth Me" in *11 Chorale Preludes.* Org. Mercury 453-00260.

Burkhardt, Michael. "Diademata" in *Five Easter Season Hymn Improvisations, Set 1.* Org.    MSM 10-403.

Callahan, Charles. "Partita on Diademata." Org.    MSM 10-409.

Callahan, Charles. "Voluntary on 'This Is the Feast'" in *This Is the Feast.* Org.    CPH 97-6575.

HANDBELL

Kinyon, Barbara B. "Good Christians All, Rejoice and Sing." 2-3 oct. L3-.    BEC HB 144.

Moklebust, Cathy. "Diademata" in *Hymn Stanzas for Handbells.* AFP 0800657330 (2-3 oct); 0800655761 (4-5 oct).

Stephenson, Valerie W. "Crown Him." 3-6 oct. L4.    ALF 18565.

PRAISE ENSEMBLE

Fitts, Bob. "Blessed Be the Lord God Almighty." SATB, kybd. MAR 301 0849 168.

Machen, Harland/arr. Tom Fettke. "Bow the Knee."    Allegis AG-1076 (SATB, kybd); MU-2446D (cass); MU 50371 (CD); OR-2446 (orch).

Paris, Twila/arr. Jack Schrader. "We Will Glorify."    HOP C5095 (SATB, kybd);  5095C (reh/perf cass); C50950 (orch).

Pethel, Stan. "Shout for Joy."    HOP GC 888 (SATB, kybd); GC 888C (cass).

201

# Tuesday, May 14

PACHOMIUS, RENEWER OF THE CHURCH, 346

Pachomius was born in Egypt about 290. He became a Christian during his service as a soldier. In 320 he went to live as a hermit in Upper Egypt, where other hermits lived nearby. Pachomius organized them into a religious community in which the members prayed together and held their goods in common. His rule for monasteries influenced both Eastern and Western monasticism through the Rule of Basil and the Rule of Benedict respectively.

The Egyptian (Coptic) church may be unfamiliar to many Western Christians. Use the commemoration of Pachomius to teach about the Egyptian church at parish gatherings this week.

# May 18, 2002

Vigil of Pentecost

## INTRODUCTION

Pentecost is one of the principal festivals of the liturgical year. Several of the festivals have the tradition of night vigils preceding them. In this night of extended prayer and silence, we anticipate being filled anew with the power of the Spirit, perhaps as the believers were in the second chapter of Acts (an alternate first reading this night). The Spirit gathers the church together. It is the same Spirit that enlightens us by the word, calls us in baptism, and sanctifies us with the bread of life and the cup of salvation. Come, Holy Spirit!

## PRAYER OF THE DAY

Almighty and ever-living God, you fulfilled the promise of Easter by sending your Holy Spirit to unite the races and nations on earth and thus to proclaim your glory. Look upon your people gathered in prayer, open to receive the Spirit's flame. May it come to rest in our hearts and heal the divisions of word and tongue, that with one voice and one song we may praise your name in joy and thanksgiving; through your Son, Jesus Christ our Lord, who lives and reigns with you and the Holy Spirit, one God, now and forever.

## READINGS

Exodus 19:1-9

God establishes the covenant with Israel at Mt. Sinai.

*or* Acts 2:1-11

Believers are filled with the Spirit to tell God's deeds.

Psalm 33:12-22

The Lord is our help and our shield. (Ps. 33:20)

*or* Psalm 130

There is forgiveness with you. (Ps. 130:3)

Romans 8:14-17, 22-27

The Spirit prays for us.

John 7:37-39

Jesus nourishes believers with living water and leads them to the Spirit of God.

## COLOR Red

## THE PRAYERS

Rejoicing in the resurrection, let us remember in prayer the church, the world, and all those in need.

*A BRIEF SILENCE.*

Fill your church with the energy of the holy and life-giving Spirit; we pray:

**Hear us, living God.**

Breathe your spirit of wisdom and peace on the leaders of nations; we pray:

**Hear us, living God.**

Reconcile races and nations divided by prejudice, fear, or warfare; we pray:

**Hear us, living God.**

Comfort with the light of your love all those who are sick or in pain (especially); we pray:

**Hear us, living God.**

Inspire us to use our gifts and to serve faithfully in the various ministries in the one body of Christ; we pray:

**Hear us, living God.**

Pour out your Spirit on this congregation, that we may be filled with new insight and noble vision; we pray:

**Hear us, living God.**

*HERE OTHER INTERCESSIONS MAY BE OFFERED.*

Unite us with the martyr Erik, king of Sweden, and with the saints of all times and places until the coming of the great and glorious day of the Lord; we pray:

**Hear us, living God.**

Receive our prayers and hopes, O God, and fill us with the risen life of Christ our Lord.

**Amen**

## IMAGES FOR PREACHING

On each of the seven mornings of the Festival of Tabernacles, priests went in solemn procession from the temple to the Gihon Spring to draw water and carry it back up to the temple. At the altar the priests then poured out the water with prayers for the autumn rain and for blessing on the harvest. Those originally agricultural prayers became prayers for the divine gift of salvation.

On the last day of the festival, Jesus cried out that all who thirsted for salvation should come to him and

202

drink (see John 4). Then he applied to himself the scripture about rivers of living water flowing from the believer's heart. The evangelist says he was speaking not of ordinary water but of the freely flowing Spirit of God. Then he adds a note that seems odd at first glance: "As yet there was no Spirit" (7:39).

Can it be that the Holy Spirit did not yet exist? It was widely thought that the spirit of prophecy had died out after Haggai, Zechariah, and Malachi. All that was left was the "daughter of the voice," a faint echo of the thunder that had once addressed Isaiah, Jeremiah, and Ezekiel. After Malachi came a time of drought that would be broken only by the advent of the Messiah. Then once more God would pour out the Spirit not only on a few but on "all flesh," on sons and daughters, on young and old, on slave and free, on male and female (Joel 2:28-29; Acts 2:17-18).

That lavishing of the Spirit upon all flesh had not yet happened when Jesus first spoke his words to the festal crowds. The gift was first given when Jesus was glorified on the cross and there yielded up his spirit (John 19:30). The evangelist sees in that glorious moment a strange and wonderful exchange: life flowed out from the side of Jesus, glorified and exalted on the cross, and it flowed into the world as a life-giving river.

## WORSHIP MATTERS

When leading the Brief Order for Confession and Forgiveness, consider standing at the baptismal font. The words of the baptismal liturgy come to mind: "In Holy Baptism our gracious heavenly Father liberates us from sin and death by joining us to the death and resurrection of our Lord Jesus Christ" (*LBW*, p. 121). By making a connection between the forgiveness of sins in the waters of baptism and our weekly confession and forgiveness as we prepare to worship, we reinforce an understanding of forgiveness as a gracious gift, not the result of our own action (not even the action of our own confession). When we return to the baptismal waters to make our

confession, we also return to the gracious gift of undeserved forgiveness that is ours in Jesus Christ.

## LET THE CHILDREN COME

The color for this day is red, a bright yet rich red. With adequate planning, children can be invited to come to worship at the Vigil or on Sunday dressed in their wildest reds! They will not quickly forget this sight. But remember this: just as the Spirit always does more than one thing, so red's vivid color is associated with more than fire or flame!

## HYMN OF THE DAY

Spirit, Spirit of gentleness   WOV 684

## OTHER HYMNS

Come down, O Love divine   LBW 508
O living breath of God   LLC 368

203

# Saturday, May 18

ERIK, KING OF SWEDEN, MARTYR, 1160

Erik, long considered the patron saint of Sweden, ruled there from 1150 to 1160. He is honored for efforts to bring peace to the nearby pagan kingdoms and for his crusades to spread the Christian faith in Scandinavia. He established a protected Christian mission in Finland that was led by Henry of Uppsala. As king, Erik was noted for his desire to establish fair laws and courts and for his concern for those who were poor or sick. Erik was killed by a Danish army that approached him at worship on the day after the Ascension. He is reported to have said to them, "Let us at least finish the sacrifice. The rest of the feast I shall keep elsewhere." As he left worship he was killed.

The commemoration of Erik could be the beginning of a discussion on the relationship between civil rule and the place of faith in the public sphere.

# May 19, 2002

The Day of Pentecost

## INTRODUCTION

On this fiftieth day of Easter, the church gathers to celebrate the ongoing life of the Holy Spirit who is its breath, vitality, and inspiration. Through the Holy Spirit, the good news unravels age-old divisions among peoples and nations. In the waters of baptism, the Spirit gives us birth as brothers and sisters of Christ and unites people of different races, tribes, and ethnic groups. In the bread and cup of the holy supper, the Spirit nourishes our unity in worship and witness. Far from celebrating its "birthday" on this day, the church offers thanksgiving to God for the very one who continues to sustain its life in each new generation and makes its prayer possible.

## PRAYER OF THE DAY

God, the Father of our Lord Jesus Christ, as you sent upon the disciples the promised gift of the Holy Spirit, look upon your Church and open our hearts to the power of the Spirit. Kindle in us the fire of your love, and strengthen our lives for service in your kingdom; through your Son, Jesus Christ our Lord, who lives and reigns with you in the unity of the Holy Spirit, one God, now and forever.

## READINGS

Acts 2:1-21

Pentecost was a Jewish harvest festival that marked the fiftieth day after Passover. After the year 70, this festival came to commemorate the covenant that God made with Israel on Mount Sinai. Still later, Luke associated the outpouring of the Holy Spirit with Pentecost as the fiftieth day after the resurrection.

or Numbers 11:24-30

The Spirit of God rests upon seventy chosen leaders in Israel who gather with Moses at the tent of meeting. Not to be contained, the Spirit also rests on two others who were not at the tent, and they too prophesy.

Psalm 104:25-35, 37 (Psalm 104:24-34, 35b [NRSV])

Alleluia or Send forth your Spirit and renew the face of the earth. (Ps. 104:31)

1 Corinthians 12:3b-13

In the church at Corinth, some Christians claimed to be more spiritual than others. Paul writes to tell them the Spirit is active in every Christian and in all the varied ministries of the church.

or Acts 2:1-21

John 20:19-23

John's gospel tells us that the experience of Easter comes to fulfillment when Jesus visits his disciples, gives them the Holy Spirit, and sends them out to continue his work of forgiving sins.

or John 7:37-39

Jesus nourishes believers with living water and leads them to the Spirit of God.

## COLOR Red

## THE PRAYERS

Rejoicing in the resurrection, let us remember in prayer the church, the world, and all those in need.

A BRIEF SILENCE.

Pour out your Spirit upon the church, that we may be a witness to the world of your grace and forgiveness in Jesus Christ; we pray:

**Hear us, living God.**

Inspire those who govern the nations to work for the good of all people; we pray:

**Hear us, living God.**

Send your peace on all who live in fear, all who suffer from loneliness, and all who are sick (especially); we pray:

**Hear us, living God.**

Fill the members of our congregation with your gifts of grace, that we may envision new ministries to serve our community; we pray:

**Hear us, living God.**

HERE OTHER INTERCESSIONS MAY BE OFFERED.

Unite us with all your Spirit-filled saints, until the coming of the great and glorious day of the Lord; we pray:

**Hear us, living God.**

204

Receive our prayers and hopes, O God, and fill us with the risen life of Christ our Lord.
**Amen**

## IMAGES FOR PREACHING

When John tells us that Jesus "breathed upon" his disciples, he uses the same word (*emphysao*) that is used in the Septuagint to describe God's action in creation. At the world's first dawning God, working like a potter (Isa. 45:9; Rom. 9:20), shaped a figure from the clay of the earth. Then God breathed into that earthen vessel, so that it became a living human being (Gen. 2:7; Wis. 15:11). The same word is used in Ezekiel's vision of the valley of dry bones, a vision in which God's breath or Spirit from the four winds of the earth breathed upon those bones, so that the vast multitude stood upright and lived (Ezek. 37:9-10).

In all four of our gospels the connection with Jesus broken by his dying, is reestablished on Easter. John describes that new beginning using carefully chosen vocabulary and imagery. In a sudden and bewildering epiphany, Jesus manifests himself in the presence of his disciples. Jesus appears to them and breathes new life into them, so that they stand up and live as a new creation.

Raymond Brown relates a story inspired by the imagery John has employed. It was long the custom for the Coptic patriarch of Alexandria in Egypt to fill a skin bag with his own holy breath, tie up that bag tightly, and then send it up river to Ethiopia. There the bag was opened, and the patriarch's breath was released onto the person who had been designated as the new abuna, or head of the Ethiopian church.

We do not know what John would have thought if he could have foreseen such a use of his narrative. He is, however, most certainly describing how the resurrected Jesus came to his own shattered community, brought that fellowship to new life, and commissioned all of them (and all of us) to be emissaries of his own peace.

## WORSHIP MATTERS

As the seasons of creation change, the signs are unmistakable: winter cold and shades of brown give way to spring warmth and sprouting green; summer heat and stillness become autumn's breezes and odors of decay. The whole creation shouts with signs of the changing seasons.

The seasons of the church year change as well but sometimes with a whisper rather than a shout. Faded paraments of one color give way to threadbare paraments of another. Yet the changing liturgical seasons are no less dramatic than those of the created order are. Advent waiting becomes Christmas fulfillment; Easter resurrection gives way to Pentecost fire.

Subtle changes in sanctuary arrangement and decoration—altar, pulpit, or baptismal font moved to a different location; banners or flowers in a different arrangement; seating shifted ever so slightly—can mark the changing of the liturgical seasons. By such variety we help our congregation to experience the changing of the seasons.

## LET THE CHILDREN COME

This great festival calls for a procession of fire and wind. Every child who wants to could be involved with very little rehearsal. Older children carry torches or large pillar candles. The danger of the fire is part of the power of the sign. Most fourth to sixth graders both know the danger and have the maturity to bear fire into the assembly.

Tie silver, white, and red streamers to the wrists of smaller children. Let them "blow where they will" as they enter dancing or skipping and twirling their arms. The procession needs to "lead the people forth in joy" at the close of the liturgy, for the fire and wind of the Spirit cannot be contained in a building.

## HYMNS FOR WORSHIP
### GATHERING

O Holy Spirit, enter in    LBW 459
Lord, you give the great commission    WOV 756

### HYMN OF THE DAY

Come, Holy Ghost, God and Lord    LBW 163

### ALTERNATE HYMN OF THE DAY

O day full of grace    LBW 161
Holy Spirit, light divine    TFF 104

### COMMUNION

Cup of blessing that we share    LBW 204
Gracious Spirit, heed our pleading    WOV 687, TFF 103
I want to be ready    TFF 41
Spirit song    TFF 105, W&P 130

205

### SENDING

Come, gracious Spirit, heavenly dove    LBW 475
Every time I feel the Spirit    TFF 241
When you send forth your Spirit    DH 43

### ADDITIONAL HYMNS AND SONGS

Send me, Jesus    WOV 773, TFF 244/245
Come down, O Love divine    LBW 508
On Pentecost they gathered    NCH 272
When God the Spirit came    RS 613
Wind who makes all winds that blow    UMI 1 538

## MUSIC FOR THE DAY

### SERVICE MUSIC

On Pentecost, a sequence hymn such as "Come, Holy Ghost, our souls inspire" (LBW 472, 473) might be added after or in place of the gospel acclamation. Choir and congregation may alternate, the choir singing stanzas 1, 3, and 5 in the chant version (LBW 472), the congregation singing stanzas 2 and 4 in the chorale version (LBW 473). The Nigerian traditional song "Wa wa wa Emimimo" (WOV 681) is another powerful invocation of the Spirit, which might accompany a gospel procession.

### PSALMODY

Bach, J.S./arr. Hill. "Alleluia, O Come and Praise the Lord." 2 pt, kybd, 2 C inst.    CGA-174.
Cooney, Rory. "Send Out Your Spirit." U, pno, gtr, fl.    OCP 5896CC.
Farlee, Robert Buckley. PW A.
Kreutz, Robert E. "Lord, Send Out Your Spirit." SATB, cong, gtr, org, inst.    OCP 9457.
Olawski.    STP, vol. 5
Saliers, Don E. "Psalm 104." Cant, cong, SATB, org, hb.    OXF 94.234.
Wright, Andrews. "Send Forth Your Spirit, O Lord" in PS 2.

### CHORAL

Bach, J.S. "Dona nobis pacem" in *Bach for All Seasons*. SATB, kybd.    AFP 080065654X.
Berger, Jean. "The Eyes of All Wait Upon Thee." SATB.    AFP 0800645596.
Burkhardt, Michael. "Come, Holy Ghost, Our Souls Inspire." 2 pt, hb.    MSM-50-5551.
Busarow, Donald. "Blessed Is the Nation." SATB, cong, opt brass qrt, org.    CPH 98-2850.
Callahan, Charles. "How Many Are Your Works, O Lord." SATB, fl, org.    CPH 98-3258.

Carlson, J. Bert. "Spirit of God, Unleashed on Earth." SATB, org, opt cong & brass quintet.    AFP 0800654692 (complete score); 0800655478 (brass pts).
Dawson, William. "Ev'ry Time I Feel the Spirit." SATB.    KJO T117.
des Prez, Josquin. "Come, O Creator Spirit, Come." SATB.    CPH 98-1994.
Diemer, Emma Lou. "And in the Last Days." SATB, org.    AFP 11-3517.
Distler, Hugo. "Come, Holy Ghost, God and Lord" in the *Chantry Choirbook*. SATB.    AFP 0800657772.
Distler, Hugo. "Creator Spirit, Heavenly Dove" in the *Chantry Choirbook*. SAB.    AFP 0800657772.
Farlee, Robert Buckley. "O Blessed Spring." SATB, ob, opt cong.    AFP 0800654242.
Gibbons, Orlando. "Come, Holy Spirit." SATB, org.    GIA G-1540.
Hassell, Michael. "Spirit, Spirit of Gentleness." SATB, pno, sax or clar.    AFP 080065711X.
Hogan, Charles. "Veni Sancte Spiritus." SATB, fl, perc.    AFP 0800657160.
How, Martin. "Hymn to the Holy Spirit." SAB, pno/org.    B&H 6078.
Jennings, Carolyn. "Creator Spirit, by Whose Aid." SATB, 3 tpts, timp.    AFP 0800646371.
Palestrina, G.P. "When Fully Came the Day of Pentecost." SSATBB.    CPH 98-3339.
Powell, Robert J. "See the Holy Flame Arise." SATB, kybd.
Schalk, Carl. "Joyous Light of Glory." SATB.    CPH 98-3354.
Schalk, Carl. "Lord God, the Holy Ghost." SATB, org.    AFP 0800646215.
Schuetky, Joseph. "Send Forth Thy Spirit." SATB, opt pno/org.    PLY SC-21.
Schwarz, May. "Come, Holy Spirit, Blow Across the Waters." SATB, org, opt brass quintet, cong.    AFP 0800657888.

### CHILDREN'S CHOIRS

Cox-Johnson, J. Phillip. "Pentecost Joy." U, kybd.    AFP 6000097905.
Kath, Maskell. "Send Down Your Spirit." 2 pt, kybd.    HAL BG2348.
Nelson, Ron. "Be Filled With the Spirit." U, kybd.    AFP 6000096674.
Ramseth, Betty Ann. "Spirit Boundless." U, kybd, fl, fc.    AFP 0800645170.
Schalk, Carl. "I Will Sing to the Lord as Long as I Live" in *Alleluia, I Will Sing*. U, org, opt hb.    AFP 0800647564.

206

## KEYBOARD/INSTRUMENTAL

Dahl, David P. "Bridegroom" in *Hymn Interpretations for Organ*. Org.
  AFP 0800658248.

Duruflé, Maurice. *Prelude, Adagio et Choral: Varié sur la theme du "Veni, Creator."* Org.   Durand 12.016.

Kohrs, Jonathan. "Spirit of Gentleness" in *Four Tunes for Piano and Two Instruments*. Pno, inst.   AFP 0800658787.

Rotermund, Donald. "Komm, heiliger Geist, Herre Gott" in *Introductions, Interludes & Codas on Traditional Hymns, vol. 2*. Org.
  MSM 10-535.

Wold, Wayne L. "Suite on 'O Day Full of Grace.'" Org.
  AFP 080065881.

Zachau, Friedrich. "Komm, heiliger Geist, Herre Gott" in *80 Chorale Preludes*. Org.   PET 11354.

## HANDBELL

Afdahl, Lee J. "Spirit in the Wind." 3-5 oct, opt perc.
  AFP 0800655443.

Hall, Jefferey A. "Come, Holy Ghost, Our Souls Inspire." 3-4 oct.
  L3.   CPH 97-6615.

Hentz, Phyllis Treby. "Meditation on 'Morecambe.'" 4-6 oct. L4.
  MSM 30-801.

Larson, Katherine Jordahl. "O Day Full of Grace." 3-5 oct. L4.
  CPH 97-6774.

Moklebust, Cathy. "Windscape." 3-5 oct. L4.   CPH 97-6833.

## PRAISE ENSEMBLE

Bible, Ken/arr. Bruce Greer. "O Mighty Breath of God."   Allegis
  AG-1066 (SATB, kybd); MU-2433 (perf cass); MU-5032T
  (CD); OR-2433 (orch).

Boerner, Connie/arr. Don Wyrtzen. "Flow, O Mighty Holy River."
  INT 01197 (SATB, kybd); 01194 (choraltrax); 01195 (orch).

Cox, Joe and Jody Lindh. "Come Holy Spirit, Heavenly Dove." SATB,
  kybd.   SMP S-464.

Fisher, Lucy. "Breathe on Me" in *Shout to the Lord 2000 Songbook*.
  SAT[B], kybd.   INT 14247.

Kensinger, Gerald. "Prayer for Pentecost." SATB, kybd.
  INT EMP-0140.

Morgan, Reuben/arr. Jay Rouse. "Eagles' Wings" in *Hillsongs Choral Collection*. SATB, kybd.   INT 16996.

Sadler, Gary. "Wind of God" in *Hosanna Music Songbook 13*. SAT[B],
  kybd.   INT 13576.

Scholtes, Peter/arr. Gregg Sewell. "By Our Love." 2 pt, kybd.
  LOR 10/2231K.

# Sunday, May 19

## DUNSTAN, ARCHBISHOP OF CANTERBURY, 988

By Dunstan's time, Viking invaders had wiped out English monasticism. Dunstan played an important role in its restoration. He was commissioned by King Edmund to reestablish monastic life at Glastonbury, which became a center for monasticism and learning. He was exiled by a later king, Edwy, whom he had publicly rebuked. After Edwy's death Dunstan was made Archbishop of Canterbury and carried out a reform of church and state. He corrected abuses by the clergy, encouraged laity in their devotional life, and was committed to concerns of justice. He was also well-known as a musician and for his painting and metal work.

# Tuesday, May 21

## JOHN ELIOT, MISSIONARY
## TO THE AMERICAN INDIANS, 1690

207

John Eliot was born in England, and his first career was as a schoolteacher. In 1631 he came to New England to preach to the Puritan settlers. In New England he developed an interest in the Algonkian Indians and learned their language and customs. He published a catechism in 1654 and in 1658 translated the scriptures into Algonkian, preparing the first complete Bible printed in the colonies. Eliot also established towns for Indians who had converted to Christianity. These towns were away from Puritan colonies and were established so that the Algonkians could preserve their own culture and live according to their own laws. Eliot also trained indigenous leaders to serve as missionaries to their own people.

Use this commemoration as an opportunity to learn of various American Indian and native Alaska tribal spiritualities and traditions.

# Thursday, May 23

LUDWIG NOMMENSEN,
MISSIONARY TO SUMATRA, 1918

Ludwig Ingwer Nommensen was born in Schleswig-Holstein, Germany. In the early 1860s he went to Sumatra to serve as a Lutheran missionary. His work was among the Batak people, who had previously not seen Christian missionaries. Though he encountered some initial difficulties, the missions began to succeed following the conversion of several tribal chiefs. Nommensen translated the scriptures into Batak while honoring much of the native culture and did not seek to replace it with a European one. At the time of World War II all missionaries were driven out, and the Batak people took over leadership of their own church.

# Friday, May 24

NICOLAUS COPERNICUS, 1543;
LEONHARD EULER, 1783; TEACHERS

Scientists such as Copernicus and Euler invite us to ponder the mysteries of the universe and the grandeur of God's creation. Copernicus is an example of a renaissance person. He formally studied astronomy, mathematics, Greek, Plato, law, medicine, and canon law. He also had interests in theology, poetry, and the natural and social sciences. Copernicus is chiefly remembered for his work as an astronomer and his idea that the sun, not the earth, is the center of the solar system. Euler is regarded as one of the founders of the science of pure mathematics and made important contributions to mechanics, hydrodynamics, astronomy, optics, and acoustics.

208

# SUMMER

*Here is beauty fair as flowers,*

*yet these blossoms grow*

*from the tree of the cross*

# Images *of the* Season

In the Eastern Orthodox liturgy, there is a point

following the kiss of peace when the priest says in a loud voice,

"The doors! The doors!" to which the people respond,

"Wisdom! Let us attend." This image of doors opening to reveal wisdom might serve us well in this summer season.

We have now completed the festival portion of the church year, when the focus is on the great events of the life of Christ, from his annunciation and birth through his passion, death, and resurrection. After the excitement and intensity of those observances, the long green season of the church year can seem anticlimactic. Attention may languish along with attendance, and sometimes the church seems to go into a dormant mode.

Nothing is wrong with enjoying a lower-key season when the sometimes frenetic pace takes a breather. Rest and recreation, too, are gifts from God. Even as we enjoy a little more time to appreciate the world around us, though, we need to remember the continuing importance of our mission in that world.

The festival seasons, with their larger turnouts, more intricate liturgies, and long-practiced movements, can be as daunting to the newcomer as observing a cricket match can be to the average American. Everyone else seems to be caught up in something obviously important, historic, and highly valued. It is hoped that congregations will welcome such uninitiated people even in the highest of holy days, yet newcomers might be too intimidated to do more than sit on the fringes and observe. During the summer, though, people might feel more comfortable approaching and opening the doors that lead into the church.

Many external factors may be at work to encourage this approach, but at the heart of it, perhaps they seek the very thing the gospels serve up so richly during this season, the very thing we all seek: the wisdom, the saving wisdom, so lacking in our society.

Ours is a culture, after all, that does a number of things well, but providing time and place for wisdom is not prominent among them. The church, though, possesses and opens the doors to just the sort of wisdom so badly needed: not simply an ethical wisdom that enables us to put matters into a pleasing and helpful order, but a spiritual wisdom.

This wisdom is not an occasional delicacy but daily, nourishing food. This wisdom is not attained by intellectual exercise or acrobatics of the soul, but is received as a gift from God. This wisdom leads to a transformation based not on our meager resources, but on the immeasurable goodness of God, revealed through the grace of Jesus Christ.

The scripture readings during summer open the doors to this wisdom. The prophets, the apostles, and above all, Christ Jesus begin with what is essentially human (doubt, pride, rebellion, injustice, and violence, as well as fledgling trust, love, and gentleness) and show us how God redeems our humanity. Beginning with common human experience, we are drawn through the doors toward God's gracious wisdom. We can see through those doors a world not so different from the one we know so well, yet one subtly transformed by the forgiving love of God, a new creation into which we are welcomed.

Even during summertime, with its often simpler pace, it is important to remember that the wisdom of God is never a light commodity that we simply acquire. One cannot simply stroll through the doors, order it "to go," and leave. The wisdom of God is not like a book to be checked out, read on the beach, and returned. It is inextricably woven in with the judgment and grace of God. Divine wisdom invites and woos us into a long-term relationship with the source of that wisdom. In an era when such lasting associations are not the norm, the church's challenge is to open wide the doors yet resist the temptation to understate the depth and the implications of an encounter with the wisdom of God. Here is food as sweet as strawberries but as enduring in its nourishment as daily bread. Here is beauty fair as flowers, yet these blossoms grow from the tree of the cross. These doors lead not merely to an hour's diversion on a summer day but to a life transformed today and forever.

With King Solomon of old, may we stand at the doors of God's house and pray: Give us wisdom. This summer, may these same wide-open doors welcome every seeking soul into the embrace of holy wisdom.

# Environment *and* Art *for the* Season

On a hot Sunday in July, Paul watered his

flowerbeds. The small boy next door played busily in his

sandbox until he noticed that his friend had come outside.

Peering through the chain link fence, the child watched Paul for a moment before asking, "Why do you like flowers so much, Mr. Moore? Is it just 'cause they're pretty?"

"I guess I never really thought about it that way," Paul replied. "Of course, the beauty of flowers is part of why I like them. But the other part is that they are living things, like us, and how I care for them makes a difference. God gives us the gift of flowers, but we have to tend the garden. I guess you could say our job is to grow the beauty that God gives us. So I like flowers because they remind me of God."

In the poem "God's Grandeur," the poet Gerard Manley Hopkins wrote: "The world is charged with the grandeur of God. / It will flame out, like shining from shook foil." In summer, the fruits of our gardens are tangible signs of God's beneficence and grandeur. With God, we are cocreators of beauty. Our gardens bring us pleasure and touch us with awe.

In the worship space, flowers are a sign of the wonder of God's creation as well as human thanksgiving and praise for this marvelous mystery. Flowers, grasses, and plants are natural elements that reveal beauty as a quality that points to the holy. The more artificial the floral setting or arrangement, the less likely it is that God's grandeur will be evoked. Artificial flowers will be downright disappointing.

The summer green season is a time to celebrate the gifts of life and growth. Summer, autumn, and November are not liturgical seasons on the same order as the preceding festival seasons. Plans for the church environment need not be as comprehensive or homogenous as they might be during the incarnation and paschal cycles of the church year. This lack of guidelines offers a nice freedom for fresh ideas during the summer months.

A church that regularly orders flowers from a florist during the summer months might ask parishioners to bring flowers from their own gardens to adorn the worship space. A parish might also consider maintaining a garden of its own. One church planned a prayer garden as part of its overall renovation project. A former parking lot will be made into a garden that invites visitors to pray and reflect. Flowers and fragrant herbs from this garden will also be brought into the worship space.

Arranging flowers is an art and should be executed with care and competence. This does not mean that to assist in decorating the church one must be an expert or professionally trained, however. It does mean that people doing the arranging should have some knowledge of basic design principles. If volunteers are planning and arranging the flowers, they might benefit from and appreciate some guidance. Perhaps the florist the church patronizes will agree to give an afternoon workshop for church volunteers on flower arranging. One of the most important considerations in the placement of flowers in the worship space is the scale of the arrangement. Often the selection of flowers, however lovely, is too small and therefore gets lost within the larger church environment.

Do not be afraid to vary flowers throughout the summer. Let the blooms of spring give way to those of summer. Have you ever brought sunflowers into the worship space? How about peppers or herbs? Grasses can be striking and can provide height and mass for floral groupings. Use blue fescue as a grassy blue accent. The July blooms of compact fountain grass are a creamy white, tinged with a hint of pink. For use in large arrangements, the variegated miscanthus is an ornamental grass that can grow as tall as nine feet. Its spiky leaves are deep green lined with white. For some marvelous textures, use the huge, fluffy plumes of compact pampas grass or the silky pink feather tips of foxtail barley.

Eucalyptus has a wonderful fragrance, and both the plant and its aroma suggest healing—an appropriate symbol for this time of the church. Yarrow, blazing star, Saint-John's-Wort, woolly verbena, black-eyed Susan, wood lily, prairie phlox, yellow star grass, and aster are just a handful of wildflowers that can be found in fields across North America. Wildflowers and grasses can offer

211

a lovely, distinctive change from more formal hothouse flowers.

The first Sunday after Pentecost we celebrate the Holy Trinity. In Genesis we will hear again the story of creation. In the gospel we will hear the words of Christ's great commission. Our Lord sends forth his disciples to draw people of all nations into the community of Christ through the saving waters of baptism. As the community of the church, we abide in the community of the Holy Trinity: we are initiated into the church in the name of the Father, and of the Son, and of the Holy Spirit. The ordinary time of the church that begins in summer with the celebration of the Holy Trinity is a fitting season, therefore, to focus on the identity of the church community.

One church commissioned a permanent clay relief installation for its gathering space. The installation is a meditation on the parish community's story. The congregation asked members to submit descriptions of the parish's values. This information was given to artist Jo Myers-Walker, who then translated the descriptions into stylized images depicting biblical narratives. The resulting clay figures grace a "story wall." Stories of forgiveness, for example, were represented by a figure that appears first turned away, then wrapped in another's embrace. Viewers will recognize the story of the prodigal son in these universal human forms.

Volunteers participated in the design of the story wall and even assisted in the actual sculpting process. The result is not only breathtaking, but the wall serves as an icon of the church's identity and mission.

How might this idea be adapted to other media or for seasonal display? The stories of remembrance incorporated in the famous AIDS quilt have been powerful symbols of hope, and a quilt could be created for celebrating a parish community's story. The information collected from the community could be translated into a quilt design that is then fabricated by church quilters and hung in an appropriate spot in the worship space.

Stained glass images of the Trinity have traditionally included the triangle, three interlocking circles, and three fish in a circle. Less well known is the shamrock. According to legend, the shamrock (or three-leaf clover) was used by the missionary Patrick in Ireland to explain the idea of the Trinity to the pagan Celts. Older churches might have stained glass images that are somewhat more

literal: often a white-haired and bearded God the Father reigns above Christ on the cross, beneath which a dove descends. Clearly, more abstract images of the Trinity are in order.

One image that might be helpful for parishioners to view and reflect on is the icon of the *Three Visitors to Abraham at Mamre.* This icon does not attempt to depict the Trinity; rather, it represents the three angels who visit Abraham as a revelation of the Trinity. Three angels sit at a table depicted as an altar with a chalice at the center. In the background are three objects—house, tree, and mountain—as if to correspond to the Holy Spirit who dwells within us, the tree of the cross, and the mountain of God. One intriguing aspect of this story is the fact that Abraham and Sarah welcomed the uninvited guests. How do we practice hospitality to visitors human and divine? An icon of the *Three Visitors* displayed near the font this year in celebration of the Holy Trinity would offer a great opportunity for deeper reflection on the meaning of the Trinity in our lives. The Sunday bulletin can be used to communicate information about the icon.

The idea of church as a community rooted in Christ is beautifully expressed in John's gospel: "I am the vine, you are the branches" (John 15:5). Seasonal vines might be used to encircle the paschal candleholder or the cross. Beautiful wreaths of vines can be put on the outside doors of the church.

This summer, we celebrate the Lord of the harvest who sends laborers into his harvest. We hear the parable of the sower and the foretelling of the end time harvest, when the righteous will be gathered into the kingdom by God's angels. Grain and other agricultural elements native to a church's locale might be worked into the worship environment. Wheat sheaves or other grains can be grouped in attractive bundles and tied with raffia or worked into other arrangements.

The sun is the most universal image of summer. An artist might be asked to work with sun imagery for a fabric installation, perhaps using sheer fabrics without any figures or embellishments other than color, texture, form, and lighting. Another option is to obtain ethnic fabrics that suggest the life and work of indigenous peoples, using sun imagery as a unifying image. This would be a fine way to suggest to the worshiping community that the work of the great commission continues today.

# Preaching *with the* Season

Summer is not just one thing. For children

and teachers, it means a break from school. Many families enjoy

weeks of vacation in the mountains, at a cabin in the woods,

or lounging along a favorite stretch of seashore. But summer does not offer a break for everyone. This is the season when Forest Service firefighters often spend long days battling flames, digging trenches, setting backfires, and putting out hot spots. Summer means more work, not less, for lots of folks.

How we experience summer also depends on where we live. In northern latitudes, summer is first a blessed relief from snow and ice that became gray and littered during winter and turned to mud in early spring. Then comes a season of fragile new growth, when a veil of pale leaves stretches over once bare tree branches. Summer gradually strengthens, the greens of field and lawn turn dark and heavy, and in some parts of the country, residents try to recall the proper procedures for responding to tornado warnings. By the end of August, Northerners suffering through the "dog days" wonder how far into September the heat and humidity will linger.

In Alaska and the Arctic slopes of Canada, "dog days" are rare, and the special feature of summer is days with twenty hours of light. In the desert Southwest, though, summer means temperatures over 100 degrees, sometimes for weeks on end, and people dash from an air-conditioned house to an air-conditioned car to an air-conditioned store or office—the way Northerners rush from one heated space to another in January. All across the South, year-round residents relax a little, because the "snow birds" have gone north, the stores are no longer crowded, and the pace of life in general is slower.

Just as we experience variety in the summer depending on our vocation and where we live, we find that the thought and mood of the Sunday lectionary readings change as we move through the weeks after Pentecost. Yes, we are observing the half-year of the church when the gospel readings present a selection of Jesus' parables, miracles, and teachings, so there is a unity to this season. But summer is not just one thing for preachers.

During these weeks, we encounter in the gospel

readings first the conclusion to Jesus' sermon on the mount, then controversies between Jesus and the Pharisees, a healing, instructions for the Twelve and for all Jesus' disciples, words of comfort, numerous parables about God's rule, a miraculous feeding and a patient rescue, the blessing of a defiant foreigner, and an affirmation of faith. Although it has been said that every preacher's sermons are essentially variations on a theme, those who pay attention to the variety provided by our lectionary will find an opportunity to explore many facets of our relationship with God.

By the end of summer, in fact, those who hear the readings and sermons based on them should be amazed by the complexity of our relationship with God. Jesus said, "Whoever does not take up the cross and follow me is not worthy of me" (Matt. 10:38), and he also said, "My yoke is easy, and my burden is light" (11:30).

When the terrified Peter pleaded for Jesus to rescue him from the sea, crying out, "Lord, save me!" Jesus challenged him, "You of little faith, why did you doubt?" (14:31). The Canaanite woman who insisted that Jesus heal her demon-possessed daughter, however, heard Jesus' reassurance, "Woman, great is your faith!" (15:28).

After Jesus healed the woman who had suffered from hemorrhages for twelve years, "the report of this spread throughout the district" (9:26). But after Peter's confession of faith, "he sternly ordered the disciples not to tell anyone that he was the Messiah" (16:20).

Jesus said, "Everyone then who hears these words of mine and acts on them will be like a wise man..." (7:24). But which words are we to act on? Are we to expect our Christian discipleship to be difficult or easy? Will the petitions of our prayers be heard as signs of doubt or indications of great faith? Are we boldly to "tell everyone what God has done," or does Jesus have some other mission strategy in mind? Might we appear to be rocky or thorny soil simply because we are not sure

213

what message we are supposed to hear? Why did Jesus make things so difficult for us?

Although we might wish Jesus had offered fewer nuances in his teaching about our relationship with God and neighbor, the seeming complexity of his message is necessary, given the human situation—our enslavement to sin, and the fact that the reign of God is "already but not yet" present among us. Lutherans have frequently summarized humanity's need for a multifaceted word from God in an understanding of law and gospel:

> We encounter God's Word as both law and gospel, and we need to hear both. Without the law, we do not know we need the gospel. Without the gospel, the law can only kill. God uses the law in two ways: to keep good order in creation and to drive sinful humans to depend on God alone. The gospel makes us, sinners who oppose the law, right with God. (Beth Ann Gaede and Margaret Marcrander, "Lutheran Basics for Teachers" [Minneapolis: Augsburg Fortress, 1998], 13.)

We find in this season's gospel readings from Matthew, in his account of Jesus' teachings, a gift from God: God's desire to meet us where we are, to speak the precise word that we need to hear at any given moment.

God knows that sometimes we need to be challenged or even scolded. Sometimes we need to be warned about the implications of following Jesus. At other times, we need reassurance and comfort, reason to have courage, hope.

We human beings are inconsistent, often well meaning, but at least as often unreliable. "For I do not do the good I want, but the evil I do not want is what I do," the apostle Paul confessed (Rom. 7:19). Given our own fickleness, uncertainty, and even wrong-headedness, we can give thanks that Jesus did not attempt to teach just one thing.

God's love for us is like a precious gem. The gem is love, through and through. When we examine that gem, however, we see it has many faces. God does not assume we will understand the message the first or even the second time. God is determined to be in relationship with us and has spoken a complex word, so that no matter what our ears are ready for, the message will get through. God loves us and sent Jesus Christ to work among us, to suffer and die, and to overcome the power of sin and death.

It is not always easy for us that God's word is not just one thing, but the message is singular. "For the Lord is good; his steadfast love endures forever, and his faithfulness to all generations" (Ps. 100:5).

# Shape *of* Worship *for the* Season

## BASIC SHAPE OF THE EUCHARISTIC RITE

- Confession and Forgiveness: see alternate worship text for summer in *Sundays and Seasons*

### GATHERING

- Greeting: see alternate worship text for summer
- Omit the Kyrie during the summer (except on the festival of the Holy Trinity)
- Omit or use the hymn of praise during the summer (use for the festival of the Holy Trinity)

### WORD

- Nicene Creed for Holy Trinity; Apostles' Creed for remaining Sundays in this season
- The prayers: see the prayers in the summer section of *Sundays and Seasons*

### MEAL

- Offertory prayer: see alternate worship text for summer
- Use the proper preface for Holy Trinity on the festival of the Holy Trinity; use the proper preface for Sundays after Pentecost for the remainder of the season
- Eucharistic prayer: in addition to four main options in *LBW,* see "Eucharistic Prayer G: Summer" in *WOV* Leaders Edition, p. 71

- Invitation to communion: see alternate worship text for summer
- Post-communion prayer: see alternate worship text for summer

### SENDING

- Benediction: see alternate worship text for summer
- Dismissal: see alternate worship text for summer

## OTHER SEASONAL POSSIBILITIES

### BLESSING FOR TRAVELERS

- Use the prayer "Before Travel" in *LBW,* p. 167, before the benediction whenever groups from the congregation set out to travel. The names of those traveling may be inserted in the prayer.

### FAREWELL AND GODSPEED

- See *Occasional Services,* pp. 151–52, for an order that is appropriate whenever people are leaving the congregation; it may be used either after the prayers or following the post-communion prayer.

215

# Assembly Song *for the* Season

Summer is a natural time for simplification

and renewal. The summer heat makes us hungry for light, cool,

fresh food. Simple picnics and barbeques replace

elegant dinner parties as the way most people gather for festive meals. The summer texts reflect on what it means to be the church in mission and ministry in the world. The summer liturgy should renew and refresh the people of God for this task. Eat the comfort food of beloved hymns and lighten the meal by focusing on the central elements of the liturgy, forgoing all the heavy appetizers, extra side dishes, and desserts.

## GATHERING

Few things renew a soul more quickly than the hearty congregational singing of a beloved hymn. This can be a challenge during the summer when choirs and musicians are scarce and worship attendance fluctuates. Instead of an instrumental prelude, a brief hymn sing could include some favorites as well as provide an opportunity to learn a few new songs over the course of the summer. Keep the accompaniments light and buoyant and the introductions clear and brief. Use the piano more often to accompany the congregation. Summer activities such as gardening, biking, camping, and hiking make us much more aware of the environment around us. Hymns with creation or environmental themes connect worship to this outdoor life. Choose a familiar entrance hymn that will enable the congregation to sing together with confidence. Omit the Kyrie and hymn of praise and move directly to the greeting and prayer of the day.

## WORD

The psalm can assume a larger musical presence in the liturgy and provide a good place to involve out-of-work choir members. Use responsorial psalms in which one or two cantors or a small schola sing the verses and the assembly sings only the refrain. The three volume collection *Psalm Songs* (AFP) and *The Psalter—Psalms and Canticle for Singing* (Westminster John Knox Press) provide a wide variety of responsorial psalm settings. As an alternative to all the alleluias of the Easter season acclamations, in-

troduce the gospel reading with "Lord, let my heart be good soil" (TFF 131, WOV 713, W&P 52) or "Santo, santo, santo" (LLC 273, TFF 203, W&P 61).

## MEAL

The summer can be a good time to teach the congregation a new musical setting of the liturgy, if the setting is musically accessible and will be used throughout the season. Concentrate on learning the eucharistic acclamations first, followed by "Lamb of God" and perhaps the offertory song. This will give the congregation the core of the new setting and the base from which to add other liturgical songs. Speak the preface dialog and proper preface to keep things simple. Congregational hymn singing during the distribution of communion can be more of a challenge in the summer if attendance fluctuates. The communion is another good place to invite choir members to offer solos or small ensemble pieces in place of congregational singing. Piano solos make a nice accompaniment to the distribution and a change of pace from hymns or vocal music. In addition to the wide range of piano literature, a variety of publishers offer collections of piano music for worship based on hymn tunes.

## SENDING

In keeping with the theme of lighter liturgical fare, omit the post-communion song and clear the table immediately following the communion of the people. Include a strong and substantial sending hymn focused on mission and ministry. Many high school and college students are at home with extra time on their hands, and they often make excellent percussionists. Recruit a few students to form a percussion ensemble. Use them to accompany "Let us talents and tongues employ" (WOV 754, TFF 232) as the dismissal hymn. Rhythm suggestions are found in the *With One Voice* accompaniment edition.

# Music *for the* Season

## VERSE AND OFFERTORY

Cherwien, David. *Verses for the Season of Pentecost, set 1.* U, kybd.
MSM 80-541.

*Gospel Acclamations.* Cant, choir, cong, inst. MAY 0862096324.

Powell, Robert. *Verses and Offertory Sentences, Part VI (Pentecost 10–18).*
CPH 97-5506.

Schiavone, J. *Gospel Acclamation Verses for Sundays of the Year, I, II, III.*
GIA G-2495, 2496, 2497.

*Verses and Offertory Sentences, Part V (Pentecost 2–9).* U/SATB, kybd.
CPH 97-5505.

## CHORAL

Armstrong, Matthew. "Savior, Like a Shepherd Lead Us." SATB,
kybd. CPH 98-3326.

Bisbee, B. Wayne. "Praise the Lord." 2 pt, org. AFP 080065970.

Callaway, Susan Naylor. "Psalms, Hymns, and Spiritual Songs."
SATB, perc. LOR 10/2084M.

Ferguson, John. "Lord of the Dance." SATB, org.
GAL, ECS 1.5260.

Jacobson, Allan S. " I Come, O Savior, to Your Table." SATB, kybd.
AFP 6000117027.

Kosche, Kenneth T. "It Is a Good Thing." SATB.
AFP 0800659635.

Leavitt, John. "Give Glory, All Creation." SATB, solo inst, perc.
CPH 98-3558.

Mendelssohn, Felix. "They That Shall Endure to the End" in *Chantry Choirbook.* SATB. AFP 0800657772.

Rutter, John. "For the Beauty of the Earth." SATB, kybd.
HIN HMC-550.

Schalk, Carl. "This Touch of Love." SATB, org, cong.
MSM-50-8301.

Schütz, Heinrich. "Sing to the Lord" in *Chantry Choirbook.* SATB,
kybd. AFP 0800657772.

Scott, K. Lee. "Let the Words of My Mouth." SATB, org.
CPH 98-2963.

Stearns, M.B. Selections: "Lift Up Your Voice." Med voice solos,
kybd. PRE.

Telemann-Nelson, Ronald A. "O Come, Holy Spirit." U, vln, cont.
AFP 11-0314.

## CHILDREN'S CHOIRS

Page, Sue Ellen. "Every Morning's Sun." U, kybd, opt glock.
CG CGA-193.

Rathmann, Dawn. "Go Forth!" U, kybd. Logia (CPH) 98-3332.

Stevens, James Michael. "Colored by God's Love." U, kybd, desc.
KIR K-138.

Tucker, Margaret. "Praise God, Creator." U, kybd. CPH 98-2773.

## KEYBOARD/INSTRUMENTAL

Callahan, Charles. *Spirituals for Keyboard.* Pno/org. MSM 10-890.

Cherwien, David. *Groundings: Five New Organ Settings.* Org.
AFP 0800659805.

Manz, Paul. "Praise God, Praise Him" in *Three Hymns for Flute, Oboe and Organ.* MSM 20-871.

Purvis, Richard. *St. Francis Suite.* Org. J. Fischer 9530-12. x

## HANDBELL

Kinney, Paul. "Vivaldi Concerto." 3-5 oct (w/fl) L3. CG CGB228.

Kinyon, Barbara. "Morning Song." 2-3 oct. L4-. BEC HB198.

Larson, Katherine Jordahl. "Be Thou My Vision." 3-4 oct. L3.
AFP 0800653661.

McChesney, Kevin. "Cantad al Señor." 5 oct. L3.
AFP 080065739X. 3

McChesney, Kevin. "Joyful Rhythm." 2-3 oct. L1+. CG CGB219.

Page, Anna Laura. "I Sing the Mighty Power of God." 3-5 oct. L2.
ALF API9013.

Thompson, Martha Lynn. "Holy Manna." 3-5 oct. L2. AG 2081.

## PRAISE ENSEMBLE

Burleigh, Glenn/arr. Jack Schrader. "Order My Steps." SATB, kybd.
HOP C 5083.

Hopson, Hal. "Amen, Sing Praises to the Lord." SATBB, soloist, opt
perc. HOP C 5057.

Kerr, Ed. "Let Your Spirit Fall Here" in *Only God for Me Songbook.*
SAT[B], kybd. INT 15297.

McPherson, Stephen/arr. Jay Rouse. "Holy Spirit, Rain Down" in
*Hillsongs Choral Collection.* SATB, kybd. INT 16996.

Pethel, Stan. "Shout for Joy." HOP GC 888 (SATB, kybd);
GC 888C (cass).

Thomas, Andrae. "I Will Sing Praises." SATB, kybd. CG A718.

217

# Alternate Worship Texts

### CONFESSION AND FORGIVENESS

Let us seek the face of God,
confessing our sin.

*Silence for reflection and self-examination.*

Holy God,
we have sinned against you and each other.
We pray for your forgiveness and healing.
The good we would do,
we often fail to do.
The evil we do not want,
we find ourselves doing.
Deliver us, O God;
save us from shame;
and guide us in your way. Amen

Nothing can separate us from the love of Christ.
While we were yet sinners, Christ died for us,
and God raised him up from death
that we too might walk in newness of life.
Almighty God have mercy on you,
forgive you all your sins through Jesus Christ,
and by the power of the Holy Spirit
keep you in eternal life.
Amen

### GREETING

The love of God,
made known in Christ Jesus our Lord,
poured into our hearts through the Holy Spirit,
be with you all.
**And also with you.**

### OFFERTORY PRAYER

God of sun and rain, farm and flower,
we praise you for your wonderful creation
and your all-sustaining love.
Calm our anxiety over the needs of this life,
that as we have freely received,
we may freely give. Amen

### INVITATION TO COMMUNION

Come to Christ, the tree of wisdom;
be sheltered, be fed.

### POST-COMMUNION PRAYER

Cultivate and nourish us, O God,
that we may be good soil.
Let the presence of Christ in word and sacrament,
planted within us now,
bring forth rich and beautiful fruit
for the life of the world.
In his name we pray.
Amen

### BLESSING

Holy eternal Majesty,
Holy incarnate Word,
Holy abiding Spirit
bless you forevermore.
Amen

### DISMISSAL

Go forth with God's blessing
to love and serve the Lord.
**Thanks be to God.**

218

# May 26, 2002

The Holy Trinity
First Sunday after Pentecost

## INTRODUCTION

Christians have held a festival in honor of the Holy Trinity since the ninth century, when it was celebrated in French monastic communities. In the fourteenth century, the festival was added to the calendar and has been celebrated throughout the world since that time.

Every celebration of baptism and eucharist is a trinitarian celebration, just as every gathering "in the name of the Father, the Son, and the Holy Spirit" is done in union with the Sacred Three.

In the power of the Holy Spirit, the church gathers on Sunday—the day of resurrection—to offer thanksgiving to the Father for Christ's saving life given to us at the table of the word and the table of the eucharist. Listen carefully to the opening greeting, the baptismal "formula," the eucharistic prayer, and the final blessing: we are accompanied in life's journey by a community of persons. We are not alone. Indeed, the church is intended to be a sign in the world of the Holy Trinity's unity-in-diversity.

## PRAYER OF THE DAY

Almighty God our Father, dwelling in majesty and mystery, renewing and fulfilling creation by your eternal Spirit, and revealing your glory through our Lord, Jesus Christ: Cleanse us from doubt and fear, and enable us to worship you, with your Son and the Holy Spirit, one God, living and reigning, now and forever.
*or*
Almighty and ever-living God, you have given us grace, by the confession of the true faith, to acknowledge the glory of the eternal Trinity and, in the power of your divine majesty, to worship the unity. Keep us steadfast in this faith and worship, and bring us at last to see you in your eternal glory, one God, now and forever.

## READINGS

### Genesis 1:1—2:4a

This creation story reached its current form during or after the crisis of the Babylonian exile of Israel. The writer makes profound declarations of faith concerning the world, human life, and God. This faith sees the world and humanity under the sovereignty of the God who redeemed Israel: it was Israel's God who was responsible for creation, not Babylon's.

### Psalm 8

How exalted is your name in all the world! (Ps. 8:1)

### 2 Corinthians 13:11-13

Paul concludes his painful letter to the troubled church at Corinth with a final appeal for these Christians to live in peace. His last words form a trinitarian benediction still used in Christian liturgy today.

### Matthew 28:16-20

After his resurrection, Jesus summons his remaining disciples and commissions them for mission in the name of the triune God.

## COLOR White

## THE PRAYERS

With the whole people of God, let us join in prayer for the church, those in need, and all of God's creation.
*A BRIEF SILENCE.*
That all humankind exercise its stewardship of creation in thoughtful, loving, and responsible ways; God of mercy,
**hear our prayer.**
That the church may grow in unity and love, bearing witness to the triune God; God of mercy,
**hear our prayer.**
That our daily labor may be good in your eyes and our days of rest may be hallowed; God of mercy,
**hear our prayer.**
That the peoples of the world may open their hearts and minds to one another and earnestly wage peace. God of mercy,
**hear our prayer.**
That all those who are sick or who grieve (especially) may be embraced in your arms of healing; God of mercy,
**hear our prayer.**
*HERE OTHER INTERCESSIONS MAY BE OFFERED.*

That we remain steadfast in our faith, following in the path of all the blessed saints who have been baptized in the name of the Holy Trinity and now dwell in your everlasting glory; God of mercy,
**hear our prayer.**
O God, give us faith to trust your promises, that our lives may glorify your name, through Jesus Christ our Lord.
**Amen**

### IMAGES FOR PREACHING

Many Christian denominations value good order. Theology and worship practices, understanding of the role of clergy, expectations for congregational and denominational organization, and other facets of Christian ecclesiastical life together are all informed by a variety of documents and traditions that produce an ordered church.

Our desire for order arises from the noblest of roots. In the beginning, when God created the heavens and the earth, God brought order out of chaos. The apostle Paul ended his second letter to the troubled church in Corinth with a plea that they "put things in order" (2 Cor. 13:11). In Matthew's gospel, Jesus provided clear instructions to his disciples as he prepared to leave them: Go, make disciples, baptize, teach, remember.

On this festival of the Holy Trinity, we are reminded both by the day's readings and by the name of the festival itself that it is the very nature of God to be orderly. We do not worship a pantheon of gods who rule over different parts of the universe and compete for our loyalty. Nor do we worship a god who terrorizes us with inconsistency, loving us one day and punishing us the next. We worship the one God—Father, Son, and Holy Spirit—who is committed to loving us in every way, by creating, redeeming, sustaining, calling, and sending us. In all that God does to strengthen our relationship with the source of life and salvation, and to sustain us in our life and ministry, God provides a gracious and inviting order.

### WORSHIP MATTERS

How can the reality of God's triune nature best be witnessed to on this festival day? This day is used most profitably as a time to focus on the praise, honor, and glory due to the God revealed in scripture and the church's life. Our confession of faith is more appropriately, and easily, sung and prayed than it is defined. But

this prayer and praise, song and glory given to the Trinity effects something in us. The truth of God as a divine community of love turned toward the world shapes us who worship. The task of leaders is to help enable the faith community through word and sacrament to reflect God's love ever more clearly in its life together, so that believers go forth from worship to serve the world in love and, by their renewed lives, help to shape God's reign among us.

### LET THE CHILDREN COME

Few people seem to know how much of the liturgy is from scripture. Not only children will benefit from a brief word about the apostolic greeting and its source in today's second reading from 2 Corinthians. Learning where things come from is a particular delight for seven- to eleven-year-olds.

### HYMNS FOR WORSHIP
GATHERING

Holy, holy, holy    LBW 165
Lord, you give the great commission    WOV 756
How majestic is your name    W&P 66

HYMN OF THE DAY

When long before time    WOV 799

ALTERNATE HYMN OF THE DAY

God, whose almighty word    LBW 400
Holy, holy    TFF 289

COMMUNION

Now the silence    LBW 205
Praise to the Father    LBW 517
I received the living God    WOV 700
Wind of the Spirit    W&P 157

SENDING

Now thank we all our God    LBW 533/534
My Lord of light    WOV 796
Go ye therefore    W&P 49

ADDITIONAL HYMNS AND SONGS

Alleluia! Let praises ring!    LW 437
Come, all you people    WOV 717, TFF 138
In the name of the Father    TFF 142

220

Many and great, O God, are your works    WOV 794
Morning has broken    W&P 98
O God, O Lord of heaven and earth    LBW 396
Who are we    DH 33

## MUSIC FOR THE DAY

### SERVICE MUSIC

Although a simpler gathering rite is appropriate for the "green" Sundays following Pentecost, this day calls for at least the trinitarian hymn of praise, "Glory to God." A setting of the Te Deum laudamus (see *LBW*, p. 139 or LLC 260) also makes a fitting hymn of praise on this day. The Sanctus, with its "thrice-holy" cry of praise, is another element worthy of embellishment on this day.

### PSALMODY

Bell, John. *Psalms of Patience, Protest and Praise.*    GIA G-4047.
Cooney, Rory. "How Glorious Is Your Name." SATB, gtr, cong, kybd.    GIA G-3412.
Geary, Patrick.    PS 3.
Haas, David.    PCY 9.
Hillert, Richard. "How Great Is Your Name."    GIA G-3187.
Shute, Linda Cable.    PW A.

### CHORAL

Bedford, Michael. "Go Therefore and Make Disciples" in *6 Scripture Anthems, Set 1.* U, org.    CPH 97-6131.
Erickson, Richard. "When Long Before Time." SATB, org, opt fl.    AFP 0800656768.
Ferguson, John. "Holy God, We Praise Your Name." SATB, cong, org, opt brass.    GIA G-3167.
Freed, Isadore. "Psalm 8." Solo, pno.    Southern Pub.
Friedell, Harold. "Draw Us in the Spirit's Tether." SATB, org.    HWG GCMR 2472.
Kosche, Kenneth T. "It Is a Good Thing." SATB.    AFP 0800659635.
Palestrina-Lundquist. "Praise Be to Thee." SATB.    Willis 5678.
Praetorius, Michael. "Praise the Lord." SATB.    GSCH 9817.
Proulx, Richard. "Te Deum Laudamus." SATB, hb.    AFP 11-1729.
Reger, Max. "We Bless the Father and the Son and the Holy Ghost" in *A Second Motet Book.* SATB, org.    CPH 97-5205.
Schalk, Carl. "Go Therefore and Make Disciples of All Nations." 2 pt mxd, kybd.    MSM-50-6200.
Scott, K. Lee. "Trinitarian Blessing" in *The Augsburg Choirbook.* SATB, kybd.    AFP 0800656784.

Sowerby, Leo. "All Hail, Adored Trinity." SATB, org.    OXF A165.
Turner, C. Kenneth. "O Trinity Most Blessed Light" in *Anthems for Choirs 1.* SATB div, org.    OXF.
Wolff, S. Drummond. "O Blessed Holy Trinity." SAB.    CPH 98-2218.
Wyton, Alec. "Go Ye Therefore." SATB, org.    HWG 2755.

### CHILDREN'S CHOIRS

Christopherson, Dorothy. "God of the Universe." 2 pt, kybd, fl, xyl, perc.    CG CGA821.
Glover, Rob. "Praise to the Trinity." U, opt gtr.    CG CGA 668.
Marcello, Benedetto/arr. Dale Grotenhuis. "O God, Creator." 2 pt, kybd.    MSM-50-9420.

### KEYBOARD/INSTRUMENTAL

Cherwien, David. "Holy God, We Praise Your Name" in *Interpretations Book VI.* Org.    AMSI SP-103.
Cherwien, David. "The Singer and the Song" in *Organ Plus One.* Org, inst.    AFP 0800656180.
Farlee, Robert Buckley. "Nicaea" in *Augsburg Organ Library: Easter.* Org.    AFP 0800659368.
Moore, David W. "Nicaea" in *Dona Nobis Pacem.* Pno, inst.    AFP 0800650300092.
Post, Piet. "Inleiding en Koraal over 'Heilig, Heilig.'" Org.    Elkan-Vogel 163-00033.

### HANDBELL

Anderson & Kramlich. "Holy, Holy, Holy." Solo.    HOP 1834.
McKlveen, Paul A. "Holy, Holy, Holy!" 3-5 oct. L3.    CPH 97-6819.
Sherman, Arnold B. "Immortal, Invisible." 3-4 oct. L1+.    Red River HB0008.
Tucker, Sondra. "Crosswind." 3-5 oct. L4.    AFP 0800659880.

### PRAISE ENSEMBLE

Hayford, Jack W./arr. Jack Schrader. "Majesty." SATB, kybd.    HOP GC 868.
Maddus, McCall, and Mukalay Mulongoy. "O Sifuni Mungu (All Creatures of Our God and King)." SATB.    HAL 40326302. Also available in SAB and 2 pt.
Smith, Byron. "Worthy to Be Praised." SATB, kybd.    WAR LG 52654.

221

# Monday, May 27

JOHN CALVIN, RENEWER OF THE CHURCH, 1564

John Calvin began his studies in theology at the University of Paris when he was fourteen. In his mid-twenties he experienced a conversion that led him to embrace the views of the Reformation. His theological ideas are systematically laid out in his *Institutes of the Christian Religion*. He is also well known for his commentaries on scripture. He was a preacher in Geneva, was banished once, and then later returned to reform the city with a rigid, theocratic discipline.

Calvin is considered the father of the Reformed churches. The ecumenical agreement the Evangelical Lutheran Church in America shares with churches of the Reformed tradition is a recent manifestation of the unity we share in Christ.

# Wednesday, May 29

JIRI TRANOVSKY, HYMNWRITER, 1637

Tranovský is considered the "Luther of the Slavs" and the father of Slovak hymnody. Trained at the University of Wittenberg in the early seventeenth century, Tranovský was ordained in 1616 and spent his life preaching and teaching in Prague, Silesia, and finally Slovakia. He produced a translation of the Augsburg Confession and published his hymn collection Cithara Sanctorum (Lyre of the Saints), the foundation of Slovak Lutheran hymnody.

Use the commemoration to pray for the Slovak church and to give thanks for the gifts of church musicians. Sing Tranovský's hymn, "Make songs of joy" (LBW 150), at parish gatherings today.

222

# Friday, May 31

THE VISITATION

The Visitation marks the occasion of Mary visiting her cousin Elizabeth. Elizabeth greeted Mary with the words, "Blessed are you among women," and Mary responded with her famous song, the Magnificat. Luke tells us that even John the Baptist rejoiced and leapt in his mother's womb when Elizabeth heard Mary's greeting. Today we are shown two women: one too old to have a child bears the last prophet of the old covenant, and the other, still quite young, bears the incarnate Word and the new covenant.

In what ways does the church bear the good news of Christ to others and remain faithful to God's call?

# Saturday, June 1

JUSTIN, MARTYR AT ROME, C. 165

Justin was born of pagan parents. At Ephesus he was moved by stories of early Christian martyrs and came under the influence of an elderly Christian man he had met there. Justin described his conversion by saying, "Straightway a flame was kindled in my soul and a love of the prophets and those who are friends of Christ possessed me." Justin was a teacher of philosophy and engaged in debates about the truth of Christian faith. He was arrested and jailed for practicing an unauthorized religion. He refused to renounce his faith and he and six of his students, one of them a woman, were beheaded.

Justin's description of early Christian worship around the year 150 is the foundation of the church's pattern of worship, East and West. His description of it is in *With One Voice* (p. 6) and helps reveal the deep roots our contemporary shape of the liturgy has in the ancient worship of the church.

# June 2, 2002

Second Sunday after Pentecost
Proper 4

## INTRODUCTION

The second half of the church's year, spanning the months from June through November, focuses upon the church's growing and building. The gospel readings flow more or less continuously from Matthew's gospel. During the summer months, we also read from the letter to the Romans. Today's readings invite us to a solid foundation for the building up of the church and of Christians: the rock of Jesus' words, the ground of faith. No flood can float away and no wind can blow down the house that is founded on this rock.

## PRAYER OF THE DAY

Lord God of all nations, you have revealed your will to your people and promised your help to us all. Help us to hear and to do what you command, that the darkness may be overcome by the power of your light; through your Son, Jesus Christ our Lord.

## READINGS

### Deuteronomy 11:18-21, 26-28

On the verge of entering the promised land, Moses invites Israel to respond to God's grace with a way of life characterized by obedience and passed on from parent to child. Living the life of faith has profound consequences for the well-being of the human family.

### Psalm 31:1-5, 19-24

Be my strong rock, a castle to keep me safe. (Ps. 31:3)

### Romans 1:16-17; 3:22b-28

In several verses from the first chapter of Romans Paul sounds the theme that is further developed in chapter three: the gospel is God's saving power for both Jews and Gentiles. All people have sinned against God but are extended the free gift of a new relationship with God through Christ Jesus, who is God's own self-offering for the life of the world.

### Matthew 7:21-29

These sayings of Jesus, which conclude the sermon on the mount in Matthew's gospel, challenge Christians in the community to trust Jesus so much that they will risk living in the ways suggested by his teachings of God's will for life together.

## SEMICONTINUOUS FIRST READING/PSALM

### Genesis 6:9-22; 7:24; 8:14-19

Through the waters of the flood, God brings judgment upon the violence of the earth; through those same waters, God delivers Noah, his family, and the animals with them to a new beginning, joined in a new covenant relationship with God.

### Psalm 46

The Lord of hosts is with us; the God of Jacob is our stronghold. (Ps. 46:4)

## COLOR Green

## THE PRAYERS

With the whole people of God, let us join in prayer for the church, those in need, and all of God's creation.
*A BRIEF SILENCE.*

When we turn from your commandments and worship gods of our making, turn us back to your way. God of mercy,

**hear our prayer.**

Build up your church and all its leaders to be a strong rock for all who seek refuge. God of mercy,

**hear our prayer.**

Make your presence and power known to all those working for justice and peace throughout the world. God of mercy,

**hear our prayer.**

As school years draw to a close, give refreshment and continued growth to teachers and students in the summer months ahead. God of mercy,

**hear our prayer.**

Strengthen and comfort those who despair, those without hope, the sick, and the grieving (especially). God of mercy,

**hear our prayer.**

*HERE OTHER INTERCESSIONS MAY BE OFFERED.*

Remembering all the saints who have served you throughout the ages, we give you thanks and pray that we will one day be reunited with them in your glory. God of mercy,

**hear our prayer.**

223

O God, give us faith to trust your promises, that our lives may glorify your name, through Jesus Christ our Lord.
**Amen**

## IMAGES FOR PREACHING

A teenage girl walks through the shopping mall with a cell phone clamped to her head, getting an update about her friends' plans for the evening. A business executive hovers over a laptop computer connected to a pay phone, determined to stay on top of things back at the office. A retired couple in Arizona downloads pictures of their new grandson through their Internet connection, thrilled to "see" the baby just hours after he was born.

Our expectation that we should easily be able to stay in touch with one another has never been more pronounced. We like to think we can communicate instantly with anyone, anywhere. We delude ourselves into thinking that if we are connected with the right people, we can stay in control of our life. We will not be left out of the loop, caught by surprise, or separated from people we care about. How firm a foundation we think we have in cell phones, personal planners, pagers, and computers!

The Bible's instructions for building a firm foundation are quite different from those our society offers, however. What matters, the deuteronomist explained, are not the words that fly over telephone lines or from one satellite dish to another. It is God's words that are important. These, we are counseled, we should put into our heart and soul (Deut. 11:18), wrap around our body, teach to our children, talk about with our friends and family, and even post at the entry to our home. The foundation for all that is life-giving is the fact that through Christ Jesus, our relationship with God has been restored. This is the solid rock on which we stand.

## WORSHIP MATTERS

Today's texts speak about obeying God's commandments, teaching them to our children, and building our lives on the rock that is Christ. Yet we are also reminded that our relationship with God rests entirely on God's grace toward us and on Christ's righteousness, which becomes our own by faith. Word and sacrament is all gift. As leaders preside and assist in worship, it is important that they do so graciously and invitingly. All present need to sense worship as a resting in the grace of God, as a place of refreshment and encouragement, and never as a performance that must be rightly done in order truly to be accepted by God.

## LET THE CHILDREN COME

Listen closely to the first reading for this day. Can you hear a child's voice proclaiming this to the assembly? To read aloud in the assembly, one must understand the text, enunciate clearly, and practice enough times so that the reading becomes lively proclamation. Surprising numbers of children are capable of this. Your task is to seek, invite, teach, and encourage them. Other children often will listen more carefully to a voice that sounds like their own.

## HYMNS FOR WORSHIP
### GATHERING

Come, thou Fount of every blessing    LBW 499
Oh, praise the gracious power    WOV 750
Awesome God    W&P 13

### HYMN OF THE DAY

My hope is built on nothing less    LBW 293, 294

### ALTERNATE HYMN OF THE DAY

Listen, God is calling    WOV 712
What God ordains is good indeed    HFW

### COMMUNION

Amazing grace    LBW 448
If you but trust in God to guide you    LBW 453
One bread, one body    WOV 710, TFF 122, W&P 111

### SENDING

The Church's one foundation    LBW 369
Go, my children, with my blessing    WOV 721, TFF 161

### ADDITIONAL HYMNS AND SONG

How firm a foundation    LBW 507
I saw water    BL
Only by grace    W&P 112
Salvation unto us has come    LBW 297
Thanksgiving to the living God    DH 3
You are mine    W&P 158

## MUSIC FOR THE DAY

### PSALMODY

*See the fifth Sunday of Easter.*

### CHORAL

Bach, J.S. "All Who Believe and Are Baptized" in *Bach for All Seasons*. SATB, kybd.  AFP 080065854X.

Bach, J.S. "Salvation Unto Us Has Come" in *Bach for All Seasons*. SATB, kybd.  AFP 080065854X.

Chemin-Petit, Hans. "Salvation Unto Us Has Come" in *The SAB Choirale Book*. SAB.  CPH 97-7575.

Ferguson, John. "Word of God Come Down on Earth." SATB, org. GIA G-3764.

Haydn, F. J. "In Thee O Lord." Sam Fox. SATB, pno/org.  PSI03.

Mendelssohn, Felix. "On God Alone My Hope I Build" in *Chantry Choirbook*. SATB.  AFP 0800657772.

Sedio, Mark. "The Thirsty Fields Drink." SATB, org. AFP 0800657063.

Walter, Johann. "I Build on God's Strong Word" in *Chantry Choirbook*. SATB.  AFP 0800657772.

### CHILDREN'S CHOIRS

Kerr, Ann. "The House of the Lord." 2 pt, kybd, fl.  CG CGA-324.

Lord, Suzanne. "Faith That's Sure." U, kybd, banjo, autoharp. CG CGA-695.

### KEYBOARD/INSTRUMENTAL

Cherwien, David. "My Hope Is Built on Nothing Less" in *Interpretations Book IX*. Org.  AMSI SP-106.

Ferguson, John. "Thy Holy Wings" in *Thy Holy Wings*. Org. AFP 0800647955.

Hassell, Michael. "Eternal Father, Strong to Save" in *Jazz Pastorale*. Pno.  AFP 0800658051.

Tryggestad, David. "Melita" in *Deo Gracias*. Org.  AFP 0800653599.

### HANDBELL

Anderson & Sherman. "Come, Thou Fount of Every Blessing." Solo. HOP 1835.

Edwards, Dan R. "Come, Thou Fount." 3 oct. L3.  CG CGB 212.

Moklebust, Cathy. "Thy Holy Wings." 3-4 oct. L3.  CPH 6518.

Sherman, Arnold B. "How Firm a Foundation." 3-5 oct. L3. CPH 97-6811.

### PRAISE ENSEMBLE

Brown, Scott Wesley and Jeff Nelson. "Grace Alone." SATB, kybd. WRD 0 80689 81027 5.

Harvill, Jamie/arr. Don Harris. "Jesus, You Are So Good." INT 09407 (SATB, kybd); 09408 (choraltrax); 09405 (orch).

Smith, Michael W. and Deborah D Smith. "Faithfulness Medley" (Great Is Thy Faithfulness and Great Is the Lord). SATB, kybd. HOP GC 4000.

Smith, Michael W./arr. Jack Schrader. "Thy Word." 2 pt (opt div), kybd.  HOP GC 960.

# Monday, June 3

### JOHN XXIII, BISHOP OF ROME, 1963

In his ministry as a bishop of Venice, John was well loved by his people. He visited parishes and established new ones. He had warm affection for the working class—he himself was the child of Italian peasants—and he worked at developing social action ministries. At age seventy-seven he was elected bishop of Rome. Despite the expectation that he would be a transitional pope, he had great energy and spirit. He convened the Second Vatican Council in order to open the windows of the church and "let in the fresh air of the modern world." The council brought about great changes in Roman Catholic worship, changes that have influenced Lutherans and many other Protestant churches as well.

# Wednesday, June 5

### BONIFACE, ARCHBISHOP OF MAINZ, MISSIONARY TO GERMANY, MARTYR, 754

Boniface (his name means "good deeds") was born Wynfrith in Devonshire, England. He was a Benedictine monk who at the age of thirty was called to missionary work among the Vandal tribes in Germany. He led large numbers of Benedictine monks and nuns in establishing churches, schools, and seminaries. Boniface was also a reformer. He persuaded two rulers to call synods to put an end to the practice of selling church offices to the highest bidder. Boniface was preparing a group for confirmation on the eve of Pentecost when he and the others were killed by Vandal warriors.

225

## Friday, June 7

### SEATTLE, CHIEF
### OF THE DUWAMISH CONFEDERACY, 1866

Noah Seattle was chief of the Suquamish tribe and later became chief of the Duwamish Confederacy, a tribal alliance. When the tribes were faced with an increase in white settlers, Seattle chose to live and work peacefully with them rather than engage in wars. After Seattle became a Roman Catholic, he began the practice of morn-ing and evening prayer in the tribe, a practice that continued after his death. On the centennial of his birth, the city of Seattle—named for him against his wishes—erected a monument over his grave.

When parish groups gather today, remember Chief Seattle and his work as a peacemaker. Consider beginning or ending parish events with a simple form of morning or evening prayer, not only today, but as a regular part of the parish life.

# June 9, 2002

### Third Sunday after Pentecost
### Proper 5

### INTRODUCTION

226

The weeks of summer coincide with the beginning of the Pentecost season. Summer brings sunny warmth, growing crops, and the promise of harvest: images of the Holy Spirit's presence and activity in our lives, the church, and the world. In our life together as a community of faith, what needs light, warmth, and watering to grow and flourish? How might we be attentive to others' needs to receive this nourishment through God's words of life and holy supper?

Today the church remembers Columba, Aidan, and Bede, three monks and missionaries in the British Isles during the seventh and eighth centuries A.D.

### PRAYER OF THE DAY

O God, the strength of those who hope in you: Be present and hear our prayers; and, because in the weakness of our mortal nature we can do nothing good without you, give us the help of your grace, so that in keeping your commandments we may please you in will and deed; through your Son, Jesus Christ our Lord.

### READINGS

#### Hosea 5:15—6:6

Because God's people have trusted in military powers and not God, today's reading begins with the surprising declaration that God will withdraw from Israel and Judah. Perhaps then, the people will recognize their sin and repent. God does not desire pious prayers apart from a life of committed action that results in the living out of the covenant.

#### Psalm 50:7-15

To those who keep in my way will I show the salvation of God. (Ps. 50:24)

#### Romans 4:13-25

In his letter to the Romans, Paul develops the idea that people are made right with God through faith rather than obedience to the law. To illustrate, he uses here the example of Abraham, whose trust in God's promise is what marks him as righteous.

#### Matthew 9:9-13, 18-26

Matthew's gospel presents Jesus as a healer of those who are sick and sinful. Through him, God's mercy overcomes exclusivism, prejudice, disease, and even death.

### SEMICONTINUOUS FIRST READING/PSALM

#### Genesis 12:1-9

This story of divine call and human response sets the pattern for those to follow. Here, God promises to bless Abram and his progeny, so that through him, "all the families of the earth" might gain blessing. Abram's response models what faith should be: a total entrusting of oneself to God's providential care.

#### Psalm 33:1-12

Happy is the nation whose God is the Lord! (Ps. 33:12)

COLOR Green

## THE PRAYERS

With the whole people of God, let us join in prayer for the church, those in need, and all of God's creation.

*A BRIEF SILENCE.*

For those who minister in the church and the priesthood of all believers, that we draw our strength from your mercy and forgiveness; God of mercy,

**hear our prayer.**

For the nations of the world and their leaders, that pride and greed give way to peace and justice in every land; God of mercy,

**hear our prayer.**

For each of us, that when we hear you calling us, we may put aside the things of this world and follow in your way; God of mercy,

**hear our prayer.**

For all who mourn and for those who suffer in body, mind, and spirit (especially), that they may find hope and healing in your presence; God of mercy,

**hear our prayer.**

*HERE OTHER INTERCESSIONS MAY BE OFFERED.*

That we may share the faith of Sarah and Abraham, of Columba, Aidan, the Venerable Bede, and all the saints, until we come with them into your promised land; God of mercy,

**hear our prayer.**

O God, give us faith to trust your promises, that our lives may glorify your name, through Jesus Christ our Lord.

**Amen**

## IMAGES FOR PREACHING

Newspaper advice columnists regularly publish letters from newlyweds who are unhappy because they suspect a wedding gift they received was secondhand. The salad bowl with more than a little telltale patina just does not seem like a real gift. Not long ago, however, a woman wrote a letter to one of the columnists that cast a different light on such gifts. "After I've had a chance to enjoy something for a while," she explained, "I like to honor others by sharing with them the treasure that has brought me so much pleasure." What matters, she reminds us, is the intention of the giver, not the gift itself.

When we offer thanks to God with our gifts of money, time, or possessions, we are giving God secondhand gifts. Everything in the world, we are frequently reminded in scripture, belongs to the Lord. Nothing we could give God appears on a heavenly gift registry. God does not need anything! God does want something, though. God desires "mercy, not sacrifice," Jesus reminded the Pharisees, who criticized Jesus' dining with tax collectors and sinners.

The people to whom God had sent several of the prophets seemed to think that they could offer sacrifices of thanks to God, even though their hearts were full of hate and their actions were unjust. The Pharisees, Jesus observed, seemed to be of a similar mind. They did not recognize that when our heart is not full of love for our neighbor, we cannot enjoy a whole relationship with God.

What matters to God is the inclination of our heart as we offer our gifts, secondhand though they are. When we ourselves desire to be in a restored relationship with God, the desire and the relationship both made possible through the death and resurrection of Jesus, whatever we bring to God will be received as a righteous and welcome gift.

## WORSHIP MATTERS

Jesus spent much of his time with those upon whom the religious establishment looked down. He welcomed all people in the name of God. When visitors worship with us, it is the task of the presider, assistants, and assembly alike warmly to welcome them in the name of God. Evaluate the congregation's communion practice. Consider whether the distribution needs to be simplified, so newcomers can easily join in. The worship folder can include a statement about how communion is received. An announcement of invitation can be made with a brief clarification of the assembly's practice. Some ushers can direct communicants to the altar, and others can stand nearby to help worshipers return to their seats. Those seated next to visitors can also extend an invitation to join them at the table. All that is done should offer an image of the joy and graciousness that will characterize the marriage feast of the Lamb.

## LET THE CHILDREN COME

What do we do in the liturgy that is done nowhere else in our society? We openly speak about sickness and pray for those who are ill, hospitalized, and home-

227

bound. Are the children invited to pray for those they know are in need of healing? We send ministers for the sick and homebound to those who are unable to be present for the Sunday worship service. Are children invited to join ministers of communion, especially if they will visit other children? Will the children be invited to participate in a service of healing and thus see the congregation supporting the sick and weak in song, prayer, and laying on of hands and anointing? After all, where will our children learn to be healers? By watching television? Or by watching their parents and the community of faith?

## HYMNS FOR WORSHIP
### GATHERING
Praise, my soul, the King of heaven   LBW 549
Gracious Spirit, hear our pleading   WOV 687, TFF 103
Morning has broken   W&P 98

### HYMN OF THE DAY
There's a wideness in God's mercy   LBW 290

### ALTERNATE HYMN OF THE DAY
By gracious powers   WOV 736
Healer of our every ill   WOV 738

### COMMUNION
My faith looks up to thee   LBW 479
I want Jesus to walk with me   WOV 660, TFF 66
Cup we bless   BL

### SENDING
How firm a foundation   LBW 507
Thy holy wings   WOV 741
The trees of the field   W&P 138

### ADDITIONAL HYMNS AND SONGS
There is a balm in Gilead   WOV 737, TFF 185
There was Jesus by the water   NCH 545
Step by step   W&P 132
Bread for the journey   GS2 40

## MUSIC FOR THE DAY
### PSALMODY
Folkening, John. "Six Psalm Settings with Antiphons." Choir, cong, kybd.   MSM 80-700.

Hopson, Hal.   TP. WJK.
Ogden, David. "Rest Your Love" in PS 2.
Shute, Linda.   PW A.

### CHORAL
Bach, J.S. "Jesus Is My Joy, My All." SATB.   ECS. 2214.
Handel, G.F. "Keep Me Faithfully in Thy Paths." SB, org.
Loosemoore, Henry. "O Lord, Increase My Faith." SATB. Broude Brothers CR11.
Mendelssohn, Felix. "I Will Sing of Thy Great Mercies" in *Sing a Song of Joy; Vocal Solos for Worship.*   AFP 0800647882 (MH); 0800652827 (ML).
Rutter, John. "I Will Worship the Lord" in *Call to Worship.* SATB, kybd.   HIN HMC-686.
Staton, Kenneth W. "There's a Wideness in God's Mercy." 2 pt mxd, kybd.   AFP 6000098367.
White, David Ashley. "There's a Wideness in God's Mercy." SATB, org.   SEL 420-243.
Zimmermann, Heinz. "Have No Fear Little Flock" in *Five Hymns.* U, SATB.   CPH 97-5131.

### CHILDREN'S CHOIRS
Dietterich, Phillip R. "Come One, Come All, Follow." U, kybd. CG CGA-553.
Edwards, Rusty/arr. Richard Drexler. "O Lord, I Worship You/Simple Song." U, kybd, opt C inst.   AFP 0800674219.
Sleeth, Natalie. "The Kingdom of the Lord." 2 pt, kybd, fl. AMSI 301.

### KEYBOARD/INSTRUMENTAL
Farlee, Robert Buckley. "Lord, Revive Us" in *Many and Great.* Org. AFP 0800658949.
Honoré, Jeffrey. "Healer of Our Every Ill" in *Augsburg Organ Library: Lent.* Org.   AFP 0800658973.
Kolander, Keith. "Healer of Our Every Ill" in *Hymn Tune Sketches, Set 1.* Org.   CPH 97-6775.
Manz, Paul. "Joyful, Joyful, We Adore Thee" in *Two Pieces for Festive Occasions.* Org.   MSM 10-840.
Pelz, Walter. *Have No Fear, Little Flock.* Org, cong.   CPH 97-5692.

### HANDBELL
Cole, Patricia Sanders. "As the Deer" in *Twelve Bells for Praise and Worship.* 3-6 ringers.   HOP 19 75.
Moklebust, Cathy, "Let All Things Now Living." 3-5 oct. L4. CG CGB 170.
Page, Anna Laura. "Fairest Lord Jesus." 2-3 oct. L1.   ALF 8659.

228

PRAISE ENSEMBLE

Martin, Joseph M. "Talitha Kum!" SATB, kybd.   GS A 7186.

Martin, Joseph M. and David Angerman. "Footprints in the Sand." SATB, kybd.   GS A 6998.

Sadler, Gary. "Wind of God" in *Hosanna Music Songbook 13.* SAT[B], kybd.   INT 13576.

## Sunday, June 9

COLUMBA, 597; AIDAN, 651; BEDE, 735; CONFESSORS

Today we commemorate three monks from the British Isles who kept alive the light of learning and devotion during the Middle Ages. Columba founded three monasteries, including one on the island of Iona, off the coast of Scotland. That monastery was left in ruins after the Reformation but today is home to an ecumenical religious community. Aidan was known for his pastoral style and ability to stir people to charity and good works. Bede was a Bible translator and scripture scholar. He wrote a history of the English church and was the first historian to date events anno domini (A.D.). Bede is also known for his hymns, including "A hymn of glory let us sing!" (LBW 157).

## Tuesday, June 11

ST. BARNABAS, APOSTLE

The Eastern church commemorates Barnabas as one of the seventy commissioned by Jesus. Though he was not among the twelve mentioned in the gospels, the book of Acts gives him the title of apostle. His name means "son of encouragement." When Paul came to Jerusalem after his conversion, Barnabas took him in over the fears of the other apostles, who doubted Paul's discipleship. Later, Paul and Barnabas traveled together on missions.

At the Council of Jerusalem, Barnabas defended the claims of Gentile Christians regarding the Mosaic law. How can his work on behalf of others and his support of other Christians serve as a model for contemporary Christians and churches?

## Friday, June 14

BASIL THE GREAT, BISHOP OF CAESAREA, 379;
GREGORY OF NAZIANZUS,
BISHOP OF CONSTANTINOPLE, C. 389;
GREGORY, BISHOP OF NYSSA, C. 385

These three are known as the Cappadocian fathers, and all three of them explored the mystery of the Holy Trinity. Basil was influenced by his sister Macrina to live a monastic life, and he settled near his home. Basil's Longer Rule and Shorter Rule for monastic life are the basis for Eastern monasticism to this day. In his rule, he establishes a preference for communal, rather than eremetical monastic life, by making the case that Christian love and service are by nature communal. Gregory of Nazianzus was sent to preach on behalf of the orthodox faith against the Arians in Constantinople, though the orthodox did not have a church there at the time. He defended orthodox trinitarian and christological doctrine, and his preaching won over the city. Gregory of Nyssa was the younger brother of Basil the Great. He is remembered as a writer on spiritual life and the contemplation of God in worship and sacraments.

229

# June 16, 2002

### Fourth Sunday after Pentecost
### Proper 6

## INTRODUCTION

In today's gospel reading, Jesus speaks of the church's mission with images drawn from daily life. The harvest is already plentiful, he says, but laborers are needed for work in the fields of daily life.

What are we to do? We are to do what the liturgy invites us to do: let our conversation be shaped by the good news, extend Christ's peace wherever we find ourselves, and share our bread with the hungry.

## PRAYER OF THE DAY

God, our maker and redeemer, you have made us a new company of priests to bear witness to the Gospel. Enable us to be faithful to our calling to make known your promises to all the world; through your Son, Jesus Christ our Lord.

## READINGS

### Exodus 19:2-8a

Upon their arrival at Mount Sinai following the great deliverance at the Reed (Red) Sea, Israel hears the marvelous story of what God has done for them. Because God has delivered them, Israel is called to live in a relationship with God—to live as a priestly people through whom God will work for all.

### Psalm 100

We are God's people and the sheep of God's pasture. (Ps. 100:2)

### Romans 5:1-8

For Paul, living in God's grace means experiencing peace with God and hope that does not disappoint. The love of God, evident in Christ's death for the undeserving, has been poured into our hearts and sustains us in our troubles.

### Matthew 9:35—10:8 [9-23]

According to Matthew's gospel, the mission of Jesus' followers is to continue the mission of Jesus himself. Here, he instructs his first disciples as to how they might proclaim the gospel through their words and deeds.

## SEMICONTINUOUS FIRST READING/PSALM

### Genesis 18:1-15 [21:1-7]

God, in the form of three messengers, announces to Sarah and Abraham that they will have a child. Sarah laughs at this seeming impossibility, for at this time she is eighty-nine years old and Abraham is ninety-nine. Yet through this "impossible" birth, the Lord fulfills his promise to Abraham to bring blessing to him and his descendants and to make him into "a great nation" (Gen. 12:2).

### Psalm 116:1, 10-17

I will call upon the name of the Lord. (Ps. 116:11)

## COLOR  Green

## THE PRAYERS

With the whole people of God, let us join in prayer for the church, those in need, and all of God's creation.

*A BRIEF SILENCE.*

Bless your church, and send us out as laborers into your harvest, proclaiming your good news. God of mercy,
**hear our prayer.**

Bless those who care for others with a father's love; send your peace into every home; bring healing to families that are divided or in crisis; and in your compassion gather the lost and scattered. God of mercy,
**hear our prayer.**

Be with those who have special need of your presence in their lives—those who are sick, homeless, grieving, or lonely (especially). Bear them up on eagles' wings, that they may know how much you treasure them. God of mercy,
**hear our prayer.**

Be with those throughout the world who suffer persecution in your name. Give them strength and grace to remain faithful in the face of suffering. God of mercy,
**hear our prayer.**

*HERE OTHER INTERCESSIONS MAY BE OFFERED.*

With apostles and martyrs, women and men of every time and place, call us one day to our eternal home. God of mercy,
**hear our prayer.**

O God, give us faith to trust your promises, that our lives may glorify your name, through Jesus Christ our Lord.

**Amen**

## IMAGES FOR PREACHING

The witness of God's people throughout scripture is that God has always looked after us. As the Israelites entered the wilderness, God called to Moses from Mount Sinai and commanded him to remind all Israel about their deliverance from Egypt, how God bore them up "on eagles' wings" (Exod. 19:4). When Jesus walked among the villagers, he saw they were broken and aimless, and appointed disciples to "cure the sick, raise the dead, cleanse the lepers, cast out demons" (Matt. 10:8).

God has left nothing to chance. So determined is God to be in relationship with us that "God's love has been poured into our hearts" (Rom. 5:5). God's love is not just "out there" and available if we decide we are interested in savoring a portion. God has placed that love right into the core of our being.

God's miraculous ways with us did not cease when Israel arrived in the promised land or even after Jesus rose from the dead. God continues to nurture us, to look after us as a most attentive parent. God has given us the gift of baptism, by which we are welcomed into the family of God, washed clean from the power of sin and death, and called to ministry in God's world. God continues to feed us with the bread and wine of eucharist, the body and blood of Jesus, through which we receive the forgiveness of sin, and life and salvation.

God has formed us into the body of Christ, where we together celebrate these sacraments and hear God's words of assurance: We are God's treasured possession. Out of all God's creation, God has chosen us, set us apart, and given us access to the "grace in which we stand" (Rom. 5:2).

## WORSHIP MATTERS

In the Sunday liturgy the members of the assembly, having lived out their vocation in daily life, gather together as one holy priesthood. One presides, many assist, and all beseech God on behalf of the world. The Christian assembly ought not to appear as if it has only one priest. All roles and actions must be held in honor and deemed important. Liturgy is work, and all are needed. All members of the assembly are "at work" as they praise God in song, give thanks for all God's gifts to humanity, become equipped by hearing the word to share the good news in daily life, and pray God that the gifts of Christ offered at worship may benefit all creation.

## LET THE CHILDREN COME

During the summer months you might have more visitors worshiping with you. How do you welcome those who bring children? Is there a nursery or cry room for the inconsolable infant? Are restrooms clearly marked? Are there books and resources for other quiet activities available for the very young? Who will assist those of any age who are unfamiliar with the liturgy?

## HYMNS FOR WORSHIP
GATHERING
This is my Father's world   LBW 554
Great is thy faithfulness   WOV 771, TFF 283
Shout to the Lord   W&P 124

HYMN OF THE DAY
The Son of God, our Christ   LBW 434

ALTERNATE HYMN OF THE DAY
Lord, you give the great commission   WOV 756
On eagle's wings   WOV 779, W&P 110

COMMUNION
Come, let us eat   LBW 214, TFF 119
Grains of wheat   WOV 708
Amazing love   W&P 8

SENDING
I love to tell the story   LBW 390, TFF 229
Father, we thank you   WOV 704
Hallelujah! We sing your praises   WOV 722, TFF 158

ADDITIONAL HYMNS AND SONGS
The care the eagle gives her young   NCH 468
We sing to you, O God   NCH 9
Come with joy   DH 41
God has called us   OBS 59

## MUSIC FOR THE DAY
### PSALMODY

All people that on earth do dwell   LBW 245

Before Jehovah's awesome throne   LBW 531

Dufford, Bob.   STP, vol. 5.

Howard, Julie. *Sing for Joy: Psalm Settings for God's Children.*   LTP.

Oh, sing jubilee to the Lord   LBW 256

Shute, Linda Cable.   PW A.

Sweelinck, Jan P. "Psalm 100." SATB, org.   ECS 2791.

Trapp, Lynn. "Psalm 100." Choir, cong, fl, org.   MSM 80-704.

### CHORAL

Bisbee, B. Wayne. "Praise the Lord." 2 pt, org.   AFP 0800659708.

Britten, Benjamin. "Jubilate Deo." SATB, org.   OXF 42.848.

Curtright, Carolee R. "Jubilate!" 2 pt, kybd.   CG CGA-582.

Head, Michael. "Make a Joyful Noise Unto the Lord."   PRE 1014 (high key); 1015 (low key), solo voice, pno, org.

Mendelssohn, Felix. "Jerusalem, Thou That Killest the Prophets" in *St. Paul.* S solo, kybd.   GSCH Ed. 321.

Mendelssohn, Felix. "They That Shall Endure to the End" in *Chantry Choirbook.* SATB.   AFP 0800657772.

Tallis, Thomas. "All People That on Earth Do Dwell" in *Anthems for Choirs 1.* SATB, org.   OXF.

Vaughan Williams, Ralph. "The Old Hundredth Psalm Tune." SATB, org.   OXF 42.953.

### CHILDREN'S CHOIRS

Heck, Lyle. "Make a Joyful Noise Unto the Lord." 2 pt, kybd, fl.   AFP 0800654773.

Kosche, Kenneth. "Make a Joyful Noise." U/2 pt, kybd.   CG CGA620.

### KEYBOARD/INSTRUMENTAL

Albrecht, Mark. "On Eagle's Wings" in *Timeless Tunes for Flute and Piano.* Pno, inst.   AFP 0800659074.

Bingham, Seth. "Festal Song" in *Hymn Preludes, set 1.* Org.   HWG GB 151.

Ferguson, John. "Old Hundredth" in *Psalm Preludes.* Org.   AFP 0800656849.

Organ, Anne Krentz. "On Eagle's Wings." Pno.   AFP 0800655524.

Purcell, Henry. "Variations on the Doxology" in *Ceremonial Music for Organ,* E. Power Biggs, ed. Org/trp.   Mercury 453-00090.

### HANDBELL

Behnke, John. "O Waly Waly." 2-3 oct, opt fl. L3.   AFP 0800657403.

Hopson, Hal H. "Psalm 100." 3-5 oct.   AFP 0800654048.

McChesney, Kevin. "Jesus Calls Us." 3-5 oct. L3.   AGEHR AG 35144.

Mendelssohn, Felix/arr. Kevin McChesney. "Lift Thine Eyes." 2 oct, quartet.   HOP CP6064.

### PRAISE ENSEMBLE

Albrecht, Sally and Jay Althouse. "Come Follow Me." ALF 4254 (SATB, kybd); 4255 (SAB); 4256 (2pt).

Fragar, Russell and Darlene Zschech/arr. J. Daniel Smith. "That's What We Came Here For" in *Hillsongs Choral Collection.* SATB, kybd.   INT 16996.

Price, Nancy and Don Besig. "Go Out and Serve Him!" SATB, kybd.   GS A 7365.

# Friday, June 21

ONESIMOS NESIB, TRANSLATOR, EVANGELIST, 1931

Onesimos was born in Ethiopia. He was captured by slave traders and taken from his Galla homeland to Eritrea, where he was bought, freed, and educated by Swedish missionaries. He translated the Bible into Galla and returned to his homeland to preach the gospel there. His tombstone includes a verse from Jeremiah 22:29, "O land, land, land, hear the word of the Lord!"

Does your congregation support mission work through synod or churchwide offerings, or do you support a specific missionary? Let the commemoration of Onesimos Nesib be a way for your congregations to focus on missions during the summer months.

# June 23, 2002

Fifth Sunday after Pentecost
Proper 7

## INTRODUCTION

In today's gospel reading, Jesus gives a brief teaching on the nature of discipleship: do not be afraid, for I am with you; tell others what you hear me say; give your life to the good news and you will discover the riches of life.

This teaching appears simple, yet it is spoken in an anxious and troubled world where it is easier to be fearful than courageous and more common to look out for oneself than to care for the neighbor in need.

## PRAYER OF THE DAY

O God our defender, storms rage about us and cause us to be afraid. Rescue your people from despair, deliver your sons and daughters from fear, and preserve us all from unbelief; through your Son, Jesus Christ our Lord.

## READINGS

Jeremiah 20:7-13

Jeremiah's message of doom earns him only contempt and persecution. Having been beaten, placed in stocks, and then released by Pashur, one of the temple priests, Jeremiah cries out in heart-wrenching lament. Nevertheless, the prophet remains confident of God's care and concludes with resounding praise.

Psalm 69:8-11 [12-17] 18-20
(Psalm 69:7-10 [11-15] 16-18 [NRSV])

Answer me, O Lord, for your love is kind. (Ps. 69:18)

Romans 6:1b-11

In the first part of his letter to the Romans, Paul says that God sent Christ to die for us while we were sinners and so, by grace, accepts us through baptism just as we are. Now, he clarifies that baptism also brings freedom from the slavery of sin and the possibility of beginning a new life.

Matthew 10:24-39

Moved by compassion for the crowds, Jesus has commissioned his twelve disciples to continue his work of preaching and healing. Now he warns them that their ministry will meet with opposition, requiring absolute trust in God and unswerving commitment to their Lord.

## SEMICONTINUOUS FIRST READING/PSALM

Genesis 21:8-21

Hagar, an Egyptian servant of Abraham's wife Sarah, is first mentioned in Genesis 16. Unable to conceive a child of her own, Sarah had selected Hagar to be a surrogate mother. Though Hagar had given birth to Ishmael, Sarah subsequently gave birth to a son of her own named Isaac, which led to the sending away of Hagar and Ishmael in this passage.

Psalm 86:1-10, 16-17

Have mercy upon me; give strength to your servant. (Ps. 86:16)

## COLOR Green

## THE PRAYERS

With the whole people of God, let us join in prayer for the church, those in need, and all of God's creation.
*A BRIEF SILENCE.*

For leaders in the church and leaders of nations, that they may carry out their office in the spirit of servanthood and discipleship; God of mercy,
**hear our prayer.**

For those who work the land and grow our food, that there may be sun and water enough to make the harvest abundant; God of mercy,
**hear our prayer.**

For families and congregations in the midst of turmoil, that they may know your reconciling love and forgiveness; God of mercy,
**hear our prayer.**

For those who carry heavy burdens—those who are addicted, those who are unemployed or homeless, those who are sick (especially); lighten their load with your love and compassion. God of mercy,
**hear our prayer.**

*HERE OTHER INTERCESSIONS MAY BE OFFERED.*

With John the Baptist and all the martyrs and saints, we give you thanks and look forward to the joy of endless life with you. God of mercy,
**hear our prayer.**

233

O God, give us faith to trust your promises, that our lives may glorify your name, through Jesus Christ our Lord.
**Amen**

## IMAGES FOR PREACHING

Worshipers in many congregations are dismissed each Sunday with the words, "Go in peace. Serve the Lord," to which they respond, "Thanks be to God." The readings for this Sunday might well leave us wondering, however, whether there really is any peace to be had.

Jeremiah lamented that he had become a laughingstock because of his prophecies, but when he tried to refrain from speaking, "Then there is something like a burning fire shut up in my bones; I am weary with holding it in, and I cannot" (Jer. 20:9). The psalmist moaned that because of his faithfulness to God, he had become an alien even to his own brothers and sisters (Ps. 69:8). Jesus warned his disciples, "I have not come to bring peace, but a sword," and "Whoever does not take up the cross and follow me is not worthy of me" (Matt. 10:34, 38).

Walking with God is not necessarily an easy journey. The ministry to which God calls us, whether in the church or in the wider world, might leave us feeling ridiculed and alone, weary and defeated, terrified about what lies ahead. Do we have the skills, the strength and stamina, the stomach to do what needs doing? Maybe we are better off simply not noticing the direction that our personal gifts and passions; friends, family, and colleagues; and opportunities seem to be taking us. If we avoid God's path, perhaps we can take one that promises to be more pleasant.

Before Jesus delivered the bad news (the warning that he did not come to bring peace), he offered his disciples some very good news: "Even the hairs of your head are all counted.... You are of more value than many sparrows" (Matt. 10:30-31). Therefore, when we go where God calls us, we walk not alone, but with God. We walk in newness of life (Rom. 6:4).

## WORSHIP MATTERS

Printed or spoken announcements at the eucharist ought to make clear to those who desire to come to the Lord's table that what they receive under the signs of bread and wine is Christ himself, risen and available to us as our spiritual food and drink. It is Christ who is the host at the meal and Christ who is the food. The one who offered himself into death for the forgiveness of our sin now offers himself—his body and blood—to us for the nourishment of the new life of faith. To invite believers to receive the real presence of Christ in the eucharist is to invite them to a deeper and more joyful relationship with God.

## LET THE CHILDREN COME

The hymn "We were baptized in Christ Jesus" (WOV 698) echoes today's second reading. The first stanza could be sung as the gospel acclamation and the last stanza at the close of the gospel. Or have an adult "line" the first stanza (sing phrase by phrase, with the children repeating each time) as the gospel acclamation.

## HYMNS FOR WORSHIP
### GATHERING
Give to our God immortal praise   LBW 520
Gather us in   WOV 718

### HYMN OF THE DAY
O Jesus, I have promised   LBW 503

### ALTERNATE HYMN OF THE DAY
Weary of all trumpeting   WOV 785
Why should I feel discouraged   TFF 252

### COMMUNION
Children of the heavenly Father   LBW 474
We come to the hungry feast   WOV 766
The summons   W&P 137

### SENDING
On our way rejoicing   LBW 260
We all are one in mission   WOV 755
Lead me, guide me   TFF 70

### ADDITIONAL HYMNS AND SONGS
Lord, listen to your children   W&P 91
I'm going on a journey   TFF 115
Waterlife   W&P 145
Christ, whose purpose is to kindle   TWC 720
Aquí del pan partido tomaré/Here would I feast   LLC 384

234

## MUSIC FOR THE DAY
### PSALMODY

Butler, Eugene. "Save Me, O God" in *The Solo Psalmist*. Solo, kybd. SMP PP98.

Dean, Stephen.  PS 3.

Haas, David.  PCY, vol. 8.

Hopson, Hal H. "You Are My Child." U, opt C inst.  CGA-480.

Kogut, Malcolm.  PCY, vol. 10.

Shute, Linda Cable.  PW A.

### CHORAL

Ahlen, Waldemar. "The Earth Adorned" in *Psalm of Summer*. SATB/solo, kybd.  WAL WH-126.

Farlee, Robert Buckley. "O Blessed Spring." SATB, org, C inst, opt cong.  AFP 0800654242.

Handel, G.F. "Since By Man Came Death" in *Messiah*. SATB, org. Various ed.

Liebhold. "Commit Your Life to the Lord" in *A Second Motet Book*. SATB, opt org.  CPH 97-5205.

Macfarlane, Will C. "Christ Our Passover." SATB, org. PRE 322.35139.

Mendelssohn, Felix. "Cast Thy Burden Upon the Lord" in *Church Choir Book*. SATB.  CPH 97-6320.

Scheidt, Samuel. "My Inmost Heart Now Raises." 2 pt mxd, kybd. CPH 98-3564.

Scott, K. Lee. "Redeeming Grace" in *Sing a Song of Joy: Vocal Solos for Worship*.  AFP 0800647882 (MH); 0800652827 (ML).

Willan, Healey. "Christ Being Raised from the Dead" in *We Praise Thee I*. SSA.  CPH CC 1032.

### CHILDREN'S CHOIRS

Gilpin, Greg. "Jubilate!" 2 pt, kybd.  BEL BSC9834.

Handel, G.F./arr. Stephen Andrews. "I Will Praise Forever." U, 2 pt. LOR 10/1443K.

### KEYBOARD/INSTRUMENTAL

Albrecht, Timothy. "Munich" in *Grace Notes, vol. V*. Org. AFP 0800656245.

Kolander, Keith. "Reflections" in *Three Arias for Piano and Solo Instruments*.  AFP 0800658175.

Miller, Aaron David. "Munich" in *Triptych for Lent and Easter*. Org. AFP 0800659457.

Pachelbel, Johann. "Alle Menschen mussen sterben" (Salzburg) in *80 Chorale Preludes*. Org.  PET 11354.

Wellman, Samuel. "Munich" in *Keyboard Hymn Favorites*. Pno. AFP 0800656814.

### HANDBELL

Anderson, Christine. "A Sacred Harp Tune." Solo.  HOP 1661.

Moklebust, Cathy. "Kyrie." 2 oct.  AFP 080064777.

Moklebust, Cathy. "Children of the Heavenly Father." 3 oct. L2. CG CGB-139.

Page, Anna Laura. "The River." 3-5 oct. L4.  ALF 8655.

### PRAISE ENSEMBLE

Burleigh, Glenn/arr. Jack Schrader. "Order My Steps" (In Your Word). SATB, kybd.  HOP C 5083.

Condon, Mark/arr. J. Daniel Smith. "Let Us Come Into This House" in *Marvelous Things Choral Collection*. SATB, kybd. INT 18256.

Williams and Mullins/arr. Russell Mauldin. "Promises One by One." SATB, kybd.  Allegis AG-1069.

# Monday, June 24
### THE NATIVITY OF ST. JOHN THE BAPTIST

The Nativity of St. John the Baptist is celebrated exactly six months before Christmas Eve. For Christians in the Northern Hemisphere, these two dates are deeply symbolic. John said that he must decrease as Jesus increased. John was born as the days are longest and then steadily decrease. Jesus was born as the days are shortest and then steadily increase. In many countries this day is celebrated with customs associated with the summer solstice. Midsummer is especially popular in northern European countries that experience few hours of darkness at this time of year.

Parishes could consider having a summer festival shaped by the pattern of the liturgical year. Consider a church picnic on or near this date, and use John's traditional symbols of fire and water in decorations and games.

# Tuesday, June 25
### PRESENTATION OF THE AUGSBURG CONFESSION, 1530;
### PHILIPP MELANCHTHON,
### RENEWER OF THE CHURCH, 1560

The University of Wittenberg hired Melanchthon as its first professor of Greek, and there he became a friend of Martin Luther. Melanchthon was a popular professor—

235

even his classes at six in the morning had as many as six hundred students. As a reformer he was known for his conciliatory spirit and for finding areas of agreement with fellow Christians. He was never ordained. On this day in 1530 the German and Latin editions of the Augsburg Confession were presented to Emperor Charles of the Holy Roman Empire. The Augsburg Confession was written by Melanchthon and endorsed by Luther. In 1580 when the Book of Concord was drawn up, the unaltered Augsburg Confession was included as the principal Lutheran confession.

In the spirit of Melanchthon's work, consider a summer ecumenical study group with a nearby Roman Catholic parish. Use the Augsburg Confession and the Joint Declaration on the Doctrine of Justification as study documents.

## Friday, June 28 .

IRENAEUS, BISHOP OF LYONS, C. 202

Irenaeus believed that the way to remain steadfast to the truth was to hold fast to the faith handed down from the apostles. He believed that only Matthew, Mark, Luke, and John were trustworthy gospels. Irenaeus was an opponent of gnosticism and its emphasis on dualism. As a result of his battles with the gnostics he was one of the first to speak of the church as "catholic." By "catholic" he meant that congregations did not exist by themselves,

but were linked to one another throughout the whole church. He also maintained that this church was not contained within any national boundaries. He argued that the church's message was for all people, in contrast to the gnostics who emphasized "secret knowledge."

What do we mean when we say that the church is catholic and apostolic? How is the apostolic faith passed down through the generations?

## Saturday, June 29

ST. PETER AND ST. PAUL, APOSTLES

These two are an odd couple of biblical witnesses to be brought together in one commemoration. It appears that Peter would have gladly served as the editor of Paul's letters: in a letter attributed to Peter, he says that some things in Paul's letters are hard to understand. Paul's criticism of Peter is more blunt. In Galatians he points out ways that Peter was wrong. One of the things that unites Peter and Paul is the tradition that says they were martyred together on this date in A.D. 67 or 68. What unites them more closely is their common confession of Jesus Christ. In the gospel reading Peter declares that Jesus is the Christ through whom the foundation of the church is established. In the second reading Paul tells the Corinthians that they are the temple of Christ. Together Peter and Paul lay a foundation and build the framework for our lives of faith through their proclamation of Jesus Christ.

# June 30, 2002

Sixth Sunday after Pentecost
Proper 8

## INTRODUCTION

Without God's loving presence, we are like a parched and waterless land. In the waters of baptism, Christ becomes our life-giving spring, quenching our thirst and pouring God's love into our hearts. In today's gospel, Christ promises that the disciple who gives a cup of cold water to the little ones serves Christ himself. Our baptism leads us to hear Jesus' words as words concerning our baptismal mission to serve the little ones of this world—with a gesture as simple as offering a cup of cold water.

Today we commemorate Johann Olof Wallin, a nineteenth-century Swedish bishop who was also a prolific hymnwriter.

## PRAYER OF THE DAY

O God, you have prepared for those who love you joys beyond understanding. Pour into our hearts such love for you that, loving you above all things, we may obtain your promises, which exceed all that we can desire; through your Son, Jesus Christ our Lord.

## READINGS

Jeremiah 28:5-9

The prophets Hananiah and Jeremiah were not at odds simply because of their differing views of upcoming events. Hananiah announces peace and restoration within two years; Jeremiah sees the path to peace as one that requires repentance—recognition of one's sins and reliance on God's forgiveness. Jeremiah knows that when Hananiah's comforting prediction does not come true, all will know that Hananiah has not been sent by God.

Psalm 89:1-4, 15-18

Your love, O Lord, forever will I sing. (Ps. 89:1)

Romans 6:12-23

Paul has told the Roman Christians that in baptism they were not only made right with God through grace, but were also made free from the slavery of sin. Thus, he now claims that those who are accepted by God as sinners may also be used by God for righteousness.

Matthew 10:40-42

When Jesus sends his disciples out as missionaries, he warns them of persecution and hardships they will face. He also promises to reward any who aid his followers and support their ministry.

## SEMICONTINUOUS FIRST READING/PSALM

Genesis 22:1-14

Today's reading portrays Abraham as the model of obedience. He is prepared to obey God's commands in the midst of extreme contradiction: the child to be sacrificed is the very child through whom Abraham is to receive descendants. This obedience prefigures the later obedience of another son through whom the world will receive blessings.

Psalm 13

I put my trust in your mercy, O Lord. (Ps. 13:5)

## COLOR  Green

## THE PRAYERS

With the whole people of God, let us join in prayer for the church, those in need, and all of God's creation.
*A BRIEF SILENCE.*

For leaders in the church and all the members of Christ's body, that we may be prophets for peace and reconciliation; God of mercy,

**hear our prayer.**

For the leaders and people of the nations, that we offer true hospitality to those who are poor, persecuted, and dispossessed; God of mercy,

**hear our prayer.**

*or*

For the leaders and people of the United States, that as we celebrate our freedom, we offer true hospitality to all those still seeking freedom; God of mercy,

**hear our prayer.**

For all who live with addiction, depression, grief, or illness (especially), that they may know your tender care; God of mercy,

**hear our prayer.**

237

For those who visit the sick, care for those in need, visit the lonely and imprisoned, and work for peace and justice, that they may be strengthened for their tasks; God of mercy,

**hear our prayer.**

For this congregation, that our lives may be a prophetic witness to your power and grace; God of mercy,

**hear our prayer.**

*HERE OTHER INTERCESSIONS MAY BE OFFERED.*

We give you thanks for Johan Olaf Wallin and all the saints who from age to age have sung of your faithfulness. Welcome us with them into the eternal light of your presence; God of mercy,

**hear our prayer.**

O God, give us faith to trust your promises, that our lives may glorify your name, through Jesus Christ our Lord.

**Amen**

### IMAGES FOR PREACHING

Matthew, working in a missionary environment, passes on Jesus' teaching that whoever welcomes Jesus' messenger welcomes Jesus himself, and God with him. At the end of today's gospel reading, we encounter one concrete image: a cup of cold water (Matt. 10:42).

We need to hear Jesus' words about a cup of cold water from two perspectives. First, Jesus' teaching is addressed to everyone who hears God's word. What we learn is that when we pay even a little attention to God's word—if we respond only by offering a drink of water to one of Jesus' disciples—that mustard-seed-size openness to a relationship with God will not be forgotten in God's presence.

Our understanding of this pericope is broadened, however, when we remember that in the previous verses from Matthew, we read Jesus' words about the challenges of Christian discipleship. It is not easy to be a follower of God; that much is clear: "Whoever does not take up the cross and follow me is not worthy of me" (Matt. 10:38). When we serve as messengers of Jesus, however, we can be hopeful, because some of those whom we encounter will be moved to respond positively to our message—will offer us a cup of cold water.

The rewards of sharing the good news are many. The image of the cup of cold water is a metaphor that describes the openness of those who hear God's word.

Those who receive that word and are moved by it will themselves be rewarded. But this passage is also about the preacher. The one who shares the good news—whether prophet, "righteous one," or "little one," that is, disciple—is blessed whenever God's word is gladly received, for there can be no greater reward than to see God's word take root in the heart of another.

### WORSHIP MATTERS

Moving out into the assembly to commune those who cannot physically come to the table can speak a word of grace to everyone present. Jesus did not require people to come to him, but rather went to those who needed to hear the good news of the reign of God. Bringing the sacrament to those who cannot physically approach the table images the love and mercy of God that is available to all through the gift of Christ's presence in the sacrament. Doing this at the outset of the distribution may offer an even more powerful sign that God cares for the neediest among us. Because we are all needy ones in various ways throughout our lives, this practical and loving gesture can have deep significance for the whole assembly.

### LET THE CHILDREN COME

You know how your ears perk up when you hear your name mentioned. Young worshipers will notice when they hear Jesus speaking about "little ones" in the gospel reading. The opening minutes of the sermon could be spoken in words even the very young could understand, and the preacher might even address the "little ones" by mentioning their names (but only with assurance that none will be omitted or forgotten).

### HYMNS FOR WORSHIP
GATHERING

Give to our God immortal praise    LBW 520

God is here    WOV 719

We bring the sacrifice of praise    W&P 150

HYMN OF THE DAY

Where cross the crowded ways of life    LBW 429, LLC 513

ALTERNATE HYMN OF THE DAY

Oh, praise the gracious power    WOV 750

Let us ever walk with Jesus    LBW 487

238

## COMMUNION

Just as I am without one plea    LBW 296

Christians, while on earth abiding    LBW 440

Jesu, Jesu, fill us with your love    WOV 765

## SENDING

God of grace and God of glory    LBW 415

The Spirit sends us forth to serve    WOV 723

## ADDITIONAL HYMNS AND SONGS

O God of mercy, God of light    LBW 425

Great is the Lord    W&P 53

Let heaven your wonders proclaim    NCH 29

O grant us, Christ, a deep humility    OBS 72

Surely it is God who saves me    WOV 635

## MUSIC FOR THE DAY

### PSALMODY

Fillmore, James. "I Will Sing of the Mercies" in SPW, 52.    WRD.

Haas, David.    PCY, vol. 8.

Powell, Robert J. "O Praise the Lord, Ye Children." 3 pt canon.
    CGA 163.

My song forever shall record    PSH 593

Shute, Linda.    PW A.

Trapp, Lynn. "Four Psalm Settings." SATB/U, kybd.    MSM 80-701.

### CHORAL

Beethoven, Ludwig van. "Prayer" in *Rejoice Now My Spirit: Vocal Solos for
    the Church Year.*    AFP 0800651081 (MH); 080065109X (ML).

Furnival, Anthony C. "Amazing Grace." SATB, org, opt brass/timp.
    HIN HMC-255.

Grieg-Overby. "God's Son Has Made Me Free." SATB.
    AFP 0800645561.

Handel, G.F. "But Thanks Be to God" in *Messiah.* SATB, kybd.
    Various ed.

Handel, G.F. "O Death, Where Is Thy Sting?" in *Messiah.* AT duet,
    kybd.    Various ed.

Sampson, Godfrey. "My Song Shall Be Alway of the Lovingkind-
    ness." U, SATB, org.    NOV 29 0244 03.

Whitaker, Howard. "I Will Sing of the Mercies." SATB, kybd.
    AFP 0800649680.

### CHILDREN'S CHOIRS

Hopson, Hal H./arr. "Rock-a My Soul." U, kybd, desc.
    CG CGA645.

Mendelssohn, Felix/arr. Gordon Blaine. "I Will Sing of Thy Great
    Mercies." 2 pt, kybd.    WAL WW1184.

### KEYBOARD/INSTRUMENTAL

Albrecht, Timothy. "Walton" in *Grace Notes VIII.* Org.
    AFP 0800658264.

Mathews, Peter. "Intermezzo for Violin and Organ."    MSM 20-969

Sadowski, Kevin. "Walton" in *Six Hymn Preludes.* Org.    CPH 97-6044.

Thayer, Eugene. "Variations on the Russian National Hymn." Org.
    MCF DM 229.

Vaughan Williams, Ralph. "Hyfrydol" in *Three Preludes for Organ on
    Welsh Hymn Tunes.* Org.    GAL 1.5987.2.

### HANDBELL

Morris, Hart. "Amazing Grace." 3-5 oct. L5-.    AGEHR AG35076.

Sherman, Arnold B. "Jesus Shall Reign." 2-3 oct. L2.    AG 1708.

Sherman, Arnold B. "Jesus Shall Reign." 4-5 oct. L2+.    AG 1709.

VaHarmony/arr. Wadsworth. "Amazing Grace." 3 oct, quartet.
    HOP CP6014.

### PRAISE ENSEMBLE

Allen, Dennis. "Trust in the Lord." SSATB, kybd.    Church Street
    (GMG) 0767396901.

Chapman, Steven Curtis/arr. Camp Kirkland. "We Trust in the
    Name of the Lord Our God."    Allegis AG 1022 (SATB,
    kybd); OR-2425 (orch); CD MU-5011T (choraltrax CD).

Sadler, Gary. "Only God for Me" in *Only God for Me Songbook.* SAT[B],
    kybd.    INT 15297.

239

# Sunday, June 30

JOHAN OLOF WALLIN, ARCHBISHOP OF UPPSALA,
HYMNWRITER, 1839

Wallin was consecrated archbishop of Uppsala and primate of the Church of Sweden two years before his
death. He was considered the leading churchman of his
day in Sweden, yet his lasting fame rests upon his poetry
and his hymns. Of the five hundred hymns in the
Swedish hymnbook of 1819, 130 were written by
Wallin, and approximately two hundred were revised or
translated by him. For more than a century the Church
of Sweden made no change in the 1819 hymnbook.

Take a look at the three Wallin hymns in *Lutheran
Book of Worship*: "All hail to you, O blessed morn!" (73),
"We worship you, O God of might" (432), and "Christians, while on earth abiding" (440). Which of these
hymns might be included in worship today as well as the
hymns of two other hymnwriters, Catherine Winkworth
and John Mason Neale, who are remembered tomorrow?

## Monday, July 1
### CATHERINE WINKWORTH, 1878;
### JOHN MASON NEALE, 1866; HYMNWRITERS

Neale was an English priest associated with the movement for church renewal at Cambridge. Winkworth lived most of her life in Manchester, where she was involved in promoting women's rights. These two hymnwriters translated many hymn texts into English. Catherine Winkworth devoted herself to the translation of German hymns, and John Mason Neale specialized in ancient Latin and Greek hymns. Winkworth has thirty hymns in *LBW,* and Neale has twenty-one. In addition, two texts by Neale are in *WOV.* Use the indexes at the back of both books to discover some of their most familiar translations.

## Saturday, July 6
### JAN HUS, MARTYR, 1415

Jan Hus was a Bohemian priest who spoke against abuses in the church of his day in many of the same ways Luther would a century later. He spoke against the withholding of the cup at the eucharist and because of this stance was excommunicated, not for heresy but for insubordination toward his archbishop. He preached against the selling of indulgences and was particularly mortified by the indulgence trade of two rival claimants to the papacy who were raising money for war against each other. He was found guilty of heresy by the Council of Constance and burned at the stake.

The followers of Jan Hus became known as the Czech Brethren and later became the Moravian Church.

240

# July 7, 2002

Seventh Sunday after Pentecost
Proper 9

### INTRODUCTION

Jesus chose to be with people who believed that they were excluded from God's mercy and love: those who were poor, sick, dying, in emotional or mental distress. Where many religious people saw only the sinful shadows in these people, Jesus recognized their need for the transforming power of mercy, forgiveness, and healing. To them he said: Come to me and find rest.

Today he comes to us in the waters of healing, in the word of mercy, in the meal of forgiveness. And he asks the church to bring these good gifts—signs of the Spirit's presence—into daily life.

### PRAYER OF THE DAY

God of glory and love, peace comes from you alone. Send us as peacemakers and witnesses to your kingdom, and fill our hearts with joy in your promises of salvation; through your Son, Jesus Christ our Lord.

### READINGS

Zechariah 9:9-12

The period after the Jews had returned from Babylonian exile was a time of extreme crisis. The return was not the glorious event announced by the prophet (Isa. 40–55). Serious social, economic, political, and religious problems confronted the people. They then looked to the future when God would intervene on their behalf.

Psalm 145:8-15 (Psalm 145:8-14 [NRSV])

The Lord is gracious and full of compassion. (Ps. 145:8)

Romans 7:15-25a

In his letter to the Romans, Paul argues that we are made right with God through Christ's action rather than through our own works. To illustrate our need for Christ, he offers us a picture of one who tries to do what is right, only to discover good intentions are not enough.

Matthew 11:16-19, 25-30

In Matthew's gospel, John the Baptist and Jesus are described as having very different approaches to ministry, though they both proclaim the same message of God's kingdom. Here, Jesus chides people who seem to find fault with all preachers as an excuse for ignoring the word of God.

SEMICONTINUOUS FIRST READING/PSALM

Genesis 24:34-38, 42-49, 58-67

The marriage of Isaac and Rebekah helped to fulfill God's covenant that Abraham would become the ancestor of many nations.

Psalm 45:11-18

God has anointed you with the oil of gladness. (Ps. 45:8)

*or* Song of Solomon 2:8-13

Arise, my love, my fair one, and come away. (Song of Sol. 2:10)

COLOR  Green

THE PRAYERS

With the whole people of God, let us join in prayer for the church, those in need, and all of God's creation.

*A BRIEF SILENCE.*

We pray for your church in every place, and for all who are scorned for what they do in your name. Show us your will, and strengthen us to do it. God of mercy,

**hear our prayer.**

We pray that the leaders of government will work with us to care for all who are poor, hungry, or homeless. God of mercy,

**hear our prayer.**

Be with those who are bowed down and falling—those in prison, those who are unemployed, those near death, those who are sick (especially). Give rest to their souls. God of mercy,

**hear our prayer.**

Watch over those who are traveling, that their way may be safe. Give vacationers rest and delight in your creation. God of mercy,

**hear our prayer.**

*HERE OTHER INTERCESSIONS MAY BE OFFERED.*

We give you thanks for all the faithful who have humbly revealed your goodness. May we celebrate with them the victory of your reign. God of mercy,

**hear our prayer.**

O God, give us faith to trust your promises, that our lives may glorify your name, through Jesus Christ our Lord.

**Amen**

IMAGES FOR PREACHING

This past week, people in the United States observed the Fourth of July. Although cynics might claim that most people view the day merely as a way to extend summer vacation, at least a few folks probably remember that July 4 is Independence Day, established to celebrate the American colonies' separation from British rule. Thanks to the spirited revolutionaries, people in the United States still proudly announce that they live in "the land of the free."

We can perhaps most clearly understand freedom, admittedly a relative and rather abstract concept, by contrasting freedom with slavery or imprisonment. A person enslaved to drugs or sex, or literally enslaved to another person, has less freedom than does someone who can walk away from these harsh taskmasters. Imprisonment of the body is torture. Freedom of the body is a privilege.

Psychiatrist Viktor Frankl, author of the classic *Man's Search for Meaning*, discovered while in a Nazi concentration camp that even a person who appears to be enslaved by suffering can transcend that suffering and find meaning in life—the root of mental, emotional, and spiritual freedom. Imprisonment of the mind and spirit, the loss of a sense of purpose in life, can mean agony. Freedom of the mind is a gift.

But it is the imprisonment of the spirit, estrangement from God, that carries the most serious consequence: death. It is in this contrast that we see the most profound experience of freedom. The "yoke" Jesus invites his followers to take up (Matt. 11:29-30) is not a yoke of imprisonment (burdensome laws), but a disciplined relationship with God that promises true freedom. Within the boundaries and commitments that define that relationship, we find a freedom that can never be taken away.

WORSHIP MATTERS

Breaking the bread before the distribution of communion is a practical necessity. Just as Jesus broke the bread at table and shared it with his followers, so we break the one loaf, a sign of our unity in the one body of Christ. Though many, we all receive from one loaf. The use of wafers makes this action both unnecessary and less clear theologically. If wafers must be used, the breaking of a large wafer can at least image the one loaf (body) and the participation of the many. The fraction (breaking) is not meant to serve as a symbolic reenactment of Jesus' actions and, thus, ought to be done not at the words "he broke it," but directly before the bread is distributed, fol-

241

lowing the Lord's Prayer. The breaking may be done in silence or accompanied by words that speak of our unity in the one body of Christ.

## LET THE CHILDREN COME

For whom do we pray? Children can be included in the work of intercessory prayer both at home and at church. John Westerhoff tells a story about one Sunday asking children to name those who needed their prayers. The children named those sick and hurting, lonely and dying. The next week he asked the children what they should do about the people for whom they were praying. "Visit them!" came the reply. So he took a group of children to the homes and hospitals and shelters where the people were staying. How shall we teach children to pray and to live the prayers they pray?

## HYMNS FOR WORSHIP

### GATHERING

Come gracious Spirit, heavenly dove    LBW 475
O day of peace    WOV 762
I will enter his gates    TFF 291

### HYMN OF THE DAY

Day by day    WOV 746

### ALTERNATE HYMN OF THE DAY

I heard the voice of Jesus say    HFW (KINGSFOLD)
I can hear my Savior calling    TFF 146

### COMMUNION

I come, O Savior, to your table    LBW 213
Eat this bread    WOV 709
Spirit of the living God    TFF 101, W&P 129
Just a closer walk with thee    TFF 253

### SENDING

Lord, dismiss us with your blessing    LBW 259
Praise to you, O God of mercy    WOV 790

### ADDITIONAL HYMNS AND SONGS

Accept, O Lord, the gifts we bring    WOV 759
Come to me, O weary traveler    NSR 66
God is compassionate    DH 46
Come unto me    DH 27
Shout to the Lord    W&P 124

## MUSIC FOR THE DAY

### PSALMODY

Folkemer, Stephen. "Psalm 145." U, tpt, kybd.    GIA G-2337.
Kemp, Helen. "God Is Always Near." U/2 pt.    CGA-31.
Makeever, Ray.    PW A.
Trapp, Lynn. *Four Psalm Settings.* SATB/U, kybd, cong.    MSM 80-701.

### CHORAL

Busarow, Donald. "O Lord, You Are My God and King." SAB, org, tpt, hb, opt cong.    AFP 080065756X.
Handel, G. F. "He Shall Feed His Flock Like a Shepherd" (Come Unto Him) in *Messiah.* S/A solo, kybd.    Various ed.
Handel, G.F. "His Yoke Is Easy" in *Messiah.* SATB, kybd.    Various ed.
Handel, G.F. "Rejoice Greatly" in *Messiah.* S solo, kybd.    Various ed.
Hayes, Mark. "Day by Day." SATB, pno.    AFP 0800658345.
Hopp, Roy. "God of Grace and God of Laughter." SATB, ob, harp/pno.    AFP 0800659570.
Killman, Daniel. "Come Unto Me." SATB, org.    MSM-50-9116.
Petzold, Johannes. "Rejoice Greatly." U, kybd.    AFP 11-1651.
Powell, Robert J. "I Will Magnify Thee." SATB, brass qrt, timp, org.    MSM-50-7019.
Willan, Healey. "Come Unto Me, All Ye That Labor." U, kybd.    CPH 98-2359.

### CHILDREN'S CHOIRS

Leaf, Robert. "Come with Rejoicing." U, kybd.    AFP 0800645758.
Perry, Dave and Jean Perry. "Come, Christians, Join to Sing." U/2 pt, kybd, 7 hb.    ALF7975.

### KEYBOARD/INSTRUMENTAL

Cherwien, David. "Softly and Tenderly Jesus Is Calling" in *Amazing Grace.* Pno.    AFP 0800659031.
Cherwien, David. "Blott en Dag" in *Eight for Eighty-Eight.* Pno, inst.    AFP 0800657322.
Porter, Rachel Trelstad. "Blott en Dag" in *Day by Day.* Pno.    AFP 0800656326.
Willan, Healey. *Slane.* Org.    PET 66034.

### HANDBELL

McChesney, Kevin. "Praise God, Praise Him." 2-3 oct. L3.    AFP 0800655060.
McChesney, Kevin. "Dona Nobis Pacem." 2 oct, quartet.    HOP CP 6058.
McFadden, Jane. "Two More Swedish Melodies for Handbells." 3-4 oct, opt ch.    AFP 0800657357.
Wagner, Douglas E. "Rondo in C." 3-4 oct. L3.    LAK HB005.

PRAISE ENSEMBLE

Bullock, Geoff/arr. Lee Poquette. "The Power of Your Love."
WRD 0 80689 80427 4; 0 80689 605246 (choraltrax cass);
0 80689 84472 (orch).

Foley, John. "Come to the Water." SATB, kybd, gtr, solo inst.
OCP 9489.

Manzo, Laura. "They Shall Soar Like Eagles." SAB, kybd, fl. Also
available in 2 pt.    FB BG 2078.

# Thursday, July 11

BENEDICT OF NURSIA,
ABBOT OF MONTE CASSINO, C. 540

Benedict is known as the father of Western monasticism.
He was educated in Rome but was appalled by the de-
cline of life around him. He went to live as a hermit, and
a community of monks came to gather around him. In
the prologue of his rule for monasteries he wrote that
his intent in drawing up his regulations was "to set down
nothing harsh, nothing burdensome." It is that moderate
spirit that characterizes his rule and the monastic communities that are formed by it. Benedict encourages a
generous spirit of hospitality in that visitors to Benedictine communities are to be welcomed as Christ himself.

Benedictine monasticism continues to serve a vital
role in the contemporary church. A summer reading
group might choose *A Share in the Kingdom* by Benet
Tvedten, OSB (Liturgical Press, 1989), to learn about
Benedict's Rule and hear this ancient voice speak to the
church today.

# Friday, July 12

NATHAN SÖDERBLOM, ARCHBISHOP OF UPPSALA, 1931

In 1930, this Swedish theologian, ecumenist, and social ac-
tivist received the Nobel Prize for peace. He saw the value
of the ancient worship of the church catholic and encouraged the liturgical movement. He also valued the work of
liberal Protestant scholars and believed social action was a
first step on the path toward a united Christianity. He organized the Universal Christian Council on Life and Work,
which was one of the organizations that in 1948 came together to form the World Council of Churches.

As you commemorate Söderblom, discuss the ecumenical situation in the church now in this new millennium. What are some of the achievements of the past
century? What hopes of Söderblom's might still wait to
be achieved?

# July 14, 2002

Eighth Sunday after Pentecost
Proper 10

## INTRODUCTION

For the next three Sundays, the gospel readings present the image of the seed. Though it is very small and seemingly insignificant, the seed contains its entire future; with light and nourishment it will grow and prosper. The seed is a vital image of faith in God, baptism, a congregation's life, the word, and the great paradox at the center of Christian faith: God brings flourishing life out of what appears to be little, dormant, even dead. It is a primary image of faith's central mystery: the dying and rising of Christ. There is ground for hope here.

## PRAYER OF THE DAY

Almighty God, we thank you for planting in us the seed of your word. By your Holy Spirit help us to receive it with joy, live according to it, and grow in faith and hope and love; through your Son, Jesus Christ our Lord.

## READINGS

### Isaiah 55:10-13

Preaching to the Babylonian exiles around 540 B.C., the prophet announces the good news that the Lord will bring the exiles home. The effectiveness of God's word is a theme that runs through chapters 40–55. What God says, will happen. Moreover, not only will the people return, the Lord will transform their path through the desert into a paradise.

### Psalm 65:[1-8] 9-14 (Psalm 65:[1-8] 9-13 [NRSV])

Your paths overflow with plenty. (Ps. 65:12)

### Romans 8:1-11

Paul has explained that, in spite of good intentions, no human being can ever please God by living in complete obedience to the law. Still, we have been reconciled to God through Christ and introduced to the new life of the Spirit.

### Matthew 13:1-9, 18-23

In Matthew's gospel, both Jesus and his disciples "sow the seed" of God's word by proclaiming the good news that "the kingdom of heaven is near." Now, in a memorable parable, Jesus explains why this good news produces different results in those who hear.

## SEMICONTINUOUS FIRST READING/PSALM

### Genesis 25:19-34

While there were obvious differences between the twins Esau and Jacob—Esau was the hunter, Jacob was the shepherd—the differences became more pronounced when Jacob persuaded his brother to sell his birthright. Suddenly what had taken generations to cultivate was sold for a mere meal.

### Psalm 119:105-112

Your word is a lantern to my feet and a light upon my path. (Ps. 119:105)

## COLOR Green

## THE PRAYERS

With the whole people of God, let us join in prayer for the church, those in need, and all of God's creation.
*A BRIEF SILENCE.*
Let your word come down like showers upon your church, so that your people may grow and the world may be blessed. God of mercy,
**hear our prayer.**
Where there is abundance in the world, let it be shared with those who are hungry. Guide our leaders, so that self-interest and political influence do not hinder the sharing of the wealth of your creation. God of mercy,
**hear our prayer.**
Give us faith, nurturing God, that when we hear your word, it may take root within us. When our hearts are hard and thorny, forgive us. God of mercy,
**hear our prayer.**
We pray for this congregation, that nourished at your table, we may grow and flourish in your grace. God of mercy,
**hear our prayer.**
You have the power to calm the seas. Calm the hearts of all who are sick and suffering (especially) with the healing power of your love. God of mercy,
**hear our prayer.**
*HERE OTHER INTERCESSIONS MAY BE OFFERED.*
We give thanks for all the saints, who in life have sown

244

the seeds of righteousness and in death have been gathered to your eternal harvest. God of mercy,
**hear our prayer.**
O God, give us faith to trust your promises, that our
lives may glorify your name, through Jesus Christ our
Lord.
**Amen**

## IMAGES FOR PREACHING

Clear thinking and sound doctrine are often claimed as
part of the heritage of Lutheran Christians. Consequently, words—especially words that describe our
human condition, God's actions throughout history, and
our proper relationship with God and neighbor—are
significant. Words that speak to the heart are quickly embraced, but there is also value placed on words that
sometimes seem to speak primarily to the head (although we hope they also touch our heart!). When
Lutheran pastors are ordained, they promise to "preach
and teach in accordance with" a great many words: not
only scripture, but the Apostles', Nicene, and Athanasian
Creeds, and the Lutheran confessions.

According to the Hebrews' understanding, however,
words are not static symbols for people, places, things,
or actions. Words are alive; they have power; they make
things happen! In fact, the Hebrew for "word," *dabar*, also
means "doing."

The power of words is never more obvious than
when we examine God's words. When God speaks, the
world changes. God spoke, and there came into being
light, water and dry land, plants and animals and fish—
and humankind. God speaks, the prophet Isaiah tells us,
and the word "shall not return to [God] empty, but it
shall accomplish" what God intends (Isa. 55:11). God
speaks, Jesus taught, and when God's words are heard by
one who understands, they bear abundant fruit.

We give thanks today for God's word for us spoken
through scripture, through the gifts of water and bread
and wine, and in the mutual conversation and consolation of the saints. God loves us with these words, and we
in response love God, ourselves, and our neighbor.

## WORSHIP MATTERS

The communion minister who serves the cup should
take care that the cup is carefully passed to and firmly
held by the communicant or held only by the minister as
the communicant guides the cup to his or her lips. Care
should be taken to wipe the cup with a clean linen and
turn it after each communicant. The linen cloth (purificator) should be turned as well so that a clean area is
used to wipe the rim of the chalice inside and out at
each rotation. Extra purificators should be available. If
the wine should spill, the minister wipes up the wine
with the purificator and replaces it with a clean one.

## LET THE CHILDREN COME

The sower and the seed, the wheat and the weeds, and
parables of the kingdom. These are featured in the
gospel readings for this and the next two Sundays. They
are parables that preach themselves to children, but you
must proclaim the readings as stories if you want to
catch the children's attention. Commit the stories to
memory. Tell them as if for the first time.

## HYMNS FOR WORSHIP
### GATHERING
Open now thy gates of beauty   LBW 250
Shout for joy loud and long   WOV 793

### HYMN OF THE DAY
We plow the fields and scatter   LBW 362

### ALTERNATE HYMN OF THE DAY
The thirsty fields drink in the rain   WOV 714
You are the seed   WOV 753, TFF 226

### COMMUNION
Break now the bread of life   LBW 235
Grains of wheat   WOV 708

### SENDING
Lord, dismiss us with your blessing   LBW 259
The Spirit sends us forth to serve   WOV 723

### ADDITIONAL HYMNS AND SONGS
Thy word   TFF 132, W&P 144
Seed, scattered and sown   W&P 121
Song of the sower   WGF 64
Aramos nuestros campos/We plow the fields   LLC 492
The word of God is source and seed   WOV 658

245

## MUSIC FOR THE DAY
### PSALMODY

Haas, David. PCY, vol. 8.

Makeever, Ray. PW A.

To bless the earth God sends us  PH 200

### CHORAL

Beebe, Hank. "Go Out with Joy." SATB, kybd.  HIN HMC-117.

Bertalot, John. "Thy Word Is a Lantern." SATB, org, opt br & perc.
AFP 0880674251 (complete); 080067726X (brass).

Clausen, René. "Seek the Lord." SATB div.  MFS MF 2009.

Cornelius, Peter. "Unto Thee I Lift Up My Soul" in *Lift Up Your Voice.*
Med voice solo, kybd.  PRE.

Ferguson, John. "Word of God Come Down on Earth." SATB, org.
GIA G 3764.

Greene, Maurice. "Thou Visitest the Earth" in *The Morningstar Choir Book I.* 2 pt, org/pno.  CPH 97-6287.

Grotenhuis, Dale. "For You Shall Go Out With Joy." SATB, org.
Heritage HRD 107.

Hopson, Hal H. "For as the Rain and Snow Come Down." SATB.
AFP 080065868X.

Young, Jeremy. "God Has Spoken, Bread Is Broken." SAB, kybd, opt cong.  AFP 0800655877.

### CHILDREN'S CHOIRS

Albrecht, Sally K. "Sing a Joyful Song." 2 pt, kybd, tpt.  ALF 7932.

Handel, G.F./arr. Spevacek, Linda. "Sing for Joy." 2 pt, kybd.
LOR 15/1286H.

Hopson, Hal H. "Song of the Mustard Seed." U, kybd.
GIA G-2239.

### KEYBOARD/INSTRUMENTAL

Callahan, Charles. "Simple Gifts." Pno/org duet.  MSM 20-870.

Lasky, David. *Trumpet Tune in C.* Org.  HWG GSTC 01050.

Organ, Anne Krentz. "The Ash Grove" in *Let It Rip! At the Piano.* Pno.
AFP 0800659066.

Wolff, S. Drummond. "Wir pflügen" in *Hymn Descants, Set IV.* Org, inst.  CPH 97-6275.

### HANDBELL

Anderson and Carter. "Morning Joy." Solo.  HOP 1378.

Afdahl, Lee J. "For as the Rain Comes Down" (Isaiah 55:10).
3-5 oct. L4.  AFP 0800658159.

McChesney, Kevin. "A Simple Celebration." 3 oct. L1+.
AGEHR AG 3073.

### PRAISE ENSEMBLE

Condon, Mark/arr. Mark Condon and J. Daniel Smith. "Giving My Best" in *Marvelous Things Choral Collection.* SATB, kybd.
INT 18256.

Smith, Michael W./arr. Emerson. "Seed to Sow." SAB, kybd, perc.
HAL 40326205.  Also available in SATB and 2 pt.

Williams/Nolan. "Teach Me, O Lord." 2 pt, kybd.  GS EA 5147.

## Monday, July 15
### VLADIMIR, FIRST CHRISTIAN RULER OF RUSSIA, 1015; OLGA, CONFESSOR, 969

Princess Olga became a Christian about the time she made a visit to Constantinople, center of the Byzantine church. She had no success persuading her son or her fellow citizens to receive the gospel. Vladimir was Olga's grandson, and he took the throne at a ruthless time and in a bloodthirsty manner: he killed his brother for the right to rule. After Vladimir became a Christian he set aside the reminders of his earlier life, including pagan idols and temples. He built churches, monasteries, and schools, brought in Greek missionaries to educate the people, and was generous to the poor. Together Vladimir and Olga are honored as the first Christian rulers of Russia.

## Wednesday, July 17
### BARTOLOMÉ DE LAS CASAS, MISSIONARY TO THE INDIES, 1566

Bartolomé de las Casas was a Spanish priest and a missionary in the Western Hemisphere. He first came to the West while serving in the military, and he was granted a large estate that included a number of indigenous slaves. When he was ordained in 1513, he granted freedom to his servants. This act characterized much of the rest of de las Casas's ministry. Throughout the Caribbean and Central America he worked to stop the enslavement of native people, to halt the brutal treatment of women by military forces, and to promote laws that humanized the process of colonization.

# July 21, 2002

Ninth Sunday after Pentecost
Proper 11

## INTRODUCTION

The parable in today's gospel reading sets forth what we may experience every day: evil coexists with the good. The conclusion to the parable—the weeds will be burned—seems simple, except for this: the one who speaks gives his life over to death, that God's mercy for all people may be revealed, and that God's power to bring good out of evil may be known. Is it possible that even weeds and thorns will be transformed into beautiful flowers and lush vines?

Here is each Christian's mission: to speak and to act with mercy and justice in a world that knows too well the presence of evil.

## PRAYER OF THE DAY

O Lord, pour out upon us the spirit to think and do what is right, that we, who cannot even exist without you, may have the strength to live according to your will; through your Son, Jesus Christ our Lord.

## READINGS

Isaiah 44:6-8

Using a dramatic courtroom scene in which God is at once prosecuting attorney, witness, and judge, this prophet of the exile introduces a radical monotheism: the Lord is not one among many gods; the Lord is the only God.

or Wisdom of Solomon 12:13, 16-19

The strength and sovereignty of God are revealed in forbearance, kindness, and care for all people.

Psalm 86:11-17

Teach me your way, O Lord, and I will walk in your truth. (Ps. 86:11)

Romans 8:12-25

Paul encourages us to experience life as more than just mortal existence, which he calls "life in the flesh." Those who are led by God's Spirit discover a hope that sustains them even in their suffering.

Matthew 13:24-30, 36-43

Jesus has just told his disciples the famous parable of the sower, which compares different responses to the word to different kinds of soil in which a seed is planted. Now he tells a second parable about sowing to illustrate the coexistence of good and evil in our world.

## SEMICONTINUOUS FIRST READING/PSALM

Genesis 28:10-19a

This story of Jacob at Beth-el ("House of God") relates how this place became an Israelite sanctuary. It also tells of the power of God's word to bring promises to fulfillment: God continues the promise of land, descendants, and blessing to Abraham even through the "cheater" par excellence, Jacob.

Psalm 139:1-11, 21-23

You have searched me out and known me. (Ps. 139:1)

## COLOR  Green

## THE PRAYERS

With the whole people of God, let us join in prayer for the church, those in need, and all of God's creation.
*A BRIEF SILENCE.*

Teach us your way, that we may walk in your truth. Guide your church in the path that leads to life. God of mercy,

**hear our prayer.**

In a world where both wheat and weeds grow, give wisdom and discernment to the nations and their leaders, that they may seek the greater good. God of mercy,

**hear our prayer.**

In the face of pollution, wastefulness, careless development, and greed, make us faithful stewards of the earth. God of mercy,

**hear our prayer.**

Comfort and support those who are sick, persecuted, grieving, and dying (especially). God of mercy,

**hear our prayer.**

*HERE OTHER INTERCESSIONS MAY BE OFFERED.*

All of creation groans in labor pains for the revealing of your glory. With your children of every time and place, bring us to the fulfillment of every hope. God of mercy,

**hear our prayer.**

247

O God, give us faith to trust your promises, that our lives may glorify your name, through Jesus Christ our Lord.
**Amen**

## IMAGES FOR PREACHING

When we read the parables of Matthew 13, we would do well to remember that Matthew says Jesus taught the crowds on a day when he had already been repeatedly challenged by the Pharisees. They had criticized Jesus for plucking and eating grain on the Sabbath, healing on the Sabbath, and then curing a man who was blind and mute. Still, even as these religious leaders plotted to destroy Jesus, they sought a sign from him.

Jesus met the Pharisees' challenges head-on. But according to Matthew, he also went directly to the people, offering them seven parables. Far better to take advantage of those with open hearts than to do battle against those with closed minds! The parable at the heart of our gospel reading for today is accompanied by an allegory, probably an interpretation provided by the early church. The message of the parable, however, is powerful enough in itself, apart from the allegory: It is God who at the end of time will separate the outcasts from the saved. It is not our job to make such judgments.

That same warning/promise appears in the reading from Isaiah, where God dares any other gods to declare their power and then, hearing no challenges, assures the people, "You are my witnesses! Is there any god besides me? There is no other rock" (Isa. 44:8).

Such are God's ways, and for this, we give thanks. In the end, our God, who alone rules over creation and alone is judge, will set all creation free, and we will be made children of God (Rom. 8:21).

## WORSHIP MATTERS

The use of one loaf for the celebration of the eucharist serves both the image of the unity of the church as one body and the sharing in a meal, the anticipation of the feast to come. Those who use a single chalice for both drinking and intinction (dipping) may be bothered by the presence of crumbs in the cup. One solution is to use a loaf that is firm and does not easily crumble. Pita and other unleavened breads work well. Recipes can also be found for leavened bread that produces a firm loaf. Using bread that is fresh and moist is also important.

Some congregations might choose to use one cup for drinking and a second for intinction only.

## LET THE CHILDREN COME

Although some children are already shopping for new school clothes, others have little to wear. Is it appropriate in your parish to begin an end-of-summer "school clothes" project? Invite children to look through their drawers and closets for good clothes they do not need. Let them help wash and prepare them to be shared with children who need them.

## HYMNS FOR WORSHIP
### GATHERING
Oh, worship the King    LBW 548
You are the seed    WOV 753, TFF 226

### HYMN OF THE DAY
For the fruit of all creation    WOV 760

### ALTERNATE HYMN OF THE DAY
O Holy Spirit, enter in    LBW 459
We plow the fields    LLC 492

### COMMUNION
Dear Lord and Father of mankind    LBW 506
As the grains of wheat    WOV 705, W&P 10
Seed, scattered and sown    W&P 121

### SENDING
Praise the Lord! O heav'ns    LBW 540
Blessed assurance    WOV 699, TFF 118

### ADDITIONAL HYMNS AND SONGS
Good soil    WOV 713, W&P 52
The thirsty fields drink in the rain    WOV 714
Lord, listen to your children    W&P 91
Come, the banquet hall is ready    GS2 14

## MUSIC FOR THE DAY
### PSALMODY
Handel, G.F./Robert Powell. "Then Will I Jehovah's Praise." U. CGA 220.
Makeever, Ray.    PW A.
Trapp, Lynn. "Four Psalm Settings." U/cant, opt SATB, cong, org. MSM 80-701.

248

## CHORAL

Bach, J.C.F. "In the Resurrection Glorious" in *Chantry Choirbook.*
SATB, org. AFP 0800657772.

Bach, J.S. "O, Mortal World" in *Lift Up Your Voice.* Med voice solo,
kybd. PRE.

Bisbee, B. Wayne. "Teach Me Your Way, O Lord." 2 pt mxd, kybd.
AFP 080065479X.

Dvořák, Antonin. "Search Me, O God" in *Lift Up Your Voice.* Med voice
solo, kybd. PRE.

Fox-Simkins. "Teach Me Thy Way, O Lord." SATB. CPH 98-2329.

Hillert, Richard. "Image of the Unseen God." SATB, org.
AFP 0880659627.

Marcello, Benedetto. "Teach Me Now, O Lord." 2 pt, kybd.
MSM-50-9418.

Mendelssohn, Felix. "Then Shall the Righteous Shine Forth" in *Vocal
Solos for Funerals and Memorial Services.* Solo, kybd.
AFP 6000001169.

Purcell, Henry. "Thou Knowest, Lord, the Secrets of Our Hearts."
SATB, org. ECS No 170 (376 Archive Reprints).

## CHILDREN'S CHOIRS

Beall, Mary Kay. "He Is There." 2 pt, kybd. Providence Press
PP123.

Burkhardt, Michael, arr. "How Can I Keep from Singing." 2 pt, kybd,
perc, tamb, tri. CG CGA795.

## KEYBOARD/INSTRUMENTAL

Albrecht, Mark. "Ar hyd y nos" in *Timeless Hymns of Faith, Volume 2.*
Kybd. AFP 0800658795.

Howells, Herbert. "Psalm Prelude 2" in *Three Psalm-Preludes for Organ,
set 2.* Org. NOV 59-0355-06.

Sedio, Mark. "If You But Trust in God to Guide You" in *A Global
Piano Tour.* Pno. AFP 0800658191.

Stoldt, Frank. "Ar hyd y nos" in *Augsburg Organ Library: November.* Org.
AFP 0800658965.

## HANDBELL

Anderson and Page. "Be Still My Soul." Solo. HOP 1983.

Sherman, Arnold. "Jubilance." 2-3 oct. L2; 4-5 oct. JEF JHS 9079.

Wagner, Douglas E. "Festival Piece on Hyfrydol" 3-5 oct. L2.
LAK HB 002.

## PRAISE ENSEMBLE

Author unknown/folk melody from India. "I Have Decided to Follow Jesus." MAR 301 0868 162 (SATB, kybd); 301 7539 083
(choraltrax).

Brown, Liles and Borop. "All God's People Said 'Amen!'" SATB, kybd.
WRD 301 0927 169.

Price, Nancy and Don Besig. "Just a Closer Walk." SATB, kybd.
GS A 7106. Also available for SAB.

# Monday, July 22

### ST. MARY MAGDALENE

The gospels report Mary Magdalene was one of the
women of Galilee who followed Jesus. She was present at
Jesus' crucifixion and his burial. When she went to the
tomb on the first day of the week to anoint Jesus' body,
she was the first person to whom the risen Lord appeared. She returned to the disciples with the news and
has been called "the apostle to the apostles" for her
proclamation of the resurrection. Because John's gospel
describes Mary as weeping at the tomb, she is often portrayed in art with red eyes. Icons depict her standing by
the tomb and holding a bright red egg.

This glimpse of Easter in the middle of summer invites us to keep our eyes open for the signs of Christ's
resurrection and new life that are always around us.

# Tuesday, July 23

### BIRGITTA OF SWEDEN, 1373

Birgitta was married at age thirteen and had four daughters with her husband. She was a woman of some standing who, in her early thirties, served as the chief lady-in-
waiting to the Queen of Sweden. She was widowed at the
age of thirty-eight, shortly after she and her husband had
made a religious pilgrimage. Following the death of her
husband the religious dreams and visions that had begun
in her youth occurred more regularly. Her devotional
commitments led her to give to the poor and needy all
that she owned while she began to live a more ascetic life.
She founded an order of monks and nuns, the Order of
the Holy Savior (Birgittines), whose superior was a
woman. Today the Society of St. Birgitta is a laypersons'
society that continues her work of prayer and charity.

249

## Thursday, July 25

ST. JAMES THE ELDER, APOSTLE

James is one of the sons of Zebedee and is counted as one of the twelve disciples. He and his brother John had the nickname "sons of thunder." One of the stories in the New Testament tells of their request for Jesus to grant them places of honor in the kingdom. They are also reported to have asked Jesus for permission to send down fire on a Samaritan village that had not welcomed them. Their nickname appears to be well deserved. James was the first of the twelve to suffer martyrdom and is the only apostle whose martyrdom is recorded in scripture.

James is frequently pictured with a scallop shell. It recalls his life as a fisherman, his call to fish for people, and the gift of our baptism into Christ.

# July 28, 2002

Tenth Sunday after Pentecost
Proper 12

## INTRODUCTION

The mission of the church and each baptized Christian is to serve the reign of God. But what is the reign of God? In today's gospel reading, Jesus offers images drawn from ordinary life that reveal something of the reign of God. It is like a tree that becomes a safe and sheltering home, like yeast that penetrates and expands, like a treasured pearl, like a net that gains a great catch. The reign of God is God's steadfast desire to unite the human family, with all its great diversity, in a justice and mercy so great and thoroughly life-giving that people will rejoice at its advent.

On July 28 we remember three musicians and composers who were influential in the life of the church: Johann Sebastian Bach, Heinrich Schütz, and George Frederick Handel.

## PRAYER OF THE DAY

O God, your ears are open always to the prayers of your servants. Open our hearts and minds to you, that we may live in harmony with your will and receive the gifts of your Spirit; through your Son, Jesus Christ our Lord.

## READINGS

### 1 Kings 3:5-12

This passage reflects a concern for leadership that is also present in the larger corpus extending from Joshua through 2 Kings. Leadership in the community that lives under the rule of God has its basis in the covenant, and leaders depend upon God's gifts of wisdom and discernment.

### Psalm 119:129-136

When your word goes forth, it gives light and understanding. (Ps. 119:130)

### Romans 8:26-39

For several chapters in his letter to the Romans, Paul argues that justification by faith produces a life in the Spirit superior to any legal obedience that might be attained through human effort. Now, in the final words of this chapter, his exuberance for this spiritual life leads to a confident hymn in praise of Christ's love.

### Matthew 13:31-33, 44-52

Throughout Matthew's gospel, Jesus and his disciples proclaim the good news that "the kingdom of heaven is near!" Here, Jesus offers several brief parables that explore the implications of this announcement for people's lives.

## SEMICONTINUOUS FIRST READING/PSALM

### Genesis 29:15-28

Jacob had earlier disguised himself as his brother Esau, thereby deceiving his father into giving him a blessing. Then it was Laban's turn to deceive Jacob by giving him his daughter Leah, after Jacob had already worked for seven years intending for Laban to give him his daughter Rachel to marry.

### Psalm 105:1-11; 45b

Make known the deeds of the Lord among the peoples. Hallelujah! (Ps. 105:1, 45) *or* Psalm 128

Happy are they who follow in the ways of the Lord. (Ps. 128:1)

COLOR Green

## THE PRAYERS

With the whole people of God, let us join in prayer for the church, those in need, and all of God's creation.
*A BRIEF SILENCE.*

Like the woman leavening flour, take your people and send us into the world as yeast, bringing life through the power of the risen Christ. God of mercy,
**hear our prayer.**

Give the leaders of the world a spirit of humility and a passion for truth and justice. God of mercy,
**hear our prayer.**

Reveal yourself to those who are searching for genuine treasure, and help us lead others to the gifts of word and sacrament that nourish us so richly. God of mercy,
**hear our prayer.**

Like the mustard seed that grows into a towering plant, may love and faith grow within all those who are in need of comfort and healing (especially). God of mercy,
**hear our prayer.**
*HERE OTHER INTERCESSIONS MAY BE OFFERED.*

We give you thanks for the gift of music and for artists who serve your church and give a glimpse of your glory in all the world. Unite us with Bach, Handel, and Schütz, with music makers of every land and culture, and with all the saints and angels in an everlasting hymn of praise. God of mercy,
**hear our prayer.**

O God, give us faith to trust your promises, that our lives may glorify your name, through Jesus Christ our Lord.
**Amen**

## IMAGES FOR PREACHING

In Matthew's gospel, we read five parables about God's loving ways among us. Only the fifth parable offers a challenge rather than an image of hope. In the first two parables, Jesus teaches that God's rule among us will spread like a mustard seed that grows into a huge tree, or like yeast through a loaf. We also learn from these parables the purpose of God's transforming rule. From small beginnings God will provide safety and nurture for all creation.

God's works are so amazing, we hear in the third and fourth parables, that a merchant or farmer would sell everything he owns in order to share in that work. We would not expect a farmer to purchase a field containing a valuable treasure, however, and then let the treasure—and the field—sit idle. The farmer would dig up the treasure and make use of both treasure and field. Likewise the merchant would not purchase the beautiful pearl and then let it sit in a glass case. The pearl, we would expect, would be used as the basis for other business. When we encounter the kingdom of heaven, then, we will certainly make use of that gift. The discovery is only the beginning of our own participation in God's rule.

Matthew closes the collection of parables with the Jesus' assurance that there is treasure to be found in both the Mosaic Law and in his new teachings. The remarkable gift God has given us through Christ Jesus our Lord is a love that sustains us in all things, a love that we will want to pass on to others.

## WORSHIP MATTERS

"Who will separate us from the love of Christ?" (Rom. 8:35). No one. Nothing! The truth that St. Paul shared with the Roman Christians is at the heart of our weekly assembly. We who are baptized into Christ are his, and he is ours. God's Spirit resides within us. We who confess our "bondage to sin" hear how, in Christ, we are forgiven and restored to new life. In the word proclaimed, we encounter the one who is always for us and woos us like a lover, refusing to let us go. And in the holy supper we again feed on Christ, our life and our salvation. As we go forth into the world to live out this good news, we are assured that God's love in Christ will always hold us fast.

## LET THE CHILDREN COME

It can be helpful to let children (and adults) know that Christ feeds us from two tables: the table of the word and the table of the eucharist. From the table of the word, the assembly moves to the table of the eucharist. You might ask how children participate in the ministries of book-bearers and gift-bearers in your worshiping assembly.

**HYMNS FOR WORSHIP**

GATHERING

Immortal, invisible, God only wise    LBW 526

When in our music God is glorified    WOV 802

HYMN OF THE DAY

You are the seed    WOV 753, TFF 226

ALTERNATE HYMN OF THE DAY

God of grace and God of glory    LBW 415

If Jesus Christ be for me    HFW

COMMUNION

Come, let us eat    LBW 214, TFF 119

Father, we thank you    WOV 704

Eat this bread, drink this cup    WOV 706, BL 4

SENDING

Sent forth by God's blessing    LBW 221

Hallelujah! We sing your praises    WOV 722

ADDITONAL HYMNS AND SONGS

Spirit, spirit of gentleness    WOV 684

As grain on scattered hillsides    CHA 491

Bless us, O God    DH 44

You, Lord    W&P 162

Spirit of the living God    W&P 129

**MUSIC FOR THE DAY**

PSALMODY

Haas, David. PCY, vol. 8.

Makeever, Ray. PW A.

*The Psalter: Psalms and Canticles for Singing.* U, kybd, cong.    WJK.

CHORAL

Attwood, Thomas. "Teach Me, O Lord." SATB, org.    GSCH 4488.

Bach, J.S. "Jesus, My Sweet Pleasure" in *Bach for All Seasons.* SATB, kybd.    AFP 080065854X.

Beck, John Ness. "Who Shall Separate Us?" SATB, org.    AMSI 261.

Handel, G.F. "If God Is for Us, Who Is against Us?" in *Messiah.* S solo, kybd.    Various ed.

Hayes, Mark. "Let the Word Go Forth." SATB, org. AFP 0800674189.

Pote, Allen. "Communion Prayer." U/2 pt, kybd.    HIN HMC-436.

Schütz, Heinrich. "Is God for Us." SATB, pno/org.    AFP 0800672119.

Schütz, Heinrich. "Sing to the Lord" in *Chantry Choirbook.* SATB. AFP 0800657772. ·

Scott, K. Lee. "Redeeming Grace" in *Sing a Song of Joy: Vocal Solos for Worship.*    AFP 0800647882 (MH); 0800652827 (ML).

Scott, K. Lee. "Teach Me, My God and King." SATB, org. AFP 0800659732.

CHILDREN'S CHOIRS

Bolt, Conway A., Jr. "The Kingdom of God." 2 pt, kybd. CG CGA677.

Schram, Ruth Elaine. "In Everything God Works for Good." 2 pt, kybd, conga, bng, tamb, tri.    Daybreak 08741991.

KEYBOARD/INSTRUMENTAL

Ferguson, John. "Children of the Heavenly Father" in *Thy Holy Wings.* Org.    AFP 600000138X.

Organ, Anne Krentz. "Te ofrecemos" in *Woven Together.* Pno, inst. AFP 0800658167.

Wold, Wayne. "Jesus, Priceless Treasure" in *Songs of Thankfulness and Praise, set 2.* Org.    MSM 10-712.

HANDBELL

Anderson, Christine. "Children of the Heavenly Father." Solo. HOP 1695.

Geschke, Susan E. "All Things Bright and Beautiful." 2-3 oct. L3-. AGEHR AG23017.

Wagner, Douglas. "Immortal, Invisible." 3 oct. L2.    AG 1238.

PRAISE ENSEMBLE

Boschman, Lamar and Tyrone Williams/arr. David Clydesdale. "Thine Is the Kingdom." SATB, kybd.    WRD 0 08689 72227 1.

Crouch, Andraé and Karen Lafferty/arr. Benjamin Harlan. "Jesus Is the Answer/Seek Ye First."    ALF 19111 (SATB, kybd); 10112 (SAB); ALF 19113 (2 pt).

Moen, Don/arr. Tom Brooks and Jay Rouse. "For All You've Done." SATB, kybd.    INT 14127.

Thomas, Andrae. "The Kingdom." SATB, kybd.    HIN HMC-1307.

# Sunday, July 28

JOHANN SEBASTIAN BACH, 1750;
HEINRICH SCHÜTZ, 1672;
GEORGE FREDERICK HANDEL, 1759; MUSICIANS

These three composers have done much to enrich the worship life of the church. Johann Sebastian Bach drew on the Lutheran tradition of hymnody and wrote about two hundred cantatas, including at least two for each Sunday and festival day in the Lutheran calendar of his day. He has been called "the fifth evangelist" for the ways that he proclaimed the gospel through his music. George Frederick Handel was not primarily a church musician, but his great work, *Messiah*, is a musical proclamation of the scriptures. Heinrich Schütz wrote choral settings of biblical texts and paid special attention to ways his composition would underscore the meaning of the words.

A musical gathering might be planned for this weekend to commemorate these and other great church composers. Remember to include a prayer of thanksgiving for organists, choir directors, composers, and all who make music in worship.

# Monday, July 29

MARY, MARTHA, AND LAZARUS OF BETHANY

Mary and Martha are remembered for the hospitality and refreshment they offered Jesus in their home. Following the characterization drawn by Luke, Martha represents the active life, and Mary, the contemplative. Mary is iden-

tified in the fourth gospel as the one who anointed Jesus before his passion and who was criticized for her act of devotion. Lazarus, Mary's and Martha's brother, was raised from the dead by Jesus as a sign of the eternal life offered to all believers. It was over Lazarus's tomb that Jesus wept for love of his friend. Congregations might commemorate these three early witnesses to Christ by reflecting on the role of hospitality in both home and church and the blessing of friendship.

# Monday, July 29

OLAF, KING OF NORWAY, MARTYR, 1030

Olaf is considered the patron saint of Norway. In his early career he engaged in war and piracy in the Baltic and in Normandy. It was there he became a Christian. He returned to Norway, declared himself king, and from then on Christianity was the dominant religion of the realm. He revised the laws of the nation and enforced them with strict impartiality, eliminating the possibility of bribes. He thereby alienated much of the aristocracy. The harshness that he sometimes resorted to in order to establish Christianity and his own law led to a rebellion. After being driven from the country and into exile, he enlisted support from Sweden to try to regain his kingdom, but he died in battle.

Olaf reminds the church of the temptation to establish Christianity by waging war, whether military or social. How might the church bear witness to the one who calls us to pray for enemies and persecutors?

253

# August 4, 2002

Eleventh Sunday after Pentecost
Proper 13

## INTRODUCTION

In the gospel reading for this day, we hear familiar words about Jesus' meal practice: he took the loaves, blessed them, broke them, and gave them for all to eat. Here the church sees the pattern of the eucharist: the gifts of God's goodness and human labor are presented, the table thanksgiving is spoken, bread is broken and wine is poured, and all are invited to the holy supper.

To this supper the church welcomes all the baptized. The gifts of God are given freely, equally, and without discrimination. How is this sacred meal a sign of what God intends for life in this world?

## PRAYER OF THE DAY

Gracious Father, your blessed Son came down from heaven to be the true bread which gives life to the world. Give us this bread, that he may live in us and we in him, Jesus Christ our Lord.

## READINGS

Isaiah 55:1-5

In both ancient Near Eastern history and literature, the building of a temple and the feast held afterward signify the establishment of the kingdom of the temple's builder. Isaiah 54 recounts God's building of a new temple following the exile. Today's reading is the invitation to the feast.

Psalm 145:8-9, 15-22 (Psalm 145:8-9, 14-21 [NRSV])

You open wide your hand and satisfy the needs of every living creature. (Ps. 145:17)

Romans 9:1-5

In his letter to the Romans, Paul proclaims the good news of Jesus Christ, through whom "nothing can separate us from the love of God." Then, his joy turns to sorrow as he considers those among God's people who have not received the gospel.

Matthew 14:13-21

After John the Baptist is murdered, Jesus desires a time of solitude. Still, his compassion for others will not allow him to dismiss those who still need him but, rather, moves him to perform a great miracle.

254

## SEMICONTINUOUS FIRST READING/PSALM

Genesis 32:22-31

After years of working for his uncle Laban, Jacob starts homeward to be reconciled to his brother Esau, whom he has cheated long before. The night before Jacob meets Esau, God (in human form) wrestles with Jacob.

Psalm 17:1-7, 16

I shall see your face; when I awake, I shall be satisfied. (Ps. 17:16)

## COLOR  Green

## THE PRAYERS

With the whole people of God, let us join in prayer for the church, those in need, and all of God's creation.
*A BRIEF SILENCE.*

As we worship this day, our eyes look to you, O God. Help us draw others to you, the source of every blessing. God of mercy,

**hear our prayer.**

As you fed the five thousand, feed us with your word and with your bread and cup, the body and blood of Christ. God of mercy,

**hear our prayer.**

As we thank you for the blessings that we have, we ask you to be with the leaders and legislators of our nation, that they work to ensure the necessities of food, shelter, clothing, and health care for all who dwell in this land. God of mercy,

**hear our prayer.**

As those who struggle with difficult decisions, unemployment, or conflicts in relationships seek your will, give them courage and strength. God of mercy,

**hear our prayer.**

As those who are sick and in any need (especially) seek strength and hope, give them the abundance of your care and compassion. God of mercy,

**hear our prayer.**
*HERE OTHER INTERCESSIONS MAY BE OFFERED.*

Bring us with all your saints to feast at the heavenly table on your never-ending love and grace. God of mercy,

hear our prayer.
O God, give us faith to trust your promises, that our lives may glorify your name, through Jesus Christ our Lord. **Amen**

## IMAGES FOR PREACHING

Thanksgiving in August! By the time we finish all the readings for this week, there is so much food on the table that it must be Thanksgiving!

The prophet Isaiah announces that a feast is ready, and even those who have no money are welcome to dine. The psalmist praises God, saying, "You open your hand, satisfying the desire of every living thing" (Ps. 145:16). Today's gospel reading contains Matthew's account of the one miracle recorded in all four gospels, the feeding of the multitude. Not only was everyone fed, but there were twelve baskets full of leftovers produced from five loaves and two fish! Scripture promises not just a meal. At God's place, they are serving an all-you-can-eat banquet!

We might actually have a difficult time appreciating the images of bounty in these readings. After all, many of us struggle to keep our weight at a healthy level, and were we to find ourselves at an endless feast, we might panic, wondering what the reading on the bathroom scale will be in the morning. At the very least, we would demurely resist, "Oh, I shouldn't! Well, maybe just one bite." But the bounty is exactly the point in these readings. God is not stingy. God not only watches over us and gives us what we need. God gives us far, far more than we could possibly want.

The fact that we have been invited to such an overwhelming feast is a profound reason to joyfully celebrate the eucharist at every Sunday worship service. God, out of infinite love for us, daily and abundantly blesses us with all that we need. In a simple meal of bread and wine, we are reminded of God's sacrificial love for us. We receive and are bound together through that love. And we are nourished for our ministry in this world and for life eternal.

## WORSHIP MATTERS

Do you ever wonder what was done with the bread that was gathered up into twelve baskets after Jesus fed the multitude? We do not know, but surely it was not wasted. What ought we to do with the leftover food from the assembly's eucharistic meal? Wine that remains in the flagon or cruet can be set aside in a separate vessel for use at the next celebration or to commune the sick and homebound. Wine from the chalice(s) should reverently be poured down the piscina (a drainpipe in many sacristies that leads to the ground) or directly onto the ground. The bread that remains can be taken from the assembly to those absent from the meal or consumed by those who communed. Care should be taken to use a loaf no larger than needed. If wafers are used, they also can be set aside in a separate vessel for communing the absent or for use at the next eucharistic celebration.

## LET THE CHILDREN COME

How do children see the connection between the eucharistic meal and the church's care for those who are hungry (and often homeless)? One way is to invite them to collect food for food shelves, pantries, and the dining rooms of homeless shelters. Another way is to invite parents and children to cook food and then bring it to a shelter where they can serve it. Teach a hymn such as "We come to the hungry feast" (WOV 766) to sing as they go.

## HYMNS FOR WORSHIP
### GATHERING
Glories of your name are spoken   LBW 358
We come to the hungry feast   WOV 766

### HYMN OF THE DAY
Praise and thanksgiving   LBW 409

### ALTERNATE HYMN OF THE DAY
Let us talents and tongues employ   WOV 754, TFF 232
Soul, adorn yourself with gladness   LLC 388

### COMMUNION
Break now the bread of life   LBW 235
I am the Bread of life   WOV 702

### SENDING
Hallelujah! We sing your praises   WOV 722
I love to tell the story   LBW 390
That we may be filled   W&P 134

### ADDITIONAL HYMNS AND SONGS
Sent forth by God's blessing   LBW 221
Unidos en la fiesta/United at the table   LLC 408

You satisfy the hungry heart    WOV 711

Just as Jesus told us    DH 29

## MUSIC FOR THE DAY

### PSALMODY

Haas, David. "I Will Praise Your Name" in PS 2.

Makeever, Ray.    PW A.

Sleeth, Natalie. "Everywhere I Go." U/2 pt, opt C inst.    CGA-171.

Trapp, Lynn. "Four Psalm Settings." U, opt SATB, cong, org.
    MSM 80-701.

### CHORAL

Barber, Todd. "What Feast of Love." AFP 0800601339. SATB, pno.

Berger, Jean. "The Eyes of All Wait Upon Thee." SATB.
    AFP 0800645596; also in *The Augsburg Choirbook*.
    AFP 0800656784.

Fleming, L.L. "Humble Service." SATB.    AFP 0800646223.

Gunderson, Jerry. "We Come to the Hungry Feast." SAB, pno, 1, 2 or
    3 C insts, opt cong.    AFP 080065871X.

Harris, William H. "The Eyes of All Wait Upon Thee, O Lord."
    SATB, org.    OXF 42.983.

Mendelssoh, Felix. "O Come, Everyone That Thirsteth" in *Elijah*.
    Vocal qrt, kybd.    GSCH ed 43.

Mozart, W. A. "Ave verum corpus." Vocal solo, kybd.    Various eds.

Proulx, Richard. "The Eyes of All." U, org.    CHA 12-109.

Smith, Robert Edward. "The Eyes of All Wait Upon Thee." SSA.
    Tetra/Continuo TC 817.

### CHILDREN'S CHOIRS

Kosche, Kenneth. "Keep Me as the Apple of Your Eye." U/2 pt,
    kybd.    CG CGA800.

Wright, Vicki Hancock. "I Will Praise God." U, kybd, hb, hc.
    CG CGA822.

### KEYBOARD/INSTRUMENTAL

Sedio, Mark. "Let Us Talents and Tongues Employ" in *Let Us Talents
    and Tongues Employ*. Org.    AFP 0800655729.

Sedio, Mark. "We Come to the Hungry Feast" in *Dancing in the Light of
    God*. AFP 0800656547. Pno.

Wasson, Laura E. "Bunessan" in *A Piano Tapestry*. Pno.
    AFP 0800656822.

### HANDBELL

McFadden, Jane. "Morning Has Broken." 3 oct, opt choir/pno.
    AFP 0800654323.

Wilson, John F. "Kum Ba Yah." 2-3 oct. L3.    AG 1650.

### PRAISE ENSEMBLE

Foley, John. "Come to the Water." SATB, kybd, gtr, and inst.
    OCP 9489.

Nuzum, Eric and Chris Springer. "Healing Waters" in *The Smithton
    Outpouring Songbook*. SAT[B], kybd.    INT 15727.

# Thursday, August 8

### DOMINIC, PRIEST, FOUNDER OF THE ORDER OF THE DOMINICANS, 1221

Dominic was a Spanish priest who preached against the Albigensians, a heretical sect that held gnostic and dualistic beliefs. Dominic believed that a stumbling block to restoring heretics to the church was the wealth of clergy, so he formed an itinerant religious order, the Order of Preachers (Dominicans) who lived in poverty, studied philosophy and theology, and preached against heresy. The method of this order was to use kindness and gentle argument, rather than harsh judgment, when bringing unorthodox Christians back to the fold. Dominic was opposed to burning Christians at the stake. Three times Dominic was offered the office of bishop, which he refused so that he could continue his work of preaching.

# Saturday, August 10

### LAWRENCE, DEACON, MARTYR, 258

Lawrence was one of seven deacons of the congregation at Rome and, like the deacons appointed in Acts, was responsible for financial matters in the church and for the care of the poor. Lawrence lived during a time of persecution under the emperor Valerian. The emperor demanded that Lawrence surrender the treasures of the church. Lawrence gathered lepers, orphans, the blind and lame. He brought them to the emperor and said, "Here is the treasure of the church." This act enraged the emperor, and Lawrence was sentenced to death. Lawrence's martyrdom was one of the first to be observed by the church.

Amid the concerns for the institutional church, reflect on what we consider the treasures of the church today. If the people on the margins of life are treasured in God's eyes, consider ways a congregation can sharpen its vision for social ministry.

# August 11, 2002

Twelfth Sunday after Pentecost
Proper 14

## INTRODUCTION

"Lord, save me." One of the most ancient prayers of the liturgy is this cry of Peter in today's gospel reading. Lord, save me. How many times in frightening moments have we not shouted or murmured this simple prayer? Faced with a threatening situation or devastating news, we recognize that left to our own devices we will not survive. Such a moment of recognition signals our deep need for God's merciful presence in our lives.

In the liturgy, we hear these words again. Lord, have mercy. Lord, to whom shall we go? Come, Lord Jesus. In our singing and speaking of these words, we ask Christ to strengthen our faith so that we might hear the cry for help in daily life and respond with Christ's own words: Take heart; do not be afraid.

## PRAYER OF THE DAY

Almighty and everlasting God, you are always more ready to hear than we are to pray, and to give more than we either desire or deserve. Pour upon us the abundance of your mercy, forgiving us those things of which our conscience is afraid, and giving us those good things for which we are not worthy to ask, except through the merit of your Son, Jesus Christ our Lord.

## READINGS

1 Kings 19:9-18

On the mountain where God had appeared to Moses with typical signs of God's presence—earthquake, wind, and fire—Elijah is now presented with a dramatic shift in the understanding of where God is to be found. God is not to be found in these signs. Rather, God is among the people, where the will of God is being lived out.

Psalm 85:8-13

I will listen to what the Lord God is saying. (Ps. 85:8)

Romans 10:5-15

Paul is discussing how we may attain the righteousness that leads to salvation. One way, he grants, would be to keep the law, but he has already shown that it is impossible. Then, he proclaims the good news about "righteousness that comes by faith."

Matthew 14:22-33

Matthew's gospel typically portrays Jesus' disciples as people of "little faith," who fail despite their best intentions. In this story, Matthew shows how Jesus comes to these disciples when they are in trouble and sustains them in their fear and doubt.

## SEMICONTINUOUS FIRST READING/PSALM

Genesis 37:1-4, 12-28

Though Joseph was Jacob's favorite son, his jealous brothers sold him into slavery. After this story, in a reversal of fortune, a famine caused Joseph's brothers to appear before him in Egypt to buy grain.

Psalm 105:1-6, 16-22, 45b

Make known the deeds of the Lord among the peoples. Hallelujah! (Ps. 105:1, 45)

## COLOR  Green

## THE PRAYERS

With the whole people of God, let us join in prayer for the church, those in need, and all of God's creation.

*A BRIEF SILENCE.*

That our minds may be silent and our hearts open to hear the voice of the Spirit in our busy and noisy world; God of mercy,

**hear our prayer.**

That all who minister in your church lead us in confessing our faith, so that we may proclaim Jesus Christ to the world; God of mercy,

**hear our prayer.**

That leaders of the world govern so that peace, truth, and righteousness may prevail; God of mercy,

**hear our prayer.**

That all who live with grief, illness, doubt, and fear (especially) may feel the hand of Jesus lifting them up; God of mercy,

**hear our prayer.**

That all who struggle with guilt, depression, abuse, poverty, and homelessness may know the abundance of your love and care; God of mercy,

257

**hear our prayer.**

*HERE OTHER INTERCESSIONS MAY BE OFFERED.*

We give thanks for Mary, mother of our Lord, and for all the faithful departed who keep the endless sabbath with you. Join their voices with ours to proclaim your praise until we meet them at your heavenly banquet. God of mercy,

**hear our prayer.**

O God, give us faith to trust your promises, that our lives may glorify your name, through Jesus Christ our Lord.

**Amen**

## IMAGES FOR PREACHING

"Let me hear what God the Lord will speak," wrote the psalmist, "for he will speak peace to his people" (Ps. 85:8). Like this poet of old, many of us are eager to hear the voice of the Lord. We long especially for words of comfort and guidance. But does God speak to us? And if so, when and how?

In Gail Godwin's novel *Evensong*, Margaret, the Episcopal priest and main character in the story, often puzzles over the matter-of-fact explanations Grace, a visitor to the community, offers for her actions. God tells her what to do, Grace firmly pronounces. Margaret, on the other hand, wishes that God would speak to her so clearly and wonders how Grace can be so certain that it is actually God speaking.

The witness of scripture is that God speaks to us "in many and various ways." The prophet Elijah heard God speak in "a sound of sheer silence" (1 Kings 19:12). Jesus' terrified disciples heard his words of comfort and admonition: "Take heart, it is I; do not be afraid" (Matt. 14:27). For the apostle Paul, our own voices are essential instruments of God: "How are they to believe in one [Christ] of whom they have never heard?" (Rom. 10:14).

The Christian community is God's gift for those trying to discern whether God is speaking to us. We hear God's word for us in the liturgy, sermons, prayers, and simple conversation. We share with fellow members of the body of Christ what we believe God is saying to us and ask for their guidance and understanding. Through baptism the Holy Spirit continually opens us to God's grace offered in scripture and the eucharist. In these and other ways, we are given courage and wisdom to answer the question, Was that God speaking to me?

## WORSHIP MATTERS

Many of the service books we use at worship include directions ("rubrics," from the Latin for "red") to help in the conduct of the liturgy. Though not to be followed slavishly, these instructions help to structure our worship, so that everything may be done in order and consistency may prevail week after week. Such consistency helps the assembly be freed to concentrate on the central matters of its worship rather than wondering what to do next. When worshipers can follow these guidelines they are not dependent on the presider but claim the liturgy as their own. The common use of rubrics from congregation to congregation also aids visitors in feeling at home in a different worship setting.

## LET THE CHILDREN COME

Tell the story of Jesus walking on the water, and make eye contact with the young listeners as you do so. During the intercessory prayers, invite children to name those in need of courage and faith and to give thanks for those who have been kind to them. Plan to help the children visit some of those for whom they prayed.

## HYMNS FOR WORSHIP

### GATHERING

Evening and morning    LBW 465

By gracious powers    WOV 736

You are my hiding place    W&P 160

### HYMN OF THE DAY

My life flows on in endless song    WOV 781

### ALTERNATE HYMN OF THE DAY

Eternal Father, strong to save    LBW 467

Will your anchor hold    TFF 255

### COMMUNION

I come, O Savior, to your table    LBW 213

Precious Lord, take my hand    WOV 731, TFF 193

### SENDING

O Jesus, I have promised    LBW 503

What a fellowship, what a joy divine    WOV 780

### ADDITIONAL HYMNS AND SONGS

Now the silence    LBW 205

Walk across the water    DH 69

258

## MUSIC FOR THE DAY

### PSALMODY

Dancing at the harvest    DH 40

Hurd, David. "Show Us Your Kindness." U, SATB, kybd, gtr.
OCP 9874CC.

Makeever, Ray.    PW A.

Smith, Alan. "Let Us See, O Lord, Your Mercy" in PS 1.

### CHORAL

Boatner, Edward. "Wade in the Water" in *The Story of the Spirituals.* Med
range solo, kybd or gtr.    MCF.

Busarow, Donald. "Forth in Thy Name." SAB, org.    AFP 11-2371.

Cherwien, David. "How Can I Keep from Singing." U, opt 2 or 3 pt,
pno.    AFP 0800658337.

Cruger-Garden. "Lord of Our Life." SATB, org.    GSCH 2887.

Handel, G.F. "How Beautiful Are the Feet" in *Messiah.* S solo.
Various ed.

Honoré, Jeffrey. "How Can I Keep from Singing." SATB, pno.
CG CGA-567.

Statham, Heathcoat. "Drop Down, Ye Heavens" in *The Oxford Easy Anthem Book.* 2 pt, org    OXF.

### CHILDREN'S CHOIRS

Behnke, John A. "Three Psalms for Unison Choir." U/2 pt, kybd.
CPH 98-3578.

Handel, G.F./arr. Peck, Richard. "How Beautiful Are the Feet."
U, kybd.    MSM-50-9505.

### KEYBOARD/INSTRUMENTAL

Sedio, Mark. "Lord, Your Hands Have Formed This World" in
*A Global Piano Tour.* Pno.    AFP 0800658191.

Wold, Wayne. "Oh, Worship the King" in *Songs of Thankfulness and
Praise, set 2.* Org.    MSM 10-712.

Young, Jeremy. "How Can I Keep from Singing?" in *At the Foot of the
Cross.* Pno.    AFP 0800655397.

### HANDBELL

Anderson and Carter. "How Firm a Foundation." Solo.
HOP 1526.

McFadden, Jane. "How Can I Keep from Singing?" 3-5 oct. L3.
AFP 0800658124.

Wiltse, Carl. "How Firm a Foundation." 4 oct. L3.    SGM 126.

### PRAISE ENSEMBLE

Courtney, Craig. "Be Not Afraid." SATB, kybd.    BEC BP 1388.

Ray, Robert. "He Never Failed Me Yet." SATB, kybd, soloist.
HAL 4478014.

# Tuesday, August 13

## FLORENCE NIGHTINGALE, 1910; CLARA MAASS, 1901; RENEWERS OF SOCIETY

When Florence Nightingale decided she would be a
nurse, her family was horrified. In the early 1800s nursing was done by people with no training and no other
way to earn a living. Florence trained at Kaiserswerth,
Germany, with a Lutheran order of deaconesses. She returned home and worked to reform hospitals in England. Nightingale led a group of thirty-eight nurses to
serve in the Crimean War, where they worked in ap-
palling conditions. She returned to London as a hero
and there resumed her work for hospital reform. Clara
Maass was born in New Jersey and served as a nurse in
the Spanish-American War, where she encountered the
horrors of yellow fever. She later responded to a call for
subjects in research on yellow fever. During the experi-
ments, which included receiving bites from mosquitoes,
she contracted the disease and died. The commemoration of these women invites the church to give thanks for
all who practice the arts of healing.

259

# Thursday, August 15

## MARY, MOTHER OF OUR LORD

The church honors Mary with the Greek title *theotokos,*
meaning God-bearer. Origen first used this title in the
early church, and the councils of Ephesus and Chal-
cedon upheld it. Luther upheld this same title in his
writings. The honor paid to Mary as *theotokos* and
mother of our Lord goes back to biblical times, when
Mary herself sang, "from now on all generations will
call me blessed" (Luke 1:48). Mary's life revealed the
presence of God incarnate among the humble and poor.
Mary's song, the Magnificat, speaks of reversals in the
reign of God: the mighty are cast down, the lowly are
lifted up, the hungry are fed, and the rich are sent away
empty-handed.

Hymns to commemorate Mary as *theotokos* might include "Sing of Mary, pure and holy" (WOV 634) or a
paraphrase of the Magnificat, such as "My soul proclaims your greatness" (WOV 730).

# August 18, 2002

Thirteenth Sunday after Pentecost
Proper 15

## INTRODUCTION

What parents would not cry out for help to someone who could save their sick or tormented children? Here, in the gospel reading, we see a mother who will not abandon her mission to find relief for her suffering daughter. She is persistent and unflinching in her request for Christ's healing.

In this Canaanite woman, the church finds an image of its mission. The world is filled with people who are tormented, sick, and oppressed. In the prayers, the church asks for God's healing in a world that is troubled and wounded. In the eucharistic meal, the church receives the strength to enter this world and bring comfort, healing, and justice to those in need.

## PRAYER OF THE DAY

Almighty and ever-living God, you have given great and precious promises to those who believe. Grant us the perfect faith which overcomes all doubts, through your Son, Jesus Christ our Lord.

## READINGS

### Isaiah 56:1, 6-8

Whereas the Israelite community, defined by early legal traditions, was expected to live the righteous and obedient life, the prophet makes a new announcement: now righteousness and obedience define who belongs to the Israelite community. In other words, commitment to the Lord makes a person a member of God's people—not race, nationality, or any other category.

### Psalm 67

Let all the peoples praise you, O God. (Ps. 67:3)

### Romans 11:1-2a, 29-32

As a Jewish Christian, Paul is dismayed that other Jews have not believed in Jesus as their Messiah. In his letter to the Romans, he discusses whether these Jews remain the chosen people of God.

### Matthew 15:[10-20] 21-28

Jesus teaches his disciples that true purity is a matter of the heart rather than outward religious observances. Almost immediately, this teaching is tested when a woman considered to be pagan and unclean approaches him for help.

## SEMICONTINUOUS FIRST READING/PSALM

### Genesis 45:1-15

Joseph, who has not been forthright with his brothers regarding his identity, finally declares, "I am Joseph!" His brothers had dealt badly with him, selling him into slavery years before. But Joseph knows that God had meant goodness in what had happened. He greets his brothers with magnanimity.

### Psalm 133

How good and pleasant it is to live together in unity. (Ps. 133:I)

## COLOR Green

## THE PRAYERS

With the whole people of God, let us join in prayer for the church, those in need, and all of God's creation.

*A BRIEF SILENCE.*

Make all peoples joyful in your house of prayer. Empower us to welcome and embrace those who are alienated from the church or feel unworthy of your love. God of mercy,

**hear our prayer.**

Guide the nations of the world and those who govern, that all may be blessed with the abundance your earth has yielded. God of mercy,

**hear our prayer.**

Bring reconciliation among Christians, Jews, and Muslims, that we may grow in understanding and respect for one another. God of mercy,

**hear our prayer.**

Heal those who are tormented by the demons of addiction, abuse, hatred, greed, and fear. God of mercy,

**hear our prayer.**

Bring comfort and consolation to those who are sick and hospitalized (especially), that they may know your loving presence. God of mercy,

**hear our prayer.**

*HERE OTHER INTERCESSIONS MAY BE OFFERED.*

We give you thanks for women and men in every age who have devoted their lives to you. Gather us with all the peoples of the world into your wide and loving embrace, here and in the life to come. God of mercy,

260

hear our prayer.
O God, give us faith to trust your promises, that our lives may glorify your name, through Jesus Christ our Lord. **Amen**

## MAGES FOR PREACHING

Depending on when we start the clock, almost everyone who lives in the United States is either a foreigner or the descendant of a foreigner. We all come from someplace else. Few of us, however, think about our status as foreigners. Even fewer have had an opportunity actually to experience being an outsider.

By the time of Jesus, the people of Israel had been foreigners for so long that we might think they would have had heightened sensitivity to the stranger in their midst. Mosaic Law specifically addressed the need for faithful Israelites to look out for the widow, the orphan, and the "sojourner," someone not of Israelite descent who lived among the Hebrews. These foreigners were under the protection of God. We read in Isaiah that they were welcome at God's holy mountain, and their sacrifices were acceptable to God (Isa. 56:7).

What we see in the gospel for today is that by Jesus' day, the Israelites' attitude toward foreigners had changed. Then a sojourner was no longer a member of a protected and welcome group but could be anyone who was simply unknown or away from home. Jesus' disciples urged him to send away a Canaanite woman who sought healing for her daughter. When Jesus appeared to do the disciples' bidding, however, the woman insisted that she, too, was a child of God. And Jesus praised her for her deep faith.

These readings call all of us to think about our own status as foreigners before God, people who were rescued from slavery to sin and adopted into God's household. We are also challenged today to think about how we treat the sojourner in our midst, anyone who lives apart from God and is in need of Christian community.

## WORSHIP MATTERS

Does the way we worship and the way we receive "outsiders" bear witness to the universality of God's grace in Jesus Christ? A clear worship folder helps visitors to join in the liturgy as they are able. Assistance in worship from those sitting nearby shows hospitality and gratitude for their presence. An open call to communion makes clear the desire of God that all the baptized come to the table of grace. A warm and personal invitation to all guests to join the community for its time of fellowship following the liturgy makes clear that the church reflects God's love and care for all people in the welcoming of newcomers.

## LET THE CHILDREN COME

The cry of the Canaanite woman reminds us of the Kyrie, our cry to the Lord for mercy on behalf of ourselves, the church, and the whole world. Let the children learn the Greek words by singing a simple Kyrie following each bid of the intercessory prayers. Consider using one from the Russian Orthodox tradition (WOV 602).

## HYMNS FOR WORSHIP
### GATHERING

God, whose almighty word    LBW 400
Here in this place    WOV 718

### HYMN OF THE DAY

Lord, whose love in humble service    LBW 423

### ALTERNATE HYMN OF THE DAY

Creating God, your fingers trace    WOV 757
In Christ there is no east or west    TFF 214

### COMMUNION

Forgive our sins as we forgive    LBW 307
One bread, one body    WOV 710, TFF 122, W&P 111

### SENDING

Lord, dismiss us with your blessing    LBW 259
Let justice flow like streams    WOV 763, TFF 48

### ADDITIONAL HYMNS AND SONGS

When in the hour of deepest need    LBW 303
Healer of our every ill    WOV 738
To God who gave the scriptures    MBW 508
We yearn, O Christ, for wholeness    NCH 179

## MUSIC FOR THE DAY
### PSALMODY

Brown, Teresa. "O God Be Gracious" in PS I.
Folkening, John. "Six Psalm Settings with Antiphons." U or SATB, opt kybd.    MSM 80-700.
May God bestow on us his grace    LBW 335
Makeever, Ray.    PW A.

261

## CHORAL

Boyle, Malcolm. "Let the People Praise Thee, O God." SATB div, org. PAR PPM08618.

Bruckner, Anton. "Locus Iste." SATB. PET 6314.

Mathias, William. "Let the People Praise Thee, O God." OXF A 331 (SATB, org); OXF A331 (SATB div, org).

Mendelssohn, Felix. "I Will Sing of Thy Great Mercies" in *Sing a Song of Joy; Vocal solos for Worship.* AFP 0800652827 (ML); 0800647882 (MH).

Rutter, John. "For the Beauty of the Earth." SA, pno. HIN HMC-469.

Schütz, Heinrich. "Lift Up Your Voice" in *Chantry Choirbook.* SATB, kybd. AFP 0800657772.

## CHILDREN'S CHOIRS

Bouman, Paul. "God Be Merciful." U, kybd. MSM-50-7039.

Powell, Robert J. "May God Be Merciful to Us." 2 pt, org. Trinitas 4528.

## KEYBOARD/INSTRUMENTAL

Albrecht, Mark. "Beach Spring" in *Early American Hymns and Tunes for Flute and Piano.* Pno, inst. AFP 0800656911.

Cherwien, David. "Lord, Whose Love in Humble Service" in *Interpretations Book VII.* Org. AMSI SP-104.

Hyslop, Scott. "Beach Spring" in *Six Chorale Fantasies for Solo Instrument and Piano.* Pno, sax. AFP 0800656601.

Porter, Rachel Trelstad. "Beach Spring" in *Day by Day.* Pno. AFP 0800656326.

Sedio, Mark. "Beach Spring" in *Dancing in the Light of God.* Pno. AFP 0800656547.

Smart, Henry. "Postlude in C" in *A Victorian Organ Album.* Org. OXF 0-19-375219-0.

## HANDBELL

Anderson & Stephenson. "Beach Spring." Solo. HOP 1707.

Angerman, David. "Fanfare on Old Hundredth." 2-3 oct. L2. ALF 12410.

Honoré, Jeffrey. "Gather Us In." 3-5 oct. L2. CPH 97-6556.

McChesney, Kevin. "Beach Spring." 2-3 oct. AFP 080065885X.

## PRAISE ENSEMBLE

Barbour, John and Anne Barbour. "I Will Follow." MAR 301 0818 165 (SATB, kybd); 301 7491 080 (choraltrax); 301 0532 253 (orch).

Harlan, Benjamin. "Lord Be Glorified" (with Glorify Thy Name). SATB, kybd. HAL 08741886.

Spencer, Linda A. "Weave Me, Lord." SATB, kybd. GS A-6332.

# Tuesday, August 20

## BERNARD, ABBOT OF CLAIRVAUX, 1153

Bernard was a Cistercian monk who became an abbot of great spiritual depth. He was a mystical writer deeply devoted to the humanity of Christ and consequently to the affective dimension of spirituality. He was critical of one of the foremost theologians of the day, Peter Abelard, because he believed Abelard's approach to faith was too rational and did not provide sufficient room for mystery. Bernard's devotional writings are still read today. His sermon on the Song of Solomon treats that book as an allegory of Christ's love for humanity. Bernard wrote several hymns, five of which are in *LBW.* Singing his hymn "Jesus the very thought of you" (316) could be a way to commemorate this monk at gatherings within the congregation today.

# Saturday, August 24

## ST. BARTHOLOMEW, APOSTLE

Bartholomew is mentioned as one of Jesus' disciples in Matthew, Mark, and Luke. The list in John does not include him but rather Nathanael, and these two are often assumed to be the same person. Except for his name on these lists of the twelve, little is known. Some traditions say Bartholomew preached in India or Armenia following the resurrection. In art, Bartholomew is pictured holding a flaying knife to indicate the manner in which he was killed.

In Bartholomew we have a model for the way many Christians live out their faith: anonymously. Like Bartholomew we are called by name to follow, though much of what we do in faith is quiet and unrecognized.

# August 25, 2002

Fourteenth Sunday after Pentecost
Proper 16

## INTRODUCTION

At any time and in any place, the Christian may ask God to forgive sin that separates one from God and others. At the same time, it is good to remember that to be a Christian is to be united to a community that bears the wounds of sin and human folly. The worshiping assembly—as a community—confesses the truth of its own unloving words, thoughts, and deeds. And throughout the liturgy, it hears and feels and tastes the merciful and forgiving love of God: in the absolution, in the waters of baptism, in receiving the body and blood of Christ, in the words of forgiveness spoken by a friend or family member, in the sharing of the peace.

These acts of confession and forgiveness in the liturgy are gifts of grace. How, then, might our words and actions extend this grace in daily life?

## PRAYER OF THE DAY

God of all creation, you reach out to call people of all nations to your kingdom. As you gather disciples from near and far, count us also among those who boldly confess your Son Jesus Christ as Lord.

## READINGS

Isaiah 51:1-6

In this text, the writer appeals to a people who seem apathetic, if not despairing. Isaiah reminds Israel that God's actions in the past (v. 2) are the basis for hope in the present.

Psalm 138

O Lord, your love endures forever. (Ps. 138:9)

Romans 12:1-8

Paul offers practical advice to the Roman Christians, suggesting new ways of relating to God, to the world, to the self, and to other believers.

Matthew 16:13-20

At a climactic point in Jesus' ministry, God reveals to Peter that Jesus is "the Messiah, the Son of the living God," and Jesus responds by revealing his vision of the church.

## SEMICONTINUOUS FIRST READING/PSALM

Exodus 1:8; 2:10

The man who would lead Israel out of bondage in Egypt began life in challenging circumstances. In order to curb the population increase of the Hebrew people, Pharaoh ordered that all male babies be killed. Moses' mother put him in a basket and hid it among reeds in the Nile River. In an ironic twist, Pharaoh's daughter found the baby, and ordered that he be nursed.

Psalm 124

We have escaped like a bird from the snare of the fowler. (Ps. 124:7)

COLOR Green

263

## THE PRAYERS

With the whole people of God, let us join in prayer for the church, those in need, and all of God's creation.
*A BRIEF SILENCE.*

That your church may rise up on the foundation of faith and never hesitate to confess the name of Jesus; God of mercy,

**hear our prayer.**

That every nation honor your gift of creation and make wise and fair use of the resources given to us and future generations; God of mercy,

**hear our prayer.**

That you would protect victims of violence, hatred, and prejudice, and that those inclined to violence would be turned to the way of peace and reconciliation; God of mercy,

**hear our prayer.**

That as we thank you for the gifts we enjoy from your hand, we set aside arrogance and entitlement, humbly receiving and generously sharing our blessings; God of mercy,

**hear our prayer.**

That all of our sisters and brothers who are suffering from abuse and who are grieving, sick, or hospitalized (especially) may be healed and restored; God of mercy,

**hear our prayer.**

*HERE OTHER INTERCESSIONS MAY BE OFFERED.*

That the faith and courage of the fathers and mothers of the church form and strengthen us until we come with them into your glory; God of mercy,

**hear our prayer.**

O God, give us faith to trust your promises, that our lives may glorify your name, through Jesus Christ our Lord.

**Amen**

## IMAGES FOR PREACHING

"Who do people say that the Son of Man is?" Jesus asked his disciples. From the disciples' answer, we see that those who knew about his preaching, teaching, and healing understood that Jesus stood on a firm foundation—the shoulders of others whom God had sent throughout the ages—John the Baptist, Elijah, Jeremiah, and other prophets.

Implicit also in Peter's response to Jesus' question—Peter's confession, "You are the Messiah"—is another expression of the firm foundation on which Jesus stood. As Messiah, Jesus did not suddenly appear out of nowhere. He is the long-promised one, the fulfillment of God's plan to restore all creation to wholeness. We might even say Jesus' foundation is the whole history of God's creation!

Peter's affirmation of faith was passed on by Matthew in order that the whole Christian church might stand on a firm foundation. We read elsewhere in the New Testament, Ephesians 2:20 and Revelation 21:14, that the faith of all the apostles and prophets provides a foundation for the church. Now we also have become part of the foundation.

When we come together to worship God, when we express our welcome for the newly baptized in our community, when we share a sign of God's reconciling peace and prepare to come together for God's holy supper, we form the foundation for one another's faith. It is on the faith of every member of the body of Christ that the church is built. It is people of faith, people called into a new relationship with God, people like Peter, whom God uses to make our foundations more sure. Now, as we are made stronger in faith, we can use our gifts, received in baptism, to answer for all the world Jesus' life-shaping question, "Who do you say that I am?"

## WORSHIP MATTERS

Those who bring communion from the liturgical assembly to those who are sick or otherwise homebound serve as representatives of the whole community of faith. They are an extension of the gathered congregation. As they leave the assembly to serve those who are absent, they go with the prayer, blessing, and authority of all the faithful. In this context the presiding minister calls them forward and gives them the food and drink of this eucharistic meal, that even the neediest within the community might be strengthened through the body and blood of Christ and reminded of their place in the church's life.

## LET THE CHILDREN COME

"We who are many are one body in Christ, and individually we are members of one another," writes the apostle Paul. "We" means all the baptized, regardless of race, gender, ability, or age. Too often we treat children as if they were part of the future church, not members of the present, living body of Christ. Take time to think of and name the particular gifts children bring to the gathering of believers where you worship. How can you evoke, honor, and strengthen those gifts?

## HYMNS FOR WORSHIP

### GATHERING

Built on a rock    LBW 365

Shout for joy loud and long    WOV 793

Faith that's sure    LS 173

We are all one in Christ    TFF 221, LLC 470

### HYMN OF THE DAY

Christ is made the sure foundation    LBW 367, WOV 747

### ALTERNATE HYMN OF THE DAY

The Church's one foundation    LBW 369

One in the bread    BL 10

### COMMUNION

Let us ever walk with Jesus    LBW 487

This is my body    WOV 707, TFF 121

How firm a foundation    LBW 507

SENDING

My hope is built on nothing less    LBW 293, 294
We all are one in mission    WOV 755

ADDITIONAL HYMNS AND SONGS

We are an offering    W&P 146
My life flows on in endless song    WOV 781
Seek ye first    WOV 783, TFF 149, W&P 122
Christ, burning Wisdom    OBS 51

**MUSIC FOR THE DAY**

PSALMODY

Butler, Eugene. "A Joyous Psalm." CGA-74. U.
Duba, Arlo. "Psalm 138" in TP.
Haas, David. PCY, vol. 3.
I will give thanks with my whole heart    PH 247
Inwood, Paul. "In the Presence of the Angels" in PS 3.
Makeever, Ray. PW A.

CHORAL

Barrett-Ayers, Reginald. "I Will Praise Thee O God." SATB, org.
NOV 20017.
Beck, John Ness. "Upon This Rock." SATB, org/pno, opt brass
sextet. GSCH 11467.
Bortniansky-Tkach. "We Thank Thee, Lord." KJO 6513
DesPres-Lovelace. "The Name of Jesus." SATB. CPH 98-1095.
Handel, G.F. "Sweet Is the Name of Jesus." U, kybd.
HOP A 391.
Mendelssohn, Felix. "On God Alone My Hope I Build" in *Chantry
Choirbook*. SATB. AFP 0800657772.
Pote, Allen. "I Will Give Thanks." SATB, opt tpts.
AFP 6000124236.

CHILDREN'S CHOIRS

Butler, Eugene. "A Joyous Psalm." U, kybd. CG CGA 74.
Lindh, Jody W. "I Give You Thanks." U, kybd, perc, synth, bass.
CG CGA-561.

KEYBOARD/INSTRUMENTAL

Albrecht, Mark. "Eden Church" in *Early American Hymns and Tunes for
Flute and Piano*. Pno, inst. AFP 0800656911.
Bisbee, B. Wayne. "Eden Church" in *From the Serene to the Whimsical*.
Org. AFP 0800654412.
Mulet, Henry. "Tu es Petra" in *Esquisses Byzantines*. Org.
Leduc B. L. 631.

Powell, Robert. "Westminster Abbey" in *Rejoice, Ye Pure in Heart*. Org.
AFP 0800653610.
Proulx, Richard. "Westminster Abbey" in *Augsburg Organ Library:
November*. Org. AFP 0800658965.

HANDBELL

Honoré, Jeffrey. "One Bread, One Body" (Glory & Praise). 3-4 oct.
L3. AG 1914.
McChesney, Kevin. "Synergy." 3-5 oct. L3. JEF RW 8127.

PRAISE ENSEMBLE

Angerman, David. "You Are the Christ." SATB, kybd. GS A-6883.
Berry, Cindy. "Seekers of Your Kingdom." SATB, kybd.
HAL 08741887.
Moen, Don and Claire Cloninger/arr. Don Harris and Dan Burgess.
"I Offer My Life." INT 46200C (SATB, kybd); 4620TX
(choraltrax); 46200R (int).

# Wednesday, August 28

AUGUSTINE, BISHOP OF HIPPO, 430

Augustine was one of the greatest theologians of the
Western church. Born in North Africa, he was a philosophy student in Carthage, where he later became a
teacher of rhetoric. Much of his young life was a de-
bauched one. As an adult he came under the influence
of Ambrose, the bishop of Milan, and through him
came to see Christianity as a religion appropriate for a
philosopher. Augustine was baptized by Ambrose at the
Easter Vigil in 387. He was ordained four years later
and made bishop of Hippo in 396. Augustine was a defender of the Christian faith and argued, against the
Donatists, that the holiness of the church did not depend on the holiness of its members, particularly the
clergy, but that holiness comes from Christ, the head of
the church. Augustine's autobiography, *Confessions*, tells
of his slow move toward faith and includes the line,
"Late have I loved thee."

# Wednesday, August 28

MOSES THE BLACK, MONK, C. 400

A man of great strength and rough character, Moses the Black was converted to Christian faith toward the close of the fourth century. Prior to his conversion he had been a thief and a leader of a gang of robbers. The story of his conversion is unknown, but eventually, he became a desert monk at Skete. The habit of his monastic community was white, though Moses is reported to have said, "God knows I am black within." The change in his heart and life had a profound impact on his native Ethiopia. He was murdered when Berbers attacked his monastery.

# Saturday, August 31

JOHN BUNYAN, TEACHER, 1688

John Bunyan had little schooling but became one of the most remarkable figures of seventeenth-century literature. He was a lay preacher who made his living as a tinker. After the restoration in England he was ordered to stop preaching, but he refused and was jailed several times. His spiritual pilgrimage is revealed in his works, particularly *The Pilgrim's Progress.* It is an allegory of a person's experience from his first awareness of sin, through a personal conversion to Christ, then on to the life of faith and then finally to the "Celestial City," the true and eternal home. His commemoration and his own journey offer strength for people to continue their own quest for spiritual truth.

# AUTUMN

*We can always be certain*

*that the Spirit and power of God*

*are at work*

# Images *of the* Season

Autumn is one of those times when the workaday

world makes its influence felt in the rhythms of the church.

Autumn is not, of course, an official season of the church year.

Rather, we are continuing the long season after Pentecost, the time of the church. This time of the year, however, does feel like a new season of beginnings. This is the time above all others when we gather our energies, restarting those programs that may have taken a summer sabbatical and breathing new life into everything else. In many parts of the continent, the weather takes on an invigorating edge; going back to school brings its own enthusiasm. What could be more natural than that same drive be applied to our life in the church? After all, we know what a good thing we have in the gospel, and we want to use every means at our disposal to bring that good news to others and to thank God for that great gift. We would like our congregational life to be faithful, to give honor to God, and to meet people's needs; but at this time we may also be looking for something especially invigorating. Young people a generation ago (that is, those now turning gray) might have called it the "dynamite" factor—as in, "That was just dynamite!"

As it happens, "dynamite" is based on a good, biblical word. The Greek term is *dunamis*, meaning "power" or "force." In the Bible, this is the power that created and still rules over the universe, the power over human affairs, the power with which Jesus was anointed by God. We associate the explosive called dynamite with one type of power, but the *dunamis*, the dynamic power of God, is something infinitely greater.

Sometimes we in mainstream denominations are a bit reticent to call on the power of God. Perhaps we recognize, with Luther, that humans who claim an immediate access to that sort of force can create precarious situations. That is why the reformer insisted on the importance of evaluating claims of special power against the witness of God's word. His counsel is still good today, when followers of new age thinking clamor for attention. We heirs of the twentieth century know how even the well-intentioned use of power can lead to regrets. It is said, for instance, that one reason that Alfred Nobel instituted the Nobel Prizes (including the Peace Prize) was that he felt the weight of responsibility for inventing dynamite and thereby providing access to such power for good and for ill.

Fortunately, we need not rely on our own judgments when we are contemplating tapping into the *dunamis* of God. Such power is, indeed, available to us, and we are encouraged to make use of it. The church is God's preeminent vehicle for bringing that force into the world. It comes to us through the means of grace: the word of God, the washing of baptism, and the Lord's supper. As long as these form the core of our worship, we can be confident that it is the Holy Spirit who provides the power.

"Ah," you say, "but we all know congregations—populated by faithful Christians, where God's word is preached and the sacraments are celebrated—that are barely alive." To that objection, a couple of responses could be made. First, "Are you sure?" That is, by what measure are you calculating life? The power of God does not always show itself in explosive growth. Sometimes it leads to a deepening of spirit, a quieter preparation of the soil for growth that may come later. We cannot always understand or even see what God is doing, but we can always be certain that the Spirit and power of God are at work.

That does not let us off the hook, however, and the second response to the above question would be to encourage faltering congregations to trust the Spirit. Look for forms of ministry that are needed in your neighborhood; then go to work providing them, again working outward from the means of grace. The power of God will lift you like a swimmer on a wave, carrying you forward until that ministry is done.

The energy of autumn is potent indeed, but it pales by comparison with the *dunamis* of God. In our worship, in our education, in our outreach—in all that we do, we look to and rely on the power unleashed by God in Jesus Christ.

# Environment *and* Art *for the* Season

Every September, the winding roads of New England

fill with visitors from across the United States. These autumn

pilgrims time their vacations to catch the crimson and gold

refulgence that blazes on the area's wooded hills. The colors of autumn leaves are a primitive, tangible sign of mortality, of the fullness of creation yielding to the inevitability of death. We know that, like the leaves, we will die. But the rich splendor of autumn harvest stirs us to thanksgiving rather than melancholy. Its beauty offers consolation rather than sadness.

In his poem *To Autumn*, John Keats captures the elegiac tone of this awareness that life's harvest bounty is a sign of death. The figure of autumn is introduced as a friend of the maturing sun who conspires with the sun "to load and bless / With fruit the vines that round the thatch-eaves run." In the next stanza, however, the figure of autumn becomes a harvester, drowsy with "the fume of poppies," while holding a hook for the cutting of grain. It is an image reminiscent of the angel reapers in Matthew's gospel (see proper 11) who are told by the master in the parable to "gather the wheat into my barn" (Matt. 13:30).

In church tradition, the end of summer and the beginning of the cold season became identified with the September 14 festival of the Holy Cross. The gospel readings this year from late September through mid-October are vineyard parables. One suggestion for the autumn worship environment, therefore, is to focus on the cross as a sign that Christ is the "first fruits" of the harvest who will be followed into heaven by the community of believers. If the central cross in the worship space is placed in a stand rather than mounted on a wall, Christ's primacy as first fruits of the harvest could be suggested by placing baskets of flowers, fruits, vegetables, and nuts on the floor surrounding the cross. Pay attention to the scale of the cross within the space. The harvest baskets will need to be sufficiently large to relate to the cross. To help achieve height, baskets and bushels might be placed on stands. The effect should not be to overwhelm the cross. The baskets should not obstruct the cross from view or restrict movement around it. An-

other option is to adorn the cross with a grapevine wreath—again, large enough in scale to make a statement but not so large as to compete with or overtake the cross. The wreath could be embellished with dried white hydrangeas and wildflowers or the bright fruit of the viburnum shrub.

Wreaths of wheat or other grains look wonderful as fall decoration. Grain stalks look beautiful gathered in simple bundles and tied with vine or other natural fibers. Gourds and corn are fine signs of the earth's fullness. Make sure that any fresh fruits or vegetables are without bruises or flaws. Fungus can spread quickly. Check also for insects. When working with corn, remove enough strands of corn silk and outer husks so that the corncob is visible and its casing is attractive. Dried corn will not rot and can be stored for future use. Replace or remove food immediately if it shows signs of decay, and watch out for mice and other animals that might enjoy midnight nibbling on the harvest feast.

Chrysanthemums, marigolds, and dahlias often remain in bloom until the first frost of the season. Even when working with dried flowers, it is best to gather them while they are fresh. Allow the flowers to dry after arranging them. Seedpods and lovely grasses can accent arrangements of dried flowers. Pink muhly grass, which blooms between September and November, has graceful pink flowers. The orange-red blades of the autumn flame miscanthus grow as high as five feet. This grass would make a striking backdrop to a large, dramatic arrangement of tall wildflowers, such as giant purple coneflowers or goldenrod. Fragrant herbs such as rosemary and basil might be included in arrangements or wreaths.

In autumn, the green Sundays of the long period after Pentecost continue. If a church owns two sets of green vestments and paraments, the darker green might be used for the green Sundays during autumn and winter, from the Sunday after Holy Cross until the last Sunday before the Transfiguration in the Epiphany season.

269

Holy Cross vesture is red, as is Reformation Sunday. A parish might consider these uses when purchasing red vestments for Pentecost.

The white festival of St. Michael and All Angels falls on Sunday, September 29, 2002. This is a festival beloved by many churches. From Revelation we hear that Michael vanquishes the dragon, the ancient serpent—Satan, throwing him down to earth along with his angels. Michael is our protector, guiding us into paradise.

Images of the archangel Michael can be found in Byzantine iconography and in Hispanic folk art. In icons, he is a winged figure, often wearing a robe of the heavenly court. In early Christian art, he became conflated with the Roman and Greek gods Mercury and Hermes and wore a winged helmet and sandals. In Mexican folk art, he is a handsome young man, clad in armor, who stands over a dragon or serpent with a spear. Since medieval times, his story has sometimes been conflated with the medieval account of St. George and the dragon.

270

Artist Nancy Chinn, in her book *Spaces for Spirit: Adorning the Church* (Chicago: LTP, 1998), displays a photograph of her "Archangel Michael" installation. The work hangs six by sixteen feet and was executed in painted and cut paper. Chinn prepared the paper (usually photographic paper that comes in rolls) by painting it with layers of acrylic paint thinned with matte medium and water. She drew on the reverse side of the paper before doing the cutting.

Chinn also includes a chapter in her book on how to make paper lace. "Paper lace," she writes, "is a term used to describe large sheets of paper that have been designed and cut to create lace-like images with pattern and shapes embedded within the structure. They are designed to be hung independent of a background, in free space, either in front of a light source, as a screen or as a canopy" (Chinn, p. 55). The resulting art is airy and elegant but is also capable of holding fine patterns. Because paper cutting is a traditional art practiced by peoples throughout the world, it offers opportunities to incorporate designs from these cultures. A church planning a

liturgy for St. Michael and All Angels might wish to consider this medium for a hanging image of the archangel on his festival day.

By mid-September, planning begins again in earnest for the new liturgical year. This is a good time to convene the art and environment committee for seasonal planning. Nancy Chinn addresses in her book some of the problems that art and environment committees might face. Well-intentioned planning by a committee sometimes results in work that appears overblown, incoherent, or otherwise compromised. Outcomes as subtle as ineffectively placed flowers or as glaring as an unsuccessful seasonal installation can be traced to problems in the committee's functioning.

Chinn offers some rules for structuring an effective meeting to do seasonal planning. She also gives pointers for successful interaction between the art and environment committee and other church committees, staff, and volunteers. Any church with an art and environment committee or any church hoping to organize a well-functioning committee will benefit from Chinn's book.

Reformation Sunday comes to us at the end of October, at a time when we both enjoy the fruits of our labors and realize their transience within life's natural order. It is a time for reflection on the reforming work in the church's past as well as on the constant rebuilding that is required of the church in the present. If the environment for worship on Reformation Sunday helps us to look back at history but not to look forward, what message about reform is being communicated? Appreciation for tradition might be melded with some contemporary touches. Be creative. As a reminder of our baptismal promises, perhaps red rose petals might be strewn artfully around the font or a wreath of red roses might encircle the paschal candle. Portraits of contemporary reformers, such as Martin Luther King Jr. and Dietrich Bonhoeffer, might be displayed along with a portrait of Martin Luther. The environment for the day can set a tone of thanksgiving for things past and of hope for things to come.

# Preaching *with the* Season

The tour group of Americans stumbled into a gala

at the Leipzig Opera House. It was a cultural hapax legomenon,

a one-time occurrence, a one-night extravaganza celebrating

the music of Robert Stolz on the twenty-fifth anniversary of his death. The name was unknown to the tourists who had somehow managed to claim prime seating in a sold-out house. The name was unknown but the music was not. The performers launched into a number we had been singing with accordion accompaniment on the tour bus, "Zwei Herzen im Dreivierteltakt." It sounded better with professional performers and full orchestra (though we did spot an accordion on the side).

> Two hearts in three-quarter time
>> May has brought them together.
> Two hearts in three-quarter time
>> In a night of waltz.
> One-quarter spring, one-quarter wine,
>> One-quarter love, one must be in love.
> Two hearts in three-quarter time,
>> Who has more to be happy about?

If May has us dancing a waltz, what is autumn's dance? We go back to school, back to what is called in church "the program year." Vacation is over. The pace picks up. Attendance is up. Expectations are up. If we have not planned adequately in August, we are lost. We are two beats behind, struggling to catch up. The dance is frantic. The rhythm is martial. Get in step. Hurry up.

May might have us dancing a waltz, but the seasons of the year beat out the rhythm of life in 4/4 time—spring, summer, autumn, winter. For the people of God the rhythm is more complicated. The four straightforward seasons of nature are overlaid with six seasons of the church year that beat out a rhythm in 6/4 time—Advent, Christmas, Epiphany, Lent, Easter, and the season after Pentecost.

The martial rhythm of 4/4 time has its accents on the first and third beats. But where does the year start? Does it begin with winter and the seed in the ground or

spring and the seed breaking ground? How does January 1 fit in? There is no clear downbeat and no snap of the baton to bring the year to an end. There is no beginning or end but endless repetition until it all comes to an end. It will all end, the scientists tell us, either in the big crunch or the big evaporation.

The 6/4 time of the church year has us dancing in time with the life of Christ, beginning with Advent preparation for his coming and culminating with Christ, the king of all creation. His movements, his rhythm, and his song become ours. With time and practice we beat out his rhythm with our lives, moving in 6/4 time in the midst of a world content with common time.

Six-four time is often comprised of two sets of three. It has a waltz feel to it. Can we dance a waltz to the time metered out by the church year? Can we live according to Christ's 6/4 time in a world that thinks 4/4 is all there is?

In an article in the May 24–31, 2000, *Christian Century*, Luke Timothy Johnson reflects on the CBS miniseries *Jesus*. He comments on the way Jeremy Sisko played the part of Jesus. Johnson writes, "It is as though in the midst of every activity, Jesus is listening for a music that is pitched beyond other ears, and his rhythms are determined more by what snatches of tune he can catch than by the din of noise around him."

No wonder Jesus appeared so odd to those around him. Small wonder Jesus' followers, those who live according to his rhythm, appear so odd to the world around us. Here is the germ of a theme for these Sundays from proper 17 to proper 25. Call the series "The Importance of Being Odd," "Called to Be Odd," or "Called to Oddness."

Life in 4/4 time says bigger is better, keep score, and get even. Each of the gospel readings for these Sundays highlights some aspect of the dance of life in 6/4 time that is at odds with what the world regards as normal.

271

# Shape *of* Worship *for the* Season

## BASIC SHAPE OF THE EUCHARISTIC RITE

- Confession and Forgiveness: see alternate worship text for autumn in *Sundays and Seasons*

### GATHERING

- Greeting: see alternate worship text for autumn
- Omit the Kyrie during autumn (except for Reformation Day)
- Omit or use the hymn of praise during autumn (use for Reformation Day; also consider using the hymn of praise "This is the feast of victory" for the festival of St. Michael and All Angels on September 29)

### WORD

- Nicene Creed for Reformation Sunday or Day and for St. Michael and All Angels; Apostles' Creed for remaining Sundays in this season
- The prayers: see the prayers in the autumn section of *Sundays and Seasons*

### MEAL

- Offertory prayer: see alternate worship text for autumn
- Use the proper preface for Sundays after Pentecost
- Eucharistic prayer: in addition to four main options in *LBW*, see "Eucharistic Prayer H: Autumn" in *WOV* Leaders Edition, p. 72
- Invitation to communion: see alternate worship text for autumn
- Post-communion prayer: see alternate worship text for autumn

### SENDING

- Benediction: see alternate worship text for autumn
- Dismissal: see alternate worship text for autumn

## OTHER SEASONAL POSSIBILITIES

- Blessing of Teachers and Students (see seasonal rites section)
- See Recognition of Ministries in the Congregation in *Occasional Services*, pp. 143–46

### DISTRIBUTION OF BIBLES

- If Bibles are publicly distributed to young readers, consider having their parents or sponsors involved in physically handing over the Bibles (as a follow-up to promises made at baptism)

### BLESSING OF ANIMALS

- Traditionally celebrated on or near October 4 (Francis of Assisi, renewer of the church, 1226); see a possible order for this celebration in the seasonal rites section

### HARVEST FESTIVAL OR HARVEST HOME

- Many congregations celebrate the harvest sometime each fall. Although readings are appointed on page 39 of *LBW* for the occasion of harvest, the gospel for proper 24 (October 20) speaks to the theme of returning to God what is God's and may be a particularly suitable occasion to celebrate the harvest.

### REFORMATION DAY

- One way to resolve the dilemma of whether to celebrate lesser festivals when they occur on Sundays or to observe the complete cycle of the Revised Common Lectionary would be to use lectionary readings for proper 25 on October 27, but to use the prayers of the day for both proper 25 and Reformation Day. Although much of the music and the prayers could reflect the lectionary for proper 25, one or more of the hymns could be chosen to reflect the Reformation festival. The color for the day could also be red.

### SERVICE OF THE WORD FOR HEALING

- See the seasonal rites section for this order, which may be used on or near the festival of St. Luke, Evangelist (October 18).

# Assembly Song *for the* Season

The renewal of summer leads to new beginnings

in Autumn. Many things in our society begin their yearly cycle

in September, including church programs. On the other hand,

nature's yearly cycle is waning in the Northern Hemisphere and the church year is in its final quarter. How do worship planners approach this situation of conflicting cycles? If you simplified the liturgy during the summer by returning to a clear focus on the central elements of the liturgy, then the liturgy is able to receive an infusion of new material, building to the final coda in November.

## GATHERING

If you began learning a new musical setting of the liturgy during the summer, now is the time to add the hymn of praise. An alternative to a singular setting of the hymn of praise is to use a variety of hymn settings such as "Now the feast and celebration" (WOV 789), "Glory to God, we give you thanks" (WOV 787), "Alabaré" (LLC 582, WOV 791), or "All glory be to God on high" (LBW 166), which is especially appropriate on Reformation Day. You might occasionally vary the traditional texts by substituting hymns such as "Oh, sing to the Lord" (LLC 598, TFF 274, WOV 795), "Praise him! Jesus, blessed Savior" (TFF 285), "Give praise to God" (LLC 577), or "The trumpets sound, the angels sing" (W&P 139).

## WORD

Propers 17, 20, and 23 provide an opportunity to use *Share Your Bread*, a lectionary-based planning guide for world hunger and worship (ELCA 6000118996). The guide includes prayers, related hymns, litanies, and reflections based on the texts for the day. If your congregation normally speaks or sings the psalm without a psalm refrain, now would be a good time to introduce the use of psalm refrains. *Psalter for Worship* (AFP) supports the settings in the lectionary inserts *Celebrate* and *Jubilate* by providing simple refrains, alternative psalm tones, and practical information on psalm singing.

## MEAL

The offertory hymn is a natural place to highlight the harvest and stewardship themes of the season. "Let the vineyards be fruitful" is always appropriate. Other options include "For the fruit of all creation" (WOV 760), "Now we offer" (TFF 129, WOV 761), "We come to the hungry feast" (WOV 766), "We give thee but thine own" (LBW 410), or "We are an offering" (W&P 146). Return to the practice of singing the preface dialog and proper preface. Add instruments to the "Holy, holy, holy Lord" on Reformation Day.

## SENDING

The use of both the post-communion song and the dismissal hymn is not necessary at this time. Various settings of "Thank the Lord/Thankful hearts" or other hymns of thanksgiving such as "Give thanks with a grateful heart" (TFF 292, W&P 41), "Praise to you, O God of mercy" (WOV 790), or "Let all things now living" (LBW 557) make appropriate post-communion song. A procession of the cross and ministers from the altar to the entrance door during the dismissal hymn can evoke a powerful image of the people moving into the world in mission and ministry. Encourage the congregation to turn and face the cross as it moves. Open the church doors wide so that the outside world can be seen from inside. Combine this procession with a strong sending hymn such as "Hallelujah! We sing your praises" (WOV 722, TFF 158), "The Spirit sends us forth to serve" (WOV 723), "Sent forth by God's blessing" (LBW 221), "The Lord now sends us forth" (LLC 415), "Send me, Jesus" (TFF 244, 245), or "Go, make disciples" (W&P 47).

273

# Music *for the* Season

## VERSE AND OFFERTORY

Busarow, Donald. *Verses and Offertories (Pentecost 21—Christ the King).*
AFP 0800648986.

*Verses and Offertory Sentences, Part VII (Pentecost 19—Christ the King).*
CPH 97-5507.

## CHORAL

Burroughs, Bob. "Jesus Loves Me." SATB, kybd.    CPH 98-3580.

Busarow, Donald. "All Creatures of Our God and King."
MSM-60-9011 (score SATB, cong, 2 tpt, org);
MSM-60-9011A (choir); MSM-60-9011B (tpt).

Handel, G.F. "All My Spirit Longs to Savor" in *Chantry Choirbook.*
SATB, kybd.    AFP 0800657772.

Hampton, Keith. "My God Is an Awesome God." SATB, pno.
AFP 0800659171.

Hassell, Michael. "Jesus Loves Me." SATB, pno, sop or alto sax.
AFP 08006 56512.

Hassler, Hans Leo. "We Give Thanks Unto Thee." SATB.
CPH 98-3378.

Mozart, W. A. "Jubilate Deo." SATB, kybd.    CPH 98-3191.

Pachelbel, Johann. "On God, and Not on Human Trust." SATB.
CPH 98-1006.

Purcell/Hopson. "Sound the Trumpet." 2 pt mxd, kybd.
CFI CM8056.

Schütz, Heinrich. "Sing Praise to Our Glorious Lord." SATB.
AFP 0800673646.

Sjolund, Paul. "Children of the Heavenly Father" in *The Augsburg
Choirbook.* SATB, org.    AFP 0800656784.

Vaughan Williams, Ralph. "At the Name of Jesus." SATB.
OXF 40-100.

White, David Ashley. "O Bread of Life from Heaven" in *The Augsburg
Choirbook.* 2 pt mxd, org.    AFP 0800656784.

## CHILDREN'S CHOIRS

Althouse, Jay. "Each and Every Day." 2 pt, kybd.    ALF 18001.

Crocker, Emily, arr. "When in Our Music God Is Glorified." 2 pt,
kybd, opt brass.    HOP 08740250.

Emerson, Roger. "Witness." 2 pt, kybd.    HAL 40326252.

## KEYBOARD/INSTRUMENTAL

Callahan, Charles. *Partita on "Diademata."* Org.    MSM 10-409.

Fields, Tim. "All Hail the Power of Jesus' Name." Org.
AFP 0800658736.

Hassell, Michael. *Jazz All Seasons.* Pno.    AFP 0800656830.

Held, Wilbur. *Hymn Preludes for the Autumn Festivals.* Org.
CPH 97-5360.

Manz, Paul. *Two Pieces for Festive Occasions.* Org.    MSM 10-840.

## HANDBELL

Afdahl, Lee J. "Lord, Dismiss us With Your Blessing" 3-5 oct. L3.
LOR 20/1193L.

McFadden, Jane. "Londonderry Air." 2-3 oct. L2.
AFP 0800656296.

Roman, Johann. "Fanfare." 3-5 oct. L2.    CPH 97-5849.

Sherman, Arnold B. "Here I Am, Lord" 3-5 oct. L2.    AG 2140.

Tucker, Sondra. "Give Me Jesus." 3 oct. L2.    AMSI HB-30.

Wagner, Douglas E. "Rondo in C." 3-4 oct. L3.    LAK HB 005.

## PRAISE ENSEMBLE

Hampton, Keith. "Praise His Holy Name." SATB, kybd.
Earthsongs.

Johnson, Ralph. "Praise the Lord (A Processional Song)." SATB,
perc.  Earthsongs.

# Alternate Worship Texts

## CONFESSION AND FORGIVENESS

Before the whole company of heaven,
in the presence of God and of one another,
let us confess our sin.

*Silence for reflection and self-examination.*

Holy and gracious God,
I confess that I have sinned against you
and done wrong to my sisters and brothers.
Some of my sin I know—
the thoughts and words and deeds
of which I am ashamed—
but some is known only to you.
In the name of Jesus Christ
I ask forgiveness.
Deliver and restore me,
and give me your peace. Amen

The almighty and merciful God
grant you pardon, forgiveness,
and remission of all your sins.
**Amen**

## GREETING

Holy people of God,
called through the gospel of Christ,
enlightened by the Spirit:
grace, mercy, and peace
be with you all.
**And also with you.**

## OFFERTORY PRAYER

Living and true God,
we return to you the things that are yours—
our time, our skills, our possessions, our selves.
Bless us and these your gifts.
Move us to works of faith and labors of love
for the good of all your people
and the wholeness of your creation;
through our Lord Jesus Christ. Amen

## INVITATION TO COMMUNION

Everything is ready;
come to the wedding banquet.

## POST-COMMUNION PRAYER

Blessed are you, God of heaven and earth.
You satisfy us with good things
as an eagle feeds her young.
Renew our strength,
that we may go with eagerness and joy
into the places where you send us
to work in Jesus' name.
**Amen**

## BLESSING

Sisters and brothers,
stand firm in one spirit;
strive side by side for the faith of the gospel;
let your gentleness be known by everyone;
and the God of peace,
the Father, the ✝ Son, and the Holy Spirit,
be with you and bless you always.
**Amen**

## DISMISSAL

Go in peace. Serve the Lord with gladness.
**Thanks be to God.**

275

# Seasonal Rites

## Blessing of Teachers and Students

### HYMN
Earth and all stars!  LBW 558

*If used on a Sunday morning the following prayer may be used during or following the prayers.*

Let us pray for all who are beginning a new school year, that both students and teachers will be blessed in their academic endeavors.

Almighty God, you give wisdom and knowledge. Grant teachers the gift of joy and insight, and students the gift of diligence and openness, that all may grow in what is good and honest and true. Support all who teach and all who learn, that together we may know and follow your ways; through Jesus Christ our Lord. **Amen**

## Blessing of Animals

*This service may be used entirely on its own, perhaps for an observance on or near the commemoration of Francis of Assisi, renewer of the church, 1226 (October 4). Various elements of this order may also be incorporated into another worship service, though this material is not intended to replace the customary Sunday worship of the congregation. Care should be used in adapting the service to the occasion and to the physical setting in which it is used. For practical reasons this service may be conducted outdoors or in a facility other than a congregation's primary worship space.*

### GREETING AND PRAYER
The grace of our Lord Jesus Christ, the love of God, and the communion of the Holy Spirit be with you all. **Amen**

Let us pray.
O merciful Creator, your hand is open wide to satisfy the needs of every living creature. Make us always thankful for your loving providence; and grant that we, remembering the account that we must one day give, may be faithful stewards of your good gifts; through your Son, Jesus Christ our Lord.
**Amen**

*OR*

Almighty God, in giving us dominion over things on earth, you made us fellow workers in your creation: Give us wisdom and reverence so to use the resources of nature, that no one may suffer from our abuse of them, and that generations yet to come may continue to praise you for your bounty; through Jesus Christ our Lord.
**Amen**

*Book of Common Prayer, prayer 41, p. 827*

### READINGS
Genesis 1:1, 20-28
Genesis 6:17-22
Psalm 8
Psalm 148
*Other readings about God's creation and the care of animals may be used. A sermon or an address appropriate to the occasion may also be included.*

### HYMN OR CANTICLE
All you works of the Lord  LBW 18
Praise and thanksgiving  LBW 409
All creatures of our God and King  LBW 527
    *or* All creatures, worship God most high
    *(see "Canticle of the Sun")*
This is my Father's world  LBW 554
Oh, that I had a thousand voices  LBW 560
All things bright and beautiful  WOV 767
Song of the Three Young Men (*Psalter for Worship*, year C, Vigil of Easter, response 12)

### BLESSING OF ANIMALS
*The leader may ask all who have brought pets or animals to the celebration to come forward for the following prayer.*

The Lord be with you.
**And also with you.**
Let us pray.
Gracious God, in your love you created us in your image and made us stewards of the animals that live in the skies, the earth, and the sea. Bless us in our care for our pets and animals *[names of pets may be added here]*. Help us recognize your power and wisdom in the variety of creatures that live in our world, and hear our prayer for all that suffer over work, hunger, and ill-treatment. Protect your creatures, and guard them from all evil, now and forever.
**Amen**

276

THE LORD'S PRAYER

BLESSING

The Lord almighty order our days and our deeds in his peace.
**Amen**

# Canticle of the Sun

All creatures, worship God most high!
Sound every voice in earth and sky: Alleluia! Alleluia!
Sing, brother sun, in splendor bright;
sing, sister moon and stars of night:
Alleluia, alleluia, alleluia, alleluia, alleluia!

Sing, brother wind; with clouds and rain
you grow the gifts of fruit and grain: Alleluia! Alleluia!
Dear sister water, useful, clear,
make music for your Lord to hear:
Alleluia, alleluia, alleluia, alleluia, alleluia!

O fire, our brother, mirthful, strong,
drive far the shadows, join the song: Alleluia! Alleluia!
O earth, our mother, rich in care,
praise God in colors bright and rare:
Alleluia, alleluia, alleluia, alleluia, alleluia!

All who for love of God forgive,
all who in pain or sorrow grieve: Alleluia! Alleluia!
Christ bears your burdens and your fears;
still make your song amid the tears:
Alleluia, alleluia, alleluia, alleluia, alleluia!

Come, sister death, your song release
when you enfold our breath in peace: Alleluia! Alleluia!
Since Christ our light has pierced your gloom,
fair is the night that leads us home.
Alleluia, alleluia, alleluia, alleluia, alleluia!

O sisters, brothers, take your part,
and worship God with humble heart: Alleluia! Alleluia!
All creatures, bless the Father, Son,
and Holy Spirit, Three in One:
Alleluia, alleluia, alleluia, alleluia, alleluia!

Text: Martin A. Seltz, based on a hymn of Francis of Assisi
Tune: LASST UNS ERFREUEN (LBW 143)

# Service of the Word for Healing

*This service may be celebrated at any time. It may be especially appropriate on or near the festival of St. Luke, Evangelist (October 18).*

## HYMN

O Christ, the healer, we have come    LBW 360
Word of God, come down on earth    WOV 716
Heal me, O Lord    TFF 189

## GREETING AND WELCOME

The grace of our Lord Jesus Christ, the love of God, and the communion of the Holy Spirit be with you all.
**And also with you.**

We gather to hear the word of God, pray for those in need, and ask God's blessing on those who seek healing and wholeness through Christ our Lord.

## PRAYER OF THE DAY

*The proper prayer of the day may be used, or the prayer for St. Luke (October 18), p. 118 in* WOV *Leaders Edition, or the following:*

Great God, our healer, by your power, the Lord Jesus healed the sick and gave hope to the hopeless. As we gather in his name, look upon us with mercy, and bless us with your healing Spirit. Bring us comfort in the midst of pain, strength to transform our weakness, and light to illuminate our darkness. We ask this in the name of Jesus Christ, our crucified and risen Lord, who lives and reigns with you and the Holy Spirit, one God, now and forever. **Amen**

## READINGS

*These readings, the readings listed for St. Luke, Evangelist (p. 118 in* WOV *Leaders Edition), or the readings listed on pp. 96–97 of* Occasional Services *may be used.*
Isaiah 61:1-3a
Psalm 23
*The Lord is my shepherd; I shall not be in want. (Ps. 23:1)*
Luke 17:11-19

## SERMON

## HYMN

Lord, whose love in humble service    LBW 423
Healer of our every ill    WOV 738
Bless the Lord, O my soul    WOV 798
Come, ye disconsolate    TFF 186

277

## THE PRAYERS

*This litany or the prayers in* Occasional Services *(pp. 91–93) may be used.*

God the Father, you desire the health and salvation of all people.
**We praise you and thank you, O Lord.**
God the Son, you came that we might have life
and might have it more abundantly.
**We praise you and thank you, O Lord.**
God the Holy Spirit,
you make our bodies the temples of your presence.
**We praise you and thank you, O Lord.**
Holy Trinity, one God,
in you we live and move and have our being.
**We praise you and thank you, O Lord.**
Lord, grant your healing grace to all who are sick, injured,
or disabled, that they may be made whole;
**hear us, O Lord of life.**
Grant to all who are lonely, anxious, or despondent
the awareness of your presence;
**hear us, O Lord of life.**
Mend broken relationships, and restore those in emotional distress to soundness of mind and serenity of spirit;
**hear us, O Lord of life.**
Bless physicians, nurses, and all others who minister
to the suffering; grant them wisdom and skill,
sympathy and patience;
**hear us, O Lord of life.**
Grant to the dying a peaceful, holy death,
and with your grace strengthen those who mourn;
**hear us, O Lord of life.**
Restore to wholeness whatever is broken in our lives,
in this nation, and in the world;
**hear us, O Lord of life.**
Hear us, O Lord of life:
**heal us, and make us whole.**

Gracious God, in baptism you anointed us with the oil of salvation, and joined us to the death and resurrection of your Son. Bless all who seek your healing presence in their lives. In their suffering draw them more deeply into the mystery of your love, that following Christ in the way of the cross, they may know the power of his resurrection; who lives and reigns forever and ever.
**Amen**

## LAYING ON OF HANDS AND ANOINTING

*Those who wish to receive the laying on of hands (and anointing) come to the altar and, if possible, kneel. The minister lays both hands on each person's head in silence, after which he or she may dip a thumb in the oil and make the sign of the cross on the person's forehead, saying:*

(Through this holy anointing) may God's love and mercy uphold you by the grace and power of the Holy Spirit.
**Amen**

*During the anointing, the assembly may sing various hymns and songs, instrumental music may be played, or a simple interval of silence may be observed.*

## PRAYER

*After all have returned to their places, the minister may say:*

As you are anointed with this oil, may God bless you with the healing power of the Holy Spirit. May God forgive you your sins, release you from suffering, and restore you to wholeness and strength. May God deliver you from all evil, preserve you in all goodness, and bring you to everlasting life, through Jesus Christ our Lord. **Amen**

## THE LORD'S PRAYER

## BLESSING AND DISMISSAL

## HYMN

Abide with us, our Savior    LBW 263
Go, my children, with my blessing    WOV 721, TFF 161
There is a balm in Gilead    WOV 737, TFF 185

278

# September 1, 2002

Fifteenth Sunday after Pentecost
Proper 17

## INTRODUCTION

Today's gospel reading reminds us that life in Christ, rather than simply comforting us or excusing us from the pain of this world, strengthens us to face what we fear most: suffering and death. Jesus does not turn from pain and loss; indeed, he offers strength and hope to his people.

God's adoption of us in the waters of baptism and our communion in Christ's body and blood—signs of healing and community—strengthen us to offer ourselves as servants to a weary and frightened world.

## PRAYER OF THE DAY

O God, we thank you for your Son who chose the path of suffering for the sake of the world. Humble us by his example, point us to the path of obedience, and give us strength to follow his commands; through your Son, Jesus Christ our Lord.

## READINGS

Jeremiah 15:15-21

The book of Jeremiah contains six personal laments or complaints. Today's reading is the second of these laments. Here the prophet complains that his faithful preaching of the word of God has brought only angry violence from his hearers. While God responds with a promise of support, note that God does not promise that Jeremiah's task will be easy or painless.

Psalm 26:1-8

Your love is before my eyes; I have walked faithfully with you. (Ps. 26:3)

Romans 12:9-21

Paul writes to the Roman Christians who have experienced rejection and ridicule as a result of their faith. He instructs them on how to live as Christians in an unfriendly world.

Matthew 16:21-28

After Peter confesses that Jesus is "the Messiah, the Son of the living God," Jesus reveals the ultimate purpose of his ministry. These words prove hard to accept even for a disciple whom Jesus has called a "rock."

## SEMICONTINUOUS FIRST READING/PSALM

Exodus 3:1-15

God is both transcendent and immanent, both beyond this world and part of it. From on high, God saw the affliction of the people. But God also promised to take part in this world's history by leading the people out of slavery into the promised land.

Psalm 105:1-6, 23-26, 45c

Make known the deeds of the Lord among the peoples. Hallelujah! (Ps. 105:1, 45)

## COLOR  Green

## THE PRAYERS

Refreshed by the living word of God, let us pray for the church, the world, and all those in need.

*A BRIEF SILENCE.*

Set the mind of your church on the things of God, that we may follow the way of Christ into paths of self-giving service. Lord, in your mercy,

**hear our prayer.**

Uphold those who govern and all who order the affairs of nations, that a spirit of compassion may guide them and sustain their labors. Lord, in your mercy,

**hear our prayer.**

Abide with those who are sick or hospitalized (especially), that they and their families may rejoice in hope, be patient in suffering, and persevere in prayer. Lord, in your mercy,

**hear our prayer.**

Uphold your people in their daily callings and labors, and use their work in blessing to others. Lord, in your mercy,

**hear our prayer.**

*HERE OTHER INTERCESSIONS MAY BE OFFERED.*

Keep us steadfast in faith until, with all the saints who have died and are at rest, we see the coming of Christ in glory. Lord, in your mercy,

**hear our prayer.**

Hear us as we pray, O God, and renew in us the joy of salvation, through Jesus Christ our Lord.

**Amen**

279

## IMAGES FOR PREACHING

The autumn preaching essay suggested "oddness" as a theme for the Sundays of September and October. In the world's view, it would be normal for Jesus to look for ways to avoid suffering and death. Jesus is odd, however. He says suffering and death are necessary. We probably think there is nothing more normal than Peter's "God-forbid-it" reaction. How odd, then, that Jesus would call him Satan for being concerned for his welfare. Jesus says if any want to be his disciples, they must take up this odd life, deny themselves, shoulder their crosses, and follow him. What odd instruction is this that "those who want to save their life will lose it and those who lose their life for my sake will find it"?

Paul describes this odd life in some detail in Romans 12:9-21, the second reading for the day. The odd reference to heaping burning coals upon the heads of enemies is not about getting even but has to do with repentance and reconciliation.

These readings fall on Labor Day weekend. Jesus' work is to suffer, die, and be raised. Our labor, he says, is to deny ourselves, take up our cross, and follow him. That is not as far removed as it might seem from the office, assembly line floor, store, school room, and home where we labor. How often in the course of the week do we say and hear others say, "This is killing me." A sermon on this Sunday might help us and our hearers explore how in our everyday struggles we take up the cross and follow. The power of Jesus' death and resurrection enables us to function in our daily lives as a part of God's redeemed new creation.

## WORSHIP MATTERS

Vessels suitable for the task of bringing communion to the sick and homebound need to be provided for communion ministers. Before ministers of communion are sent out from the assembly, the presiding minister places the bread and wine in the vessels to be used and delivers them to the communion ministers after an appropriate prayer is spoken. Guidelines for this ministry are available in *Ministers of Communion from the Assembly: A Worship Handbook* (AFP 0806642807).

## LET THE CHILDREN COME

Some scholars would suggest that in the background behind Jesus' admonition to "carry the cross" was the first-century Jewish practice of tracing a *T* or "tau" (+ or x) on the forehead (see Ezek. 9:4-6). The one who received this cross was branded as one whose heart was open to God, ready to receive the word and act on it. Perhaps this Jewish practice entered early Christian baptismal practice and was reinterpreted in light of the death and resurrection of Christ. The cross of Christ is traced on the forehead signifying that this person has been claimed and anointed by Christ for a mission (see Luke 4:18). This gesture, tracing the cross on the forehead, is one of the identifiable marks of the Christian family.

## HYMNS FOR WORSHIP

### GATHERING

Lift high the cross    LBW 377

Shout for joy loud and long    WOV 793

Lord, my strength    W&P 93

### HYMN OF THE DAY

"Take up your cross," the Savior said    LBW 398, HFW (Wareham)

### ALTERNATE HYMN OF THE DAY

Son of God, eternal Savior    LBW 364

The summons    W&P 137

### COMMUNION

Now the silence    LBW 205

O Jesus, I have promised    LBW 503

Stay with us    WOV 743

### SENDING

Blest be the tie that binds    LBW 370

Bind us together    WOV 748, TFF 217, W&P 18

Step by step    W&P 132

### ADDITIONAL HYMNS AND SONGS

"Come, follow me," the Savior spake    LBW 455

When Israel was in Egypt's land    WOV 670, TFF 87

Day by day    WOV 746

We will glorify    W&P 154, TFF 281

This bread that we break    DH 30

## MUSIC FOR THE DAY

### PSALMODY

Becker, John.    PW A.

Bender, Mark. "O Lord, I Love the Habitation of Your House." 2 pt. CPH 98-2859.

Gerike, Henry. "Psalm 26." U, cong, acc.    GIA G-2632.

280

## CHORAL

Ashdown, Franklin. "Jesus, the Very Thought of Thee." STB, org, opt
C inst.   AFP 0800657500.

Bender, Mark. "O Lord, I Love the Habitation of Your House." 2 pt
mxd, org.   CPH 98-2859.

Hopson, Hal H. "A Lenten Walk" in *The Augsburg Choirbook*. 2 pt mxd,
org/pno, opt timp, opt hb.   AFP 0800656784.

Leavitt, John. "Come, Follow Me." SAB, oboe, kybd.   GIA G-3028.

Lindley, Simon. "O God, My Heart Is Ready." SS or SA, org.
Banks Music Pub ECS 162.

Martin, Gilbert. "When I Survey the Wondrous Cross." SAB, org.
PRE 312-41467.

Parry, Charles H. "Dear Lord and Father." SATB, org.   NOV 29 0247.

Scott, K. Lee. "Who at My Door Is Standing?" 2 pt mxd, kybd.
HIN HMC-728.

Scott, K. Lee. "So Art Thou to Me." SATB, kybd.   AFP 0800674308.

## CHILDREN'S CHOIRS

Christopherson, Dorothy, arr. "Followers of the Lamb." U, kybd, fl,
xyl, tamb, fc.   CG CGA672.

Nagy, Russell. "Follow Me." 2 pt, kybd.   High Street Music JH545.

## KEYBOARD/INSTRUMENTAL

Jongen, Joseph. *Petit Prelude.* Org.   OXF 0-19-375495-9.

Organ, Anne Krentz. "The Summons" in *Come to Us, Creative Spirit.*
Pno.   AFP 08065904X.

Petersen, Lynn L. "I Want Jesus to Walk with Me" in *Spiritual Sounds
for Trombone and Organ.*   CPH 97-6887.

Wold, Wayne. "Blest Be the Tie That Binds" in *Songs of Thankfulness and
Praise, set 2.* Org.   MSM 10-712.

## HANDBELL

Farm, Edie. "The Ash Grove." 3 oct. L2+.   JEF JHS 9244.

Moklebust, Cathy. "O For a Thousand Tongues to Sing." 3-5 oct. L3.
CG CGB 205.

Tucker, Sondra. "Make Me a Channel of Your Peace." 3-5 oct.
AFP 0800659864.

## PRAISE ENSEMBLE

Founds, Rick/arr. Gary Rhodes. "Jesus, Draw Me Close" (with I Am
Thine, O Lord).   WRD 301 0965 168 (SATB, kybd); 301
7647 080 (choraltrax); 301 0681 259 (orch).

Gordon, Nancy and Jamie Harvill. "I Love to Be with You" in
*Hosanna Music Songbook 13.* SAT[B], kybd.   INT 13576.

Temple, Sebastian/arr. Mark Hayes. "Make Me a Channel of Your
Peace." ALF 18316 (SATB, kybd); 18317 (SAB); 18318 (2 pt);
18320 (inst); 18319 (perf cass).

# Monday, September 2

### NIKOLAI FREDERIK SEVERIN GRUNDTVIG, BISHOP, RENEWER OF THE CHURCH, 1872

Grundtvig was one of two principal Danish theologians
of the nineteenth century; the other was Søren
Kierkegaard. Grundtvig's ministry as a parish pastor had
a difficult start. He was officially censured after his first
sermon, though he did receive approval a year later to be
ordained. He served with his father for two years but was
unable to receive a call for seven years after that. In 1826
he was forced to resign after he attacked the notion that
Christianity was merely a philosophical idea rather than
God's revelation made known to us in Christ and
through word and sacrament. This belief would be a
hallmark of Grundtvig's writing. He spent the last
thirty-three years as a chaplain at a home for elderly
women. From his university days he was convinced that
poetry spoke to the human spirit better than prose, and
he wrote more than a thousand hymns. Eight of his
hymns are in *LBW.*

281

# Wednesday, September 4

### ALBERT SCHWEITZER, MISSIONARY TO AFRICA, 1965

Schweitzer was a philosopher, theologian, and an ordained Lutheran minister. He wrote *The Quest for the Historical Jesus.* He was also an organist who published a
study of Johann Sebastian Bach. But he set aside careers
as a university lecturer and musician, went to medical
school, and became a missionary in the Gabon province
of French Equatorial Africa. He believed that the solution to the world's problems was simple: have reverence
for life. His style of practicing medicine shocked some,
but he was a humanitarian who served Christ by serving
his neighbors in need.

Now that school is resuming in many places,
parishes can hold up Schweitzer as an example of someone who used vast knowledge for service and ministry to
others.

# September 8, 2002

## Sixteenth Sunday after Pentecost
## Proper 18

### INTRODUCTION

Life in community is a precious thing, but it easily breaks down if rumors and idle talk are given free reign. In today's gospel, Jesus prescribes a manner for dealing with conflict in community life, a procedure reflected in many congregations' constitutions. The intent of such a form of church discipline is to restore people to community life.

May all who come to hear and to taste the presence of Christ in word and sacrament today also find communities that seek to understand one another in truth and in love.

### PRAYER OF THE DAY

Almighty and eternal God, you know our problems and our weaknesses better than we ourselves. In your love and by your power help us in our confusion and, in spite of our weakness, make us firm in faith; through your Son, Jesus Christ our Lord.

### READINGS

#### Ezekiel 33:7-11

Shortly before the fall of Jerusalem, the Lord commissions Ezekiel to serve as a sentinel. The role of watchman is crucial in the hills of Palestine, where early detection of approaching danger can mean the difference between victory and defeat. The prophet's task is also crucial: warn the wicked of the danger of retaining wicked ways.

#### Psalm 119:33-40

I desire the path of your commandments. (Ps. 119:35)

#### Romans 13:8-14

Although Paul insists that we are reconciled to God through faith rather than through works of the law, he encourages Christians to practice God's law of love while we wait for the salvation that is to come.

#### Matthew 18:15-20

Jesus has just said that God's concern for every individual is like that of a shepherd who will leave the entire herd to look for one sheep that is lost. Now, he says, the church should reach out to and welcome members who sin.

### SEMICONTINUOUS FIRST READING/PSALM

#### Exodus 12:1-14

Israel celebrated its deliverance from slavery in Egypt by keeping the festival of Passover. This festival included the slaughter, preparation, and consumption of the Passover lamb, whose blood was used to protect God's people from the threat of death. The early church described the Lord's supper using imagery from the Passover, especially in portraying Jesus as the lamb who delivers God's people from sin and death.

#### Psalm 149

Sing the praise of the Lord in the congregation of the faithful. (Ps. 149:1)

### COLOR  Green

### THE PRAYERS

Refreshed by the living word of God, let us pray for the church, the world, and all those in need.

*A BRIEF SILENCE.*

Let us pray for the church, that through its ministry of reconciliation in Jesus Christ, your gracious love may be revealed in every place. Lord, in your mercy,

**hear our prayer.**

Let us pray for regions of the world where there is civil strife, and for all refugees and displaced people, that they may find lasting shelter and new hope. Lord, in your mercy,

**hear our prayer.**

Let us pray for those enduring any injury or illness (especially), that your healing power would lift their spirits and speed their recovery. Lord, in your mercy,

**hear our prayer.**

Let us pray for those who are separated by sin from you, that they may come to know the peace of reconciliation and take their place at your table. Lord, in your mercy,

**hear our prayer.**

*HERE OTHER INTERCESSIONS MAY BE OFFERED.*

We give thanks for the faithful departed who have made known to us your good and gracious ways. Gather us with them at the last into your loving rule. Lord, in your mercy,

**hear our prayer.**
Hear us as we pray, O God, and renew in us the joy of salvation, through Jesus Christ our Lord.
**Amen**

## IMAGES FOR PREACHING

An odd business is spelled out in the gospel reading. It is the Christian business, the ministry of reconciliation. We live in a culture that is both litigious and conflict avoidant, and members of the church reflect that culture. People resort to litigation when they do not know how to be responsible for and accountable to each other. Or is the problem that they actually refuse to be responsible and accountable?

There is good reason one might refuse to attempt reconciliation. Our lives, well-being, or reputation might be threatened. The ministry of reconciliation is needed when a wrong has been committed. The confrontation over some wrong done, no matter how gently phrased, bears the echo of God's accusation leveled against us. No wonder some people avoid conflict and may even seek a legal defense when an accusation is brought.

This is not to be the model for the Christian community. We will not walk away, either from a congregation, a group, or an individual, because our feelings are hurt. We will not nurse a grudge. We will not engage in scorekeeping and paybacks. Jesus died and rose to reconcile us to God. We are adopted into the family by baptism. Reconciliation is the family business.

Sometimes this gospel reading has been used as the basis of a bureaucratic program to expel unwanted people from the church. That procedure might seem like it ought to work—until we get to the punch line: "Let such a one be to you as a Gentile and a tax collector" (Matt. 18:17). How did Jesus treat Gentiles and tax collectors? He ate dinner with them, ministered to them, and called them to be disciples.

## WORSHIP MATTERS

When we are in the presence of God in worship, we want both to listen and to respond. Prayer is conversation with God, so we allow time to discern what God might be saying to us. Silence in the liturgy serves this purpose. After listening to a scripture reading, we can use silence to apply these words to our own life. Following the sermon, silence allows time for the word to take root in our heart,

so that we might begin a conversation with God throughout the week concerning what was spoken. Silence between prayer petitions provides space for us to add our own petitions to what was offered or to let the words sink deeply into our hearts. Ample silence before the benediction is a time to rest in the Lord, gaining strength for the work of ministry in the week to come.

## LET THE CHILDREN COME

Today's gospel reading provides an opportunity to encourage people to engage in the process of confessing sin in order to receive comfort and to strengthen faith. We lay our sins at the foot of the cross, where Christ has redeemed us, in order to receive from the crucified and risen Lord his gifts of forgiveness, healing, and restoration. Children can begin to understand the gift of reconciliation when they acknowledge behavior that has been hurtful to another. Leading a child to a genuine "I'm sorry" takes special care. Encourage a child to respond to these words with "I forgive you," not simply "That's OK."

## HYMNS FOR WORSHIP
### GATHERING
Joyful, joyful we adore thee   LBW 551
Lord, you give the great commission   WOV 756
Sing out, earth and skies   W&P 126

### HYMN OF THE DAY
In all our grief   WOV 739

### ALTERNATE HYMN OF THE DAY
Where charity and love prevail   LBW 126, TFF 84
Seek ye first   WOV 783, TFF 149, W&P 122

### COMMUNION
At the Lamb's high feast we sing   LBW 210
We come to the hungry feast   WOV 766
The Lamb   TFF 89

### SENDING
Let all things now living   LBW 557
What wondrous love is this   LBW 385
Awake, o sleeper   WOV 745

### ADDITIONAL HYMNS AND SONGS
When twilight comes   WOV 663

283

God! When human bonds are broken   WOV 735

Help us accept each other   UMH 560

Step by step   W&P 132

## MUSIC FOR THE DAY

### PSALMODY

Becker, John.   PW A.

Guimont, Michel. "Ps 119: Happy Are They" in RS.

Haas, David.   PCY, vol. 8 & 9.

Hurd, David. "Teach Me, O Lord." SATB, org, cong.   GIA G-2715.

### CHORAL

Attwood, Thomas. "Teach Me, O Lord." SATB, kybd.   GIA G-3045.

Bach, J.S. "Sing Praise to Christ." SATB, org.   CPH 98-1377.

Friedell, Harold W. "Draw Us in the Spirit's Tether." SATB, org.
HWG CMR 2472.

Holst, Gustav. "Turn Back O Man." SATB, kybd.   GAL S & B 2152.

Marcello, Benedetto. "Teach Me Now, O Lord." 2 pt mxd, kybd.
MSM-50-9418.

Scott, K. Lee. "Teach Me, My God and King." SATB, org.
AFP 080065973.

### CHILDREN'S CHOIRS

Horman, John D. "Small Deeds." U/2 pt, kybd.   CG CGA-562.

Martin, Joseph. "Sing a New Song." 2 pt, kybd, perc.   ALF 5862.

Pearson, Brian and Sherry. "Life Together." U, kybd, opt inst & perc.
AFP 0800674197.

### KEYBOARD/INSTRUMENTAL

Bernthal, John. "Fredericktown" in *Lift High the Cross*. Org.
AFP 0800657314.

Cherwien, David. "In All Our Grief" in *Organ Plus One*. Org, inst.
AFP 11-10759.

Cherwien, David." "Fredericktown" in *O God, Beyond All Praising*. Org
AFP 0800657241. .

Organ, Anne Krentz. "Fredericktown" in *Woven Together*. Pno, inst.
AFP 0800658167.

Sedio, Mark. "Jesu, Jesu, Fill Us with Your Love" in *Dancing in the Light of God*. Pno.   AFP 0800656547.

### HANDBELL

Cherwien, David/arr. William Mathis. "Let Us Talents and Tongues Employ/We Come to the Hungry Feast." 3-5 oct, opt perc & ch.
AFP 0800658884.

Dobrinski, Cynthia. "Come, Christians, Join to Sing." 3-5 oct. L3.
AG 1420.

Leavitt, John. "A Joyful Flourish." 3 oct. L2.   CPH 97-6867.

Sherman, Arnold B. "Joyful, Joyful, We Adore Thee." 2-3 oct. L2.
AG 1652.

### PRAISE ENSEMBLE

Beethoven/Smith and Rhoades. "Joyful, Joyful We Adore Thee (with Cry of My Heart)." SATB, orch.   WRD 0 80689 34327 8.

Burleigh, Glenn/arr. Jack Schrader. "Order My Steps."
HOP C5083 (SATB, kybd); C5083 C (reh/perf cass);
C5083R (rhythm chart).

Fragar, Russell/arr. J. Daniel Smith. "I Believe the Promise" in *Hillsongs Choral Collection*. SATB, kybd.   INT 16996.

Medema, Ken/arr. Jack Schrader. "Lord, Listen to Your Children Praying."   HOP GC 850; GC 850C (cass).

Moen, Don and Paul Overstreet. "God Is Here."   INT 14647 (SATB, kybd); 14648 (choraltrax); 14645 (orch).

Phillips, Don. "Share Your Faith." SATB, kybd.   HOP GC 946.

# Monday, September 9

## PETER CLAVER, PRIEST, MISSIONARY TO COLOMBIA, 1654

Peter Claver was born into Spanish nobility and was persuaded to become a Jesuit missionary. He served in Cartagena (in what is now Colombia) by teaching and caring for the slaves. The slaves arrived in ships, where they had been confined in dehumanizing conditions. Claver met and supplied them with medicine, food, clothing, and brandy. He learned their dialects and taught them Christianity. He called himself "the slave of the slaves forever." Claver also ministered to the locals of Cartagena who were in prison and facing death.

Claver's advocacy on behalf of the rights of slaves is a witness to a gospel that is for all people. Pray for contemporary ministries and for persons who offer care and compassion to people living in substandard living conditions.

284

# Friday, September 13

JOHN CHRYSOSTOM, BISHOP OF CONSTANTINOPLE, 407

John was a priest in Antioch and an outstanding preacher. His eloquence earned him the nickname "Chrysostom" ("golden mouth") but it also got him into trouble. As bishop of Constantinople he preached against corruption among the royal court. The empress, who had been his supporter, sent him into exile. His preaching style emphasized the literal meaning of scripture and its practical application. This interpretation stood in contrast to the common style at the time, which emphasized the allegorical meaning of the text.

Chrysostom's skill in the pulpit has led many to describe him as the patron of preachers. This week at gatherings of parish groups, include prayers for pastors and all who proclaim the gospel through preaching.

# Saturday, September 14

HOLY CROSS DAY

Helena, the mother of Constantine, made a pilgrimage to Israel to look for Christian holy sites. She found what she believed were the sites of the crucifixion and burial of Jesus, sites that modern archaeologists believe may be correct. Here Constantine built two churches. The celebration of Holy Cross Day commemorates the dedication of the Church of the Resurrection in 335.

This day gives the church a chance to celebrate the victory of the cross with a festivity that would be out of place on Good Friday. Today alleluias are sung in thanksgiving for the tree of the cross, which Andrew of Crete described as "the trophy of God's victory." This week sing the hymn "Lift high the cross" (LBW 377).

# September 15, 2002

Seventeenth Sunday after Pentecost
Proper 19

285

## INTRODUCTION

In today's gospel reading, Jesus invites us to forgive one another. His invitation, however, is not an optional activity for Christians. It is the heart of the gospel and the distinctive character of Christian life. Out of love for us in our weakness and sin, God forgives us, heals us, and strengthens us to be a forgiving people. The sign of the cross invites us to the ministry of reconciliation in word and sacrament. The cross, marked on our foreheads at baptism and traced over our bodies at the funeral liturgy, assures us of Christ's victory over death and the promise of eternal life.

## PRAYER OF THE DAY

O God, you declare your almighty power chiefly in showing mercy and pity. Grant us the fullness of your grace, that, pursuing what you have promised, we may share your heavenly glory; through your Son, Jesus Christ our Lord.

## READINGS

Genesis 50:15-21

The story of Joseph is a wisdom story. In it, Joseph plays the role of a wise man. Portrayed in a situation of oppression, he provides an important model of how the wise should act.

Psalm 103:[1-7] 8-13

The Lord is full of compassion and mercy. (Ps. 103:8)

Romans 14:1-12

The Christians in Rome came from a diversity of cultural backgrounds: some Jewish, some Gentile. Here Paul urges them to respect one another's opinions on various religious matters, even though he himself believes that some of the ideas are held by people weak in faith.

Matthew 18:21-35

Jesus has been instructing his disciples about confronting other people who live in ways that are sinful. Now, Peter's question about forgiveness elicits a parable that clarifies this issue. Although the community of faith should challenge sinners to repent, it should also proclaim a forgiveness that reflects the bountiful mercy of God.

## SEMICONTINUOUS FIRST READING/PSALM

Exodus 14:19-31

Having already decided to let the Israelites go from Egypt, Pharaoh had second thoughts and sent his army after them. Though the passage through the Red Sea became a sign of salvation for the people of Israel, Pharaoh's forces drowned in the waters, convincing the Israelites that God was on their side.

Psalm 114

Tremble, O earth, at the presence of the Lord. (Ps. 114:7)

## COLOR Green

## THE PRAYERS

Refreshed by the living word of God, let us pray for the church, the world, and all those in need.

*A BRIEF SILENCE.*

God of might, sweep aside the brokenness of sin, cleansing your people throughout the world. Make the church a sign of your steadfast love and an agent of your compassion. Lord, in your mercy,

**hear our prayer.**

God of peace, in the midst of conflict and inequity around the world, lift up all who work for justice and uphold their cause. Lord, in your mercy,

**hear our prayer.**

God of hopefulness, the needs of all your children are known to you. Help those who are distressed in any way (especially), that they know the comfort of your loving and ever present hands. Lord, in your mercy,

**hear our prayer.**

God of mercy, give to each of us a mindfulness of your deep, forgiving love, that we may let go of old hurts and be ready to forgive. Lord, in your mercy,

**hear our prayer.**

*HERE OTHER INTERCESSIONS MAY BE OFFERED.*

God of salvation, we give thanks for family members and friends who have recently died. Keep us in communion with them and with all the saints. Lord, in your mercy,

**hear our prayer.**

Hear us as we pray, O God, and renew in us the joy of salvation, through Jesus Christ our Lord.

**Amen**

## IMAGES FOR PREACHING

The parent came to the principal of the school, irate over something the teacher had done. "That's three strikes," the parent said. "That's it."

The principal commented on the unfairness of it. "One of those strikes is from two years ago, the other is from last year. Don't we ever get a new inning around here?"

In human relationships and even in the legal system, baseball has been a source of metaphor for counting transgressions. Three strikes and you're out! Yet this is a selective use of baseball metaphor. After all, there are three outs per inning. The batter who is out the first time up will probably have another two or three at-bats. And the teams come back to play the next day, and the next, throughout the long season.

Peter had a discussion with Jesus about the rules for forgiveness. Seven strikes and you're out! Does that sound generous enough, Jesus? Jesus' first response suggests to Peter that there is more than one inning. The parable he tells goes even farther: forgiveness is not a game with scorekeeping. In baseball, in forgiveness based on keeping score, the focus is on getting people out. The focus for Christians is on getting and keeping people in.

The focus for the people of God is not on limits but on a new way of life. This old era is limited on all sides by the grave. Life under its aegis cannot help but set limits. Jesus breaks through all limitations with his dying and rising. He is the firstborn of a whole new creation. Under the jurisdiction of our Lord Jesus, forgiveness is the norm. It is the way we live together. In the reign of God, mercy is the ethos and forgiveness the ethic by which we live. That is the point of the parable Jesus tells. God's forgiveness is not dependent on our forgiving others. Rather, when we do not forgive, we are operating as a part of the old order. How can we stay there, when a whole new way of life beckons?

## WORSHIP MATTERS

Providing each worshiper with a well-prepared worship folder allows each person to take responsibility for her or his own part in the liturgy. When a folder is unclear, the assembly is forced to rely on the presider as a type of liturgical emcee. Constant announcements concerning page numbers, hymn choices, body position, and the like, foster the assembly's dependency on the presider and

286

gives the impression that it is the presider's liturgy that the assembly attends. A well-prepared worship folder enables worshipers to see that their participation is just as crucial to the assembly's life as that of the presider. The presider's hospitable gestures and words will be more attentively received when they are well-placed and necessary than when they become a chatty narration.

### LET THE CHILDREN COME

We hear in the words of absolution that our sins are forgiven. Faith in Christ Jesus has saved us. "Go in peace," the assisting minister declares. "Serve the Lord." Perhaps it isn't only because this signals the "end of church" that children respond enthusiastically, "Thanks be to God!"

### HYMNS FOR WORSHIP
#### GATHERING

When morning gilds the skies    LBW 545, 546
O God beyond all praising    WOV 797
I will sing, I will sing    W&P 73

#### HYMN OF THE DAY

Where charity and love prevail    LBW 126, TFF 84

#### ALTERNATE HYMN OF THE DAY

Forgive our sins as we forgive    LBW 307
If I have wounded any soul today    TFF 170

#### COMMUNION

Now the silence    LBW 205
Great God, your love has called us    WOV 666
Alleluia    W&P 6

#### SENDING

Jesus shall reign    LBW 530
In thee is gladness    LBW 552
Go, my children, with my blessing    WOV 721, TFF 161

#### ADDITIONAL HYMNS AND SONGS

Bless the Lord, O my soul    WOV 798
Here is bread    W&P 58
Sing unto the Lord    DH 47
God of love, have mercy    DH 10
Pues si vivimos/When we are living    LLC 462

### MUSIC FOR THE DAY
#### PSALMODY

Becker, John.    PW A.
Bless the Lord    DH 42
Dufford, Bob.    STP, vol. 4.
Folkening, John. "Six Psalm Settings with Antiphons."    MSM 80-700.
Haugen, Marty. "Psalm 103: The Lord Is Kind and Merciful" in RS.
My soul, now praise your maker!    LBW 519
Praise, my soul, the King of heaven    LBW 549
Praise to the Lord, the Almighty    LBW 543

#### CHORAL

Bush, Gladys Blakely. "With What Shall I Come Before the Lord."    SATB.    CPH 98-3398.
Collins, Dori Erwin. "Offering." SATB, U, pno, fl, opt hb.    AFP 0800659694.
Duruflé, Maurice. "Ubi caritas." SATB.    PRE 312-41253.
Ehret, Walter. "O My Soul, Bless God the Father." SATB pno/org.    FLA A-680.
Griglak, Robert G. "Where Charity and Love." SAB.    AFP 080064994X.
Lovelace, Austin. "Like as a Father." 3 pt mxd.    CG A-156.
Mendelssohn, Felix. "Not Unto Him" in *St. Paul.* SATB, kybd.    GSCH Ed 321.
Organ, Anne Krentz. "Love One Another." SATB.    AFP 0800659643.
Peter, Johann F. "Praise the Lord, O My Soul." SATB, kybd.    B&H 5891.

#### CHILDREN'S CHOIRS

Henderson, Ruth Watson. "Bless the Lord, O My Soul." U, kybd.    HIN HMC-1171.
Hopson, Hal H. "O Bless the Lord, My Soul. 2 pt, org.    HIN HMC-1339.
Powell, Robert. "Awake, Awake." 2 pt, pno.    AFP 0800674022.

#### KEYBOARD/INSTRUMENTAL

Behnke, John. "Variations on *Kum Ba Yah.*" Org.    MSM 10-893.
Biery, Marilyn. "Ubi caritas" in *Augsburg Organ Library: Lent.* Org.    AFP 0800658973.
Brahms, Johannes. "Herzlich tut mich verlangen" in *Eleven Chorale Preludes.* Org.    Mercury 453-00260.
Burkhardt, Michael. "Twenty-Fourth" in *Four Hymn Improvisations for Holy Week.* Org.    MSM 10-318.
Callahan, Charles. "Twenty-Fourth" in *Rhapsody on American Folk Hymns.* Kybd, fl.    MSM 20-870.

287

Cherwien, David. "Holy Manna" in *Groundings: Five New Organ Settings.*
Org. AFP 0800659805.

Wold, Wayne L. "St. Magnus" in *A November to Remember.* Org.
AFP 080065983X.

## HANDBELL

Hopson, Hal. "Be Thou My Vision." 3 oct. L2. PRE 494-42004.

McFadden, Jane. "The Londonderry Air." 2-3 oct, opt ch & inst.
AFP 0800656296.

Rogers, Sharon Elery. "God, Who Stretched the Spangled Heavens."
3-5 oct. L2. AFP 0800657373.

## PRAISE ENSEMBLE

Machen, Harland/arr. Tom Fettke. "Bow the Knee."
Allegis AG-1076 (SATB, kybd); MU-2446D (cass);
MU-50371 (CD); OR-2446 (orch).

Martin, Joseph. "I Will Sing Praise." SATB, kybd. LOR 10/1144.

Parker/Lantz. "Bless the Lord O My Soul." STB, kybd. HAL
0874222.

288

# Monday, September 16

## CYPRIAN, BISHOP OF CARTHAGE, MARTYR, C. 258

Cyprian worked for the unity of the church and cared for his flock in North Africa during a time of great persecution. During Cyprian's time as bishop many people had denied the faith under duress. In contrast to some who held the belief that the church should not receive these people back, Cyprian believed they ought to be welcomed into full communion after a period of penance. Cyprian insisted on the need for compassion in order to preserve the unity of the church. His essay *On the Unity of the Catholic Church* stressed the role of bishops in guaranteeing the visible, concrete unity of the church. Cyprian was also concerned for the physical well-being of the people under his care. He organized a program of medical care during a severe epidemic in Carthage.

# Wednesday, September 18

## DAG HAMMARSKJÖLD, PEACEMAKER, 1961

Dag Hammarskjöld was a Swedish diplomat and humanitarian who served as Secretary General of the United Nations. He was killed in a plane crash on this day in 1961 in what is now Zambia while he was on his way to negotiate a cease-fire between the United Nations and the Katanga forces. For years Hammarskjöld had kept a private journal, and it was not until that journal was published as *Markings* that the depth of his Christian faith was known. The book revealed that his life was a combination of diplomatic service and personal spirituality, a combination of contemplation on the meaning of Christ in his life and action in the world.

To commemorate Hammarskjöld, pray for the work of the United Nations and for all peacemakers. Here is an example of a person whose quiet contemplation led to visible action in the world.

# Friday, September 20

## NELSON WESLEY TROUT, BISHOP, 1996

Trout was born in Columbus, Ohio, and attended the Evangelical Lutheran Theological Seminary in Columbus. Ordained in 1952, he served parishes in Montgomery, Alabama; Los Angeles, California; and Eau Claire, Wisconsin. Trout also served in staff positions with the American Lutheran Church, Lutheran Social Services of Dayton, and the Columbus seminary. In 1983 Trout was elected bishop of the South Pacific District of the American Lutheran Church, the first African American to serve in such a capacity.

# Saturday, September 21

## ST. MATTHEW, APOSTLE AND EVANGELIST

Matthew was a tax collector for the Roman government in Capernaum. Tax collectors were distrusted because they were dishonest and worked as agents for a foreign ruler, the occupying Romans. In the gospels, tax collectors are mentioned as sinful and despised outcasts, but it was these outcasts to whom Jesus showed his love. Matthew's name means "gift of the Lord."

In the gospels Jesus tells his disciples to treat notorious sinners as Gentiles and tax collectors. That has often been taken as a mandate for the church to avoid such people. But Jesus brought his ministry to these very people. In what ways might the church not shun "tax collectors" and sinners but extend its ministry to them and see them as gifts of the Lord?

# September 22, 2002

Eighteenth Sunday after Pentecost
Proper 20

## INTRODUCTION

People like to keep score. If our team wins by a point, we rejoice and claim victory. But our relationships begin to dissolve when we count up little mistakes, losing trust and patience.

We learn today that God is not interested in playing counting games. In the reign of God, mercy is freely given to those who come late, as well as to those who have labored for many hours or years. Any claim to partiality, any impulse to keep score, is undercut by the grace of God received in word and sacrament. In the presence of God's mercy, wrote Luther, we are all beggars.

## PRAYER OF THE DAY

Lord God, you call us to work in your vineyard and leave no one standing idle. Set us to our tasks in the work of your kingdom, and help us to order our lives by your wisdom; through your Son, Jesus Christ our Lord.

## READINGS

Jonah 3:10—4:11

Unlike all other prophetic books, the book of Jonah focuses on the person of the prophet rather than on the prophet's message. The main story begins when Jonah flees God's call to announce destruction of the city of Nineveh, which symbolizes all that is hated by the Israelites. This story of a reluctant prophet highlights the very nature of God, the creator of the universe, who "is gracious and merciful…and abounding in steadfast love." In the end, every reader must answer the question: should this God not have pity on Nineveh?

Psalm 145:1-8

The Lord is slow to anger and of great kindness. (Ps. 145:8)

Philippians 1:21-30

Paul writes to the Philippians from prison, knowing that he may soon suffer martyrdom for his faith.

Matthew 20:1-16

Jesus tells his disciples a shocking parable about God's generosity, which reverses human expectations and offends those who believe God gives people only what they deserve.

## SEMICONTINUOUS FIRST READING/PSALM

Exodus 16:2-15

Exodus 16 recounts the second of three tests for Israel in the wilderness (see also 15:22-27 and 17:1-7). In this reading, a food crisis becomes a faith crisis. The hunger of the wandering Israelites moves the people to deny God's saving work in the exodus. At least they had food when they were in Egypt! Nevertheless, God meets their need day by day.

Psalm 105:1-6, 37-45

Make known the deeds of the Lord among the peoples. Hallelujah! (Ps. 105:1, 45)

## COLOR  Green

289

## THE PRAYERS

Refreshed by the living word of God, let us pray for the church, the world, and all those in need.
*A BRIEF SILENCE.*

Let us pray for the church throughout the world, that we may grow together in your service and invite others to work with us in your vineyard. Lord, in your mercy,
**hear our prayer.**

Let us pray for church schools and colleges, that all who teach and learn may grow in wisdom and faith. Lord, in your mercy,
**hear our prayer.**

Let us pray for those in charge of world affairs, that they may be careful stewards of the gifts of creation and the labor of your people. Lord, in your mercy,
**hear our prayer.**

Let us pray for those who are unemployed and for those who labor for a living, that all might be able to find work and be justly compensated. Lord, in your mercy,
**hear our prayer.**

Let us pray for all who are homebound, hospitalized, or ill (especially), that they may know our compassionate care. Lord, in your mercy,
**hear our prayer.**

Let us pray for ourselves, that nourished at the Lord's table we may go forth to serve, not desiring reward, but giving thanks for your grace and invitation. Lord, in your mercy,

**hear our prayer.**
*HERE OTHER INTERCESSIONS MAY BE OFFERED.*
For all the holy ones who have died, we give you thanks. Make us faithful stewards of all your gifts until we join them at the endless feast of joy. Lord, in your mercy,
**hear our prayer.**
Hear us as we pray, O God, and renew in us the joy of salvation, through Jesus Christ our Lord.
**Amen**

## IMAGES FOR PREACHING

This gospel reading teaches an odd business ethic. Are we really to run a business by paying the same wage to the person who works one hour as to the person who works twelve? No. But God does run God's business this way. God's business with us is not based on what we earn. It is based on God's generosity.

In the world in which we live, we think we are supposed to we get what we have coming to us. If we work hard and apply ourselves, we should get ahead. We should get the grade, the promotion, or the money. We should receive recognition. If we lead irresolute lives, however, we should also suffer the consequences. When life does not work this way, we think an injustice has been done. An old Texas swing song has a lyric something like, "Little bee collects the nectar; big bee gets the honey. Little man does the work; big man gets the money." The economics of this horizontal realm, a realm bounded by birth and death, the law of gravity, and the rules of quid pro quo, demand fairness. When we experience life as unfair, we bristle.

The economics of God's realm are different. God does not deal with us according to the Fair Labor Relations Act. The currency in God's kingdom is not what we earn. Our merits cannot be spent. Legal tender in God's realm is God's generosity. God first does the spending. On us. God spent God's own lifeblood in Jesus Christ. God lavishes us with mercy, forgiveness, and eternal life. God calls us freely to spend this currency. There is nothing more compelling than spending someone else's money!

## WORSHIP MATTERS

Those who preside at the assembly's liturgy are not performers. It is not necessary that they memorize their lines as if our worship were a play or a dramatic reenactment. Yet it assists communication when certain words of the ministers are memorized, so they can be spoken directly to the people. This is especially the case with those texts spoken in dialog or in the place of Christ. Such texts include the absolution, the greeting, the salutation before prayer, the peace, the preface dialogue, Christ's words of institution in the eucharistic prayer, the words spoken at the distribution of communion, the benediction, and the dismissal.

## LET THE CHILDREN COME

"Knock, knock." "Who's there?" "Your children!" The assisting minister ends each intercessory prayer, "O God, your children are knocking." Invite the children to knock twice on the back of the pew in front of them or another hard surface. Then, all the people respond, "Hear our prayer." Or have the children sing "Lord, listen to your children praying" (WOV 775) following each petition.

## HYMNS FOR WORSHIP
### GATHERING
O God of earth and altar   LBW 428
Listen, God is calling   WOV 712, TFF 130
Great is the Lord   W&P 53

### HYMN OF THE DAY
Salvation unto us has come   LBW 297

### ALTERNATE HYMN OF THE DAY
Great God, your love has called us   WOV 666
Stand in the congregation   W&P 131

### COMMUNION
For the bread which you have broken   LBW 200
Thine the amen, thine the praise   WOV 801
We are all one in Christ   TFF 221, LLC 470

### SENDING
Lord of all hopefulness   LBW 469
Alleluia, alleluia, give thanks   WOV 671

### ADDITIONAL HYMNS AND SONGS
Softly and tenderly Jesus is calling   WOV 734, TFF 155
Come, labor on   HFW
Precious Lord, take my hand   WOV 731, TFF 193
O sacred River   OBS 74

290

## MUSIC FOR THE DAY
### PSALMODY

Becker, John.   PW A.

Haas, David. "I Will Praise Your Name" in PS 2.

Haas, David.   PCY, vol. I, 8 & 9.

Kogut, Malcolm.   PCY, vol. 10.

Smith, Timothy R.   STP, vol. 4.

Trapp, Lynn. "Four Psalm Settings." Cant/choir, cong, org.
    MSM 80-701.

### CHORAL

Adelmann, Dale. "Steal Away." SSAATTBB, A solo.
    PAR PPM09512.

Adelmann, Dale. "Swing Low Sweet Chariot." SATTBB div, B solo.
    PAR PPM09522.

Bach, J.S. "Bist du bei mir" in *Sing Solo Sacred.* High or low voice, kybd.
    OXF.

Busarow, Donald. "Forth in Thy Name." SAB, org, trbl inst, opt cong.
    AFP 11-2371.

Carnahan, Craig. "Bring Bread, Bring Wine." 2 pt mxd, kybd, opt hb.
    AFP 0800674049.

Distler, Hugo. "Salvation Unto Us Has Come" in *Chantry Choirbook.*
    SATB.   AFP 080065854X.

Fedak, Alfred V. "I Will Extol Thee." SATB, org.   SEL 410-845.

Koshe, Kenneth K. "It Is a Good Thing." SATB.   AFP 0800659635.

Nelson, Ronald A. "Whoever Would Be Great Among You." SAB, gtr,
    opt kybd.   AFP 0800645804.

Sateren, Leland. "O Lord, Thou Art My God and King." SATB, org.
    AFP 6000108966.

### CHILDREN'S CHOIRS

Courtney, Craig. "Praise Him!" 2 pt, kybd.   BEC BP1350.

Martin, Joseph M. "Jonah." 2 pt, kybd.   FB BG2237.

Perry and Perry. "Lead Me to a Brighter Day." 2 pt.   ALF 4747.

Tucker, Margaret. "Each Day." U/2 pt, kybd, fl.   CG CGA 770.

### KEYBOARD/INSTRUMENTAL

Bach, J.S. "Es ist das Heil" in *Orgelbüchlein.* Org.   PET 10635.

Behnke, John. "Es ist das Heil" in *Variations for Seven Familiar Hymns.*
    Org.   AFP 0800655605.

Billingham, Richard. "Give Me Jesus" in *Seven Reflections on African American Spirituals.* Org.   AFP 0800656229.

Kolander, Keith. "Es ist das Heil" in *All Things Are Thine.* Org.
    AFP 0800658000.

Wasson, Laura E. "Alleluia No. 1" in *A Piano Tapestry.* Pno.
    AFP 0800658183.

### HANDBELL

Bach, J.S./arr. Roy Emiliani. "CelloMosso." 3-5 oct.
    AFP 0800655435.

Hopson, Hal. "Antiphon." 3-5 oct. L2.   LAK HB003.

Nelson, Susan T. "Give Me Jesus." 3 oct. L2.   AFP 0800658132.

### PRAISE ENSEMBLE

Smith, Byron. "Worthy to Be Praised."   WAR LG 52654. SATB,
    kybd.

Smith, Michael W./arr. Gary Rhodes. "Great Is the Lord." SSATB,
    kybd (choraltrax and orch available).   WRD 301 02061 6X.

# Wednesday, September 25

### SERGIUS OF RADONEZH,
### ABBOT OF HOLY TRINITY, MOSCOW, 1392

The people of Russia honor Sergius as the most beloved of all their saints and a model of Russian spiritual life at its best. At the age of twenty he began to live as a hermit, and others joined him. From their monastery in the forest, Sergius led the renewal of Russian monastic life. His monastery, the Monastery of the Holy Trinity, was a center for pilgrimage where people came to worship and receive spiritual support. Sergius was also a peacemaker whose influence stopped four civil wars between Russian princes. Sergius left no writings, but his disciples founded seventy-five monasteries and spread his teachings.

The commemoration of Sergius is an opportunity to consider the traditions of Russian Orthodoxy.

# Saturday, September 28

### JEHU JONES, MISSIONARY, 1852

A native of Charleston, South Carolina, Jones was ordained by the New York Ministerium in 1832, and was the Lutheran church's first African American pastor. Upon returning to South Carolina he was arrested under a law prohibiting free blacks from reentering the state, so was unable to join the group of Charlestonians he had been commissioned to accompany to Liberia. For nearly twenty years Jones carried out missionary work in Philadelphia in the face of many difficulties. There he led the formation of the first African American Lutheran congregation, St. Paul's, and the construction of its church building.

291

# September 29, 2002

## St. Michael and All Angels

### INTRODUCTION

Angels visited Abraham at Mamre; the angel Gabriel announced to Mary that she would be the mother of Jesus; a great company of angels sang at Jesus' birth. Michael the archangel, captain of the heavenly hosts and protector of Christians, is remembered on this day with all the angels of God.

### PRAYER OF THE DAY

Everlasting God, you have ordained and constituted in a wonderful order the ministries of angels and mortals. Mercifully grant that, as your holy angels always serve and worship you in heaven, so by your appointment they may help and defend us here on earth; through your Son, Jesus Christ our Lord, who lives and reigns with you and the Holy Spirit, one God, now and forever.

### READINGS

Daniel 10:10-14; 12:1-3

Daniel trembles in the presence of an angel. That angel tells the prophet about the good and terrible future when the dead will be resurrected and the archangel Michael will usher in the deliverance of the nation.

Psalm 103:1-5, 20-22

Bless the Lord, you angels of the Lord. (Ps. 103:20)

Revelation 12:7-12

Armed with the power of God, Michael and the angels of God fight those armed with the power of evil, the devil and the devil's angels. The "blood of the Lamb," our crucified Lord Jesus, gives Michael the power to force the devil from a place in heaven.

Luke 10:17-20

The missionary church ("the seventy-two") is given magnificent power. Greater than this gift of power over the enemy, however, is the gift of salvation: their names are written in heaven.

### COLOR White

### THE PRAYERS

Refreshed by the living word of God, let us pray for the church, the world, and all those in need.

*A BRIEF SILENCE.*

Let us pray that all the baptized, raised with Christ in his victory over Satan and every evil, may be renewed for lives of discipleship. Lord, in your mercy,

**hear our prayer.**

Let us pray that the earth, sea, and all creatures may benefit from wise stewardship by humankind, to the blessing of generations yet to come. Lord, in your mercy,

**hear our prayer.**

Let us pray that those who are poor in any circumstance of body or spirit may know the providence of God and the abundance of the Holy Spirit. Lord, in your mercy,

**hear our prayer.**

Let us pray that all students of God's word may rejoice in the great drama of salvation and be bearers of the good news of Jesus Christ. Lord, in your mercy,

**hear our prayer.**

*HERE OTHER INTERCESSIONS MAY BE OFFERED.*

Let us pray in thanksgiving for St. Michael and all the holy angels, that with the great host of witnesses we may join in singing the victory song of the Lamb. Lord, in your mercy,

**hear our prayer.**

Hear us as we pray, O God, and renew in us the joy of salvation, through Jesus Christ our Lord.

**Amen**

### IMAGES FOR PREACHING

The volunteer gardener who took care of the church courtyard set masonry angels, fat baby cherubs, in front of the flowerbeds. They looked nothing like what the prophet Daniel saw. He saw a man whose "body was like beryl, his face like lightning, his eyes like flaming torches, his arms and legs like the gleam of burnished bronze, and the sound of his words like the roar of a multitude" (Dan. 10:6). When Daniel saw that celestial being, he did what we would do: he fainted dead away.

As the first reading begins, Daniel has fallen into a trance, his face to the ground. A hand touches him and raises him. He gets up like a felled boxer trying to rise. First he gets to his hands and knees. "Stand on your feet," says the man. Then he begins to deliver his message: "Do not fear." We know the speaker must be an angel. Angels said "do not fear" to Joseph and Mary and the shepherds and to the women who come early to the tomb. This angel tells Daniel he has nothing to fear because "Michael, the great prince, the protector of your people, shall arise" (12:1). Michael fights for you, the messenger promises Daniel.

Michael is also the one doing battle in the vision of St. John. It is interesting that God is only secondarily involved. The evil one is no threat to God. God sends a lieutenant to lead the fight. The archangel is victorious. Is this the same victory Jesus tells the seventy about upon their return from their first missionary venture?

Martin Luther ends both his morning and evening prayers, "Let your holy angels have charge of us, that the wicked one have no power over us." Do we need a crucified and risen Savior if we have such guardian angels on our side? Note by what means Michael and all angels win the victory. It is by the blood of the Lamb that the evil foe has no power over us. The evil one is as dangerous as any mortally wounded animal. But his wounds are mortal. His days are numbered.

## WORSHIP MATTERS

The festival of St. Michael and All Angels provides a wonderful opportunity for worship leaders to emphasize that when we gather around word and sacrament, we do not do so alone. We are surrounded by "angels and archangels and the whole company of heaven." Our assembly is part of a great chorus of praise before God and we, with all the saints, are recipients of God's love and grace, which exceeds anything we can ever imagine. This realization encourages us to lead worship in such a way that the awe and mystery of the whole company of heaven is imaged in our midst. With proper preparation, this day might be one to consider introducing incense in worship. Make reference to the song of the seraphim surrounding the divine throne in Isaiah 6:3, which we sing whenever we sing the Sanctus, "Holy, holy, holy Lord."

## LET THE CHILDREN COME

Angels and dragons, snakes and scorpions, lightning and a heavenly battle! Children will naturally be captivated by the vivid imagery in today's scripture readings. On this festival day sing "Ye watchers and ye holy ones" (LBW 175) with its references to seraphim, cherubim, and archangels. Teach children these words, and have

them listen for other places angels are named in the liturgy today.

## HYMNS FOR WORSHIP
### GATHERING
Holy God, we praise your name   LBW 535
Praise, my soul, the King of heaven   LBW 549
The trumpets sound, the angels sing   W&P 139

### HYMN OF THE DAY
Ye watchers and ye holy ones   LBW 175

### ALTERNATE HYMN OF THE DAY
God, my Lord, my strength   LBW 484
On eagle's wings   WOV 779, W&P 110

### COMMUNION
Let all mortal flesh keep silence   LBW 198
Eat this bread, drink this cup   WOV 706
We will glorify   TFF 281, W&P 154

### SENDING
Rejoice, O pilgrim throng!   LBW 553
Thine the amen, thine the praise   WOV 801

### ADDITIONAL HYMNS AND SONGS
Isaiah in a vision did of old   LBW 528
God is truly present   HFW
Lord, my strength   W&P 93
God of love, have mercy   DH 10
We see the Lord   W&P 153

## MUSIC FOR THE DAY
### PSALMODY
Bless the Lord, O my soul   WOV 798 (Ps. 103:1)
Dufford, Bob.   STP, vol. 4.
Moore, Bob. Cong, gtr.   GIA G-3858.
Organ, Anne Krentz.   PW C.
Walker, E.   STP, vol. 2.

### CHORAL
Bach, J.S. "Blessing, Glory and Wisdom." SATB, pno/org. KJO 5140.
Busarow, Donald. "Lord, Thee I Love with All My Heart." SATB or 2 pt mxd, opt cong, oboe/tpt/cl, org.   CPH 98-3429.
Haan, Raymond. "They Shall Shine Like Stars." SATB, org. AFP 0800674014.

293

Shepperd, Mark. "Bless His Holy Name." SATB, kybd, opt U, cong, hb. AFP 0800674030.

Williams, David H. "Sing Alleluia Forth." SATB, org. HWG CMR 2390.

## CHILDREN'S CHOIRS

Cobb, Nancy Hill. "Bless the Lord, O My Soul." 2 pt, kybd. KIR 10/1339K.

Kosche, Kenneth. "Bless God's Holy Name." 2 pt, kybd, hb. CG CGA766.

## KEYBOARD/INSTRUMENTAL

Carter, John. "Lasst uns erfreuen" in *Contemplative Folk Tunes for Piano.* Pno. AFP 0800659775.

Dahl, David P. "Lasst uns erfreuen" in *Hymn Interpretations for Organ.* Org. AFP 0800658248.

Dupré, Marcel. "Thou Splendor and Power" in *Sixteen Chorales.* Org. BEL GB 197.

Farlee, Robert Buckley. "God, My Lord, My Strength" *Gaudeamus!* Org. AFP 0800655389.

Johnson, David. *Trumpet Tune in D Major.* Org. AFP 0800645499.

Near, Gerald. "Prelude on the Hymntune PICARDY." Org. AUR AE 78.

## HANDBELL

Behnke, John A. "My Lord, What a Morning." 3-5 oct. L3. AG 1877.

Hopson, Hal H. "All Creatures of Our God and King." 3-4 oct. L2. AG 1546.

Moklebust, Cathy. "Festival Sanctus." 4-5 oct. L5. AFP 0800601185.

## PRAISE ENSEMBLE

Clydesdale, David T. "I Stand in Awe." WRD 0 80689 71727 7 (SATB, kybd); 0 80689 66924 8 (choraltrax); 0 80689 71747 5 (orch).

Stonehill, Randy/arr. Mark Hayes. "Shut De Door." SATB, opt perc. WRD 301 10212 167.

# September 29, 2002

Nineteenth Sunday after Pentecost
Proper 21

## INTRODUCTION

As we gather today around the table of the word, we become more than a collection of individuals. We have been united to each other in the waters of baptism and welcomed by Christ to his holy supper. While some may be strangers to us, we are invited to recognize the deep communion we share in Christ Jesus. The liturgy does not protect us from others; it teaches us to be a people of hospitality, generous in faith, hope, and love.

## PRAYER OF THE DAY

God of love, you know our frailties and failings. Give us your grace to overcome them; keep us from those things that harm us; and guide us in the way of salvation; through your Son, Jesus Christ our Lord.

## READINGS

Ezekiel 18:1-4, 25-32

The prophet Ezekiel challenges an old proverb that would see the exile as punishment for the sins of the exiles' ancestors. Rather, he says, God insists that individuals are responsible for their own sin and their own repentance.

Psalm 25:1-8 (Psalm 25:1-9 [NRSV])

Remember, O Lord, your compassion and love. (Ps. 25:5)

Philippians 2:1-13

Paul quotes from an early Christian hymn to describe the attitude of humble self-sacrifice displayed in Christ Jesus. Although Christians may disagree on many things, he urges them to be of one mind with regard to emulating Christ's self-giving love.

Matthew 21:23-32

Shortly after arriving in Jerusalem, Jesus drives the moneychangers out of the temple, heals the sick, and begins teaching there. These activities are challenged by the religious leaders who are in charge of the temple.

## SEMICONTINUOUS FIRST READING/PSALM

Exodus 17:1-7

Today's reading is one of several that tell of experiences during the wilderness wandering. In this case, the people complain because they have a legitimate need and God responds by providing for them. Later in their wanderings, when the people complain because of their wants, God responds with anger.

Psalm 78:1-4, 12-16

We will recount to generations to come the power of the Lord. (Ps. 78:4)

## COLOR  Green

## THE PRAYERS

Refreshed by the living word of God, let us pray for the church, the world, and all those in need.

*A BRIEF SILENCE.*

Let us pray for the church, that it may have the mind of Christ and empty itself for the sake of the world. Lord, in your mercy,

**hear our prayer.**

Let us pray for civic leaders, that they may discern your will and wisdom amid the pressures of this world and be upheld in every good work. Lord, in your mercy,

**hear our prayer.**

Let us pray for those suffering from physical abuse, mental anguish, or broken relationships, that they may know the peace and healing of your presence. Lord, in your mercy,

**hear our prayer.**

Let us pray for victims of war and violence, and for those living with poverty, anxiety, or illness (especially), that they may know your compassion and love. Lord, in your mercy,

**hear our prayer.**

Let us pray for this congregation, that we may grow in faith and service, living out our baptismal promises with joy. Lord, in your mercy,

**hear our prayer.**

*HERE OTHER INTERCESSIONS MAY BE OFFERED.*

We give thanks for all the faithful departed who have confessed Jesus as Lord, and we pray that we may follow them in the way of righteousness. Lord, in your mercy,

295

**hear our prayer.**
Hear us as we pray, O God, and renew in us the joy of salvation, through Jesus Christ our Lord.
**Amen**

## IMAGES FOR PREACHING

Standing in a long line for lunch at a tourist-infested location, people became increasingly anxious when a half dozen more people arrived on the scene. Would these newcomers mistake the space between me and the person in front of me for the end of the line? I moved up a bit, closed the gap, and turned my back to the new arrivals to edge them out. The group stood by, talking, trying to look innocent and nonchalant. They moved when the line moved. They merged their way into the line like so much rush hour traffic. Someone said to them, "The line starts back there." They looked where the man pointed. It was a good distance away. They shrugged their shoulders. They stayed where they were. Those in line around them seethed. We had invested a great deal of time and energy in that line. We resented these interlopers.

Jesus entered the temple, says the gospel reading. He came upon those who were already standing in line for the reign of God. They had invested a great deal of time and much energy in their quest for a place with God. "Who is this interloper, and by what authority does he cut in line?" they asked.

Jesus does not claim authority merely to cut in line. He claims authority over the whole enterprise. The line begins with me, he says. "The tax collectors and the prostitutes are going into the kingdom of God ahead of you" (Matt. 21:31).

Lines and queues are an inescapable part of the linear world of this horizontal realm. The realm of God is more like an all-embracing circle. Where such a line begins or ends is not important, only that Jesus is its center.

## WORSHIP MATTERS

Acolytes can be assigned a number of different tasks to perform. In addition to lighting and extinguishing the candles and assisting with receiving the offering, they can serve the presider by holding the book and freeing the presider for gestures. They can also receive the gifts of bread and wine from the ushers and assist in the distribution of communion. Acolytes can serve in the procession as crucifer, bookbearer, torchbearer, or thurifer. Though children or young adults serve ably in this role, age ought not be the only criterion for service. Acolytes should be vested in the common baptismal garment, the alb, and seated close to the presiding and assisting ministers.

## LET THE CHILDREN COME

Teach the children how and when to make the sign of the cross. If this is an unfamiliar gesture to most members of the worshiping community, then let the children teach the adults. Tell them that this sign first was made upon them when they were baptized into the name of the Holy Trinity. Show them how to touch their foreheads with the fingers of their right hand, then to touch their chest, one shoulder, the other shoulder, and their chest again at the words, "Father, Son, and Holy Spirit."

## HYMNS FOR WORSHIP
### GATHERING

Look, the sight is glorious   LBW 156
God himself is present   LBW 249
Here in this place   WOV 718

### HYMN OF THE DAY

O God, my faithful God   LBW 504

### ALTERNATE HYMN OF THE DAY

At the name of Jesus   LBW 179
Take the name of Jesus with you   TFF 159

### COMMUNION

What wondrous love is this   LBW 385
Now we offer   WOV 761, TFF 129
Jesus, name above all names   W&P 77

### SENDING

For the bread which you have broken   LBW 200
Bind us together   WOV 748

### ADDITIONAL HYMNS AND SONGS

He is exalted   W&P 55
May the mind of Christ my Savior   CEL 568
Christ the victorious   H82 358

296

## MUSIC FOR THE DAY
### PSALMODY

Becker, John.   PW A.

Haas, David.   PCY 9.

Haugen, Marty. "To You, O Lord." Cant, cong, opt 2 pt, kybd.
   GIA G-2653.

Joncas, Michael.   STP, vol. 5.

Maeker, Nancy and Don Rotermund. "Sing a New Song" in *Five Psalms/Anthems, set 2.* Speech choir, perc.   CPH 97-6041.

Pelz, Walter. "Show Me Thy Ways." SATB, gtr, ob/fl.
   AFP 0800645421.

Wellicome, Paul.   PS 1.

### CHORAL

Englert, Eugene. "I Lift Up My Soul." SATB, fl, org.
   AFP 6000117078.

Gallus-Handl, Jacob. "At the Name of Jesus." SATB.
   CPH 98-1051.

Handel, G.F. "Let Thy Hand Be Strengthened" in *Coronation Anthems.* SAATB, kybd.   OXF.

Hampton, Keith. "My God Is an Awesome God." SATB, pno.
   AFP 0800659171.

Nelson, Ronald. "To You, O Lord, I Lift Up My Soul." U, kybd.
   CPH 98-2928.

Pelz, Walter. "Show Me Thy Ways." SATB, ob, gtr.
   AFP 0800645421.

Rachmaninoff, Sergei. "To Thee O Lord" in *Anthems for Choirs 1.* SATB.   OXF.

Vaughan Williams, Ralph. "At the Name of Jesus." SATB, org, cong.
   OXF A158.

Young, Jeremy. "God Has Spoken, Bread Has Broken." SAB, kybd, opt cong.   AFP 0800655877.

### CHILDREN'S CHOIRS

Bock, Fred. "God Is at Work in You." 2 pt, kybd.
   FB BG2367.

Hobby, Robert A. "Thy Holy Wings—I Lift Up My Soul."
   U, kybd, fl.   MSM-50-9453.

Wetzler, Robert. "Take of the Wonder." U or SATB, cong, kybd, opt gtr/inst.   AFP 0800655222.

### KEYBOARD/INSTRUMENTAL

Beck, Theodore. "Was frag' ich nach der Welt" in *Basic Hymn Accompaniments,* vol. 4. Kybd.   CPH 97-5553.

Powell, Robert. "At the Name of Jesus" in *Augsburg Organ Library: November.*   AFP 0800658965.

Tambling, Christopher. "Postlude on a Theme by Orlando Gibbons" in *Festival Finales.* Org.   MAY 0862093538.

Trapp, Lynn. "Pan de vida" in *Laudate, vol. 6.* Org.   CPH 97-6792.

### HANDBELL

Dare, John C. "Fugue in F." 3 oct. L2.   FLA HP5383.

Dobrinski, Cynthia. "Come, Thou Fount." 3 oct.   CG CGB 66.

Gramann, Fred. "Fantasy on KING'S WESTON." 3-6 oct. L5.
   AG 1671.

### PRAISE ENSEMBLE

Albrecht, Carl and Leann Albrecht. "In the Arms of His Love" in *Extravagant Grace Songbook.* SAT[B], kybd.   INT 16737.

Berry, Cindy. "United in His Love." SATB, kybd.   HAL 08741785.

Condon, Mark/arr. J. Daniel Smith. "Holy Is Thy Name" in *Marvelous Things Choral Collection.* SATB, kybd.   INT 18256.

Price, Nancy and Don Besig. "United in Christ." SATB, kybd, tpt.
   FLA A7302.

297

# Sunday, September 29

ST. MICHAEL AND ALL ANGELS
*See pages 292–294.*

# Monday, September 30

JEROME, TRANSLATOR, TEACHER, 420

Jerome is remembered as a biblical scholar and translator. Rather than choosing classical Latin as the basis of his work, he translated the scriptures into the Latin that was spoken and written by the majority of people in his day. His translation is known as the Vulgate, which comes from the Latin word for "common." While Jerome is remembered as a saint, he could be anything but saintly. He was well known for his short temper and his arrogance, although he was also quick to admit to his personal faults.

Thanks to the work of Jerome, many people received the word in their own language and lived a life of faith and service to those in need.

## Friday, October 4

FRANCIS OF ASSISI, RENEWER OF THE CHURCH, 1226

Francis was the son of a wealthy cloth merchant. In a public confrontation with his father he renounced his wealth and future inheritance and devoted himself to serving the poor. Francis described this act as being "wedded to Lady Poverty." Under his leadership the Order of Friars Minor (Franciscans) was formed, and they understood literally Jesus' words to his disciples that they should take nothing on their journey and receive no payment for their work. Their task in preaching was to "use words if necessary." Francis had a spirit of gladness and gratitude for all of God's creation. This commemoration has been a traditional time to bless pets and animals, creatures Francis called his brothers and sisters. A prayer attributed to St. Francis is included in *LBW* (p. 48) and could be used at gatherings in the congregation today.

## Friday, October 4

THEODORE FLIEDNER, RENEWER OF SOCIETY, 1864

Fliedner's work was instrumental in the revival of the ministry of deaconesses among Lutherans. While a pastor in Kaiserswerth, Germany, he also ministered to prisoners in Düsseldorf. Through his ministry to prisoners he came in contact with Moravian deaconesses, and it was through this Moravian influence that he was convinced that the ministry of deaconesses had a place among Lutherans. His work and writing encouraged women to care for those who were sick, poor, or imprisoned. Fliedner's deaconess motherhouse in Kaiserswerth inspired Lutherans all over the world to commission deaconesses to serve in parishes, schools, prisons, and hospitals. At this motherhouse in Kaiserswerth, Florence Nightingale received her training as a nurse (see August 13).

298

# October 6, 2002

Twentieth Sunday after Pentecost
Proper 22

### INTRODUCTION

In today's gospel reading, Jesus tells a parable of the vineyard, an image of Israel, the prophets' mission, and Christ's death. For Christians, the vineyard also speaks of God's love poured out in the blood of Christ, given to us for the forgiveness of sin. Grafted onto Christ the vine at baptism, we are nourished with his blood and drawn to each other by his love.

October 6 is the commemoration of William Tyndale, one of the first translators of the Bible into English.

### PRAYER OF THE DAY

Our Lord Jesus, you have endured the doubts and foolish questions of every generation. Forgive us for trying to be judge over you, and grant us the confident faith to acknowledge you as Lord.

### READINGS

Isaiah 5:1-7

The prophet sings a sad, parable-like love song about the relationship between God and Israel. Israel is likened to a promising vineyard that now must be destroyed. Despite God's loving care, Israel has brought forth "wild grapes" of injustice and distress where fine grapes of justice and righteousness were expected. Having failed to uphold the covenant, Israel will bear the Lord's judgment.

Psalm 80:7-14 (Psalm 80:7-15 [NRSV])

Look down from heaven, O God; behold and tend this vine. (Ps. 80:14)

Philippians 3:4b-14

Paul has warned the Philippians about Christian leaders who may have impressive credentials but do not witness to the gospel of Christ. Now he offers his own list of credentials, only to reject them all in favor of what he considers truly significant.

Matthew 21:33-46

Jesus tells a parable to the religious leaders who are plotting his death, revealing that their plans will ironically bring about the fulfillment of scripture.

SEMICONTINUOUS FIRST READING/PSALM

Exodus 20:1-4, 7-9, 12-20

After escaping from slavery, the Israelites come to Mount Sinai where God instructs them how to live together in community. The Ten Commandments recognize that God is the creator of all things. Flowing from God, the life of the community flourishes when marked by the basic building blocks recounted in today's reading: honesty, trust, fidelity, and respect for life, family, and property.

Psalm 19

The statutes of the Lord are just and rejoice the heart. (Ps. 19:8)

COLOR  Green

THE PRAYERS

Refreshed by the living word of God, let us pray for the church, the world, and all those in need.

*A BRIEF SILENCE.*

O God of hosts, plant the vineyard of the church in every place, and gather your harvest of righteousness from all the nations of the world. Lord, in your mercy,

**hear our prayer.**

O Lord of creation, teach us to preserve and wisely use this earth, fashioned by your hands, that its abundant goodness may be a blessing to many. Lord, in your mercy,

**hear our prayer.**

O Bread of life, you supply all who hunger with the food that is unfailing. Be with all in need, and sustain with your presence those who are sick and hospitalized (especially). Lord, in your mercy,

**hear our prayer.**

O gracious God, we thank you for the great variety of gifts shared in this community. Bless our serving, that it may bring praise to you and be a joy to all your people. Lord, in your mercy,

**hear our prayer.**

*HERE OTHER INTERCESSIONS MAY BE OFFERED.*

O Lord of love, help us press toward the goal of your heavenly call in Christ Jesus until we stand in the company of all your saints in light. Lord, in your mercy,

**hear our prayer.**

Hear us as we pray, O God, and renew in us the joy of salvation, through Jesus Christ our Lord.

**Amen**

IMAGES FOR PREACHING

When the young man turned sixteen, his father put a set of car keys in his hands and said, "Happy birthday, son." The father had looked forward to seeing the joy on his son's face when the son realized the keys were not to the family sedan. The father was not disappointed.

In the first six months of driving on his own, however, the young man was involved in three accidents and received two tickets. When the young man came home with the second ticket, his father took the car keys from him. The young man protested, "But it is my car. You gave it to me. I'm working to pay for the insurance. I'm maintaining the car."

The father answered, "I placed the keys in your hand. I referred to it as your car. But whose name is on the title? It is my car. Now I am taking the keys and placing them in your sister's hand. We will now refer to it as her car."

Jesus tells a similar story about tenants of a vineyard. The tenants' sedition goes beyond protesting the ownership. They attempt to depose the owner and for that, if Jesus' listeners are correct, they themselves will be deposed.

Is there any good news here? After we read the gospel, how can we proclaimers say, "The gospel of the Lord," and expect the congregation to respond, "Praise to you, O Christ"?

Such an acclamation is possible because we know the story does not end there. Jesus always goes to "the least, the last, and the lost," as the phrase goes. Jesus travels out to those who are deposed from the land of the living. Hell is as far as a person can be deposed. Jesus goes even there. Those outside the vineyard are the ones to whom Jesus goes. They are the ones to whom we go in his name. Praise to you, O Christ.

WORSHIP MATTERS

Our worship as the baptized people of God ought to provide an image of the priesthood of all believers. Worship that is led by only one or two persons leaves the impression that the rest are an audience, looking on as a few conduct the liturgy. To image the full participation of all the baptized in the "work of the people," leadership should be shared as widely as possible. Others besides the presider can minister by lighting candles, assisting in singing the liturgy, offering the prayers, reading

299

the scriptures, distributing the sacrament, leading the procession cross, candles, or thurible, and serving as ministers of music (choir members, cantors, and instrumentalists) and hospitality (ushers, greeters). Those serving in these positions should reflect the whole congregation in age, gender, race, and longevity in the congregation.

### LET THE CHILDREN COME

From the fruit of the vineyard comes wine. In this harvest season, let the wine be visible and audible. Use a crystal or simple glass flagon. When preparing the table, the assisting minister can hold the flagon high enough that the children can see and hear the wine flowing into the chalice. Watch! Listen! Taste! See! The wine of the eucharist is a sign of God's future.

### HYMNS FOR WORSHIP

#### GATHERING

300

Open now thy gates of beauty    LBW 250
Christ is made the sure foundation    WOV 747, LBW 367
Thy word    TFF 132, W&P 144

#### HYMN OF THE DAY

There in God's garden    LBW 668

#### ALTERNATE HYMN OF THE DAY

Amid the world's bleak wilderness    LBW 378
When I survey the wondrous cross    LBW 482, TFF 79

#### COMMUNION

We who once were dead    LBW 207
I want Jesus to walk with me    WOV 660, TFF 66
Taste and see    BL 12

#### SENDING

Children of the heavenly Father    LBW 474
Send me, Jesus    WOV 773, TFF 244
May you run and not be weary    W&P 97

#### ADDITIONAL HYMNS AND SONGS

Amazing love    W&P 8
My hope is built on nothing less    LBW 293, 294
Open our lives to the Word    DH 8
How clear is our vocation, Lord    PH 419
A single unmatched stone    W3 574

### MUSIC FOR THE DAY

#### PSALMODY

Becker, John.    PW A.
Behold and tend this vine    DH 39
Hughes, Howard/Joseph Gelineau.    TP.
Kogut, Malcolm.    PCY 10.
Smith, Timothy.    STP, vol. 4.

#### CHORAL

Ashdown, Franklin D. "Jesus, the Very Thought of Thee." SATB, org, opt C inst.    AFP 0800657500.
Bairstow, Edward. "Jesu, the Very Thought of Thee." SATB.    OXF 43.003.
Gardner, John. "Fight the Good Fight with All Thy Might." SATB, pno, opt orch.    OXF 42.874.
Handel, G. F. "Glory and Worship" in *Coronation Anthems*. SAATBB, kybd.    OXF.
Handel, G. F. "Since By Man Came Death" in *Messiah*. SATB, kybd. Various ed.
Isaac, Heinrich. "O Bread of Life from Heaven" in *Chantry Choirbook*. SATB.    AFP 0800657772.
Keesecker, Thomas. "The Song of the Vineyard." SA, hb/kybd.    AFP 0800651006.
Lenel, Ludwig. "When I Survey the Wondrous Cross." U, kybd.    RME.
Petker, Allan Robert. "Lamb of God, What Wondrous Love." SATB, kybd.    Gentry JG2029.
Young, Jeremy. "Taste and See." U, kybd, opt cong.    APF 0800657608.

#### CHILDREN'S CHOIRS

Barnard, Mark. "Sing Alleluia to Our King." 2 pt, kybd, opt cong.    UNI 10/1399U.
Ferguson, John. "For the Beauty of the Lord." U, opt inst.    CG CGA 558.
Jothen, Michael. "You Are the Branches." U, opt gtr, inst, hb.    CG CGA 755.

#### KEYBOARD/INSTRUMENTAL

Cherwien, David. "There in God's Garden" in *O God Beyond All Praising*. Org.    AFP 0800657241.
Leavitt, John. "With High Delight" in *A Little Easter Suite*. Org.    CPH 97-6646.
Organ, Anne Krentz. "Shades Mountain" in *Woven Together*. Pno, inst.    AFP 0800658167.
Young, Jeremy. "Shades Mountain" in *At the Foot of the Cross*. Pno.    AFP 0800655397.

HANDBELL

Dicke, Martin. "Rondo for Bells." 2 oct. L3.    AFP 0800659945.

Moklebust, Cathy. "Children of the Heavenly Father." 3 oct, opt ch.
CG CGB 139.

Sherman, Arnold B. "When I Survey the Wondrous Cross." L2+.
Red River HB00010A (2-3 oct); HB00010B (4-5 oct).

Thompson, Martha Lynn. "Promised Land." 3-5 oct. L2.    AG 2082.

PRAISE ENSEMBLE

Founds, Rick/arr. Gary Rhodes. "Jesus, Draw Me Close" (with I Am
Thine, Lord).    WRD 301 0965 168 (SATB, kybd);
301 7647 080 (choraltrax); 301 0681 259 (orch).

Machen, Harland/arr. Tom Fettke. "Bow the Knee."    Allegis
AG-1076 (SATB, kybd); MU-2446D (cass); MU 50371
(CD); OR-2446 (orch).

# Sunday, October 6

WILLIAM TYNDALE, TRANSLATOR, MARTYR, 1536

William Tyndale was ordained in 1521, and his life's
desire was to translate the scriptures into English.
When his plan met opposition from Henry VIII,
Tyndale fled to Germany, where he traveled from city
to city and lived in poverty and constant danger. He
was able to produce a New Testament in 1525. Nine
years later he revised it and began work on the Old Testament, which he was unable to complete. He was tried
for heresy and burned at the stake. Miles Coverdale
completed Tyndale's work, and the Tyndale-Coverdale
version was published as the "Matthew Bible" in 1537.
The style of this translation has influenced English
versions of the Bible such as the King James (Autho-
rized Version) and the New Revised Standard Version
for four centuries.

# Monday, October 7

HENRY MELCHIOR MUHLENBERG,
MISSIONARY TO NORTH AMERICA, 1787

Muhlenberg was prominent in setting the course for
Lutheranism in this country. He helped Lutheran
churches make the transition from the state churches of
Europe to independent churches of America. Among
other things, he established the first Lutheran synod in
America and developed an American Lutheran liturgy.
His liturgical principles became the basis for the Common Service of 1888, used in many North American
service books for a majority of the past century.

The commemoration of Muhlenberg invites congregations to look back on what has shaped their identity,
worship, and mission in the past and to look ahead to
what might shape it in the future.

# Thursday, October 10

MASSIE L. KENNARD, RENEWER OF THE CHURCH, 1996

Massie L. Kennard was a native of Chicago, Illinois.
He was a major figure in supporting and working toward ethnic and racial inclusiveness in the former
Lutheran Church in America. Ordained in 1958, he
served the church in various staff positions, including
work as the director for Minority Concerns of the Division for Mission in North America.

# October 13, 2002

Twenty-first Sunday after Pentecost
Proper 23

## INTRODUCTION

Three sets of meals cluster around the readings today: the meals of Jesus; the church's celebration of the holy supper; and the wedding feast of heaven. In each meal, the invitation is given to all who hunger for God's love: Come to the banquet.

Come and feast on the bread of heaven; come and drink God's mercy; come and be strengthened for service to the needy. As Augustine once said to his congregation, Become the bread that you hold in your hand. Come to the holy supper and learn what it means to be a Christian.

## PRAYER OF THE DAY

Almighty God, source of every blessing, your generous goodness comes to us anew every day. By the work of your Spirit lead us to acknowledge your goodness, give thanks for your benefits, and serve you in willing obedience; through your Son, Jesus Christ our Lord.

## READINGS

### Isaiah 25:1-9

Today's reading begins with a hymn of thanksgiving and concludes with the promise of the banquet celebrating the day in which the Lord's sovereignty is fully established. This banquet symbolizes not only the establishment of God's reign on earth, it also symbolizes the joy, companionship, and prosperity characteristic of God's reign.

### Psalm 23

You spread a table before me, and my cup is running over. (Ps. 23:5)

### Philippians 4:1-9

Paul's letter to the Philippians is written from prison at a time when the apostle faced possible martyrdom. Nevertheless, his words reveal concern for the needs of others and convey an attitude of joy, hope, gratitude, and peace.

### Matthew 22:1-14

Jesus tells a parable to the religious leaders of his day, indicating that even though God's kingdom is a great feast open to all, its coming will prove disastrous for some.

## SEMICONTINUOUS FIRST READING/PSALM

### Exodus 32:1-14

Prior to this chapter, Moses received instructions from God on Mount Sinai. Meanwhile, the people grew rebellious and decided to make a golden calf. Today's reading suggests a court setting in which God acts as prosecuting attorney and Moses as defense attorney in a lawsuit against the people.

### Psalm 106:1-6, 19-23

Remember, O Lord, the favor you have for your people. (Ps. 106:4)

## COLOR Green

## THE PRAYERS

Refreshed by the living word of God, let us pray for the church, the world, and all those in need.

*A BRIEF SILENCE.*

Let us pray that the church will embrace Jesus' mission of inviting and welcoming all people to the supper of life. Lord, in your mercy,

**hear our prayer.**

Let us pray for international organizations and relief agencies that work to improve the health, education, and welfare of people throughout the world. Lord, in your mercy,

**hear our prayer.**

Let us pray that those who are sick or in any kind of need (especially) may know your peace that surpasses all understanding. Lord, in your mercy,

**hear our prayer.**

Let us pray for those who mourn, that they may know the consolation of your love and care. Lord, in your mercy,

**hear our prayer.**

Let us pray for artists, musicians, and all whose skill glorifies the Creator, that your abundant grace and beauty may be impressed upon our hearts. Lord, in your mercy,

**hear our prayer.**

Let us pray that our participation in the eucharistic feast may lead us to share your blessings with those who hunger or are in need. Lord, in your mercy,

**hear our prayer.**

Let us pray that we may follow the blessed saints in lives of faith and service until we join them at the wedding feast of Christ. Lord, in your mercy,

**hear our prayer.**

Hear us as we pray, O God, and renew in us the joy of salvation, through Jesus Christ our Lord.

**Amen**

## IMAGES FOR PREACHING

The word from a member of a neighboring church is that the congregation I serve includes people who are confirmed Lutherans and comfortable in the church but not sure they believe in Jesus.

When I first heard that comment, my thought was, "Good. This is where they belong. In church. Hearing week after week about the wonders God does in the world and in our lives through Jesus Christ. I want unbelievers in the pews."

Then I realized the judgment was aimed not so much at the person in the pew as at the parson in the pulpit. The accusation is that the people do not hear the clear gospel from this preacher. That's obvious, because look, here is an unbeliever in their midst. What sort of congregation allows such a thing? My answer: a faithful congregation.

Jesus expects there to be unbelievers in our midst. Jesus' parable in the gospel today has some similarities with the parables of Matthew 13. Like the fisherman (Matt. 13:47-50) and the householder with weeds and wheat growing together (Matt. 13:24-30), the king's servants gather everyone in sight. No questions are asked. There is no doctrinal quiz. No one judges whether they are sufficiently schooled in social graces. That sweeping invitation no doubt resulted in there being some odd company at the wedding banquet for the king's son. Keep odd company, Jesus advises in his parable. It is not up to us to make judgments about those who answer the gospel invitation to faith.

When the king arrives, he removes one guest, because he was not dressed in a wedding garment. We do not quite know what to make of this. It is possible that Jesus' hearers were acquainted with a social custom of the host providing each guest a wedding garment, so that the guest's refusal would constitute a rejection of the host's gift. In any case, it is the king who makes the judgment. Not us. We, the king's servants, invite.

## WORSHIP MATTERS

Processions for worship can be varied depending on the day and the context. A basic order for the procession would be crucifer, choir, and ministers, with the presider at the end. To this procession could be added a thurifer (incense bearer) to lead the procession, torches to flank the crucifer, a bookbearer following the cross, and banner bearers between different groups within the procession. A second crucifer might precede the ministers, especially if the procession is long.

## LET THE CHILDREN COME

Who is invited to the banquet? Jesus' parables invite us to look again at our table hospitality. Who is invited to the table? How do we extend hospitality to baptismal candidates and others who do not receive the bread and wine? How are children welcomed to the feast?

## HYMNS FOR WORSHIP

### GATHERING

Now we join in celebration   LBW 203

God is here!   WOV 719

This is the feast of victory   W&P 142

### HYMN OF THE DAY

At the Lamb's high feast we sing   LBW 210

### ALTERNATE HYMN OF THE DAY

Now the feast and celebration   WOV 789

The trumpets sound, the angels sing   W&P 139

### COMMUNION

Here, O my Lord, I see thee   LBW 211

The King of love my shepherd is   LBW 456

What feast of love   WOV 701

### SENDING

O Savior, precious Savior   LBW 514

Thine the amen, thine the praise   WOV 801

### ADDITIONAL HYMNS AND SONGS

Grains of wheat   WOV 708

Give thanks   TFF 292, W&P 41

We come to the hungry feast   WOV 766

Rejoice in Christ Jesus   NSR 75

## MUSIC FOR THE DAY

### PSALMODY

*See the fourth Sunday in Lent.*

### CHORAL

Anon (Attrib. John Redford). "Rejoice in the Lord Always." SATB. OXF 43.243. (Also in *The Second Motet Book.* CPH 97-5205.)

Jacob, Gordon. "Brother James's Air." SATB. OXF 94P316.

Mendelssohn, Felix. "I Praise Thee" in *St. Paul.* B solo, SATB, kybd. GSCH ed 321.

Purcell, Henry. "Rejoice in the Lord Always." CPH 97-6344 (SATB, solo ATB, org.); CPH 97-4472 (str, cont).

Rachmaninoff, Sergei. "Today Hath Salvation Come" from *All Night Vigil* in *Songs of the Church.* SSAATTB. HWG GB640.

Rutter, John. "The Lord Is My Shepherd" in *Requiem.* SATB, org/pno, ob. HIN HMB-164.

Schalk, Carl. "The God of Love My Shepherd Is." SATB, 2 vlns, org. MSM-50-8812.

Schütz, Heinrich. "O Lord, I Trust Your Shepherd Care" in *Chantry Choirbook.* SATB, cong. AFP 0800657772.

Thomson, Virgil. "My Shepherd Will Supply My Need." SATB. HWG 2046.

Zimmerman, Heinz Werner. "Psalm 23" in *The Augsburg Choirbook.* SATB, str bass. AFP 0800656784.

### CHILDREN'S CHOIRS

Carter, John. "The Shepherd Psalm." 2 pt, kybd. HOP A555.

Fauré, Gabriel/arr. Richard Wegner. "Blessed Jesus." U, org. CPH 98-2580.

Shute, Linda Cable. "Feed My Lambs." 2 pt, kybd. AFP 0800674111.

### KEYBOARD/INSTRUMENTAL

Burkhardt, Michael. "Rejoice, O Pilgrim Throng" in *Praise and Thanksgiving, set 5.* Org. MSM 10-755.

Carter, John. "Holy Manna" in *Contemplative Folk Tunes for Piano.* Pno. AFP 0800659775.

Cherwien, David. "Now We Join in Celebration" in *Interpretations Book VI.* Org. AMSI SP-103.

Dahl, David P. "Sonne der Gerechtigkeit" in *Hymn Interpretations for Organ.* Org. AFP 0800658248.

Martin, Gilbert. "The Good Shepherd." Org. SMP/LOR.

Organ, Anne Krentz. "Sonne der Gerechtigkeit" in *Reflections on Hymn Tunes for Holy Communion.* Pno. AFP 0800654978.

Schack, David. "At the Lamb's High Feast We Sing" in *Augsburg Organ Library: Easter.* Org. AFP 0800659368.

### HANDBELL

Afdahl, Lee J. "The Lord's My Shepherd." 3-5 oct, opt ch. L3. AFP 0800659902.

Behnke, John. "Fantasy on St. Columba." 3-5 oct. L2+. JEF JHS 9227.

McChesney, Kevin. "Jubilance." 2-3 oct. L3. CG CGB188.

### PRAISE ENSEMBLE

Albrecht, Sally Althouse. "Step by Step." SATB, kybd. ALF 18700.

Morgan, Reuben. "My Heart Will Trust" in *Shout to the Lord 2000 Songbook.* SAT[B], kybd. INT 14247.

Paris, Twila/arr. Bruce Greer. "How Beautiful." WRD 301 0830 165 (SATB, kybd); 301 7505 081 (choraltrax); 301 0546 254 (orch).

# Monday, October 14

## DAY OF THANKSGIVING (CANADA)

*See Day of Thanksgiving (U.S.A.), November 28, 2002.*

# Tuesday, October 15

## TERESA OF JESUS, TEACHER, RENEWER OF THE CHURCH, 1582

Teresa of Jesus is also known as Teresa of Avila. She may be commemorated with John of the Cross on December 14. Teresa chose the life of a Carmelite nun after reading the letters of Jerome. She was frequently sick during her early years as a nun and found that when she was sick her prayer life flowered, but when she was well it withered. Steadily her life of faith and prayer deepened, and she grew to have a lively sense of God's presence with her. She worked to reform her monastic community in Avila, which she believed had strayed from its original purpose. Her reforms asked nuns to maintain life in the monastic enclosure without leaving it and also to identify with those who are poor by not wearing shoes. Teresa's writings on devotional life are widely read by members of various denominations.

# Thursday, October 17

IGNATIUS, BISHOP OF ANTIOCH, MARTYR, C. 115

Ignatius was the second bishop of Antioch in Syria. It was there that the name "Christian" was first used to describe the followers of Jesus. Ignatius is known to us through his letters. In them he encouraged Christians to live in unity sustained with love while standing firm on sound doctrine. Ignatius believed Christian martyrdom was a privilege. When his own martyrdom approached, he wrote in one of his letters, "I prefer death in Christ Jesus to power over the farthest limits of the earth. . . . [D]o not stand in the way of my birth to real life."

Ignatius and all martyrs are a reminder that even today "standing firm in the Lord" (Phil. 4:1) may lead to persecution and death.

# Friday, October 18

ST. LUKE, EVANGELIST

Luke is identified as the author of both Luke and Acts. Luke is careful to place the events of Jesus' life in both their social and religious contexts. Some of the most loved parables, including the good Samaritan and the prodigal son, are found only in this gospel. Luke's gospel has also given the church some of its most beautiful songs: the Benedictus sung at morning prayer, the Magnificat sung at evening prayer, and the Nunc dimittis sung at the close of the day. These songs are powerful witnesses to the message of Jesus Christ.

Paul calls Luke the "beloved physician," and some congregations use the day of St. Luke to remember and pray for those in healing professions. See the seasonal rites for an order of service.

# October 20, 2002

Twenty-second Sunday after Pentecost
Proper 24

305

## INTRODUCTION

In today's gospel reading, Jesus' words are more than a clever response to a trap set by his opponents. Give the tax that is due to the ruler, he says, but offer to God what is God's: the very life given you by the Creator.

These words of Jesus remind us that no earthly authority can claim the church's ultimate allegiance to God; its life comes from God so that it might serve the world in the labor of love.

## PRAYER OF THE DAY

Almighty and everlasting God, in Christ you have revealed your glory among the nations. Preserve the works of your mercy, that your Church throughout the world may persevere with steadfast faith in the confession of your name; through your Son, Jesus Christ our Lord.

## READINGS

Isaiah 45:1-7

The prophet announces a radical vision in today's reading. Late in the period of exile in Babylon, the Persian king Cyrus has taken power in the East and threatens the great Babylonian empire. Seeing this, the prophet announces that God is using Cyrus to accomplish God's purpose of freeing the exiles. Amazingly, God calls Cyrus "his anointed" (a translation of "messiah"), a title earlier reserved solely for Davidic kings.

Psalm 96:1-9 [10-13]

Ascribe to the Lord honor and power. (Ps. 96:7)

1 Thessalonians 1:1-10

Paul's first letter to the Thessalonians is probably the earliest of any of his writings. He opens with a prayer of thanksgiving for the witness these Christians have provided for others to whom he ministers.

Matthew 22:15-22

After Jesus comes to Jerusalem and begins teaching in the temple, the religious leaders try to trap him with trick questions. The first of these questions tries to force him to make an arbitrary choice between devotion to religion or politics.

## SEMICONTINUOUS FIRST READING/PSALM

Exodus 33:12-23

God was determined not to accompany the Israelites

into the land of promise, but Moses interceded to the point that God relented. Moses also expressed a desire to see God face-to-face, but was only allowed to view God from behind.

Psalm 99

Proclaim the greatness of the Lord our God. (Ps. 99:5)

COLOR Green

THE PRAYERS

Refreshed by the living word of God, let us pray for the church, the world, and all those in need.

*A BRIEF SILENCE.*

Let us pray that preachers, evangelists, and missionaries may boldly proclaim the message of the gospel in every circumstance of life. Lord, in your mercy,

**hear our prayer.**

Let us pray that all local officers of government— mayors and managers, council members and attorneys— may be blessed in their serving and promote the welfare of communities. Lord, in your mercy,

**hear our prayer.**

Let your blessing rest upon the seedtime and harvest, the business and enterprise of your people, that your good gifts may be shared among all. Lord, in your mercy,

**hear our prayer.**

Let us pray that all who are hospitalized or ill (especially) may be renewed by the Spirit's healing power and remain steadfast in hope. Lord, in your mercy,

**hear our prayer.**

Let your blessing rest upon us as we commit our time, energy, and income to serve the mission and ministry of Christ in months to come. Lord, in your mercy,

**hear our prayer.**

*HERE OTHER INTERCESSIONS MAY BE OFFERED.*

We give thanks for all the saints who have revealed your generosity and grace. Help us to offer our lives in gratitude to your never-ending love. Lord, in your mercy,

**hear our prayer.**

Hear us as we pray, O God, and renew in us the joy of salvation, through Jesus Christ our Lord.

**Amen**

## IMAGES FOR PREACHING

Today's gospel reading is regularly used on both sides of debates about whether to support the government. How

the text is applied depends on who is marshalling the story. But how can there be more than one interpretation? The emperor's image may be on the coin, but does not even that belong to God?

One edition of the Boy Scout chaplain's resource book contains a devotion that instructed the leader first to show the scouts an unimpressive coin, a penny. The point of the devotion was to talk about four little words, "In God We Trust," imprinted on our nation's lowest-denomination coin. With those twelve letters, we acknowledge that there is an authority beyond civil authority. The laws we make and the governments we elect are not ultimately sovereign.

The slogan on our national currency can give us the opportunity to talk about how God rules. In the civil realm God rules through governments and laws. Cyrus is God's unwitting tool (Isa. 45:1-7). Luther said he would rather be governed by a smart Turk than by a stupid Christian. We might say that rendering to "a smart Turk" would be rendering to God. When Caesar usurps God's authority, however, we must render to God, not Caesar.

God rules the eternal commonwealth of God through the gospel. Mercy is the ethos, forgiveness the standard. Here is power that is at odds with the world's understanding. It looks weak and ineffective but it is the ultimate in power. Law works by restricting and constricting: the civil realm is bounded by death. But the gospel is expansive and freeing. God's eternal realm has no boundaries; those who find their home here are bound only for life.

## WORSHIP MATTERS

More congregations are using incense in worship on certain days and occasions. The practice is described both in the Bible and through much of the church's history. Incense represents the prayers of the people ascending to God and symbolizes the cleansing of ourselves and our worship as we come into the divine presence. Traditionally, the altar, the gospel book, the communion elements, the ministers, and the people were censed using a thurible, a container with openings in the cover that holds hot coals onto which a bit of incense is placed. Recently, open incense bowls have become available and are carried with both hands rather than swung on a chain. Care must be taken not to place too much incense on the coals at one time.

## LET THE CHILDREN COME

How can we involve children in the time of offering? Encouraging them to put coins in the plate is the beginning of a good discipline, but unless the children have earned the money, they may have less of a sense of what it means to give it away. Today's gospel allows us to consider how the ritual action of giving an offering becomes translated into giving "to God the things that are God's."

## HYMNS FOR WORSHIP

### GATHERING

When morning gilds the skies   LBW 545, 546
O God beyond all praising   WOV 797
We bow down   W&P 149

### HYMN OF THE DAY

God is here!   WOV 719

### ALTERNATE HYMN OF THE DAY

Sing praise to God, the highest good   LBW 542
Lift every voice and sing   LBW 562, TFF 296

### COMMUNION

O Bread of life from heaven   LBW 222
Let us talents and tongues employ   WOV 754, TFF 232

### SENDING

You servants of God   LBW 252
For the fruit of all creation   WOV 760

### ADDITIONAL HYMNS AND SONGS

Evening and morning   LBW 465
Glory and praise to our God   W&P 43
You, Lord   W&P 162
I come with joy to meet my Lord   H82 304

## MUSIC FOR THE DAY

### PSALMODY

Becker, John.   PW A.
Burkhardt, Michael. "Three Psalm Settings."   MSM 80-705.
Foley, John.   PCY 7.
Hassler, Hans Leo/arr. Norman Greyson. "Cantate Domino." SATB.
    BRN ES18.
Lindh, Jody. "Come, Let Us Sing." U, kybd.   CGA-478.

### CHORAL

Berger, Jean. "This Is the Covenant." SATB, opt org.   AFP 11-1677.
Butler, Eugene. "Sing to the Lord a Marvelous Song." SATB,
    pno/org.   HOP A 451.
Jennings, Carolyn. "God's Word Is Our Great Heritage." SATB,
    brass/kybd.   AFP 0800646495.
Purcell, Henry. "O Sing Unto the Lord." SATB, SATB soli, org, opt
    str.   NOV 29 0146 03.
Schein, Johann. "Sing to the Lord." SAB, org.   RME.
Scott, K. Lee. "Sing Aloud to God Our Strength." SATB, org or brass
    qrt.   AFP 0800659716.
Sweelinck, Jan Peiterszoon. "Sing to the Lord, New Songs Be Raising" in *Chantry Choirbook*. SATB.   AFP 0800657772.
Tye, Christopher. "Give Almes of Thy Goods" in *Anthems for Choirs 1*.
    SATB.   OXF.

### CHILDREN'S CHOIRS

Bates, William H. "O Sing to the Lord a New Song." 2 pt, kybd.
    HIN HMC-1737.
Ogasapian, John. "Psalm 96." U, kybd.   AFP 11-4607.

### KEYBOARD/INSTRUMENTAL

Hobby, Robert. "Fanfare and Chorale on 'Abbot's Leigh'" in *Two
    English Hymntune Settings*. Org.   MSM 10-856.
Kallman, Daniel. "Three Hymns for Two Violins and Piano."
    MSM 20-971.
Manz, Paul. "Abbot's Leigh" in *Three Hymn Improvisations*. Org.
    MSM 10-867.
Martinson, Joel. "Miriam's Dance." Org.   CPH 97-6490.
Wold, Wayne. "O God of Earth and Altar" in *Boundless Grace*. Org.
    AMSI OR 26.

### HANDBELL

Afdahl, Lee J. "Abbot's Leigh." 3-5 oct. L2+.   HOP 2103.
Morris, Hart. "Cantad al Señor." 3-5 oct. L3.   CPH 97-6827.
Organ, Anne Krentz. "Earth and All Stars." 3 oct. L2.
    AFP 0800658086.

### PRAISE ENSEMBLE

Baloche, Paul and Gary Sadler. "Rise Up and Praise Him" in *Hosanna
    Music Songbook 13*. SAT[B], kybd.   INT 13576.
Pote, Allen. "Psalm 139." SATB, kybd.   CGA 610.
Spencer, Linda A. "Wings of the Dawn." SATB, kybd.   GS A6183.

## Wednesday, October 23

JAMES OF JERUSALEM, MARTYR

James became an early leader of the church in Jerusalem. He is described in the New Testament as the brother of Jesus, and secular historian Josephus calls James, the brother of Jesus, "the so-called Christ." Little is known about him, but Josephus reported that the Pharisees respected James for his piety and observance of the law. His enemies had him put to death.

Was James a blood brother of the Lord? It is difficult to answer that question because the Aramaic word for brother can also mean cousin. Jesus also said, "Whoever does the will of God is my brother and sister and mother." The commemoration of James and his connection to Jesus as "brother" can spark further discussion about how we all share Christ as our brother through baptism into his death and resurrection.

# October 27, 2002

Reformation Sunday

## Saturday, October 26

PHILIPP NICOLAI, 1608; JOHANN HEERMANN, 1647; PAUL GERHARDT, 1676; HYMNWRITERS

These three outstanding hymnwriters all worked in Germany in the seventeenth century during times of war and plague. When Philipp Nicolai was a pastor in Westphalia, the plague killed thirteen hundred of his parishioners. One hundred seventy people died in one week. His hymns "Wake, awake, for night is flying" (LBW 31) and "O Morning Star, how fair, how bright" (LBW 76) were included in a series of meditations he wrote to comfort his parishioners during the plague. The style of Johann Heermann's hymns moved away from the more objective style of Reformation hymnody toward expressing the emotions of faith. Three of his hymns are in *LBW*, including his plaintive text, "Ah, holy Jesus" (123). Paul Gerhardt lost a preaching position at St. Nicholas's Church in Berlin, because he refused to sign a document stating he would not make theological arguments in his sermons. Some have called him the greatest of Lutheran hymnwriters.

## INTRODUCTION

This day invites the daughters and sons of the Reformation to celebrate the perennial source of reform in the church: the word of God and the sacraments of forgiveness and new life. Indeed, when the church welcomes a new member in baptism or gathers around the table of communion, the Holy Spirit's reforming labor continues among us.

On this day, we acknowledge that our souls are captive to the word of God, that we share the life of Christ with other Christians through baptism, and that we are urged by the Holy Spirit to pray for the ongoing renewal of the church in our day.

## PRAYER OF THE DAY

Almighty God, gracious Lord, pour out your Holy Spirit upon your faithful people. Keep them steadfast in your Word, protect and comfort them in all temptations, defend them against all their enemies, and bestow on the Church your saving peace; through your Son, Jesus Christ our Lord, who lives and reigns with you and the Holy Spirit, one God, now and forever.

## READINGS

Jeremiah 31:31-34

In contrast to Judah's sin, which Jeremiah describes as "engraved on the tablet of their hearts" (17:1), the prophet envisions a future day when the law will be written "on their hearts" (31:33). To know God in this way is to have a direct and profound connection to God. Forgiveness of sins, which is so complete as to be forgotten, is the motivating force for keeping the law.

Psalm 46

The Lord of hosts is with us; the God of Jacob is our stronghold. (Ps. 46:4)

**Romans 3:19-28**

Martin Luther and other leaders of the Reformation believed the heart of the gospel was found in these words of Paul written to the Romans. All people have sinned, but God offers forgiveness of sins through Christ Jesus. We are justified, or put right with God, through faith in Jesus.

**John 8:31-36**

True freedom is not related to ethnic distinctions or social class. Only Jesus can free us from slavery to sin, and he does this through the truth of the gospel.

COLOR Red

THE PRAYERS

Refreshed by the living word of God, let us pray for the church, the world, and all those in need.

*A BRIEF SILENCE.*

Let us pray for the church throughout the world, that our unity in Christ may carry the good news of salvation to people in every place. Lord, in your mercy,

**hear our prayer.**

Let us pray for those who serve in ministries of word, sacrament, and service, and for all who proclaim the gospel, that the word of Jesus Christ may be written on the hearts of all people. Lord, in your mercy,

**hear our prayer.**

Let us pray for good government in those regions of the world torn by conflict, that the justice of God may prevail. Lord, in your mercy,

**hear our prayer.**

Let us pray for those who are assailed by anxiety, guilt, loneliness, poverty, or illness (especially), that they find in you their refuge and strength. Lord, in your mercy,

**hear our prayer.**

Let us pray with the children and youth of our congregation, that they may grow in wisdom from above and discover in Christ the truth that sets us free. Lord, in your mercy,

**hear our prayer.**

Let us pray for the family of faith gathered here, and for our friends and loved ones, that where there is discord, we may receive grace to forgive and be forgiven. Lord, in your mercy,

**hear our prayer.**

*HERE OTHER INTERCESSIONS MAY BE OFFERED.*

We give you thanks for all who have died in the faith, especially Martin Luther and all who have worked for renewal in the church. May their bold witness to the gospel inspire us to walk in grace and to strive for justice. Lord, in your mercy,

**hear our prayer.**

Hear us as we pray, O God, and renew in us the joy of salvation, through Jesus Christ our Lord.

**Amen**

IMAGES FOR PREACHING

In a scene from the movie *Martin Luther: Heretic*, Martin Luther is shown instructing his students. He is a professor at the University of Wittenberg in Germany, and he is teaching the students about the meaning of *repentance*. He shows them the Latin, which means "do penance." This seems to require action on our part. Luther points out, however, that the Greek says "change your mind." Repentance is not our action, he says, but an inward transformation of mind and heart worked by the Holy Spirit.

A student objects. "You mean we don't have to do anything to be a Christian, just believe in our hearts?"

"That's right," says Luther.

"Then we can do whatever we want," presses yet another student.

"Yes," agrees Luther. "But what do you want to do?"

Yes, what do we want to do? The new covenant is tattooed on our hearts, as Jeremiah said it would be. The righteousness of God is established apart from the law, as Paul says. We are declared righteous by God's grace through the redemption that is in Christ Jesus. We continue in Jesus' word by faith and are set free from sin. We have a place in God's household. So, what do we want to do? How shall we live?

A good outline for how we shall live is provided in the rite of Affirmation of Baptism in *Lutheran Book of Worship* (p. 198). We declare our intent to continue in the covenant God made with us in baptism by

- living among God's faithful people,
- hearing God's word and sharing Christ's holy supper,
- proclaiming the good news of God in Christ through word and deed,
- serving all people, following the example of our Lord Jesus, and
- striving for justice and peace in all the earth.

That's what we want to do.

309

## WORSHIP MATTERS

The worship of the assembly on this day ought to be a clear sign that the central reforms of the sixteenth century are carried out in our churches to the present day. The proclamation of the word may be highlighted in several ways. This could be done by processing with the lectionary or Bible and reading the gospel in the midst of the people and then lifting (or even kissing) the book when saying, "The gospel of the Lord." The eucharistic liturgy should be used in its fullness, and hymns should celebrate the real presence of Christ in word and sacrament. The cross should be central to the celebration and, if possible, used in procession. The grounding of our faith in baptism should be emphasized and, again if possible, a font filled with water centrally located. A wide variety of people should be asked to serve as worship leaders to image the priesthood we all share in Christ Jesus.

## LET THE CHILDREN COME

310

Attach red streamers to dowels for children to wave in the procession. Whether there are many children or few, the streamers will add color and movement to this festive day. Have the children "plant" the beribboned dowels in a heavy-based container in front of the ambo and then retrieve them at the beginning of the sending hymn to process out of the church. A few children, instructed in advance, could help with a gospel procession.

## HYMNS FOR WORSHIP

### GATHERING

Rise shine, you people!   LBW 393
Here in this place   WOV 718
We are all one in Christ   TFF 221, LLC 470

### HYMN OF THE DAY

A mighty fortress is our God   LBW 228, 229

### ALTERNATE HYMN OF THE DAY

Oh, praise the gracious power   WOV 750
By grace we have been saved   W&P 25

### COMMUNION

If you but trust in God to guide you   LBW 453
Seek ye first   WOV 783, TFF 149, W&P 122
As the grains of wheat   WOV 705

### SENDING

The Church's one foundation   LBW 369
We all are one in mission   WOV 755

## ADDITIONAL HYMNS AND SONGS

What a mighty word God gives!   W&P 155
I will sing, I will sing   W&P 73
Sun of righteousness, arise   MBW 521
Rise, O church, like Christ arisen   OBS 76

## MUSIC FOR THE DAY

### SERVICE MUSIC

The Chorale Service of Holy Communion (*LBW*, p. 120), with its roots in the Lutheran reformation, is an option for this day. Although the athletic tunes may be challenging for many congregations, make an effort to keep in the repertoire at least one or two of these. Other hymn paraphrases from various churches of the Reformation may keep this from becoming a German fest.

### PSALMODY

A mighty fortress is our God   LBW 228, 229
Bertalot, John. "God Is Our Hope." 2 pt.   CGA-444.
Cherwien, David. "God Is Our Refuge." U, cong, org.   MSM 80-800.
Folkening, John. "Six Psalm Settings with Antiphons."   MSM 80-700.
Hopson, Hal H. "The Lord of Hosts Is with Us." SATB, org, cong, cant.   GIA G-3253.
Wood, Dale.   PW A.
Ziegenhals, Harriet Isle. *Sing Out! A Children's Psalter.*   WLP 7191.

### CHORAL

Berger, Jean. "This Is the Covenant." SATB, opt org.   AFP 11-1677.
Bertalot, John. "Thy Word Is a Lantern." SATB, org, opt brass, timp, perc.   AFP 0800674251 (comp); 080067726X (brass).
Buxtehude, Dietrich. "Lord, Keep Us Steadfast in Thy Word." SATB, 2 vlns, cont.   CPH 97-6331.
Distler, Hugo. "Salvation Unto Us Has Come" in *Chantry Choirbook.* SATB.   AFP 0800657772.
Ferguson, John. "Psalm 46." SATB, org.   AFP 0800656067.
Grieg-Overby. "God's Son Has Made Me Free." SATB, opt kybd.   AFP 0800645561.
Hassler, Hans Leo. "A Mighty Fortress Is Our God" in *Chantry Choirbook.* SATB.   AFP 0800657772.
Hayes, Mark. "Let the Word Go Forth." SATB, org.   AFP 0800674189.
Keesecker, Thomas. "Remember." SATB, kybd, 2 trbl inst, opt cong.   AFP 0800656016.

Pote, Allen. "God Is Our Refuge." SATB, kybd.    HOP A583.

Proulx, Richard. "You, Lord, We Praise." 2 pt mxd, 5 hb.
CPH 98-3448.

Walter, Johann. "Lord, Keep Us Steadfast in Thy Word." SATB.
CPH 98-3509.

Walter, Johann. "I Build on God's Strong Word" in *Chantry Choirbook*.
SATB.    AFP 0800657772.

Weber, Paul. "I Will Sing the Story of Your Love." SATB, kybd, opt
cong.    AFP 0800657004.

CHILDREN'S CHOIRS

Bertalot, John. "God Is Our Hope." 2 pt, kybd.    CG CGA-444.

Cherwien, David M. "God Is Our Refuge and Strength." U, org.
MSM-80-800.

Sleeth, Natalie. "God Is Like a Rock." U.    CG CGA 395.

KEYBOARD/INSTRUMENTAL

Bender, Jan. "Ein feste Burg" in *Augsburg Organ Library: November*. Org.
AFP 0800658965.

Nelhybel, Vaclav. "A Mighty Fortress." Org, brass.    HOP 533.

Peeters, Flor. "Ein feste Burg" in *30 Chorale Preludes op. 69*. Org.
Peters 6024.

Pelz, Walter. *Triptych on "Lord, Keep Us Steadfast."* Org.    MSM 10-808.

Wellman, Samuel. "A Mighty Fortress" in *Keyboard Hymn Favorites*. Pno.
AFP 0800656814.

Wold, Wayne. "O Praise the Gracious Power" in *Child of the Light*. Org.
AFP 0800657993.

HANDBELL

Kinyon, Barbara. "God Ever Glorious." 2-3 oct, opt ch. L3+.
HOP 2094.

McChesney, Kevin. "The Church's One Foundation." 3-5 oct. L2.
AFP 0800658078.

Page, Anna Laura. "A Mighty Fortress Is Our God." 3-5 oct. L2.
AFP 0800658841.

Wiltse, Carl. "A Mighty Fortress." 4-5 oct. L2.    SGM 102.

PRAISE ENSEMBLE

Chapman, Steven C./arr. Tom Fettke. "Be Still and Know."
AG-1073 (SATB, kybd), MU-2442D (choraltrax cass);
MU-5036T (CD); OR-2442 (orch).

Choplin, Pepper. "Family of Faith." SATB, kybd.    LOR 10-1657M.

Luther, Martin/arr. Dennis Allen. "A Mighty Fortress Is Our God."
Allegis AG-1020 (SATB, kybd); MU-23210 (choraltrax); MU-
5010T (CD); OR-2321 (orch).

Noblitt, Kim/arr. Tom Brooks and Jay Rouse. "Be Still My Soul."
INT 14147 (SATB, kybd); 14148 (choraltrax); 14145 (orch).

Pote, Allen. "God Is My Refuge and Strength." SATB, kybd, opt
brass.    HOP A-583.

311

# October 27, 2002

Twenty-third Sunday after Pentecost
Proper 25

INTRODUCTION

In the era of "sound bites" and headline news, Jesus' summary of the entire law and the prophets to just two commandments is no doubt quite appealing. But what commandments they are! Love God with all your heart, soul, and mind. And love your neighbor as yourself. These are easy commandments to speak, but they will take more than a lifetime for any of us to be able to put into practice. So we have gathered here this day to deepen our desire and our commitment to love God and to love our fellow human beings. May the words we hear and our communion in the body of Christ strengthen us to do those very things.

PRAYER OF THE DAY

Almighty and everlasting God, increase in us the gifts of faith, hope, and charity; and, that we may obtain what you promise, make us love what you command; through your Son, Jesus Christ our Lord.

READINGS

Leviticus 19:1-2, 15-18

God's people exercise justice and love in their dealings with one another.

Psalm 1

Their delight is in the law of the Lord. (Ps. 1:2)

1 Thessalonians 2:1-8

The apostle Paul demonstrates how he had ministered gently and tenderly among the Thessalonians. He not only shared the gospel, but gave of his very self.

Matthew 22:34-46

Jesus displays his great wisdom among the Pharisees by summing up the entirety of the Hebrew scriptures in just two commandments. He furthermore confounds the Pharisees by demonstrating that the Messiah is far more than simply the son of David.

## SEMICONTINUOUS FIRST READING/PSALM

Deuteronomy 34:1-12

Israel regarded Moses as its greatest prophet. The people saw him perform many wonders, and he led them out of slavery in Egypt and gave them God's law from Mount Sinai. Though he may not enter the promised land, Moses is shown by the Lord a vision of that land.

Psalm 90:1-6, 13-17

Show your servants your works, and your splendor to their children. (Ps. 90:16)

COLOR Green

## THE PRAYERS

Refreshed by the living word of God, let us pray for the church, the world, and all those in need.

*A BRIEF SILENCE.*

Let us pray for the baptized people of God, that the praise of our hearts, souls, and minds may deepen with each passing day. Lord, in your mercy,

**hear our prayer.**

Let us pray for towns, cities, and people of every community, that justice may be established there and your church lift high the saving name of Christ. Lord, in your mercy,

**hear our prayer.**

Let us pray for all social service and helping agencies, that their work may be strengthened by your steadfast love. Lord, in your mercy,

**hear our prayer.**

Let us pray for those who struggle with addiction, grief, or despair, and for all living with illness (especially), that we may embrace them with your love and care. Lord, in your mercy,

**hear our prayer.**

Let us pray for this community, that our outreach to neighbors may be an extension of your gracious love for the whole human family. Lord, in your mercy,

**hear our prayer.**

*HERE OTHER INTERCESSIONS MAY BE OFFERED.*

For all the saints, who loved you in life and death, we give you thanks and pray that we may model for others the way of Jesus Christ. Lord, in your mercy,

**hear our prayer.**

Hear us as we pray, O God, and renew in us the joy of salvation, through Jesus Christ our Lord.

**Amen**

## IMAGES FOR PREACHING

Among the principles J.R. Averill proposes in his monograph "The Rules of Hope" is an action rule: People are inclined to act on behalf of their hopes. In an adult study group one person responded to this rule by paraphrasing James 2:17: "Does that mean hope without works is dead?" Another said, "It means hope without works is wishful thinking."

We hope for the redemptive reign of God. When that reign is brought to fulfillment, we will love the Lord our God with all our heart, soul, and mind. We will also love our neighbor as ourselves.

The reign of God for which we hope will look like the life of Christ and all that happened in his wake—the blind see, the lame walk, the deaf hear, and those imprisoned are set free. Forgiveness is the ethic and mercy the ethos of Christ's kingly rule. Death and devil yield to Christ.

This is our hope. It is not wishful thinking. Our hope is tied to Jesus' works. When Jesus turned the tables on the questioning Pharisees, he made it quite clear that he is the one upon whom our hope depends. Our hope depends on God's work to place everything under his feet. More precisely, our hope depends on God's cross work.

Our hope in Christ is tied to the work we do in his name. We do not bring about the kingdom. Our works, however, are a prolepsis of the kingdom. We give witness to and lean into the kingdom of God by acting on behalf of our hope. With every splash of baptismal water, we celebrate the extension of God's jurisdiction and the part we have to play in it.

## WORSHIP MATTERS

The rite of Farewell and Godspeed (*Occasional Services*, p. 151) is an opportunity to give thanks for the presence and ministry of an individual or family within the life of the congregation. It is often used as people move to a new town and join another Christian community. It may also be used for students leaving to attend a school away from home, members entering the military, or those leaving for long periods to travel or live elsewhere for a season. The use of such a service is important not only for those who leave, but also for those who remain, that all might know both those who leave and those who remain will continue to be united in one body and kept in prayer.

## LET THE CHILDREN COME

At the beginning of the liturgy, a small ensemble of children or a children's choir can sing one of the Kyrie settings in *With One Voice*. Have the assembly simply repeat each petition after the children sing it. Make sure that the ensemble or the choir is well-rehearsed and, before the liturgy begins, placed so that they can be heard. If the children will sing only this litany, let them return to their seats after the prayer of the day and before the first reading is proclaimed.

## HYMNS FOR WORSHIP

### GATHERING

Joyful, joyful we adore thee   LBW 551
O God beyond all praising   WOV 797

### HYMN OF THE DAY

Great God, your love has called us   WOV 666

### ALTERNATE HYMN OF THE DAY

Come, my way, my truth, my life   LBW 513
Jesu, Jesu, fill us with our love   WOV 765, TFF 83

### COMMUNION

For the bread which you have broken   LBW 200
Lord, thee I love with all my heart   LBW 325
Draw us in the Spirit's tether   WOV 703

### SENDING

Love divine, all loves excelling   LBW 315
My Lord of light   WOV 796

## ADDITIONAL HYMNS AND SONGS

O God of love, enable me   BH 580
Come, let us join with faithful souls   NCH 383
By your streams of living waters   NSR 61
Around the Great Commandment   DH 93
Beloved, God's chosen   OBS 48

## MUSIC FOR THE DAY

### PSALMODY

Cooney, Rory. "Psalm 1: Roots in the Earth." U, cong, gtr, kybd. GIA G-3969.

Haas, David.   PCY, vol. 3.

How blest are they who, fearing God   TWC 342

Howard, Julie. *Sing for Joy: Psalm Settings for God's Children.* LTP.

Organ, Anne Krentz.   PW A.

Schoenbachler, Tim. "Happy Are They."   STP, vol. 2.

### CHORAL

Bach, J.S. "Lord, Thee I Love with All My Heart" in *Bach for All Seasons.* SATB, kybd.

Busarow, Donald. "Lord, Thee I Love with All My Heart." SATB or 2 pt mxd, opt cong, ob/tpt, org.   CPH 98-3429.

Byrd, William. "Lord, Make Me to Know Thy Ways." SATB, opt org. CPH 98-2935.

Christiansen, F.M. "My God, How Wonderful Thou Art." SATB. AFP 6000106106.

Hassell, Michael. "Beloved, God's Chosen." SATB, kybd. AFP 0800659139.

Shute, Linda Cable. "If You Can Walk." SAB, org.   AFP 0800659619.

Stanford, C.V. "O For a Closer Walk with God." SATB, org. Collegium.

Vaughan Williams, Ralph. "The Call" in *Five Mystical Songs.* B solo, kybd.   GAL 1.5038.

### CHILDREN'S CHOIRS

Eggert, John, arr. "Is There Anybody Here." U, kybd.   0800651995.
Hruby, Dolores, arr. "Help Us Accept Each Other." U, kybd, fl, gtr. CG CGA-713.

### KEYBOARD/INSTRUMENTAL

Callahan, Charles. *Partita on "Duke Street."* Org.   CPH 97-5998.
Manz, Paul. "Praise, My Soul, the King of Heaven" in *2 Pieces for Festive Occasions.* Org.   MSM 10-840.
Sedio, Mark. "Chereponi" in *Dancing in the Light of God.* Pno. AFP 0800656547.
Sedio, Mark. "Ryburn" in *Organ Tapestries*, vol. 1. Org.   CPH 97-6812.

313

## HANDBELL

Helman, Michael. "Jesu, Jesu, Fill Us with Your Love." 3-5 oct.
AFP 0800658876.

Stephenson, Valerie W. "Passacaglia No. 1 in C." 3-5 oct. L2.
CPH 97-6832.

Wagner, Douglas E. "Joyful, Joyful, We Adore Thee." 3 oct. L3.
LOR HB 302.

## PRAISE ENSEMBLE

DeShazo, Lynn and Gary Sadler. "Mercy" in *Only God for Me Songbook.*
SAT[B], kybd.  INT 15297.

Espinosa, Eddie. "Change My Heart, O God." SATB, kybd.
MAR 301 0813 163.

Fragar, Russell. "Love You So Much" in *Shout to the Lord 2000 Songbook.*
SAT[B], kybd.  INT 14247.

Martin, Joseph M. "Trust in the Lord." SATB, kybd.  GS A 7378.

314

# Monday, October 28

## ST. SIMON AND ST. JUDE, APOSTLES

We know little about Simon and Jude. In New Testament lists of the apostles, Simon the "zealot" or Cananean is mentioned, but he is never mentioned apart from these lists. Jude, sometimes called Thaddeus, is also mentioned in lists of the twelve. At the last supper Jude asked Jesus why he had chosen to reveal himself to the disciples but not to the world. A traditional story about Simon and Jude says that they traveled together on a missionary journey to Persia and were both martyred there.

The prayer of the day for this lesser festival asks that as Simon and Jude "were faithful and zealous in their mission, so we may with ardent devotion make known the love and mercy of our Lord and Savior Jesus Christ."

# Thursday, October 31

## REFORMATION DAY

*See Reformation Sunday, October 27, 2002.*

# NOVEMBER

*Peace at the last*

# Images *of the* Season

November is a deeply evocative time of the year.

Beginning with All Saints Day and continuing through the festival of

Christ the King, we are led into a contemplation of last things.

That reflection encompasses remembrances of past loved ones and our own inevitable death as well as the end of all things when the entire cosmos is reconciled through Christ to its creator. This season, with its religious and cultural observances relating to death and (in the Northern Hemisphere) its ever-shortening days, has the power to bring such thoughts of death to the fore.

It is a blessing, then, that in the church we have a framework for such musings, one that guides us in helpful ways past mere morbid sentiment to a more hopeful anticipation. Yes, there is melancholy in recalling the great spirits who have died and who are dearly missed. And many of us have a sense that our own lives are moving much too quickly toward their end. But we who follow Christ also possess the assurance that all of our lives are in the Lord's keeping. This does not remove the desire to contemplate last things, but rather puts them in perspective.

One of the collects for Prayer at the Close of the Day deals with just this sort of meditation:

> O Lord, support us all the day long of this troubled life, until the shadows lengthen and the evening comes and the busy world is hushed, the fever of life is over, and our work is done. Then, Lord, in your mercy, grant us a safe lodging, and a holy rest, and peace at the last; through Jesus Christ our Lord. (*LBW*, p. 158)

Peace at the last—that is the reason for focusing on death and its attendant issues during this month. Yes, we could ignore the near certainty of death. ("Near" only because there is always the chance that our Lord will return before then!) We could simply barge full steam ahead with life until death forces us to stop. But what such an approach lacks is purpose and completion. We are not to live aimlessly but with direction—from God and toward God. Our learning, our work, our relationships—all of these potentially point beyond themselves and even beyond ourselves to the one by whose grace they are accomplished, God our creator and redeemer.

That means that they have meaning beyond their significance for our transitory earthly life. These accomplishments, meager though they may seem, are celebrated around the heavenly banquet table.

Yet what about those things that often seem to outweigh our accomplishments—our shortcomings, faults, sins? Many people, nearing the end of their life, are haunted by thoughts of the wrongs they have committed. More than anything else, those thoughts rob them of longed-for peace. Even if they recognize that salvation comes only through the grace of God in Christ Jesus, still the regrets linger. Such is the insinuating power of sin.

In some societies, the notion that ghosts haunt the living is, in part, a way of acknowledging how sin can block the path to peace at the last. It is important to bring the haunting of guilt and sin into the light, for in our modern society, we can easily delude ourselves into believing that we are too sophisticated to worry about sin and other spiritual intangibles. Once the truth of sin is acknowledged, however, the door is opened to the light of Christ shining from that safe lodging spoken of in the prayer. His life and death gained the victory over all the forces that torment us. Our sins are taken up with him on the cross and there put to death. Sin's power to condemn us, to haunt us, is ended. Now we who have been baptized into Christ's death are freed of all chains and are lifted up with him into the new resurrection life. "Peace at the last" is, indeed, attainable through our Savior.

So we, in the presence of all the departed faithful, move beyond mere remembrance. There is that, but there is also thanksgiving, and supplication, and mission. And at the end, as our Lord reigns, so shall we. The feast of which we now have merely taste, the banquet of companionship, gladness, and participation in the fullness of God's presence, that banquet will envelop us completely, and we will be home.

316

# Environment *and* Art *for the* Season

Five-year-old Rebecca loved her great-grandmother

and treasured her family's visit each summer to Great-grandma's

house, a thousand miles away from Rebecca's home.

But this summer, the summer of Great-grandma's nineti-eth birthday, Rebecca told her parents she did not want to return home with them. "I need to stay here with Great-grandma," she said, as tears fell from her big, dark eyes. "If she dies in the winter, I'll never see her again."

The child knew intuitively that winter signals death. To bridge the separation of death and mollify grief, the little girl would need to stay close to her great-grand-mother. In November, the church attends to the very human feelings surrounding death and helps us to re-member that those who have died remain with us in the community of saints.

Although November is still within the North Amer-ican season of autumn, in its northern starkness, it has a feel all its own. The same trees that arrested us with the painted glory of their leaves now appear forlorn or naked, shorn of their majesty. Statistics tell us that more people in the Northern Hemisphere die at this time of year than at any other. The stark natural world reminds us that there is a time for everything, including death. As the growing season ends and we begin to store for win-ter, our thoughts turn to our loved ones who have died. We become aware of our own mortality and the fulfill-ment of all things in Christ.

The festival of All Saints sets the tone for this month. With few, if any, modifications, the environment for All Saints will be appropriate throughout November, including Christ the King and Thanksgiving.

An important, beloved custom is the display of the church's book of the dead. The book can be displayed on All Saints Sunday and throughout the month of No-vember. Issues surrounding the display of this book are often analogous to those related to the Advent wreath. Neither is required in liturgy, and yet members may ex-pect both to be present in the worship space.

How will the book be used? If people are invited to write in their own hand the names of the dead, then they will need sufficient space to gather around the book, ad-equate lighting, and a place to keep pens. If the font is moveable, consider placing the book on a stand near the font (and paschal candle) in the gathering space or an area where people can linger. Some parishes ask a skilled calligrapher to enter names each year, so that the book has a formal elegance. While this removes the need for keeping pens nearby, the book will still need to be in a well-lit area, with sufficient space for people to stand as they look through its pages.

Another option is to create a space away from the font and the central actions of the liturgy for display of the book and photos of the dead. This can be done somewhat informally, in the tradition of a Mexican Day of the Dead altar. Parishioners can be invited to bring photos and other memorabilia to the church. These can be displayed on a table featuring the book of the dead as the focal point, perhaps using a distinctive white or em-broidered fabric as a backdrop for the book. (A good image for embroidery is one or two deer drinking from the river of living water that flows from the cross.) Flow-ers and votive candles can be arranged to create a beauti-ful setting for the memorial to the dead. Although some-one would need to maintain the table, people could freely add to it throughout the month.

A more formal display of the book of the dead sur-rounded by carefully arranged photos might be appropri-ate by the font, but such an arrangement would not lend itself to spontaneous changes and additions by parish-ioners. If the book and photos are placed near the font, the paschal candle, rather than smaller votive candles, would be the focal point.

Is the church's book of the dead beautiful? The art of bookmaking is being revived in Western culture. Many graphic and fine artists study bookmaking as part of their education. Artists skilled in bookmaking can produce stunning works that would add meaning to the display of names. If the church prefers to purchase a book, make sure it is handsome and of fine quality. The

317

paper used for recording the names should be acid-free, so that the pages will not yellow.

In the white imagery of All Saints we see the tablecloth of the heavenly banquet, the baptismal robes of those in the New Jerusalem, the celestial cloud of the witnesses who have gone before us. This is rich, profound imagery for a time in the church year that looks out on a darkening and bare natural world. This environment, combined with unresolved grief over death and loss, leaves many people vulnerable during this time of year. This vulnerability is intensified by our cultural awareness of Thanksgiving as the threshold of the holiday season. The holiday expectations of good cheer and warm relations may trigger deep feelings of abandonment and isolation. The church has an opportunity in November to create an environment in which people can acknowledge and explore the dimensions of loss, both individually and as part of a larger community of the living and the dead.

What can be done to engage people during this time as members of a community that includes a cloud of faithful witnesses? Artist Nancy Chinn, in her book *Spaces for Spirit: Adorning the Church* (Chicago: LTP, 1998), tells of an experience working with St. Mark's Episcopal Cathedral in Minneapolis. Although Chinn's project was not planned around the festival of All Saints, the process and outcome are a good model for an art installation in November. Chinn gave participating parishioners each a strip of sheer cloth. The people were asked to reflect on a particular relationship in their lives. After praying about this relationship, each person was invited to use the cloth to make an artifact of prayer. The people used writing instruments, paint, or thread to individualize the prayer cloths. Chinn then wove the cloth pieces into a huge canopy that hung over the assembly in the worship space. Imagine how powerful such a cloud of prayer over the people might be for All Saints Day. It is also appropriate to the environment of Christ the King and Thanksgiving. The image even presages Christ's coming in a cloud in Advent.

The gospel readings in November offer rich images that might be worked with during this month. Whether the church celebrates All Saints Sunday with a gospel proclamation of the beatitudes or chooses the green Sunday reading for proper 26, the theme of humility is central. An environment that is gracious and hospitable,

not fussy or overdone, communicates this theme. The following Sunday we hear the story of the wise and foolish bridesmaids. The use of votive candles, in remembrance of the dead and in vigilant anticipation of our fulfillment among them, might be effective. The parable of the talents on the following Sunday suggests we explore the ways in which we are stewards of our gifts and resources. Again, the environment reveals the values of the church community. What does the church wish to communicate about its values and identity? Consider this question throughout the year as the worship environment is planned.

The gospel for Christ the King in Matthew tells of the final judgment, of Christ separating the sheep from the goats. We hear Christ declare that he is present in the "least of these"—the hungry, the thirsty, the naked, and the stranger. This year Christ the King falls on the Sunday before Thanksgiving. The church has an opportunity to emphasize social outreach to the needy as an integral part of its celebration of thanksgiving. A station for year-round collection of food might be set apart. Use attractive baskets or bins and create a dignified atmosphere, adding flowers, greens, or harvest fruits to relate this area, most likely in the narthex, to the larger church environment.

Resist the temptation to create a distinctive church environment for Thanksgiving. If the environment created for All Saints and lasting through Christ the King is visually effective, harvest and thanksgiving themes can be given attention within this context throughout the month.

The New Jerusalem is a profound and appropriate image for the month of November. One way to evoke an image of the church as the New Jerusalem is to create an arch above the main doorway from the outside. The color of the fabric is less important than its ability to withstand the weather and to maintain its shape. The arch should communicate a sense of triumph without being in any way exclusive or inhospitable. A deep forest green awning or bunting accented with white and gold might be handsome. Grapevine wreaths can hang on every door. Although flowers no longer fare well outdoors in many November climates, chrysanthemums in pots or arranged with fruits of the harvest will be a welcoming sight for visitors stepping inside the church.

# Preaching *with the* Season

Richard Bernstein begins a recent *New York Times*

book review of Andre Aciman's memoir *False Papers* by saying,

"Someone once said that nostalgia was the most beautiful

word in any language. Like the cruelest month, it mixes memory and desire."

The reference to the cruelest month is from T.S. Eliot's poem *The Wasteland.* Eliot names April as the cruelest. Asked to name the cruelest month, those living in the north might be expected to name February. In the tropical south August is cruelest for its unrelenting heat. Not so according to the poet. April is cruel because it causes us to remember what was and what we so desired. We cannot have it. It is history. It is cruel because we look at springtime and everything else is coming to life and we are not.

April may be the cruelest month but November is awash in nostalgia. Could the remnant of memory for All Hallows' Eve contribute to the nostalgia? Is a longing for the blessed dead so woven into the fabric of our lives that no amount of commercialism or cultural forgetfulness can completely erase it?

The role of nostalgia at Thanksgiving is more easily recognizable than on All Hallows' Eve. It has been pointed out that Thanksgiving is the one day of the year when the vast majority of Americans sit down to the same menu. Memories of Thanksgivings past dominate us. From our memories we conjure an ideal for the Thanksgiving Day looming before us. It is an ideal that perhaps never was and is seldom achieved. Even if we achieve the perfect Thanksgiving, it is all too quickly over. And long before Thanksgiving we are inundated with the build-up to the next letdown, the perfect Christmas.

Perhaps nostalgia is inevitable, given nature's cycle. In November much of North America sees the last of the leaves turning their brilliant colors and falling to the ground. People from the South plan trips north for the fall foliage. Rites of passage from this season, football games and homecomings, have great emotive power over us, much more so than those from other seasons. November has a strong presence and odor. But isn't the scent of November, after all, the smell of decay and the presence of death?

Bernstein says Aciman's memoir gives the questions about what we remember and desire "deep, lyrical and melancholy reflection, melancholy because nostalgia in this rumination is connected to the quest to make sense out of a life, even though 'we know there is no sense to be made.'" Such is one strand of modern "wisdom": there is no sense to be made out of our lives.

Nostalgia is melancholy not only in Aciman's rumination. By definition nostalgia is the confluence of memory and desire. The melancholic power of nostalgia is its memory and desire for what we cannot again have or be. What sense could one possibly find for one's life in this endeavor? No other conclusion is possible.

This is the temptation of our time, to believe there is no sense to be made of our lives. It is a sign of our time, the self-pitying, self-indulgent age in which we live. It is the essence of idolatry that a person would look to his or her own life to find meaning. That makes each of us god of a very small, fragile, and short-lived universe, even if we live five score years.

November may be awash in nostalgia, yearning for what was. The end of the long Pentecost season, however, is filled with yearning for what will be. The scripture readings and themes for these Sundays also mix memory and desire, yet they do not engender nostalgia. They rather lead us to the future. A survey of the prayers of the day for these Sundays bears witness. On All Saints we pray, "Grant us grace to follow [into the future] your blessed saints in lives of faith…"; proper 26, "Stir up, O Lord, the wills of your faithful people to seek…"; proper 27, "Lord, when the day of wrath comes …Make us so to watch…"; proper 28, "that, always keeping in mind the end…we may be stirred up to holiness of life here and may live with you forever…"; Thanksgiving, "your generous goodness comes to us new every day"; Christ the King, "God, whose will it is to restore all things…Grant that all…may be united under the glorious and gentle rule of your Son.…"

How can one mixture of memory and desire yield a backward-looking melancholy and another mixture of memory and desire cause us to yearn for what will be? In the first mixture, the assumption is there is no sense to be made of life. In the second, godly mixture of memory and desire, the fact that life makes sense is assumed.

How can these two mixtures of memory and desire yield such different results? It is a matter of who is god in each endeavor. In the former a person looks inwardly for meaning and can come up with nothing that transcends the grave. In the latter endeavor all eyes are on God.

# Shape *of* Worship *for the* Season

## BASIC SHAPE OF THE EUCHARISTIC RITE

- Confession and Forgiveness: see alternate worship text for November in *Sundays and Seasons*

### GATHERING

- Greeting: see alternate worship text for November
- Omit the Kyrie during November (except on the festivals of All Saints and Christ the King)
- Use the hymn of praise throughout November (or use "This is the feast of victory" just for the festivals of All Saints and Christ the King)

### WORD

- Use the Nicene Creed for the festivals of All Saints and Christ the King, use the Apostles' Creed for the remainder of the month
- The prayers: see the prayers in the November section of *Sundays and Seasons*
- Incorporate the names of those who have died into one of the prayer petitions on All Saints Sunday

### BAPTISM

- Consider observing All Saints Sunday (November 3) as a baptismal festival

### MEAL

- Offertory prayer: see alternate worship text for November
- Use the proper preface for Sundays after Pentecost; for the festival of All Saints, use the proper preface for All Saints; *WOV* Leaders Edition provides a proper preface for Christ the King
- Eucharistic prayer: in addition to four main options in *LBW*, see "Eucharistic Prayer I: November" in *WOV* Leaders edition, p. 73
- Invitation to communion: see alternate worship text for November
- Post-communion prayer: see alternate worship text for November

### SENDING

- Benediction: see alternate worship text for November
- Dismissal: see alternate worship text for November

# Assembly Song *for the* Season

As the church year comes to a conclusion, it is

helpful to think of this yearly pilgrimage as a journey around a

continuous circle. November is a time of paradoxical themes.

We remember our loved ones who have died and at the same time anticipate the resurrection. The earthly harvest intersects with the themes of God's harvest at the end of time. The music of the season sings the songs of faith that sustain us on this journey through a time when God's reign is here but not yet. We look forward to the end days with uncertain eagerness. We await the second coming of Jesus Christ—a journey continued and begun again in Advent.

## GATHERING

Use both the Kyrie and "This is the feast" on All Saints Day and Christ the King. Sing only "This is the feast" on the Sundays in between. On All Saints Day, "A Litany of the Saints" from *Welcome to Christ: Lutheran Rites for the Catechumenate* could replace the entrance hymn and Kyrie. A slow procession into the church, perhaps beginning at the font or the church cemetery, could accompany the litany.

## WORD

Alleluias should again resound to remind us of the hope of salvation through the resurrection of Jesus Christ. If in the previous Easter season you used gospel acclamations based on alleluias from an Easter hymn, use them again in November. If not, see the Easter Assembly Song for the Season for ideas on how to compose this type of acclamation. Congregational responses to the prayers of the people may be sung. Prayer petitions ending in phrases such as "Let us pray to the Lord" or "We pray" could be followed by "O Lord, hear our prayer (W&P 108) or "O Lord, hear my prayer" (WOV 772).

## MEAL

Use "As the grains of wheat" (WOV 705) or "Shall we gather at the river" (TFF 179, WOV 690) as an alternate to "Let the vineyards be fruitful." "Holy, holy, holy Lord" (WOV 616a) and "Acclamations and Amen" (WOV 616b) are based on the tune LAND OF REST, "Jerusalem, my happy home" (LBW 331). Sing both of these on All Saints Day and continue singing WOV 616a and b through Christ the King. During the distribution on All Saints Day, consider remembering with thanksgiving the names of the faithful departed. Invite people to write the names of loved ones who have died on a list prior to the service. Divide the list into four equal parts. Following the refrain and before stanzas 2–5 of "Blest are they" (WOV 764), read the names aloud. The pianist may improvise lightly while the names are read. This act serves as a reminder of our communion with all God's saints—past, present and future—and can be a source of healing for those mourning recent losses.

## SENDING

On the remaining Sundays in November, sing the refrain of "Blest are they" (WOV 764) several times while the table is cleared as a reminder of our communion with all the saints. "Thine the amen, thine the praise" (WOV 801) or "Soon and very soon" (WOV 744, TFF 38, W&P 128) could serve as sending hymns for the season.

# Music *for the* Season

## VERSE AND OFFERTORY

Hobby, Robert. "Offertory for All Saints Day." 2 pt mxd.
MSM 80-811.

Hobby, Robert. "Verse for All Saints Day." 2 pt mxd.  MSM 80-810.

*See also Music for the Season for Autumn.*

## CHORAL

Bach, J.S. "Now Thank We All Our God" in *Bach for All Seasons.*
SATB, kybd.

Berger, Jean. "The Eyes of All Wait Upon Thee." SATB.
AFP 0800645596. Also in *The Augsburg Choirbook*
AFP 0800656784.

Brahms, Johannes. "How Lovely Is Thy Dwellingplace" in *Chantry
Choirbook.* SATB, org.  AFP 0800657772.

Campbell, Sidney. "Sing We Merrily Unto God Our Strength."
SATB, org.  NOV 29 0253.

Carter, John. "Shall We Gather at the River." SATB, kybd.
BEC BP1119.

Forsberg, Charles. "Fairest Lord Jesus." SATB, pno.
AFP 0800656962.

Handel, G.F. "But Who May Abide the Day of His Coming?" in
*Messiah.* A or B solo, kybd.  Various ed.

Handel, G.F. "The Trumpet Shall Sound" in *Messiah.* B solo, kybd,
opt tpt.  Various ed.

Hobby, Robert A. "Lord, Let Us Listen." 2 pt trbl, pno.
AFP 0800659236.

Johnson, Ralph M. "Be Thou a Smooth Way." SATB, pno.
AFP 0800659325.

Kosche, Kenneth T. "Bring Us, O Lord God." SATB.
MSM-50-8103.

Lovelace, Austin C. "How Lovely Is Thy Dwelling Place." SATB, org.
AFP 0800650948.

Manz, Paul. "E'en So, Lord Jesus, Quickly Come." SATB.
MSM 50-900.

Martinson, Joel. "By All Your Saints." 2 pt, mxd, org.
AFP 080065160X.

Schalk, Carl. "O Lord, Thou Hast Been Our Dwelling Place." SATB.
AFP 0800650441.

Shute, Linda Cable. "Who Are These Like Stars Appearing." SATB,
org.  AFP 0800658507.

## CHILDREN'S CHOIRS

Jothen, Michael. "I Will Give Thanks." U, kybd, fl.  BEC BP1101.

Leaf, Robert. "To the Glory of Our King." U, kybd.  CG CGA-173.

Powell, Robert J. "We Give Thee Thanks Today." 2 pt, kybd.
AFP 6000102666.

## KEYBOARD/INSTRUMENTAL

*Augsburg Organ Library: November.* Org.  AFP 0800658965.

Oldroyd, George. *Three Liturgical Improvisations.* Org.
OXF OUP 31-261.

Peeters, Flor. *Aria.* Org.  PRE EH 265.

Wellman, Samuel. *Keyboard Hymn Favorites.* Pno.  AFP 0800656814.

West, John. "Fanfare on Sine Nomine." Org.  AFP 0800659473.

Wold, Wayne L. *A November to Remember.* Org.  AFP 080065983X.

## HANDBELL

Behnke, John A. "The Promise" (Jeremiah 29:11). 3-5 oct. L3.
AG 2133.

Edwards, Dan R. "Let Us Break Bread Together." 3 oct. (w/fl). L2.
CG CGB227.

McChesney, Kevin. "Ring Together Church Year." 2-3 oct. L1+.
JEF JHS 9241.

McFadden, Jane. "In Heaven Above." 3-5 oct.  AFP 0800659929.

Simpson, Thomas F. "A Trumpet Chorale" (J.S. Bach). 2-3 oct. L2.
AG 2137.

Tucker, Margaret R. "Beach Spring." 4 oct. L3.  BEC HB48.

## PRAISE ENSEMBLE

Joncas, Michael and Mark Hayes. "On Eagle's Wings." SATB, orch.
ALF 16104.

Mollicone, Henry. "Hear Me, Redeemer." SATB, solo, and pno.
ECS.

# Alternate Worship Texts

## CONFESSION AND FORGIVENESS

Before God, our rock and our refuge,
let us keep silence, confessing our sin.

*Silence for reflection and self-examination.*

Most merciful God,
you know our failings better than we do;
our sins are revealed in the light of your face.
Our days and years pass by;
the things we trust fade like grass.
Be gracious to us, O God.
Guide us again to the water of life,
and renew in us the grace of baptism;
through Jesus Christ, our Lord. Amen

You are all children of the light and of the day;
you are God's children now.
In the mercy of God,
Jesus Christ was given to die for you,
and for his sake,
God forgives you all your sin.
With all the faithful in heaven and on earth,
rejoice and be glad!
**Amen**

## GREETING

May the hope to which God has called you,
the power of God at work in Christ,
and the wisdom of the Holy Spirit
be with you all.
**And also with you.**

## OFFERTORY PRAYER

God of every generation,
we offer you our songs
of praise and thanksgiving;
we bring you these tokens
of our talents and our lives.
Help us to use our gifts
so that justice rolls down like waters,
and righteousness like an ever-flowing stream. Amen

## INVITATION TO COMMUNION

Saints of God,
taste and see that the Lord is good.

## POST-COMMUNION PRAYER

Shepherd of Israel,
you have gathered us and fed us richly
with the bread of life and cup of blessing.
Turn our hearts to all who hunger and thirst
for food and for justice,
that in them we may see Christ,
who lives and reigns with you and Holy Spirit,
one God, forever and ever.
**Amen**

## BLESSING

God's blessing be with you,
Christ's peace be with you,
the Spirit's outpouring be with you,
now and always.
**Amen**

## DISMISSAL

Surrounded by God's people of every time and place,
go in peace to love and serve the Lord.
**Thanks be to God.**

323

# Seasonal Rites

## Vigil of All Saints

*This order of worship may be used on All Hallows Eve, October 31, or the evening before All Saints Sunday.*

### SERVICE OF LIGHT
#### PROCESSION

*All stand as the lighted paschal candle is carried in procession to its stand in front of the assembly. The people may light hand-held candles from its flame.*

In the new Jerusalem there will be no need of | sun or moon,
**for the glory of God will be its | light.**
Before the Lamb is a multitude from | every nation,
**and they worship God night and | day.**
Surely he is | coming soon.
**Amen. Come, Lord | Jesus.**

### HYMN OF LIGHT

*As this hymn is sung, the candles on and near the altar are lighted from the flame of the paschal candle.*

Joyous light of glory:
**of the immortal Father;**
**heavenly, holy, blessed Jesus Christ.**
**We have come to the setting of the sun,**
**and we look to the evening light.**
**We sing to God, the Father, Son, and Holy Spirit:**
**You are worthy of being praised**
**with pure voices forever.**
**O Son of God, O Giver of light:**
**The universe proclaims your glory.**

### THANKSGIVING FOR LIGHT

The Lord be with you.
**And also with you.**
Let us give thanks to the Lord our God.
**It is right to give our thanks and praise.**
Blessed are you, O Lord our God, king of the universe,
who led your people Israel by a pillar of cloud by day
and a pillar of fire by night:
Enlighten our darkness by the light of your Christ;
may his Word be a lamp to our feet and a light to our path;
for you are merciful, and you love your whole creation,
and we, your creatures, glorify you, Father, Son, and Holy Spirit.
**Amen**

### LITURGY OF THE WORD

#### FIRST READING
Genesis 12:1-8
Psalm 113

#### SECOND READING
Daniel 6:[1-15] 16-23
Psalm 116

#### THIRD READING
Hebrews 11:32—12:2
Psalm 149

#### FOURTH READING
Revelation 7:2-4, 9-17

#### CANTICLE
This is the feast of victory

#### GOSPEL
Matthew 5:1-12

#### SERMON

#### HYMN OF THE DAY

### THANKSGIVING FOR BAPTISM

*If possible, the people may gather around the font. After the prayer each person may dip a hand in the water and make the sign of the cross in remembrance of baptism.*

The Lord be with you.
**And also with you.**
Let us give thanks to the Lord our God.
**It is right to give our thanks and praise.**
Holy God and mighty Lord, we give you thanks,
for you nourish and sustain us and all living things
with the gift of water.
In the beginning your Spirit moved over the waters,
and you created heaven and earth.
By the waters of the flood you saved Noah and his family.
You led Israel through the sea out of slavery
into the promised land.
In the waters of the Jordan
your Son was baptized by John and anointed with the Spirit.

By the baptism of his death and resurrection
your Son set us free from sin and death
and opened the way to everlasting life.
We give you thanks, O God,
that you have given us new life in the water of baptism.
Buried with Christ in his death,
you raise us to share in his resurrection
by the power of the Holy Spirit.
Through it we are united to your saints
of every time and place
who proclaim your reign
and surround our steps as we journey
toward the new and eternal Jerusalem.
May all who have passed through the waters of baptism
continue in the risen life of our Savior.
To you be all honor and glory, now and forever.
**Amen**

## LITURGY OF THE EUCHARIST

*After all have returned to their places, the liturgy continues with
the preparation of the altar and the presentation of the gifts.*

## NOTES ON THE SERVICE:

*- The opening verses in the procession of the paschal candle
may be sung using the musical setting found in LBW, p. 142.*
*- The hymn of light is found in LBW, p. 143. An alternate hymn
is "O Light whose splendor thrills" (WOV 728).*
*- The thanksgiving for light (LBW, p. 144) may be sung or spoken
by the leader.*
*- The psalm responses to the readings may be sung or spoken
by the assembly.*
*- The canticle is sung using one of the available musical settings
of this text.*
*- For the hymn of the day, one of the following hymns is sug-
gested: "Sing with all the saints in glory" (WOV 691) or "Who is
this host arrayed in white" (LBW 314).*
*- If the people cannot gather at the font, the worship leaders
may process there during the singing of the hymn of the day.*

325

## Friday, November 1
### ALL SAINTS DAY

The custom of commemorating all of the saints of the church on a single day goes back at least to the third century. Our All Saints Day celebrates the baptized people of God, living and dead, who make up the body of Christ. Today, or on this upcoming All Saints Sunday, many congregations will remember the faithful who have died during the past year.

Our liturgy abounds with references to the saints and to our continual relationship with them. The preface for All Saints describes the relationship this way: "that moved by their witness and supported by their fellowship, we may run with perseverance the race that is set before us and with them receive the unfading crown of glory." Today and this week invite people to reflect on others—living and dead—who have moved and supported us in our lives of faith.

# November 3, 2002

### All Saints Sunday

### INTRODUCTION

As November heralds the dying of the landscape in many northern regions, the readings and liturgy call us to remember those who have died in Christ. As the liturgical year draws to a close, we hear warnings about the end of time, stories of crisis and judgment, and parables of loss and death. The Christian community speaks honestly about human frailty and mortality.

At the same time, we confess our faith in the risen Lord, in the communion of saints, the resurrection of the body, and life everlasting. While we may face dying or death with fear, the liturgy calls us to hear the Lord's promise that he is with us in life and in death.

Christ has claimed us in baptism and nourishes us in the communion of his body and blood. He leads us to the new Jerusalem. There we shall join all the saints in praise of God, who has turned our graves into the doorway to eternal life.

### PRAYER OF THE DAY

Almighty God, whose people are knit together in one holy Church, the body of Christ our Lord: Grant us grace to follow your blessed saints in lives of faith and commitment, and to know the inexpressible joys you have prepared for those who love you; through your Son, Jesus Christ our Lord, who lives and reigns with you and the Holy Spirit, one God, now and forever.

### READINGS

#### Revelation 7:9-17

The book of Revelation is written to seven churches in western Asia Minor during a time of great oppression (in A.D. 95 or 96). Today's reading provides a response to the question asked in 6:17: "Who is able to stand?" The writer responds to the faithful with the assurance of God's protection and a vision of eventual victory.

#### Psalm 34:1-10, 22

Fear the Lord, you saints of the Lord. (Ps. 34:9)

#### 1 John 3:1-3

John encourages us to hope in God's love and trust the promise that we shall see God's face.

#### Matthew 5:1-12

In the beatitudes, Jesus provides a unique description of those who are blessed with God's favor. His teaching is surprising and shocking to those who seek wealth, fame, and control over others.

### COLOR White

### THE PRAYERS

Surrounded by a great cloud of witnesses, let us offer our prayers before God's throne of grace.

*A BRIEF SILENCE.*

Let us pray for God's holy church throughout the world, that we may faithfully proclaim the blessedness of new life in Christ. In your great mercy,

**hear us, O God.**

Let us pray for the leaders of nations, that they may work tirelessly as peacemakers and ambassadors of good-will among all people. In your great mercy,

**hear us, O God.**

Let us pray for all who will vote in elections, that you give them wisdom in their deliberations and bless the outcome of their decisions. In your great mercy,

**hear us, O God.**

Let us pray for the meek and pure in heart and for those weighed down by trial and distress, that the example of the saints may give them endurance and courage. In your great mercy,

**hear us, O God.**

Let us pray for those who live with poverty or who are poor in spirit, and for all who are homebound, hospital-ized, or sick (especially), that you fill them with hope. In your great mercy,

**hear us, O God.**

Let us pray for those who mourn the loss of loved ones, that they would find comfort in the promise of eternal life. In your great mercy,

**hear us, O God.**

*HERE OTHER INTERCESSIONS MAY BE OFFERED.*

We give thanks for all the saints who now rest from their labors and dwell in your eternal light. With affection and love we remember those dear to us who have died (especially). May their memory stir our imagination and deepen our hope of sharing with you the endless feast of victory. In your great mercy,

**hear us, O God.**

Rejoicing in the communion of all the saints, let us commend ourselves, one another, and our whole life to Jesus Christ our Lord.

**Amen**

## IMAGES FOR PREACHING

A day to commemorate all the martyrs was observed at least as far back as the mid-300s. In the great vision of St. John the Divine, one of the elders identifies the great multitude. "These are they who have come out of the great ordeal," he says. "They have washed their robes and made them white in the blood of the Lamb" (Rev. 7:14). They are the ones who died for the faith. What imagery! Blood-washed robes come out white. It is not their own blood in which their robes are washed, although their robes were stained with it when they died for the faith. It is the blood of Christ that cleanses.

In the first letter of John, we hear the promises of that same cleansing for us who are in the midst of the great ordeal. "All who have this hope in him purify themselves" (I John 3:3), he writes. The ordeal is the pressure put on us to renounce or water down the faith. Sometimes the pressure is violent. Sometimes the pressure is subtle.

On All Saints Sunday, we remember those who have died for the faith and those who have died in the faith. We also recognize on All Saints Sunday all the baptized. We are sinners. Remember that the next time you look in the mirror. We are saints, as well. Remember that, too, when you look yourself over. We are sinners in our own right and saints by virtue of Christ's death and resurrection for us.

In the sermon on the mount, Jesus speaks his blessing on all his saints. On All Saints Sunday, as every Sunday, we saints on earth join the saints in heaven in singing God's praises. We join them at the meal, as well, keeping in mind that what we receive here is but an appetizer from the heavenly banquet table.

## WORSHIP MATTERS

The festival of All Saints is a celebration of the whole people of God, the church in heaven and on earth. Those who departed this life since last All Saints Day may be remembered in the prayers. Their names may be read from a memorial book, flanked by candles, that has been placed prominently in the assembly. A bell might be rung and a moment of silence allowed after each name is read. Names of others among the faithful to be remembered can be added as well. Hymns of hope, celebration, and resurrection should mark this day. Incense might be used to symbolize the prayers of the saints ascending to the throne of God. Worship leadership by many of various ages, races, and backgrounds helps convey an image of the inclusive nature of the innumerable company of saints.

## LET THE CHILDREN COME

Let the children help with a watery reminder of the baptismal grace that joins us with all the saints in light. In advance, teach older children how to sprinkle the people with water from the font, using evergreen or other

327

branches. Invite the people to make the sign of the cross as the water touches them. Let the water rain upon the people like grace, refreshing and unearned, as they confess the creed. Little children will await and delight in this moment.

## HYMNS FOR WORSHIP

### GATHERING

O God, our help in ages past   LBW 320

Come, we that love the Lord   WOV 742, TFF 135

Oh, when the saints go marching in   TFF 180

### HYMN OF THE DAY

Sing with all the saints in glory   WOV 691

### ALTERNATE HYMN OF THE DAY

Who is this host arrayed in white   LBW 314

Blest are they   WOV 764

### COMMUNION

Come, my way, my truth, my life   LBW 513

I am the bread of life   WOV 702

Taste and see   BL 12

### SENDING

Rejoice, O pilgrim throng!   LBW 553

Rejoice in God's saints   WOV 689

### ADDITIONAL HYMNS AND SONGS

The trumpets sound, the angels sing   W&P 139

I will sing, I will sing   W&P 73

Deep river   TFF 174

Behold a host   HFW

Death be never last   DH 102

## MUSIC FOR THE DAY

### PSALMODY

I will bless you, O God   DH 34

Eat this bread, drink this cup   WOV 706

Cooney, Rory. "Taste and See." Cant, kybd, gtr, ft.   OCP 5290CC.

Currie, Randolph. "Taste and See." U or 2 pt, cong, org.   GIA G-2824.

Hobby, Robert. "I Will Bless the Lord." U, cong, org.   MSM 80-707.

Kreutz, Robert. "Jesu dulcis" (The Taste of Goodness). SATB, cong.   GIA G-2304.

Organ, Anne Krentz.   PW A.

Taste and see   TFF 5, TFF 126

Walker, Christopher. "Taste and See."   PS 3.

### CHORAL

Bach, Johann Christian Friedrich. "In the Resurrection Glorious" in *Chantry Choirbook.* SATB, org.   AFP 0800657772.

Bairstow, Edward C. "Jesu, the Very Thought of Thee." SATB.   OXF A5.

Bisbee, B. Wayne. "In Heavenly Love Abiding." SATB.   AFP 0800649575.

Ferguson, John. "Holy God We Praise Your Name." SATB, cong, org, opt brass.   GIA G-3167.

Franklin, Cary John. "Behold, I Make All Things New." SATB, org.   AFP 11-2276.

Harris, William. "Faire Is the Heaven" in *Anthems for Choirs 4.* SSAATTBB.

Hassell, Michael. "I Sing a Song of the Saints of God." 2 pt trbl, pno, fl.   AFP 0800658515.

McIver, Robert H. "Pie Jesu." 2 pt, pno, fl, ob/cl, opt strs.   CG CGA814.

Rachmaninoff, Sergei. "Blessed Is the Man" from *All Night Vigil* in *Songs of the Church.* SSAATTBB div.   HWG GB 640.

Roberts, William Bradley. "In All These You Welcomed Me/Sing with All the Saints in Glory." U, org, opt ob or other B-flat or C inst.   AFP 6000001207.

Schalk, Carl. "Blessed Are the Dead Who Die in the Lord." SATB.   CPH 98-3214.

Schulz-Widmar, Russell. "Give Rest O Christ." SATB, org.   GIA G-3819.

Svedlund, Karl-Erik/ed. Bruce Bengtson. "There'll Be Something in Heaven." SATB.   AFP 0800657616.

Vaughan Williams, Ralph. "O Taste and See." SATB, org.   OXF 43 909.

### CHILDREN'S CHOIRS

Agozin, Charlotte. "Come, Join Your Hands." 2 pt, kybd.   CG CGA729.

Phillips, Craig. "Psalm 34." 2 pt, org.   ECS 5364.

Price and Besig. "Chariots Comin'!" 2 pt, kybd.   ALF 4751.

### KEYBOARD/INSTRUMENTAL

Biery, James. "Mississippi" in *Tree of Life.* Org.   AFP 0800655370.

Daniel-Lesur. "In Paradisum" in *Augsburg Organ Library: November.* Org.   AFP 0800658965.

Howells, Herbert. "Psalm-Prelude I" in *Three Psalm-Preludes for Organ, Set One.* Org.   NOV 59-0353-10.

Kohrs, Jonathan. "Mississippi" in *Four Tunes for Piano and Two Instruments*. Kybd, inst.  AFP 0800658787.

Vierne, Louis. "Requiem Aeternam" in *Augsburg Organ Library: November*. Org.  AFP 0800658965.

West, John. "Fanfare on Sine Nomine." Org.  AFP 0800659473.

### HANDBELL

Afdahl, Lee J. "Rejoice in God's Saints." 3-5 oct. L3.  AFP 0800656695.

Chatfield, Frederick. "Shall We Gather at the River." LOR 20/1143L (3 oct. L3); 20/1145L (5 oct. L3).

McFadden, Jane. "In Heaven Above." 3-5 oct, opt ch. L2.  AFP 0800659929.

### PRAISE ENSEMBLE

Baroni, David. "Blessed Are the Broken" in *Hosanna Music Songbook 13*. SAT[B], kybd.  INT 13576.

Haas, David. "Blest Are They." SATB, kybd, gtr, C inst.  GIA G-2958.

Hayes, Mark. "Swingin' with the Saints."  SHW A-1637 (SATB, inst.); D-367 (SAB).

Mohr, Jon. "Find Us Faithful." SATB, orch.  GS A-6462.

Rambo, Dottie. "We Shall Behold Him" in *Hosanna Music Songbook 13*. AT[B], kybd.  INT 13576. S

Smith, Paul. "Every Good Thing" in *Only God for Me Songbook*. SAT[B], kybd.  INT 15297.

# November 3, 2002

Twenty-fourth Sunday after Pentecost
Proper 26

329

## INTRODUCTION

As we come to the final month of a liturgical year, the scripture readings become more urgent, encouraging us to think about things of ultimate importance. Today's readings strongly urge us to obey God's teachings and to act fairly and charitably in our dealings with others. The church, especially, is called into forms of humble service and justice for the sake of the world.

On November 3 the church remembers Martin de Porres, seventeenth-century renewer of society.

## PRAYER OF THE DAY

Stir up, O Lord, the wills of your faithful people to seek more eagerly the help you offer, that, at the last, they may enjoy the fruit of salvation; through our Lord Jesus Christ.

## READINGS

Micah 3:5-12

Judgment shall be heaped upon the prophets and the rulers who act unjustly and fail to do what the Lord has commanded.

Psalm 43

Send out your light and truth that they may lead me. (Ps. 43:3)

1 Thessalonians 2:9-13

The apostle Paul shows how his kind fatherly dealings with the Thessalonians aided in their receiving the word of God.

Matthew 23:1-12

Jesus encourages his disciples to obey religious teaching, but not to act like some of their teachers who desire privileged positions or seats of honor.

## SEMICONTINUOUS FIRST READING/PSALM

Joshua 3:7-17

Leadership of Israel passed from Moses to Joshua. At long last the people of Israel crossed the Jordan into the land of promise, with the ark of the covenant preceding them.

Psalm 107:1-7, 33-37

Give thanks to the Lord, all those whom the Lord has redeemed. (Ps. 107:1-2)

COLOR  Green

## THE PRAYERS

Surrounded by a great cloud of witnesses, let us offer our prayers before God's throne of grace.
*A BRIEF SILENCE.*

God of grace, bless your church throughout the world, that it may be a living sign of Jesus Christ and a source

of hope for the world. In your great mercy,
**hear us, O God.**
God of righteousness, we ask your blessing upon the trade and commerce of all nations, that relationships among people may reflect your goodwill for their lives. In your great mercy,
**hear us, O God.**
God of truth, we pray for all who will vote in elections, that you give them wisdom in their deliberations and bless the outcome of their decisions. In your great mercy,
**hear us, O God.**
God of all comfort, we pray for those living with anxiety, guilt, loneliness, poverty, or illness (especially), that you would be their refuge and strength. In your great mercy,
**hear us, O God.**
God of all generations, we pray for parents, youth workers, caregivers, and all who love and nurture children, that they may be blessed in their work. In your great mercy,
**hear us, O God.**
*HERE OTHER INTERCESSIONS MAY BE OFFERED.*
God of hope, we give you thanks for Martin de Porres and all the faithful ones who followed Christ in life and death. Help us to walk by faith and to look to you, our hope for years to come. In your great mercy,
**hear us, O God.**
Rejoicing in the communion of all the saints, let us commend ourselves, one another, and our whole life to Jesus Christ our Lord.
**Amen**

### IMAGES FOR PREACHING

A layperson spoke to a gathering of clergy. He began his presentation by trying to disarm the assembled troops. He said, "I know that half of you sitting out there will be thinking 'I could have said it better than that.'" The group chuckled. You could almost hear a few knives being sheathed and revolvers holstered.

The speaker continued, "I was raised in a congregation where the ministers regularly quoted Jesus from the King James Version saying, 'Let him who would be greatest among you be your minister.'" This time the laughter was loud and appreciative. The speaker had won us over.

We knew the speaker had our number. Lack of ego is generally not a problem among the clergy. One profes-

sor told us in seminary, "Don't try to deny that you have big egos. Just make sure you subject those big egos to Christ and Christ's service."

The speaker at the clergy gathering was paraphrasing the King James translation of Jesus' words in today's gospel reading. Jesus is instructing us about the great reversal that will take place when those who exalt themselves will be humbled and vice versa. Jesus is the kind of Lord who does not lord it over others. He is not an overlord. He is an underlord; he lords it under us. God exalts him for it. So do we.

What we have to look forward to is the culmination of this great reversal. Looking forward to it, we live even now by the rubrics of the great reversal. We may be ambitious, but we will make the distinction Winston Churchill noted. Some people, he pointed out, are ambitious to be. Others are ambitious to do. Our ambition is to serve the gospel of Christ and Christ's people.

### WORSHIP MATTERS

One method of tying rope cinctures for clergy locates the knot in the front center. Small loops are created to the right and left when the extra rope is draped to each side and allowed to fall evenly over the pockets. The stole is then slipped through the loops and held in place. Or, you may prefer this simpler look: Double the cincture and fold the looped end back on itself to create a second, small loop. Bring the knotted ends around the waist and place them through this loop to create an adjustable knot. Let the knotted ends fall to one side. Remember that a cincture is not essential. Depending on the alb design, the graceful flow of fabric may not need the addition of the cincture.

### LET THE CHILDREN COME

We are reminded today that there is no place in the reign of God for big shots and nobodies. We are all students of the one teacher, Christ Jesus. In him we are sisters and brothers to one another. Perhaps the presider could share the peace in this way, "Sisters and brothers, the peace of the Lord be with you always." Then the members of the assembly, regardless of age or earthly kinship, could greet one another in like manner.

## HYMNS FOR WORSHIP
### GATHERING
Lord, whose love in humble service   LBW 423

Come to us, creative Spirit   WOV 758

As the deer   W&P 9

### HYMN OF THE DAY
Oh, praise the gracious power   WOV 750

### ALTERNATE HYMN OF THE DAY
Praise the Almighty   LBW 539

Here in this place   WOV 718

### COMMUNION
Come down, O Love divine   LBW 508

Father, I adore you   W&P 37

In the morning when I rise   WOV 777, TFF 165

### SENDING
Guide me ever, great Redeemer   LBW 343

All my hope on God is founded   WOV 782

Glory and praise to our God   W&P 43

### ADDITIONAL HYMNS AND SONGS
Lead me, guide me   TFF 70, W&P 84

Let your heart be broken   BH 611

We are called to be God's people   TWC 710

We are your people   NCH 309

We are an offering   W&P 146

## MUSIC FOR THE DAY
### PSALMODY
Haas, David.  PCY 9.

Hopson, Hal H. *Psalm Refrains and Tones.*   HOP 425.

Organ, Anne Krentz.   PW A.

### CHORAL
Bach, J.S. "Bring Low Our Ancient Adam" in *Bach for All Seasons.* SATB, kybd.   AFP 080065854X.

Bach, J.S. "Lord Jesus Christ, Thou Prince of Peace." SATB/S, vln, cont.   CPH 98-1955.

Fleming, Larry L. "Humble Service." SATB.   AFP 0800646223.

Handel, G.F. "Ev'ry Valley" in *Messiah.* T solo, kybd.   Various ed.

Lynn, George. "Come, Let Us Use the Grace Divine." SATB.   ABI APM-139.

Mendelssohn-Ziemer. "Judge Me, O God." SSAATBB, pno/org.   WAL W2157.

Moe, Daniel. "O Jesus Christ to Thee May Hymns Be Rising." SATB, org.   AFP 6000103263.

Nelson, Ronald A. "Whoever Would be Great Among You." SAB, gtr/kybd.   AFP 0800645804.

Rogers, Sharon Elery. "Come, Dearest Lord, Descend and Dwell." 2 or 3 pt mxd, kybd, opt fl.   MSM-50-8110.

### CHILDREN'S CHOIRS
Cox, Joe. "Put Your Trust in God" from *Psalms for the People of God.* Cant, choir, cong, kybd.   SMP 45/1037S.

Hobby, Robert A. "Lord, Let Us Listen." 2 pt. trbl, pno.   AFP 0800659236.

Willan, Healey. "Oh, Send Out Thy Light" in *Psalms for the People of God.* Cant, choir, cong, kybd.   SMP 45/1037S.

### KEYBOARD/INSTRUMENTAL
Langlois, Kristina. "Down Ampney" in *Eight Miniatures: Lent, Easter, Pentecost.* Org.   MSM 10-345.

Martinson, Joel. "Cwm Rhondda" in *Madison Organ Book.* Org.   HWG GB 9513.

Stoldt, Frank. "Come Down, O Love Divine." Org, inst.   MSM 20-540.

Vann, Stanley. "Exsultate" in *Festival Finales.* Org.   MAY 0-86209-353-8.

Wold, Wayne L. "Christpraise Ray" in *Child of the Light.* Org.   AFP 0800657993.

### HANDBELL
Kinyon, Barbara. "A Joyful Ring." 2-3 oct. L2.   AG 1397.

Nelson, Susan T. "Give Me Jesus." 3 oct.   AFP 0800658132.

Tucker, Sondra K. "Here I Am, Lord." 3-5 oct. L4.   CPH 97-6756.

### PRAISE ENSEMBLE
Temple, Sebastian/arr. Mark Hayes. "Make Me a Channel of Your Peace."   ALF 18316 (SATB, kybd); 18317(SAB); 18318 (2 pt); 18320 (inst); 18319 (perf cass).

Ziegenhals, Harriet, arr. "Since I Laid My Burden Down." SATB, kybd, soloists.   CGA 796.

331

## Sunday, November 3

MARTIN DE PORRES, RENEWER OF SOCIETY, 1639

Martin was the son of a Spanish knight and Ana Velázquez, a freed black slave from Panama. Martin apprenticed himself to a barber-surgeon in Lima, Peru, and was known for his work as a healer. Martin was a lay brother in the Order of Preachers (Dominicans) and engaged in many charitable works. He was a gardener as well as a counselor to those who sought him out. He was noted for his care of all the poor, regardless of race. His own religious community described him as the "father of charity." His work included the founding of an orphanage, a hospital, and a clinic for dogs and cats. He is recognized as an advocate for Christian charity and interracial justice.

## Thursday, November 7

JOHN CHRISTIAN FREDERICK HEYER, MISSIONARY TO INDIA, 1873

Heyer was the first missionary sent out by American Lutherans. He was born in Germany and came to the United States after his confirmation. He was ordained in 1820, established Sunday schools, and taught at Gettysburg College and Seminary. Heyer became a missionary in the Andhra region of India. During a break in his mission work he received the M.D. degree from what would later be Johns Hopkins University. He later served as chaplain of the Lutheran seminary at Philadelphia until his death.

Because of his work as a pastor, missionary, and medical doctor, his commemoration can lead us to be mindful of all who work for healing of both body and spirit.

# November 10, 2002

332

Twenty-fifth Sunday after Pentecost
Proper 27

## INTRODUCTION

Why does the bridegroom come so late to the wedding celebration? Why, asked the early Christians, does Christ seemingly delay his promised return? And we, who live in an unjust and violent world may ask, Where is the Lord when we need him?

We do not know the hour of his final advent. But we do know that Christ has claimed us in baptism as his servants in this world. We have the witness of the word and sacrament to enlighten our path in life. We are strengthened in the eucharist as heralds of the coming reign of God's justice and peace. Between his first advent and his final coming, the church is called to serve the Lord Jesus in faith, hope, and love.

## PRAYER OF THE DAY

Lord, when the day of wrath comes we have no hope except in your grace. Make us so to watch for the last days that the consummation of our hope may be the joy of the marriage feast of your Son, Jesus Christ our Lord.

## READINGS

### Amos 5:18-24

In this speech, Amos takes up one of the central themes of Israel's faith and turns it against his Israelite audience. The Day of the Lord was understood to be a day of disaster and judgment for the Lord's enemies, but one of salvation and deliverance for the Lord's people. Now, Amos declares, because the people have turned away from God and failed to pursue justice and righteousness, Israel will be numbered among the Lord's enemies.

### or Wisdom of Solomon 6:12-16

Wisdom is not hidden. Those who seek her will find her, for she graciously seeks them first.

### Psalm 70

You are my helper and my deliverer; O Lord, do not tarry. (Ps. 70:6)

### or Wisdom of Solomon 6:17-20

The beginning of wisdom is the most sincere desire for instruction. (Wisd. of Sol. 6:17)

### 1 Thessalonians 4:13-18

The Thessalonian Christians were eagerly awaiting the return of Christ and became distressed when loved ones died before this occurred. Paul's words about the second coming offer hope to all who grieve.

Matthew 25:1-13

In this chapter, Jesus tells three parables about the second coming. The first of these emphasizes the need for readiness at all times.

## SEMICONTINUOUS FIRST READING/PSALM

Joshua 24:1-3a, 14-25

In the ancient Near East *covenant* meant "agreement" or "alliance." It described relationships and was the primary word used to characterize the relationship between the Lord and Israel. By delivering Israel, God had already begun the relationship. In today's reading, Joshua called upon the people to respond.

Psalm 78:1-7

We will recount to generations to come the power of the Lord. (Ps. 78:4)

## COLOR Green

## THE PRAYERS

Surrounded by a great cloud of witnesses, let us offer our prayers before God's throne of grace.

*A BRIEF SILENCE.*

Let us pray for the church, that through its proclamation and witness it may be a lamp of hope for all who live with darkness and despair. In your great mercy,

**hear us, O God.**

Let us pray for political leaders, that they may be watchful and responsible, and so give the light of peace to a world threatened by war and violence. In your great mercy,

**hear us, O God.**

Let us pray for those oppressed and treated unfairly, that your justice may roll down like waters and your righteousness like an everflowing stream. In your great mercy,

**hear us, O God.**

Let us pray for those without food, shelter, or clothing and for those whose spirits are broken, that your light may give them hope. In your great mercy,

**hear us, O God.**

Let us pray for those living with illness or who may find it difficult to face the future (especially), that they may be encouraged by the promise of your coming reign. In your great mercy,

**hear us, O God.**

Let us pray for ourselves, that we may seek to be wise, living with our eyes open, watchful and alert to the signs of your grace in the world and in our lives. In your great mercy,

**hear us, O God.**

*HERE OTHER INTERCESSIONS MAY BE OFFERED.*

We give you thanks for all the saints who surround us as we celebrate this eucharistic banquet. May their memory enliven our faith and deepen our hope. In your great mercy,

**hear us, O God.**

Rejoicing in the communion of all the saints, let us commend ourselves, one another, and our whole life to Jesus Christ our Lord.

**Amen**

## IMAGES FOR PREACHING

A roof with multiple leaks is a device used in one old film to comment on the character of those who live under that roof. As the rain pours in, the residents scurry about putting pots and pans under the drips. A visitor inquires "Why don't you repair the roof?"

The head of the house replies, "We can't fix the roof; it's raining."

The visitor persists, "Well, why don't you fix the roof when the rain stops and the sun is shining?"

The head of the house will have none of that logic. She says, "When the sun is shining, the roof does not leak."

The obvious conclusion is that the residents of that house are foolish. "Foolish" is the label Jesus gave the bridesmaids who took no oil beyond what was in their lamps. The difference between being wise and foolish has to do with preparation and vision. The foolish cannot see beyond the moment. The wise attempt to peer into the future and to prepare for it.

This is the stuff not only of biblical wisdom. Secular stories tell the same cautionary tale. The ant works to lay in food for the long winter. The grasshopper plays all summer long. The tortoise keeps his eye on the finish line. The hare is a layabout. Two of the three little pigs take the easy way out when it comes to home construction. The foolish two have to run for shelter to the wise pig's house when the wolf arrives on the scene.

The difference between the parable and these cau-

333

tionary tales is that the parable is not about industry and
wakeful persistence. All ten maidens slept when the
bridegroom delayed. The parable is about hope. One of
the characteristics of hope is that we are willing to take
action, action such as carrying an extra flask of oil, because we have hope.

## WORSHIP MATTERS

The use of flowers in the worship space is not merely ornamental. Flowers point us to the beauty of the Creator's ongoing work and remind us that all creation is meant to pay
tribute to the one from whom all things come. Either living
plants that symbolize the growth and continuation of life
in God or cut flowers, sacrificed to serve the worship of
God, can be placed in the worship space. The altar table is
reserved for the elements of the eucharistic meal and is not
a place for flowers.

## LET THE CHILDREN COME

334

The children could sing the first stanza of "Let justice
flow like streams" (WOV 763) following the first reading, before the reader closes by saying, "The word of the
Lord," and the assembly responds, "Thanks be to God."

## HYMNS FOR WORSHIP
### GATHERING

Oh, happy day when we shall stand    LBW 351
Come away to the skies    WOV 669
Lift up your heads    W&P 88

### HYMN OF THE DAY

Rejoice, rejoice, believers    LBW 25

### ALTERNATE HYMN OF THE DAY

Wake, awake, for night is flying    LBW 31, HFW (revised)
Blessed assurance    WOV 699, TFF 118

### COMMUNION

When peace, like a river    LBW 346, TFF 194
Let justice flow like streams    WOV 763
That Christ be known    W&P 133

### SENDING

Rise up, O saints of God    LBW 383
What a fellowship, what a joy divine    WOV 780, TFF 220

## ADDITIONAL HYMNS AND SONGS

Children of the heavenly Father    LBW 474
Immortal, invisible, God only wise    LBW 526
My Lord, what a morning    WOV 627, TFF 40
Keep your lamps trimmed and burning    NCH 369
Let justice roll like a river    W&P 85

## MUSIC FOR THE DAY
### PSALMODY

Hallock, Peter. "Psalm 70" in TP.
Hopson, Hal H. *Psalm Refrains and Tones.*    HOP 425.
Organ, Anne Krentz.    PW A.

### CHORAL

Bach, J.S. "Wake, Awake, for Night Is Flying" in *Bach for All Seasons.*
SATB.    AFP 0800659546.
Bach, J.S. "Zion Hears the Watchmen Singing" in *Bach for All Seasons.*
U, kybd.    AFP 0800659546.
Bouman, Paul. "Rejoice, Rejoice Believers." SATB, org.
MSM 50-0004.
Johnson, Ralph M. "Be Thou a Smooth Way." SATB, pno.
AFP 0800659325.
Leaf, Robert. "Rise Up, You Heirs of Glory." SATB, org.
AFP 0800646835.
Mendelssohn, Felix. "Sleepers Wake!" in *Anthems for Choirs 1.* SATB,
org.    OXF.
Powell, Robert J. "O Day of Peace." SATB, org.    CPH 98-3565.
Purcell, Henry. "Thou Knowest, Lord, the Secrets of Our Hearts."
SATB, org.    ECS No 170 (376 Archive Reprints).
Thomas, Andre. "Keep Your Lamps!" SATB, conga drm.
HIN HMC-577.

### CHILDREN'S CHOIRS

Makeever, Ray. "It Won't Be Long" in DH. U, kybd.    AFP.
Sleeth, Natalie. "Fear Not for Tomorrow" in LS. U, kybd.    AFP.

### KEYBOARD/INSTRUMENTAL

Albrecht, Timothy. "Assurance" in *Grace Notes IX.* Org.
AFP 0800659813.
Bach, J.S. "Wachet auf" in *Six Organ Chorales/Schübler.* Org.
PRE 78332-97.
Ferguson, John. "Bred dina vida vingar" in *Thy Holy Wings.* Org.
AFP 0800647955.
Langlais, Jean. *Te Deum.* Org.    Herelle p.32.317.
Sedio, Mark. "Bred dina vida vingar" in *Dancing in the Light of God.* Pno.
AFP 0800656547.

## HANDBELL

McChesney, Kevin. "Praise to the Lord, the Almighty." 2-3 oct. L3.
AG 1499.

McFadden, Jane. "Bred dina vida vingar" in *Two More Swedish Melodies for Handbells*. 3-4 oct, opt ch.  AFP 0800657357.

Morris, Hart. "O The Deep, Deep Love of Jesus." 3-5 oct. L3.
ALF 12396.

## PRAISE ENSEMBLE

Christensen, Chris. "Let Justice Roll Down" in *Hosanna Music Songbook 13*. SAT[B], kybd.  INT 13576.

Condon, Mark/arr. J. Daniel Smith. "We Seek Your Face" in *Marvelous Things Choral Collection*. SATB, kybd.  INT 18256.

Day, Greg and Chuck Day/arr. Tom Fettke. "Midnight Cry." SATB, kybd.  LIL AN-1839.

Thomas, Andre. "When the Trumpet Sounds." SATB, kybd.
MF 261.

# Monday, November 11

## MARTIN, BISHOP OF TOURS, 397

Martin's pagan father enlisted him in the army at age fifteen. One winter day, a beggar approached Martin for aid, and he cut his cloak in half and gave a portion to the beggar. Later, Martin understood that he had seen the presence of Christ in that beggar, and this ended his uncertainty about Christianity. He soon asked for his release from his military duties, but he was imprisoned instead. After his release from prison he began preaching,

particularly against the Arians. In 371 he was elected bishop of Tours. As bishop he developed a reputation for intervening on behalf of prisoners and heretics who had been sentenced to death.

Today, at the same time as we remember this soldier turned peacemaker, we remember the end of World War I and veterans of war. Let these commemorations together move us to pray and work for peace in our families, congregations, and nation.

# Monday, November 11

## SØREN AABYE KIERKEGAARD, TEACHER, 1855

Kierkegaard, a nineteenth-century Danish theologian whose writings reflect his Lutheran heritage, was the founder of modern existentialism. Though he was engaged to a woman he deeply loved, he ended the relationship because he believed he was called to search the hidden side of life. Many of his works were published under a variety of names, so that he could reply to arguments from his own previous works. Kierkegaard's work attacked the established church of his day. He attacked the church's complacency, its tendency to intellectualize faith, and its desire to be accepted by polite society.

Kierkegaard's work makes room for doubt in the life of faith. He also served as a prophetic challenge to churches that may want to set aside paradox for an easy faith and the gospel for cultural acceptability.

335

# November 17, 2002

### Twenty-sixth Sunday after Pentecost
### Proper 28

## INTRODUCTION

In a world marked by much suspicion and backbiting, those who offer encouragement, trust, and hope are like an oasis of green-growing life. In a world wounded by rugged individualism, cutthroat competition, and much greed, the Holy Spirit blesses each Christian with the ability to use one's gifts for the greater and common good, to build up the body of Christ, and to serve those who suffer injustice.

The gospel reading for this day encourages us to use our God-given talents wisely while we still have time to do so. Elizabeth of Thuringia, whom the church remembers this day, offers an example of one who was eager to share earthly possessions as well as the riches of God's love with those in need.

## PRAYER OF THE DAY

Lord God, so rule and govern our hearts and minds by your Holy Spirit that, always keeping in mind the end of all things and the day of judgment, we may be stirred up to holiness of life here and may live with you forever in the world to come, through your Son, Jesus Christ our Lord.
*or*
Almighty and ever-living God, before the earth was formed and even after it ceases to be, you are God. Break into our short span of life and let us see the signs of your final will and purpose, through your Son, Jesus Christ our Lord.

## READINGS

### Zephaniah 1:7, 12-18

Like last week's reading, today's reading revolves around the concept of the Day of the Lord, the day of destruction of the Lord's enemies and of salvation for the Lord's faithful. This little-known prophet declares to the people of Jerusalem that sin without repentance will lead to destruction.

### Psalm 90:1-8 [9-11] 12

So teach us to number our days, that we may apply our hearts to wisdom. (Ps. 90:12)

### 1 Thessalonians 5:1-11

Paul encourages the Thessalonian Christians to look forward to the return of Christ as a day of salvation.

### Matthew 25:14-30

In the second of three parables concerning the second coming, Jesus indicates that merely maintaining things as they are is not sufficient. As Christians await his return, we are to use wisely the gifts of God.

## SEMICONTINUOUS FIRST READING/PSALM

### Judges 4:1-7

Deborah was a military general who, with her general Barak, led a victorious battle against a stronger Canaanite force from the north.

### Psalm 123

Our eyes look to you, O God, until you show us your mercy. (Ps. 123:3)

## COLOR  Green

## THE PRAYERS

Surrounded by a great cloud of witnesses, let us offer our prayers before God's throne of grace.
*A BRIEF SILENCE.*

Let us pray that the church may faithfully proclaim the day of the Lord, inviting all people to live each day with integrity and wisdom. In your great mercy,
**hear us, O God.**

Let us pray that those who have received blessings in abundance may share their resources with those in need. In your great mercy,
**hear us, O God.**

Let us pray that nations beset by storms, earthquakes, and calamities may be sustained by the help of other nations and the sharing of our gifts. In your great mercy,
**hear us, O God.**

Let us pray that all who are troubled, fearful, or ill (especially) may find refuge and hope in God, the source of all healing. In your great mercy,
**hear us, O God.**

*HERE OTHER INTERCESSIONS MAY BE OFFERED.*

Let us pray that we follow all the saints in light until we come with them to the great and promised day of the Lord. In your great mercy,
**hear us, O God.**
Rejoicing in the communion of Elizabeth of Thuringia and all the saints, let us commend ourselves, one another, and our whole life to Jesus Christ our Lord.
**Amen**

## IMAGES FOR PREACHING

In the conclusion to the parable of the talents, Jesus seems to reverse the great reversal. So often, we hear that the last will be first and the first last, and that those who exalt themselves will be humbled and those who humble themselves will be exalted. Here Jesus says, "For to all those who have, more will be given…but from those who have nothing, even what they have will be taken away" (Matt. 25:29).

This parable was read and the conclusion quoted by a teacher of preaching at a weeklong course. He said, "From my experience at doing this sort of thing, I know without knowing you that you are all good preachers to begin with. You already get many compliments on your preaching. You work hard at it. You are noted among your peers and envied by more than a few of them for your reputation as preachers. Those whose congregations wish they would take a course like this are not here and never will be. 'For to all those who have, more will be given.' That's just the way it is."

The master had entrusted the man in this parable with riches. He did not even benefit from them himself, let alone invest them. What is even worse, he concluded that the master was hard and bitter, although the master lavished such wealth upon him.

The other two servants in the parable embrace both the riches and the responsibility. They invest, and the return is inevitable. To faithful stewards of the gospel, even more will be given.

## WORSHIP MATTERS

The readings at the end of the church year focus on the eschaton, the last things. Though the impending Christmas season makes this focus somewhat difficult, the shortening of daylight and the withering of flowers and leaves in the Northern Hemisphere all help to set the stage for us to give our attention to the end times. The worship of the church should also reflect the church year's focus. Banners, paraments, and flowers can reflect deeper, earthier tones of green and brown. Instrumental and choral music might be more reflective in nature than it was earlier in the season. Whatever is done should present a clear contrast to the grand celebration of the reign of Christ on the last Sunday of the church year, thus reflecting both an awareness of human mortality as well as the ultimate triumph and victory of Christ.

## LET THE CHILDREN COME

We are about to begin the church year anew. Make note of the ways you have tried to welcome children into worship. What worked? What did not? What would you like to try in the year to come? Do not try something only once. Children learn by repetition and love to sing "by heart." Let the children come deeply into the worship of the church.

## HYMNS FOR WORSHIP
### GATHERING

O God, our help in ages past   LBW 320
All my hope on God is founded   WOV 782
In the morning   W&P 75

### HYMN OF THE DAY

Lord of light   LBW 405

### ALTERNATE HYMN OF THE DAY

God, whose giving knows no ending   LBW 408
O Christ the same   WOV 778

### COMMUNION

Stand up, stand up for Jesus   LBW 389
I want to walk as a child of the light   WOV 649
Listen, God is calling   WOV 712, TFF 130

### SENDING

Lead on, O King eternal   LBW 495
Let us talents and tongues employ   WOV 754, TFF 232

### ADDITIONAL HYMNS AND SONGS

Soon and very soon   WOV 744, TFF 38, W&P 128
O day of God, draw near   UMH 730
As the deer   W&P 9
Rich in promise   OBS 75

337

## MUSIC FOR THE DAY
### PSALMODY

Farrell, Bernadette.   STP, vol. 2.

Folkening, John. "Six Psalm Settings with Antiphon."   MSM 80-700.

Gelineau, Joseph. "In Every Age" in RS.

Kogut, Malcolm.   PCY 10.

Organ, Anne Krentz.   PW A.

### CHORAL

Bairstow, Edward. "Lord, Thou Hast Been Our Refuge." SATB div, org.   NOV 14430.

Bach, J.S./arr. Hal H. Hopson. "The Lord Will Soon Appear." SATB, kybd.   AFP 080065752.

Ferguson, John. "A Song of Thanksgiving." SATB, org. AFP 0800653858.

Ferguson, John. "O God, Our Help in Ages Past." SATB, cong, brass, org.   GIA G-3892.

Landes, Rob. "Lord, Thou Hast Been Our Dwelling Place." SATB, T solo, org.   MSM-50-9097.

Manz, Paul. "E'en So, Lord Jesus, Quickly Come." SATB. MSM 50-900.

Vaughan Williams, Ralph. "Lord, Thou Hast Been Our Refuge." SATB, soli or semi-chorus, org.   GSCH 9720.

Walter, Johann. "Rise Up! Rise Up!" in Chantry Choirbook. SATB. AFP 0800657772.

### CHILDREN'S CHOIRS

Berry, Cindy. "Deborah—Chosen of God." 2 pt, kybd. FB BG2320.

Exner, Max. "I Didn't Make a Sound." U, kybd.   AFP 6000108427.

### KEYBOARD/INSTRUMENTAL

Callahan, Charles. "Two English Voluntaries on English Hymn Tunes." Org.   CPH 97-6274.

Near, Gerald. "Final," from Suite for Organ. Org.   HWG GB 278.

Stanford, C.V. "Intermezzo Founded Upon an Irish Air" in A Victorian Organ Album. Org.   OXF 0-19-375219-0.

### HANDBELL

Kinyon, Barbara Baltzer. "Londonderry Air." 3-6 oct. L2.   BEC HB186.

Moklebust, Cathy. "Abbot's Leigh" in Hymn Stanzas for Handbells. AFP 0800655761 (4-5 oct); 0800657330 (2-3 oct.).

Rogers, Sharon Elery. "How Great Thou Art." 3-5 oct, opt ch. L2. AFP 0800659910.

Wagner, Douglas E. "Ring for Joy." 3 oct. L3-.   AGEHR AG 3035.

338

### PRAISE ENSEMBLE

Bullock, Geoff. "The Power of Your Love."   WRD 0 80689 80427 4 (SATB, kybd); 0 80689 60524 6 (choraltrax); 0 80689 84472 (orch).

Condon, Mark/arr. Mark Condon and J. Daniel Smith. "All of Our Praise" in Marvelous Things Choral Collection. SATB, kybd. INT 18256.

Himes. "All That I Am." SATB, kybd.   HOP GC 963.

# Sunday, November 17
ELIZABETH OF THURINGIA, PRINCESS OF HUNGARY, 1231

This Hungarian princess gave away large sums of money, including her dowry, for relief of the poor and sick. She founded hospitals, cared for orphans, and used the royal food supplies to feed the hungry. Though she had the support of her husband, her generosity and charity did not earn her friends within the royal court. At the death of her husband, she was driven out. She joined a Franciscan order and continued her charitable work, though she suffered abuse at the hands of her confessor and spiritual guide. Her lifetime of charity is particularly remarkable when one remembers that she died at the age of twenty-four. She founded two hospitals and many more are named for her.

# Saturday, November 23
CLEMENT, BISHOP OF ROME, C. 100

Clement was the third bishop of Rome and served at the end of the first century. He is best remembered for a letter he wrote to the Corinthian congregation still having difficulty with divisions in spite of Paul's canonical letters. Clement's writing echoes Paul's. "Love...has no limits to its endurance, bears everything patiently. Love is neither servile nor arrogant. It does not provoke schisms or form cliques, but always acts in harmony with others." Clement's letter is also a witness to early understandings of church government and the way each office in the church works for the good of the whole.

Clement's letter reminds us that divisions within the church are a sad part of our history and that pastoral love for people must be present amid our differing views of authority, scripture, and ministry.

## Saturday, November 23

### MIGUEL AGUSTIN PRO, PRIEST, MARTYR, 1927

Miguel Agustín Pro grew up among oppression in Mexico, where revolutionaries accused the church of siding with the rich. He was a Jesuit priest who served during a time of intense anticlericalism, and therefore he carried out much of his ministry in private settings. He worked on behalf of the poor and homeless. Miguel and his two brothers were arrested, falsely accused of throwing a bomb at the car of a government official, and assassinated by a firing squad. Just before the guns fired he yelled, "Viva Christo Rey!" which means "Long live Christ the king!"

Make plans for work that can be done on behalf of the poor in the upcoming weeks. Raise questions about what long-term solutions may bridge the gap between rich and poor.

# November 24, 2002

Christ the King
Last Sunday after Pentecost/Proper 29

### INTRODUCTION

The Lord Jesus was not wealthy or famous. He did not promise his followers that they would possess riches, power, or prestige. He was named a king only in his death. He reigned from the cross, leaving his disciples the treasure of his body and blood.

Today we gather at the table of Christ, our merciful and loving ruler. We wear the crown of baptism and trace his royal sign—the holy cross—over our brows and bodies. We leave here strengthened to serve those who are hungry, thirsty, strangers, naked, sick, and imprisoned. We look for the day when all earth's people will see him coming with the scepter of peace and the crown of justice.

### PRAYER OF THE DAY

Almighty and everlasting God, whose will it is to restore all things to your beloved Son, whom you anointed priest forever and king of all creation: Grant that all the people of the earth, now divided by the power of sin, may be united under the glorious and gentle rule of your Son, our Lord Jesus Christ, who lives and reigns with you and the Holy Spirit, one God, now and forever.

### READINGS

**Ezekiel 34:11-16, 20-24**

The term *shepherd*, which was another image for "king" in the ancient Near East, was suggestive of the care, concern, and protection that a shepherd/king was to show on behalf of his flock of citizens. When Israel's kings prove to be bad shepherds, Ezekiel declares from exile in Babylon that the Lord will assume the role of shepherd.

**Psalm 95:1-7a**

We are the people of God's pasture and the sheep of God's hand. (Ps. 95:7)

**Ephesians 1:15-23**

On Christ the King Sunday, we read this prayer of thanksgiving for the Ephesian Christians, a prayer that exalts Christ as head of the church and Lord of the universe.

**Matthew 25:31-46**

Jesus tells three stories about the second coming in this chapter. The final story—today's gospel—contains a surprise: when he does return, people will discover he has come to them before, in ways they did not recognize.

### SEMICONTINUOUS FIRST READING/PSALM

**Ezekiel 34:11-16, 20-24**

God will shepherd Israel.

**Psalm 100**

We are God's people and the sheep of God's pasture. (Ps.100:3)

### COLOR White

### THE PRAYERS

Surrounded by a great cloud of witnesses, let us offer our prayers before God's throne of grace.

*A BRIEF SILENCE.*

God our shepherd, guide your church into ways of loving service, that the blessing of your abundant life may come to those who are hungry, sick, and in prison. In your great mercy,

**hear us, O God.**

God of justice, guide the leaders of government and make them responsive to your will, that those who live in scarcity and distress may have their hope renewed. In your great mercy,

**hear us, O God.**

God of comfort, uphold with the word of life all who are sick or hospitalized (especially), that they may give thanks to you. In your great mercy,

**hear us, O God.**

God of grace, bless all developing and mission congregations, that they may be communities of lively fellowship, service, and witness in their neighborhoods. In your great mercy,

**hear us, O God.**

*HERE OTHER INTERCESSIONS MAY BE OFFERED.*

God of resurrection, bring us with all your saints to the promised day of judgment and mercy, before the throne of Christ our Savior. In your great mercy,

**hear us, O God.**

Rejoicing in the communion of all the saints, let us commend ourselves, one another, and our whole life to Jesus Christ our Lord.

**Amen**

### IMAGES FOR PREACHING

Christ the King is a Johnny-come-lately to the schedule of festivals and observances on the church calendar. It has neither the biblical warrant of Easter nor the antiquity of the forty days of Lent. Christ the King Sunday is the invention of a twentieth-century pope, Pius XI. Yet Christ the King Sunday is on the calendars of all the Protestant churches that keep a church calendar. No doubt the appeal of the day is rooted in the need Pius XI saw in 1925. Europe was still reeling from World War I, and economic uncertainty abounded. People were bending the knee and doing obeisance to human saviors and political parties that promised to rescue them. Religion was increasingly relegated to the

private sphere. In response to this, Pius XI called for an annual Sunday feast day to assert the "Kingship of our Savior." He called for a day on which people would gather to bend their knees to Christ and do obeisance to him as a witness to the day when every knee in heaven and on earth and under the earth will bend to Christ and confess him as Lord. In 1925 the observance of Christ the King proclaimed that no earthly ruler is lord. The day proclaimed Jesus is king not only of our hearts and our private moments and personal salvation but of all time and space.

That continues to be the message of Christ the King Sunday. Paul makes clear the cosmic and personal significance of this cross-enthroned king. Note the places in the second reading where the word "all" occurs. Christ is seated far above all rule, authority, and power. All things have been put under his feet. Christ is the head over all things for the church, which is his body. Christ fills all things. For us personally, Christ's rule means we are rescued from the power of death and transferred into Christ's jurisdiction. Christ is the king to whom we bend the knee, the very one who bent the knee to become a servant on our behalf. Indeed, it is when we kneel to serve the hungry, the thirsty, the sick, the imprisoned, that we bend the knee to this servant king.

### WORSHIP MATTERS

This festival of the reign of Christ over all creation is a fitting conclusion to the church year. Though every Sunday is a celebration of the resurrection, on this Sunday we seek to view the Easter event from its ultimate perspective. The Risen One is the one who now rules, as both human brother and holy God, in God's gentle and gracious realm of love. The worship celebration needs to image this victory over sin and evil, and the new world for which we are destined. Processions, special music, and the abundant use of paradoxical images in the liturgy (for example, the crucified Christ is Christ the king) should be the rule of the day.

### LET THE CHILDREN COME

"Jesus, remember me" (WOV 740) is an easy song for children to learn. Have the cantor sing it first, then the children, next add women's voices, then men's, ending with children alone. This hymn could be used during a gospel procession on this feast day, and could be sung before and after the reading of the gospel.

## HYMNS FOR WORSHIP

### GATHERING

Crown him with many crowns   LBW 170

Glory to God, we give you thanks   WOV 787

Majesty   W&P 94

### HYMN OF THE DAY

Thine the amen, thine the praise   WOV 801

### ALTERNATE HYMN OF THE DAY

The head that once was crowned   LBW 173

Come now, you blessed   LS 141

### COMMUNION

Jesus, the very thought of you   LBW 316

Lord, whose love in humble service   LBW 423

Jesus, remember me   WOV 740, LLC 457, W&P 78

What feast of love   WOV 701

### SENDING

Beautiful Savior   LBW 518

Soon and very soon   WOV 744, TFF 38, W&P 128

### ADDITIONAL HYMNS AND SONGS

Lord of glory, you have bought us   LBW 424

For he alone is worthy   TFF 284

We bow down   W&P 149

Strange King   DH 61

## MUSIC FOR THE DAY

### SERVICE MUSIC

The Kyrie and "This is the feast of victory" are strong acclamations of the sovereign Christ; this may be one of the days when both are used.

### PSALMODY

Dobry, Wallace. "A Trio of Psalms."   MSM 80-706.

Geary, Patrick. "Listen to the Voice of the Lord" in PS 2.

Joncas, Michael. "Come, Let Us Sing." SATB, cong, kybd.
GIA G-3473.

Oh, come, let us worship   DH 5

Organ, Anne Krentz.   PW A.

### CHORAL

Benson, Robert. "O Lord Most High." SATB, org.
AFP 0-800674200.

Busarow, Donald. "O Lord You Are My God and King." SATB, org, tpt, hb, opt cong.   AFP 080065756X.

Ferguson, John. "The Head That Once Was Crowned with Thorns." SATB, org, brass qrt.   GIA G-3750.

Forsberg, Charles. "Fairest Lord Jesus." SATB, pno.
AFP 0800656962.

Handel, G.F. *Coronation Anthems*, SAATBB, opt. soli, kybd, opt orch.

"Glory and Worship" (Second Reading)

"Kings Shall Be Thy Nursing Fathers" (First Reading)

"Let Justice and Judgment" (Gospel)

"Let Thy Hand Be Strengthened" (Gospel)

"My Heart Is Inditing" (Psalm)

"The King Shall Rejoice" (Second Reading)

Handel, G.F. "He Shall Feed His Flock" in *Messiah*. S solo, kybd. Various ed.

Mathias, William. "Let All the World in Every Corner Sing." SATB, org.   OXF A352.

Mendelssohn/Christiansen, O.C. "The Lord Is a Mighty God." SATB, pno/org.   KJO 9.

Pelz, Walter L. "Come, You Have My Father's Blessing." SAB, org. AFP 11-1761.

Rachmaninoff, Sergei. "O Come Let Us Worship" from *All Night Vigil* in *Songs of the Church*. SSAATTBB (Psalm).   HWG GB 640.

Scott, K. Lee. "The Glory of Christ." SATB, org, hb, opt brass. CPH 98-2982.

Scott, K. Lee. "You Will I Love." SATB, org.   CPH 98-3360.

Tye, Christopher. "Give Almes of Thy Goods" in *Anthems for Choirs 1*. SATB. (Gospel)   OXF.

### CHILDREN'S CHOIRS

Leaf, Robert. "Singing Alleluia." U/2 pt, org.   AFP 6000104871.

Leaf, Robert. "To the Glory of Our King." U.   CG CGA 173.

Liebergen, Patrick M./arr. "Simple Canon of Thanks." 2 pt/3 pt, kybd, fl.   ALF 19034.

Ziegenhals, Harriet. "Sing, Dance, Clap Your Hands." U, kybd. CG CGA 625.

### KEYBOARD/INSTRUMENTAL

Biery, James. "Thine" in *Tree of Life*. Org.   AFP 0800646126.

Langlais, Jean. "Acclamations" in *Suite Medievale*. Org.
Salabert R. L. 12360.

Martinson, Joel. *Postlude for a Festival Day*. Aureole AE 50. Org.

Wold, Wayne L. "St. Magnus" in *A November to Remember*. Org.
AFP 080065983X.

341

## HANDBELL

Kerr, J. Wayne. "Crown Him with Many Crowns." 4-5 oct. L3.
CPH 97-6125.

Kinyon, Barbara B. "All Hail the Power of Jesus' Name." 2-3 oct. L3.
AG 1658.

Larson, Katherine Jordahl. "Beautiful Savior." 3-4 oct. L2.
AFP 0800653963. .

Moklebust, Cathy. "Ring to the Lord a New Song." 4 oct. L3.
AFP 0800647874.

## PRAISE ENSEMBLE

Hayford, Jack/arr. Jack Schrader. "Majesty" SATB, kybd.
HOP GD 868.

Paris, Twila/arr. Jack Schrader. "We Will Glorify." SATB, kybd.
HOP C 5095.

Thomas, Andrae. "The Kingdom." SATB, kybd.    HIN HMC 1307.

# Monday, November 25

## ISAAC WATTS, HYMNWRITER, 1748

Isaac Watts was born in England to a nonconformist family, people who thought the Church of England had not carried its reforms far enough. As a youth, Watts complained to his father about the quality of hymnody in the metrical psalter of his day. That was the start of his hymnwriting career. He wrote about six hundred hymns, many of them in a two-year period beginning when he was twenty years old. Some of Watts's hymns are based on psalms, a nonconformist tradition, but others are not. When criticized for writing hymns not taken from scripture, he responded that if we can pray prayers that are not from scripture but written by us, then surely we can sing hymns that we have made up ourselves.

342

# November 28, 2002

## Day of Thanksgiving (U.S.A.)

## INTRODUCTION

While North Americans celebrate one day of thanksgiving each year, Christians gather frequently to celebrate a thanksgiving meal at the table of Christ. In the eucharist, the church receives the body and blood of Christ, the food and drink of the promised land. His abundant grace is the reason for our thanksgiving. Indeed, when we gather at the holy supper, there is always enough for everyone. No one is turned away.

At the same time, many people in our rich country go without food, shelter, and clothing. Here, in the eucharist with enough for everyone, we find the source of our service in the world to those who have little or nothing. As Christ has blessed us with the riches of his life, so we are called to give ourselves freely to all in need.

## PRAYER OF THE DAY

Almighty God our Father, your generous goodness comes to us new every day. By the work of your Spirit lead us to acknowledge your goodness, give thanks for your benefits, and serve you in willing obedience; through your Son, Jesus Christ our Lord.

## READINGS

### Deuteronomy 8:7-18

Giving thanks begins with remembering. Even when God's people are well settled in the land, they are to remember the mighty deeds by which God brought them on their pilgrimage to a place of plenty.

### Psalm 65

You crown the year with your goodness, and your paths overflow with plenty. (Ps. 65:12)

### 2 Corinthians 9:6-15

Paul was placed in charge of collecting an offering from among the early Christian communities on behalf of Jerusalem church during a time of need. Here, Paul encourages the Corinthians to express their thanksgiving to God by donating to this collection.

### Luke 17:11-19

A Samaritan leper becomes a model for thanksgiving. He

does not take for granted the kindness shown to him but takes time to thank Jesus and to glorify God.

COLOR  White

THE PRAYERS

Filled with gratitude for all God's blessings, let us remember our nation, the church, and all those in need.
*A BRIEF SILENCE.*

God of peace, we give you thanks for the bounty of this fair land and ask that you bless all its people with freedom and justice. Lord, in your mercy,
**hear our prayer.**

God our provider, nourish the church at the Lord's supper, and let this communion be a sign of thanksgiving and hope in the world. Lord, in your mercy,
**hear our prayer.**

God of all comfort, give us generous hearts that we may share the abundance of your blessings with those who are poor, hungry, or in need. Lord, in your mercy,
**hear our prayer.**

God of healing, bless all those who are sick or suffering this day (especially), and fill them with the bounty of your grace. Lord, in your mercy,
**hear our prayer.**

God of all generations, we thank you for family, home, and all the circles of human relationships. Keep our loved ones in your tender care. Lord, in your mercy,
**hear our prayer.**
*HERE OTHER INTERCESSIONS MAY BE OFFERED.*

God of everlasting life, raise us with all your saints to the heavenly harvest, where we will join the angels' song of praise. Lord, in your mercy,
**hear our prayer.**

Crown the year with your goodness, O God, that our lives may overflow with thanksgiving, through Jesus Christ our Lord.
**Amen**

IMAGES FOR PREACHING

When my children were small I had a song for each of them. To my daughter I sang "Summertime." One line goes, "Your daddy's rich, and your momma's good looking; so hush, little baby, don't you cry."

My wife cautioned me, "Don't sing that to her. You know how children are. She'll repeat it to others, and they will think we are rich." (You note she did not object to the "your momma's good looking" part.)

"But we are rich," I replied. I was thinking "rich" in terms of the daughter in my arms, the son and spouse by my side. But North Americans are also rich in ways that are more conventional, richer than ninety-eight percent of the people in this world. Human nature being what it is, however, we compare ourselves with those who have more and find ourselves in need.

Was that why the nine lepers did not return to give thanks? Did they look at their health but immediately turn their eyes to all they did not have, all they missed out on because of their years of illness? Did they start wondering how to make up for those lost earnings?

The road most often traveled in preaching on this text is the guilt trip. "Were not ten made clean? But the other nine, where are they?" (Luke 17:17). Guilt does not work to motivate either thanksgiving or thanks-living, however. The road better traveled this Thanksgiving would be to celebrate the abundance that comes from the hand of a gracious Lord who lavishes healing indiscriminately on those who asked him. Jesus did not inquire into the lepers' worthiness. Jesus' indiscriminate gifts form the basis for calling people to live generously and hospitably out of the abundance that God gives.

Such abundance can begin with the meal the congregation shares. On this day many people sit down to a meal and menu that is similar from one end of the continent to the other. Any given Sunday, Christians all over the world celebrate the same thanksgiving meal, a eucharist that gives witness to far more abundance than we can even imagine.

WORSHIP MATTERS

The North American celebration of Thanksgiving in the church combines both a harvest theme and a time to give thanks for all the many blessings of life. Decorations such as cornucopia and flower arrangements help to emphasize the harvest theme, but the theme of thanksgiving is more difficult to image. For Christians, our thanksgiving centers on the one who is our life and our salvation, Jesus Christ. When our thanksgiving is centered in him, it spills out into all of life, especially in service to God and our neighbor. The eucharist is the event around which we gather as Christians to give thanks to God for all that the divine love has done for us in Christ. Here,

343

around the sharing of God's good gifts and the fruit of human labor, we make our thanksgiving by feeding together on Christ and then becoming what we eat: the body of Christ for the world.

## LET THE CHILDREN COME

Parents and teachers are constantly reminding children, "Did you say thank you?" Worship on this day is a time to remember that our thanks is always directed to someone, and ultimately to God. Saying thanks is not merely a social duty; it draws us closer to the person we are thanking. Children can learn that the good feeling of receiving a gift is surpassed by the joy and fulfillment of a relationship in which thanks is naturally and freely expressed. Children can learn to say simple "Thank you" prayers to God in the middle of their daily experiences. Children can learn to shout at the end of the liturgy, "Thanks be to God."

## HYMNS FOR WORSHIP

### GATHERING

All creatures of our God and King    LBW 527
O God beyond all praising    WOV 797
Glory and praise to our God    W&P 43

### HYMN OF THE DAY

Let all things now living    LBW 557

### ALTERNATE HYMN OF THE DAY

Great is thy faithfulness    WOV 771
Praise to you, O God of mercy    WOV 790

### COMMUNION

Come, you thankful people, come    LBW 407
How great thou art    LBW 532
As the grains of wheat    W&P 10
Give thanks    TFF 292, W&P 41

### SENDING

For the fruit of all creation    LBW 563, WOV 760
Now thank we all our God    LBW 533, 534

### ADDITIONAL HYMNS AND SONGS

Praise and thanksgiving    LBW 409
Accept, O Lord, the gifts we bring    WOV 759

Living thanksgiving    DH 99
What have we to offer    W&P 156

## MUSIC FOR THE DAY

### PSALMODY

Guimont, Michel. "The Seed That Falls on Good Ground" in RS.
Haas, David.    PCY, vol. 8.
Organ, Anne Krentz.    PW A.
To bless the earth, God sends us    PH 200
Ridge, M.D. "The Seed That Falls on Good Ground." SAB, cant, cong, desc, kybd, gtr, solo inst.    OCP 9460.

### CHORAL

Bach, J.S. "Now Thank We All Our God" in *Bach for All Seasons*. SATB, org.    AFP 080065854X.
Britten, Benjamin. "Jubilate Deo." SATB, org.    OXF 42.848.
Goemanne, Noel. "Hymns of Thanks." SATB, org, opt tpts.    GIA G-1543.
Head, Michael. "Make a Joyful Noise Unto the Lord." Solo, org/pno.    PRE 1014 (high); 1015 (low).
Hopson, Hal H. "A Canon of Thanks." SATB, org.    AG HH3943.
Kremser, Eduard. "Prayer of Thanksgiving." SATB, pno, org.    GSCH 4345.
Pachelbel, Johann. "Now Thank We All Our God." SATB, cong.    CPH 98-1944.
Prower, Anthony. "For the Fruits of All Creation." SATB, org, opt cong.    AFP 0800649524.
Sweelinck, Jan Pieterszoon. "Sing to the Lord, New Songs Be Raising" in *Chantry Choirbook*. SATB.    AFP 0800657772.
Vaughan Williams, Ralph. "The Old Hundredth Psalm Tune." SATB, org.    OXF 42.953.
Willan, Healey. "Sing to the Lord of Harvest." CPH 98-2013.

### CHILDREN'S CHOIRS

Jothen, Michael. "I Will Give Thanks." U, kybd.    BEC BP1101.
Smith, Henry/arr. John F. Wilson. "Give Thanks." 2 pt, kybd.    HOP C5090.

### KEYBOARD/INSTRUMENTAL

Albrecht, Mark. "Three for Piano and Sax."    AFP 0800657977.
Bernthal, John. "The Ash Grove" in *Lift High the Cross*. Org, tpt.    AFP 0800657314.
Cherwien, David. "Now Thank We All Our God" in *Postludes on Well Known Hymns*. Org.    AFP 0800656563.

344

Cherwien, David. "Triptych on The Ash Grove." Org. AFP 0800658256.

Groom, Lester. "Prelude on 'St. George's, Windsor'" in *Six Preludes*. Org. HWG GB 654.

Hovland, Egil. "Nun danket alle Gott" in *A New Liturgical Year*. Org. AFP 0800656717.

Wold, Wayne L. "Kremser" in *A November to Remember*. Org. AFP 080665983X.

## HANDBELL

Ingram, Bill. "Three Hymns of Praise." 2-3 oct. L1. CG CGB224.

Moklebust, Cathy. "Morning Dance." 3-5 oct. L3. CG CGB218.

Rogers, Sharon Elery. "Now Thankful People, Come." 2-3 oct. L3. AFP 0800656652.

Smith, James. "Pilgrims and Praise A la Carte." 3-4 oct. L2. JEF RO2339.

Stephenson, Valerie. "Now Thank We All Our God." 3-6 oct. L3. CPH 97-6798.

## PRAISE ENSEMBLE

Maddus, McCall, and Mukalay Mulongoy. "O Sifuni Mungu" (All Creatures of Our God and King). SATB. HAL 40326302. Also available in SAB and 2 pt.

Martin, Joseph M. "I Will Give Thanks." SATB, kybd. LOR 10/1281P.

Patterson, Mark. "We Will Give Thanks." LOR 10/2171M (SATB, kybd); 10/2190M (2 pt.).

Smith, Henry/arr. Tom Brooks. "Give Thanks." INT 41040C (SATB, kybd); 4104TX (choraltrax); INT 41040R (orch).

# Saturday, November 30

## ST. ANDREW, APOSTLE

Andrew was the first of the twelve. He is known as a fisherman who left his net to follow Jesus. As a part of his calling, he brought other people, including Simon Peter, to meet Jesus. The Byzantine church honors Andrew as its patron and points out that because he was the first of Jesus' followers, he was, in the words of John Chrysostom, "the Peter before Peter." Together with Philip, Andrew leads a number of Greeks to speak with Jesus, and it is Andrew who shows Jesus a boy with five barley loaves and two fish. Andrew is said to have died on a cross saltire, an X-shaped cross.

We too are called to invite others to the life of Christ that we will celebrate during Advent and Christmas. In what ways will the church that bears the light of Christ lead others to meet Jesus?

345

# Bibliography

## CHOIRBOOKS

*Augsburg Choirbook, The.* Minneapolis: Augsburg Fortress, 1998. Kenneth Jennings, ed. Sixty-seven anthems primarily from twentieth-century North American composers.

*Bach for All Seasons.* Minneapolis: Augsburg Fortress, 1999. Richard Erickson and Mark Bighley, eds. Offers movements from cantatas and oratorios presented with carefully reconstructed keyboard parts and fresh English texts.

*Chantry Choirbook.* Minneapolis: Augsburg Fortress, 2000. Choral masterworks of European composers spanning five centuries, many with new English translations, and indexed for use in the liturgical assembly throughout the year.

*100 Carols for Choirs.* Oxford and New York: Oxford University Press, 1987. David Willcocks and John Rutter, eds. One hundred classic choral settings of traditional Christmas carols.

## COMPUTER RESOURCES

*Icon: Visual Images for Every Sunday.* Minneapolis: Augsburg Fortress, 2000. Contains over 600 images by liturgical artist Tanja Butler that are based on the church year and lectionary gospel readings for use in congregational bulletins and other self-published materials.

Lutheran Resources for Worship Computer Series. *Lutheran Book of Worship Liturgies; With One Voice Liturgies; Words for Worship: 2002,* Year A; *Graphics for Worship; Hymns for Worship;* Minneapolis: Augsburg Fortress, 1997–2001. Newly published, *Hymns for Worship* contains over one thousand hymn texts and music graphics with multiple search functions.

## DAILY PRAYER RESOURCES

*Book of Common Worship: Daily Prayer.* Louisville, Ky.: Westminster John Knox Press, 1993. Presbyterian.

*For All the Saints.* 4 vols. Frederick Schumacher, ed. Delhi, N.Y.: American Lutheran Publicity Bureau, 1994.

Haugen, Marty. *Holden Evening Prayer.* Chicago: GIA Publications, Inc., 1990.

Makeever, Ray. *Joyous Light Evening Prayer.* Minneapolis: Augsburg Fortress, 2000.

Weber, Paul. *Music for Morning Prayer.* Minneapolis: Augsburg Fortress, 1999. Setting of liturgical music for morning prayer.

*Welcome Home: Year of Matthew.* Minneapolis: Augsburg Fortress, 1995. Scripture, prayers, and blessings for the household.

## ENVIRONMENT AND ART

Chinn, Nancy. *Spaces for Spirit: Adorning the Church.* Chicago: Liturgy Training Publications, 1998. Imaginative thinking about ways to treat visual elements in the worship space.

*Clothed in Glory: Vesting the Church.* David Philippart, ed. Chicago: Liturgy Training Publications, 1997. Photos and essays about liturgical paraments and vestments.

Huffman, Walter C., S. Anita Stauffer, and Ralph R. Van Loon. *Where We Worship.* Minneapolis: Augsburg Publishing House, 1987. Written by three Lutheran worship leaders, this volume sets forth the central principles for understanding and organizing space for worship. Study book and leader guide.

Mauck, Marchita. *Shaping a House for the Church.* Chicago: Liturgy Training Publications, 1990. The author presents basic design principles for worship space and the ways in which the worship space both forms and expresses the faith of the worshiping assembly.

Mazar, Peter. *To Crown the Year: Decorating the Church through the Seasons.* Chicago: Liturgy Training Publications, 1995. A contemporary guide for decorating the worship space throughout the seasons of the year.

Stauffer, S. Anita. *Altar Guild and Sacristy Handbook.* Minneapolis: Augsburg Fortress, 2000. Revised and expanded edition of this classic on preparing the table and the worship environment.

## HYMN AND SONG COLLECTIONS

*As Sunshine to a Garden: Hymns and Songs.* Rusty Edwards. Minneapolis: Augsburg Fortress, 1999. Forty-six collected hymns from the author of "We all are one in mission."

*Borning Cry: Worship for a New Generation.* Compiled by John Ylvisaker. Waverly, Iowa: New Generation Publishers, 1992.

*Bread of Life: Mass and Songs for the Assembly.* Minneapolis: Augsburg Fortress, 2000. Jeremy Young's complete eucharistic music based on *With One Voice* setting five and twelve of his worship songs.

*Dancing at the Harvest: Songs by Ray Makeever.* Minneapolis: Augsburg Fortress, 1997. Over one hundred songs and service music items.

*O Blessed Spring: Hymns of Susan Palo Cherwien.* Minneapolis: Augsburg Fortress, 1997. New hymn texts set to both new and familiar hymn tunes.

*Worship & Praise.* Minneapolis: Augsburg Fortress, 1999. A collection of songs in various contemporary and popular styles, with helps for using them in Lutheran worship.

## LEADING WORSHIP

Adams, William Seth. *Shaped by Images: One Who Presides.* New York: Church Hymnal Corporation, 1995. An excellent review of the ministry of presiding at worship.

Hovda, Robert. *Strong, Loving and Wise: Presiding in Liturgy.* Collegeville, Mn.: The Liturgical Press, 1981. Sound, practical advice for the worship leader from a beloved advocate of social justice and liturgical renewal.

Huck, Gabe. *Liturgy with Style and Grace,* rev. ed. Chicago: Liturgy Training Publications, 1984. The first three chapters offer a practical, well-written overview of the purpose of worship, the elements of worship, and liturgical leadership.

Huffman, Walter C. *Prayer of the Faithful: Understanding and Creatively Leading Corporate Intercessory Prayer,* rev. ed. Minneapolis: Augsburg Fortress, 1992. A helpful treatment of communal prayer, the Lord's Prayer, and the prayers of the people.

*Singing the Liturgy: Building Confidence for Worship Leaders.* Chicago: Evangelical Lutheran Church in America, 1996. A demonstration recording of the chants assigned to leaders in *LBW* and *WOV.*

## LECTIONARIES

*Lectionary for Worship* (A). Minneapolis: Augsburg Fortress, 1995. The Revised Common Lectionary. Includes first reading, psalm citation, second reading, and gospel for each Sunday and lesser festival. Each reading is "sense-lined" for clearer proclamation of the scriptural texts. New Revised Standard Version.

*Lectionary for Worship, Ritual Edition.* Minneapolis: Augsburg Fortress, 1996. Large print, illustrated, hardbound edition that includes the complete three-year Revised Common Lectionary and lesser festival scriptural readings.

*Readings and Prayers: The Revised Common Lectionary.* Minneapolis: Augsburg Fortress, 1995. Scripture citations for the Revised Common Lectionary in use within the Evangelical Lutheran Church in America.

*Readings for the Assembly* (A). Gordon Lathrop and Gail Ramshaw, eds. Minneapolis: Augsburg Fortress, 1995. The Revised Common Lectionary. Emended NRSV with inclusive language.

## LECTIONARY-BASED RESOURCES

Life Together. Minneapolis: Augsburg Fortress. A comprehensive series of Revised Common Lectionary resources that integrates the primary activities of congregational life: worship, proclamation, and learning.

*Faith Life Weekly.* Reproducible weekly handouts to guide conversations, prayer, and activities in the home.

*Kids Celebrate.* Reproducible children's bulletins.

*LifeSongs* (children's songbook, leader book, and audio cds). A well-rounded selection of age-appropriate songs, hymns, and liturgical music that builds a foundation for a lifetime of singing the faith.

*Life Together: Faith Nurturing Resources for Children.* Quarterly teaching and learning resources for three age levels: pre-elementary, lower elementary, upper elementary.

*Living and Learning.* A quarterly (except summer) guide for educational planning using the resources of *Life Together.*

*Word of Life.* Weekly devotional studies for adults based on the lectionary texts.

*Share Your Bread: World Hunger and Worship.* A Lectionary-Based Planning Guide. Chicago: Evangelical Lutheran Church in America, 2000. Worship materials, activity ideas, and devotional reflections that relate worship and the three-year lectionary to the church's mission in the areas of world hunger and social justice.

## PERIODICALS

*Assembly.* Notre Dame Center for Pastoral Liturgy. Chicago: Liturgy Training Publications. Published five times a year. Each issue examines a particular aspect of worship. (800) 933-1800.

*Catechumenate: A Journal of Christian Initiation.* Chicago: Liturgy Training Publications. Published bimonthly with articles on congregational preparation of older children and adults for the celebration of baptism and eucharist. (800) 933-1800.

*Cross Accent.* Journal of the Association of Lutheran Church Musicians. Publication for church musicians and worship leaders in North America. (800) 624-ALCM.

*Faith & Form.* Journal of the Interfaith Forum on Religion, Art and Architecture. Editorial office. (617) 965-3018.

*Grace Notes.* Newsletter of the Association of Lutheran Church Musicians. (708) 272-4116.

*Liturgy.* Quarterly journal of The Liturgical Conference, Washington, DC Each issue explores a worship-related issue from an ecumenical perspective. (800) 394-0885.

*Plenty Good Room.* Chicago: Liturgy Training Publications. Published bimonthly. A magazine devoted to African American worship within a Roman Catholic context. Helpful articles on the enculturation of worship. (800) 933-1800.

*Procession.* Published periodically by the Office of Worship of the Evangelical Lutheran Church in America. Articles and annotated bibliographies on a range of worship topics. (800) 638-3522.

347

*Worship.* Collegeville, Mn: The Order of St. Benedict, published through The Liturgical Press six times a year. Since the early decades of this century, the primary promoter of liturgical renewal among the churches. (800) 858-5450.

## PLANNING TOOLS

*Church Year Calendar 2002.* Minneapolis: Augsburg Fortress, 2001. A one-sheet calendar of lectionary citations and liturgical colors for each Sunday and festival of the liturgical year. Appropriate for bulk purchase and distribution.

*Choosing Contemporary Music: Seasonal, Topical, Lectionary Indexes.* Minneapolis: Augsburg Fortress, 2000. *Indexes for Worship Planning: Revised Common Lectionary, Lutheran Book of Worship, With One Voice.* Minneapolis: Augsburg Fortress, 1996. *Choosing Contemporary Music* provides references to multiple collections of contemporary praise and liturgical songs; *Indexes for Worship Planning* indexes the hymns and songs in *Lutheran Book of Worship* and *With One Voice.* Both include extensive scripture and topic indexes.

*Calendar of Word and Season 2002: Liturgical Wall Calendar.* Minneapolis: Augsburg Fortress, 2001. Date blocks note Revised Common Lectionary readings for Sundays and festivals and identify seasonal or festival color. A reference tool for home, sacristy, office.

*Worship Planning Calendar 2002.* Minneapolis: Augsburg Fortress, 2001. A two-page per week calendar helpful for worship planners, with space to record appointments and notes for each day. Specially designed to complement *Sundays and Seasons.*

## PREPARING MUSIC FOR WORSHIP

Cherwien, David. *Let the People Sing! A Keyboardist's Creative and Practical Guide to Engaging God's People in Meaningful Song.* St. Louis: Concordia Publishing House, 1997. Emphasis on the organ.

Cotter, Jeanne. *Keyboard Improvisation for the Liturgical Musician.* Chicago: GIA Publications, Inc. Practical tips for keyboard improvisation.

Farlee, Robert Buckley, gen. ed. *Leading the Church's Song.* Minneapolis: Augsburg Fortress, 1998. Articles by various contributors, with musical examples and audio cd, giving guidance on the interpretation and leadership of various genres of congregational song.

*Handbells in the Liturgy: A Practical Guide for the Use of Handbells in Liturgical Worship Traditions.* St. Louis: Concordia Publishing House, 1996.

Haugen, Marty. *Instrumentation and the Liturgical Ensemble.* Chicago: GIA Publications, Inc., 1991.

Hopson, Hal H. *The Creative Use of Handbells in Hymn Singing.* Carol Stream: Hope Publishing Co. Specific handbell techniques to be used in accompanying congregational singing.

*Let It Rip at the Piano* and *Pull Out the Stops.* Minneapolis: Augsburg Fortress, 2000–2001. Collections for piano and organ respectively, each containing introductions and varied musical accompaniments by various composers for over 100 widely used hymns and songs. Emphasis on current musical styles including blues, gospel, new age, jazz, and rolling contemporary.

Rotermund, Donald. *Intonations and Alternative Accompaniments for Psalm Tones.* St. Louis: Concordia Publishing House, 1997. (*LBW* and *LW* versions available separately.)

Weidler, Scott, and Dori Collins. *Sound Decisions.* Chicago: Evangelical Lutheran Church in America, 1997. Theological principles for the evaluation of contemporary worship music.

Westermeyer, Paul. *The Church Musician,* rev. ed. Minneapolis: Augsburg Fortress, 1997. Foundational introduction to the role and task of the church musician as the leader of the people's song.

———. *Te Deum: The Church and Music.* Minneapolis: Fortress Press, 1998. An historical and theological introduction to the music of the church.

Wilson-Dickson, Andrew. *The Story of Christian Music.* Minneapolis: Fortress Press, 1996. An illustrated guide to the major traditions of music in worship.

Wold, Wayne. *Tune My Heart to Sing.* Minneapolis: Augsburg Fortress, 1997. Devotions for choirs based on the lectionary.

## PROCLAIMING THE WORD

Brueggemann, Walter, et al. *Texts for Preaching: A Lectionary Commentary Based on the NRSV.* Cycles A, B, C. Louisville, Ky.: Westminster John Knox Press, 1993–95.

Craddock, Fred, et al. *Preaching through the Christian Year.* Three volumes for Cycles A, B, C. Valley Forge, Pa.: Trinity Press International, 1992, 1993. In three volumes, various authors comment on the Sunday readings and psalms as well as various festival readings.

*Days of the Lord: The Liturgical Year.* 7 vols. Collegeville, Mn.: The Liturgical Press, 1991–94. Written by French biblical and liturgical experts, this series provides helpful commentary useful also with the Revised Common Lectionary.

*Homily Service: An Ecumenical Resource for Sharing the Word.* Silver Spring, Md.: The Liturgical Conference. A monthly publication with commentary on Sunday readings (exegesis, ideas and illustrations, healing aspects of the word, a preacher's reflection on the readings).

*New Proclamation,* Year A. Minneapolis: Augsubrg Fortress, 2001–2002. Various authors. A sound and useful series of commentaries on year A readings. In two volumes, Advent–Holy Week and Easter–Pentecost.

## PSALM COLLECTIONS

*Anglican Chant Psalter, The.* Alec Wyton, ed. New York: Church Hymnal Corporation, 1987.

Daw, Carl P., and Kevin R. Hackett. *A Hymn Tune Psalter.* New York: Church Publishing, 1999.

*Grail Gelineau Psalter, The.* Chicago: GIA Publications, Inc., 1972. 150 psalms and eighteen canticles.

*Plainsong Psalter, The.* James Litton, ed. New York: Church Hymnal Corporation, 1988.

*Psalm Songs.* David Ogden and Alan Smith, eds. Minneapolis: Augsburg Fortress, 1998. Three volumes of responsorial psalm settings by various composers.

*Psalms for the Church Year.* Various volumes by different composers. Chicago: GIA Publications, Inc., 1983–present.

*Psalter, The.* International Commission on English in the Liturgy (ICEL). Chicago: Liturgy Training Publications, 1995.

*Psalter for Worship.* Martin Seltz, ed. Minneapolis: Augsburg Fortress, 1995 and continuing. Settings of psalm antiphons by various composers with *LBW* and other psalm tones. Psalm texts included. Revised Common Lectionary.
    *Psalter for Worship (A).*
    *Psalter for Worship (B).*
    *Psalter for Worship (C).* Includes all lesser festivals.

*The Psalter: Psalms and Canticles for Singing.* Louisville, Ky.: Westminster John Knox Press, 1993. Various composers.

*Singing the Psalms.* Various volumes with various composers represented. Portland: Oregon Catholic Press, 1995–present.

## REFERENCE WORKS

*Concordance to Hymn Texts: Lutheran Book of Worship.* Robbin Hough, compiler. Minneapolis: Augsburg Publishing House, 1985.

Foley, Edward. *Worship Music: A Concise Dictionary.* Collegeville: The Liturgical Press, 2000.

*New Dictionary of Sacramental Worship, The.* Peter Fink, ed. Collegeville, Mn.: Michael Glazier/Liturgical Press, 1990.

*Praying Together.* English Language Liturgical Consultation. Nashville: Abingdon Press, 1988. Core ecumenical liturgical texts with annotation and commentary.

Pfatteicher, Philip. *Festivals and Commemorations.* Minneapolis: Augsburg Publishing House, 1980.

———. *Commentary on Occasional Services.* Philadelphia: Fortress Press, 1983.

———. *Commentary on Lutheran Book of Worship.* Minneapolis: Augsburg Fortress, 1990.

Pfatteicher, Philip, and Carlos Messerli. *Manual on the Liturgy: Lutheran Book of Worship.* Minneapolis: Augsburg Publishing House, 1979.

Stulken, Marilyn Kay. *Hymnal Companion to the Lutheran Book of Worship.* Philadelphia: Fortress Press, 1981.

———. *With One Voice Reference Companion.* Minneapolis: Augsburg Fortress, 2000.

Van Loon, Ralph, and S. Anita Stauffer. *Worship Wordbook.* Minneapolis: Augsburg Fortress, 1995.

## SEASONS AND LITURGICAL YEAR

Huck, Gabe. *The Three Days: Parish Prayer in the Paschal Triduum,* rev. ed. Chicago: Liturgy Training Publications, 1992. For worship committees, it is an excellent introduction to worship during the Three Days: Maundy Thursday, Good Friday, and Holy Saturday/Easter Sunday.

Hynes, Mary Ellen. *Companion to the Calendar.* Chicago: Liturgy Training Publications, 1993. An excellent overview of the seasons, festivals and lesser festivals, and many commemorations. Written from an ecumenical/Roman Catholic perspective, including commemorations unique to the Lutheran calendar.

## WORSHIP BOOKS

*Libro de Liturgia y Cántico.* Minneapolis: Augsburg Fortress, 1998. A complete Spanish-language worship resource including liturgies and hymns, some with English translations.

*Lutheran Book of Worship.* Minneapolis: Augsburg Publishing House; Philadelphia: Board of Publication, Lutheran Church in America, 1978.

*Lutheran Book of Worship,* Ministers Edition. Minneapolis: Augsburg Publishing House; Philadelphia: Board of Publication, Lutheran Church in America, 1978.

*Occasional Services: A Companion to Lutheran Book of Worship.* Minneapolis: Augsburg Publishing House; Philadelphia: Board of Publication, Lutheran Church in America, 1982.

*Ritos Ocasionales.* Minneapolis: Augsburg Fortress, 2000. Spanish language translation of rites from *Occasional Services.*

*This Far by Faith: An African American Resource for Worship.* Minneapolis: Augsburg Fortress, 1999. A supplement of worship orders, psalms, service music, and hymns representing African American traditions and developed by African American Lutherans.

*With One Voice: A Lutheran Resource for Worship.* Minneapolis: Augsburg Fortress, 1995. Pew, leader, and accompaniment editions; instrumental parts, organ accompaniment for the liturgy, cassette.

## WORSHIP STUDIES

Foley, Edward. *From Age to Age: How Christians Have Celebrated the Eucharist.* Chicago: Liturgy Training Publications, 1991. An excellent survey of Christian worship, music, environment, and theological concerns.

*Gathered and Sent: An Introduction to Worship.* Participant book by Karen Bockelman. Leader guide by Roger Prehn. Minneapolis: Augsburg Fortress, 1999. Basic worship study course for inquirers and general adult instruction in congregations.

*Inside Out: Worship in an Age of Mission.* Thomas Schattauer, gen ed. Minneapolis: Fortress Press, 1999. Multiple authors who teach at North American Lutheran seminaries address the mission of the church as it pertains to various aspects of worship.

Open Questions in Worship. Gordon Lathrop, gen. ed. Minneapolis: Augsburg Fortress, 1994–96. Eight volumes of essays on matters of current conversation and concern regarding Christian worship.

*What are the essentials of Christian worship?* vol. 1 (1994).

*What is "contemporary" worship?* vol. 2 (1995).

*How does worship evangelize?* vol. 3 (1995).

*What is changing in baptismal practice?* vol. 4 (1995).

*What is changing in eucharistic practice?* vol. 5 (1995).

*What are the ethical implications of worship?* vol. 6 (1996).

*What does "multicultural" worship look like?* vol. 7 (1996).

*How does the liturgy speak of God?* vol. 8 (1996).

Ramshaw, Gail. *Every Day and Sunday, Too.* Minneapolis: Augsburg Fortress, 1996. An illustrated book for parents and children. Daily life is related to the central actions of the liturgy.

———. *1-2-3 Church.* Minneapolis: Augsburg Fortress, 1996. An illustrated rhyming primer and number book. For parents with young children, this book presents the fundamental actions of worship through numbered rhymes. A song for singing at home or in church school is included.

———. *Sunday Morning.* Chicago: Liturgy Training Publications, 1993. A book for children and adults on the primary words of Sunday worship.

Senn, Frank. *Christian Liturgy: Catholic and Evangelical.* Minneapolis: Fortress Press, 1997. A comprehensive historical introduction to the liturgy of the Western church with particular emphasis on the Lutheran traditions.

*Use of the Means of Grace: A Statement on the Practice of Word and Sacrament, The.* Chicago: Evangelical Lutheran Church in America, 1997. Also available in Spanish and Mandarin versions.

*Welcome to Christ: A Lutheran Catechetical Guide.* Minneapolis: Augsburg Fortress, 1997.

*Welcome to Christ: A Lutheran Introduction to the Catechumenate.* Minneapolis: Augsburg Fortress, 1997.

*Welcome to Christ: Lutheran Rites for the Catechumenate.* Minneapolis: Augsburg Fortress, 1997.

*What Do You Seek? Welcoming the Adult Inquirer.* Minneapolis: Augsburg Fortress, 2000. An introduction to a congregational process for welcoming Christians through affirmation of their baptism, using the resources of catechumenal formation.

Worship Handbook Series. Minneapolis: Augsburg Fortress, forthcoming. Brief guides to liturgical ministries and celebrations for those who lead and participate in worship.

*Acolytes and Servers.* Gerald Spice. A guide for acolytes and servers as they prepare the worship space, participate in processions, and carry out other worship leadership roles.

*Assisting Ministers and Readers.* Gerald Spice. A guide for those who read the scriptures, offer prayer, and carry out other roles of assisting ministers in worship.

*Christian Burial.* Karen Bockelman. An invitation into the funeral liturgy, written to those preparing for worship in the time of death.

*Marriage.* Karen Bockelman. An invitation into the marriage liturgy, written to those planning for a wedding or the renewal of marriage vows.

*Ministers of Communion from the Assembly.* Donald Luther. Encouragement and practical helps for the ministry of carrying communion to those who are sick or otherwise absent from the worshiping assembly.

*Musicians in the Assembly.* Robert Buckley Farlee. Essentials of making music for worship, written for those who inspire congregational song and lead ensembles of voices or instruments in a variety of styles.

*Preparing the Assembly's Worship.* Craig Mueller. An overview of the work of the worship committee or other group that organizes and leads the congregation in a vibrant worship life.

*Preparing the Worship Folder.* Techniques for building a hospitable and effective aid to assembly participation in worship.

*Presiding in the Assembly.* Essentials of presiding and preaching within the assembly gathered around word and sacrament.

*Sponsors and Baptism.* Elaine Ramshaw. Encouragement and suggestions for those who serve as sponsors or godparents (especially for children) in the baptismal liturgy and in the ongoing life of the baptized.

*Welcome to Worship.* Karen Bockelman. In leaflet form for pew or tract rack, a brief and very basic introduction to the essential pattern of worship.

# The Art

*Sundays and Seasons* presents image selections from *Icon: Visual Images for Every Sunday*, an electronic library of illustrations for all three cycles of the liturgical year. The Icon artwork, sampled here, is a series of papercuttings, a technique associated with folk art that employs incisive lines and bold contrasts.

Tanja Butler is a painter and printmaker whose work has been displayed in many solo and group exhibitions across the United States. Her artwork is included in the collection of the Vatican Museum of Contemporary Religious Art and the Armand Hammer Collection of Art. Her illustrations have been published in a variety of publications and worship resource materials. She currently teaches art at Gordon College in Wenham, Massachusetts, and lives in Lynn, Massachusetts, and Averill Park, New York.

# The Design

The design elements of *Sundays and Seasons* are elemental in form and structure, expressing a simplicity of means. Silver metallic ink, chosen to fill the intimately sized icons, reflects the precious nature of both image and word. The cover's striped and solid fields of color provide a sense of serenity and order. The typeface Centaur, modeled on letters cut by the fifteenth-century printer Nicolas Jenson, expresses a beauty of line and proportion that has been widely acclaimed since its release in 1929. The book's contents use a combination of the typefaces Centaur (body text) and Univers (subtexts).

The Kantor Group, based in Minneapolis, provides communication design solutions to its clients nationwide.